# Globalization and the Decolonial Option

This is the first book in English profiling the work of a research collective that evolved around the notion of 'coloniality', understood as the hidden agenda and the darker side of modernity and whose members are based in South America and the United States. The project called for an understanding of modernity not from modernity itself but from its darker side, coloniality, and proposes the de-colonization of knowledge as an epistemological restitution with political and ethical implications.

Epistemic decolonization, or de-coloniality, becomes the horizon to imagine and act toward global futures in which the notion of a political enemy is replaced by intercultural communication and towards an-other rationality that puts life first and that places institutions at its service, rather than the other way around.

This book is profoundly inter- and trans-disciplinary, with authors writing from many intellectual, transdisciplinary, and institutional spaces.

This book was published as a special issue of *Cultural Studies*.

**Walter D. Mignolo** is William H. Wannamaker Professor of Romance Studies, Professor in the Program of Literature and Adjunct in Cultural Anthropology. He is also Director of the Center for Global Studies and the Humanities at Duke University and Associated Researcher, Universidad Andina Simón Bolívar, Quito, Ecuador.

**Arturo Escobar** is Kenan Distinguished Professor of Anthropology, and Adjunct in the Department of Geography and of Communication, at the University of North Carolina in Chapel Hill.

# Globalization and the Decolonial Option

Edited by Walter D. Mignolo and
Arturo Escobar

Routledge
Taylor & Francis Group
LONDON AND NEW YORK

First published 2010 by Routledge
2 Park Square, Milton Park, Abingdon, Oxon, OX14 4RN

Simultaneously published in the USA and Canada
by Routledge
711 Third Avenue, New York, NY 10017

*Routledge is an imprint of the Taylor & Francis Group, an informa business*

First issued in paperback 2013



Typeset in Perpetua by Value Chain, India



*British Library Cataloguing in Publication Data*
A catalogue record for this book is available from the British Library

ISBN13: 978-0-415-54971-4

# CONTENTS

## IV (De)Coloniality at Large



## V On Empires and Colonial/Imperial Differences

# Notes on contributors

**Manuela Boatcă** is currently an Assistant Professor in the Department of Sociological Theory at the University of Eichstat in Germany. Her research interests include political sociology, world-system analysis, gender and violence, and postcolonial studies. Among her recent publications are *From Neoevolutionism to World-Systems Analysis: The Romanian theory of 'Forms Without Substance'* (2003); 'Peripheral Solutions to Peripheral Development', *Journal of World-Systems Research,* vol. 11, no. 1, 2005; and 'Knocking in Europe's Door: Romanian Academia Between Communist Censorship and Western Neglect', *SAQ*, vol. 105, no. 3, 2006. Semiperipheries in the World-System. Reflecting Eastern European and Latin American Experiences, in *Journal of World-Systems Research,* vol. XII, no. 2, 2006.

**Santiago Castro-Gómez** is Associate Professor of Philosophy at the Universidad Javeriana in Bogotá, Colombia. He is also Associate Researcher at the Insituto PENSAR at the same university. He received his PhD in philosophy from the Johann Wolfgang Goethe Universitat in Frankfurt, Germany. Among his recent books are *Crítica de la razón latinoamericana* (1996); *La postcolonialidad explicada a los niños* (2005) and *La hybris del punto cero* (2005).

**Arturo Escobar** is Professor of Anthropology and Director, Institute of Latin American Studies, University of North Carolina, Chapel Hill. His main interests are: political ecology, the anthropology of development, social movement theory, and science and technology studies. Over the past ten years, he has worked closely with several social movements in the Colombian Pacific and with the Rome-based Society for International Development (SID) on projects on globalization, culture, women, environment, and place.

**Ramón Grosfoguel** is a Sociologist and a Professor in the Ethnic Studies Department at UC-Berkeley. He has published many articles on the Political Economy of the World-System and on Caribbean Migrants in Western Europe and the United States. He is the author of *Colonial Subjects* (University of California Press, 2003).

**Zilkia Janer** is working on a critical history of culinary thought from a translocal perspective. She has published 'The Geopolitics of Culinary Knowledge' (New Delhi) and 'In Search of a High-Cuisine' (Kathmandu). Janer is also preparing a manuscript on Latino food culture for Greenwood Press. She is the author of *Puerto Rican Nation-Building Literature: Impossible Romance* (University Press of Florida, 2005) and teaches Latin American literature and culture at Hofstra University.

**Agustin Lao-Montes** teaches at the Department of Sociology of the University of Massachusetts at Amherst where he is also affiliated with the Center for Latin American, Caribbean, and Latino Studies, and with the Afro-American Studies Program. He has written extensively in a variety of fields including world-historical sociology, decolonial critique, social movements, cultural studies, and urban studies. He co-edited *Mambo Montage: The Latinization of New York* and is working on a manuscript tentatively titled 'Afro-Latina/o Diasporas: Black Movements and Racial Politics in the Americas'.

**María Lugones** is Professor of Philosophy and Director of the Interdisciplinary Research Center in Philosophy, Interpretation and Culture at the University of New York at Binghamton, focussing on "Decolonial Thinking" (http://cpic.binghamton.edu/decolonial.html). She is a popular educator and philosopher and teaches also at the Escuela Popular Norteña, a popular education center and in the Comparative Literature department, at Binghamton. Lugones is the author of *Pilgrimages/Peregrinajes: Theorizing Resistance Against Multiple Oppressions* (Rowman and Littlefield, 2003). She is finishing two books, I*ntimate Interdependencies: Theorizing Collectivism;* and *Radical Multiculturalism*.

**Nelson Maldonado-Torres** is Assistant Professor of Comparative Ethnic Studies in the Department of Ethnic Studies at the University of California, Berkeley and former Postdoctoral Fellow in the Center for Global Studies and the Humanities at Duke University. He works on theories and philosophies that address problems and questions related to the intersection of knowledge, ethics and politics on the one hand, and race, gender, nation, and empire on the other, particularly in connection with critical theory, phenomenology, postcolonial studies, and modern religious thought. He has published several articles and is working on two book-length projects: *Against War: Views from the Underside of Modernity* (forthcoming with Duke University Press), and *Fanonian Meditations*. He is also co-editor with Ramón Grosfoguel and José David Saldívar of *Latin@s in the World-System: Decolonization Struggles in the 21st U.S. Empire* (Paradigm Press).

**Walter D. Mignolo** is William H. Wannamaker Professor and Director of the Center for Global Studies and the Humanities at Duke University. In the recent past he has explored geo-politics and the body-politics of knowledge in the context of the colonial matrix of power; border thinking and the decolonial option. Among his recent publications *Local Histories/Designs: Coloniality, Subaltern Knowledges and Border Thinking* (2000); *The Idea of Latin America* (2005). The forthcoming *I Am Where I Think: Globalization, Epistemic Disobedience and the Decolonial Option* is the third part of a trilogy composed by

*The Darker Side of the Renaissance* (1995) and *Local Histories/Global Designs*. With Madina Tlostanova he co-edited *Double Critique: Scholars and Knowledge at Risk in Post-Soviet Societies* (2006).

**Aníbal Quijano** is a Professor of Sociology at the Universidad de San Marcos in Lima and at the State University of New York in Binghamton. Professor Quijano had an influential role to originally formulate dependency theory in Latin America and introduced the key-concept of 'coloniality of power' in the late 80s. Since then, his research has focused and examines the 'coloniality of power' and its implications for the formation of the modern world-system. Among his more recent and influential publications are: 'Coloniality of Power, Eurocentrism and Latin America', *Nepantla: Views from South* (2003); 'Colonialidad del poder y clasificación social', *Festschrift for Immanuel Wallerstein* (2000); 'Estado-nación y 'movimientos indígenas' en la región Andina: cuestiones abiertta' in *Observatorio Social de América Latina (Revista OSAL,* 2006).

**José David Saldívar** is the Class of 1942 Professor of Ethnic Studies and English at the University of California, Berkeley. He is the author T*he Dialectics of Our America: Genealogy, Cultural Critique, and Literary History* (Duke 1991) and *Border Matters: Remapping American Cultural Studies* (California 1997).

**Javier Sanjinés** is Associate Professor of Latin American Literature and Cultural Studies at the University of Michigan, Ann Arbor. His work relates racial issues with the construction of nation in the Andes, particularly in Bolivia. In *Mestizaje Upside-Down. Aesthetic Politics in Modern Bolivia* (University of Pittsburgh Press, 2004), his most recent book, Sanjinés argues that present-day indigenous movements in Bolivia have inverted the imaginary under which the Bolivian nation was constructed by mestizo elites during the twentieth century. Contending that mestizaje is not a true merging of equals, but representative of a fundamentally Western perspective that excludes indigenous ways of viewing the world, Sanjinés grounds his argument in an examination of fiction, political essays, journalism, and visual art. At present, Sanjinés is exploring the connections between history and difference in Andean modernity. He concentrates on Bolivian historicism as a transition narrative which is incomplete due to a national struggle remained unfulfilled.

**Freya Schiwy** is Assistant Professor at the University of California, Riverside. Her teaching combines Cultural and Film with Latin American Studies. Schiwy is currently completing a book manuscript on indigenous media, decolonization and the Andes. She is co-editor (with Catherine Walsh and Santiago Castro-Gómez) of *(In)disciplinar las ciencias socials* (Quito, 2002). She has published articles on cultural theory and on indigenous media in Latin America, Germany, England, and the USA. With Michael Ennis, Schiwy

co-edited a special dosser 'Knowledge and the Known: Andean Perspectives on Capitalism and Epistemology', *Nepantla,* vol. 3, no. 1, 2002.

**Madina Tlostanova** is Professor in the Department of Comparative Politics at the People's Friendship University of Russia. Her current interests include globalization's effects in contemporary culture, post-national, post-colonial and comparative studies; the post-Soviet cultural imaginary; and trans-cultural subjectivity and aesthetics. Tlostanova authored two books in Russian and two in English. The most recent ones, *Post-Soviet Literature and Transcultural Aesthetics* (2004, in Russian) and *The Sublime of Globalization: Sketches on Transcultural Subjetivity and Aesthetics* (2005, in English). Among her recent articles in English, 'The Imagined Freedom: Post-Soviet Intellectuals Between the Hegemony of the State and the Hegemony of the Market', in *SAQ*, vol. 105, no. 3, 2006. She is currently writing a book on gender and sexuality in a 'rootless' world.

**Catherine Walsh** is Professor and Director of the doctoral program in Latin American Cultural Studies at the Universidad Andina Simon Bolivar in Quito, Ecuador, where she also directs the Fondo Documental Afro-Andino, a project dedicated to the recuperation of knowledge in Afro-Ecuadorian communities, and the Intercultural Workshop which has been actively engaged in work with indigenous mayors in several municipalities. Her recent publications include, among others, *Pensamiento critico y matriz (de)colonial* (2005), *Estudios culturales latinoamericanos: retos desde y sobre la región andina* (2003), *Indisciplinar las ciencias sociales. Geopolíticas del conocimiento y colonialidad del poder. Perspectivas desde lo andino* (co-edited with F. Schiwy and S. Castro-Gómez, 2002)), 'Interculturality and the Coloniality of Power. An 'Other' Thinking and Positioning from the Colonial Difference', (in *Coloniality of Power, Transmodernity, and Border Thinking,* R. Grosfóguel, J.D. Saldívar, and N. Maldonado-Torres (eds.), forthcoming), and 'The (Re)Articulation of Political Subjectivities and Colonial Difference in Ecuador: Reflections on Capitalism and the Geopolitics of Knowledge', *Nepantla,* vol. 3, no. 1, 2002.

Walter D. Mignolo

# Introduction: Coloniality of power and de-colonial thinking

## I About the Book

This book the reader has in her/his hands is the outcome of one of the workshops of the project modernity/coloniality/decoloniality, held at Duke-UNC in May of 2004, and organized by the volume editors. The workshop stressed the shift that the project was taking, by moving from the analytic of modernity/coloniality to the emphasis places in de-coloniality, as Aníbal Quijano mapped in the opening article.

The workshop focused on the following question: what are the differences between existing critical projects and de-colonization of knowledge and other contemporary critical projects (an outline of this scenario in section III, below). We decided to focus on Max Horkheimer's formulation of 'critical theory' for several reasons. The first was that the project of the Frankfurt School and the early works of Horkheimer in particular were meaningful for some of the participants in the project modernity/coloniality (chiefly Enrique Dussel and Santiago Castro-Gómez, both philosophers from Argentina and Colombia, respectively).[1] Secondly, because the Frankfurt School condensed a tradition of Jewish critical thinkers in Germany during the early years of Hitler's regime that although Marxist in spirit was entangled with racism and coloniality in the body. As Aimé Césaire noted, half a century ago, the Holocaust was a racial crime perpetrated against racialized whites in Europe, applying the same logic that the colonizer had applied to people of color outside of Europe (Césaire 2000). While de-coloniality names critical thoughts emerging in the colonies and ex-colonies, Jewish critical traditions in Europe, since the nineteenth century, materialized as the internal responses to European formation of imperial nation-states.[2]

This volume intends to be a contribution to the advancement of de-colonial thinking as a particular kind of critical theory and to the de-colonial option as a specific orientation of doing.[3] We assume that critical theory in the Marxist genealogy of thought, as articulated by Max Horkheimer, is also a particular kind of critical theory and not the norm or the master paradigm against which all other projects should be compared, measured, evaluated and judged.[4] Master paradigms are just but options dressed with universal clothes. One of the consequences of de-colonial options is to make clear precisely that master paradigms and abstract universals (left, right and center) are still

caught in imperial desires. We also assume that 'history' is not only linear; and that 'historical awards' are only endowed to those who get there first, in the uni-linear chronology of events. There are several histories, all simultaneous histories, inter-connected by imperial and colonial powers, by imperial and colonial differences. The volume is also intended as a contribution to the de-colonial option in epistemology and politics. The de-colonial option requires a different type of thinking (Catherine Walsh theorizes it as an-other-thinking), a non-linear and chronological (but spatial) epistemological break; it requires border epistemology (e.g., epistemic disobedience), a non-capitalist political economy, and a pluri-national (that is, non-mono-national) concept of the state. The de-colonial option opens up as de-linking and negativity from the perspective of the spaces that have been silenced, repressed, demonized, devaluated by the triumphant chant of self-promoting modern epistemology, politics and economy and its internal dissensions (honest liberals, theologians of liberation, post-moderns and post-structuralists, Marxists of different brands).

Section I features the seminal article by Peruvian sociologist, Aníbal Quijano, published at the beginning of the 90s, when the dust of a crumbling Soviet Union was still in everybody's eyes.[5] At the beginning of this century, Arturo Escobar (an anthropologist from Colombia currently residing in the US) wrote a critical review of what he called 'the modernity/coloniality research program'. This article is included here, following the one by Quijano. The rest of the articles reflect part of the research and publications of many of us participating in the project, who continue to meet yearly and exchange views, articles, opinions and information. Ramón Grosfoguel (a sociologist and activist, from Puerto Rico residing in the US) reviews world-system analysis from the perspective of coloniality. A former student of Immanuel Wallerstein, Grosfoguel's contribution to the epistemic shift opened up, in the social sciences, by modernity/coloniality research program starts and departs from dependency theory and world-system analysis. His contribution in this volume is part of his larger argument to transcend the basic economic model in which dependency theory and world-system analysis rest. Catherine Walsh (scholar, activist and resident of Ecuador), has in the past eight years, developed a critical discourse based on her political work with Indigenous and Afro-intellectuals and communities, in Ecuador; as well as in her role as founder and director of the program in cultural studies at the Universidad Andina Simón Bolívar. Here Walsh strongly argues for an 'other thought' to avoid the modern trap of putting everything in one temporal line, in one highway that is already being patrolled and guarded by gate-keepers making sure that 'other thoughts' do not cross the borders.

In section II Nelson Maldonado-Torres and Freya Schiwy engage in explorations that each have been pursuing in the past five or so years and

that expand the modernity/coloniality/decolonialilty project to the sphere of philosophy and cultural critique. Maldonado-Torres (a Puerto Rican philosopher and historian of religions), has been exploring the concept of 'coloniality of being', that was implied but not clearly stated in all its consequences, in Quijano's notion of 'subjectivity and knowledge'. In Quijano's germinal article the colonial matrix of power has been described in four interrelated domains: control of economy (land appropriation, exploitation of labor, control of natural resources); control of authority (institution, army); control of gender and sexuality (family, education) and control of subjectivity and knowledge (epistemology, education and formation of subjectivity). Furthermore, implanting the colonial matrix of power (either in sixteenth century Anahuak [Valley of Mexico] or in today's Iraq) implies to dismantle, simultaneously, existing forms of social organization and ways of life. 'Coloniality of being' as unfolded by Maldonado-Torres brings forward what has been silenced beyond Heideger and Levinas: the 'being' of Frantz Fanon's 'damnés de la terre'. Freya Schiwy (a cultural critic from Germany residing in the US) has distinguished herself within the research program, for her original investigation of Indigenous video making and her interrogation of the roles of gender in the colonial matrix of power. While Maldonado-Torres explores the intersection of coloniality and subjectivity in the domain of philosophy and in the tradition of the concept of 'being', Schiwy explores coloniality and subjectivity in the domain of cultural studies and in the debate on gender issues. In Quijano's colonial matrix of power, gender and sexuality is one sphere in which coloniality of power is articulated. Quijano's has concentrated himself in the spheres of the control of economy (mainly exploitation of labor) and authority articulated with the coloniality of knowledge. Maldonado-Torres and Schiwy are contributing to unfold the question of being and gender entangled with the coloniality of knowledge.

In section III, ethnicity, nation-state and racism come into prominent focus. Where do these issues fit in the colonial matrix of power? Where is the nation-state in the colonial matrix of power?; in the sphere of control of authority, for sure. The emergence of 'modern nation-states' in Europe, means two things: that the state became the new central authority of imperial/colonial domination and that the 'nation' in Europe was mainly constituted of one ethnicity, articulated as 'whiteness'. Chronologically, South America and the Caribbean were the first cases of 'colonial nation-states' and in the process of their appearance and materialization, the colonial matrix of power was re-articulated in what has been described as 'internal colonialism': a Creole elite (e.g., white elite from European descent), took the power from the hands of Spanish and Portuguese monarchies, and re-enacted it in their own hands. In the case of Haiti, it was the Black Creole and ex-Slaves who took power. However, and as history demonstrated, a Black colonial state was not

allowed to occupy the same position in the modern/colonial world, than the White colonial state. The co-existence of the modern nation-state with colonial nation-states is one of the key points in the transformation of racism and the colonial matrix of power since the beginning of the nineteenth century.

Javier Sanjinés (a Bolivian cultural critic and former political theorist, who splits his time between Bolivia and the US) takes Brazilian essayist and intellectual Euclides da Cunha, *Os Sertões* (1902) in order to explore the tensions and conflicts between race and nation in the formation of the colonial state. At the beginning of the twentieth century, Brazil was no longer a direct colony of Portugal. But it was, like the rest of Latin America, an indirect colony of the French civilizing mission and of the British Empire economy. Brazilian critical intellectuals (as it became the case all around the colonial world), torn between the exemplarity of European modern states and the miseries of mentally, economically, and politically dependent colonial states, were the visible cases of a new subjectivity, the subjectivity of the colonial citizens of the colonial nation-states. Sanjinés describes the particular form that the colonial state took in South America as the 'oligarchic-liberal States' and contrasts those who trumpeted the European model (like Argentinean Domingo Faustino Sarmiento), with those critical of it (as Sarmiento's counterpart in Brazil, Euclides De Cunha).

In the same vein, Agustin Lao-Montes (a sociologist from Puerto Rico, residing in the US) explores the past (in)visibility of Afro-Latinos and their growing demographic and political presence. What does it mean to be Afro-Latinos and Afro-Latinas? Where are they coming from? They are entangled, woven, trapped in the colonial matrix of power of the modern/colonial world? The situation today is directly linked with, on the one hand, the formation of colonial nation states, in the nineteenth century and, on the other hand, with the imperial/colonial differences that unfolded between the colonial nation state in the US and the colonial nation states in South America and the Caribbean. The modern/colonial imaginary and increasing US imperial prominence during Cold War and the Civil Rights Movement, produced the impression that Afros in the Americas were mainly located in the US and in the Caribbean former colonies of France (Guadalupe, Martinique) and England (Jamaica, Barbados). That is, Afro-Americans are people who speak English or French but not Spanish or Portuguese! Afro-Latinos as are becoming visible not only in the US but also in South America—in the ex-colonies of Spain and Portugal—those places where Spanish and Portuguese were relegated to second class Latin languages, after French. Lao-Montes explores Afro-Latinidad in the US which is both a consequence of migration from the South, and of the US pushing the Southern frontiers farther South, in 1848, and leaving thousands of Mexicans inside US expanded territory.

At this junction, José Saldívar intervenes in an effort to link a strand of Latino/a critical and theoretical reflection, in dialogue with the modernity/coloniality research program. The strength of Saldívar's reflection is to make clear that Latinos and Latinas are not just a social phenomenon that shall be studied from the perspective of the social sciences modeled from the perspective of White Europeans and US scholars. It means that Latinos and Latinas are finding a locus of enunciation from where White Europeans and US social phenomenon shall be studied. This is a process in which a radical epistemic shift is taking place and the hubris of the zero point (see Castro-Gómez in this volume) that anchors the social sciences became under siege and denounced for the universal pretension of an epistemology that is founded, as Quijano observes in his contribution, on the experience of one particular ethnicity, White Euro-Americans. Saldívar's contribution helps us (the readers) in looking at the coloniality of power from the perspective of experiences similar to those that brought the concept of 'coloniality' into existence; experiences that generate the need of border thinking and de-colonial projects; experiences that disengage from the 'obligation' to see the world according to the ethnical experiences hidden behind the epistemic universality of the hubris of the zero point. Going back to the moment in which, in the US, Deleuze and Guatari's concept of 'minor literature' (Kafka) was translated into 'minority discourse' in the US (that is, the discourse emerging from the colonial wound – both racial and patriarchal – of people of color in the US, Saldívar casts a wide net and connects theoretical and political intellectual production with Afro-US, South America (coloniality of power) and South Asia (subaltern studies; connectors is a fundamental concept to link de-colonial projects coming from different colonial experiences). His essays continue to show that de-colonial thinking is the pluri-versal epistemology of the future; an epistemology that de-links from the tyranny of abstract universals (Christians, Liberals or Marxists).

Section IV takes up where section III left off: the inter-connections between the peripheries and the geo-political and body-political location of border thinking and de-colonial projects. Coloniality of power, in other words, it is not just a question of the Americas for people living in the Americas, but it is the darker side of modernity and the global reach of imperial capitalism. While Saldívar connected the interior periphery of Latinos, Latinas and Afro-Americans in the US with activists in British India, Manuela Boatcă (a Romanian trained as sociologist in the US and currently residing in Germany) looks at the effects and consequences of the Western colonial matrix of power in a place like Romania, ex-colony of non-Western empires (the Ottomans and the Soviets and now becoming a colony - as many others - of the European Union). Building on the metaphor center/periphery introduced by Argentinean economist Raúl Prebisch in the early 50s and developed by US

sociologist, Immanuel Wallerstein in the 70s, Boatcă reflects on the borders of Romanian principalities of Transylvania, Wallachia and Moldavia surrounded by the Habsburg, the Ottoman and the Tsarist empires. Boatcă focuses on the nineteenth century when Romania entered European modernity through the back door. She suggests an epistemic de-colonial shift by looking at the empires from the perspective of Romania rather than looking at Romania from the perspective of the empires. Centers and peripheries do not exist any more, progressive intellectuals would argue today. That is a traditional distinction of the seventies. Neo-liberalism shuffled all the cards, no more center and periphery, no more left and right. And yet, there are equally progressive intellectuals who dwell in the borders (not just of the US and Mexico!!); in the imperial/colonial borders of the modern/colonial world. These pluri-versal borders are the consequences of pluri-versal histories (e.g., India or Bolivia, Algeria or Romania, Russia or China) dealing with the global designs of Euro-American local histories.

Zilkia Janer (a cultural critic from Puerto Rico residing in the US) returns to the New World while joining the global reach of coloniality revealed by Boatcă and Madina Tlostanova: the question here is not so much the New World, as it is the question of the commercialization of nature and of food and the assault to human health in the name of science for the purpose of capital accumulation. The colonial difference here is articulated in between the 'superiority of modern transgenic seeds' and the 'sophistication of modern French cuisine' and traditional ways of harvesting (having to deal with weeds and insects) and the inferiority of world-cuisine compared with French culinary history and global image. In between, food chains like McDonald's points toward the commercialization of food disregarding human health. Janer uncovers a very important dimension of the colonial matrix of power: the variegated spectrum of food, from basic nourishment, to its transformation into the commodity of high cuisine and also as a locus of inhuman profit invocating the advances in science in the production transgenic seeds. Janer looks at food, and explains in a way the coloniality of Nature (that Escobar points out as lacking consideration within the modernity/coloniality project). Although Janer doesn't make an explicit connection, it is obvious that the direction of her argument joins the direction that Native Americans are following (Mishehuah) and the struggle for the democratization of food that Vandana Shiva argued at the end of her book on 'stolen harvests'. The fight that is currently being fought by transnational organizations such as the International Federation of Organic Agriculture Movements and Via Campesina, are a case in point.[6] The control of food supply is one of the most terrifying aspects of today's uncontrolled capitalism (e.g., Monsanto) and as such one of the most salient aspect of the reproduction of coloniality of power. De-linking, civil des-obedience and a reversal of the way production

and distribution of food is conceived are all aspect of de-colonization at large. De-linking, once again, implies work at the fringes, at the border between hegemonic and dominant forms of knowledge, of economic practices, of political demands. Using the system but doing something else, moving in different directions: peaceful civil disobedience, as Mahatma Gandhi and Martin Luther King insisted upon, toward a truly democratic organization instead of using the rhetoric of democracy to control authority by violence and war.

Madina Tlostanova (a cultural critic originally from Kabardino-Balkaria – a republic of the Russian Federation – in the Caucasus and resident of Moscow) follows suit and explores three imperial/colonial chronotopes and brings aesthetics into the conversation. Although feeling and sensing is a phenomenon common to all living organisms, the hegemonic concept of 'aesthetics' was conceptualized and exploited from the European Renaissance to the European Enlightenment. Aesthetics became a crucial component of the colonial matrix of power in the control and management of subjectivities. There is a long history of imperial looting of 'aesthetic' objects from the colonized world, as well as Western artists 'borrowing' from the colonial world (e.g. Picasso, Gauguin, etc.). But what about writers and artists who dwell in the borders of the imperial/colonial differences? What emerges from that experience is a new aesthetic, a trans-cultural aesthetic that, like in Saldívar, connects people through the worlds that have suffered, one way or another, the colonial wound. Tlostanova dwells in and thinks from the imperial/colonial differences that makes of Russia/Soviet Union—a second class empire and, consequently, in control of second class colonies—take center stage. For Tlostanova, trans-cultural aesthetics - in the imperial/colonial city chronotope - fly off the handle of writers who dwell in the cultural, linguistic, ethnic, and religious Spirit (we are using Hegel's concept of Spirit intentionally here) of the imperial/colonial in between-ness. In this regard, writers like Pamuk, Volos and Memedov are de-colonizing aesthetics, in a way parallel and complementary to the de-colonization of being and of gender, explored by Maldonado-Torres and Freya Schiwy. Tlostanova finds in the imperial/colonial borders the energy and the creativity that Kant imagined in the territory of European national communities.[7]

We assume that most readers familiar with Cultural Studies as well as with the modernity/coloniality research program, will be familiar also with Istanbul. But perhaps a little bit less with Baku, in Azerbaijan, and with Khurramabab, a fictional city in Tajikistan. On that assumption, let us indulge in some basic information that would be helpful in following Tlostanova's argument. Baku is one of the holy centers of Zoroastrianism, invaded by the Mogols and a home for the expansion of Islam after the ninth century. The city became an important commercial center after the discovery of oil in

Azerbaijan, in a very short historical period, and now in the middle of the Trans-Caucassian corridor. Khurramabab is located, by Volos, in Tajikistan. Tajik territory began to form around the ninth and tenth century and was conquered by the Mogols in the thirteenth century. Russia took control of the Tajik lands in the 1880s and 90s, but the Tajiks remained split among several administrative-political entities, and their territories were economically backward and were exploited for their raw materials. In the aftermath of the 1917 Russian Revolution, the Tajiks rebelled against Russian rule. The Red Army did not establish control over them until 1921. Tajikistan was made an autonomous republic within Uzbekistan in 1924; in 1929 it became a constituent republic of the USSR. In the 1930s canals and other irrigation projects vastly increased cultivated acreage as agriculture was more thoroughly collectivized; population also increased rapidly. Further expansion of irrigated agriculture occurred after World War II, especially in the late 1950s, as the area became increasingly important as a cotton producer. In 1978 there were anti-Russian riots in the republic and after the collapse of the Soviet Union, life for Russians in Tajikistan became difficult. Khurramabad is the scenario of several of these stories. The way that Tlostanova made sense of the logic of coloniality is by focusing on the imperial and colonial differences construed by the dominant imaginary of Western empires: the imperial differences account for the location of the Russian/Soviet and Ottoman empires in relation to Western capitalism; and the location of Azerbaijan and Tajiskistan as Russian and Soviet colonies first and independent nations-states after the collapse of the Soviet Union brings forward the colonial difference, first, in their relation to the Russian and Soviet empires and, secondly, with Western neo-liberal imperial expansion after the collapse of the Soviet Union.

Section V closes the volume with the interventions of Santiago Castro–Gómez, Walter Mignolo and María Lugones. The three articles in this section return to the very foundation of the project: the decolonization of knowledge that was articulated by Quijano in the seminal article reproduced here. Castro-Gómez returns here to one of his outstanding reflections on the 'hubris of the zero point'. Modern epistemology, Castro-Gómez proposes, was historically founded on the assumption that is obtained from a zero-point-of-observation. The formation of the modern/colonial world went hand in hand, in the sixteenth century, with theology; the eyes of God as the ultimate warranty of knowing. Secularization displaced the eyes of God for the eyes of Reason and the authority of the modern subject. The zero-point-of-observation was and continues to be, in both forms, disembodied and un-located. God is everywhere and Reason is immaterial, doesn't have color, sex, gender and it is beyond any singular memory. It is assumed, however that the memory that goes back to Greece and back to Rome and the modern

six European imperial and capitalist nations of the Atlantic world is the memory of the entire world. For that reason, the 'hubris of the zero point' is untouchable. Coloniality of knowledge is precisely the affirmation of the zero point and the success in silencing or relegating other epistemologies to a barbarian margins, a primitive past or a communist or Muslim evil. Thus, Castro-Gómez is contributing to unfold the coloniality of knowledge, and bringing its historical foundation in the sixteenth century, to its continuing implementation in the twenty-first century.

Walter Mignolo (trained in semiotics and philosophy in France; from Argentina and currently residing in the US) unfolds one of the basic assumptions of the project modernity/coloniality: the assumption that there is no modernity without coloniality, that coloniality is constitutive of modernity. That is, modernity/coloniality. Mignolo shows that while modernity is presented as the rhetoric of salvation, it hides coloniality, which is the logic of oppression and exploitation. Modernity, capitalism and coloniality are aspects of the same package of control of economy and authority, of gender and sexuality of knowledge and subjectivity. To understand how tangled up the rhetoric of modernity and logic of coloniality are with each other, the reader should consider two recent examples: that of Monsanto, a leading provider of agricultural products and solutions, while its implementation deploys a logic of control that kills all other alternatives as traditional and anti-modern. Consider former President George W. Bush's recent appeal to the United Nations to control the possibility of Iran's developing nuclear energy. The West said that to build atomic bombs in Iran endangers democracy and global peace. To implement that content of that rhetoric, the Bush administration is looking for the support of Russia, China and India in order to maintain the imperial/colonial control of authority and, consistently with neo-liberal doctrine, the control of economy. The president of Iran insists on the right of Iran to advance knowledge for the well-being and protection of the society. Iran's President Mahmoud Ahmadinejad, knows that Bush's rhetoric hides the logic of coloniality: to keep control of authority. Unlike the peasants in India and in Africa that suffer the aggression of Monsanto, their protests are not carried on by international media, Mahmoud Ahmadinejad is the chief of a State sitting on oil and making his voice heard. In any case, Monsanto and the quarrel with USA-Iran are two examples of the entanglements between the rhetoric of modernity and the logic of coloniality as it relates to the control of economy and control of authority. Finally, in 'the grammar of de-coloniality' Mignolo outlines one of the strategies, in intellectual projects and social movements confronting modernity/coloniality, unveils its hidden complicity and sustain the claim that other worlds are possible.

María Lugones (a philosopher and Latina cultural critic) closes the volume with a ground breaking article on coloniality, gender and sexuality. In her chapter, Lugones commences the important task of articulating the concept of coloniality with feminist perspectives on gender. She does so by establishing a conversation between the feminist work on intersectionality and Quijano's notion of coloniality of power,; her goal is to arrive at a conceptualization of 'the modern/colonial gender system.' In tandem with recent contributions by Native American intellectuals, and some feminist and African anthropologists, among others, on non-gendered egalitarianism and gynocentric societies, Lugones raises questions about the validity of patriarchy as an intercultural category; this is clearly the case with African societies prior to colonization by the West, for which gender was not a central organizing principle of social life, or with some Native American groups, for whom there existed a 'gynecratric spiritual plurality.' To narrow the scope of gender to the control of sex and resources, as in much Western scholarship, is itself an aspect of gender domination. The "woman" of the Western imperial/colonial experience is not to be found in non-Western civilizations before 1500. This does not mean either that non-Western societies were non-patriarchal. It just means that in non-Western societies before 1500, patriarchal or not, the concept of "woman" –that assumes a white bourgeois subject— did not exist. Lugones' contribution to the larger debate on gender and sexuality lies in her linking it with colonialty, and vice versa. In this way, Lugones mutually enriches both frameworks; she does so by looking at the inter-connections not just between race, gender, and sexuality but by placing them in the imperial construction of the modern/ colonial world and the ongoing debates not only to decolonize imperial knowledge but also, and more importantly, to generate de-colonial knowledge. Lugones thus properly brings the volume to its closure.

In summary, the volume is a show-case of almost two decades of work since the publication of Quijano's article. The project, however, did not emerge with the publication of the article but about 8 years later when a group of us (Aníbal Quijano, Fernando Coronil and Walter Mignolo, convened by Edgardo Lander, met in Montreal, in August of 1998, in two panels at the meeting of the International Sociological Association. Independently of this meeting, another one took place in Binghamton, convened by Ramón Grosfoguel and Agustin Lao-Montes around the concepts of "historical capitalism, coloniality and transmodernity." Immanuel Wallerstein, Aníbal Quijano and Enrique Dussel speaking on each of the concepts they introduced in the vocabulary of the social sciences and the humanities. These two meetings formed, by serendipity, a research, intellectual and political project known as modernity/colonialilty/decoloniality.

The volume traces also the itinerary that formed and transformed the project MCD during the past two decades. The common thread of all the

contributions is the concept of coloniality (e.g., patron colonial de poder or colonial matrix of power). The volume also shows further unfolding of the trajectory. Early on Edgardo Lander pressed the question of "nature" (which did not have a distinctive place in Quijano's article) early on[8] and Escobar comes back to it in this issue. The question of gender was also raised by Freya Schiwy (this volume) an more recently by María Lugones (this volume). Both Schiwy and Lugones saw a residue of patriarchal underpinning in the original formulation of gender and sexuality in the colonial matrix of power. On the other hand, Quijano's original article prompted the introduction of new concepts: coloniality of knowledge (Lander), geopolitics of knowledge (Mignolo), coloniality of being (Mignolo and Maldonado-Torres in this book); interculturalidad (introduced by Indigenous leaders in Ecuador and Bolivia and explored in further details by Catherine Walsh); the hubris of the zero point (Castro-Gómez in this collection) and above all, the concept of de-coloniality (common to all) that has its roots also in Quijano's foundational article formulated as "decolonization of knowledge" (Quijano, this volume). Furthermore, "coloniality" has been taken as a guided principle by scholars who were not originally associated with the project (see Boatcă, Janer and Tlostanova). And it was also picked up dialogically by Latino/as scholars and intellectuals (see Saldívar, Lugones, Maldonado-Torres).

Additionally, coloniality (e.g., colonial matrix of power) shall not be taken as a model, a theory or an object of study. Quijano's formulation is clear in this regard: it is necessary to detach oneself from the hegemonic and Eurocentered matrix of knowledge. The very concept of "coloniality" implies thinking de-colonially (and not for example, "thinking about coloniality") it is not intended to map a territory to be "studied" from the perspective of sociology, political science, economy, cultural studies or postcolonial studies. Thinking de-colonially means, precisely, to delink from thinking "disciplinarily" (e.g., sociologically, economically, anthropologically, artistically, etc.). In that regard, thinking de-colonially and the de-colonial option are not "new interpretive tools" but an-other thinking grounded in border epistemology rather than in Greek philosophy (Mignolo 2000, 313-338). Such detachment (that Mignolo explores here as "de-linking") shall be understood as one aspect of a decolonial energy, a force that permeates all the disciplines as well as common sense guiding global struggles not just "against capitalism" but toward the making of a world no longer ruled by the colonial matrix of power (Lander 2002). It is not an interdisciplinary tool but, rather, a trans-disciplinary horizon in which de-coloniality of knowledge and de-colonial knowledge places life (in general) first and institutions at the service of the regeneration of life. In terms of Evo Morales, it will amount to a horizon in which the prime concern is to well being for all rather than living better for some. The "natural" order of capital has put the cart in front

of the horse: to save institutions (the state, capitalism, democracy) define the horizon and life comes in second place. As a result, we are living in a world in which human lives are dispensable and life of the planet secondary. Bio-technology is not a solution, since it is caught in the "natural" order of capital. It aims to help in redressing current social orientations having the cart in front of the horse: institutions comes first, they should be saved (the state, capitalism, democracy,etc.) at the expenses of life, of human beings, all living organism and the planet itself. Redressing the horizon means to place life in first place and the institutions at their service. Is that simple, but of course it will not be understood or accepted by the agencies that at this point control both authority and economy. For what would be their life if not devoted to increase gain and decrease cost and to be head of a State that controls all other States in the name of international sovereignty and democracy? Life has to be sacrificed to the survival of institutions working toward the happiness of humanity at large, while destroying everything that prevents the perfection of final institutional goals.

Last but not least, missing from this volume is the significance of "trans-modernity," for the project MCD., a concept introduced and explored by Enrique Dusell.[9] Like coloniality, trans-modernity introduces a non-Eurocentric critique to Eurocentrism. It claims that "modernity" is a European narrative but the historical events that sustain are not only constituted by the internal history of Europe but of Europe and its colonial world since 1500. Clearly, the concept introduces a detour in global history: the history of Europe seen from the colonies. But it also introduces a horizon to imagine global futures: modernity can no longer be superseded within the history of Europe itself, either by postmodernity or altermodernity; in that regard, asserts and reclaims what has been denied to the non-European world: their capacity to think, to govern themselves, to prosper without the guidance of modern, post-modern or alter-modern agents and institutions. We are witnessing already the emergence of transmodern futures. Trans-modern futures today are being enacted in two directions: de-westernization (de-centering the control of economy and authority (e.g., China, India, Indonesia, the South American Union) and de-colonization (the emergence of the global political society).

## II. Locating decolonial thinking and the decolonial option within current geopolitics and scholarly and intellectual debates

Lewis Gordon closes his article on "Fanon and Development" with the following reflection:

> The ideas, many of which will unfold through years of engaged political work, need not be perfect. For in the end, it will be the hard, creative work of communities that take them on. That work is the concrete manifestation of political imagination.
>
> Fanon described this goal as setting afoot a new humanity. He knew how terrifying such an effort is, for we do live in times where such a radical break appears as no less than the end of the world. In the meantime, the task of building infrastructures for something new must be planned, and where there is some room, attempted, as we all no doubt already know, *because given the sociogenic dimension of the problem, we have no other option but to built the options on which the future our species rest.*[10]

The statement should be read in relation to Gordon's foundation of the *Caribbean Philosophical Association*, and with his project on Africana Philosophy: "that we do not have other option but to built the options on which the future of the species rest" is a line that runs throughout and connects all de-colonial projects across the globe in spite of their different local histories, languages, religions, subjectivities and temporalities on their imperial/colonial interactions with Western political, economic and cultural institutions.

The perspective presented in this volume –known until 2006 as "modernity/coloniality" and since then as "modernity/coloniality/decoloniality, or MCD—has been closely associated with researchers in a number of South America (chiefly in the Andean region), Caribbean and US locations, (see Escobar, this volume, for a description of the perspective and the groups associated with it; see also Castro-Gómez and Grosfogel, eds. 2007, for a recent statement on the perspective as a whole). It makes sense to locate this research, then, within the momentous events in contemporary (South and Central) America, the world as a whole, and in various scholarly trends.

### *a) Geopolitical locations*

This section thus reopens the debate by placing de-colonial thinking in the geopolitics of various world regions. The workshop that originated the volume of *Cultural Studies* (21/2-3, 2007) took place in May of 2004. Today, at the time of writing this new introduction to the book edition, the consequences of 9/11 have been expanding and the recent collapse of Wall Street compounded the political crisis of the US, nationally and internationally, with the economic one. The imperial control of authority and of the economy (two domains or spheres of the colonial matrix of power in the hands of the US since the end of WWII), entered a severe process of crisis.

Conversely, planetary history has been witnessing, with surprises and horrors, growing political forces acting toward de-linking from the control of authority in national and international law and from a single sources of economic planning (IMF, World Bank, US and the European Union). This includes from Islamic radicalism (labeled "terrorism" in the vocabulary of agents and institutions who enact imperial control) in a variety of forms (from suicidal bombs, to elected organizations, e.g., Hamas, Hezbollah), to radical Islamic intellectuals who are unfolding new global futures no longer "opposed" to Western modernity but on the contrary, appropriating it in order to build their own future instead of having their future mortgaged (economically, politically, subjectivity) and controlled by Western institutions and designs.

In the sphere of the economy, not only had China taken a lead in East Asian economies, but a powerful discourse emerged in South East and East Asia, convincingly arguing for a radical global shift, from five centuries of Atlantic centrality, to the Eastern Hemisphere. Building on the legacies of Lee Kuan Yew's views of capitalism with an Asian face, brought to light in the West through the much discussed interview with Fareed Zakaria, published in *Foreign Affairs* in 1994, Kishore Mahbubani has advanced strong arguments (in books, interviews, op-ed articles) describing and advocating the shift to the Western Hemisphere. London weekly *The Economist* is not enthusiastic about it.[11]. The shift to the Eastern Hemisphere doesn't mean that China will be the next "hegemon" in world affairs, as Giovanni Arrighi saw as a possibility in 1995 (the long twentieth century) and explored more recently (Arrighi 2007). It means that the unilateral control of the economy and of authority that grew out of the Atlantic economy, in the past five centuries, is being mutated into ONE global economy (that both liberals and Marxists agree to describe as "capitalism", and assign different values to it), but in a poly-centric world order.

Mahbubani's arguments on de-westernization should be taken seriously. They are powerful and convincing evidence (in other words, his arguments constitute evidence, and we are not talking about the evidence in supporting his arguments): the awareness, and the consciousness, that the West has neither the rights, nor the obligation to "develop" Asians and that Asians can think for themselves and take care of themselves, is uncontroversial and should be applauded and admired. It doesn't have to be followed by everyone though. A poly-centric world means that there is not just one UNI-versal solution but pluri-versal futures: "*The difficulty lies, not in new ideas but in detaching (de-linking) from the old ones, which ramify, for those brought up with them as most of us have been, into every corner of our minds.*"[12]

We are not advocating either that Kishore Mahbubani shall be "the guiding light" instead of, say, Milton Friedman, Giorgio Agamben, Carl Schmitt, or

Sir John Maynard Keynes. We do not think within the mind-frame of modernity, looking for the last gadget to replace the old ones. We are suggesting that the decolonization of the mind is also necessary among thinkers and doers who do not reject Western contributions to world civilizations. They only question the self-attributed legitimacy of the West, that is, its self-appointment to rule, to decide and manage the entire world. We are just saying that we have to pay close attention to the powerful articulation of players that have been reduced to the silence of the barbarians for five hundred years of Western political theology (meaning, theological and secular), in the sense Schmitt has it. We are not advocating either that Mahbubani is de-colonial or that de-colonial projects shall follow Mahbubani's lead. We are just saying that we are facing a garden of forking paths: the forced hand of neoliberal globalization to follow just one path, the Western neo-liberal path, is gone, new players are entering the game, learning from and thanking the West for what they learned. In summary, the colonial matrix of power, established in the Atlantic in the sixteenth and seventeenth centuries, transformed and expanded through five centuries, and controlled by Western imperial power, is now escaping Western imperial control. The polycentric world order is organized around the dispute for the control of the colonial matrix, which is being played out at different and interconnected levels: control and management of knowledge and subjectivity, of gender and sexuality, of authority and of the economy. You can expand each domain and see, for example, how the exhaustion of natural resources, food crisis, bio-technological dreams of "reproducing nature artificially", etc, are all new aspects of a basic imperial/colonial structure: the colonial matrix of power (see section I for more details about it).

### *b) Some scholarly contexts*

What does the decolonial option offer, and where does it fall in the spectrum of available options to imagine, think and engage in making global futures? Let's look first at disciplinary formations and dissenting world views. Where does modernity/coloniality research program and de-colonial thinking stand——vis-à-vis postcolonial studies (or postcoloniality), Marxism and cultural studies? These are commonly asked questions. The reader will find some answers to these questions as she reads through. But let us put three flags that would be helpful in looking for answers to these questions. The de-colonial option is an option among existing ones both in the academy and in the spheres of political theory, political economy, and social practice. We will limit ourselves here to sketch the de-colonial option in the academy. It will require another volume to address the de-colonial option in the terrain of political theory and economy. However, the current situation in Bolivia,

under the leadership of Evo Morales, and the discourse that is being constructed there, clearly shows the potential of the de-colonial option in economy and politics.[13]

The radical difference between post-colonial theory and pos-coloniality in general—on the one hand—and de-colonial projects, on the other, lies in the genealogy of the thoughts and experiences of the scholars and intellectuals engaged in each of them, and in which each project finds its energy and its vision. The volume asserts the end of epistemic ownership and disciplinary private properties. It rejects the principle of "who was the first in saying or doing what", the principle of "newness" that so much contributed to colonizing knowledges and beings.

Post-coloniality emerged from the extension of Michel Foucault, Antonio Gramsci, Jacques Derrida and Jacques Lacan to the colonization of Palestine by Israel, and its Oriental underpinning (Edward Said) and to the post-colonial situation of India as an ex-colony of the British Empire (Ranajit Guha, Homi Bhabha and Gayatri Spivak). We (the participant members of MCD) do not claim to be "first" although we highlight the de-colonial projects that emerged in intellectual debates from the critical foundation established, in Latin America, by José Carlos Mariátegui, in Perú (in the 1920s), and by dependency theory and philosophy of liberation, in the 70's, and that spread all over Latin America. We are not "first" (a claim that reproduced modern chronology rather than de-colonial geographies), we just *are* in a different track in tracing de-colonial options to globalization, since 1500. Once the foundation of the de-colonial project emerged (as Quijano states in the article reprinted here: de-colonization as epistemological reconstitution), the history of de-colonial thinking can be traced back. And we find, in that genealogy, two pillars: individual thinkers and activists like Waman Puma de Ayala in colonial Peru, Ottabah Cugoano, in British Caribbean and then in London, in the eighteen century; Mahatma Gandhi in nineteenth-twentieth century India; Amilcar Cabral in the Portuguese colonies of Africa; Aimé Césaire and Frantz Fanon in the French Caribbean; W.E.B Dubois and Gloria Anzaldúa in the US. On the other hand, countless uprising and social movements that, today, have in the Zapatistas and the indigenous movements in Ecuador, Bolivia as well as Indigenous activists in New Zealand, Australia, Canada and the US. a continuous source of inspiration.

The difference between de-colonial thinking and Marxism has been laid out by Quijano in several places, but chiefly in Quijano (2000). [18] In relation to our previous argument, Marxism is a critical and liberating project dwelling in the local history of Europe, in a relatively homogeneous community where workers and factory owners belonged to the same ethnicity and, therefore, Marxism relied on class oppression and the exploitation of labor. However, as European economy and political theory expanded and conquered the world,

the tools that Marx offered in the analysis of capital are of course useful beyond Europe. However, subjectivities and knowledge in the colonial and ex-colonial world are as important as are divergent from European experiences. From those subjectivities, experience, religions, histories, everyday life, emerged border thinking and de-colonial liberating projects. Marxism is then subsumed and incorporated into parallel but different projects. De-colonial thinking highlights racial discrimination (the hierarchy of human beings, since the sixteenth century, that justified economic and political subordination of people of color and women) and of course also in class exploitation, in the sense that "class" acquired in Europe after the Industrial Revolution. In the colonies workers are colonial subjects of color. In the heart of the empire (Western Europe and the US), workers are the racialized minorities. Certainly, neo-liberalism is bringing the "celebration" to the white middle class in the US, Germany, and elsewhere and of course, more than ever, to the once existing middle class in some ex-colonial countries. Marxism and de-colonial projects point toward the same direction, but each has quite different agendas. De-colonial projects cannot be subsumed under Marxist ideology; Marxism should be subsumed under de-colonial projects. Why should it be like that? Look at the directionality of the coloniality of power (e.g., the colonial matrix of power), and you will soon realize that Marxism would be an imperial ideology from the left, by imagining that Marxism, instead of Neo-Liberalism or Islamism a la Bin-Laden, is the good abstract universal for the entire humanity.

Last but not least, the differences between Cultural Studies and de-colonial projects lie—like in the case of postcoloniality—in the genealogy of thoughts that anchor and nourish each project.[14] The historical experience and the history of Marxism that brought Cultural Studies to England in the late fifties and early sixties had a parallel in Argentina. Dissidents of the Communist Party, following the lead of Antonio Gramsci, founded *Pasado and Presente* (1963-73)). The founders of the journal (José Aricó, Oscar del Barco, "Toto" Smuchler) did not come up with an institutional name but with a political project of which *Punto deVista* (founded in 1974 and edited since the seventies by Beatriz Sarlo, currently still alive and well), was a main vehicle. When a Latin American version of Cultural Studies emerged in the horizon, with the works of Néstor García Canclini and Jesús Martín Barbero, among others, this was a different project. This project focused on cultural production, for instance, in the media, urban popular cultures, and the technological transformations in Latin America. This important critical work remained within the perspective of modernity, even if a peripheral one as in the case of Latin America. The modernity/coloniality research program, and its necessary consequence, de-coloniality places itself in another, different arena: on the darker side of modernity. De-colonial projects dwell in the borders,

are anchored in double consciousness, in mestiza consciousness. It is a colonial subaltern epistemology in and of the global and the variegated faces of the colonial wound inflicted by five hundred years of the historical foundation modernity as a weapon of imperial/colonial global expansion of Western capitalism.

Beyond the academy, de-colonial options are being enacted by indigenous as well as by social movements emerging in the process not just of being-anti imperial, but of undoing the logic of coloniality and imagining de-colonial societies. This orientation informs to some extent the government of Evo Morales confronted by the landowners of the low land and in tension with Marxists orientations within his government. De-colonial thinking has been already engaged by Iranian intellectuals reunited around the book series *Decolonial Studies, Postcolonial Horizons*, published by Pluto Press. In the indigenous realm,world wide, from the Americas to New Zealand and Australia the orientation is well defined. Aymara intellectual Marcelo Fernández-Osco outlined the principles underlying the thoughts and actions of indigenous people. In a nutshell:

> [...] indigenous protests and mobilizations are not merely about opposition or resistance to specific policies or political leaders. Rather, they express an indigenous episteme, a system of understanding the world that has a completely different basis for thinking about socio-political relations and practices, based on a model of horizontal solidarity that extends not only to all humans but also to non-humans in the natural and cosmological world. In contrast, mainstream knowledge, rooted in European colonial understandings of the world, is structured along vertical, hierarchical lines. That is, certain groups of people and certain ways of acting and thinking are deemed to be superior to others. This difference is the key to understanding Andean politics, because it is in the indigenous episteme that the concept of (an) other autonomy is located. The versions of autonomy currently understood in mainstream politics (and promoted by nation-states) provide indigenous groups limited opportunities for decision making but only within the same body of laws that existed before. This notion of autonomy for Indigenous peoples places them under the same subjugation that they have been experiencing since colonization.[15]

But, above all, de-colonial options is what have informed the politics of liberation of the so called "Third World" after WWII. Today, the focus of de-colonial thinking is no longer sending the colonizers home but to de-link, in thought and action, in thinking and doing, from the colonial matrix of power. *La vía campesina* as well as the tireless work of Vandana Shiva are other cases in which de-colonial thinking informs the analytic of globalization and the

horizon for future non-imperial societies (see Escobar's "Afterword" to this volume for more detail).

## III. Towards genealogies of decolonial thoughts and practices of decoloniality

The concept of 'decoloniality' broadens the project of critical thinking (rather than critical theory, old or new) in various ways. De-colonial projects are, of course, constitutive of modernity and of transforming modernity. Intra Euro-American critical thought, however, while seeing the consequences of coloniality on subalternized peoples, is not well placed to understand, or even see, the decolonial impetus as a challenge to dominant modernities. To achieve this aim, as this volume suggests, requires of a veritable 'de-colonial turn,' one that highlights and makes possible epistemic decolonization, opening up to a *pensamiento otro*, an-other-thought.[17]

De-colonial thought has a dense planetary history; it does not manifest itself only in South, Central America and the Caribbean, but also in the US and in Canada. De-colonial thinking, sensing and doing are a common thread around world, including now the European Union and the US who are being "invaded" by the force of immigration that Europe and the US created. Constructing de-colonial projects at the level of critical thinking thus entails three efforts: first, to construct genealogies of decolonial thought in many world locations; this was already hinted a with references to Waman Puma de Ayala, Ottabah Cugoano, Gandhi, the Caribbean thinkers of liberation like Césaire and Fanon, W.E.B. Dubois, and Anzaldúa (see also Mignolo 2008). But this is just the tip of the iceberg; the task is just beginning, and this volume is an invitation to engage in this mapping of de-colonial turns world-wide and at many moments of history, with attention to situations of coloniality of knowledge, gender, nature, and being. The result at this first level would be an archive of decolonial texts, words, events, memories, narrations.

Second, it is important to look at concrete experiences and practices of decoloniality going on today world wide. As we mentioned, MCD means that modernity, coloniality, and decoloniality are world-wide affairs – decoloniality meaning also the existence of something other-than-modern, at least in the sense of dominant Euro-modernities. Even if there might be subjects who, because of their historical location within the MCD complex are potentially more directly located on the side of de-colonial experiences, it is important to avoid going back to an essentialized notion of agency.

Third, to the extent that social movements –as some current Central/South American and Caribbean experiences suggest—might be more likely to articulate decolonial projects, it is crucial that we pay attention to them,

that is, that we think with them theoretically and politically. More clearly than ever before, social movement activist are sophisticated knowledge producers, like where before Gandhi, Césaire, Fanon, Amilcar Cabral, Dolores Caguango, among many others (Patzi Paco 2008; Nina Pacari 2008; Escobar 2008). This volume is also aimed at conveying the importance of thinking within, and in the perspective of, these movements.

## Notes

1 Enrique Dussel's critical positions in his unfolding of philosophy of liberation, are summarized in 'Critical Theory, Poststructuralism and the Philosophy of Liberation' by Douglas Kellner (2001) and Santiago Castro-Gómez (2000). Critical Theory edited by David Rasmussen (2004) is a good case of regional experiences propelled globally as if what is good for Germany and Europe will be good for Korea and Tanzanía. The logic is the same than the logic of IMF and World Bank, only the content differs. Valuable as it is, this volume makes necessary other kinds of theories, given the extreme Eurocentrism to which Horkheimer has been taken. This volume portraits indeed a regional and particular view of critical theory (narrowly focused in the history, experience and *existential Europaen* as it "critical theory" would have an universal import. A good example also of coloniality of knowledge and imperial designs in the academy. Notice the title: "THE Handbook..."

2 Luis Mates conceptualizes the singularity of the Jewish experience in a way similar to the ways, for instance, Lewis Gordon does it with the Africana experience and Gloria Anzaldúa and Jacqueline Martinez with the Chicana and lesbian experience. Common to all three is the politic of identity rather than identity politics. 'It matters little, says Mates, that the thinkers who pursue this path (the Jewish question) be Jewish. What matters is their experience as Jews' (p. 4). Further on he further specifies: 'For Emmanuel Levinas [...] 'to be Jewish in our time means not just believing in Moses and the prophets: it means recovering the right to judge history, recovering the place of consciousness that affirms itself unconditionally (p. 107) (Mates 2004; Slabodsky 2009); Gordon (2003) and Martinez (2000).

3 See Dussel (2002) and Lander (2002).

4 Similar arguments can be developed for many other key words in contemporary life. Take 'democracy' for example. Drives toward democratic societies are not a privilege of Europe or the US. France or the US have their concepts and application of the word based on their own histories, subjectivities, economy and the political theories that emerged therein. Democracy means a different thing in Bolivia and in Palestine,

although they are all striving for equality. And in Bolivia and Palestine, equality means to overcome the imperial violence and domination of Western Europe and the US, for example.

5 Quijano continued to refine and clarify his foundational statement throughout the nineties. Two substantial pieces are 2000a and 2000b.

6 Shiva (2000). For the International Federation of Food Suply http://www.ifoam.org/about_ifoam/index.html; and for La via campesina see http://viacampesina.org/en/index.php; for Native Americans struggle in the same direction, Devon Abbot Mishehuah, 'Decolonizing our Diets by Recovering our Ancestor's Garden', http://muse.jhu.edu/journals/american_indian_quarterly/v027/27.3mihesuah.html.

7 Tlostanova (2003) has developed this argument and showed that an-other-aesthetic is possible and necessary beyond, next and countering Kant's.

8 Lander (2002),

9 See Enrique Dussel's article launching the concept of "transmodernity" ( Dussel,1995). This article, originally published in 1992, became next to Quijano's in this volume, a basic concept in the project MCD. See also Dussel (2002). For an overview and the links between coloniality and transmodernity, Grosfóguel (2008)..

10 Lewis Gordon (2004).

11 Mahbubani (2008). See also, in constrast with Mabhbubani, the special section of *The Economist,* http://www.economist.com/books/displaystory.cfm?story_id=10640560

12 John Maynard Keynes used as epigraph by Mahbubani. The argument that follows the epigraph shows that Keynes is a starting point to quickly depart from it; http://www.npr.org/templates/story/story.php?storyId=90132165

13 see, for instance, http://www.counterpunch.org/mignolo05082006.html

14 See Walter D. Mignolo (2003).

15 Marcelo Fernández-Osco (2008). For the link between decolonial knowledge and social transformation, see the classic book by Linda T. Smith (1999). .

17 There is notable video reflecting on video-making as political doing (which is the same assumption that animates decolonial thinking), authored by Grzinick and Smid 2008.

18 For current debates see the special section, *Palestra*, in Revista Tabula Rasa, edited by Heriberto Cairo (2008)

# Aníbal Quijano

## COLONIALITY AND MODERNITY/RATIONALITY

With the conquest of the societies and the cultures which inhabit what today is called Latin America, began the constitution of a new world order, culminating, five hundred years later, in a global power covering the whole planet. This process implied a violent concentration of the world's resources under the control and for the benefit of a small European minority – and above all, of its ruling classes. Although occasionally moderated when faced with the revolt of the dominated, this process has continued ever since. But, now during the current crisis, such concentration is being realized with a new impetus, in a way perhaps even more violent and on a much larger, global scale. The 'Western' European dominators and their Euro-North American descendants are still the principal beneficiaries, together with the non-European part of the world not quite former European colonies, Japan mainly, and mainly their ruling classes. The exploited and the dominated of Latin America and Africa are the main victims.

A relation of direct, political, social and cultural domination was established by the Europeans over the conquered of all continents. This domination is known as a specific Eurocentered colonialism. In its political, above all the formal and explicit aspect, this colonial domination has been defeated in the large majority of the cases. America was the first stage of that defeat, and afterwards, since the Second World War, Asia and Africa. Thus the Eurocentered colonialism, in the sense of a formal system of political domination by Western European societies over others seems a question of the past. Its successor, Western imperialism, is an association of social interests between the dominant groups ('social classes' and/or 'ethnies') of countries with unequally articulated power, rather than an imposition from the outside.

However, that specific colonial structure of power produced the specific social discriminations which later were codified as 'racial', 'ethnic', 'anthropological' or 'national', according to the times, agents, and populations involved. These intersubjective constructions, product of Eurocentered colonial domination were even assumed to be 'objective', 'scientific', categories, then of a historical significance. That is, as natural phenomena, not referring to the history of power. This power structure was, and still is, the framework within which operate the other social relations of classes or estates.

In fact, if we observe the main lines of exploitation and social domination on a global scale, the main lines of world power today, and the distribution of

resources and work among the world population, it is very clear that the large majority of the exploited, the dominated, the discriminated against, are precisely the members of the 'races', 'ethnies', or 'nations' into which the colonized populations, were categorized in the formative process of that world power, from the conquest of America and onward.

In the same way, in spite of the fact that political colonialism has been eliminated, the relationship between the European – also called 'Western' – culture, and the others, continues to be one of colonial domination. It is not only a matter of the subordination of the other cultures to the European, in an external relation; we have also to do with a colonization of the other cultures, albeit in differing intensities and depths. This relationship consists, in the first place, of a colonization of the imagination of the dominated; that is, it acts in the interior of that imagination, in a sense, it is a part of it.

In the beginning colonialism was a product of a systematic repression, not only of the specific beliefs, ideas, images, symbols or knowledge that were not useful to global colonial domination, while at the same time the colonizers were expropriating from the colonized their knowledge, specially in mining, agriculture, engineering, as well as their products and work. The repression fell, above all, over the modes of knowing, of producing knowledge, of producing perspectives, images and systems of images, symbols, modes of signification, over the resources, patterns, and instruments of formalized and objectivised expression, intellectual or visual. It was followed by the imposition of the use of the rulers' own patterns of expression, and of their beliefs and images with reference to the supernatural. These beliefs and images served not only to impede the cultural production of the dominated, but also as a very efficient means of social and cultural control, when the immediate repression ceased to be constant and systematic.

The colonizers also imposed a mystified image of their own patterns of producing knowledge and meaning. At first, they placed these patterns far out of reach of the dominated. Later, they taught them in a partial and selective way, in order to co-opt some of the dominated into their own power institutions. Then European culture was made seductive: it gave access to power. After all, beyond repression, the main instrument of all power is its seduction. Cultural Europeanisation was transformed into an aspiration. It was a way of participating and later to reach the same material benefits and the same power as the Europeans: viz, to conquer nature – in short for 'development'. European culture became a universal cultural model. The imaginary in the non-European cultures could hardly exist today and, above all, reproduce itself outside of these relations.

The forms and the effects of that cultural coloniality have been different as regards to times and cases. In Latin America, the cultural repression and the colonization of the imaginary were accompanied by a massive and gigantic extermination of the natives, mainly by their use as expendable labor force, in

addition to the violence of the conquest and the diseases brought by Europeans. Between the Aztec- Maya-Caribbean and the Tawantinsuyana (or Inca) areas, about 65 million inhabitants were exterminated in a period of less than 50 years. The scale of this extermination was so huge that it involved not only a demographic catastrophe, but also the destruction of societies and cultures. The cultural repression and the massive genocide together turned the previous high cultures of America into illiterate, peasant subcultures condemned to orality; that is, deprived of their own patterns of formalized, objectivised, intellectual, and plastic or visual expression. Henceforth, the survivors would have no other modes of intellectual and plastic or visual formalized and objectivised expressions, but through the cultural patterns of the rulers, even if subverting them in certain cases to transmit other needs of expression. Latin America is, without doubt, the most extreme case of cultural colonization by Europe.

In Asia and in the Middle East, the high cultures could never be destroyed with such intensity and profundity. But they were nevertheless placed in a subordinate relation not only in the European view, but also in the eyes of their own bearers. Through the political, military and technological power of its foremost societies, European or Western culture imposed its paradigmatic image and its principal cognitive elements as the norm of orientation on all cultural development, particularly the intellectual and the artistic. That relationship consequently became a constitutive part of the conditions of reproduction of those societies and cultures that were pushed into Europeanisation of everything or in part.

In Africa, cultural destruction was certainly much more intensive than in Asia, but less than in America. Nor did the Europeans there succeed in the complete destruction of the patterns of expression, in particular of objectification and visual formalization. What the Europeans did was to deprive Africans of legitimacy and recognition in the global cultural order dominated by European patterns. The former was confined to the category of the 'exotic'. That is, doubtless, what is manifested, for example, in the utilization of the products of African plastic expression as motive, starting-point, source of inspiration for the art of Western or Europeanized African artists, but not as a mode of artistic expression of its own, of a rank equivalent to the European norm. And that exactly identifies a colonial view.

Coloniality, then, is still the most general form of domination in the world today, once colonialism as an explicit political order was destroyed. It doesn't exhaust, obviously, the conditions nor the modes of exploitation and domination between peoples. But it hasn't ceased to be, for 500 years, their main framework. The colonial relations of previous periods probably did not produce the same consequences, and, above all, they were not the corner stone of any global power.

## 'Race' and coloniality of power

Coloniality of power was conceived together with America and Western Europe, and with the social category of 'race' as the key element of the social classification of colonized and colonizers. Unlike in any other previous experience of colonialism, the old ideas of superiority of the dominant, and the inferiority of dominated under European colonialism were mutated in a relationship of biologically and structurally superior and inferior.[1]

The process of Eurocentrification of the new world power in the following centuries gave way to the imposition of such a 'racial' criteria to the new social classification of the world population on a global scale. So, in the first place, new social identities were produced all over the world: 'whites', 'Indians, 'Negroes', 'yellows', 'olives', using physiognomic traits of the peoples as external manifestations of their 'racial' nature. Then, on that basis the new geocultural identities were produced: European, American, Asiatic, African, and much later, Oceania. During European colonial world domination, the distribution of work of the entire world capitalist system, between salaried, independent peasants, independent merchants, and slaves and serfs, was organized basically following the same 'racial' lines of global social classification, with all the implications for the processes of nationalization of societies and states, and for the formation of nation-states, citizenship, democracy and so on, around the world. Such distribution of work in the world capitalist system began to change slowly with the struggles against European colonialism, especially after the First World War, and with the changing requirements of capitalism itself. But distribution of work is by no means finished, since Eurocentered coloniality of power has proved to be longer lasting than Eurocentered colonialism. Without it, the history of capitalism in Latin America and other related places in the world can hardly be explained.[2]

So, coloniality of power is based upon 'racial' social classification of the world population under Eurocentered world power. But coloniality of power is not exhausted in the problem of 'racist' social relations. It pervaded and modulated the basic instances of the Eurocentered capitalist colonial/modern world power to become the cornerstone of this coloniality of power.

## Eurocentrism, cultural coloniality and modernity/rationality

During the same period as European colonial domination was consolidating itself, the cultural complex known as European modernity/rationality was being constituted. The intersubjective universe produced by the entire Eurocentered capitalist colonial power was elaborated and formalized by the Europeans and established in the world as an exclusively European product and

as a universal paradigm of knowledge and of the relation between humanity and the rest of the world. Such confluence between coloniality and the elaboration of rationality/modernity was not in anyway accidental, as is shown by the very manner in which the European paradigm of rational knowledge was elaborated. In fact, the coloniality of power had decisive implications in the constitution of the paradigm, associated with the emergence of urban and capitalist social relations, which in their turn could not be fully explained outside colonialism and coloniality particularly not as far as Latin America is concerned. The decisive weight of coloniality in the constitution of the European paradigm of modernity/rationality is clearly revealed in the actual crisis of that cultural complex. Examining some of the basic questions of that crisis will help to illuminate the problem.

## The question of the production of knowledge

For a start, in the current crisis of the European paradigm of rational knowledge, the latter's fundamental presupposition is questioned: vis. knowledge as a product of a subject-object relation. Apart from the problems of validation of knowledge implied, that presupposition raises other problems worthy of a brief presentation here.

First, in that presupposition, the 'subject' is a category referring to the isolated individual because it constitutes itself in itself and for itself, in its discourse and in its capacity of reflection. The Cartesian 'cogito, ergo sum', means exactly that. Second, the 'object' is a category referring to an entity not only different from the 'subject'! individual, but external to the latter by its nature. Third, the 'object' is also identical to itself because it is constituted by 'properties' which give it its identity and define it, i.e., they demarcate it and at the same time position it in relation to the other 'objects'.

What is in question in this paradigm is, firstly, the individual and individualist character of the 'subject', which like every half-truth falsifies the problem by denying intersubjectivity and social totality as the production sites of all knowledge. Secondly, the idea of 'object' is incompatible with the results of current scientific research, according to which the 'properties' are modes and times of a given field of relations. Therefore there is not much room for an idea of identity as ontologically irreducible originality outside the field of relations. Thirdly, the externality of the relations between the 'subject' and the 'object', founded on differences of nature, is not only an arbitrary exaggeration of the differences, since current research rather leads to the discovery that there exists a deeper communication structure in the universe. Much more important and decisive, is that in such a cognitive perspective it is implied a new radical dualism: divine reason and nature. The 'subject' is

bearer of 'reason', while the 'object', is not only external to it, but different nature. In fact, it is 'nature'.

One can, of course, recognize in the idea of 'subject' as an isolated individual, an element and an instance of the process of liberation of the individual with respect to the adscriptive social structures that imprisoned it in Europe. The latter condemned the individual to one single place and social role during its entire life, as happens in all societies with rigidly fixed hierarchies sustained by violence and by ideologies and corresponding imagery. This was the case of the premodern European cultures/societies. That liberation was a social and cultural struggle associated with the emergence of social relations of capital and ofurban life. But, on the other hand, that proposal is today inadmissible in the current field of knowledge. The differentiated individual subjectivity is real', but it is not an entity, so it doesn't exist only *vis-a-vis* itself or by itself. It exists as a differentiated part, but not separated, of an intersubjectivity or intersubjective dimension of social relationship. Every individual discourse, or reflection, remits to a structure of intersubjectivity. The former is constituted in and vis a vis the latter. Knowledge in this perspective is an intersubjective relation for the purpose of something, not a relation between an isolated subjectivity, and that something.

Probably it is not accidental that knowledge was considered then in the same way as property – as a relation between one individual and something else. The same mental mechanism underlies both ideas at the point when modern society was emerging. Nevertheless, property, like knowledge, is a relation between people for the purpose of something, not a relation between an individual and something. These phenomena differ in that the property relation exists in a material as well as in an intersubjective manner; knowledge, on the other hand, only as an intersubjective relationship.

It seems, then, that one can demonstrate the association between individualism/dualism and the European social and cultural conflicts at the time when the main European paradigm of rationality was elaborated. But in that individualism/dualism there is another component, the explanation of which is not exhausted in the internal context of Europe: the 'other' is totally absent; or is present, can be present, only in an 'objectivised' mode.

The radical absence of the 'other' not only postulates an atomistic image of social existence in general; that is, it denies the idea of the social totality. As European colonial practice was to show, the paradigm also made it possible to omit every reference to any other 'subject' outside the European context, i.e., to make invisible the colonial order as totality, at the same moment as the very idea of Europe was establishing itself precisely in relation to the rest of the world being colonized. The emergence of the idea of the 'West' or of 'Europe', is an admission of identity – that is, of relations with other cultural experiences, of differences with other cultures. But, to that 'European' or 'Western' perception in full formation, those differences were admitted

primarily above all as inequalities in the hierarchical sense. And such inequalities are perceived as being of nature: only European culture is rational, it can contain 'subjects' – the rest are not rational, they cannot be or harbor 'subjects'. As a consequence, the other cultures are different in the sense that they are unequal, in fact inferior, by nature. They only can be 'objects' ofknowledge or/and of domination practices. From that perspective, the relation between European culture and the other cultures was established and has been maintained, as a relation between 'subject' and 'object'. It blocked, therefore, every relation of communication, of interchange of knowledge and of modes of producing knowledge between the cultures, since the paradigm implies that between 'subject' and 'object' there can be but a relation of externality. Such a mental perspective, enduring as practice for five hundred years, could only have been the product of a relation of coloniality between Europe and the rest of the world. In other terms, the European paradigm of rational knowledge, was not only elaborated in the context of, but as part of, a power structure that involved the European colonial domination over the rest of the world. This paradigm expressed, in a demonstrable sense, the coloniality of that power structure.

As has been widely discussed, especially since the Second World War, the formation and the development of certain disciplines, such as Ethnology and Anthropology, have always shown that kind of 'subject-object' relations between the 'Western' culture and the rest. By definition, the other cultures are the 'object' of study. Such studies about the Western cultures and societies are virtually non existeni except as ironical parodies ('The ritual among the Nacirema' – a anagram of 'American' – is a typical example).

## The question of totality in knowledge

In spite of its absence in the Cartesian paradigm, the intellectual necessity of the idea of totality, especially in relation to social reality was present in the European debate; early on in the Iberian countries (Victoria, Suárez) and in the preservation of power defended by the Church and the Crown, and in France somewhat later (eighteenth century), and then already as a key element of social criticism and of alternative social proposals. Above all, from Saint-Simon, the idea of social totality was spread together with proposals of revolutionary social change, in confrontation with the atomistic perspective of social existence then predominant among the empiricists and among the adherents of the existing social and political order. In the twentieth century, totality became a perspective and a category generally admitted in scientific investigations – especially those about society.

European-Western rationality/modernity is constituted not only in a disputatious dialogue with the church and with religion, but also in the very

process of restructuration of power, on the one hand, in capitalist and urban social relations and nation-states; and, on the other, in the colonization of the rest of the world. This was probably, not divorced from the circumstance that the idea of social totality was developed according to an organicist image, which led to adopting a reductionist vision of reality.

In fact, that perspective was certainly useful to introduce and to fix the idea of social totality, i.e., society. But it was also instrumental in making the same with two other ideas: one, society as a structure of functional relations among each and every one of the parts, and therefore linked to the action of one sole logic, and therefore, a closed totality. It led later to a systemic idea of totality in structural- functionalism. The other idea was society as an organic structure, where the parts are related according to the same rules of hierarchy between the organs, as the image we have of every organism, and in particular the human one. Where there exists a part ruling the rest (the brain) – though it cannot expunge them in order to exist – the rest (in particular the extremities) cannot exist without being subordinately related to the ruling part of the organism.

It is an image diffused with the enterprise and the relations between entrepreneurs and workers, prolonging the legend of Menenius Agrippa's ingenious discourse in the beginning of the Roman Republic, which was to dissuade the first strikers in history: the owners are the brain, and the workers are the arms which form society together with the rest of the body. Without the brain, the arms would be meaningless, and without the latter the brain could not exist. Both are necessary in order to keep the rest of the body alive and healthy without which neither the brain nor the arms could exist. Kautsky' proposal, adopted by Lenin, is a variant of this image, where the proletarians are unable by themselves to elaborate their class-consciousness, and the bourgeois intelligentsia and/or the petite bourgeoisie are the ones who have to teach it to them. Not by accident Lenin explicitly argued already in his polemic with the Russian Populists ('Who are the Friends of the People'), that society is an organic totality. In Latin America, the image has been used repeatedly. Recently, for instance, by Jaime Paz Zamora, in a journalist interview, referring to the relation between the political parties and the trade unions, between the intellectuals and the workers in Bolivia: the parties are the head, the unions are the feet. This idea frequently impregnates the practices of most of the political parties and their popular 'bases'.

This organicist concept of social totality, of society, is not incompatible with the general paradigm of knowledge as a subject-object relation – nor its systemic variant. They are an alternative option in the atomistic perspective of reality, but they sustain themselves in the same paradigm. However, during the ninetennth century and a great part of the twentieth, social criticism and the proposals of social change could be propped up by the organic view, because the latter made manifest the existence of power as articulator of

society. It thus contributed to establishing and to debating the question of power in society.

On the other hand, those organicist ideas, imply the presupposition of an historically homogenous totality, in spite of the fact that the order articulated by colonialism was not homogenous. Hence, the colonized part was not, at bottom, included in that totality. As is well known, in the Europe of the Enlightenment the categories of' humanity' and 'society' did not extended to the non-Western peoples, or only in a formal way, in the sense that such recognition had no practical effects. In any case, in accord with the organic image of reality, the ruling part, the brain of the total organism, was Europe, and in every colonized part of the world, the Europeans. The well-known claptrap that the colonized peoples were the 'white mans' burden' (Kipling), is directly associated with that image.

In this way, finally, the ideas of totality, which elaborated an image of society as a closed structure articulated in a hierarchic order with functional relations between its parts, presupposed a unique historical logic to the historical totality, and a rationality consisting in the subjection of every part to that unique total logic. This leads to conceiving society as a macro-historical subject, endowed with a historical rationality, with a lawfulness that permits predictions of the behavior of the whole and of all its part, as well as the direction and the finality of its development in time. The ruling part of the totality incarnated, in some way, that historical logic, with respect to the colonial world – i.e. Europe. Not surprisingly then, history was conceived as a evolutionary continuum from the primitive to the civilized; from the traditional to the modern; from the savage to the rational; from pro-capitalism to capitalism, etc. And Europe thought of itself as the mirror of the future of all the other societies and cultures; as the advanced form of the history of the entire species. What does not cease to surprise, however, is that Europe succeeded in imposing that 'mirage' upon the practical totality of the cultures that it colonized; and, much more, that this chimera is still so attractive to so many.

## The epistemological reconstitution: de-colonization

The idea of totality in general is today questioned and denied in Europe, not only by the perennial empiricists, but also by an entire intellectual community that calls itself postmodernist. In fact, in Europe, the idea of totality is a product of colonial/modernity. And it is demonstrable, as we have seen above, that the European ideas of totality led to theoretical reductionism and to the metaphysics of a macro-historical subject. Moreover, such ideas have been associated with undesirable political practices, behind a dream of the total rationalization of society.

It is not necessary, however, to reject the whole idea of totality in order to divest oneself of the ideas and images with which it was elaborated within European colonial/modernity. What is to be done is something very different: to liberate the production of knowledge, reflection, and communication from the pitfalls of European rationality/modernity.

Outside the 'West', virtually in all known cultures, every cosmic vision, every image, all systematic production of knowledge is associated with a perspective of totality. But in those cultures, the perspective of totality in knowledge includes the acknowledgement of the heterogeneity of all reality; of the irreducible, contradictory character of the latter; of the legitimacy, i.e., the desirability, of the diverse character of the components of all reality – and therefore, of the social. The idea of social totality, then, not only does not deny, but depends on the historical diversity and heterogeneity of society, of every society. In other words, it not only does not deny, but it requires the idea of an 'other' – diverse, different. That difference does not necessarily imply the unequal nature of the 'other' and therefore the absolute externality of relations, nor the hierarchical inequality nor the social inferiority of the other. The differences are not necessarily the basis of domination. At the same time – and because of that – historical-cultural heterogeneity implies the co-presence and the articulation of diverse historical 'logic' around one of them, which is hegemonic but in no way unique. In this way, the road is closed to all reductionism, as well as to the metaphysics of an historical macro- subject capable of its own rationality and of historical teleology, of which individuals and specific groups, classes for instance, would hardly be carriers or missionaries.

The critique of the European paradigm of rationality/modernity is indispensable – even more, urgent. But it is doubtful if the criticism consists of a simple negation of all its categories; of the dissolution of reality in discourse; of the pure negation of the idea and the perspective of totality in cognition. It is necessary to extricate oneself from the linkages between rationality/modernity and coloniality, first of all, and definitely from all power which is not constituted by free decisions made by free people. It is the instrumentalisation of the reasons for power, of colonial power in the first place, which produced distorted paradigms of knowledge and spoiled the liberating promises of modernity. The alternative, then, is clear: the destruction of the coloniality of world power. First of all, epistemological decolonization, as decoloniality, is needed to clear the way for new intercultural communication, for an interchange of experiences and meanings, as the basis of another rationality which may legitimately pretend to some universality. Nothing is less rational, finally, than the pretension that the specific cosmic vision of a particular ethnie should be taken as universal rationality, even if such an ethnie is called Western Europe because this is actually pretend to impose a provincialism as universalism.

The liberation of intercultural relations from the prison of coloniality also implies the freedom of all peoples to choose, individually or collectively, such relations: a freedom to choose between various cultural orientations, and, above all, the freedom to produce, criticize, change, and exchange culture and society. This liberation is, part of the process of social liberation from all power organized as inequality, discrimination, exploitation, and as domination.

## Notes

Translated from the Spanish original by Sonia Therborn. This essay was originally published in *Globalizations and Modernities. Experiences, Perspectives and Latin America*, Stockholm, FRN-Report, 99: 5, 1.

1 Here is not the place for a more detailed discussion on the origins of the idea of 'race'. See Quijano (1992).

2 As for Latin America, see Quijano (1993).

## References

Quijano, Anibal (1992) 'Raza, Etnia y Nacion: Cuestiones Abiertas', in *Jose CarlosMariateguiyEuropa*, ed. Roland Forgues, La otracaradelDescubrimiento, Liina, Amauta, Peru.

——(1993) 'America Latina en Ia Economia Mundial', in *Problemas dcl Desarrollo, Revista del Instituto de Investigaciones de Ia Facultad de Econornja*, UNAM, vol. XXIV, no. 95, Mexico.

**Arturo Escobar**

# WORLDS AND KNOWLEDGES OTHERWISE[1]

## The Latin American modernity/coloniality research program

### Introduction: *Cruzando Fronteras* and the borders of thought

*Cruzando Fronteras*, the timely organizing theme for the 2002 CEISAL Congress celebrated in Amsterdam on 3–6 July, sought to signal, and rethink, the ever increasing relevance of 'borders' to the construction of political, social, and cultural imaginaries from, and about, Latin America at the dawn of the new millennium. The present paper focuses on a 'border' that is gaining salience in recent years, particularly as a result of the work of an increasingly interconnected group of researchers in Latin America and the United States, with smaller branches elsewhere. I am referring to the concepts of 'border thinking' and 'border epistemologies' associated with a larger effort that I will call here 'the modernity/coloniality research program'. I am using the concept of research program loosely (not in a strict Lakatosian sense) to refer to what seems to be an emergent but already significantly cohesive perspective that is fueling a series of researches, meetings, publications, and so forth around a shared – even if course contested – set of concepts. In keeping with the spirit of the group, I would argue that this body of work, still relatively unknown in the English speaking world for reasons that go beyond language and that speak to the heart of the program, constitutes a novel perspective from Latin America but not only for Latin America but for the world of the social and human sciences as a whole. By this I do not mean that the work of this group is just *of interest* to allegedly universal social and human sciences, but that that the group seeks to make a decisive intervention into the very discursivity of the modern sciences in order to craft another space for the production of knowledge – an other way of thinking, *un paradigma otro*, the very possibility of talking about 'worlds and knowledges otherwise'. What this group suggests is that an other thought, an other knowledge (and another world, in the spirit of Porto Alegre's World Social Forum), are indeed possible.

A proper contextualization and genealogy of the modernity/coloniality research program (MC from now on) would have to await future studies. It suffices to say, for now, that there are a number of factors that could plausibly enter into the genealogy of this group's thinking, including: liberation theology from the 1960s and 1970s; debates in Latin American philosophy and social

science around notions of liberation philosophy and autonomous social science (e.g., Enrique Dussel, Rodolfo Kusch, Orlando Fals Borda, Pablo Gonzales Casanova, Darcy Ribeiro); dependency theory; the debates on Latin American modernity and postmodernity in the 1980s, followed by discussions on hybridity in anthropology, communications and cultural studies in the 1990s; and, in the United States, the Latin American Subaltern Studies group. The modernity/coloniality group certainly finds inspiration in a number of sources, from European and North American critical theories of modernity and postmodernity to South Asian subaltern studies, Chicana feminist theory, postcolonial theory, and African philosophy; many of its members operate within a modified world systems perspective. Its main driving force, however, is a continued reflection on Latin American cultural and political reality, including the subaltern knowledge of exploited and oppressed social groups. If dependency theory, liberation theology, and participatory action research can be said to have been the most original contributions of Latin American critical thought in the twentieth century (with all the caveats that may apply to such originality), the MC research program emerges as heir to this tradition. As we shall see, however, there are significant differences. As Walter Mignolo puts it, MC should be seen as *un paradigma otro*. Rather than a new paradigm 'from Latin America' (as it could have been the case with dependency), the MC project does not fit into a linear history of paradigms or epistemes; to do so would mean to integrate it into the history of modern thought. On the contrary, the MC program should be seen as an other way of thinking that runs counter to the great modernist narratives (Christianity, liberalism, and Marxism); it locates its own inquiry in the very borders of systems of thought and reaches towards the possibility of non-eurocentric modes of thinking.

Part I of the paper presents an overview of the current MC landscape. I must emphasize that this is my own particular reading of this group's work, from my limited engagement with it and my equally limited understanding. This paper should be read as a 'report from the field', so to speak. Part II deals with open and unresolved questions facing the MC research program. Among these questions, I will highlight gender, nature, and the need to think about alternative economic imaginaries.

## I The modernity/coloniality research program

Why, one may ask, do these group of Latin Americans and Latin Americanists feel that a new understanding of modernity is needed? To fully appreciate the importance of this question, it is instructive to begin by discussing the dominant tendencies in the study of modernity from what we can call 'intra-modern perspectives' (the term will become clear as we move along). I am very much aware that the view of modernity to be presented below is terribly partial and contestable. I am not presenting it with the goal of 'theorizing

modernity', but rather in order to highlight, by way of contrast, the stark difference that the MC program poses in relation to the dominant inquiries about modernity. In the last instance, the goal of this brief excursus into modernity is political. If, as most intra-modern discussion suggest, globalization entails the universalization and radicalization of modernity, then what are we left with? How can we think about social change? Does radical alterity become impossible? More generally, what is happening to development and modernity in times of globalization? Is modernity finally becoming universalized, or is it being left behind? The question is the more poignant because it can be argued that the present is a moment of transition: between a world defined in terms of modernity and its corollaries, development and modernization, and the certainty they instilled – a world that has operated largely under European hegemony over the past two hundred years if not more; and a new (global) reality which is still difficult to ascertain but which, at opposite ends, can be seen either as a deepening of modernity the world over or, on the contrary, as a deeply negotiated reality that encompasses many heterogeneous cultural formations – and of course, the many shades in between. This sense of a transition is well captured by the question: Is globalization the last stage of capitalist modernity, or the beginning of something new? As we shall see, intra-modern and MC perspectives on modernity give a very different answer to this set of questions.

### *Globalization as the radicalization of modernity. An intra-modern view of modernity*

The idea of a relatively single globalization process emanating out of a few dominant centers remains prevalent. It is useful to review succinctly how this image arose in the most recent period and why it seems so difficult to dispel. From a philosophical and sociological perspective, the root of the idea of an increasingly overpowering globalization lies in a view of modernity as essentially an European phenomenon. Recent challenges to this view from peripheral locations have questioned the unexamined assumption – found in thinkers like Habermas, Giddens, Taylor, Touraine, Lyotard, Rorty, etc., as much as in Kant, Hegel, and the Frankfurt School philosophers before them – that modernity can be fully explained by reference to factors internal to Europe. The views of Habermas and Giddens have been particularly influential, having given rise to a veritable genre of books on modernity and globalization. From this perspective, modernity may be characterized as follows:

1 *Historically*, modernity has identifiable temporal and spatial origins: seventeenth century northern Europe (especially France, Germany, England), around the processes of Reformation, the Enlightenment, and the French Revolution. These processes crystallized at the end of the

eighteenth century (Foucault's modern episteme) and became consolidated with the Industrial Revolution.

2 *Sociologically*, modernity is characterized by certain institutions, particularly the nation state, and by some basic features, such as *self-reflexivity* (the continuous feedback of expert knowledge back into society, transforming it); the *dismembedding* of social life from local context and its increasing determination by translocal forces; and *space/time distantiation*, or the separation of space and place, since relations between 'absent others' become more important than face to face interaction (Giddens 1990).

3 *Culturally*, modernity can be further characterized in terms of the increasing appropriation of previously taken for granted cultural backgrounds by forms of expert knowledge linked to capital and state administrative apparatuses (Habermas 1973). Habermas (1987) describes this process as the increasing rationalization of the life-world, accompanied by universalization and individuation. Modernity brings about an order on the basis of the constructs of reason, the individual, expert knowledge, and administrative mechanisms linked to the state. Order and reason are seen as the foundation for equality and freedom, and enabled by the language of rights.

4 *Philosophically*, one may see modernity in terms of the emergence of the notion of 'Man' as the foundation for all knowledge and order of the world, separate from the natural and the divine (a pervasive anthropocentrism; Foucault 1973, Heidegger 1977, Panikkar 1993). On the other, modernity is seen in terms of the triumph of metaphysics, understood as a tendency – extending from Plato and some of the pre-Socratics to Descartes and the modern thinkers, and criticized by Nietzsche and Heidegger among others – that finds in logical truth the foundation for a rational theory of the world as made up of knowable (and hence controllable) things and beings (e.g., Vattimo 1991). For Vattimo, modernity is characterized by the idea of history and its corollary, progress and overcoming. Vattimo emphasizes the logic of development – the belief in perpetual betterment and overcoming – as crucial to the philosophical foundations of the modern order.

On the critical side, the disembeddedness of modernity is seen to cause what Paul Virilio (1999) calls global de-localization, including the marginalization of place (the here and now of social action) in the definition of social life. The underside of order and rationality is seen in various ways, from the domination and disenchantment that came about with secularization and the predominance of instrumental reason to the normalization of life and the disciplining of populations. As Foucault put it, 'the Enlightenment, which discovered the liberties, also invented the disciplines' (1979, p. 222). Finally, modernity's anthropocentrism is related to logocentrism and phallogocentrism, defined here simply as the cultural project of ordering the world according to

rational principles from the perspective of a male eurocentric consciousness – in other words, building an allegedly ordered, rational, and predictable world. Logocentrism has reached unprecedented levels with the extreme economization and technification of the world (Leff 2000). Modernity of course did not succeed in constituting a total reality, but enacted a totalizing project aimed at the purification of orders (separation between us and them, nature and culture), although inevitably only producing hybrids of these opposites along the way (thus Latour's dictum that 'we have never been modern', 1993).

Is there a logical necessity to believe that the order so sketchily characterized above is the only one capable of becoming global? For most theorists, on all sides of the political spectrum, this is exactly the case. Giddens (1990) has made the argument most forcefully: globalization entails the radicalization and universalization of modernity. No longer purely an affair of the West, however, since modernity is everywhere, the triumph of the modern lies precisely in its having become universal. This may be call 'the Giddens effect': *from now own, it's modernity all the way down, everywhere, until the end of times*. Not only is radical alterity expelled forever from the realm of possibilities, all world cultures and societies are reduced to being a manifestation of European history and culture. The 'Giddens effect' seems to be at play, directly or indirectly, in most works on modernity and globalization at present. No matter how variously qualified, a 'global modernity' is here to stay. Recent anthropological investigations of 'modernity at large' (Appadurai 1996) have shown modernity to be seen as de-territorialized, hybridized, contested, uneven, heterogenous, even multiple, or in terms of conversing with, engaging, playing with, or processing modernity; nevertheless, in the last instance these modernities end up being a reflection of a eurocentered social order, under the assumption that modernity is now everywhere, an ubiquitous and ineluctable social fact.[2]

Could it be, however, that the power of Eurocentered modernity – as a *particular local history* – lies in the fact that is has produced *particular global designs* in such a way that it has 'subalternized' other local histories and their corresponding designs? If this is the case, could one posit the hypothesis that radical alternatives to modernity are not a historically foreclosed possibility? If so, how can we articulate a project around this possibility? Could it be that it is possible to think about, and to think differently from, an 'exteriority' to the modern world system? That one may envision alternatives to the totality imputed to modernity, and adumbrate not a different totality leading to different global designs, but a network of local/global histories constructed from the perspective of a politically enriched alterity? This is precisely the possibility that may be gleaned from the work of a group of Latin American theorists that in refracting modernity through the lens of coloniality engage in a questioning of the spatial and temporal origins of modernity, thus unfreezing the radical potential for thinking from difference and towards the constitution

of alternative local and regional worlds. In what follows, I present succinctly some of the main arguments of these works.[3]

### *The modernity/coloniality research program*

The conceptualization of modernity/coloniality is grounded in a series of operations that distinguish it from established theories of modernity. Succinctly put, these include the following: (1) an emphasis on locating the origins of modernity with the Conquest of America and the control of the Atlantic after 1492, rather than in the most commonly accepted landmarks such as the Enlightenment or the end of the eighteenth century;[4] (2) a persistent attention to colonialism and the making of the capitalist world system as constitutive of modernity; this includes a determination not to overlook the economy and its concomitant forms of exploitation; (3) consequently, the adoption of a world perspective in the explanation of modernity, in lieu of a view of modernity as an intra-European phenomenon; (4) the identification of the domination of others outside the European core as a necessary dimension of modernity, with the concomitant subalternization of the knowledge and cultures of these other groups; (5) a conception of eurocentrism as the knowledge form of modernity/coloniality – a hegemonic representation and mode of knowing that claims universality for itself, and that relies on 'a confusion between abstract universality and the concrete world hegemony derived from Europe's position as center' (Dussel 2000, p. 471, Quijano 2000, p. 549).

A number of alternative notions emerge from this set of positions: (a) a decentering of modernity from its alleged European origins, including a debunking of the linear sequence linking Greece, Rome, Christianity and modern Europe; (b) a new spatial and temporal conception of modernity in terms of the foundational role of Spain and Portugal (the so-called first modernity initiated with the Conquest) and its continuation in Northern Europe with the industrial revolution and the Enlightenment (the second modernity, in Dussel's terms); the second modernity does not replace the first, it overlaps with it, until the present; (c) a focus on the peripheralization of all other world regions by this 'modern Europe', with Latin America as the initial 'other side' of modernity (the dominated and concealed side); and (d) a re-reading of the 'myth of modernity', not in terms of a questioning of the emancipatory potential of modern reason, but of modernity's 'underside', namely, the imputation of the superiority of European civilization, coupled with the assumption that Europe's development must be followed unilaterally by every other culture, by force if necessary –what Dussel terms 'the developmentalist fallacy' (e.g., 1993, 2000). Some additional consequences include the re-valuing of landmark experiences of decolonization, from the Tupac Amaru rebellion and the 1804 Haitian revolution to the 1960s anti-colonial movements, as sources of visions for the future, as opposed to the

conventional sources such as the French and American revolutions; and, in general, the need to take seriously the epistemic force of local histories and to think theory through from the political praxis of subaltern groups.

The main conclusions are, first, that the proper analytical unit for the analysis of modernity is modernity/coloniality – in sum, there is no modernity without coloniality, with the latter being constitutive of the former (in Asia, Africa, Latin America/Caribbean). Second, the fact that 'the colonial difference' is a privileged epistemological and political space. The great majority of European theorists (particularly those 'defenders of the European patent on modernity', as Quijano mockingly calls them (2000, p. 543)) have been blind to the colonial difference and the subalternization of knowledge and cultures it entailed. A focus on the modern/colonial world system also makes visible, besides the internal conflicts (conflicts within powers with the same world view), those that take place at the exterior borders of the modern/colonial system – i.e., the conflicts with other cultures and world views.[5]

### *Key notions and themes of the modernity/coloniliaty research program*

Some of the key notions that make up the conceptual corpus of this research program are thus: the *modern colonial world system* as the ensemble of processes and social formations that encompass modern colonialism and colonial modernities; although it is structurally heterogeneous, it articulates the main forms of power into a system. *Coloniality of power* (Quijano), a global hegemonic model of power in place since the Conquest that articulates race and labor, space and peoples, according to the needs of capital and to the benefit of white European peoples. *Colonial difference* and *global coloniality* (Mignolo) which refer to the knowledge and cultural dimensions of the subalternization processes effected by the coloniality of power; the colonial difference brings to the fore persistent cultural differences within global power structures. *Coloniality of being* (more recently suggested by Nelson Maldonado-Torres in group discussions) as the ontological dimension of colonialty, on both sides of the encounter; based on Levinas, Dussel and Fanon, it points at the 'ontological excess' that occurs when particular beings impose on others and, beyond that, the potential or actual effectivity of the discourses with which the other responds to the suppression as a result of the encounter (Maldonado-Torres 2003). *Eurocentrism,* as the knowledge model that represents the local European historical experience and which became globally hegemonic since the seventeenth century (Dussel, Quijano); hence the possibility of *non-eurocentric thinking* and epistemologies. Each of these notions are in themselves rooted in complex conceptualizations that represent decades of research; even thus, they are of course debatable. There are some other notions, more peculiar to specific authors but which are gaining currency within the group, that it is also important to introduce. These include Dussel's

notion of exteriority and transmodernity and Mignolo's concept of border thinking, pluritopic hermeneutics, and pluriversality.

The question of whether there is an 'exteriority' to the modern/colonial world system is somewhat peculiar to this group, and easily misunderstood. It was originally proposed and carefully elaborated by Dussel in his classic work on liberation philosophy (1976) and reworked in recent years. In no way should this exteriority be thought about as a pure outside, untouched by the modern. The notion of exteriority does not entail an ontological outside; it refers to an outside that is precisely constituted as difference by a hegemonic discourse. This notion of exteriority arises chiefly by thinking about the Other from the ethical and epistemological perspective of a liberation philosophy framework: the Other as oppressed, as woman, as racially marked, as excluded, as poor, as nature. By appealing from the exteriority in which s/he is located, the Other becomes the original source of an ethical discourse vis à vis a hegemonic totality. This interpellation of the Other comes from outside or beyond the system's institutional and normative frame, as an ethical challenge. This challenge might only be 'quasi-intelligible' at first (Dussel 1996, p. 25), given the difficulties in establishing meaningful interpellation that exploited peoples have with respect to a hegemonic system (contra Habermas' notion of a communication free of domination). There are degrees of exteriority; in the last instance, the greater challenge comes from

> the interpellation which the majority of the population of the planet, located in the South, raises, demanding their right to live, their right to develop their own culture, economy, politics, etc. . . . There is no liberation without rationality; but there is no *critical* rationality without accepting the interpellation of the excluded, or this would inadvertently be only the rationality of *domination*. . . . From this negated Other departs the praxis of liberation as 'affirmation' of the Exteriority and as origin of the movement of negation of the negation'.
>
> (Dussel 1996, pp. 31, 36, 54)[6]

This is precisely what most European and Euro-American theorists seem unwilling to consider: that it is impossible to think about transcending or overcoming modernity without approaching it from the perspective of the colonial difference. Both Mignolo and Dussel see here a strict limit to deconstruction and to the various eurocentered critiques of eurocentrism – in short, these continue to be thought about from within eurocentric categories (of, say, liberalism, Marxism, poststructuralism), not from the border thinking enabled by the colonial difference. . . . Critiques of modernity, in short, are blind to the (epistemic and cultural) colonial difference that becomes the focus of modernity/coloniality.

Dussel's notion of *transmodernity* signals the possibility of a non-eurocentric and critical dialogue with alterity, one that fully enables 'the negation of the negation' to which the subaltern others have been subjected, and one that does not see critical discourse as intrinsically European. Integral to this effort is the rescuing of non-hegemonic and silenced counter-discourses, of the alterity that is constitutive of modernity itself. This is the ethical principle of liberation of the negated Other, for which Dussel coins the term, 'trans-modernity', defined as a project for overcoming modernity not simply by negating it but by thinking about it from its underside, from the perspective of the excluded other. Trans-modernity is a future-oriented project that seeks the liberation of all humanity (1996, p. 14, Ch. 7), 'a worldwide ethical liberation project in which alterity, which was part and parcel of modernity, would be able to fulfill itself' (2000, p. 473), 'in which both modernity and its negated alterity (the victims) co-realize themselves in a process of mutual fertilization' (1993, p. 76). In short, trans-modernity cannot be brought about from within modernity, but requires of the action – and the incorporative solidarity – of the subalternized groups, the objects of modernity's constitutive violence embedded in, among other features, the developmentalist fallacy. Rather than the rational project of a discursive ethics, transmodernity becomes the expression of an ethics of liberation.

Mignolo's notions of *border thinking*, *border epistemology*, and *pluritopic hermeneutics* are important in this regard. They point at the need 'for a kind of thinking that moves along the diversity of historical processes' (Mignolo 2001, p. 9). There are, to be sure, no original thinking traditions to which one can go back. Rather than reproducing Western abstract universals, however, the alternative is a kind of border thinking that 'engages the colonialism of Western epistemology (from the left and from the right) from the perspective of epistemic forces that have been turned into subaltern (traditional, folkloric, religious, emotional, etc.) forms of knowledge' (2001, p. 11). Resituating Anzaldúa's metaphor of the border into the domain of coloniality, Mignolo adumbrates the possibility of ''thinking otherwise', from the interior exteriority of the border. That is, to engage in border thinking is to move beyond the categories created an imposed by Western epistemology' (p. 11). This is not just a question of changing the contents but the very terms of the conversation. It is not a question of replacing existing epistemologies either; these will certainly continue to exist and as such will remain viable as spaces of, and for, critique. Instead, what he claims 'is the space for an epistemology that comes from the border and aims toward political and ethical transformations' (p. 11). Finally, while Mignolo acknowledges the continued importance of the monotopic critique of modernity by Western critical discourse (critique from a single, unified space), he suggests that this has to be put into dialogue with the critique(s) arising from the colonial difference, which constitutes border thinking. The result is a 'pluritopic hermeneutics' (a term he seemingly

adapts from Pannikar's 'diatopic hermeneutics'), a possibility of thinking from different spaces which finally breaks away from eurocentrism as sole epistemological perspective. This is the double critique of modernity from the perspective of coloniality, from the exterior of the modern/colonial world system. Let it be clear, however, that border thinking entails both 'displacement and departure' (2000, p. 308), double critique and positive affirmation of an alternative ordering of the real. To sum up,

> Border thinking points towards a different kind of hegemony, a multiple one. As a universal project, diversity allows us to imagine alternatives to universalism (we could say that the alternative to universalism in this view is not particularism but multiplicity). 'The 'West and the rest' in Huntington's phrase provides the model to overcome, as the 'rest' becomes the sites where border thinking emerges in its diversity, where 'mundialización' creates new local histories remaking and readapting Western global designs . . . and transforming local (European) histories from where such designs emerged . . . . 'Interdependence' may be the word that summarizes the break away from the idea of *totality* and brings about the idea of *networks* whose articulation will require epistemological principles I called in this book 'border thinking' and 'border gnosis', as a rearticulation of the colonial difference: 'diversality as a universal project', which means that people and communities have the right to be different precisely because 'we' are all equals'
>
> (2000, pp. 310, 311).

'There is no question', writes Mignolo (2000), p. 59), 'that Quijano, Dussel and I are reacting not only to the force of a historical imaginary but also to the actuality of this imaginary today'. The corollary is the need to build narratives from the perspective of modernity/coloniality 'geared towards the search for a different logic' (p. 22). This project has to do with the rearticulation of global designs by and from local histories; with the articulation between subaltern and hegemonic knowledge from the perspective of the subaltern; and with the remapping of colonial difference towards a worldly culture – such as in the Zapatista project, that remaps Marxism, thirdworldism, and indigenism, without being either of them, in an excellent example of border thinking. While 'there is nothing outside of totality . . . totality is always projected from a given local history', it becomes possible to think of 'other local histories producing either alternative totalities or an alternative to totality' (p. 329). These alternatives would not play on the 'globalization/civilization' couplet inherent to modernity/coloniality; they would rather build on a '*mundialización*/culture' relation centered on the local histories in which colonial global designs are necessarily transformed, thus transforming also the local histories that created them. Unlike globalization, *mundialización* brings to the fore the

manifold local histories that, in questioning global designs (e.g., neo-liberal globalization), aim at forms of globality that arise out of 'cultures of transience' that go against the cultural homogeneity fostered by such designs. The diversity of *mundialización* is contrasted here with the homogeneity of globalization, aiming at multiple and diverse social orders.

In short, the perspective of modernity/coloniality provides an alternative framework for debates on modernity, globalization and development; it is not just a change in the description of events, it is an epistemic change of perspective. By speaking of the colonial difference, this framework brings to the fore the power dimension that is often lost in relativistic discussions of cultural difference. More recent debates on interculturality, for instance in Ecuador's current political and cultural scene, deepens some of these insights (Walsh 2003). In short, the MC research program is a framework constructed from the Latin American periphery of the modern colonial world system; it helps explain the dynamics of eurocentrism in the making of modernity and attempts to transcend it. If it reveals the dark sides of modernity, it does not do it from an intra-epistemic perspective, as in the critical European discourses, but from the perspective of the receivers of the alleged benefits of the modern world. Modernity/coloniality also shows that the perspective of modernity is limited and exhausted in its pretended universality. By the same token, it shows the shortcomings of the language of alternative modernities in that this latter incorporates the projects of the non-moderns into a single project, losing the subaltern perspectives and subordinating them, for even in their hybridity subaltern perspectives are not about being only modern but are heteroglossic, networked, plural. In highlighting the developmentalist fallacy, lastly, modernity/coloniality not only re-focuses our attention on the overall fact of development, it provides a context for interpreting the various challenges to development and modernity as so many projects that are potentially complementary and mutually reinforcing. Beyond Latin America, one may say, with Mignolo (2000), p. 309), that this approach 'is certainly a theory *from/of* the Third World, *but not only for the Third World*. . . . Third World theorizing is also *for* the First World in the sense that critical theory is subsumed and incorporated in a new geocultural and epistemological location'.[7]

Finally, there are some consequences of this group's work for Latin American Studies in the US, Europe, and elsewhere. The MC perspective moves away from viewing 'Latin America' as an object of study (in relation to which US-based Latin American Studies would be the 'knowing subject'), towards an understanding of Latin America as a geo-historical location with and within a distinct critical genealogy of thought. Modernity/Coloniality suggests that globalization must be understood from a geo-historical and critical Latin American perspective. With this the MC approach proposes an alternative to the genealogy of the modern social sciences that are still the foundation of Latin American Studies in the US. In this way, *Latin American*

*Studies* in, say, North America and Europe, and *Critical Social Thought* in Latin America (which offers the epistemic grounding for the MC group) emerge as two *complementary but distinct* paradigms.[8] This also means that, as an epistemic perspective, the MC research program is not associated with particular nationalities or geographical locations. To occupy the locus of enunciation crafted by the MC project, in other words, one does not need to be a Latin American nor live in the continent. 'Latin America' itself becomes a perspective that can be practiced from many spaces, if it is done from counter-hegemonic perspectives that challenge the very assumption of Latin America as fully constituted object of study, previous to, and outside of, the often imperialistic discourses that construct it.

## II Some trends, open questions, and tasks ahead

So far I have presented some of the main lines of inquiry and concepts of the loose collective I have referred to as the MC research program. I also focused on the commonly agreed upon main intellectual sources of the group – chiefly, Enrique Dussel, Aníbal Quijano, and Walter Mignolo. My purpose has been to provide an overview of the shared ground on which the group has been constituted. This story, of course, leaves out much that is of interest to the project, including valuable contributions by other participants, as well as the most collective aspects of the current phase of joint inquiry. There are certainly disagreements and tensions among the group, which makes for lively exchanges and debates, but an 'ethnography' of this 'community of argumentation' (as Brazilian anthropologist Gustavo Lins Ribeiro would call it) will have to await for another opportunity. For now, a further brief characterization of the group might suffice; this will be followed by a sketch of what I believe are some open questions, trends, and promising tensions.

### *The modernity/coloniality group*

The MC research program group can be tentatively characterized as follows (note: this characterization is a more a straightforward sociology of knowledge exercise than, say, an analysis of the discursive formation being mapped by MC):

1 It is largely interdisciplinary or, rather, transdisciplinary. Although philosophy, political economy, and literary theory have been salient, disciplines such as history, sociology and anthropology are increasingly important. Other fields, such as feminist theory and political ecology, already begin to make inroads into the program. It is transdisciplinary to the extent that disciplinary inquiries are set into dialogue with those of other fields, sometimes by the same author, leading to new forms of inquiry. There is an explicit attempt at 'un-disciplining' the social sciences

(*indisciplinar las ciencias sociales*; see Walsh *et al.* 2002) and at building *teorías sin disciplina* (Castro-Gómez & Mendieta 1998).

2 While firmly anchored in 'Latin America', the group cannot be said to be of the geographical Latin America, but rather made up of a network of sites, some of which are most stabilized by particular practices than others (e.g, the sites mentioned in Quito, Bogotá, Durham-Chapel Hill, México City and more recently Berkeley). This goes with the suggestion that Latin America be understood more as a 'perspective' or epistemic space than as a region. It is an approach that, again, while it can be said to have roots in the Latin American experience, finds sustenance globally; hence the appeal to many critical theories, especially those emerging from similar subaltern epistemic locations. This differentiates it sharply from earlier 'Latin American paradigms', such as dependency and liberation theology (even if these also had a transnational dimension).

3 The group can be said to be a community of argumentation that works collectively on concepts and strategies; up to a certain point, it can be said to practice the critical border thinking it proposes; hence the emphasis on questions of knowledge. In other words, there is an explicit collective dimension to the conceptual work that, although around a set of formative concepts, is significantly open ended. This sense of collectivity is strengthened by the feeling of the radical potential of the project – the fact that what is at stake is 'not only to change the content but the very terms of the conversation' (Mignolo). The goal is to craft new forms of analysis, not to contribute to already established (eurocentric) systems of thought, no matter how critical these might be. This could be related to what Boaventura de Sousa Santos (2003) has called 'epistemologies of the South' in his analysis of the World Social Forum.

4 The group's participants tend to share a political position that is seemingly consistent with this radical emphasis, even if their practice continues to have a primary (if not exclusive) site in the academy (see discussion below). At this level, there can be said to be three privileged sites and agents of radical change: subaltern social actors and movements (and to this extent the political practice of the group's members is seen as aligned with subaltern actors); intellectual-activists in mixed spaces, from NGOs to the state; and the universities themselves, to the extent that, taken to their logical conclusions, the MC approach is bound to constitute a challenge to normative academic practices and canons.

### *Open-ended questions, sites of tension*

To end, I would like to briefly sketch out three areas the importance that have remained largely outside the purview of the project, but which are of great relevance to the very experiences that the project theorizes. The first, and

perhaps most pressing, is gender; the second nature and the environment; the third the need to construct new economic imaginaries capable of supporting concrete struggles against neo-liberalism and designs for alternative economies. If the group's efforts can be said to have remained largely academic (or academic-intellectual), and to this extent largely at the level of disembodied abstract discourse, these dimensions are likely to add 'flesh and blood', so to speak, into it (the flesh and blood of women's bodies, nature, and place-based economies, for instance), and to contribute to ward off the risks of logocentrism. This should also be of consequence for the strategies of dissemination of this work into particular political arenas.[9] In other words, an engagement with feminism and environmentalism would be fruitful in terms of thinking the non-discursive side of social action (Flórez 2003). It would be equally important to theorize further notions that are central to the group and to feminist theory alike, such as epistemology, power, identity, subjectivity, agency, and everyday life.

A final area of potential work would be ethnographies of modernity/coloniality. Conceived within the framework presented here, these ethnographies would avoid the epistemological traps of the studies of modernity reviewed in the first part of the paper. They would also be useful to ascertaining instances of the colonial difference and border thinking from the ground up, so to speak, for instance by engaging with gender, ecological, or economic difference as explained below. This is, however, an epistemological and methodological issue, and as such it will not be elaborated upon further here.

## Engendering modernity/coloniality

It is clear that the treatment of gender by the MC group so far has been inadequate in the best of cases. Dussel was among the very few male Latin American thinkers to discuss at length the issue of women early on, as one of the important categories of excluded others. Mignolo has paid attention to some of the works by Chicana feminists, particularly the notion of borderlands/*la frontera*. These efforts, however, hardly get at the potential contributions of feminist theory to the MC framework. The Finnish theologian and feminist theorist Elina Vuola has pioneered the identification of this silence, particularly in connection with Dussel's work as a liberation theology scholar and other liberation theology frameworks (Vuola 2000, 2002, 2003, in press). Vuola (2002) finds hopeful Dussel's move to defining the object of liberation as the 'Other' (more than just the poor, and thus going beyond class), but she finds less encouraging the theologians' inability to identify the race and gender position of their theorizing and to respond to the challenges that arise when the objects become subjects in their own right. The Other, in other words, is subsumed in a new kind of totality, a male-centered one, thus denying the existence of women in their alterity and difference.

In a more recent text, and building on post-colonial and feminist theory, Vuola (2003) renews her call for taking seriously the heterogeneity and multiplicity of the subject of liberation (theology and philosophy), namely 'the poor' – and, one may add, the subaltern, in the MC project. In other words, she is calling for a politics of representation of the poor and the subaltern that fully acknowledges this multiplicity; in the case of women, this means addressing themes that have been absent from the discussion, such as violence against women, reproductive rights and sexuality, and giving complete visibility to the agency of women. In other words, the subject of the colonial difference is not an undifferentiated, gender-neutral subject (or differentiated only in terms of race and class); there are differences in the way subaltern groups are objects of power and subjects of agency. To acknowledge this might change, to paraphrase, not only the contents but also the terms of the conversation. That women are other in relation to men – and certainly treated as such by phallogocentric social and human sciences – certainly should have consequences for a perspective centered precisely on exteriority and difference. What Vuola points at is the fact that whereas the discourse of the (mostly male still) MC group is illuminating and radical in so many ways, and as such taken seriously by feminists, *it largely excludes women and women's theoretical and political concerns.* There seems to be a conflict here between discourse and practice as far as women is concerned. Finally, the feminist deconstruction of religious fundamentalism, something that is not well known in either feminist social science or the MC project, is also of relevance to the engendering of the MC project. As a broad political movement, transnational feminism(s) is developing new approaches to formulating inter-cultural criteria for human rights, especially women's rights, and for analyzing the truth claims on which these are based (Vuola 2002). New works on transnational feminism deal with race, gender and culture issues in ways that resonate with the concerns of the MC project (see e.g, Shohat 1998, Bahavani *et al.* 2003).

There are, actually, many points of actual or potential convergence between feminism and the theory of MC (this discussion is by no means exhaustive, but intended to show some possible points of connection). First, they both share the radical suspicion of universalist discourse; at this level, what needs to be understood is that modern discourse is also a masculinist discourse, as feminist philosophers and political theorist have shown since at least the late 1980s (see, e.g., the well-known collection by Nicholson (1990)). There is convergence also at the level of the situated character of all knowledge; yet in the feminist theory version (e.g., Haraway's famous 1988 article) the situated knowledge comes with the realization of the necessarily partial character of all perspectives – MC included. In other words, the critical subject position of the modernity/coloniality scholar is not beyond the scholar's gender. In refusing to locate himself/herself within feminism, the scholar is also missing the chance to engage in an other thought, another

subjectivity, or subjectivity otherwise. To paraphrase Ranajit Guha, the scholar would be reducing women's agency to another history with another (male) subject; he would then be complicit with the prose of counter-insurgency. As Vuola puts it, in speaking of Walter Mignolo's notions of pluritopic hermeneutics and pluriversality as goals to be embraced, 'it is easy to see how this project has been present in liberation theology from its beginning . . . however, it is less clear how liberation theologians have been able to conceptualize and differentiate that *from where* . . . One should always be willing to look at one's own truth claims and positions with the critical eyes of others' (2003, p. 7). Beyond liberation theology, what would 'opting for women' bring to the MC research program? Of course, it should be clear that talking about women is only part of the story. A gender perspective demands situating this talk in contexts of power, particularly power relations between women and men, including power relations within the academy. Given the relationality of gender, it has to be recognized that the subject of the colonial difference is not autonomous but relational. This pertains as much to women as to men.

At stake here is the possibility of deepening the MC project's concern with epistemology through an engagement with the sophisticated and politically-minded debate on feminist epistemology and positionality (e.g., Alcoff 1988, 1991). The notion of women's positionality suggests that women utilize their subject positions for the construction of meaning in ways that cannot be fully ascertained from another perspective. The emphasis on epistemology and positionality is of course linked to a reflection on gender inequality – an aspect that, again, is fully consistent with MC theory. Feminist ethnography has taken on these challenges in an interesting direction by articulating the analysis of women's dis/empowerment with tactics of voicing, writing, and representation (see, e.g, Behar & Gordon 1995). Besides and beyond the more established modes of academic writing (which are necessarily entangled with logocentric practices?), can one write differently about the subjects whose non-eurocentric perspectives one expects to contribute bringing into light? And how do we put our writings into circulation in those very spaces where the colonial difference is being re-worked daily through social practices? In doing so, feminist ethnography has taken clues from post-structuralism and also from writings by women of color in the US and elsewhere, particularly the work of Gloria Anzaldúa and Cherrie Moraga. *This Bridge We Call Home*, the recent volume in this tradition (Anzaldúa & Keating 2003), poses new challenges for feminist theory and MC theory alike. Moving from victimhood to agency, and recognizing the persistent condition of living *entremundos* (hence the need for bridge building which is also a home building and community building), the *nepantleras* in this volume are border thinkers that make connections for social change; they do so out of an act of will and an act of love, and as 'a promise to be present with the pain of others without losing

themselves in it' (Anzaldúa 2003, p. 4). Their 'technologies of crossing' are technologies for recognizing power and for going beyond, for shifting to other modes of consciousness and being, for a new hermeneutics of love (Sandoval 2003). Strategies of knowledge, writing and representation are again central to this internationalist feminist project now focused on agency, connection, and re/construction of social, cultural and natural worlds.[10]

Besides issues of power and epistemology, feminist theory's concerns with subjectivity and identity would be crucial areas of engagement. No contemporary theory has radicalized these concepts as much as queer theory; this theory has eloquently shown that the constituent elements of gender and sexual identities are never monolithic, but more the result of weavings, overlaps, dissonances, gaps and possibilities. 'Queer' names the radical contestation of the norm – and here I am suggesting the norm of heterosexism, patriarchy, modernity, and coloniality. It can be said that 'queer' signals the identity without essence par excellence, and it thus becomes the site of both historical analysis and future imaginings. If not necessarily always in a position of subversive exteriority, the queer subject shows that the borders (in this case the heterosexual norm) can be redrawn so that it becomes possible to envision identities and knowledges otherwise (e.g, Halperin 1995). The de-essentializatioon of identity means taking all identities seriously. Feminist identities, as some theorists emphasize, are also constructed through pleasure and desire, and here lies another possibility for a critique of 'Man the Modern', to use Donna Haraway's happy (and devastating) expression – the Man that constructs himself as both object and subject of all knowledge. There is no autonomous subject of knowledge; all knowledge has a relational dimension and a materiality. Who is the subject of knowledge, and how is s/he enabled in her everydayness? Who can be a 'critical border thinker, and how? Who can afford to be in a border position and a position of resistance, and what is the sexual and political economy that authorizes this privilege? Finally, the researcher too is a subject of desire, and this too needs to be acknowledged (Flórez 2003).[11]

To speak about Latin America: The very fact that sexism continues to be one of the most pervasive, and seemingly intractable, problems in Latin American societies should be reason enough to engage with feminism. Latin American feminists have pointed at the fact that women are also the Other of modernity. Beyond discussions of divisions of labor and epistemology, this has visible consequences for the analysis of key processes of coloniality, including nation building, race, and eurocentric patriarchal formations (see, e.g., Rojas 2001). It is fitting to end this section with a brief mention of the speech by Comandante Ester, delivered before Congress in Mexico City at the end of *La Marcha del Color de la Tierra* in March 2001. It was expected that Sub-comandante Marcos would deliver the speech; instead, it was an Indian woman, the comandante Ester. After initial hesitancy and difficulties in incorporating the voices and demands of women so that women were still

constructed as supplements (Belaustiguigoitia 1998), it seemed that the Zapatista had finally arrived at the recognition of the central place of indigenous women in both society and the struggle. A few days earlier, in Juchitán, Comandante Ester had already referred to the triple discrimination confronted by Indian women – as Indian, woman, and poor. Engaging in a double critique in her México City speech, Comandante Ester discussed the *Leyes Revolucionarias de la Mujer*, intended to eliminate all discriminatory practices form within and from without. She spoke at length of the forms of discrimination of women in daily life arising from booth the communities and the nation, as well as of the indigenou cultural practices that need to be preserved. In this way, 'the march made visible the invisible, and representable the unrepresentable: Indian women speaking and demanding 'before the law' . . . . Is it possible for the law to hear them? In which language, through which discourse do they have to make clear what they want: to be Indian, to be women and to be Mexican?' (Belausteguigoitia 2002, p. 52). There are, again, clear implications from this call for the modernity/coloniality research program. The crucial question is: can the subaltern woman speak through MC theorizing? If not, what is the cost of this silence? What sort of translations and mediations are at stake?

Some of the questions raised here could easily emerge from the MC framework. To this extent, it would be important for feminists to think about the contributions that the MC project could make to theorizing gender and difference. It is true that after the critiques by women of color and third world women in the 1980s allegedly universal feminisms have been more aware of the race and culture dimensions in the dynamic of gender; however, varieties of eurocentrism continue to be pervasive in a number of feminist positions. The language of 'colonial difference' brings this issue into new light. It complicates, for instance, assumptions about gender that are still informed by Eurocentric notions of liberation and equality; it might help explain subaltern coalitions that do not necessarily embrace gender demands or follow a logic of solidarity among women (above say, class and ethnic solidarity). Looking forward, one may say that MC contributes to establish conversations between class, gender and race/ethnicity in Latin America that could be of great interest to feminists that do not speak from this position. This promise is already shown by the few works within the MC group that are already conceived from this perspective (particularly Freya Schiwy's work on race and gender in Bolivia), and by the interpellation of some feminists, such as those reviewed here.

## Nature and the colonial difference

Like feminism, ecology and environmentalism present the MC project with similar challenges and possibilities. Ecology and environmentalism imply

different ways of thinking (necessarily relational, situated and historical); ways of reading modernity; an acute concern with epistemology (particularly a critique of reductionist science and logocentric discourse); and an articulation of the question of difference (ecological and cultural difference) that can easily be linked to coloniality, and vice versa. All of these are potential points of convergence with the MC project, and some members of the group have begun to broach these questions (e.g., Coronil 1997, Escobar 1999, Lander 2002). Environmentalism's orientation towards social movements can also be seen as a shared aspect with the MC project. More is yet to be done, however.

There is, actually, an ongoing effort at developing a Latin American political ecology framework that similarly purports to develop a unique geopolitical perspective on the question of nature; the brief comments below are purposely written from this vantage point.[12] To begin with, political ecology underscores the civilizational character of the current environmental crisis; this crisis is, bluntly put, is a crisis of modernity, to the extent that modernity has failed to enable sustainable worlds. It is also a *crisis of thought*, to the extent that logocentric thought has fueled the ecologically destructive practices of modernity (Leff 2000, Boff 2002). (As some feminists convincingly argue, the domination of women and nature are at the basis of the modern patriarchal project enacted by fallogocentric thought.) It is difficult for those not accustomed to thinking in ecological terms to realize that today's environmental crisis is not only a generalized crisis but perhaps the central contradiction and limit to capital today. More readily accepted is the idea that modernity is structured around the split between nature and culture, even if it is rarely acknowledged that this split might be equally formative of modernity than the civilized/other (us/them) binary. Nature then appears at the other side of the colonial difference, with certain natures (colonial/third world natures, women's bodies, dark bodies) located in the exteriority to the Totality of the male eurocentric world. The environmental crisis thus signals the limits of modern, instrumental rationality; it reflects modernity's failure to articulate biology and history save through the capitalization of nature and labor. What ensued was a regime of capitalist nature that subalternized all other articulations of biology and history, of nature and society, particularly those that enact – through their local models and practices of the natural – a culturally-established continuity (as opposed to a separation) between the natural, human, and supernatural worlds. These local models of the natural are at the basis of environmental struggles today. In this way, these struggle need to be seen as *struggles for the defense of cultural, ecological, and economic difference* (Leff 2000, Escobar 1999). Ethno-ecological social movements are very clear about this. Here lies another type of critical border thinking that needs to be taken into account.

In a more prospective way, the Latin American political ecology effort attempts to construct an ethics and culture of sustainability; this entails the

rethinking of production towards a new environmental rationality; and a dialogue among forms of knowledge towards the construction of novel environmental rationalities. This ecology's ethical perspective on nature, life, and the planet entails a questioning of modernity and development, indeed an irrefutable indictment of the developmentalist fallacy. By privileging subaltern knowledges of the natural, this political ecology articulates in unique ways the questions of diversity, difference, and inter-culturality – with nature, of course, occupying a role as actor and agent. At stake here is a cultural politics of difference that goes beyond the deconstruction of anthropo-logocentrism; it aims at the cultural re-appropriation of nature through political strategies such as those of social movements. According to this group, there is an emergent Latin American environmental thought that builds on the struggles and knowledges of indigenous, peasants, ethnic and other subaltern groups to envision other ways of being with a multiplicity of living and non-living beings, human and not. Respecting the specificity of place-based cultures and peoples, it aims at thinking about the re/construction of local and regional worlds in more sustainable ways.

## Rethinking the economy, in the concrete

The combined processes of modernity and coloniality can be seen as projects for the radical reconversion of human and biophysical ecologies world wide. One may speak about a systematic project of cultural, ecological, and economic reconversion along eurocentric lines. Conversely, one may consider the need to build on *practices of cultural, ecological, and economic difference* for concrete projects of world transformation – for worlds and knowledges otherwise. This helps give flesh and blood to the colonial difference and global coloniality. While these processes have to be advanced at the same time, there seems to be a pressing need to come up with new economic imaginaries, imaginaries that enable effective and practical resistance to the seemingly overpowering imaginary of the market sanctified by neo-liberal globalization (Hinkelamert's age of the total market). Ethnographically, we can follow in the wake of ecological anthropologists documenting practices of ecological difference, which, coupled with the political-intellectual strategies of social movements, could feed into concrete projects of alternative eco-cultural designs and world construction. Theoretically, we are ill equipped for the task. Part of the answer lies in the fact that political economy analyses have made invisible practices of economic difference, given the totalizing and capitalocentric tendencies of their discourses; these analyses have, in short, tended to reduce all economic forms to the terms of the Same, namely, capital itself (Gibson-Graham 1996).

That ecology and the body are ineluctably attached to place (even if not place-bound) seems easy to accept. Less clear is that thinking about economic

difference and alternative economic imaginaries should also have a place-based dimension. Let us see why, in a way that enables us to introduce a place-based dimension to the coloniality of power and the colonial difference. Place, after all, is the site of the subaltern par excellence, the excluded dimension of modernity's concern with space, universality, movement, and the like. It would then make sense to 'emplace' the MC project in more than a metaphorical way. This point is driven home by a project on Women and the Politics of Place that brings together gender, ecology and economy into one theoretical-political framework.[13] In writing about this project, Julie Graham and Katherine Gibson introduce the notion of economic difference and the idea of emplacement, building on the decentered and disorganized (but globally emplaced) political imaginary of second wave feminism, in the following way:

> Women and the Politics of Place (Harcourt & Escobar 2002) builds on that ground [of feminist politics], extending the idea of a politics of ubiquity by emphasizing its ontological substrate: a vast set of disarticulated 'places' – households, social communities, ecosystems, workplaces, organizations, bodies, public arenas, urban spaces, diasporas, regions, occupations – related analogically rather than organically and connected through webs of signification. If *women* are everywhere, *a woman* is always somewhere, and those somewheres are what the project is interested in: places being created, strengthened, defended, augmented, transformed by women. It is as though the identity category, woman, were to be addressed through contextualization or emplacement, and the feminist question had become 'What might a politics of the emplacement be?' Not a politics of the category, or of identity per se, but a politics of the production of subjects and places. A politics of becoming in place.
> (Gibson-Graham 2003).

From an MC perspective, it can be said that 'place' here serves as an epistemic perspective that can be occupied by many subjects. The Women and the Politics of Place project indeed aims at asserting a logic of difference and possibility against the homogenizing tendencies of globalization and political economy; it seeks to make visible a landscape of cultural, ecological and economic differences; to this extent, there is certain convergence here between the projects of feminism, ecology, and alternative economies and this convergence is articulated around the politics of place. I am not arguing that this is the only space of convergence for projects of feminist, economic, and ecological futures. I am arguing for a dialogue between the MC project and projects such as those reviewed in this section. The notion of place-based (although, again, not place-bound) practices of identity, nature, and economy allows us to go beyond a view of subaltern places as just subsumed in a global logic or as a site in a global network, unable to ground any significant

resistance, let alone an alternative construction. At the level of the economy, one may realize that places are never fully capitalist, but are inhabited by economic difference, with the potential for becoming something other, an other economy. It is about rethinking difference from the perspective of the economy, and the economy from the perspective of difference. By emplacing the MC project, one might thus be able to link global coloniality to projects that have potential for concrete, real transformations. These may take place in conjunction with social movements. This revaluing of local politics might be one of most important contributions we can make at present, in a moment when nobody seems to give any credence to local actions.

## Conclusion

In his retrospective look at critical discourses on identity in Latin American philosophy and social sciences since the end of the nineteenth century to the present, *Crítica de la Razón Latinoamericana*, Santiago Castro-Gómez (1996) concludes that all such discourses of identity – from Alberdi to Martí and Rodó and to Zea and Roig – have been complicit with a modernist logic of alterization, and have thus amounted to counter-modernist proposals in the best of cases. In other words, most accounts of identity in liberation discourses in philosophy and other fields have relied on postulating a foundational alterity and a transcendental subject that would constitute a radical alternative in relation to an equally homogenized modern/European/North American Other. Whether appealing to Latin American indigenous, mestizo, catholic, primordialist, anti-imperialist, or vitalist identities – in contradistinction to white, protestant, instrumental, disenchanted, individualist, patriarchal, etc. Euro/American identity – these strategies of alterization, in Castro-Gómez archaeological analysis, are doomed to failure. To acknowledge the partial, historical, and heterogeneous character of all identities is to begin to correct this flaw, and to begin the journey towards views of identity that emerge from an *episteme posilustrada*, or post-Enlightment episteme. To the counter-modernist logic of alterization, Castro-Gómez opposes a logic of the historical production of difference.

It remains to be seen whether the MC project will fully bypass the modernist logic of alterization insightfully analyzed by Castro-Gómez. Conceived as an epistemic decolonization, this project would certainly seem to go beyond a politics of representation based on identifying an exclusive space of enunciation 'of one's own' that is blind to its own constructedness; it would also avoid comprehensive allegations of inclusion under a single umbrella (all 'Latin Americans'), and would resist the idea that those included would be fully outside the colonialist totality. Such dreams are in the process of being abandoned. The notion of border thinking (or 'critical border positioning', as Catherine Walsh has recently called it, 2003) seems to provide, by itself, some insurance against the older logic. As we have seen,

engaging with gender, environment and economy might afford further guarantees that the important insights of this group will not run into the traps described by Castro-Gómez. No longer an 'absolute other' in relation to modernity, and so no longer condemned to the perpetual solitude of which Octavio Paz and García Márquez were so enamored, the Latin America that emerges from the project so sketchily reviewed here would however continue to enact a politics of difference, precisely because it has become newly aware of the constitutive difference that inhabits it and the history that has produced it. Perhaps it is indeed the case that an other Latin America(s) is possible.

## Notes

1 This paper is revised from a version presented at the Tercer Congreso Internacional de Latinoamericanistas en Europa, Amsterdam, 3–6 July 2002. It was previously published in *Cuadernos del CEDLA* 16, pp. 31–67, in 2003. The title, 'Worlds and Knowledges Otherwise', comes from a discussion at the meeting of the editorial collective of the journal *Nepantla Views from South* (Duke University, 4 April 2003). This journal has published a number of articles by the authors featured in this text. As the journal moves from a printed to an electronic format, the journal's character has changed somewhat; the new subtitle (this paper's title) reflects the new orientation. I would like to thank Annelies Zoomers for her initial invitation to the Congress and for her generous interest in the paper. I would also like to thank Walter Mignolo, Eduardo Restrepo, Juliana Flórez, and Nelson Maldonado-Torres for our engaging conversations over the 2002–03 academic year, and Santiago Castro-Gómez, Elina Vuola, Freya Schiwy, Catherine Walsh and Edizon León for their stimulating participation and ideas in our Spring workshops, all in Chapel Hill and Duke.

2 Although I have not done an exhaustive search, I believe a *eurocentered* view of modernity is present in most conceptualizations of modernity and globalization in philosophy, geography, anthropology, and communications, and on all sides of the political spectrum. Many of these works, to be sure, are important contributions to the understanding of modernity, yet their eurocentrism has theoretical and political consequences. Some of these works explicitly engage with Giddens' work and develop an elegant and coherent conceptualization of globalization from this perspective (e.g., Tomlinson 1999); others follow a more ethnographic orientation (e.g., Englund and Leach 2000, and Kahn 2001 for reviews; Appadurai 1996, plus the works inspired by this author's work), or a cultural-historical orientation (e.g., Gaonkar, ed. 2001). Some assert the plurality of globalization (i.e., globalizations) yet go on to explain such plurality in political and economic terms, taking for granted a dominant cultural matrix (see the special issue of *International Sociology* on 'Globalizations', Vol. 15, Number 2, June 2000; e.g., Wallerstein 2000). A eurocentered and eurocentric notion of modernity is also at play in most of the works on the Left, such as Hardt

and Negri (2000). These authors' reinterpretation of the European history of sovereignty in light of current bio-political structures of rule, as well as their elaboration of resistance in the Western philosophy of immanence, are novel element for rethinking modernity. However, their eurocentrism becomes particularly problematic in their identification of the potential sources for radical action, and in their belief that there is no outside to modernity (again, a la Giddens). To the view that 'there is no outside' the MC perspective counter-poses a notion of exteriority to modernity/coloniality not entertained by any of the authors that follow in the tradition of Eurocentered modernity.

Recent anthropological reflection on modernity has also seen major changes. In the United States, anthropology of modernity has focused again on both 'modernity abroad', and on people's (largely non-experts) engagement with it. This approach has been important in grounding the understanding of modernity in ethnographic cases. As Kahn (2001) put it in a recent review, taken as a whole these works have pluralized the accepted understanding of modernity as a homogenous process. The various ways in which modernity is 'pluralized', however, need to be taken into account. Most discuss 'alternative modernities' (with 'hybrid', 'multiple', 'local', etc. as other qualifiers) as emerging from the dynamic encounter of dominant (usually Western) and non-dominant (e.g., local, non-Western, regional) forms (e.g., Pred & Watts 1992, Gupta 1998, Sivaramakrishnan & Agrawal c. 1999, Arce & Long 2000). There is no unified conception in these works, however, on what exactly constitutes modernity. References range from Baudelaire to Kant, Weber, Giddens, and Habermas. Kahn is right in saying that stating that modernity is plural, and then showing ethnographically the ways in which it is localized, has limitations in terms of theory. However, his appeal for an anthropology of modernity based on the theories of, say, Hegel, Weber, and Habermas compounds the problem, given the eurocentrism of most of these thinkers (see Dussel 1993 for an analysis of the deep ethnocentrism of Hegel and Habermas, whose works 'take on something of the sonority of Wagner's trumpets' (p. 71)). As Ribeiro says in his commentary to Kahn, 'modernity is subject to indigenization, but this does not amount to saying that it is a native category' (2001, p. 669). What is lost in these debates, it seems to me, is the very notion of difference as both a primary object of anthropology and an anchoring point for theoretical construction and political action. In the last instance, the limits of pluralizing modernity lie in the fact that it ends up reducing all social practice to being a manifestation of a European experience and will, no matter how qualified. Englund and Leach (2000) make a related argument in their critique of the ethnographic accounts of multiple modernities; they argue, correctly in my mind, that these works re-introduce a metanarrative of modernity in the analysis, be it 'the dialectic', a (European) core that remains invariant, or a self-serving appeal to 'wider context' or 'larger scale perspective'. The result is a weak relativism and a

pluralization of modernities that reflects the ethnographer's own assumptions. Englund and Leach's call is for a renewed attention to ethnographic knowledge as a domain for ascertaining the very contexts that are relevant to investigation, before such a context is imputed to this or that version of modernity. From this perspective, a question remains: *What other kinds of theoretical and political claims can we possibly make with the insights of the ethnographies of modernity,* that are not considered by their authors? In short, it seems to me that in many recent anthropological works modernity is, first, redefined in a way that dissolves it and deprives it of any semblance of historical coherence, let alone unitary, social and cultural logic and then, second, found ethnographically everywhere, always plural, changing and contested. A new balance seems necessary. After all, *why are we so ready still to ascribe to capitalism powerful and systematic effects*, with a coherent and for many a totalizing logic, *while denying modernity any significant connection with a coherent cultural logic, let alone a project of domination*?

3 This is a very sketchy presentation of this group's ideas in the best of cases. Broadly speaking, this group is associated with the work a few central figures, chiefly, the Argentinean/Mexican philosopher Enrique Dussel, the Peruvian sociologist Aníbal Quijano and, more recently, the Argentinean/US semiotician and cultural theorist Walter Mignolo. There are, however, a growing number of scholars associated with the group (e.g., Edgardo Lander in Venezuela; Santiago Castro-Gómez, Oscar Guardiola and Eduardo Restrepo in Colombia; Catherine Walsh in Quito; Zulma Palermo in Argentina; Jorge Sanjinés in Bolivia; Freya Schiwy, Fernando Coronil, Ramón Grosfogel, Jorge Saldivar, Ana Margarita Cervantes-Rodríguez, Agustín Lao Montes, Nelson Maldonado-Torres, and myself in the United States. More loosely associated with members of the group are: Linda Alcoff and Eduardo Mendieta (associated with Dussel); Elina Vuola (Institute of Development Studies, Helsinki); Marisa Belausteguigoitia in Mexico City; Cristina Rojas (Canada/Colombia). A number of PhD students are now working within the MC program at various universities in Quito, Mexico, and Duke/UNC. My first contact with some of the members of this group took place in Caracas in 1991 at a seminar on critical theory, where I met Lander and Quijano. This was followed by a joint session on 'Alternatives to Eurocentrism' at the 1998 World Congress of Sociology in Montreal, which resulted in a collective volume (Lander 2000). In more recent years, the group has gathered around several projects and places: the PhD Program on *Estudios de la Cultura* at the Universidad Andina Simón Bolivar in Quito, headed by Catherine Walsh; the doctoral Program on *Pensamianto Crítico en América* Latina at the new Universidad de la Ciudad de México in Mexico City; the geopolitics of knowledge project shared by Instituto Pensar (Universidad Javeriana, Bogotá), the Universidad Andina (Quito), and Duke University and University of North Carolina at Chapel Hill in the USA; and the Ethnic Studies department at Berkeley. For the main ideas presented here, see Dussel ([1975] 1983, 1992, 1993, 1996, 2000), Quijano (1988,

1993, 2000), Quijano & Wallerstein 1992), Mignolo (2000, 2001a,b), Lander (2000), Castro-Gómez (1996), Coronil (1996, 1997), Rojas (2001). Little of these debates have been translated into English. See Beverly and Oviedo, eds. (1993) for some of these authors' works in English. A volume in this language has been recently devoted to Dussel's work under the apposite title, *Thinking from the Underside of History* (Alcoff & Mendieta 2000). The journal *Nepantla. Views from South*, recently founded at Duke University, has a partial focus on the works of this group. See especially the Vol. 1, No. 3 issue of 2000, with contributions by Dussel and Quijano among others. Other collective volumes already produced by the group include: Castro-Gómez & Mendieta (1998), Castro-Gómez (2002), Mignolo (2001), Walsh *et al*. (2002). Another volume in English, by Grosfogel and Saldívar, is in preparation.

4 The choice of origin point is not a simple matter of preference. The conquest and colonization of America is the formative moment in the creation of Europe's Other; the point of origin of the capitalist world system, enabled by gold and silver from America; the origin of Europe's own concept of modernity (and of the first, Iberian, modernity, later eclipsed with the apogée of the second modernity); the initiation point of Occidentalism as the overarching imaginary and self-definition of the modern/colonial world system (which subalternized peripheral knowledge and created, in the eighteenth century, Orientalism as Other). The sixteenth century also saw crucial debates on 'the rights of the people', especially the legal-theological debates in Salamanca, later suppressed with the discourse of the 'rights of man' in the eighteenth century. Finally, with the Conquest and colonization, Latin America and the Caribbean emerged as 'the first periphery' of European modernity.

5 Different authors emphasize different factors in the making and functioning of modernity/coloniality. For Quijano, for instance, the key process in its constitution is the colonial classification and domination in terms of race. Coloniality is at the crux of modernity precisely because of the persistence of the idea of race. The second key process is the constitution of a structure of control of labor and resources. Dussel emphasizes the original violence created by modernity/coloniality (see also Rojas 2001), the importance of the first (Iberian) modernity for the structure of coloniality, and of course the concealment of the non-European (the negation of its alterity), particularly Latin America as modernity's first periphery. Mignolo also appeals to sources outside Iberian-America for his conceptualization of 'border thinking', the kind of thinking that brings about the de-subalternization of knowledge and rationality. Mignolo's project is that of conducting a genealogy of local histories leading to global designs, so as to enable other designs from other local histories to emerge from border thinking and the colonial difference. Some of these differences are explained by somewhat different frameworks, emphases and aims – political economy for Quijano, a philosophy of liberation for Dussel, literature and

epistemology for Mignolo. For most of these authors, however, Marxism and the question of the economy remain paramount.

6 Dussel's notion of exteriory has several sources, chiefly Levinas' concept of the contradiction Totality-Exteriority caused by the ethical interpellation of the Other (say, as poor). It also finds inspiration in Marx's notion of living labor as radical Other with respect to capital. Dussel spells out his views through the use of the theory of speech acts and communication (especially Apel's but also Habermas and Searle). Above all, Dussel introduces the concepts of Exteriory and Alterity as essential to his liberation philosophy; Exteriority becomes a negativity from which the domination of the Other can be discovered. There is a clear political bent to Dussel's intervention, which can thus be seen as an original theory and a radicalization of the work of Levinas and others. For Mignolo, as for Quijano', the modern world system looks different from its exteriority' (2000, p. 55). Mignolo builds on Dussel and also on other sources, from Fanon and W.E.B. Du Bois to Anzaldúa and writers from the Caribbean and the Maghreb such as Glissant, Béji, and Khatibi. Theories of 'double consciousness', double critique, an other thinking, crealization, and cultures of transience become equivalent to his own notion of border thinking. Mignolo's theory of exteriority is related to Dussel's but has a different emphasis. Mignolo differentiates between the 'interior borders' of the modern/colonial world system (imperial conflicts, say, between Spain and England) and its 'exterior borders' (imperial conflicts with cultures being colonized, e.g., between Spain and the Islamic world, between Spain and the Aztecs, or between the Britain and the India in the nineteenth century). The colonial difference becomes visible only from the exterior of the universal history of the modern world system; it makes possible breaking away from eurocentrism as epistemological perspective. Without this exteriority in which subaltern knowledges dwell, 'the only alternative left is a constant reading of the great thinkers of the West in search of new ways to imagine the future' (2000, p. 302).

Mignolo develops his notion of border thinking as 'thinking from another place, imagining an other language, arguing from another logic' (p. 313). It is a subaltern knowledge conceived from the borders of the colonial/modern world system that strives to break away from the dominance of eurocentrism. Border thinking refers to 'the moments in which the imaginary of the world system cracks' (2000, p. 23), 'an epistemology of and from the border' (p. 52), a kind of 'double critique' (Khatibi) that is critical of both Occidentalism/eurocentrism and of the excluded traditions themselves; this ability stems from its location in the borderlands (Anzaldúa). Border thinking is an ethical way of thinking because, in its marginality, it has no ethnocidal dimension. Its aim is not to correct lies and tell the truth, but 'to think otherwise, to move toward 'an other logic' – in sum to change the terms, not just the content of the conversation' (p. 70). Border thinking enables a new view of the diversity and alterity of the world, one that does not fall into the traps of a culturalist (essentialist) rhetoric but rather highlight the irreducible

differences that cannot be appropriated by the monotopic critique of modernity (the radical critique of Western logocentrism understood as a universal category), and that does not conceive of difference as antithesis in search of revanchism. Border thinking is complementary to deconstruction (and to all critical discourses of modernity); it sees decolonization as a particular kind of deconstruction but moves towards a fragmented, plural project instead of reproducing the abstract universals of modernity (including democracy and rights). Border thinking, finally, is an attempt to move beyond eurocentrism by revealing the coloniality of power embedded in the geopolitics of knowledge – a necessary step in order to 'undo the subalternization of knowledge and to look for ways of thinking beyond the categories of Western thought' (p. 326).

7 Elsewhere I have introduced the notion of *alternatives to modernity* to refer imagine an explicit cultural-political project of transformation from the perspective of modernity/coloniality – more specifically, an alternative construction of the world from the perspective of the colonial difference. The dimension of alternatives to modernity contributes to a weakening of modernity as logocentrism, as some of the philosophers of end of modernity would have it (e.g., Vattimo 1991), but from a different position. We should be clear also about what this concept is not: It does not point towards a *real* pristine future where development or modernity no longer exist; it is intended rather to intuit the possibility of *imagining* an era where development and modernity cease to be the central organizing principles of social life – a moment when social life is no longer so permeated by the constructs of economy, individual, rationality, order, and so forth that are characteristic of Eurocentered modernity. Alternatives to modernity is a reflection of a political desire, a desire of the critical utopian imagination, not a statement about the real, present or future. Operating in the cracks of modernity/coloniality, it gives content to the Porto Alegre Global Social Forum slogan, *another world is possible*. Alternative development, alternative modernities, and alternatives to modernity are partially conflicting but potentially complementary projects. One may lead to creating conditions for the others.

8 This perspective is at the heart of the Andean Studies Working Group: Development, Modernity and Coloniality, that Walter Mignolo and I co-facilite within the UNC-Duke Latin American Studies Consortium.

9 I am indebted to Juliana Flórez (Department of Social Psychology, Universitat Autonoma de Barcelona; Visiting Scholar at Chapel Hill for Spring 2003) for this point, and for comments below on some of the contributions from the sociology of knowledge and from feminist theory in social psychology, particularly in the work of Margot Pujal. Some of the ideas also come from discussions at a meeting of the some of the group's members in Chapel Hill and Duke in February 2000, facilitated particularly by Freya Schiwy's presentation and the discussion on liberation theology, and by discussions at LASA Congress (Dallas, March 2003).

10 I thank Nelson Maldonado for bringing this important book to our attention and speaking enthusiastically about it in one of our recent meetings in Chapel Hill and Duke.

11 These issues also emerged in conversations with Juliana Flórez concerning the work of feminist theory in social psychology (Chapel Hill, April 2003).

12 I am referring to the collective work of the Grupo de Trabajo de Ecología Poliíica established by CLACSO, and coordinated by Hector Alimonda. Of particular interest here are the *Manifesto. Por Una Etica de la Sustentabilidad* (PNUMA, 2002), at www.rolac.unep.mx, and the recent draft for discusión by Enrique Leff (2003).

It should be mentioned that this important initiative is also still to be 'engendered'.

13 See the Women and the Politics of Place Project at www.sidint.org and the special issue of *Development* devoted to the project, 45(1), March 2002). I have co-organized this project with Wendy Harcourt, Society for International Development. See also Julie Graham and Katherine Gibson's project web page, www.communityeconomies.org.

## References

Alcoff, Linda (1991) 'The Problem of Speaking for Others', *Critical Inquiry*, vol. 20, pp. 5–32.

—— (1988) 'Cultural Feminism versus Poststructuralism: The Identity Crisis in Feminist Theory', *Signs*, vol. 13, pp. 405–36.

Alcoff, Linda & Mendieta, Eduardo, eds. (2000) *Thinking from the Underside of History. Enrique Dussel's Philosophy of Liberation*. Lanham: Rowman and Littelfield.

Anzaldúa, Gloria & Analouise Keating, eds. (2003) *This Bridge We Call Home. Radical Visions for Social Transformation*. New York: Routledge.

Anzaldúa, Gloria (2003) 'Preface. (Un)natural bridges, (Un)safe spaces', in *This Bridge We Call Home. Radical Visions for Social Transformation*, eds G. Anzaldúa and A. Keating, New York: Routledge, pp. 1–5.

Appadurai, Arjun (1996) *Modernity at Large.* Minneapolis: University of Minnesota Press.

Arce, Alberto & Long, Norman, eds. (2000) *Anthropology, Development, and Modernities.* London: Routledge.

Behar, Ruth, & Gordon, Deborah, eds. (1995) *Women Writing Culture*. Berkeley: University of California Press.

Belausteguigoitia, Marisa (2002) 'The Color of the Earth: Indigenous Women "Before the Law"', *Development*, vol. 45, no. 1, pp. 47–53.

—— (1998) 'Visualizing Places: 'She Looks, therefore . . . Who Is?'', *Development*, vol. 41, no. 2, pp. 44–52.

Beverly, John & Oviedo, José, eds. (1993) *The Postmodernism Debate in Latin America*. Durham: Duke University Press.

Bhavani, Kum-Kum, Foran, John & Kurian, Priya, eds. (2003) *Feminist Futures: Re-Imagining Women, Culture and Development*. London: Zed Books.

Boff, Leonardo (2002) *El Cuidado Esencial*. Madrid: Editorial Trotta.

Castro-Gómez, Santiago (1996) *Crítica de la razón latinoamericana*. Barcelona: Puvill Libros.

—— ed. (2002) *La reestructuración de las ciencias sociales en América Latina*. Bogotá: Universidad Javeriana.

Castro-Gómez, Santiago, & Mendieta, Eduardo, eds. (1998) *Teorías sin disciplina, latinoamericanismo, poscolonialidad y globalización en debate*. Mexico, DF: Miguel Angel Porrúa/University of San Francisco.

Coronil, Fernando (1997) *The Magical State: Nature, Money and Modernity in Venezuela*. Chicago: University of Chicago Press.

—— (1996) 'Beyond Occidentalism: Toward Nonimperial Geohistorical Categories', *Cultural Anthropology*, vol. 11, no. 1, pp. 52–87.

Dussel, Enrique (2000) 'Europe, Modernity, and Eurocentrism', *Nepantla*, vol. 1, no. 3, pp. 465–478.

—— (1996) *The Underside of Modernity*. Atlantic Highlands, NJ: Humanities Press.

—— (1993) 'Eurocentrism and Modernity', in *The Postmodernism Debate in Latin America*, eds J. Beverly and J. Oviedo, Durham.: Duke University Press, pp. 65–76.

—— (1992) *1492. El encubrimiento del Otro*. Bogotá: Antropos.

—— (1983) [1975]. *Introducción a la Filosofía de la Liberación* (2ª. Edición). Bogotá: Editorial Nueva América.

—— (1976) *Filosofía de la Liberación*. Mexico: Editorial Edicol.

Englund, Harri & Leach, James (2000) 'Ethnography and the Meta-Narratives of Modernity', *Current Anthropology*, vol. 41, no. 2, pp. 225–248.

Escobar, Arturo (1999) 'After Nature: Steps to an Anti-essentialist Political Ecology', *Current Anthropology*, vol. 40, no. 1, pp. 1–30.

Flórez, Juliana (2003) 'Notas sobre teoría feminista y modernidad/colonialidad'. Documento de trabajo sin publicar, University of North Carolina, Chapel Hill, April.

Foucault, Michel (1979) *Discipline and Punish.* New York: Vintage Books.

—— (1973) *The Order of Things.* New York: Vintage Books.

Gaonkar, Dilip P., ed. (2001) *Alternative Modernities*. Durham: Duke University Press.

Gibson-Graham, J.K. (2003) 'Politics of Empire, Politics of Place'. Unpublished manuscript.

—— (1996) *The End of Capitalism (As We Knew It)*. Oxford: Blackwell.

Giddens, Anthony (1990) *The Consequences of Modernity*. Stanford: Stanford University Press.

Gupta, Akhil (1998) *Postcolonial Developments.* Durham: Duke University Press.

Habermas, Jurgen (1987) *The Philosophical Discourse of Modernity*. Cambridge: MIT Press.

—— (1973) *Legitimation Crisis*. Boston: Beacon Press.

Halperin, David (1995) *Saint Foucault: Toward a Gay Hagiography*. New York: Oxford University Press.
Haraway, Donna (1988) 'Situated Knowledges: The Science Question in Feminism and the Privilege of Partial Perspective', *Feminist Studies*, vol. 14, no. 3, pp. 575–599.
Harcourt, Wendy & Escobar, Arturo (2002) 'Lead Article: Women and the Politics of Place', *Development*, vol. 45, no. 2, pp. 7–14.
Hardt, Michael & Negri, Antonio (2000) *Empire*. Cambridge: Harvard University Press.
Heidegger, Martin (1977) 'The Age of the World Picture', in *The Question Concerning Technology*, ed. M. Heidegger, New York: Harper and Row, pp. 115–154.
Kahn, Joel (2001) 'Anthropology and Modernity', *Current Anthropology*, vol. 42, no. 5, pp. 651–680.
Lander, Eduardo (2002) 'Los derechos de propiedad intelectual en la geopolítica del saber de la sociedad global', in *Interdisciplinar las ciencias sociales*, eds C. Walsh, F. Schiwy and S. Castro-Gómez., Quito: Universidad Andina/Abya Yala, pp. 73–102.
—— ed. (2000) *La colonialidad del saber: eurocentrismo y ciencias sociales*. Buenos Aires: CLACSO.
Latour, Bruno (1993) *We Have Never Been Modern*. Cambridge: Harvard University Press.
Leff, Enrique (2003) 'La Ecología Política en América Latina: Un Campo en Construcción (Borrador para discusión)'. CLACSO Grupo de Trabajo en Ecología Política. Manuscrito sin publicar.
—— (2000) *Saber Ambiental*. Mexico: Siglo XXI.
Maldonado-Torres, Nelson (2003) 'Imperio y colonialidad del ser'. Presented at the XXIV International Congress, Latin American Studies Association, LASA, Dallas, March 27–29.
Mignolo, Walter (2001a) 'Local Histories and Global Designs: An Interview with Walter Mignolo', *Discourse*, vol. 22, no. 3, pp. 7–33.
—— (2000) *Local Histories/Global Designs*. Princeton: Princeton University Press.
—— ed. (2001b) *Capitalismo y geopolítica del conocimiento*. Buenos Aires: Ediciones del Signo.
Nicholson, Linda, ed. (1999) *Feminism/Postmodernims*. New York: Routledge.
Panikkar, Raimon (1993) *The Cosmotheandric Experience*. New York: Orbis Books.
Pred, Alan & Watts, Michael (1992) *Reworking Modernity*. New Brunswick: Rutgers University Press.
Quijano, Aníbal (2000) 'Coloniality of Power, Ethnocentrism, and Latin America', *Nepantla*, vol. 1, no. 3, pp. 533–580.
—— (1993) 'Modernity, Identity, and Utopia in Latin America', in *The Postmodernism Debate in Latin America*, eds J. Beverly and J. Oviedo., Durham: Duke University Press, pp. 140–155.
—— (1988) *Modernidad, Identidad y Utopía en América Latina*. Lima: Sociedad y Política Ediciones.

Quijano, Aníbal & Wallerstein, Immanuel (1992) 'Americanity as a Concept, or the Americas in the Modern World-System', *International Social Science Journal*, vol. 134, pp. 459–559.

Rojas, Cristina (2001) *Civilization and Violence. Regimes of Representation in Nineteenth Century Colombia*. Minneapolis: University of Minnesota Press.

Sandoval, Chela (2003) Foreword: AfterBridge: Technologies of Crossing, in *This Bridge We Call Home. Radical Visions for Social Transformation*, eds G. Anzaldúa and A. Keating, New York: Routledge, pp. 21–26.

Santos, Boaventura de Sousa (2003) 'The World Social Forum: Toward a Counter-Hegemonic Globalization'. Presented at the XXIV International Congress, Latin American Studies Association, LASA, Dallas, March 27–29. See also at: http://www.ces.fe.uc.pt/bss/fsm.php

Shohat, Ella, ed. (1998) *Talking Visions. Multicultural Feminism in a Transnational Age*. Cambridge: MIT Press.

Sivaramakrishnan, K. & Agrawal, Arun, eds. (2003) *Regional modernities: the cultural politics of development in India.* Stanford: Stanford University Press.

Tomlinson, John (1999) *Globalization and Culture.* Chicago: University of Chicago Press.

Vattimo, Gianni (1991) *The End of Modernity*. Baltimore: Johns Hopkins University Press.

Virilio, Paul (1999) *Politics of the Very Worst*. New York: Semitext(e).

Vuola, Elina (In press) 'Option for the Poor and the Exclusion of Women: The Challenge of Postmodernism and Feminism to Liberation Theology', in *Opting for the Margins. Theological and Other Challenges in Posmodern and Postcolonial Worlds*, ed. Joerg Rieger, Oxford: Oxford University Press.

—— (2003) 'Radical Eurocentrism. The Crisis and Death of Latin American Liberation Theology and Recipes for its Improvement', in *Interpreting the Postmodern. Responses to Radical Orthodoxy*, eds Rosemary Ruether & Marion Grau, New York: T & T Clark International, pp. 57–75.

—— (2002) 'Remaking Universals? Transnational Feminism(s) Challenging Fundamentalist Ecumenism', *Theory, Culture, Society*, vol. 19, no. 1–2, pp. 175–195.

——(2000) 'Thinking *Otherwise*: Dussel, Liberation Theology, and Feminism', in *Thinking from the Underside of History*, eds L. Alcoff and E. Mendieta, Lanham: Rowman and Littlefield, pp. 149–180.

Wallerstein, Immanuel (2000) 'Globalization, or the Age of Transition? A long-Term View of the Trajectory of the World System', *International Sociology*, vol. 15, no. 2, pp. 249–265.

Walsh, Catherine (2003) 'Ecuador 2003: Promises and Challenges'. Presented at the UNC-Duke Latin American Studies 'Burning Issues' Series, April 25.

Walsh, Catherine, Schiwy, Freya, & Castro-Gómez, Santiago, eds. (2002) *Interdisciplinar las ciencias sociales*. Quito: Universidad Andina/Abya Yala.

**Ramón Grosfoguel**

# THE EPISTEMIC DECOLONIAL TURN

## Beyond political-economy paradigms[1]

In October 1998, there was a conference/dialogue at Duke University between the South Asian Subaltern Studies Group and the Latin American Subaltern Studies Group. The dialogue initiated in this conference eventually resulted in the publication of several issues of the journal NEPANTLA. However, this conference was the last time the Latin American Subaltern Studies Group met before their split. Among the many reasons and debates that produced this split, there are two that I would like to stress. The Latin American Subaltern Studies Group composed primarily by Latinamericanist scholars in the USA. Despite their attempt at producing a radical and alternative knowledge, they reproduced the epistemic schema of Area Studies in the United States. With a few exceptions, they produced studies *about* the subaltern rather than studies *with* and *from* a subaltern perspective. Like the imperial epistemology of Area Studies, theory was still located in the North while the subjects to be studied are located in the South. This colonial epistemology was crucial to my dissatisfaction with the project. As a Puerto Rican in the United States, I was dissatisfied with the epistemic consequences of the knowledge produced by this Latinamericanist group. They under-estimated in their work ethnic/racial perspectives coming from the region, while giving privilege to Western thinkers. This is related to my second point: they gave epistemic privilege to what they called the 'four horses of the apocalypse',[2] that is, Foucault, Derrida, Gramsci and Guha. Among the four main thinkers they privilege, three are Eurocentric thinkers while two of them (Derrida and Foucault) form part of the poststructuralist/postmodern Western canon. By privileging Western thinkers as their central theoretical apparatus, they betrayed their goal to produce subaltern studies.

Among the many reasons for the split of the Latin American Subaltern Studies Group, one of them was between those who read subalternity as a postmodern critique (which represents a Eurocentric critique of eurocentrism) and those who read subalternity as a decolonial critique (which represents a critique of eurocentrism from subalternized and silenced knowledges) (Mignolo 2000, pp. 183–186, pp. 213–214). For those of us that took side with the decolonial critique, the dialogue with the Latin American Subaltern Studies Group as well as with the South Asian Subaltern School made evident the need to epistemologically transcend, decolonize the Western canon and epistemology. South Asian Subaltern School main project is a

critique to Western European colonial historiography about India and to Indian nationalist eurocentric historiography of India. But by using a Western epistemology and privileging Gramsci and Foucault, constrained and limited the radicality of their critique to eurocentrism. Although they represent different epistemic projects, the South Asian Subaltern School privilege of Western epistemic canon overlapped with the sector of the Latin American Subaltern Studies Group that sided with postmodernism. However, with all its limits, South Asian Subaltern Studies Group was part of an intellectual movement known as postcolonial critique (a critique of modernity from the Global South) as opposed to the Latin American Subaltern Studies Group postmodern critique (a critique of modernity from the Global North) (Mignolo 2000). These debates made clear to us the need to decolonize not only Subaltern Studies but also Postcolonial Studies (Grosfoguel 2006).

This is not an essentialist, fundamentalist, anti-European critique. It a perspective that is critical of both Eurocentric and Third World fundamentalisms, colonialism and nationalism. What all fundamentalisms share (including the Eurocentric one) is the premise that there is only one sole epistemic tradition from which to achieve Truth and Universality. However, my main points here are three: (1) that a decolonial epistemic perspective requires a broader canon of thought than simply the Western canon (including the Left Western canon); (2) that a truly universal decolonial perspective cannot be based on an abstract universal (one particular that raises itself as universal global design), but would have to be the result of the critical dialogue between diverse critical epistemic/ethical/political projects towards a pluriversal as oppose to a universal world; (3) that decolonization of knowledge would require to take seriously the epistemic perspective/cosmologies/insights of critical thinkers from the Global South thinking *from* and *with* subalternized racial/ethnic/sexual spaces and bodies. Postmodernism and postructuralism as epistemological projects are caught within the Western canon reproducing within its domains of thought and practice a coloniality of power/knowledge.

However, what I have said about the Latin American Subaltern Studies Group applies to the paradigms of political-economy. In this article, I propose that an epistemic perspective from racial/ethnic subaltern locations has a lot to contribute to a radical decolonial critical theory beyond the way traditional political-economy paradigms conceptualize capitalism as a global or world-system. The idea here is to decolonize political-economy paradigms as well as world-system analysis and to propose an alternative decolonial conceptualization of the world-system. The first part is an epistemic discussion about the implications of the epistemological critique of feminist and subalternized racial/ethnic intellectuals to western epistemology. The second part is the implications of these critiques to the way we conceptualize the global or world system. Finally, the last part is a discussion of global coloniality today.

## Epistemological critique

The first point to discuss is the contribution of racial/ethnic and feminist subaltern perspectives to epistemological questions. The hegemonic Eurocentric paradigms that have informed western philosophy and sciences in the 'modern/colonial capitalist/patriarchal world-system' for the last 500 hundred years assume a universalistic, neutral, objective point of view. Chicana and black feminist scholars (Moraga & Anzaldua 1983, Collins 1990) as well as thirdworld scholars inside and outside the United States (Dussel 1977, Mignolo 2000) reminded us that we always speak from a particular location in the power structures. Nobody escapes the class, sexual, gender, spiritual, linguistic, geographical, and racial hierarchies of the 'modern/colonial capitalist/patriarchal world-system'. As feminist scholar Donna Haraway (1988) states, our knowledges are always situated. Black feminist scholars called this perspective 'afro-centric epistemology' (Collins 1990) (which is not equivalent to the afrocentrist perspective) while Latin American Philosopher of Liberation Enrique Dussel called it 'geopolitics of knowledge' (Dussel 1977) and following Fanon (1967) and Anzaldúa (1987) I will use the term 'body-politics of knowledge'.

This is not only a question about social values in knowledge production or the fact that our knowledge is always partial. The main point here is the locus of enunciation, that is, the geo-political and body-political location of the subject that speaks. In Western philosophy and sciences the subject that speaks is always hidden, concealed, erased from the analysis. The 'ego-politics of knowledge' of Western philosophy has always privilege the myth of a non-situated 'Ego'. Ethnic/racial/gender/sexual epistemic location and the subject that speaks are always decoupled. By delinking ethnic/racial/gender/sexual epistemic location from the subject that speaks, Western philosophy and sciences are able to produce a myth about a Truthful universal knowledge that covers up, that is, conceals who is speaking as well as the geo-political and body-political epistemic location in the structures of colonial power/knowledge from which the subject speaks.

It is important here to distinguish the 'epistemic location' from the 'social location'. The fact that one is socially located in the oppressed side of power relations, does not automatically mean that he/she is epistemically thinking from a subaltern epistemic location. Precisely, the success of the modern/colonial world-system consist in making subjects that are socially located in the oppressed side of the colonial difference, to think epistemicaly like the ones on the dominant positions. Subaltern epistemic perspectives are knowledge coming from below that produces a critical perspective of hegemonic knowledge in the power relations involved. I am not claiming an epistemic populism where knowledge produced from below is automatically an epistemic subaltern knowledge. What I am claiming is that all knowledges

are epistemically located in the dominant or the subaltern side of the power relations and that this is related to the geo- and body-politics of knowledge. The disembodied and unlocated neutrality and objectivity of the ego-politics of knowledge is a Western myth.

Rene Descartes, the founder of Modern Western Philosophy, inaugurates a new moment in the history of Western thought. He replaces God, as the foundation of knowledge in the Theo-politics of knowledge of the European Middle Ages, with (Western) Man as the foundation of knowledge in European Modern times. All the attributes of God are now extrapolated to (Western) Man. Universal Truth beyond time and space, privilege access to the laws of the Universe, and the capacity to produce scientific knowledge and theory is now placed in the mind of Western Man. The Cartesian 'ego-cogito' ('I think, therefore I am') is the foundation of modern Western sciences. By producing a dualism between mind and body and between mind and nature, Descartes was able to claim non-situated, universal, God-eyed view knowledge. This is what the Colombian philosopher Santiago Castro-Gomez called the 'point zero' perspective of Eurocentric philosophies (Castro-Gomez 2003). The 'point zero' is the point of view that hides and conceals itself as being beyond a particular point of view, that is, the point of view that represents itself as being without a point of view. It is this 'god-eye view' that always hides its local and particular perspective under an abstract universalism. Western philosophy privileges 'ego politics of knowledge' over the 'geopolitics of knowledge' and the 'body-politics of knowledge'. Historically, this has allowed Western man (the gendered term is intentionally used here) to represent his knowledge as the only one capable of achieving a universal consciousness, and to dismiss non-Western knowledge as particularistic and, thus, unable to achieve universality.

This epistemic strategy has been crucial for Western global designs. By hiding the location of the subject of enunciation, European/Euro-American colonial expansion and domination was able to construct a hierarchy of superior and inferior knowledge and, thus, of superior and inferior people around the world. We went from the sixteenth century characterization of 'people without writing' to the eighteenth and nineteenth century characterization of 'people without history', to the twentieth century characterization of 'people without development' and more recently, to the early twenty-first century of 'people without democracy'. We went from the sixteenth century 'rights of people' (Sepulveda versus de las Casas debate in the school of Salamanca in the mid-sixteenth century), to the eighteenth century 'rights of man' (Enlightment philosophers), and to the late twentieth century 'human rights'. All of these are part of global designs articulated to the simultaneous production and reproduction of an international division of labor of core/periphery that overlaps with the global racial/ethnic hierarchy of Europeans/non-Europeans.

However, as Enrique Dussel (1994) has reminded us, the Cartesian 'ego cogito' ('I think, therefore I am') was preceded by 150 years (since the beginnings of the European colonial expansion in 1492) of the European 'ego conquistus' ('I conquer, therefore I am'). The social, economic, political and historical conditions of possibility for a subject to assume the arrogance of becoming God-like and put himself as the foundation of all Truthful knowledge was the Imperial Being, that is, the subjectivity of those who are at the center of the world because they have already conquered it. What are the decolonial implications of this epistemological critique to our knowledge production and to our concept of world-system?

## Coloniality of power as the power matrix of the modern/colonial world

Globalization studies, political-economy paradigms and world-system analysis, with only a few exceptions, have not derived the epistemological and theoretical implications of the epistemic critique coming from subaltern locations in the colonial divide and expressed in academia through ethnic studies and woman studies. They still continue to produce knowledge from the Western man 'point zero' god-eye view. This has led to important problems in the way we conceptualize global capitalism and the 'world-system'. These concepts are in need of decolonization and this can only be achieved with a decolonial epistemology that overtly assumes the decolonial geopolitics and body-politics of knowledge as points of departure to a radical critique. The following examples can illustrate this point.

If we analyze the European colonial expansion from a Eurocentric point of view, what we get is a picture in which the origins of the so-called capitalist world-system is primarily produced by the inter-imperial competition among European Empires. The primary motive for this expansion was to find shorter routes to the East, which let accidentally to the so-called discovery and, eventual, Spanish colonization of the Americas. From this point of view, the capitalist world-system would be primarily an economic system that determine the behavior of the major social actors by the economic logic of making profits as manifested in the extraction of surplus value and the ceaseless accumulation of capital at a world-scale. Moreover, the concept of capitalism implied in this perspective privileges economic relations over other social relations. Accordingly, the transformation in the relations of production produces a new class structure typical of capitalism as oppose to other social systems and other forms of domination. Class analysis and economic structural transformations are privileged over other power relations.

Without denying the importance of the endless accumulation of capital at a world scale and the existence of a particular class structure in global capitalism,

I raise the following epistemic question: How would the world-system looks like if we move the locus of enunciation from the European man to an Indigenous women in the Americas, to, say Rigoberta Menchu in Guatemala or to Domitila in Bolivia? I do not pretend to speak for or represent the perspective of these indigenous women. What I attempt to do is to shift the location from which these paradigms are thinking. The first implication of shifting our geopolitics of knowledge is that what arrived in the Americas in the late fifteenth century was not only an economic system of capital and labor for the production of commodities to be sold for a profit in the world market. This was a crucial part of, but was not the sole element in, the entangled 'package'. What arrived in the Americas was a broader and wider entangled power structure that an economic reductionist perspective of the world-system is unable to account for. From the structural location of an indigenous woman in the Americas what arrived was a more complex world-system than what political-economy paradigms and world-system analysis portrait. A European/capitalist/military/christian/patriarchal/white/heterosexual/male arrived in the Americas and established simultaneously in time and space several entangled global hierarchies that for purposes of clarity in this exposition I will list below as if they were separate from each other:

1 a particular global class formation where a diversity of forms of labor (slavery, semi-serfdom, wage labor, petty-commodity production, etc.) are going to co-exist and be organized by capital as a source of production of surplus value through the selling of commodities for a profit in the world market;
2 an international division of labor of core and periphery where capital organized labor in the periphery around coerced and authoritarian forms (Wallerstein 1974);
3 an inter-state system of politico-military organizations controlled by European males and institutionalized in colonial administrations (Wallerstein 1979);
4 a global racial/ethnic hierarchy that privileges European people over non-European people (Quijano 1993, 2000);
5 a global gender hierarchy that privileges males over females and European patriarchy over other forms of gender relations (Spivak 1988, Enloe 1990);
6 a sexual hierarchy that privileges heterosexuals over homosexuals and lesbians (it is important to remember that most indigenous peoples in the Americas did not consider sexuality among males a pathological behavior and has no homophobic ideology);
7 a spiritual hierarchy that privileges Christians over non-Christian/non-Western spiritualities institutionalized in the globalization of the Christian (Catholic and later Protestant) church;

8 an epistemic hierarchy that privileges Western knowledge and cosmology over non-Western knowledge and cosmologies, and institutionalized in the global university system (Mignolo 1995, 2000, Quijano 1991).
9 a linguistic hierarchy between European languages and non-European languages that privileges communication and knowledge/theoretical production in the former and subalternize the latter as sole producers of folklore or culture but not of knowledge/theory (Mignolo 2000).

It is not an accident that the conceptualization of the world-system, from decolonial perspectives of the South will question its traditional conceptualizations produced by thinkers from the North. Following Peruvian Sociologist, Aníbal Quijano (1991, 1998, 2000), we could conceptualize the present world-system as a historical-structural heterogeneous totality with a specific power matrix that he calls a 'colonial power matrix' ('patrón de poder colonial'). This matrix affects all dimensions of social existence such as sexuality, authority, subjectivity and labor (Quijano 2000). The sixteenth century initiates a new global colonial power matrix that by the late nineteenth century came to cover the whole planet. Taking a step further from Quijano, I conceptualize the coloniality of power as an entanglement or, to use US Third World Feminist concept, intersectionality (Crenshaw 1989, Fregoso 2003) of multiple and heterogeneous global hierarchies ('heterarchies') of sexual, political, epistemic, economic, spiritual, linguistic and racial forms of domination and exploitation where the racial/ethnic hierarchy of the European/non-European divide transversally reconfigures all of the other global power structures. What is new in the 'coloniality of power' perspective is how the idea of race and racism becomes the organizing principle that structures all of the multiple hierarchies of the world-system (Quijano 1993). For example, the different forms of labor that are articulated to capitalist accumulation at a world-scale are assigned according to this racial hierarchy; coercive (or cheap) labor is done by non-European people in the periphery and 'free wage labor' in the core. The global gender hierarchy is also affected by race: contrary to pre-European patriarchies where all women were inferior to all men, in the new colonial power matrix some women (of European origin) have a higher status and access to resources than some men (of non-European origin). The idea of race organizes the world's population into a hierarchical order of superior and inferior people that becomes an organizing principle of the international division of labor and of the global patriarchal system. Contrary to the Eurocentric perspective, race, gender, sexuality, spirituality, and epistemology are not additive elements to the economic and political structures of the capitalist world-system, but an integral, entangled and constitutive part of the broad entangled 'package' called the European modern/colonial capitalist/patriarchal world-system (Grosfoguel 2002). European patriarchy and European notions of sexuality, epistemology and spirituality were exported to the rest of the world through colonial expansion

as the hegemonic criteria to racialize, classify and pathologize the rest of the world's population in a hierarchy of superior and inferior races.

This conceptualization has enormous implications that I can only briefly mention here:

1 The old Eurocentric idea that societies develop at the level of the nation-state in terms of a linear evolution of modes of production from pre-capitalist to capitalist is overcome. We are all encompassed within a capitalist world-system that articulates different forms of labor according to the racial classification of the world's population (Quijano 2000, Grosfoguel 2002).
2 The old Marxist paradigm of infrastructure and superstructure is replaced by a historical-heterogeneous structure (Quijano 2000), or a 'heterarchy' (Kontopoulos 1993), that is, an entangled articulation of multiple hierarchies, in which subjectivity and the social imaginary is not derivative but constitutive of the structures of the world-system (Grosfoguel 2002). In this conceptualization, race and racism are not superstructural or instrumental to an overarching logic of capitalist accumulation; they are constitutive of capitalist accumulation at a world-scale. The 'colonial power matrix' is an organizing principle involving exploitation and domination exercised in multiple dimensions of social life, from economic, sexual, or gender relations, to political organizations, structures of knowledge, state institutions, and households (Quijano 2000).
3 The old division between culture and political-economy as expressed in post-colonial studies and political-economy approaches is overcome (Grosfoguel 2002). Post-colonial studies conceptualize the capitalist world-system as being constituted primarily by culture, while political-economy place the primary determination on economic relations. In the 'coloniality of power' approach, what comes first, 'culture or the economy', is a false dilemma, a chicken-egg dilemma that obscure the complexity of the capitalist world-system (Grosfoguel 2002).
4 Coloniality is not equivalent to colonialism. It is not derivative from, or antecedent to, modernity. Coloniality and modernity constitute two sides of a single coin. The same way as the European industrial revolution was achieved on the shoulders of the coerced forms of labor in the periphery, the new identities, rights, laws, and institutions of modernity such as nation-states, citizenship and democracy were formed in a process of colonial interaction with, and domination/exploitation of, non-Western people.
5 To call 'capitalist' the present world-system is, to say the least, misleading. Given the hegemonic Eurocentric 'common sense', the moment we use the word 'capitalism' people immediately think that we are talking about the 'economy'. However, 'capitalism' is only one of the multiple entangled constellations of colonial power matrix of the

'European modern/colonial capitalist/patriarchal world-system'. It is an important one, but not the sole one. Given its entanglement with other power relations, destroying the capitalist aspects of the world-system would not be enough to destroy the present world-system. To transform this world-system it is crucial to destroy the historical-structural heterogenous totality called the 'colonial power matrix' of the 'world-system'.

6 Anti-capitalist decolonization and liberation cannot be reduced to only one dimension of social life. It requires a broader transformation of the sexual, gender, spiritual, epistemic, economic, political, linguistic and racial hierarchies of the modern/colonial world-system. The 'coloniality of power' perspective challenges us to think about social change and social transformation in a non-reductionist way.

## From global colonialism to global coloniality

We cannot think of decolonization in terms of conquering power over the juridical-political boundaries of a state, that is, by achieving control over a single nation-state (Grosfoguel 1996). The old national liberation and socialist strategies of taking power at the level of a nation-state are not sufficient because global coloniality is not reducible to the presence or absence of a colonial administration (Grosfoguel 2002) or to the political/economic structures of power. One of the most powerful myths of the twentieth century was the notion that the elimination of colonial administrations amounted to the decolonization of the world. This led to the myth of a 'postcolonial' world. The heterogeneous and multiple global structures put in place over a period of 450 years did not evaporate with the juridical-political decolonization of the periphery over the past 50 years. We continue to live under the same 'colonial power matrix'. With juridical-political decolonization we moved from a period of 'global *colonialism*' to the current period of 'global *coloniality*'. Although 'colonial administrations' have been almost entirely eradicated and the majority of the periphery is politically organized into independent states, non-European people are still living under crude European/Euro-American exploitation and domination. The old colonial hierarchies of European versus non-Europeans remain in place and are entangled with the 'international division of labor' and accumulation of capital at a world-scale (Quijano 2000, Grosfoguel 2002).

Herein lies the relevance of the distinction between 'colonialism' and 'coloniality'. Coloniality allow us to understand the continuity of colonial forms of domination after the end of colonial administrations, produced by colonial cultures and structures in the modern/colonial capitalist/patriarchal world-system. 'Coloniality of power' refers to a crucial structuring process in

the modern/colonial world-system that articulates peripheral locations in the international division of labor with the global racial/ethnic hierarchy and Third World migrants' inscription in the racial/ethnic hierarchy of metropolitan global cities. In this sense, there is a periphery outside and inside the core zones and there is a core inside and outside the peripheral regions.

Peripheral nation-states and non-European people live today under the regime of 'global coloniality' imposed by the United States through the International Monetary Fund (IMF), the World Bank (WB), the Pentagon and NATO. Peripheral zones inside and outside core zones remain in a colonial situation even though are not any longer under a colonial administration.

'Colonial' does not refer only to 'classical colonialism' or 'internal colonialism', nor can it be reduced to the presence of a 'colonial administration'. Quijano distinguishes between colonialism and coloniality. I use the word 'colonialism' to refer to 'colonial situations' enforced by the presence of a colonial administration such as the period of classical colonialism, and, following Quijano (1991, 1993, 1998), I use 'coloniality' to address 'colonial situations' in the present period in which colonial administrations have almost been eradicated from the capitalist world-system. By 'colonial situations' I mean the cultural, political, sexual, spiritual, epistemic and economic oppression/exploitation of subordinate racialized/ethnic groups by dominant racialized/ethnic groups with or without the existence of colonial administrations. Five hundred years of European colonial expansion and domination formed an international division of labor between Europeans and non-Europeans that is reproduced in the present so-called 'post-colonial' phase of the capitalist world-system (Wallerstein 1979, 1995). Today the core zones of the capitalist world-economy overlap with predominantly White/European/Euro-American societies such as Western Europe, Canada, Australia and the United States, while peripheral zones overlap with previously colonized non-European people. Japan is the only exception that confirms the rule. Japan was never colonized nor dominated by Europeans and, similar to the West, played an active role in building its own colonial empire. China, although never fully colonized, was peripheralized through the use of colonial entrepots such as Hong Kong and Macao, and through direct military interventions such as the opium wars in the nineteenth century.

The mythology about the 'decolonization of the world' obscures the continuities between the colonial past and current global colonial/racial hierarchies and contributes to the invisibility of 'coloniality' today. For the last fifty years, peripheral states that are today formally independent, following the dominant Eurocentric liberal discourses (Wallerstein 1991a, 1991b, 1995), constructed ideologies of 'national identity', 'national development', and 'national sovereignty' that produced an illusion of 'independence', 'development', and 'progress'. Yet their economic and political systems were shaped by their subordinate position in a capitalist world-system organized around a

hierarchical international division of labor (Wallerstein 1979, 1984, 1995). The multiple and heterogeneous processes of the world-system, together with the predominance of Eurocentric cultures (Said 1979, Wallerstein 1991b, 1995, Lander 1998, Quijano 1998, Mignolo 2000), constitute a 'global coloniality' between European/Euro-American peoples and non-European peoples. Thus, 'coloniality' is entangled with, but is not reducible to, the international division of labor. The global racial/ethnic hierarchy of Europeans and non-Europeans, is an integral part of the development of the capitalist world system's international division of labor (Wallerstein 1983, Quijano 1993, Mignolo 1995). In these 'post-independence' times the 'colonial' axis between Europeans/Euro-Americans and non-Europeans is inscribed not only in relations of exploitation (between capital and labor) and relations of domination (between metropolitan and peripheral states), but in the production of subjectivities and knowledge. In sum, part of the Eurocentric myth is that we live in a so-called 'post'-colonial era and that the world and, in particular, metropolitan centers, are in no need of decolonization. In this conventional definition, coloniality is reduced to the presence of colonial administrations. However, as the work of Peruvian sociologist Anibal Quijano (1993, 1998, 2000) has shown with his 'coloniality of power' perspective, we still live in a colonial world and we need to break from the narrow ways of thinking about colonial relations, in order to accomplish the unfinished and incomplete twentieth century dream of decolonization. This proposal invite us to examine new decolonial utopian alternatives beyond Eurocentric and 'Thirdworldist' fundamentalisms.

## Notes

1 The notion of 'Decolonial Turn' is a notion elaborated by Puerto Rican fanonian philosopher Nelson Maldonado-Torres. See his forthcoming book *Against War* (Duke University Press, 2006).

2 See the discussion of this term coined by Florencia Mallon (1994) in Ileana Rodriguez's (2001) introductory essay to the The Latin American Subaltern Studies Reader.

## References

Anzaldúa, Gloria (1987) *Borderlands/La Frontera: The New Mestiza*. San Francisco: Spinsters/Aunt Lute.

Castro-Gomez, Santiago (2003) 'La Hybris del Punto Cero: Biopolíticas imperiales y colonialidad del poder en la Nueva Granada (1750–1810)'. Unpublished manuscript. Bogotá, Colombia: Instituto Pensar, Universidad Javeriana.

Collins, Patricia Hill (1990) *Black Feminist Thought: Knowledge, Consciousness and the Politics of Empowerment*. New York: Routledge, Chapman and Hall.

Crenshaw, Kimberle (1989) 'Demarginalizing the Intersection of Race and Sex: A Black Feminist Critique of Antidiscrimination Doctrine, Feminist Theory, and Antiracist Politics', in *Feminism in the Law: Theory, Practice, and Criticism*. University of Chicago Legal Forum, pp. 139–67.

Dussel, Enrique (1977) *Filosofía de Liberación*. México: Edicol.

—— (1994) *1492: El encubrimiento del Otro: Hacia el origen del 'mito de la modernidad'*. La Paz, Bolivia: Plural Editores.

Enloe, Cythia (1990) *Banana, Beaches and Bases: Making Sense of International Politics*. Berkeley: University of California Press.

Fanon, Frantz (1967) *Black Skin, White Masks*. New York: Grove Press.

Fregoso, Rosa Linda (2003) *MeXicana Encounters: The Making of Social Identities in the Borderlands*. Berkeley: University of California Press.

Grosfoguel, Ramón (1996). 'From Cepalismo to Neoliberalism: A World-System Approach to Conceptual Shifts in Latin America', *REVIEW,* vol. 19, no. 2, pp. 131–154.

—— (2002) 'Colonial Difference, Geopolitics of Knowledge and Global Coloniality in the Modern/Colonial Capitalist World-System', *Review*, vol. 25, no. 3, pp. 203–224.

—— (2006) 'World-System Analysis in the Context of Transmodernity, Border Thinking and Global Coloniality', *Review*, vol. 29, no. 2, pp. 167–187.

Haraway, Donna (1988) 'Situated Knowledges: The Science Question in Feminism and the Privilege of Partial Perspective', *Feminist Studies*, vol. 14, pp. 575–599.

Kontopoulos, Kyriakos (1993) *The Logic of Social Structures*. Cambridge: Cambridge University Press.

Lander, Edgardo (1998) 'Eurocentrismo y colonialismo en el pensamiento social latinoamericano', in *Pueblo, época y desarrollo: la sociología de América Latina*, eds Roberto Briceño-León and Heinz R. Sonntag, Caracas: Nueva Sociedad, pp. 87–96.

Mallon, Florencia (1994) 'The Promise and Dilemma of Subaltern Studies: Persepctives from Latin American History', *American Historical Review*, vol. 99, pp. 1491–1515.

Moraga, Cherrie & Anzaldúa, Gloria (eds) (1983) *This Bridge Called my Back: Writing by Radical Women of Color*. New York: Kitchen Table/Women of Color.

Mignolo, Walter (1995) *The Darker Side of the Renaissance: Literacy, Territoriality and Colonization*. Ann Arbor: The University of Michigan Press.

—— (2000). *Local Histories/Global Designs: Essays on the Coloniality of Power, Subaltern Knowledges and Border Thinking*. Princeton: Princeton University Press.

Quijano, Aníbal (1991) 'Colonialidad y Modernidad/Racionalidad', *Perú Indígena*, vol. 29, pp. 11–21.

—— (1993) 'Raza','Etnia' y'Nación' en Mariátegui: Cuestiones Abiertas, in *José Carlos Mariátgui y Europa: El Otro Aspecto del Descubrimiento*, ed. Roland Forgues, Lima, Perú: Empresa Editora Amauta S.A, pp. 167–187.

——. (1998). 'La colonialidad del poder y la experiencia cultural latinoamericana', in *Pueblo, época y desarrollo: la sociología de América Latina*, eds Roberto Briceño-León and Heinz R, Sonntag, Caracas: Nueva Sociedad, pp. 139–155.

—— (2000) 'Coloniality of Power, Ethnocentrism, and Latin America', *NEPANTLA*, vol. 1, no. 3, pp. 533–580.

Quijano, Aníbal & Wallerstein, Immanuel (1992) Americanity as a Concept, or the Americas in the Modern World-System, *International Journal of Social Sciences*, vol. 134, pp. 583–591.

Robertson, Roland (1992) *Globalization*. London: Sage Publications.

Said, Edward (1979) *Orientalism*. New York: Vintage Books.

Rodriguez, Ileana (2001) Reading Subalterns Across Texts, Disciplines, and Theories: From Representation to Recognition, in *The Latin American Subaltern Studies Reader*, ed. Rodriguez Ileana, Durham and London: Duke University Press.

Spivak, Gayatri (1988) *In Other Worlds: Essays in Cultural Politics*. New York: Routledge, Kegan and Paul.

Wallerstein, Immanuel (1974) *The Modern World-System*. New York: Academic Press.

—— (1979) *The Capitalist World-Economy*. Cambridge and Paris: Cambridge University Press and Editions de la Maison des Sciences de l'Homme.

—— (1983) *Historical Capitalism.* New York: Monthly Review Press.

—— (1984) *The Politics of the World-Economy*. Cambridge and Paris: Cambridge University Press and Editions de la Maison des Sciences de l'Homme.

—— (1991a) *Unthinking Social Science*. Cambridge: Polity Press.

—— (1991b) *Geopolitics and Geoculture*. Cambridge and Paris: Cambridge University Press and Editions de la Maison des Sciences de l'Homme.

—— (1995) *After Liberalism*. New York: The New Press.

**Catherine Walsh**

# SHIFTING THE GEOPOLITICS OF CRITICAL KNOWLEDGE

## Decolonial thought and cultural studies 'others' in the Andes

> Let's go comrades,
> the European game is definitely finished,
> it is necessary to find something else.
>
> (Frantz Fanon, 1963)

As most everywhere in the globe, the production of knowledge in Latin America has long been subject to colonial and imperial designs, to a geopolitics that universalizes European thought as scientific truths, while subalternizing and invisibilizing other epistemes. This dominant geopolitics of knowledge extends to both the Right and the Left, present even in the theoretical and ideological frames that orient many of those recognized (by the academy) as the producers and proponents of critical thought and theory.

Of course, the problem is not with the existence of such frames but rather with the ways they have historically worked to subordinate and negate 'other' frames, 'other' knowledge, and 'other' subjects and thinkers. That is to say, the problem is in the ways that critical thought in Latin America tends to reproduce the meta-narratives of the West while discounting or overlooking the critical thinking produced by indigenous, Afro, and mestizos whose thinking finds its roots in other logics, concerns, and realities that depart not from modernity alone but also from the long horizon of coloniality.

Such was the case even with José Carlos Mariategui, considered one of the fathers of twentieth century Latin American critical thought. For Mariategui, the central concerns in Latin America were the struggles of nationhood, culture, and class, understood from the frame of Marxism, applied and thought from the particularity of the Andes. The attention Mariategui gave to the plight of the peasantry afforded a visibility previously negated. Yet, by elevating the struggles of class over race, converting indigenous peoples to *campesinos* or peasants, and denouncing blacks as barbarians with nothing to contribute to these struggles,[1] Mariategui not only reproduced Marxism's racial blindness,

but also the racist sentiments propagated by many key European thinkers, most notably Kant and Hegel.[2]

Of course the issue here is not to debate with Mariategui or discount his critical contribution. Rather it is to place in tension, and in dialogue with Fanon, the historical and present-day nature of critical thought or theory; that is to say its centeredness in western paradigms, frameworks, and theory. As such, we can ask: How is one to understand critical theory in Latin America today? Is it true, as some claim, that critical theory (or at least postmodernist critical theory) has reached its twilight? And if this is so, should we abandon it or rather reconstruct it from other conceptual and political frameworks and other subjects, frameworks and subjects not considered by the European fathers such as Marx or Horkheimer, nor by Latin American (neo)marxists and (pos)modernists neither in the past nor today? What might it mean to think critical theory from other places – not simply from the West and from modernity, but from what has occurred in its margins or borders, and with a need to shed light on it's underside, that is on coloniality? To recognize and take seriously the critical intellectual production of those historically denied the category of 'thinkers' – that is, of indigenous and blacks – including the knowledge produced collectively in the context and struggles of social movements? Could such perspectives and contributions shape a distinct critical theory and thought – a critical thought otherwise or of an 'other' mode – and why? That is to say, a critical thought whose purposes or goals point not just to other possible worlds (in the spirit of the World Social Forum) but also to de-coloniality? Finally, what might this 'other' thought afford to the construction of 'other' cultural studies, that is to say, a cultural studies of decolonial orientation?

These questions orient the reflections that follow. As such, the interest of this article is to make visible debates, discussions, and projects in Latin America and particularly in the Andes that are concerned with a shifting of the geopolitics of critical knowledge, shifts that work towards the building of decolonial thought and the building of spaces for its positioning and construction.

## The geopolitics of critical thought in the frame of modernity/coloniality

To speak of the geopolitics of knowledge and the geopolitical locations of critical thought is to recognize the persistence of a Western hegemony that positions Eurocentric thought as 'universal', while localizing other forms of thought as at best folkloric. For Frantz Fanon but also for Fausto Reinaga,[3] a Bolivian quechua-aymara intellectual whose thought found its base and reason in Andean indigenous struggles, the hegemony, universality, and violence of

Western thinking must be confronted and a different thought constructed and positioned from 'other' histories and subjectivities. As both made clear in their writings, the problem is with the intimate entanglement of Western thought to the processes and projects of modernity and coloniality.[4] In fact, it is with the initiation of both in Latin America in 1492 as part and parcel of European expansionism and capital accumulation that the struggle begins. As Reinaga states in the introduction to his book *La Revolución India*:

> . . . Our struggle comes from afar, from the same instance that the Spanish hordes invaded the Confederation of Amer-Indian Peoples. Our struggle is against all European vestiges . . . Roman Law, the Napoleonic Code, French democracy, Marxism-Leninism, all that maintains us in dependence, in mental colonialism, in blindness without finding the light.
> (Reinaga 1970/2001, p. 15)

For Reinaga, the concern was to recognize and construct other theoretical and conceptual frames: 'neither Marx nor Christ, we need to think with our own heads'. Such legacy, struggle, and need are made more complicated when one takes into account the naturalization and intransigence of this eurocentricity, of mental colonialism and blindness even amongst the Left and the proponents of so-called 'critical' theory; a naturalization and intransigence that continues to mark critical thought in Latin America, if not in the globe.

Of course this critique is not meant to discount the existence in Latin America of alternatives to Eurocentric-colonial thought, alternatives that in the 60s and 70s questioned both modernity as the universal model of civilization, and the continued force of imperial and colonial relations (see Lander 2000). The theology and philosophy of liberation, dependency, pedagogy of the oppressed, structural heterogeneity, internal colonialism, participatory action research, among other intellectual productions and schools of thought are representative. Yet, as Lander (2000, p. 521) points out,

> This theoretical production remained within the limits of the universal metanarrative of modernity and progress. Only timidly did it explore the enormous implications of the plurality of histories, subjects, and cultures that characterizes Latin America.

However, in the last several decades, these attempts to 'rethink South America from within' have taken a reverse turn (ibid.); neoliberalism, postmodernism, and a strengthening of Eurocentric narratives are now what orient most university programs, particularly in the social sciences.[5] It is in this context that the dominant geopolitics of knowledge, including with regards to critical theory, assumes an ever increasing force, including within contemporary Leftist thinking – both in the academy and politics. Here one can witness a renewed centrality of certain European thinkers and schools of thought and a

conspicuous absence of the colonial experience. This was made clear in the working tables on the 'Reconstruction of Critical-Revolutionary Thought' during the Social Forum of the Americas held in Quito, Ecuador in July 2005. As a summary of the meetings published in the alternative press noted:

> In the vacuum provoked by Marxism, the richness of theoretical formulations that occupy the intellectual scene of critical theory, such as the thesis of Foucault, Deleuze, Lacan, and feminist and ecological critique, have opened a horizon of critical currents, the dialogue around which is proving to be extremely positive.
>
> (Moreano 2004).

The reference to these 'critical currents' without consideration of Latin American critical currents of thought including those produced within, in relation to, and by indigenous and afro social movements and their intellectuals,[6] raises question such as: who produces critical knowledge, for what purposes, and with what recognition? Asked differently: Whose critical knowledge? For whom? Why and for what uses? And, what in fact is meant by 'critical'? With reference to this latter question, Horkheimer's influence continues to be central.

Horkheimer's contribution in 1937 was to the distinction between traditional and critical theory. Specifically, Horkheimer helped elucidate the alienation in traditional theory between value and research, subject and object, knowledge and action. His argument was for a 'critical attitude', including a change in the subject and function of knowledge, in the relation between being and consciousness, and between the theorist and the oppressed sectors of humanity, all aimed at 'the suppression of social injustice', radical transformation, and the construction of a new society (1937, pp. 76–77). By placing attention to the structures in which social reality, as well as the theories that seek to understand this reality, were constructed, Horkheimer challenged the positivism of his era, establishing a relation between critical theory and issues of social justice and transformation. Theory in this sense became more than an activity of contemplation and 'pure thought'; it also became a tool of struggle.

Many Latin American critical theorists continue to find usefulness in Horkheimer both for his challenge to positivism and his distinction between traditional and critical theory. This is the case in Santiago Castro-Gomez's (2000) important article which applies this distinction between the traditional and the critical to a present-day mapping of theories of culture.

For Horkheimer as well as for Marx the struggle, of course, was that of the proletariat[7] understood in the context of central Europe, a struggle marked by class, not by color, and by modernity, not coloniality.[8] It is in the application or traveling of this context to other places – in this case Latin America – that

a geopolitical problem begins to takes form. As the Afro-Colombian intellectual Manuel Zapata Olivella (1989) notes, here in Latin America the concepts of race and class are inseparable, part and parcel of the colonialist phase of capitalism that created a new economic-racial relation: 'the technological development of white oppressors and the backwardness of pigmented, subordinated peoples. Without these biological and socioeconomic premises, the assumptions that are made about race, class, and culture in America are reduced to mere "elucubrations" that hide the true essence of the racist colonial system' (p. 14).

In fact, Castro-Gomez (2000) takes this concern into account in his discussion of postcolonialism as a critical theory of culture, making clear that in the modern world-system in general and in the processes of colonization in particular, 'race' played a key role not only in the relations of production and the market, but also in the natural and social sciences. In fact, what Castro-Gomez works to show is the intrinsic relation between the colonial idea of 'race' and the traditional concept of 'culture', again using Horkheimer's distinction as points of departure and reference. Yet one could ask, what might it mean to shift this geopolitics of critical theory, that is to say, to depart not from Horkheimer but from the critical production in Latin America, including by those who have lived and struggled within the racist and patriarchal colonial system? By starting from this vantage point and locus of enunciation, and later placing it in dialogue with Horkheimer, Wallerstein and other Western thinkers, might the weight of Eurocentric applications be lightened? Said differently, might such a shift help make visible other referents for defining and understanding what can be meant by 'critical', referents for whom the concern is not just with modernity but with its other face, that is coloniality?

Different consequences arise from this geopolitical shift in interpretation and reasoning. In fact,

> The implications for non-Western societies and for subaltern and excluded subjects around the world would be quite different if colonialism, imperialism, racism, and sexism were thought of not as regretful by-products of modern Europe, but as part of the conditions that made the modern West possible.
>
> (Lander 2000, p. 525).

## Decolonial thought, 'other' thought, and 'other' critical theory

Coloniality as both a concept and lived reality provides a foundational context for understanding this 'other' intellectual production in Latin America in general

and in the Andes in particular. While colonialism ended with independence, coloniality is a model of power that continues. Central to the establishment of this model was the codification of differences in ways that construct and establish a domination and inferiority based on race, serving as a fundamental criterion for the distribution of the population in ranks, places and roles within the social structure of power (Quijano 2000). While this codification was installed with colonialism and with the naming of a hierarchal ordering of social identities: whites, mestizos, '*indios*' and '*negros*', the latter two erasing the cultural differences that existed before colonialization, its efficacy remains ever present. Such efficacy in fact extends to the 'coloniality of knowledge'; that is, the hegemony of Eurocentrism as *the* perspective of knowledge, and an association of intellectual production with 'civilization', the power of the written word, and with the established racial hierarchy (Quijano 2000). In this construction and its maintenance over more that 500 years, indigenous and black peoples are still considered (by dominant society but also by the white-mestizo Left) as incapable of serious 'intellectual' thinking. It is in this context that the eurocentricity and racialized character of critical thought takes form.

Still, the construction, logic, and use of a critical thought have long existed amongst indigenous and Afro-descendent peoples, although Latin American philosophers, social scientists, and leftist intellectuals have seldom recognized or valued its existence.[9] Of course the logic of such thought has most often been of a very different kind. For the Nasa intellectual Manuel Quintín Lame (1883–1967), this logic comes not from books but from nature: 'nature educated me under its shadows . . . she taught me to think; . . . *pensar el pensar* – to think thought . . . (Quintín Lame 2004, p. 236).[10] By describing nature as the place of knowledge and wisdom, Quintín Lame in fact established its epistemological logic and condition (Romero 2004), a logic and condition opposed to that of the white world:

> It is not true that only those who have studied 15 or 20 years and have learned to think are the ones that have the vocation for thought, even if they have climbed from the Valley to the Mountain. I was born and raised in the Mountain, and from the Mountain I descended to the Valley to write this work . . . The Indian Quintin Lame was able to interpret the thought of the ant and of the various insects that nature cultivates. The thought of the smallest ant is the same as that of the condor when it was finishing to dress in the cave; it is the same as that of the offspring of the tiger, it is the same as that of the son of man. The ant to unwrap its wings and leave its nest does not follow the path of the others, instead it climbs up on the sand and flaps its wings, infinitely challenging because it feels itself to be big and powerful. But in crossing the path it is attacked by its enemy, and it is in this same way, that the error of man is assailed.
>
> (Quintín Lame 2004, p. 151)[11]

Yet and as the Quechua-Aymara intellectual Fausto Reinaga argued, Western thought distorts this nature by positioning a singular 'human nature' as a unitary, eternal, and absolute power.

> The 'human nature' of the 'white' man of the West is one; and that of the man (sic) colonized by the West is other. The 'human nature' of the 'white European beast' is ferocity; and that of the colonized 'indigenous-natural', of the black, yellow, and *indio,* is the struggle for freedom.
>
> (Reinaga 1970/2001, p. 91)

It is this struggle for liberty and freedom that in fact has long guided the 'critical' thinking of the peoples of Abya Yala[12] as well as of African descendents. From this struggle, one can question, as does the contemporary Aymara intellectual Esteban Ticona (2005a), the utility of Eurocentric theories, particularly for understanding the colonial condition. 'The indigenous, afro and poor mestizo America is an example of this feeling, because after more than 500 years, it continues to think with 'its own head', trying to crystallize a *'pensamiento propio'* – a thought of one's own- that definitely helps our liberation'.

In fact, the recognition, crystallization, and use of a '*pensamiento propio*' has in very recent years become a visible component in the struggles of both indigenous and Afro groups in the region, struggles that as I have argued elsewhere are not just social and political but also epistemic in nature.[13] As CRIC – the Indigenous Council of Cauca (Popayan, Colombia) – (2004), makes clear, this work towards the building and articulation of a *pensamiento propio* or indigenous thought is recent, part of a moving from struggles around language and culture to struggles instead centered in the construction and 'generating of philosophies or epistemologies of our own' (p. 27). Such process is not limited to CRIC but also evident in Ecuador's indigenous movement, including in debates about the need to move beyond a simple focus on bilingualism in educational programs to the application of a scientific or epistemic interculturality. It is also evident in the conceptual model of *Amawtay Wasi*, the Intercultural University of Indigenous Nationalities and Peoples of Ecuador, conceived and thought from the perspective not of the West but of an Abya Yala cosmology and philosophy (see Walsh 2002, Walsh forthcoming). *Amawtay Wasi* describes its task as one that:

> Responds from epistemology, ethics and politics to the decolonialization of knowledge (...), a space of reflection that proposes new ways of conceiving the construction of knowledge (...) potentializing local knowledges and building sciences of knowledge, as an indispensable requirement to work not from the answers to the epistemological, philosophical, ethical, political, and economic order, but from a proposal based on [Andean] philosophical principles.
>
> (*Amawtay Wasi* 2004).

Essential to such constructions among indigenous organizations and groups have been the guiding notion of autonomy – of freedom of control from the Church, landowners, commercial intermediaries, political parties, including those of the Left, and dominant state institutions and models – and of the grounding of a political project that directs action in a host of realms, including in the social, political, economic, and epistemic spheres. In this sense, '*pensamiento propio*' and the building of a cosmology and epistemology are the results of historical transformations in the movement, their moving from demands and vindications to the building of a critical thought that has within its site radical transformations and the creation of new social arrangements or orderings not just for indigenous peoples but for all of society. *'Propio',* then, is not understood as meaning separation or isolation from other processes or tendencies in society, or an attention only to indigenous cultures, perspectives, and interpretations. Rather and as CRIC (2004, p. 67) argues 'it requires a dialogue with other cultures and the development of a political conscience'.

The 'political conscience' here is not the same as that conceived by Marxism or by Eurocentric critical thought. Instead it is a consciousness whose roots derive from the lived experience of colonial histories and millenary struggles to confront the social, political, epistemic, racialized, and existential effects of these histories. It is what the Afro-Ecuadorian intellectual Juan García refers to as the building of a collective sense of belonging, an unlearning of what the dominant society has inculcated and a relearning of past and present ancestral knowledge, a focus on the social, political, and epistemic work that needs to be done within (Walsh and León forthcoming).

In this sense '*pensamiento propio*' is suggestive of a different critical thought, one that seeks to mark a divergence with dominant 'universal' thought (including in its 'critical', progressive, and leftist formations). Such divergence is not meant to simplify indigenous or black thought or to relegate it to the category or status of localized, situated, and culturally specific and concrete thinking; that is to say, as nothing more than 'local knowledge' understood as mere experience. Rather it is to put forward its political and decolonial character, permitting a connection then among various '*pensamientos propios*' as part of a broader project of 'other' critical thought and knowledge. Khatibi (2001) refers to this broader project as the 'complot' of 'other' thought. For indigenous and black intellectuals such as Quintín Lame (2004), Muyolema (2001), García (see Walsh and García 2002 and Walsh and León forthcoming), Reinaga (2001) and Zapata Olivella (1989) such project opens the possibility of a different universalization of radical and subversive character.

'Other', in this sense, is not meant to refer to one thought more or to the anthropological other of alterity. It is instead to bring forward and relate histories, struggles, experiences, and knowledges lived and constructed within and marked by the context of colonialism and its processes of subalternization and racialization; that is by the common connector of coloniality (Mignolo

2003). Its use here engages that introduced by the Arab-Islamic intellectual Abdelkebir Khatibi (2001). That is, a signifying of a collective mode of thinking that is produced and thought from difference, towards liberation. It is a thought that demands a radical elucidation, a strategical use, and a play with the political; a thought that opens decolonial possibilities, not just in the social and political spheres but also in terms of existence. In this sense and as I have argued elsewhere (Walsh 2005a), 'other' thought becomes a strategical tool in the struggle to confront non-existence, dominated existence and dehumanization – key referents, it seems, in rethinking critical thought or critical knowledges from other spaces and places – spaces and places that modernity or intellectuals like Horkheimer never could have imagined.

To speak of an 'other' critical thought then is to give credence to ongoing struggles – struggles that are epistemic as well as political in character – to confront coloniality, thus marking a positioning radically distinct from that which locates critical theory simply within the histories and experiences of modernity and the narratives these histories and experiences have fostered and created. Such shift is important for what it helps reveal, including the subjects left out or marginalized by much of critical theory and their socio-political and epistemic agency, but also the association between thought and social and political intervention. Said differently, what this 'other' thought brings to light is both a political use of knowledge and an epistemic acting on the political from the colonial difference. It is an intellectual production not aimed at individual accomplishment or limited to the confines of the academy, but rather at the shared need to confront the colonial-racist structures, systems, and institutions of society through a collective praxis that finds its meaning in the condition of the colonial difference.[14] And it is *this* difference that marks a distinction with the anti-colonial thinking predominant in Latin America in the 60s and 70s, a thinking typically associated with the Left and white-mestizo intellectuals.

What does this difference afford in terms of a rethinking of 'critical' intellectual work, including for the building of spaces and places of thought of an 'other' kind even within the university?

## Decolonial shifts and cultural studies 'others'

Discussions in the United States about cultural studies in Latin America typically depart from associations with Nestor García Canclini and Jesús Martin Barbero on the one hand and Nelly Richard and Beatriz Sarlo on the other, although these latter two more often refer to their work as cultural critique and not 'cultural studies'. In fact, it is the work and perspectives of these four authors that have had the widest circulation both within Latin America and without; they have also served as the basis for critique for treatises on the problems of cultural studies.[15]

Of course the naming of cultural studies itself is part of the predicament, raising questions about the reproduction of British and US models in the south and the negation or subalternization of the trajectory of cultural production here, thus contributing in some sense to the dominant geopolitics of knowledge (see Walsh 2003). However what interests me here is not this debate as such, but rather the socialization of our experience in Ecuador to both indiscipline the human and social sciences and rethink and reconstruct cultural studies from the political and ethical perspectives of knowledge (including subalternized knowledges) and from the borders of modernity/coloniality. The reference here is to the specific experience of the Doctoral program in Latin American Cultural Studies at the Universidad Andina Simón Bolívar in Quito, the overall goal of which is to build new critical communities of thought, interpretation, and intervention.[16]

This effort is conceived as a space of encounter between disciplines and intellectual, political, and ethical projects, projects constructed in different historical moments and epistemological places and concerned with the search for ways to think, know, and act toward a more socially just world and towards the comprehension and change of structures of domination – epistemological as well as social, cultural, and political. As such, it is directed toward a renovation and reconstruction of critical thought in ways that take into account the present-day relations between culture, politics, and economy, challenge the hegemony of Eurocentric perspectives, and promote dialogues and *thinking with* thought and knowledge 'others', including that of Afro and indigenous social movements and intellectuals.

The interest is thus, in part, with intellectual projects and the building of a space and place of thought concerned with the consequences of the colonial difference and the epistemic racism of modernity; projects, spaces, and places that are directed toward local histories that are simultaneously global, reflections of the present-day cultural logic of late capitalism and the installation of new forms of global coloniality.[17] In this sense, *a thinking from* Latin America (but with relation as well to other parts of the globe) gives importance to the place of enunciation, and to what Arturo Escobar (2000) refers to as the relation between the creation of place and the creation of people. It is the 'place' of Latin America that helps to make visible 'the forms of subaltern thought and the local and regional modalities that configure the world' (Escobar 2000, p. 116) that Western theory (including in its metropolitan postcolonial versions) and the dominant geopolitics of knowledge tends to hide.

The fact that the students who participate in this doctorate (now in its second promotion) come from the various countries of the Andean region and have, for the most part, a strong base of experience in the social and political realms (including in and with social movements and community-based processes and struggles), enables a level of dialogue and exchange not typical in most academic settings, this further strengthened by the presence of

indigenous and Afro intellectuals within the group.[18] It is this base, combined with efforts to build dialogue and shared (rather than simply individual) knowledge production that is what gives substance and credence to the idea of an 'other' space and place of thought.[19] The majority of faculty share these interests and goals. More than coming to 'teach', their contributions have been to further extend critical dialogue through theoretical, conceptual, and thematic explorations and reflection, thus forming part of these emergent communities of critical thought, interpretation, and intervention.

Overall, this experience along with the others in which we are engaged in Ecuador, are less concerned with the institutionalization of programs (that is, with the establishment of a new place of study) than with the building of spaces and places (within the university but not limited to it) for the generation and production of non eurocentric and decolonial thought. These efforts mark the urgency to construct more systematic articulations and bridges among intellectual, political, and ethical projects, both those that come from intellectuals within the academy and those outside of it, particularly those associated with social movements.[20] But they also mark the need to promote new critical and decolonial projects, and to extend existing projects to epistemological and educational restructuring and intervention. In essence, they form part of the search for other possible knowledges and worlds.

## As a way of conclusion

In a recent work, Arturo Escobar (2003) makes the argument for the need to take seriously the epistemic force of local histories and the need to think theory through the political praxis of subaltern groups. What such argument points to is not the incorporation or inclusion of the histories, praxis, and 'other' thought of subaltern groups as new objects of study – a kind of *critical cultural studies of the other*. Rather and as I have argued here, it suggests the building of new places and new communities of thought, interpretation, and intervention that seek to generate and build intersections among critical forms of decolonial thought and political-epistemic projects grounded in the histories and lived experiences of coloniality – what we might instead refer to as *cultural studies 'others'* or a *cultural studies of decolonial orientation.*

Of course the issue is much deeper than the naming or conceptualization of spaces and places of critical thought. As I have attempted to make clear here, it is an issue grounded in the ways coloniality and the geopolitics of knowledge have worked to enable modernity as *the* 'civilization' project of the West, a project that has systematically worked to subordinate and negate 'other' frames, 'other' knowledges, and 'other' subjects and thinkers. The location of critical thought and the meta-narratives that have directed it within this project, including that critical thought associated with the Left in Latin

America, is demonstrative of the complexity of the problem and its simultaneously local and global nature.

To begin to 'think thought' from 'other' places and with intellectuals for whom the point of departure is not the academy but political-epistemic projects of decoloniality, might open paths that enable shifts in the geopolitics of critical knowledge as well as the building of a shared praxis of a very different kind, a praxis that attempts to confront what the Afro-Colombian intellectual and *ekobio mayor* Manuel Zapata Olivella once affirmed: 'The chains are not on our feet, but on our minds'.

## Notes

1 'The contribution of the negro that arrived as a slave seems less valuable and negative [in comparison to the indigenous]. The negro brought with him his sensuality, superstition, and primitive nature. He is not in conditions to contribute to any culture, but rather threatens to obstruct culture through the crude and living influence of his barbarianism (Mariategui 1995).

2 See Eze (2001) and Walsh (2004).

3 Interesting to note is the dialogic relation that Reinaga, a Bolivian quechua-aymara intellectual, established with Fanon in his texts. Such dialogue is the only one of which I am aware in which an Andean radical indigenous intellectual looks for points of relation with a radical black thinker.

4 For a detailed discussion of the relation between knowledge and the projects of modernity/coloniality, see Mignolo (2001).

5 The query of a professor to graduate students in a Latin American university program centered on critical thought and Latin American cultural studies makes evident this intellectual hegemony: how is it possible to understand Latin America and the social sciences if one has not read Foucault, Bourdieu, Deleuze and Lacan?

6 This was also made evident in the 2005 meeting of the World Social Forum in Porto Alegre. Here the voices of black and indigenous movements remained absent in the major spaces of debate of the Left (spaces overwhelming represented by white men of Euro-American origin). And while indigenous movements were given for the first time their own territorial space, this was physically and programmatically marginalized from the main space of the Forum.

7 For Horkheimer (1937), the situation of the proletariat afforded no guarantees in terms of critical knowledge or consciousness. '. . . The clarity of class consciousness shows itself in the always open possibility of a tension between the theoretician and the class that directs his thought (p. 50). Both were understood as interactive processes in which the critical theorist could play a key role in helping expose social contradictions not just as an expression of a concrete historical situation but also as a stimulating and transformative factor.

8 For a discussion regarding the position of the pre-sub Comandante Marcos Rafael Guillen in this configuration see Walsh (2005).

9 This is despite the existence of written texts and publications, the distribution of which for the same reasons argued here, have had limited circulation.

10 As Romero (2004, 114) notes, Quintín Lame's objective in *pensar el pensar* was to 'offer a point of view with regard to the milestones of the catholic religion and his own version of this religion, and analyze and argue, using both neo-tomist philosophy and an indigenous perspective, diverse philosophic problems about nature, education and knowledge, themes at the center of discussion during the end of the nineteenth and beginning of the twentieth centuries in Colombian society'.

11 Originally written in 1939 when the author was 56 years old.

12 *Abya Yala* is the name coined by the *cunas* in Panama to refer to the territory and the indigenous nations of the Americas, 'land in full maturity', a name now generally assumed by these nations to refer to the Americas. For Muyulema (2001), this naming has a double siginificance: as a political positioning and as a place of enunciation, that is to say as a way to confront the colonial weight present in 'Latin America' understood as a cultural project of westernization, ideologically articulated in *mestizaje.* As such and as Ticona (2005b) points out (in conversation with Muyulema), 'the 'recategorizing' of names, such as *Abya Yala,* means a rethinking of decolonialization from the experience of kichua and aimara peoples and from their ethical-political values'. Of course the problem is that while *Abya Yala* recuperates indigenous roots, it leaves out the presence and struggles of African descendents.

13 See Walsh (2005a, forthcoming).

14 Reinaga (2001, p. 95) makes this clear: 'Our philosophy, motor and goal of our thought, is directed toward liberty'.

15 See, for example, Reynoso (2000) and Follari (2002).

16 While the doctoral program is the center of reflections here, this program is only one of several sites where we are working to build these communities of thought, interpretation, and intervention. The others include the spaces devoted to work around the Afro-Andean diaspora, both in graduate level programs, with Afro organizations, groups, and communities, and through the *Fondo Documental Afro-Andino.* This latter space, part of a collaborative agreement between the organization *Proceso de comunidades negras – PCN* and the university, was formed in 2002 when PCN placed in the university's trust over 3000 hours of taped oral histories and testimonies from Afro-Ecuadorian communities (complied over a 35 year time frame) and over 8000 photographs with the goal of systematizing this material and putting it in useable forms for schools and communities.

17 With regard to this latter point see Mignolo (2002).

18 Given the intellectual and academic isolation among Andean and Latin American countries and the present-day economic crisis, an academic

institutionalization of this 'space and place' is in fact strategically necessary for the structure and financing it affords. In this sense, institutionalization serves as a strategy that helps enable the construction and promotion not of a program but of an intellectual project of a clearly political nature. Such project has its resonance outside Quito and the university as such, serving as a base for the building of a network of projects in other spaces and places in the region.

19 Examples include two published collections: Pensamiento crítico y matriz (de) colonial (Walsh 2005b) and Texiendo textos. Cinco hilos para pensar los estudios culturales, la colonialidad y la interculturalidad (Kowii *et al.* 2005).

20 Of course in Latin America, these inside and outside distinctions are less evident than they are in the United States or Europe. In Latin America it is fairly common for intellectuals who work in the university to have strong ties to social movements. Less common, however, is the incorporation within the university of the knowledge produced by these movements as 'knowledge' and not merely as examples of 'ethnographic experience'.

## References

*Amawtay Wasi* (2004) 'Aprender en la sabiduría y el buen vivir', Quito: Universidad Intercultural Amawtay Wasi/UNESCO.

Castro-Gómez, Santiago (2000) 'Teoría tradicional y teoría crítica de la cultura', in *La reestructuración de las ciencias sociales en América Latina*, eds. Santiago Castro-Gómez. Bogotá: Instituto Pensar/Centro Editorial Javeriana, pp. 94–107.

CRIC (2004) *Qué pasaría si la esculea . . .? 30 años de construcción de una educación propia*. Popayán: Consejo Regional Indígena de Cauca.

Escobar, Arturo (2000) 'El lugar de la naturaleza y la naturaleza del lugar: ¿globalización o posdesarrollo?, in *La colonialidad del saber: eurocentrismo y ciencias sociales. Perspectivas latinoamericanas.* Buenos Aires: CLASCO, pp. 113–143.

Eze, Emmanuel Chukwudi (2001) 'El color de la razón. Las ideas de 'raza' en la antropología de Kant', in *Capitalismo y geopolítica del conocimiento*, Walter Mignolo (comp.). Buenos Aires: Ediciones del signo.

Fanon, Frantz (1963) *The Wretched of the Earth*. NY: Grove.

Follari, Roberto (2002) *Teorías debiles (para una crítica de la deconstrucción y de los estudios culturales*. Rosario: Homo Sapiens ediciones.

García, Jesus (2002) 'Encuentro y desencuentros de los 'saberes'. En torno a la africana latinoamericana', in *Estudios y otras prácticas intelectuales latinoamericanas en cultura y poder*, Daniel Mato (comp.). CLACSO/Faces: Caracas.

Horkheimer, Max (1937) *Teoría tradicional y teoría crítica.* Barcelona: Paidós, 2000.

Khatibi, Abdelkebir (2001) 'Maghreb plural', in *Capitalismo y geopolítica del conocimiento. El eurocentrismo y la filosofía de la liberación en el debate intelectual*

*contemporáneo*, Walter Mignolo (comp.). Buenos Aires: Ediciones del signo, pp. 71–92.

Kowii, Ariruma, Garcés, Fernando, Noboa, Patricio, Lamus, Doris & Albán, Adolfo (2005) *Texiendo textos. Cinco hilos para pensar los estudios culturales, la colonialidad y la interculturalidad*. Popayán: Universidad de Cauca.

Lander, Edgardo (2000) 'Eurocentrism and Colonialism in Latin American Thought', *Nepantla. Views from South*, vol. 1, no. 3, pp. 519–532.

Mariategui, José Carlos (1995) 'El problema de las razas en la América Latina', in *Textos Básicos.* Jose Carlos Mariategui, México: Fondo de Cultura Económica, pp. 210–257.

Mignolo, Walter (2003) 'Prefacio a la edición castellana', in *Historias locales/diseños globales. Colonialidad, conocimientos subalternos y pensamiento fronterizo*. Madrid: Akal, pp. 19–110.

—— (2002) 'Colonialidad global, capitalismo y hegemonía epistémica', in *Indisciplinar las ciencias sociales. Geopolíticas del conocimiento y colonialidad del poder. Perspectivas desde lo andino,* eds C. Walsh, F. Schiwy y S. Castro-Gómez. Quito: Universidad Andina Simón Bolívar/Abya Yala, pp. 215–243.

—— (2001) *Local Histories, Global Designs*. Princeton: Princeton University Press.

Moreano, Alejandro. (2004) 'La reconstrucción del pensamiento crítico-revolucionario', *Tintají* (special edition of the Social Forum of the Americas), July, e.

Muyulema, Armando (2001) 'De la ′cuestión indígena′ a lo ′indígena′como cuestionamiento', in *Convergencia de tiempos: estudios subalternos/contextos latinoamericanos. Estado, cultura y subalternidad,* I. Rodríguez (editor). Amsterdam/Atlanta, GA, Rodopi, pp. 327–364.

Quintín Lame, Manuel (2004) *Los pensamientos del indio que se educó dentro de las selvas colombianas*. Popayán: Editorial Universidad de Cauca.

Quijano, Aníbal (2000) 'Coloniality of Power, Eurocentrism, and Latin America', *Nepantla. Views from South*, vol. 1, no. 3, pp. 533–580.

Reinaga, Fausto (1970/2001) *La revolución indio*. La Paz: Ediciones Fundación Amaútica 'Fausto Reinaga'.

Reynoso, Carlos (2000) *Apogeo y decadencia de los estudios culturales. Una visión antropológica*. Barcelona: Gedisa.

Romero, Fernando (2004) 'Aspectos pedagógicos y filosóficos en *Los pensamientos del indio que se educó dentro de las selvas colombianas* de Manuel Quintín Lame', in Quintín Lame, Manuel. *Los pensamientos del indio que se educó dentro de las selvas colombianas*. Popayán: Editorial Universidad de Cauca, pp. 111–138.

Ticona, Esteban (2005a) 'El estado, el poder y la dominación y el pensamiento occidental. Una crítica desde Abya Yala-América', unpublished essay, Doctoral Program in Latin American Cultural Studies, Universidad Andina Simón Bolívar, Quito, Ecuador.

—— (2005b) 'Una *Yapita* en perspectiva', unpublished essay, Doctoral Program in Latin American Cultural Studies, Universidad Andina Simón Bolívar, Quito, Ecuador.

Walsh, Catherine (forthcoming) 'Interculturality and the Coloniality of Power.An 'Other' Thinking and Positioning from the Colonial Difference', in *Coloniality of Power, Transmodernity, and Border Thinking*, eds R. Grosfoguel, J.D. Saldivar, and N. Maldonado-Torres. Durham: Duke University Press.

—— (2005a) '"Other" Knowledges, "Other" Critiques. Reflections on the Politics and Practices of Philosophy and De-coloniality in the "Other" America', paper presented at the conference *Mapping the Decolonial Turn. Post/Trans-Continental Inventions in Philosophy, Theory, and Critique*, University of California Berkeley, April 21–23.

—— (ed.) (2005b) *Pensamiento critico y matriz (de)colonial. Reflexiones latinoamericanas*. Quito: Universidad Andina Simón Bolívar/Abya Yala.

—— (2004) 'Colonialidad, conocimiento y diáspora afro-andina: Construyendo etnoeducación e interculturalidad en la universidad', in *Conflicto e (in)visibilidad. Retos en los estudios de la gente negra en Colombia*, eds Axel Rojas y Eduardo Restrepo. Popayán, Editorial Universidad del Cauca, Colección Políticas de la Alteridad.

—— (2003) 'Introducción. ¿Qué saber, qué hacer y cómo ver? Los desafíos y predicamientos disciplinares, políticos y éticos de los estudios (inter)culturales *desde* América Andina', in *Estudios culturales latinoamericanos, retos desde y sobre la región andina*, ed. Catherine Walsh, Quito: UASB/Abya Yala, pp. 11–30.

—— (2002) 'The (Re)articulation of Political Subjectivities and Colonial Difference in Ecuador: Reflections on Capitalism and the Geopolitics of Knowledge', *Nepantla*, vol. 3, no. 1, pp. 61–98.

Walsh, Catherine & García Juan (2002) 'El pensar del emergente movimiento afroecuatoriano: Reflexiones (des)de un proceso', in *Estudios y otras prácticas intelectuales latinoamericanas en cultura y poder*, Daniel Mato (comp.). Caracas: CLACSO/Faces, pp. 317–326.

Walsh, Catherine and León, Edizon (forthcoming) 'Afro Andean Thought and Diasporic Ancestrality', in *Shifting the Geography of Reason, Gender, Science and Religion*, Marina Banchetti and Clevis Headley (eds.). London: Cambridge Scholars Press.

Zapata Olivella, Manuel (1989) *Las claves mágicas de América*. Bogotá: Plaza y Janes.

**Nelson Maldonado-Torres**

# ON THE COLONIALITY OF BEING

## Contributions to the development of a concept[1]

The concept of coloniality of Being emerged in discussions of a diverse group of scholars doing work on coloniality and decolonization.[2] More particularly, we owe the idea to Walter D. Mignolo, who reflected on it in writing as early as 1995.[3] I do not remember exactly when it was that I heard or read the term for the first time – I believe that it was in 2000 in a talk given by Mignolo at Boston College – but I do know that since I heard it, it caught my attention in an unusual way.[4] The reason was that when I heard it I had already spent some time working on the thought of Martin Heidegger and some of his critics who engaged his work from the perspective of questions related to race and the colonial experience. Heidegger, who is considered by many one of the two most original European philosophers of the twentieth century (the other being Ludwig Wittgenstein), left an indelible mark in European philosophy by continuing Nietzsche's frontal attack of modernity and epistemologically-centered philosophy with an elaboration of what he referred to as fundamental ontology. Heidegger's formulation of a new starting point for philosophy consisted in a rearticulation of the question of Being, which influenced many other intellectuals thereafter, the most notable perhaps being the French-Algerian philosopher Jacques Derrida.

I was introduced to Heidegger by Joan Stambaugh who spent some time working with him in Germany. She translated several of his works in English, including Heidegger's magnus opus *Being and Time*.[5] After I read Heidegger with her, I began to engage the phenomenological tradition and particularly the work of Jean-Paul Sartre, Edmund Husserl, and eventually also Jacques Derrida. I gradually became aware, at least to the extent that a young scholar can be, of the varied accents, the original approaches, and the different questions that were at the center of these and other philosophers who drew ideas from phenomenology. But it was not until I read the work of the Lithuanian Jewish thinker Emmanuel Lévinas that I woke up from what I would call my 'phenomenological and ontological slumber'. Lévinas's work was not only a variation of European philosophy or the phenomenological theme. In Lévinas I found a more radical subversion of Western philosophy. He thought through not only Greek and European, but also Judaic sources. Jewish concepts and ideas replaced Greek and Christian concepts in key parts

of the philosophical armoire. This subversion allowed him to present a different picture of philosophy and conception of the vocation of the human: instead of the act of thinking or the encounter between human beings and nature, it was ethics and the face-to-face (the subject-Other) encounter which became the starting point for his philosophy. His work also makes explicit reference to Jewish ideas and illustrates the difference of thinking with sources that have been to some extent marginalized by the West. I was fascinated and surprised. After having read with some detail key works of the masters of suspicion (Marx, Nietzsche, and Freud), my horizon of conceptual possibilities did not contain the idea of a rupture such as his. I wanted to know more about Lévinas, but my main interest did not reside so much in becoming an expert of sorts in Lévinas's intellectual work, but in learning in some way more about his method and approach. I was sure that the path that he opened for himself was as rich and productive as the Euro-Christian and Euro-secular traditions that he contested, and that it was necessary to expand it by discovering new themes and other thinkers who would make similar kind of heretical interventions.

In addition to Levinas's heretical gesture, there were other elements in his project which resonated with interests that I had. Lévinas was a survivor of the Jewish Holocaust, an event that marked all his thinking. Heidegger, on the other hand, had been a supporter of the Nazi regime and saw in the *Führer* a leader that would take the people (*Völk*) to the path of national authenticity.[6] While Heidegger's affiliation with the Nazi regime was not long, it was firm and strong, and while his alliance apparently did not extend to the years of the Jewish Holocaust, he never made an apology to the Jewish people for his support of whom it was clear from the beginning that was an anti-Semitic leader.[7] Lévinas, who became enchanted with Heidegger's thought while he spent a year in Freiburg in the 1920s, later became perhaps the most radical opposer of Heideggerianism. He made the point that Heidegger's affiliation with the Nazi regime was not only a matter of personal preference, but that in some way involved his philosophical project as well. A dark cloud encompassed for Lévinas Heidegger's ontological project. Ontology became equal for him to a philosophy of power.[8] That is, ontology as *first philosophy* is for Lévinas ultimately complicit with violence. Conversely, a new starting point presented itself for him, one that would make by all means sure that philosophy would not lead, be complicit, or provoke blindness in respect to dehumanization and suffering. That is another reason why ethics and the face-to-face occupies center stage in Lévinas's thought.

Little did I know at that point that a similar encounter with Lévinas stood behind the emergence of liberation philosophy in Latin America with Enrique Dussel and Juan Carlos Scannone, among other young Argentineans. Lévinas also woke up Dussel from his ontological slumber and inspired him to articulate a critical philosophy of Being as Totality that not only considered the

experience of anti-Semitism and the Jewish Holocaust, but also that of colonized peoples in other parts of the world, particularly Latin America. If Levinas made the link between ontology and power, Dussel made the connection between Being and the history of colonial enterprises, thus leading to the door of the coloniality of Being. It was, however, as I mentioned before, a different Argentinean (Mignolo), who came up with the concept years later for the first time. The concept of coloniality of being was born in conversations about the implications of the coloniality of power in different areas of society.[9] The idea was that colonial relations of power left profound marked not only in the areas of authority, sexuality, knowledge and the economy, but on the general understanding of being as well.[10] And, while the coloniality of power referred to the interrelation among modern forms of exploitation and domination (power), and the coloniality of knowledge had to do with impact of colonization on the different areas of knowledge production, coloniality of being would make primary reference to the lived experience of colonization and its impact on language. Mignolo makes it clear in his own reflections on the topic:

> 'Science' (knowledge and wisdom) cannot be detached from language; languages are not just 'cultural' phenomena in which people find their 'identity'; they are also the location where knowledge is inscribed. And, since languages are not something human beings have but rather something of what humans beings are, coloniality of power and of knowledge engendered the coloniality of being [*colonialidad del ser*]'.[11]

The emergence of the concept 'coloniality of Being' responded to the need to thematize the question of the effects of coloniality in lived experience and not only in the mind. From here that the idea resonated so strong with me, who was working on phenomenological and existential philosophy and critiques to such approaches from the perspective of racial and colonial 'sub-alterity'. When one reflects on the term 'coloniality of being' in the context of Lévinas and Dussel's debate with Heidegger, it provides an important clue to clarify the specific ties between what Heidegger referred to as Being and the colonial project.

There is still a crucial figure that I was studying whom I have not mentioned, and whose work offers demand an elucidation of coloniality in connection with the question of lived experience and language: Frantz Fanon.[12] Fanon's critique of Hegel's ontology in *Black Skin, White Masks* not only provide the basis for an alternative depiction of the master/slave dialectic, but also contributes to a more general rethinking of ontology in light of coloniality and the search for decolonization. If Dussel spells out the historical dimension of the coloniality of Being, Fanon deploys the existential expressions of coloniality in relation to the colonial experience in its racial and, to some

extent as well, its gendered dimensions. And if Lévinas's point of departure is the anarchic moment of the constitution of subjectivity in its encounter with the Other, Fanon concentrates his attention in the trauma of the encounter with the imperial and racist Other. 'Look a Negro!' That is the point of departure for Fanon to begin to elaborate what might be referred to as the existentialia of the 'subject' of the coloniality of Being. A consistent effort in this direction would lead to an exploration of language, history, and existence. Coloniality of Being raises the challenge of connecting the genetic, the existential, and the historical dimensions where Being shows most evidently its colonial side and its fractures.[13] Hopefully I can make some steps here in this direction. This essay is divided in four main sections, each of which focuses on answering a question. The first is What is coloniality?, the second is What is being?, the third is What is the coloniality of being?, and lastly What is the decolonization of being and the *des-gener-acción del ser*?

## What is coloniality?

Coloniality is different from colonialism. Colonialism denotes a political and economic relation in which the sovereignty of a nation or a people rests on the power of another nation, which makes such nation an empire. Coloniality, instead, refers to long-standing patterns of power that emerged as a result of colonialism, but that define culture, labor, intersubjective relations, and knowledge production well beyond the strict limits of colonial administrations.[14] Thus, coloniality survives colonialism. It is maintained alive in books, in the criteria for academic performance, in cultural patterns, in common sense, in the self-image of peoples, in aspirations of self, and so many other aspects of our modern experience. In a way, as modern subjects we breath coloniality all the time and everyday.

Coloniality is not simply the aftermath or the residual form of any given form of colonial relation. Coloniality emerges in a particular socio-historical setting, that of the discovery and conquest of the Americas.[15] For it was in the context of this massive colonial enterprise, the more widespread and ambitious in the history of humankind yet, that capitalism, an already existing form of economic relation, became tied with forms of domination and subordination that were central to maintaining colonial control first in the Americas, and then elsewhere. Coloniality refers, first and foremost, to the two axes of power that became operative and defined the spatio-temporal matrix of what was called America. According to Anibal Quijano these two axes were:

> The codification of the differences between conquerors and conquered in the idea of 'race', a supposedly different biological structure that placed some in a natural situation of inferiority to the others. The conquistadors

> assumed this idea as the constitutive, founding element of the relations of domination that the conquest imposed. . . . The other process was the constitution of a new structure of control of labor and its resources and slavery, serfdom, small independent commodity production and reciprocity, together around and upon the basis of capital and the world market.[16]

The project of colonizing America did not have only local significance. Quite the contrary, it became a model of power, as it were, or the very basis of what was then going to become modern identity, inescapably framed by world capitalism and a system of domination structured around the idea of race. This model of power is at the heart of the modern experience. Modernity, usually considered to be a product of the European Renaissance or the European Enlightenment, has a darker side, which is constitutive of it.[17] Modernity as a discourse and as a practice would not be possible without coloniality, and coloniality continues to be an inevitable outcome of modern discourses.

How did the coloniality of power emerged? Quijano locates it in discussions about whether the Indians had souls or not. New identities were created in the context of European colonization: European, white, Indian, black, and mestizo.[18] A characteristic feature of this type of social classification is that the relation between the subjects is not horizontal but vertical in character. That is, some identities depict superiority over others. And such superiority is premised on the degree of humanity attributed to the identities in question. The 'lighter' one's skin is, the closer to full humanity one is, and viceversa.[19] As the conquerors took on the role of mapping the world they kept reproducing this vision of things. The whole world was practically seen in the lights of this logic. This is the beginning of 'global coloniality'.[20]

It is true that in 1537 the Pope declared the Amerindians as human. Yet as Quijano points out 'from then on, the idea that non-Europeans have a biological structure that is not only different from that of Europeans but also inferior, was imprinted on intersubjective relations and social practices of power'.[21] It is clear that the meaning of race has changed throughout the centuries, and that 'raza' did not mean in the sixteenth century what it came to mean at the height of the biological revolution in the nineteenth century that produced taxonomies based on a formal biological category of race. Yet, there was a commonality between nineteenth century racism and the attitude of the colonizers in regard to differences in degrees of humanity. In some ways, scientific racism and the very idea of race were the most explicit expressions of a widespread and general attitude regarding the humanity of colonized and enslaved subjects in the Americas and Africa in the sixteenth century. I'd like to suggest that what was born in the sixteenth century was something more pervasive and subtle than what at first transpires in the concept of race: it was an attitude characterized by a permanent suspicion. Enrique Dussel states that Hernán Cortés gave expression to an ideal of subjectivity that could be defined

as the *ego conquiro*, which predates René Descartes's articulation of the *ego cogito*.[22] This means that the significance of the Cartesian *cogito* for modern European identity has to be understood against the backdrop of an unquestioned ideal of self expressed in the notion of the *ego conquiro*. The certainty of the self as a conqueror, of its tasks and missions, preceded Descartes's certainty about the self as a thinking substance (*res cogitans*) and provided a way to interpret it. I am suggesting that the practical conquering self and the theoretical thinking substance are parallel in terms of their certainty. The *ego conquiro* is not questioned, but rather provides the ground for the articulation of the *ego cogito*. Dussel suggests as much: 'The 'barbarian' was the obligatory context of all reflection on subjectivity, reason, the *cogito*'.[23] But the true context was marked not only by the existence of the barbarian, or else, the barbarian had acquired new connotations in modernity. The barbarian was a racialized self, and what characterized this racialization was a radical questioning or permanent suspicion regarding the humanity of the self in question. Thus, the 'certainty' of the project of colonization and the foundation of the *ego conquiro* stand, just like Descartes's certainty about the *cogito*, on doubt or skepticism. Skepticism becomes the means to reach certainty and provide a solid foundation to the self. The role of skepticism is central for European modernity. And just like the *ego conquiro* predates and precedes the *ego cogito*, a certain skepticism regarding the humanity of the enslaved and colonized sub-others stands at the background of the Cartesian certainties and his methodic doubt. Thus, before Cartesian methodic skepticism (the procedure that introduced the heuristic device of the evil demon and which ultimately led to the finding of the *cogito* itself) became central for modern understandings of self and world, there was another kind of skepticism in modernity which became constitutive of it. Instead of the methodical attitude that leads to the *ego cogito*, this form of skepticism defines the attitude that sustains the *ego conquiro*. I characterize this attitude as racist/ imperial Manichean misanthropic skepticism. It could also be rendered as the *imperial attitude*, which gives definition to modern Imperial Man.[24]

Unlike Descartes's methodical doubt, Manichean misanthropic skepticism is not skeptical about the existence of the world or the normative status of logics and mathematics. It is rather a form of questioning the very humanity of colonized peoples. The Cartesian idea about the division between *res cogitans* and *res extensa* (consciousness and matter) which translates itself into a divide between the mind and the body or between the human and nature is preceded and even, one has the temptation to say, to some extent built upon an anthropological colonial difference between the *ego conquistador* and the *ego conquistado*. The very relationship between colonizer and colonized provided a new model to understand the relationship between the soul or mind and the body; and likewise, modern articulations of the mind/body are used as models to conceive the colonizer/colonized relation, as well as the relation between

man and woman, particularly the woman of color.[25] This difference translates itself into European and non-European and into lighter and darker peoples, or what W.E.B. Du Bois refers to as the color-line.[26] If the *ego conquiro* anticipates in some ways the subjective turn and solipsism of the *ego cogito*, then Manichean skepticism in some ways opens the door and shapes the reception of Cartesian skepticism. This point of view also leads to the idea that it would be impossible to provide an adequate account of the crisis of modern Europe without reference, not only to the limits of a Cartesian view of the world, but also to the traumatic effects of Manichean misanthropic skepticism and its imperial ethos.

Misanthropic skepticism doubts in a way the most obvious. Statements like 'you are a human' take the form of cynical rhetorical questions: Are you completely human? 'You have rights' becomes 'why do you think that you have rights?' Likewise 'You are a rational being' takes the form of the question 'are you really rational?' Misanthropic skepticism is like a worm at the very heart of modernity. The achievements of the *ego cogito* and instrumental rationality operate within the logic that misanthropic skepticism helped to established. That is why the idea of progress always meant in modernity progress for a few and why the Rights of Man do not apply equally to all, among many other such apparent contradictions. Misanthropic skepticism provides the basis for the *preferential option for the ego conquiro*, which explains why security for some can conceivably be obtained at the expense of the lives of others.[27] The *imperial attitude* promotes a fundamentally genocidal attitude in respect to colonized and racialized people. Through it colonial and racial subjects are marked as dispensable.

Ideas of war, conquest, and genocide here bring up another fundamental aspect of coloniality.[28] The question about whether the indigenous peoples of the Americas had soul or not was framed around the question of just war. In the debates that took place in Valladolid in the sixteenth century Sepúlveda argued against Las Casas that the Spanish had the obligation to engage in a just war against subjects who, in their inferiority, would not adopt by themselves the superior Christian religion and culture.[29] Once more, just like it happens in respect to the question about the humanity of the so called Amerindians, the outcome of the discussion is not as important as the question itself. The 'discovery' and conquest of the Americas was no less than an ontological event with many implications, the most dramatic of which were established by the attitudes and questions that emerged in the context. By the time when the question about engaging in a just war against the Amerindians was answered the conquerors had already established a particular way of relating to the peoples that they encountered. And the way in which they pursued such relations did not correspond to the ethical standards that were followed in their countries of origin. Indeed, as Sylvia Wynter argues, Columbus's redefinition of the purpose of land as being one *for us*, whereby *for us* meant *for*

*us* who belong to the realm of Man vis-à-vis those outside the human oecumene, already introduces the exceptional character that ethics is going to take in the New World.[30] As we know, such exceptional situation gradually lost its exceptionality and became normative in the modern world. But before it gained such a widespread acceptance and became constitutive of a new reigning episteme, the exceptionality was shown in the way in which colonizers behaved in relation to the indigenous peoples and black slaves. And this behavior coincided more with the kind of actions shown at war, than with the ethics that regulated live with other European Christians.

When the conquerors came to the Americas they did not follow the code of ethics that regulated behavior among subjects of the crown in their kingdom.[31] Their actions were regulated by the ethics or rather the non-ethics of war. One cannot forget that while early Christians criticized slavery in the Roman Empire, later Christians considered that vanquished enemies in war could legitimately be enslaved.[32] Indeed, in the Ancient world and the Middle Ages it was for the most part legitimate to enslaved some people, particularly prisoners of war and the vanquished. What happens in the Americas is a transformation and naturalization of the *non-ethics of war*, which represented a sort of exception to the ethics that regulate normal conduct in Christian countries, to a more stable and long-standing reality of *damnation*. Damnation, life in hell, refers here to modern forms of colonialism which constitute a reality characterized by the naturalization of war by means of the naturalization of slavery, now justified in relation to the very physical and ontological constitution of people – by virtue of 'race' – and not to their faith or belief.[33] That human beings become slaves when they are vanquished in a war translates in the Americas to the suspicion that the conquered people, and then non-European peoples in general, are constitutively inferior and that therefore they should assume a position of slavery and serfdom. Sepúlveda draws on Aristotle to justify this position, but he was more than anything translating into categories ideas that were already becoming common sense. Later the idea was going to be solidified in respect to the slavery of people from Africa and become stable until today under the tragic reality of different forms of racism.

Coloniality, I am suggesting here, can be understood as a radicalization and naturalization of the non-ethics of war. This non-ethics included the practices of eliminating and slaving certain subjects – e.g., indigenous and black – as part of the enterprise of colonization. The hyperbolic expression of coloniality includes genocide, which is the paroxysm of the ego cogito – a world in which the ego cogito exists alone. War, however, is not only about killing or enslaving. War includes a particular treatment of sexuality and of feminity: rape. Coloniality is an order of things that put people of color under the murderous and rapist sight of a vigilant ego. And the primary targets of rape are women. But men of color are also seeing through these lenses. Men of color are feminized and become for the *ego conquiro* fundamentally penetrable

subjects.[34] I will expand more on the several dimensions of murder and rape when I elaborate the existential aspect of the analytics of the coloniality of Being. The point that I want to make here is that racialization works through gender and sex and that the ego conquiro is constitutively a *phallic ego* as well.[35] Enrique Dussel, who submits the thesis of the phallic character of the ego cogito, also makes links, albeit indirectly, with the reality of war.

> And thus, in the beginning of modernity, before Descartes discovered . . . a terrifying anthropological dualism in Europe, the Spanish conquistadors arrived in America. The phallic conception of the European-medieval world is now added to the forms of submission of the vanquished Indians. 'Males', Bartolomé de las Casas writes, are reduced through 'the hardest, most horrible, and harshest serfdom'; but this only occurs with those who have remained alive, because many of them have died; however, 'in war typically they only leave alive young men (mozos) and *women*.[36]

Joshua Goldstein complements this account by depicting conquest as an extension of the rape and exploitation of women in wartime.[37] He argues that to understand conquest one needs to examine: (1) male sexuality as a cause of aggression; (2) the feminization of enemies as symbolic domination, and (3) dependence on exploiting women's labor. My argument is that these three things come together in the idea of race that began to emerge in the conquest and colonization of the Americas. Misanthropic skepticism posits its targets as racialized and sexualized subjects. Once vanquished, they are said to be inherently servants and their bodies come to form part of an economy of sexual abuse, exploitation, and control. The ethics of the *ego conquiro* ceased to be only a special code of behavior for periods of war and becomes in the Americas – and gradually the modern world – by virtue of misanthropic skepticism, the idea of race, and the coloniality of power, a standard of conduct that reflects the way things are – a way of things whose naturalization reaches its climax with the use of natural science to validate racism in the nineteenth century. The way things supposedly are emerge from the idea of how a world is conceived to be in conditions of war and the code of behavior that is part of it. What happens in modernity is that such a view of the world and code of conduct is transformed – through the idea of race – and becomes naturalized. Thus, the treatment of vanquished peoples in conditions of war is perceived as legitimate long after war is over. Later on, it won't be their aggression or opposition, but their 'race' which justifies continued serfdom, slavery, and rape. This represents a break with the European medieval tradition and its ethical codes. With the initial exploitation of Africa and the colonization of the Americas in the fifteenth century, the emerging modernity comes to be shaped by a paradigm of war.[38]

Building on the work of Dussel, Gordon, Quijano, and Wynter I articulated in this section what I see as three contributions to the understanding of coloniality and race: (1) the understanding of race as misanthropic skepticism, (2) the interrelation of race and gender, and (3) the understanding of race and gender conceptions in modernity as the result of the naturalization of the ethics of war. The lived experience of racialized people is deeply touched by the encounter with misanthropic skepticism and by the constant encounter with violence and death. The language that they use has also already being shaped by understanding of the world as a battle field in which they are permanently vanquished. Now that we have an idea about the basic conditions of life in the colonial side of the modern world or in the dark side of the color-line we can try to find a more precise philosophical articulation of these experiences and thus to lay out the fundamentals for a discourse about the coloniality of being. But, while we have explored to some extent the meaning of the idea of coloniality, we haven't done the same with the idea of 'being'. We shall do that next.

## What is being?

As I made clear at the outset, Heidegger's fundamental ontology informs the conception of Being that I want to elaborate here. His work, particularly his 1927 magnus opus, *Being and Time* is not the point of departure to think about the coloniality of Being but it is, at least when spelled out in the context of the phenomenological tradition and its heretic expressions, an inescapable reference point. I do not think that Heidegger's conception of ontology and the primacy that he gives to the question of being necessarily provide the best basis for the understanding of coloniality or decolonization, but his analyses of being-in-the-world serve as a starting point to understanding some key elements of existential thought, a tradition that has made important insights into the lived experience of colonized and racialized peoples.[39] Returning to Heidegger can provide new clues about how to articulate a discourse on the colonial aspects of world making and lived experience.

Heidegger's ontology is characterized by the idea that Being is not a being, an entity, or a thing, but the Being of beings, that is, something like the general horizon of understanding for all beings.[40] He refers to the distinction between Being and beings as the *ontological difference*.[41] According to Heidegger, Western philosophy, particularly Western metaphysics, is characterized by the forgetfulness of Being and by a denial of the ontological difference. Western metaphysics has equally betrayed the understanding of Being by conceiving Being in terms of the godhead or divinity. He calls this tendency onto-theology, which is for him what fundamental ontology needs to overcome.[42]

In addition to arguing for the crucial importance of the ontological difference, Heidegger makes the point that the answer to the question of the

meaning of Being necessitates a new radical point of departure. God cannot stand as the beginning of ontology anymore. Things as such are of not much help either, since their meaning is partly independent of them, and surely they do not grasp their own meaning. In fact there is only one being for whom the question of Being is significant: the human being. Since Heidegger's aim is to begin philosophy anew, he does not want to use Man or any known concept to refer to human beings. They all carry the trace of metaphysics and of epistemologically-centered philosophy, which would vitiate his efforts to escape from them. The concept that he uses to refer to human beings-qua-beings for whom their own being is in question is *Dasein*. Dasein literally means 'being there'. Thus, *Dasein* is simply the being who is there. For Heidegger, fundamental ontology needs to elucidate the meaning of 'being there' and through that, articulate ideas about Being itself.

Heidegger's first reflection about Dasein is that it ek-sist, which means that it is projected to the future.[43] But Dasein is also 'thrown there'. Dasein ek-sist in a context which is defined by a history and where there are laws and established conceptions about social interaction, subjectivity, the world, and so on. Now, through the analysis of Dasein, Heidegger discovers that for the most time its subjectivity takes the shape of a collective anonymous figure: the One or the They. The They could be compared to what Nietzsche referred to as the herd or the mass of people.[44] Once Heidegger has elaborated his view of the They the rest of part I of *Being and Time* takes on the question of how can Dasein relate authentically to itself by projecting its ownmost possibilities – not those defined by the They. Heidegger's response is that authenticity can only be achieved by resoluteness, and that resoluteness can only emerge in an encounter with the possibility which is inescapably one's own, that is, death. In death one is fully irreplaceable: no one can die for one, or one for another. Death is a singular individualizing factor. The anticipation of the death and the accompanying anxiety allow the subject to detach herself from the They, to determine her ownmost possibilities, and to resolutely define her own project of ek-sistence.[45]

While the anticipation of death provides the means for the achievement of authenticity at an individual level, a *Fuhrer* or leader became for Heidegger the means to achieve authenticity at a collective level. Resoluteness at a collective level could only emerge by virtue of a leader. From here that Heidegger came to praise Hitler's role in Germany and became an enthusiastic participant in the Nazi administration. War in some way provided a way to connect these two ideas: the wars of the *volk* (people) in the name of their leader provide the context for a confrontation with death, and thus, to individual authenticity. The possibility of dying for the country in a war becomes a means for individual and collective authenticity.[46] This picture, to be sure, seems to reflect more the point of view of the victor in war, than that of the vanquished. But it could be said that the vanquished can also achieve authenticity through the confrontation with death in war. Anybody can. Yet, the missing factor here

is the following: if the previous account of coloniality in relation to the non-ethics of war is plausible then it must be admitted that the encounter with death is no extra-ordinary affair, but a constitutive feature of the reality of colonized and racialized subjects. The colonized is thus not ordinary Dasein, and the encounter with the possibility of death does not have the same impact or results than for someone whose mode of alienation is that of depersonalization by the One or They. Racialized subjects are constituted in different ways than those that form selves, others, and peoples. Death is not so much an individualizing factor as a constitituve feature of their reality. It is the encounter with daily forms of death, not the They, which afflicts them. The encounter with death always comes too late, as it were, since death is already beside them. For this reason, decolonization, deracialization, and des-gener-acción (in sum, decoloniality) emerge not through an encounter with one's own mortality, but from a desire to evade death, one's own but even more fundamentally that of others. In short, while a vanquished people in war could achieve authenticity, for subjects who are not considered to be part of 'the people' the situation is different. For some subjects modernity changed the way of achieving authenticity: they already live with death and are not even 'people'. What Heidegger forgot is that in modernity Being has a colonial side, and that this has far-reaching consequences. The colonial aspect of Being, that is, its tendency to submit everything to the light of understanding and signification, reaches an extreme pathological point in war and its naturalization through the idea of race in modernity. The colonial side of Being sustains the color-line. Heidegger, however, looses from view the particular predicament of subjects in the darker side of this line and the significance of their lived experience for theorization of Being and the pathologies of modernity. Ironically, Heidegger recognizes the existence of what he calls 'primitive Dasein', but in no way he connected it with colonized Dasein.[47] Instead, he took European Man as his model of Dasein, and thus the colonized appeared as a 'primitive'. He forgot that if the concept of Man is a problem, is not only because it is metaphysical, but also because it does away with the idea that, in modernity, what one finds is not a single model of human being, but relations of power that create a world with masters and slaves. He needed to break with the idea of Europe and the European as models, in order to uncover the complex dynamics of Dasein in the modern period – both of European and colonized Dasein, to which we will refer here as the *damné*. But we are already in the territory of discourse on the coloniality of being.

## What is the coloniality of being?

The concept of the coloniality of Being is best understood in light of the discussion of the *ego conquiro* and Manichean misanthropic skepticism in the

first section. I argued that the ego conquiro and misanthropic skepticism remained unquestioned by Descartes's formulation of the ego cogito and his methodic doubt. He could imagine an evil demon who deceives people about their apparent certainties, but could not observe an *ego conquiro* at work in the consciousness of the European (and, if we follow Dussel and Quijano, in his own presuppositions as well) and how it made everyone to take for granted the inhumanity of colonized peoples.

How does this relate to ontology and Being? Heidegger's critical response to the subjective and epistemological turn of modern philosophy achieved by Descartes consisted in pointing out an alleged forgetfulness in Descartes's thought. Heidegger correctly suggests that Descartes and basically all of modern philosophy after him focused rather exclusively on the question of the *ego cogito*. 'Cogito, ergo sum', 'I think, therefore I am', however, introduced, what was for Heidegger a more fundamental notion than the cogito itself: the very concept of Being. 'I THINK, therefore I am' turned for him into 'I think, therefore I AM'. The question of Being appears in the second part of the Cartesian formulation – the I AM.[48] Focusing on the second part of the expression, Heidegger wanted to oppose the modern tradition of philosophy as epistemology with his own fundamental ontology. Now, in light of what has been said about the *ego conquiro* and the misanthropic doubt that remains unquestioned in Descartes's formulation, it is possible to point out what both Descartes and Heidegger missed in their philosophical views. If the *ego cogito* was built upon the foundations of the *ego conquiro*, the 'I think, therefore I am' presupposes two unacknowledged dimensions. Beneath the 'I think' we can read 'others do not think', and behind the 'I am' it is possible to locate the philosophical justification for the idea that 'others are not' or do not have being. In this way we are led to uncover the complexity of the Cartesian formulation. From 'I think, therefore I am' we are led to the more complex and both philosophically and historically accurate expression:

> 'I think (others do not think, or do not think properly), therefore I am (others are-not, lack being, should not exist or are dispensable)'.

The Cartesian formulation privileges epistemology, which simultaneously hides both what could be regarded as the coloniality of knowledge (others do not think) and the coloniality of Being (others are not). Heidegger's ontological turn missed these two unacknowledged components of Descartes's formulation. Cartesian epistemology and Heideggerian ontology presuppose the coloniality of knowledge and the coloniality of Being. In what was unmentioned and presupposed in Descartes's formulation we find thus the fundamental link between the 'colonialidad del saber' (coloniality of knowledge) and the 'colonialidad del ser' (coloniality of being). The absent of rationality is articulated in modernity with the idea of the absence of Being in

others. Misanthropic skepticism and racism work together with ontological exclusion. It is in this way that we better understand Frantz Fanon's idea that in a colonial anti-black world the Black does not have ontological resistance or ontological weight in the eyes of the white.[49] He also says that when the black person is going to speak with whites, reason flees away and irrationality imposes the terms of the conversation.[50] The lack of ontological resistance is linked with the absence of rationality and viceversa.

For Fanon, the black is not a being or simply nothingness. The Black is something else. The enigma of blackness appears as the very radical starting point to think about the coloniality of Being. While Heidegger's focus on Being required reflection on Dasein's comportment and existentialia, reflection on the coloniality of Being requires elucidation of the fundamental existential traits of the black and the colonized. In this way, from Descartes's *Meditations* we move to the territory of 'Fanonian meditations'.[51] The Black, people of color, and the colonized become the radical points of departure for any reflection on the coloniality of Being. Following Fanon, I will use a concept that refers to the colonial subject, equivalent in some way to Dasein but marking the aspects of the coloniality of Being: the *damné* or condemned of the earth. The *damné* is for the coloniality of Being what Dasein is for fundamental ontology, but, as it were, in reverse. The *Damné* is for European Dasein the being who is 'not there'. I want to argue that they are not independent of each other but that, without awareness of coloniality, reflection on Dasein and Being involve the erasure of the *damné* and the coloniality of Being. If there has been a problem in modern Western civilization it has not been so much forgetfulness of Being, as Heidegger believed, but suppression of the understanding of coloniality in all its aspects and lack of recognition of the efforts by the *damnés* to overcome the imposed limits by the cruel reality of damnation or the naturalization of war. This is part of what a project of Fanonian meditations would aim to elucidate. Fanonian meditations would articulate new categories for philosophical disquisition. For the purpose of clarity and consistency, I will only introduce and briefly discuss some of the elements that stand as parallels to Heidegger's efforts.

One of the most basic distinctions that Heidegger elaborates is that of the ontological difference, or the difference between Being and beings. Elucidation of the coloniality of Being entails reflection on this and other two kinds of fundamental differences: the trans-ontological difference and the sub-ontological difference. Fanonian meditations would be guided by these three categories:

**Trans-ontological difference**
(difference between Being and what is beyond Being; or Being and exteriority)

**Ontological difference**
(difference between Being and beings)

## Sub-ontological or ontological colonial difference

(difference between Being and what lies below Being or that which is negatively marked as dispensable as well as a target of rape and murder)

We owe a more or less explicit discourse about the trans-ontological difference to Emmanuel Lévinas. The sub-ontological difference has been elaborated, although implicitly, by Fanon. The coloniality of being makes reference to the two of them – since ultimately what lies 'beyond' is what is put in a lower position – but I will focus here on the second.

The ontological difference allows one to think clearly about Being and not to confuse it with beings or entitites or God. Likewise the sub-ontological or ontological colonial difference brings into view the reality that is defined by a differentiation between selves and subjects without ontological resistance. The sub-ontological difference relates to what Walter Mignolo has referred to as the colonial difference. But while his notion of colonial difference is primarily epistemic, sub-ontological difference refers primarily to being. Thus it would be best to distinguish between an epistemic colonial difference that allows one to perceive the contours of the coloniality of knowledge, and an ontological colonial difference which reveals the presence of the coloniality of being. Or else, one can say that there are different aspects to the colonial difference: epistemic and ontological, both of whom are related to power (exploitation, domination, and control). In short, sub-ontological or ontological colonial difference relates to the coloniality of Being in a way similar to how the epistemic colonial difference is related to the coloniality of knowledge. Colonial difference in general is indeed the first by-product of the coloniality of power, of knowledge, and being. Ontological colonial difference is more specifically the product of the coloniality of being.

Now, what kind of questions should orient our inquiry of the coloniality of Being. While Heidegger bases his reflections on an existential analysis of Dasein, the elucidation of the coloniality of Being requires an analysis of the existential modalities of the *damné*. For Heidegger Dasein ek-sist, that is, it is thrown toward the future, and it achieves authenticity when it anticipates his own mortality, that is, the very end of his future. This position contrasts sharply with Fanon's description of the existential reality of the *damné*. In *A Dying Colonialism* he writes,

> There is, first of all, the fact that the colonized person, who in this respect is like men in underdeveloped countries or the disinherited in all parts of the world, perceives life not as a flowering or a development of an essential productiveness, but as a permanent struggle against an omnipresent death. This ever-menacing death is experienced as endemic famine, unemployment, a high death rate, an inferiority complex and the absence of any hope for the future. All this gnawing at the existence of the

> colonized tends to make of life something resembling an incomplete death.[52]

While Dasein is lost in the They and achieves authenticity when it anticipates its own death, the *damné* confronts the reality of its own finitude as a day to day adventure. That is why Fanon writes in *Black Skin, White Masks* that the black lacks the opportunity to descend into hell.[53] As Lewis Gordon puts it, the reason is because the black already lives in hell.[54] The extraordinary event of confronting mortality turns into an ordinary affair.

Hellish existence in the colonial world carries with it both the racial and the gendered aspects of the naturalization of the non-ethics of war. *Indeed, coloniality of Being primarily refers to the normalization of the extraordinary events that take place in war.* While in war there is murder and rape, in the hell of the colonial world murder and rape become day to day occurrences and menaces. 'Killability' and 'rapeability' are inscribed into the images of the colonial bodies. Lacking real authority, colonized men are permanently feminized. At the same time, men of color represent a constant threat and any amount of authority, any visible trace of the phallus is multiplied in a symbolic hysteria that knows no limits.[55] Mythical depiction of the black man's penis is a case in point. The Black man is depicted as an aggressive sexual beast who desires to rape women, particularly White. The Black woman, in turn, is seeing as always already sexually available to the raping gaze of the White and as fundamentally promiscuous. The Black woman is seeing as a highly erotic being whose primary function is fulfilling sexual desire and reproduction. To be sure, any amount of 'penis' in both represents a threat. But in its most familiar and typical forms the Black man represents the act of rape – 'raping' – while the Black woman is seeing as the most legitimate victim of rape – 'being raped'. Women deserve to be raped and to suffer the consequences – in terms of lack of protection from the legal system, further sexual abuse, and lack of financial assistance to sustain herself and her family – just as black man deserve to be penalized for raping, even without committing such an act. Both 'raping' and 'being raped' are attached to Blackness as if they were part of the essence of Black folk, which is seeing as a dispensable population. Black bodies are seeing as excessively violent and erotic, as well as the legitimate recipients of excessive violence, erotic and otherwise. 'Killability' and 'rapeability' are part of their essence – understood in a phenomenological way. The 'essence' of Blackness in a colonial anti-black world is part of a larger context of meaning in which the non-ethics of war gradually becomes a constitutive part of an alleged normal world. In its racial and colonial connotations and uses, Blackness is an invention and a projection of a social body oriented by the non-ethics of war. The murderous and raping social body projects the features that define it to sub-Others, in order to be able to legitimate the same behavior that is allegedly descriptive of them. The same ideas that inspire perverted acts

in war, particularly slavery, murder and rape, are legitimized in modernity through the idea of race and gradually are seeing as normal to a great extent thanks to the alleged obviousness and non-problematic character of Black slavery and anti-Black racism. To be sure those who suffer the consequences of such a system are primarily Blacks and indigenous peoples, as well as all of those who appear as colored. In short, this system of symbolic representations, the material conditions that in part produce it and continue to legitimate it, and the existential dynamics that occur therein, which are also at the same time derivative and constitutive of such a context, are part of a process that naturalizes the non-ethics of war. The sub-ontological difference is the result of such naturalization. It is legitimized through the idea of race. In such a world, ontology collapses into a Manicheism, as Fanon suggested.[56]

Fanon offered the first phenomenology of the Manichean colonial world, understood properly as a Manichean reality and not solely as ontological.[57] In his analysis, he investigated not only the relation between whites and blacks, but also those between black males and black females. Much can be added to his discussion, but that is not my purpose here. What I wish is first to provide a way to understand the Fanonian breakthrough in light of the articulation of sub-ontological difference and the idea of the naturalization of the non-ethics of war. This is important because, among other things, we can see now that when Fanon called for a war against colonialism, what he was doing was to politicize social relations which were already premised on war. Fanon was not only fighting against anti-black racism in Martinique, or French colonialism in Algeria. He was countering the force and legitimacy of a historical system (European modernity) which utilized racism and colonialism to naturalize the non-ethics of war. He was doing a war against war oriented by 'love', understood here as the desire to restore ethics and to give it a proper place to trans-ontological and ontological differences.[58]

For Fanon, in the colonial context, ontological colonial difference or sub-ontological difference profoundly marks the day to day reality. If the most basic ontological question is 'why are things rather than nothing', the question that emerges in this context and that opens up reflection on the coloniality of Being is 'Why go on?' As Lewis Gordon has put it, 'why go on?' is a fundamental question in the existential philosophy of the African diaspora and it illuminates the plight of the *wretched of the earth*.[59] Why go on? is preceded only by one expression, which becomes the first instance that revels the coloniality of Being, that is, the *cry*.[60] The cry, not a word but an interjection, is a call of attention to one's own existence. The cry is the pre-theoretical expression of the question – Why go on? – which for the most part drives theoretical reflection in the peoples of the African diaspora. It is the cry that animates the birth of theory and critical thought. And the cry points to a peculiar existential condition: that of the condemned. The *damné* or condemned is not a 'being there' but a non-being or rather, as Ralph Ellison

so eloquently elaborated, a sort of an invisible entity.[61] What is invisible about the person of color is its very humanity, and this is in fact what the cry tries to call attention to. Invisibility and dehumanization are the primary expressions of the coloniality of Being. The coloniality of Being indicates those aspects that produce exception from the order of Being; it is as it were, the product of the excess of Being that in order to maintain its integrity and inhibit the interruption by what lies beyond Being produces its contrary, not nothing, but a non-human or rather an inhuman world. The coloniality of Being refers not merely to the reduction of the particular to the generality of the concept or any given horizon of meaning, but to the violation of the meaning of human alterity to the point where the alter-ego becomes a sub-alter. Such a reality, typically approximated very closely in situations of war, is transformed into an ordinary affair through the idea of race, which serves a crucial role in the naturalization of the non-ethics of war through the practices of colonialism and (racial) slavery. The coloniality of Being is not therefore an inevitable moment or natural outcome of the dynamics of creation of meaning. Although it is always present as a possibility, it shows itself forth when the preservation of Being (in any of its determinations: national ontologies, identitarian ontologies, etc.) takes primacy over listening to the cries of those whose humanity is being denied. The coloniality of Being appears in historical projects and ideas of civilization which advance colonial projects of various kinds inspired or legitimized by the idea of race. The coloniality of Being is therefore co-extensive with the production of the color-line in its different expressions and dimensions. It becomes concrete in the appearance of *liminal* subjects, which mark, as it were, the limit of Being, that is, the point at which Being distorts meaning and evidence to the point of dehumanization. The coloniality of Being produces the ontological colonial difference, deploying a series of fundamental existential characteristics and symbolic realities. I have sketched out some. An ample discussion will require another venue. What I would like to do here is to show the relevance of the categories that have been introduced so far for the project of decolonization, which is, ultimately, the positive dimension that inspires this analysis. Like I did in this section, let me begin once more with what we have discovered as our radical point of departure: the *damné*.

## Decolonization and 'des-gener-acción' of being[62]

What is the meaning of *damné*? The *damné* is the subject that emerges in a world marked by the coloniality of Being. The *damné*, as Fanon put it, has non-ontological resistance in the eyes of the dominant group. The *damné* is either invisible or excessively visible. The *damné* exists in the mode of not-being there, which hints at the nearness of death, at the company of death. The *damné* is a concrete being but it is also a transcendental concept. Emile

Benveniste has shown that the term *damné* is etymologically related to the concept of *donner*, which means, to give. The *damné* is literally the subject who cannot give because what he or she has has been taken from him or her.[63] This means that the *damné* is a subject from whom the capacity to have and to give have been taken away from her and him. The coloniality of Being is thus fundamentally an ontological dynamic that aims to obliterate – in its literal sense of doing away completely so as to leave *no trace* – gift-giving and generous reception as a fundamental character of being-in-the-world.

Emmanuel Lévinas argues that gift-giving and reception are fundamental traits of the self. Giving is first and foremost for Lévinas a metaphysical act that makes possible the communication between a self and an Other – as trans-ontological – as well as the sharing of a common world. Without giving to an Other there would be no self just as without receiving from the Other there would be no reason. In short, without a trans-ontological moment there would be no self, no reason, and no Being. The trans-ontological is the foundation of the ontological. For Lévinas, the ontological, the realm of being, comes to exist out of the introduction of justice into the trans-ontological relation, which introduces measure and synchronicity in the order of the fundamentally diachronic.[64] The ontological comes to be at the expense of the trans-ontological. The ontological thus carries with it the marks of both positive achievement and betrayal of the trans-ontological relation, a relation of radical givenness and reception.

According to Lévinas, ontology is a philosophy of power. It is a discourse that, when taken as foundation or ultimate end, it gives priority to an anonymous Being over and beyond the self-Other relation – it gives priority to the ontological rather than to the trans-ontological, and to authenticity rather than to radical responsibility. When ontology is conceived as fundamental, the self-Other relation becomes a secondary dimension of the subject. It is also seen as a source of the potential *forgetfulness* of Being and thus as a departure from authenticity. Lévinas argues precisely the contrary: it is the forgetting of the self-Other relation that characterizes the return of ontology as fundamental, which can lead, not to lacking authenticity, but to a renunciation of responsibility and justice. That is so because being is always already a betrayal of sorts of the trans-ontological relation (of gift and reception between self and Other), and it tends to *forgetting*. That is, being presents itself as the foundation of reality when it is not. This happens because once being is born, it tends to preserve itself and to present itself as autonomous foundation. But, preservation and autonomy can be achieved at the expense of the trans-ontological. Being thus aims to eliminate the *traces* of the trans-ontological. This is done, both, by philosophical accounts that attempt to reduce the self-Other relation to knowledge or being, and by ways of thinking, concrete policies, and historical projects that reduce the significance of givenness, generosity, hospitality, and justice. Clearly enough, Lévinas saw Nazism and

the Jewish Holocaust as radical betrayals of the trans-ontological dimension of human reality, and thus, of the very meaning of the human as such. Thus, Nazism represented not only a threat to European nations and many minorities within Europe, but also a crucial moment in the history of being. The presence of anti-Semitism, Aryanism, and other forms of racial prejudices in Nazism, make clear that race and racism occupy an special place in that history.

Race and caste, along with gender and sexuality, are perhaps the four forms of human differentiation that have served most frequently as means to transgress the primacy of the self-Other relation and to obliterate the traces of the trans-ontological in the concrete world. In modernity, racial differentiation alters the way in which the other forms of human differentiation work in modernity, as the entire globe is divided according to races, which alter the existing caste, gender, and sexual relations. To be sure, race is not totally independent of gender or sexuality, as feminization and eroticism are always part of it. I have argued that the emergence of race and its entanglement with gender and sexuality can be explained in part by their relation to war ethics and their naturalization in the colonial world. Lévinas did not go into these matters. He focused on the analysis of the trans-ontological dimension of human reality and in the rescue and philosophical reconstruction of the Jewish conceptual and ethical legacy, which for him provided an alternative to the Euro-Greek tendency to privilege knowledge and being. He nonetheless provided important considerations for understanding the meaning and significance of the *damné* and the coloniality of being. The appearance of the *damné* is not only of social significance but of ontological significance as well. It indicates the emergence of a world structured on the basis of the lack of recognition of the greater part of humanity as givers, which legitimizes dynamics of possession, rather than generous exchange. This is in great part achieved through the idea of race, which suggests not only inferiority but also dispensability. From here that not only poverty, but also the nearness of death – in misery, lack of recognition, lynching, and imprisonment among so many other ways – characterize the situation of the *damné*. It is this situation that we refer to here as coloniality. And the ways by virtue of which the world comes to be shaped by the excess of being and its obliteration of the trans-ontological we call the coloniality of being. Coloniality of being refers to a process whereby the forgetfulness of ethics as a transcendental moment that founds subjectivity turns into the production of a world in which exceptions to ethical relationships become the norm. That being has a colonial aspect means that in addition to posit itself as autonomous and be driven by preservation, it tries to obliterate the traces of the trans-ontological by actually giving birth to a world in which lordship and supremacy rather than generous interaction define social dynamics in society. The *damné* is the product of these tendencies. Colonization and racialization are the concrete and conceptual ways by virtue of which the *damné* emerges as an idea and mode of being. Colonization and

racialization are expressions of the dark side of being, that is, they represent radical betrayals of the trans-ontological. Colonization and racialization are not only political and social events or structures. They also have metaphysical and ontological significance.

War is the opposite of the an-archical relation of absolute responsbility for the Other that gives birth to human subjectivity. The obliteration of the trans-ontological takes the tendency of producing a world in which war becomes the norm, rather than the exception. That is the basic meaning of the coloniality of being: the radical betrayal of the trans-ontological by the formation of a world in which the non-ethics of war become naturalized through the idea of race. The *damné* is the outcome of this process. Her agency needs to be defined by a consistent opposition to the paradigm of war and the promotion of a world oriented by the ideals of human generosity and receptivity. This is the precise meaning of decolonization: restoration of the logic of the gift. Fanon suggests as much in the conclusion of *Black Skin, White Masks*:

> Superiority? Inferiority?
>
> Why not the quite simple attempt to touch the other, to feel the other, to explain the other to myself?
>
> Was my freedom not given to me then in order to build the world of the *You*?[65]

Fanon's message is clear: decolonization should aspire at the very minimum to restore or create a reality where racialized subjects could give and receive freely in societies founded on the principle of receptive generosity.[66] Receptive generosity involves a break away from racial dynamics as well as from conceptions of gender and sexuality that inhibit generous interaction among subjects. In this sense, a consistent response to coloniality involves both decolonization and 'des-gener-acción' as projects, both of which are necessary for the YOU to emerge. Only in this way the trans-ontological can shine through the ontological, and love, ethics, and justice can take the role that the non-ethics of war have occupied in modern life.

Decolonization and 'des-gener-acción', different from authenticity, are not based on the anticipation of death, but on the aperture of one's self to the racialized other *to the point of substitution*.[67] Substitution occurs when one's identity is teleologically suspended and when one offers one's life to the task of achieving decolonial justice: that is, a justice oriented by the trans-ontological dimension of the human. Decolonial justice opposes the preferential option for imperial Man by the preferential option for the *damné* or condemned of the earth. Such justice is inspired by a form of love which is also decolonial. 'Decolonial love' – a concept coined and developed by the Chicana theorist Chela Sandoval – gives priority to the trans-ontological over the claims of

ontology.[68] Decolonization and 'des-gener-acción' are the active products of decolonial love and justice. They aim to restore the logics of the gift through a decolonial politics of receptive generosity.[69]

In order to be consistent, the discourse of decolonization and 'des-gener-acción' would have to be understood according to the very logics that they open. They cannot take the form of a new imperial universal. Decolonization itself, the whole discourse around it, is a gift itself, an invitation to engage in dialogue. For decolonization, concepts need to be conceived as invitations to dialogue and not as impositions. They are expressions of the availability of the subject to engage in dialogue and the desire for exchange. Decolonization in this respect aspires to break with monologic modernity. It aims to foment transmodernity, a concept which also becomes an invitation that has to be understood in relation to the decolonial paradox of giving and receiving.[70] Transmodernity is an invitation to think modernity/coloniality critically from different epistemic positions and according to the manifold experiences of subjects who suffer different dimensions of the coloniality of Being. Transmodernity involves radical dialogical ethics – to initiate a dialogue between humans and those considered subhumans – and the formulation of a decolonial and critical cosmopolitanism.[71]

Decolonization is an idea that is probably as old as colonization itself. But it only becomes a project in the twentieth century. That is what Du Bois suggested when he stated that the problem of the twentieth-century is the problem of the color-line. The idea was not that the color-line was unique to the twentieth century, but that critical and violent confrontations with it were unavoidable then. With decolonization I do not have in mind simply the end of formal colonial relations, as it happened throughout the Americas in the late eighteenth and the nineteenth centuries. I am instead referring to a confrontation with the racial, gender, and sexual hierarchies that were put in place or strengthened by European modernity as it colonized and enslaved populations through the planet. In short, with decolonization I am thinking of oppositions to the coloniality of power, knowledge, and being – it may be more consistent to refer to it as 'decoloniality', as Chela Sandoval and Catherine Walsh suggest.[72] Such opposition existed before the twentieth century, but only reached interconnected global articulations then. If Du Bois announced the project of systematic opposition to the color-line, it was perhaps intellectuals after the Second World War who most consistently expressed the ambitions of decolonization as project. We owe some of the most important early formulations to authors such as Aimé Césaire and Frantz Fanon. They are key thinkers of what could very well be considered a de-colonial turn in theory and critique.

The de-colonial turn refers to a shift in knowledge production of similar nature and magnitude to the linguistic and pragmatic turns.[73] It introduces questions about the effects of colonization in modern subjectivities and modern

forms of life as well as contributions of racialized and colonized subjectivities to the production of knowledge and critical thinking. As mentioned above, the decolonial turn was announced by figures such as W.E.B. Du Bois in the early twentieth century. Du Bois was trying to see what was produced as invisible. He was trying to look at the pathology of the world from the position of those regarded as most pathological and in some way non-human. The very enunciation of the 'problem of the color-line' was predicated on at least a partial solution, which involved a shift in the theoretical attitude of the knower. The theoretical attitude requires detachment and wonder; the *decolonial attitude*, which Du Bois advances, demands responsibility and the willingness to take many perspectives, particularly the perspectives and points of view of those whose very existence is questioned and produced as insignificant.[74] The Decolonial Turn is about making visible the invisible and about analyzing the mechanisms that produce such invisibility or distorted visibility in light of a large stock of ideas that must necessarily include the critical reflections of the 'invisible' people themselves. Indeed, one must recognize their intellectual production as thinking – not only as culture or ideology.[75] DuBois was implicitly suggesting as much when he explore the meaning of the question 'How does it feel to be a problem?'[76] But, while much is talked about the idea that the problem of the twentieth century is the problem of the color-line, much less discussed are his own responses to the problems, which not only involved the creation of black institutions in the United States as well as furthering Pan-African visions and struggles, but also a fundamental shift in perspective that leads one to see the world anew in a way that allows one to target its evils in a new way and that gives us a better sense of what to do next. If the problem of the twentieth and the twenty-first century, and indeed, the problem of the entire modernity is the problem of the color-line, the solution for the twentieth century is, at least in part, the decolonial turn, which promotes a shift away from the *imperial attitude* (both natural and theoretical; Eurocentric, Americancentric, or otherwise) and the *decolonial attitude* in politics, theory, and critique. The decolonial turn marks the definitive entry of enslaved and colonized subjectivities into the realm of thought at before unknown institutional levels.

The de-colonial turn involves interventions at the level of power, knowledge, and being through varied actions of decolonization and 'des-gener-acción'. It opposes the paradigm of war which has driven modernity for more than five hundred years, with a radical shift in the social and political agent, the attitude of the knower, and the position in regards to whatever threatens the preservation of being, particularly the actions of the *damné*s. The transition from modernity to transmodernity lies first and foremost in the political and epistemic interventions and creations of the *damné*s, not the 'people' (of the nation) or the 'multitude' (of Empire). Michael Hardt and Antonio Negri describe the 'project of the multitude' as the expression of a

desire for a world of equality and freedom as well as for global democracy.[77] The 'project of the *damnés*' incorporates such ideals but is more precisely defined by the opposition to the scandal of death and the naturalization of war and by the search for love and human filiality which can only be achieved through decolonization and 'des-gener-acción'.[78] The 'unfinished democratic project of modernity' which the multitude assumes gives way in this picture to the 'unfinished project of decolonization' that aims at transmodernity as a goal. The *damnés* or condemned of the earth become primary agents of such transformations. The *damnés* have the potential of transforming the modern/colonial into a transmodern world: that is a world where war does not become the norm or the rule, but the exception.[79]

## Notes

1 Sections of this essay were presented in talks at the John Hope Franklin Center at Duke University on 5 November 2003 and in the Critical Theory and Decolonization Conference at Duke University and the University of North Carolina, Chapel Hill on 30 May 2004.

2 They include Fernando Coronil, Santiago Castro-Gómez, Oscar Guardiola, Edgardo Lander, Walter Mignolo, Anibal Quijano, Freya Schiwy, Catherine Walsh, and others.

3 See Walter Mignolo (1995). For a more recent source see Walter Mignolo (2003). The concept also appears in a recent essay by Sylvia Wynter (2003).

4 It seems that Mignolo was presenting the idea in different places in the year 2000. He offered a presentation entitled 'Thinking Possible Future: The Network Society and the Coloniality of Being' in a Joan Carlisle-Irving Lecture at the University of British Columbia on 30 March 2000. Unfortunately the text of this presentation is missing.

5 See Martin Heidegger (1996).

6 For discussion about Heidegger's involvement with Nazism, including primary sources, see Wolin (1991).

7 Lévinas judges Heidegger very negatively for not offering an apology to the Jewish people. See Lévinas (1989).

8 See Emmanuel Lévinas (1969).

9 On the 'coloniality of power' see Quijano (2000, 1991, 1992).

10 The idea of the coloniality of knowledge ('colonialidad del saber') becomes the organizing theme of Edgardo Lander (2000).

11 Mignolo (2003, p. 669).

12 Mignolo takes Fanon as a major source for his own articulation of the coloniality of Being. See Mignolo (2003, p. 669).

13 For a clarification on the relation between genetic, existential, and genealogical/historical levels of analysis see Nelson Maldonado-Torres (forthcoming). In this book I articulate genetic, existential, and genealogical/historical reflections on modernity on the basis of Lévinas, Fanon, and

Dussel's work. This essay represents a transition between *Against War* and a new book project preliminarily entitled *Fanonian Meditations*.

14 See Aníbal Quijano (2001).

15 See Aníbal Quijano and Immanuel Wallerstein (1992).

16 Quijano (2000, p. 533).

17 See Walter Mignolo (2003).

18 See Quijano (1992, n.p.).

19 See Gordon (1995, 2000), Nelson Maldonado-Torres (2006) and Wynter (1995).

20 On 'global coloniality' see Georas (1997), Grosfoguel (2003), and Mignolo (2002, 2000).

21 Translation of 'desde entonces, en las relaciones intersubjetivas y en las prácticas sociales del poder, quedó formada, de una parte la idea de que los no-europeos tienen una estructura biológica no solamente diferente a la de los europeos; sino, sobre todo, perteneciente a un tipo o a un nivel 'inferior'.' See Quijano (1992, n.p.).

22 Dussel (1996, p. 133).

23 Dussel (1996, p. 133).

24 The model or paradigm of existence referred to with the concept Imperial Man has more concrete manifestation: European and American Man. I have referred to the overcoming of these modes of selfhood in terms of the 'death' of Imperial Man. See Maldonado-Torres (2005, 2002).

25 See Quijano's comments on modern dualism in Quijano (2000, pp. 554–6).

26 Recall Du Bois's sentence about the twentieth century: 'The problem of the twentieth century is the problem of the color line, the relation of the lighter and darker races in Asia, Africa, America and the islands of the sea' (Du Bois 1999, p. 17).

27 The preferential option for the ego conquiro would be contested later on by liberation theology's emphasis on the preferential option for the poor and dispossessed. On the preferential option for the poor and other central ideas in liberation theology see Ellacuría and Sobrino (1993).

28 The rest of this section reproduces a discussion that I develop more in the six chapter of Maldonado-Torres (forthcoming).

29 On the debates in Valladolid see Lewis Hanke (1974).

30 Wynter (1995, pp. 5–57).

31 See Todorov (1992, pp. 144–5).

32 On the early Christian conception of slavery and their relationship with the Roman Empire see Horsley (1997).

33 I take the notion of damnation from Fanon (1991).

34 On this point see the chapter on 'The Negro and Psychopathology' in Fanon (1968, pp. 141–209). See also 'Sex, Race, and Matrices of Desire in an Antiblack World', in Gordon (1997, pp. 73–88).

35 In this respect, Dussel writes: 'El *sujeto* europeo que comienza por ser un 'yo conquisto' y culmina en la 'voluntad de poder' es un sujeto *masculino*. El *ego cogito* es el *ego* de un varón'. [The European *subject* who begins in the

mode of 'I conquer' and reaches its climax in the 'will to power' is a *masculine* subject. The *ego cogito* is the *ego* of a male.] (Dussel 1977, p. 50). Dussel also comments in this text on the ways in which the colonized male subject repeats the same behavior toward colonized women.

36 Dussel (1977, p. 99).

37 Goldstein (2001, p. 332).

38 This idea is the basis of Maldonado-Torres (forthcoming).

39 See the work of Lewis Gordon, the most prominent black existentialist today. See, among others, Gordon (1995, 2000, 1997). Even though Gordon's existentialism is mainly Fanonian and Sartrean, his phenomenological explorations of the meaning of blackness in the modern world greatly inform my critical assessment of Heidegger's categories and the overall discourse on the coloniality of being articulated here.

40 My description here is based on Heidegger (1962).

41 See Heidegger (1962, pp. 28–35).

42 For a Heideggerian critique of theology see Heidegger (1962, pp. 74–5).

43 On Dasein's existential character see Heidegger (1962, pp. 32–35).

44 See Nietzche's reflections on herd morality in Nietzsche (1989).

45 For reflections on being-toward-death and authenticity see Heidegger (1962, pp. 279–304).

46 On the relation between war and authenticity see, among others, Gray (1959) and Losurdo (2001).

47 Heidegger (1962, p. 76).

48 See Heidegger (1962, pp. 46, 71–2).

49 Fanon (1968, p. 110).

50 Fanon (1968, pp. 119–20).

51 Fanonian meditations refers to a decolonial horizon of re-thinking the idea of first philosophy, just as Descartes did in his *Meditations on First Philosophy*. It is also the title of a book project in progress.

52 Fanon (1965, p. 128). See also Fanon (1988, pp. 13–4).

53 See Fanon (1968, p. 8).

54 Gordon (2005, p. 4).

55 This analysis is informed by Lewis Gordon description of sexual and racial dynamics. See Gordon (2005, pp. 73–88). Gordon writes: 'For, in an antiblack world, a black penis, whatever its size, represents a threat. Given our discussion of the black signifying the feminine, the underlying nature of the threat should be obvious: the black penis is feared for the same reason that a woman with a penis is feared. She represents a form of revenge' (p. 83).

56 See Fanon (1991).

57 I am referring to Fanon (1968).

58 The idea of 'love' appears in several parts of *Black Skin*, particularly in the conclusion.Gordon (2000, pp. 13–15).

59 Gordon (2000, pp. 13–15).

60 For an analysis of the meaning of the 'cry' from the perspective of the coloniality of being and decolonization see Maldonado-Torres (2001, pp. 46–60).
61 Ellison (1999).
62 I owe the concept of 'desgeneración' to Laura Pérez.
63 Benveniste (1997, pp. 34, 40).
64 See Lévinas (1974).
65 Fanon (1968, pp. 231–2), bold mine.
66 On the concept of receptive generosity see Coles (1997).
67 Decolonization and 'des-gener-acción' characterize forms of thought and action that are central to what Mignolo refers as the geo-politics and the body-politics of knowledge in his contribution to this volume. They are the privileged forms of action that emerge and are characteristic of the Decolonial Turn (see below).
68 Sandoval (2000).
69 See Coles (1997).
70 For an elucidation of the concept of transmodernity see Dussel (1995, 1996, 1999, 2002). Also see Dussel's contribution in this volume.
71 On critical cosmopolitanism see Mignolo, (2000) and Saldívar (1991).
72 See Sandoval (2000) and Walsh (2005).
73 See Nelson Maldonado-Torres (2005). This conference was organized by Ramón Grosfoguel, Nelson Maldonado-Torres, and José David Saldívar.
74 For reflections on the decolonial attitude see Maldonado-Torres (forthcoming, n.p., 2005, 2006, n.p.).
75 This is a point incessantly made other figures of the Decolonial Turn: Lewis Gordon, Walter Mignolo Chela Sandoval, and Sylvia Wynter, among others.
76 Du Bois, 1999, p. 9. See an acute analysis of this question in Gordon (2000, pp. 62–95).
77 See Hardt & Negri (2004, p. xi).
78 I develop this point more in Maldonado-Torres (forthcoming).
79 For references to the unfinished project of decolonization see Grosfoguel (2005); Ramón Grosfoguel *et al.* (2005), Maldonado-Torres (forthcoming) and Mignolo (2000).

## References

Benveniste, Émile (1997) 'Gift and Exchange in the Indo-European Vocabulary', in *The Logic of the Gift: Toward an Ethic of Generosity*, ed. Alan D. Schrift, New York: Routledge, pp. 33–42.

Coles, Romand (1997) *Rethinking Generosity: Critical Theory and the Politics of Caritas*. Ithaca, N.Y.: Cornell University Press.

Du Bois, W.E.B. (1999) *The Souls of Black Folk. Authoritative Text. Contexts. Criticisms*. Eds Henry Louis Gates Jr. and Terri Hume Oliver. New York: W. W. Norton & Co.

Dussel, Enrique (1977) *Filosofía ética de la liberación*. 3rd edn. V vols. Vol. III. Niveles concretos de la ética latinoamericana. Buenos Aires, Arg.: Ediciones Megápolis.

—— (1995) *The Invention of the Americas: Eclipse of 'the Other' and the Myth of Modernity*. Trans. Michael D. Barber. New York: Continuum.

—— (1996) 'Modernity, Eurocentrism, and Trans-Modernity: In Dialogue with Charles Taylor', in *The Underside of Modernity: Apel, Ricoeur, Rorty, Taylor, and the Philosophy of Liberation*, ed. Eduardo Mendieta, Atlantic Highlands, NJ: Humanities, pp. 129–59.

—— (1999) *Posmodernidad y transmodernidad: diálogos con la filosofía de Gianni Vattimo*. Puebla, Mex.: Universidad Iberoamericana, Golfo Centro; Instituto Tecnológico y de Estudios Superiores de Occidente; Universidad Iberoamericana, Plantel Laguna.

—— (2002) 'World System and 'Trans'-Modernity'. Trans. Alessandro Fornazzari. *Nepantla: Views from South* 3, no. 2, pp. 221–44.

Ellacuría, Ignacio & Sobrino, Jon (eds) (1993) *Mysterium Liberationis: Fundamental Concepts of Liberation Theology*. Maryknoll, N.Y.: Orbis Books; North Blackburn, Victoria, Australia: Collins Dove.

Ellison, Ralph (1999) *Invisible Man*. Philadelphia: Chelsea House Publishers.

Fanon, Frantz (1968) *Black Skin, White Masks*. TranS. Charles Lam Markmann. New York: Grove Press.

—— (1965) *A Dying Colonialism*. Trans. Haakon Chevalier. New York: Grove Press.

—— (1988) *Toward the African Revolution: Political Essays*. Trans. Haakon Chevalier. New York: Grove Press.

—— (1991) *The Wretched of the Earth*. Trans. Constance Farrington. New York: Grove Press.

Georas, Chloe S. (1997) 'From Colonial Empire to Culture Empire: Re-reading Mitterand's Paris'. MA thesis, Binghamton University.

Goldstein, Joshua S. (2001) *War and Gender: How Gender Shapes the War System and Vice Versa*. Cambridge: Cambridge University Press.

Gordon, Lewis R. (1995) *Bad Faith and Antiblack Racism*. Atlantic Highlands, N.J.: Humanities Press.

—— (2000) *Existentia Africana: Understanding Africana Existential Thought*. New York: Routledge.

—— (1997) *Her Majesty's Other Children: Sketches of Racism from a Neocolonial Age*. Lanham, MD: Rowman & Littlefield.

—— (2005) 'Through the Zone of Nonbeing: A Reading of Black Skin, White Masks in Celebration of Fanon's Eightieth Birthday', *The C.L.R. James Journal*, vol. 11, no. 1, pp. 1–43.

—— (ed.) (1997) *Existence in Black: An Anthology of Black Existential Philosophy*. New York: Routledge.

Gray, J. Glenn (1959) *The Warriors: Reflections on Men in Battle*. New York: Harper & Row.

Grosfoguel, Ramón (2003) *Colonial Subjects: Puerto Ricans in a Global Perspective*. Berkeley: University of California Press.

—— (2005) 'Subaltern Epistemologies, Decolonial Imaginaries and the Redefinition of Global Capitalism'. *Review*, vol. 28, n.p.

Grosfoguel, Ramón, Maldonado-Torres, Nelson and Saldívar, José David (2005) 'Latin@s and the'Euro-American' Menace: The Decolonization of the US Empire in the 21st Century'. In *Latin@s in the World-System*, eds Ramón Grosfoguel, Nelson Maldonado-Torres and José David Saldívar. Boulder, Co: Paradigm Press.

Hanke, Lewis (1974) *All Mankind is One: A Study of the Disputation between Bartolome de Las Casas and Juan Gines de Sepulveda in 1550 on the Intellectual and Religious Capacity of the American Indians*. DeKalb: Northern Illinois University Press.

Hardt, Michael & Negri, Antonio (2004) *Multitude: War and Democracy in the Age of Empire*. New York: The Penguin Press.

Heidegger, Martin (1962) *Being and Time*. Trans. John Macquarrie and Edward Robinson. San Francisco: Harper Collins.

—— (1996) *Being and Time: A Translation of Sein und Zeit*. Trans. Joan Stambaugh. Albany: State University of New York Press.

Horsley, Richard A., ed. (1997) *Paul and Empire: Religion and Power in Roman Imperial Society*. Harrisburg, Pennsylvania: Trinity Press International.

Lander, Edgardo (ed.) (2000) *La colonialidad del saber: eurocentrismo y ciencias sociales: perspectivas latinoamericanas*. Caracas, Ven.: Facultad de Ciencias Económicas y Sociales (FACES-UCV); Instituto Internacional de la UNESCO para la Educación Superior en América Latina y el Caribe (IESALC).

Lévinas, Emmanuel (1989) 'As if Consenting to Horror'. Translated by Paula Wissing, *Critical Inquiry*, vol. 15, pp. 485–8.

—— (1974) *Otherwise than Being or, Beyond Essence*. Trans. Alphonso Lingis. Pittsburgh, PA, Duquesne University Press, 1998. Reprint, Trans. of *Autrement qu'être ou, Au-delà de l'essence*.

—— (1969) *Totality and Infinity: An Essay on Exteriority*. Trans. Alphonso Lingis. Pittsburgh: Duquesne University Press.

Losurdo, Domenico (2001) *Heidegger and the Ideology of War: Community, Death and the West*. Trans. Marella and Jon Morris. Amherst, NY: Humanity Books.

Maldonado-Torres, Nelson (forthcoming) *Against War: Views from the Underside of Modernity*. Durham: Duke University Press.

—— (2001) 'The Cry of the Self as a Call from the Other: The Paradoxical Loving Subjectivity of Frantz Fanon', *Listening: Journal of Religion and Culture*, vol. 36, no. 1, pp. 46–60.

—— (2005) 'Decolonization and the New Identitarian Logics after September 11: Eurocentrism and Americanism against the Barbarian Threats', *Radical Philosophy Review*, vol. 8, no. 1, pp. 35–67.

—— (forthcoming) 'Intervenciones filosóficas al proyecto inacabado de la descolonizacion'. In *Filosofía y liberación. Homenaje a Enrique Dussel*, eds

Juan Manuel Contreras Colín and Mario Rojas, n.p. México, D.F.: Universidad de la Ciudad de México.

—— (2005) 'Post-continental Philosophy and the Decolonial Turn: Introduction to Conference Mapping the Decolonial Turn: Post/Trans-Continental Interventions in Philosophy, Theory, and Critique', University of California at Berkeley, 21 April.

—— (2002) 'Post-imperial Reflections on Crisis, Knowledge, and Utopia: Transgresstopic Critical Hermeneutics and the'Death of European Man', *Review: A Journal of the Fernand Braudel Center for the Study of Economies, Historical Systems and Civilizations*, vol. 25, no. 3, pp. 277–315.

—— (2006) 'Reconciliation as a Contested Future: Decolonization as Project or Beyond the Paradigm of War'. in *Reconciliation: Nations and Churches in Latin America*, ed. Iain S. Maclean, London: Ashgate, n.p.

Mignolo, Walter (2003) *The Darker Side of the Renaissance: Literacy, Territoriality, and Colonization*. 2nd edn. Ann Arbor: The University of Michigan Press.

—— (2002) 'Colonialidad global, capitalismo y hegemonía epistémica'. in *Indisciplinar las ciencias sociales: geopolíticas del conocimiento y colonialidad del poder: perspectivas desde lo andino*, eds Catherine Walsh, Freya Schiwy and Santiago Castro-Gómez, Quito: Universidad Andina Simón Bolívar, and Abya Yala, pp. 215–44.

—— (1995) 'Decires fuera de lugar: sujetos dicentes, roles sociales y formas de inscripción', *Revista de crítica literaria latinoamericana*, vol. 11, pp. 9–32.

—— (2000) *Local Histories/Global Designs: Coloniality, Subaltern Knowledges, and Border Thinking*. Princeton, NJ: Princeton University Press.

—— (2000) 'The Many Faces of Cosmo-polis: Border Thinking and Critical Cosmopolitanism', *Public Culture*, vol. 12, no. 3, pp. 721–48.

—— (2003) 'Os esplendores e as misérias da << ciência >> : colonialidade, geopolítica do conhecimento e pluri-versalidade epistémica'. In *Conhecimento Prudente para uma Vida Decente: Um Discurso sobre as Ciências' revistado*, ed. Boaventura de Sousa Santos, Edições Afrontamento, pp. 667–709.

Nietzsche, Friedrich (1989) *On the Genealogy of Morals and Ecce Homo*. Trans. Walter Kaufmann and R.J. Hollingdale. New York: Vintage Books.

Quijano, Aníbal (2000) 'Colonialidad del poder y clasificación social'. *Journal of World-Systems Research*, vol. XI, no. 2, pp. 342–86. Accesible en http://jwsr.ucr.edu.

—— (1991) 'Colonialidad y modernidad/racionalidad', *Perú indígena*, vol. 29, pp. 11–20.

—— (2000) 'Coloniality of Power, Eurocentrism, and Latin America', *Nepantla: Views from South*, vol. 1, no. 3, pp. 533–80.

—— (2001) 'Globalización, colonialidad y democracia'. In *Tendencias básicas de nuestra época: globalización y democracia*, ed. Instituto de Altos Estudios Diplomáticos 'Pedro Gual', Caracas, Ven.: Instituto de Altos Estudios Diplomáticos 'Pedro Gual', pp. 25–61.

——(1992) ''Raza,'etnia, y'nación': cuestiones abiertas'. In *José Carlos Mariátegui y Europa: la otra cara del descubrimiento*, ed. Roland Forgues, n.p. Lima, Peru: Amauta.

Quijano, Aníbal & Immanuel, Wallerstein (1992) 'Americanity as a Concept, or the Americas in the Modern World-System', *International Social Science Journal*, vol. 44, pp. 549–57.

Saldívar, José David (1991) *Dialectics of Our America: Genealogy, Cultural Critique, and Literary History*. Durham: Duke University Press.

Sandoval, Chela (2000) *Methodology of the Oppressed*. Minneapolis: University of Minnesota Press.

Todorov, Tzvetan (1992) *The Conquest of America: The Question of the Other*. Trans. Richard Howard. New York: HarperCollins, HarperPerennial.

Walsh, Catherine (ed.) (2005) *Pensamiento crítico y matriz (de)colonial: reflexiones latinoamericanas*. Quito, Ec., Editorial Universidad Andina Simón Bolivar.

Wolin, Richard (ed.) (1991) *The Heidegger Controversy: A Critical Reader*. New York: Columbia University Press.

Wynter, Sylvia (1995) '1492: A New World View'. In *Race, Discourse, and the Origin of the Americas: A New World View*, ed. Vera Lawrence Hyatt and Rex Nettleford, Washington, D.C.: Smithsonian Institution Press, pp. 5–57.

—— (2003) 'Unsettling the Coloniality of Being/Power/Truth/Freedom: Towards the Human, After Man, Its Overrepresentation–An Argument', *The New Centennial Review*, vol. 3, no. 3, pp. 257–337.

**Freya Schiwy**

# DECOLONIZATION AND THE QUESTION OF SUBJECTIVITY

## Gender, race, and binary thinking

*The construction and performance of gender and gender relations has been paramount to the process of Decolonization. Gender has permeated the discourses and enactments of colonization and is an inseparable part of the casting of subjectivity through the coloniality of power. The notions of femininity and masculinity are themselves colonial constructs that have pressed more complex notions of gender, sexuality, and desire into a binary. The treatment of gender in three approaches to decolonization (Nelly Richard's cultural theory,* Mujeres Creando*'s lesbian street performance, indigenous movement's written and audiovisual discourse) help to discern how gender and the coloniality of power are articulated and in how far these efforts at decolonization unwork colonial legacies. Richard challenges the geopolitics of knowledge. As she claims the specificity of Latin American heterogeneity as a place from which to theorize she also guards against essentialist notions of gender. The conflicts underlying gender heterogeneity, however, are glossed over. The discourses of indigenous movements debate concepts of gender complementarity while, at the same time, using gender complementarity as a template for thinking decolonized relations. Yet, gender here remains caught in the Andean paradigm of duality.* Mujeres Creando *call attention to the conflicts underlying heterogeneity without essentializing notions of woman and man. Rather, their performances, publications and graffitties challenge the idea of gender binaries as they expose lingering racial and gender imaginaries that connect with state power and NGO solidarity. Their performances, however, remain isolated from the networks of decolonization that indigenous movements have established and run the risk of turning into a shock commodity.*

Gender has been paramount to the process of Decolonization. In Latin America, indigenous intellectuals such as Fausto Reinaga have held forth the idea of gender complementarity as an illustration of the colonial difference, that is, as an element that distinguishes Aymara gender relations from western patriarchy (1981, pp. 89–90). While for Reinaga gender complementarity is a

reality, for María Eugenia Choque Quispe gender complementarity is an ideal that the colonial experience itself has compromised (1998, p. 12). For many indigenous women, questioning gender paradigms in the process of decolonization has helped to constitute indigenous cultures as dynamic practices that are in need of re-invention rather than offering a return to an idealized past (Cervone 1998, Mujeres Indígenas de la CONAIE 1994). Documentary and fiction videos, directed and produced by members of indigenous communities frequently cast women as the guardians of tradition; they enact the transmission of social memory and perform gender complementarity on screen. At the same time, videomakers foster debates over the links between gender and the colonial subalternization of knowledge. For some indigenous videomakers gender complementarity itself has become a metaphor for thinking decolonized relations between indigenous communities and national society (Schiwy 2002).

Social memory and subalternized knowledge is embodied and transmitted in gendered ways but the enactment and representation of such links between knowledge and the female body in the discourse of decolonization has been a central point of debate not only for indigenous movements in Latin America. In postcolonial discussions focused on India and Northern Africa, scholars such as Partha Chatterjee asked whether decolonization mustn't 'include within it a struggle against the false essentialism of home/world, spiritual/material, feminine/masculine propagated by nationalist ideology' (1990, p. 252). While gender concepts are clearly crucial to decolonization, the heterosexual model through which complementarity is thought affirms Andean duality and hides those subjectivities and forms of desire that would challenge binary thinking itself. Indeed, as, the literary critic Michael Horswell argues, the Andean gender binary is itself a modern/colonial construct (2003).

Decolonization and gender also intersect in feminist criticism of the geopolitics of knowledge. The Chilean cultural critics Nelly Richard (1996) and Kemy Oyarzún (1992) have frowned on Latin American and feminist scholars studying Latin America for essentializing the concepts of man and woman in Latin America, thus issuing a critique of the geopolitics of knowledge that resonates with Chandra Mohanty's well known arguments about the making of the theoretical subject of feminism (1988). As Richard and Oyarzún call for a deconstruction of gender categories, they themselves, however, rely on a problematic notion of heterogeneity that fails to interrogate how gender and colonial legacies congeal in the process of theorizing in Latin America across different social classes, ethnicities, and technologies of knowledge. The Bolivian performance activists Julia Paredes and Maria Galindo who have worked with urban Aymara women, in turn, have countered the dense interrelations of colonial legacies and heterosexual normativity through graffitti, street performance, and audiovisual media.

All of these approaches to decolonization share a need to address the intersection of gender relations and colonial subalternization. Posing the question of gender allows to discern added complexities of the constitutive elements of the coloniality of power. Asking how modern/colonial constructs of gender are perpetuated and contested also helps to better understand the ways decolonization pushes against the building blocks of coloniality and where, at times inadvertently, decolonization recreates these.

## Coloniality and the question of subjectivity

Despite the meshing together of anticolonial discourse with gender imaginaries the construction and relevance of gender to the coloniality of power has been difficult to accommodate. Approaches to thinking the power of coloniality in the modern world as well as in the seemingly re-born world of global social movements, commodified multiculturalism, and deterritorialized capitalism are interdisciplinary but they still follow lines of inquiry traced out by the kind of research questions asked. The question of gender is usually set aside, not however the construction of subjectivity. The concept of coloniality is three-dimensional; it encompasses the study of economical and political relations in their constitutive role for the process of globalization and emphasizes the qualitative difference these relations have ushered in since the conquest of the Americas, differences that mark the present global world-system inaugurated in 1492 from prior economic relations and imperial desires (Quijano and Wallerstein 1992, Mignolo 2000, p. 37). No less foundational are the epistemic relations that have given way to a hegemonic order of knowledge which for many continues to form the way globalization is thought. A shorthand for this order of knowledge has been the concept of Eurocentrism, again inaugurated with the chronicles and reports issued about the Spanish imperial experience in the fifteenth and sixteenth century (Quijano 2000, p. 53, Mignolo 2000). The study of epistemic relations of power also comprises research on epistemologies that were subalternized in the process of colonization and its aftermath. In the colonial past as well as in the present, the focus here lies on how these epistemic traditions have been negotiated and might intersect in novel and more democratic ways, creating a border thinking (e.g., Mignolo 2000, Escobar forthcoming). Thinking about epistemology and about the construction of subjectivity has also involved reflecting on the technologies of representation, de-centering literacy as the technology of the intellect (Mignolo 1995, Schiwy 2003). For many involved in thinking coloniality a crucial step has been to think from subalternized perspectives that may be enunciated through multiple media and bodily enactments.

The construction of subjectivity is the third dimension of the coloniality of power; it has been thought as a naturalization of colonial relations articulated around the idea of race. For Quijano, the principle of race

> has proven to be the most effective and long-lasting instrument of universal social domination, since the much older principle – gender or intersexual domination – was encroached upon by the inferior/superior racial classifications. So the conquered and dominated peoples were situated in a natural position of inferiority and, as a result, their phenotypic traits as well as their cultural features were considered inferior. In this way, race became the fundamental criterion for the distribution of the world population into ranks, places, and roles in the new society's structure of power.
>
> (2000, p. 535)

When gender has entered into reflections on the coloniality of power and processes of decolonization it has been as an afterthought, for instance when Mignolo draws attention to the blindness of so-called white feminism to the coloniality of power (Mignolo 2000, pp. 124–26, 314–15). Or, more recently, gender has been taken as a short-hand for 'woman' leading some to ask about the participation of women in decolonization efforts (Escobar forthcoming, chapter five). How gender imaginaries themselves have entered colonial constructs and their aftermath, however, has not received the same attention. Instead, the invention of race – through discourses and practices – has been privileged as a marker of the coloniality of power, precisely as a part of what distinguishes this globalization (1492 to the present) from other forms of imperial rule and expansion.

Certainly, racial thinking has been transformed since the sixteenth century, moving from a focus on purity of blood and religious difference, to biological racism, to the multicultural acknowledgement of different ethnicities structured in relation to the market and parallel to the remobilizing of religious and ethnic differences (Mignolo 2000, pp. 27–33). The idea of race has been inscribed and enacted through social practices and performances exercised since the colonial period. It has evolved from the representation of otherness and debates over the humanity of the people the conquerors and clerics encountered in the early chronicles to more contemporary literary, photographic and audiovisual texts that recreate racial otherness and 'colonial looking relations' (Kaplan 1997). Certainly the meanings and parameters attributed to race have also been constructed in intellectual and academic treatises that at once explain and produce our understanding of the world. The construction of racial subjectivity has served as a bodily metaphor for ordering economic, political as well as epistemic relations, while at the same time creating lived exclusions and abuses as well as forms of organized and quotidian

resistance and subversion. Yet, constructs of masculinity and femininity, relations between women and men as well as those who do not fit smoothly into these binary categories have been crucial to all of these dimensions. As Anne McClintock put it in her analysis of British colonialism, 'race, gender and class are not distinct realms of experience, existing in splendid isolation from each other; nor can they be simply yoked together retrospectively like armatures of Lego. Rather, they come into existence *in and through* relation to each other' (1995, p. 5, emphasis in the original). She adds that 'imperialism cannot be fully understood without a theory of gender power. Gender power was not the superficial patina of empire, an ephemeral gloss over the more decisive mechanics of class or race. Rather, gender dynamics were, from the outset, fundamental to the securing and maintenance of the imperial enterprise' (pp. 6–7).

Obviously, gender does not refer only to women. It is a construct that regards the ideas we hold about masculinity and femininity, about appropriate roles and about power relations. Gender is a historical and social category that is continuously enacted albeit under the constraints of existing norms and imaginaries that differ across 'geopolitical boundaries and cultural constraints on who is imagining whom, and for what purpose' (Butler 2004, p. 10). When debates about gender abstract from the colonial making of social relations (among women, among ethnicities and classes) they risk perpetuating colonial relations. But if gender is no more primary than race and ethnicity, then surely the construction of race cannot bee seen to supplant the construction of gender with the onset of global coloniality. Rather, both concepts interact, coalescing into gender specific forms of oppression and meshing longstanding imaginaries in order to justify hierarchies of subjectivity, economical and political as well as epistemic orders associated with these subjectivities. When gender analyses abstract from racial paradigms they tend to recreate geopolitical power relations inaugurated with the colonization of the Americas. When discussions of the coloniality of power abstract from gender, they risk re-inscribing foundational elements of the coloniality power where gender binaries and gender imaginaries have been naturalized.

The colonial imaginary has employed gender as a metaphor and means of subalternization, a metaphor that resulted not only in the representation of territories as female virgin lands that the conquerors penetrated with the sword in hand. The gendering of colonial imaginaries has operated as a means of rendering European masculinity through Othering. That is, European and Caucasian men have thought themselves in opposition to colonized (or postcolonial) men who have been represented as effeminate or as part of an irrational nature where nature itself is also bound up with tropes of femininity (Shohat 1991, pp. 53–5). The emasculation of indigenous men in Latin America has prefigured and paralleled that of other colonized peoples, enacted and inscribed through rape, both real and in the imaginary of colonial texts,

and later in indigenista literature and film. The force of this tool of war has relied not only on the harm inflicted on women it also enacts the inability of colonized men to protect 'their women'. Rape, the founding act and trope of *mestizaje* re-enforces patriarchal relations where women are reduced to objects and their abuse comes to signify damage to male honor. It thus inscribes a heterosexual order and may lead to an urgent need to affirm male power in the process of decolonization.

Early modernity itself was a time when Europe sought to fix a four-fold and more dynamic notion of gender and sexuality into the binary categories of man and woman. George Mariscal argues that 'virtually all forms of subjectivity in this period depended on different degrees and kinds of 'maleness' rather than on the historically more recent male/female binomial' (1991, p. 27). Not only gender – sociohistorically constructed and enacted ideas and roles but sex itself was seen as dynamic, subject to change according to levels of body heat and humidity (Jones and Stallybrass 1991, p. 84). Chronicles telling of encounters with indigenous peoples betray the renaissance anxiety about gender indeterminacy as the conquerors saw themselves battling monsters and virile Amazons (Mott 1992, Montrose 1991). Similarly, precolonial Andean cultures seem to have held the idea of a third gender, a central mediating force that was subalternized with the growing emphasis on gender duality during the colonial period (Horswell 2003). Today, medical practices police the sexual morphology of newborns, at times without the consent of parents, in order to assure an anatomical correspondence between bodies and the idea of a sexual binary, a practice to which the intersex movement in the US is drawing increasing attention (Anne Fausto-Sterling 2000, Butler 2004, pp. 7–16).

Decolonization under current conditions of multicultural capitalism no longer necessarily involves working with binaries of colonizer and colonized or with countering the dominant tropes and logic of colonial power with oppositional categories. Rather, in the context of commodified multiculturalism and revamped imperial discourses on the presumed coexistence of medieval and postmodern culture, decolonization challenges received notions of identity, temporal unevenness as well as knowledge and forms of representation. Decolonization transforms and indianizes established codes and creates novel forms of translation/transculturation (Mignolo and Schiwy 2003, Schiwy 2003). Yet, this does not mean that decolonization can fully disregard the tropes that have categorized the colonized. The emphasis on gender in the projects of decolonization hence comes as no surprise. The way gender concepts are engaged shows different angles and depths of transformation. The remainder of this article will thus not dwell further on the different ways colonial discourse has enacted racial and gender constructs but look at three different efforts to challenge colonialism's aftermath.

## Feminism, the geopolitics of knowledge, and the problem of heterogeneity

Nelly Richard and Kemy Oyarzún have been among the most outspoken feminist critics of the geopolitics of knowledge in Latin America. While Oyarzún approaches the question of power and subalternity in the production of knowledge between North and South America from the perspective of feminist literary criticism, Nelly Richard has elaborated her arguments engaging both feminist and poststructuralist theory in her readings of vanguard anti-dictatorship theater and installations by the *Escena Avanzada*. Resonating with Chandra Mohanty's critique of First World white feminism (1998), Richard challenged Latin American studies (the study of Latin America by those located in other places) stating that

> también dentro del feminismo opera este ideologema del cuerpo (realidad concreta, vivencia práctica) que soporta la fantasía de una América Latina animada por la energía salvadora del compromiso social y de la lucha comunitaria, cuyo valor popular y testimonial es juzgado políticamente superior a cualquier elaboración teórico-discursiva.
>
> (1996, p. 738)

> the ideology of the body (a concrete reality and lived practice) is also at work within the feminism that supports the fantasy of a Latin America animated by the salvational energy of social commitment and communal struggle, the value of which is considered testimonial and close to the people and judged as politically superior to any kind of theoretical-discoursive elaboration.
>
> (1996, p. 739, my translation)

For Richard colonial legacies are crucial and express themselves at an international level in the geopolitics of knowledge where Northern academics disdain the theory produced in the South in favor of cultural manifestations to be theorized.[1] Her criticism is certainly warranted (although Richard herself has perhaps been the most widely read and translated feminist critic working in Chile). Richard defends the process of theorizing, however, as a process that cannot abstract from particular lived experiences without repeating the gesture of Eurocentrism. She thus emphasizes the importance of place. Richard invokes the geopolitics of knowledge and their colonial becoming in order to argue against the subalternization of Latin American theorists. At the same time she opposes the easy essentialism and anti-theoretical approach, which she sees as underlying much of Latin America's own feminist critique. For many Latin American feminists, says Richard,

> las condiciones materiales de explotación, miseria y opresión de las que se vale el patriarcado para redoblar su eficacia en tramar la desigualdad en América Latina nos exigiría . . . más acción que discurso, más compromiso político que sospecha filosófica, más denuncia testimonial que arabescos descontructivos.
>
> (1996, p. 735)

> the material conditions of exploitation, misery and oppression which patriarchy deploys in order to double its efficiency in laying out inequality in Latin America demands from us ... more activism than discourse, more political commitment than philosophical suspicion, more testimonial denunciation than arabesque deconstruction.
>
> (1996, p. 735, my translation)

For Richard, this political-action oriented approach expresses an unreflected essentialism that ends up affirming the categories of femininity and masculinity instead of questioning their historical making. Feminism thus cements the discourses and imaginaries that have naturalized gender concepts and equipped them with unequal meanings. Against this position, Richard sustains that feminist labor must involve the deconstruction of notions of gender, again an argument that resonates with that of Partha Chatterjee quoted earlier.

Richard's emphasis on the importance of place in the process of theorizing targets a geopolitical structure that places theories from the South and in languages other than English, French, and German at a disadvantage. Place is important because it informs the kind of theorizing we do. Thus, for Richard, the notion of heterogeneity is vital, both in terms of the multiplicity of feminist activists in Latin America as well as with regard to the social heterogeneity of Latin American women. According to Richard, Latin America is marked by 'una pluralidad disímil de voces y estratos de identidad que derivan de espacios y tiempos irregulares, de memorias y tradiciones híbridas' (p. 743)/'a dissimilar plurality of voices and layers of identity that derive from irregular spaces and temporalities, from memories and hybrid traditions' (p. 743, my translation). The heterogeneity of place is precisely what allows theoretical production to destabilize the dominant construction of knowledge as objective and disembodied. Quoting Kemy Oyarzún, Richard thus suggest that

> sólo reinscribiendo lo femenino en un contexto de lecturas suficientemente múltipiles e interactivas, es posible dar cuenta de la heterogeneidad de posiciones culturales que asumen los signos de identidad en América Latina donde 'cohabitan diosas y dioses precolombinos, vírgenes y brujas, oralidad, escritura y otras grafías; voces indígenas, mestizas y europeas; retazos de máquinas sociales, rituales, semifeudales o burguesas; pero

también dioses del consumismo, voces de la ciudad y de la calle, fragmentos de cultura libresca.

(p. 743)

only reinscribing the feminine in a context of readings that is sufficiently multiple and interactive is it possible to understand the heterogeneity of cultural positions that the signs of identity assume in Latin America. Here 'precolumbian goddesses and gods coexists with virgins and witches; orality with writing and other graphic systems; indigenous with mestizo and European peoples; remnants of ritual, semifeudal and bourgeois social machines; but also the gods of consumerism with the voices of the city and the streets and fragments of book culture.

(p. 743)

As Richard list the differences that illustrate heterogeneity, however, she does not interrogate the legacies of colonial power relations in shaping this heterogeneity. The internal conflicts fracturing heterogeneity in Latin America are glossed over as Richard fails to distinguish between the multicultural, the hybrid, and the heterogeneous. In other words, multicultural diversity is not deconstructed in terms of its own colonial history, in terms of its embedded power differences, incompatible and contradictory arguments issued by those thinking from different perspectives (feminist or otherwise) within the heterogeneous make-up of Latin America. Neither does Richard question the colonial construction of value regarding different technologies of the intellect, such as those of orality print media, audiovisual technology, performance, and other complex forms of transmitting knowledge through media means other than literacy.

Technologies themselves have been subalternized in the process of colonization as they have become associated with racial and gendered bodies.[2] Storytelling and the embodied transmission of social memory has been associated not only with indigenous cultures but more precisely with indigenous women; weaving, an Andean technology of knowledge, has also come to be largely equated with femininity. The pen and the movie-camera, in turn, have symbolized and produced phallic power.

Kemy Oyarzún's text from which Richard quotes does understand heterogeneity as a product of colonial history. Referencing Antonio Cornejo Polar, Oyarzún arrives at the conclusion that cultural production reveals heterogeneity in terms of 'concepciones del mundo conflictivas, contradictorias' (1992, p. 35)/ conflicting and contraditory conceptions of the world (p. 35, my translation); cultural production for that reason is often more polyphone than theoretical criticism. Nevertheless, by linking her vindication of the subversive potential of literature written by women with Bajtin, Oyarzún avoids exploring these conflicts, leveling them through recourse to

dialogue, which presumes the possibility of communication in an ideal democratic setting where power relations are relatively absent and subjects interact on the basis of an a priori common ground.[3] When heterogeneity is converted into hybridity and dialogics there is no need to distinguish between the critique and negotiation of power in different voices such as those of Laura Esquivel and Rigoberta Menchú, two examples that Oyarzún herself mentions.

A critique of essentialism must include a critique of colonial legacies. If we refrain from interrogating the coloniality of power not only at a geopolitical level but also in the context of Latin America itself, we limit our understanding of the geopolitical relations that constitute heterogeneity. Latin American heterogeneity is reduced to multiculturalism, emptied of its contradictions and incommensurabilities as well as its potentials to think modernity otherwise. The body remains coded in terms of sex and race instead of leading us to questioning the ways gender and racial constructs go hand in hand.

By emphasizing that theory is largely considered to take place in the media and contexts that colonialism itself has privileged, that is in academic spaces and in the technology of the alphabet, Richard also defines what counts as thinking and as sustainable knowledge. Although she affirms the need to 'elaborar formas locales de producción teórica' para frenar el 'nomadismo postmodernista' (p. 739)/'elaborate local forms of theoretical production' in order to brake 'postmodern nomadism' (p. 739, my translation), the opportunity for questioning where and how thinking might take place otherwise is lost, reduced to a critique of the folkloric curiosity exhibited by theorists (and tourists) from the North. The potential of this other thinking, the possibility of reflecting from other angles on what it could mean to deconstruct naturalized identities and power relations framed by these identities demands an approach that engages with subalternized discourses without reducing them to colorful objects of study or consumption. For Richard, however, deconstruction is limited to those forms of academic writing and artistic expression that resist their own commodification. The line between commodity, cultural object of study, and the creation of meaning and knowledge needs to be negotiated differently by those seeking to democratize decolonization.

*Mujeres Creando* is a group of radical Bolivian lesbians and performance activists that brought together urban Aymara women and *Mestizas*.[4] One of the most accomplished street performances or *acciones callejeras* by *Mujeres Creando*, was a critique of feminist NGOs. The performance took place in El Alto, the mostly Aymara city on the highland rim above La Paz and was then edited into a video, put up for sale, and televised on the cable channel P.A.T. The video begins with a fictitious testimony of a young feminist working in an NGO whose salary now enables her to employ a maid, followed by footage of the *acción callejera* itself. In this performance young blond women with their faces painted united-nations-blue play with the globe, an inflated balloon that ends up lifeless and cast aside. They metaphorically drink the blood of the poor as

the video cuts to a close-up of miniature figurines representing Andean women perched on the open palm of a hand. The camera follows their fall into the dirt where they join coins lying in a pool of blood (red wine). Audience participation in the performance is exemplary as young children scramble to pick up the money while women bend to recover the figurines.

The video argues that the funds offered by NGOs exacerbate class differences among women and the exploitation of women by women, strengthening the middle class and its reliance on domestic service, itself a colonial relation that the market has only cosmetically transformed. At the same time global power relations are seen as representing patronizing and exploitative relations that prolong those formed through colonialism. The piece allows for an optimistic reading of Andean solidarity as the women of El Alto recover the figurines so carelessly cast to the ground by the UN blondes but also calls attention to a heterogeneity based on colonial legacies that demands questioning and transforming these legacies. The documentary also foregrounds the differences among women by questioning international NGO solidarity. This is a critique of the geopolitics of knowledge, where because of ignorance, prejudice or for personal gain, economic and intellectual concepts of the North are imported without worrying too much about whether these models actually serve to solve the problems in the South. Although this performance might be seen to complement Richard and Oyarzún's critique of the geopolitics of knowledge it enacts not only a critique of global power relations but also of internal colonialism where racism fractures the concept of gender. This performance is only one of a series of other *acciones callejeras* that target the racism and class differences among women in Bolivia (e.g. KETAL), criticize the racist patriarchy of the Bolivian state (e.g. Prólogo), while also enacting lesbian desire (e.g. Dos mujeres besandose en el Prado) and thus questioning heteronormativity.[5]

The videos by *Mujeres Creando* echo the famous critique of white feminism that Domitila Barrios de Chungara voiced in the First International Feminist Congress in Mexico City 1975 (1991, pp. 216–27) as well as the testimonies of Chilean women collected by Jo Fisher (1993, pp. 17–44, 177–200). Yet the videos go not only beyond Richard and Oyarzun's critique of the geopolitics of knowledge but also beyond Barrios de Chungara's dismissal of questioning sexuality *Mujeres Creando* destabilize the Andean paradigm of duality. This duality also underwrites the process of decolonization by indigenous movement organizations.

## Indigenous video – decolonization and the body

Indigenous movements in Latin America have been engaged in a long process of anti-colonial resistance that has gained renewed momentum and has

continued to change face and forms since the 1960s. Today, decolonization involves political struggle, working with NGOs and UN level organizations, and rethinking concepts of human, cultural, and intellectual property rights. Indigenous movement organizations have also made use of audiovisual technology, communicating diverse indigenous and peasant populations and thereby creating new spaces for intercultural debate and exchange of ideas.[6] One fundamental aspect of this work has been the effort to decolonize the soul, that is, to counter the effects of ethnic self-denigration that the pressure to assimilate has exacerbated. What role and importance indigenous culture can play in bettering the economic situation of indigenous populations here has been just as important as figuring out what resources indigenous ethics and epistemologies hold for thinking modernity otherwise.

Indigenous filmmakers organized in CAIB (Coordinadora Audiovisual Indígena y Originaria de Bolivia/Bolivian Association of Indigenous Communicators) and collaborating with a center for training in cinematography, CEFREC (Centro de Formación y Realización Cinematográfica) in Bolivia have maintained some of the most prolific and varied video production in the continent. As these indigenous communicators represent the problems and issues their communities face their documentaries and fiction shorts highlight the way indigenous traditions have been transmitted in embodied ways. Storytelling, weaving, even clothing, are not exclusively but more frequently associated with women than with men. Indeed, several of the fiction shorts explicitly frame the problem of the colonization of the soul in a gendered way: women become the guardians of tradition, their death or suffering redeeming those middle aged men, who have come to doubt the traditional stories and belief systems in favor of more secular and rational perspectives that coincide with a long standing colonial discourse that disqualifies indigenous belief systems as superstitions.[7]

*Qati Qati*, a complex thirty-five minute fiction short, signed responsible by Reynaldo Yujra and produced by CAIB and CEFREC, is perhaps the most telling example.[8] It places the relation between gender, epistemology, and economic practice into the center of the frame. In this film, the male protagonist is accused by his wife and by a community elder of having lost respect, not only for the traditional tale of the woman who is converted into a flying head (the story of the *q'ati q'ati*) but also for the spirits of mountains and lakes, manifested in the surrounding landscape, the 'pathways of memory' as Thomas Abercrombie would call it (1998). The video ends with the mysterious death of the protagonist's wife Valentina (Ofelia Condori), herself converted into a *q'ati q'ati* and the protagonist Fulo (Pedro Gutiérrez) declaring that it might have been better to believe.

*Qati Qati* constructs a male cinematic gaze that never quite comes into its own. At the level of narrative, the topic is the redemption of man through woman's death. By implication, Fulo's initial lack of belief is characteristic of a

world order marked by robbery and selfishness, rather than by reciprocity, community solidarity, and traditional forms of administering justice. Reciprocity and community solidarity are enacted on screen by female actors, just as the practice of story-telling itself. Aymara policing and justice, in turn, are embodied by men, keeping with a traditional gendered division of labor but not fully undermining the predominant embodiment of culture by women on screen. At the same time, the camera seeks to maintain a neutral perspective, avoiding point of view shots, in order to embody the eyes of a female and male indigenous viewership. But the video, like so many other indigenous fiction pieces, creates an identification with the male protagonist. The seemingly neutral camera gaze is then indeed rendered male, a perspective that acquires force through the emotions it evokes: as Fulo laughs at his wife's superstitions and at the flying head he sees in his dreams, humor locates the children and the spectators on his side. Nevertheless, the video proposes the female body and mind as the principal site for the reinvention of an indigenous ethics, thus not affirming a masculine order or oedipal allegory. Unlike the anticolonial cinema of Jorge Sanjinés and the Ukamau group, indigenous videomakers do not frame a confrontation between colonizer and colonized and racial discrimination is not the primary topic of their productions.

Encouraged by the context of community screenings and the presence of audiovisual (indigenous) facilitators organized in the Network, the viewers debate the survival and relevance of alternative ethics and social order across different indigenous cultures. These debates re-evaluate not only a colonized epistemology but also one associated with femininity. The power of the colonization of the soul goes hand in hand with patriarchal designs, where those seeking masculinity are seen as rejecting a colonized order identified with women.

Parallel to the epistemic argument, the video frames multiple instances of a gendered division of labor. Fulo braids the ropes for constructing a shelter; Valentina trades potatoes in the market place; she also takes care of the children and small animals. Fulo, in turn cuts wood and guards their potato field against a robber. The argument of the film ultimately ends up endorsing gender complimentarity, itself rendered on screen as a successful gendered division of labor between the protagonist and his wife that is based on their equal importance for sustaining their nuclear family and by extension, the social relations within the *ayllu* itself. The video claims – against the western patriarchal order – that Aymara gender relations are based on complementarity and this gender complementarity sustains both an outside to western epistemology and the vestiges of an alternative economic order and ethics. The claim not only recalls Fausto Reinaga's assertions in the late sixties but has also been prevalent in contemporary Aymara politics, from the enactment of gender duality by the populist and media savvy Palenquismo (Archondo 1991,

p. 139) to one of Bolivia's current most vociferous political leaders, Felipe Quispe (1999, p. 15).

This notion of complementarity is crucial to decolonization because it links an epistemic and economic regime with gendered subjectivity. It provides simultaneously the pattern for three types of relations. First, relations between different indigenous traditions; second, relations between diverse indigenous knowledge traditions and western epistemology; and third, for an alternative idea of economy that combines a critique of the unchecked profit principle while vindicating market relations.

Film, however, is not only a form of representation. Social relations are enacted in front of the camera and filmmaking itself is a social practice. On screen *Qati Qati* highlights the market place as dominated by women and by forms of exchange based on barter. At the level of production, the videomakers insist that the videos are collective productions that entail complicated notions of property rights. Thus, not all of the videos produced by CEFREC/CAIB are sold in the free market place. Sometimes buyers will be screened (as to their intended use of the video) and prompted to enter into relations of reciprocity that go beyond the purchase of the video and the exchange of money for a product. On the one hand, although employing a vastly different film aesthetic, the social practice of videomaking transforms economic relations and builds on the legacy of the Latin America's revolutionary anticolonial cinema of the sixties and seventies that sought to transform cinema from a capitalist art form into a revolutionary tool. On the other hand, the attempt to control reception and distribution is no longer linked to the effort to create a socialist revolution. Rather, it invokes a pan-indigenous economic order based on reciprocity, not profit maximization, into which video production and exchange is integrated.[9] Complementarity, derived from idealized gender relations and the principle of duality, thus becomes one model for thinking an alternative modernity.

Gender complementarity, however, is a contested concept in the politics of decolonization. If western 'traditional' gender roles are idealized constructs, shaped since the Renaissance and hardened during the European enlightenment, these constructs do not exactly correspond to gender role ideals in Quechua and Aymara communities. The gendered division of labor and space among Quechuas and Aymaras are not the same as western notions of private (associated with the feminine) and public sphere (associated with masculinity), although the pressures of developmental policies, migration and internal colonialism are increasingly shaping the gendered divisions of labor in indigenous communities as well (Rivera Cusicanqui 1996). Even where traditional indigenous labor divisions are still dominant, the roles of men and women are, however, not interchangeable. Corresponding to a complex ordering of space in terms of female and male attributes Aymara and Quechua

subjectivity is also conceived of as the result of interacting male and female elements as well as other factors.[10]

Allison Spedding suggests that Aymara gender ideals in the Bolivian Yungas region are differentiated by age. For 15–45 year old women they include the ability to work, to bear children, active sexual desire, although to be addressed solely to the legitimate partner – (the same, by the way goes for males), and a penchant for economic calculus. Women are encouraged to travel (to markets), but their status does not depend on the ability to be articulate which, in contrast, is one of the measuring sticks for male status (1997, pp. 337–38).[11] The issue of oral eloquence, however, has become crucial for women political representatives (Cervone *et al.* 1998). Opting to be active in political organization or in videomaking contradicts traditional notions of women's roles and responsibilities in the low and high lands (both according to transculturated indigenous social orders as well as to the patriarchal western ideal) unless this activity is explicitly framed as 'helping' men and of temporary nature.

Unlike in the video *Qati Qati*, the Aymara historian María Eugenia Choque Quispe claims the ideal of complementarity in order to challenge Aymara patriarchy. Choque Quispe invokes the image of the colonizers as those who 'obsessed with gold and silver, raped, kidnapped, and defiled, bringing dishonor to Indian women'. She asserts that 'the imposition of colonial order meant the institutionalization not only of the irrational exploitation of the people and resources of this continent but also of gender relations between indigenous women, indigenous men, and the Spanish, marking them with conflict and violence' (Choque Quispe 1998, p. 12). Gender complimentarity has therefore not necessarily meant equality or equal value. Basing herself on Palma Milagro's work, Choque Quispe affirms that

> the declining indigenous population and the appearance of castes (in colonial times), transformed the indigenous woman into a commodity whose value hinged on her reproductive abilities as the primary resource for a new identity; for Indian males the possession and control of the Indian woman acquired dramatic significance. The creation of a new prevailing order prompted indigenous thought to make women responsible for their suffering and problems.
>
> (1998, p. 12)

Much has been written about the political representation and contacts with the outside lying in the hands of indigenous men. Women have been seen as, at best, playing an indirect role of exerting influence. Both low and high land cultures have been characterized as patriarchal and even mysogenist.[12] In CEFREC/CAIB's indigenous video production, viewers glimpse the problem of violence, such as in *Qulqi Chaliku*, when the avaricious husband physically

threatens his wife, or in the melodrama *Llanthupi Munakuy/Loving Each Other in the Shadows* where the young woman falls for romantic love and tries to escape an arranged marriage only to be killed, though inadvertently, by her father. These are exceptions, however. Issues such as rape, violence against women, or spatial confinement, have not been at the center of most indigenous videos.

Enacting indigenous tradition in gendered ways thus addresses the collusion of racial and gender constructs in the coloniality of power in a creative though not unproblematic way. On one hand, as Madhu Dubey suggested for the postcolonial resolution of nation building, 'decolonizing nationalist discourses summon the metaphorical figure of "woman" to resolve the inescapable contradiction of their project, which is to lay claim to post-Enlightenment European categories of progress and modernity, while reviving precolonial traditions to safeguard the nation's cultural difference from the West (Dubey 1998, p. 2). To be more specific, these 'post-Enlightenment Categories of progress and modernity' here entail the risk of a male dominance that would guard the reinvention of indigenous cultures from a transformation of gender relations and concepts of duality.

The ideology of complementarity and the gendered division of labor create mutual dependency between men and women but this does not imply a lack of hierarchy and processes of subordination. Rather, hierarchies operate in terms of gender and ethnicity where women considered 'misti' or 'mestiza' are above men considered '*indio*' and indigenous women are at the lowest rung (De la Cadena 1992, p. 186). In Bolivia, Rivera Cusicanqui suggests that the peculiar articulation of ethnicity, class and gender in Bolivian society at large has lead to a '"cadena de estratificación postcolonial" muy compleja ... privilegiando a los sectores masculinos y occidentalizados en las capas con mayores ingresos, mayor calificación y educación formal, y relegando a las mujeres y a los/as migrantes indígenas a las ocupaciones más rutinarias, peor pagadas y con menor prestigio y reconocimiento social' (1996, pp. 51–52)/a complex chain of postcolonial stratification...that privileges westernized masculine sectors with greater economic income and formal education while relegating women and idigenous migrants to the less demanding and worst paid occupations that hold the least amount of prestige and social acknowledgement (1996, pp. 51–2, my translation). As De la Cadena puts it, 'si el proyecto colonizador supuso la femeneización de los pueblos que llamaron indígenas, el entrampamiento del proyecto patriarcal contemporáneo es la indianización de las mujeres' (1997, p. 149)/ 'if the colonizing project supposed the feminization of the peoples they called 'indigenous', the entrapment of the patriarchal project is the indianization of women' (1997, p. 149, my translation). De la Cadena as well as Rivera Cusicanqui address here two crucial aspects of the way coloniality is intertwined with gender: the

'feminization of indigenous peoples' and 'the indianization' of indigenous women.

The videomakers working with CAIB and CEFREC are acting precisely against the devalorization of indigeneity that is bound to the hierarchies of gender and ethnicity that de la Cadena analyzed. Yet, casting women as the guardians of indigenous traditions and as a resource for thinking an alternative modernity, runs the risk of leaving the gender constructs underlying the coloniality of power unchallenged and reaffirming male dominance as those in charge of elaborating from the raw material of feminized culture.

When gender complementarity serves as an ideal for imagining decolonized epistemic relations with the West the colonial subalternization of knowledge, perspectives, genealogies and technologies of the intellect gives way to a fruitful coexistence where all traditions shed mutual light on each other. But even here, diversity does not simply dissolve itself in multicultural coexistence. Rather like gender relations epistemic relations require a process of de-subalternization. Although indigenous discourse has created debates around gender roles and hierarchies, the relation between colonial subalternization and gender stereotypes itself is still conceived in terms of a gender binary. Homosexuality and third gender remain tabu. Colonial history, nevertheless, is also bound up with creating the well-known duality that anthropologists and indigenous communities have come to see as paradigmatic of Andean cosmovision.

## Decolonizing the gender binary

Based on a detailed analysis of different kinds of colonial texts (written, drawn, woven and orally transmited), Michael Horswell has argued that Andean duality is indeed based on the notion of a third space, that is, on the ritual enactment of third gender. Duality is negotiated by a liminal zone that corresponds to a third gender which itself was subalternized with colonial discourse. Colonialism itself entailed the creation of the idea of only two genders (2003). While Horswell seeks to avoid the imposition of contemporary categories of identity, such as homosexuality, on the past, his work points to a significant transformation in the understanding of gender and colonialism.

In the last fifteen years, *Mujeres Creando* has been paramount in questioning not only the colonial legacies underlying feminist geopolitics of knowledge and the patriarchal discourses meshed with racism but also its normative heterosexism. Like indigenous videomakers, *Mujeres Creando* create knowledge and debates through technologies of knowledge that do not primarily rely on literacy. In their performances and publications, the group enacts homosexuality without creating the figure of the homosexual as an exclusive identity.

Rather, the variety of desires and identifications becomes a cornerstone of their critique of the intricate construct of power, gender and racial subjectivity. While indigenous movement approaches to decolonization debate gender roles and the subalternization of epistemic regimes by association with femininity, *Mujeres Creando* go a step further, undoing the binary of normative heterosexuality, not only in their famous graffities that have covered the walls of La Paz.

The performance Prógolo lead by María Galindo, linked virility, state power, and the Bolivian tabu of discussing sexuality by contrasting flaccid penises being painted in different colors with the erect obelisk on La Paz's main artery. The audiovisual edition of this *acción callejera* obliges its viewers to maintain their gaze on phallic power and its desacralization through a long sequence with little cross-cutting among the close-ups. The performance attests to its power to disturb by including footage of enraged audience responses and the performers' arrest by the police. At the same time, this video enacts a critique of the geopolitics of knowledge and of gender concepts. The shots combine through the on-screen narrative of a lower class urban woman who does not fit easily into the Andean categories of subjectivity. The narrator/commentator of the events fails to correspond to the concepts of man and woman as she becomes a public commentator and is neither *de vestido* (wearing a western dress or costume) nor *de pollera* (the outfit donned by urban migrants that has created the identity of the chola). Her image is reflected back through the video's use of extreme angles, split and tilted frames. The video thus enhances the destabilizing effects of the performance, unsettling the conventions of looking and thinking.

By destabilizing Andean duality *Mujeres Creando* criticizes not only essentialist feminism and bourgeois morality but also the discourses of indigenous movements who deploy gender duality in their efforts to decolonize without opening up possibilities for interrogating the joint history of colonialism and gender. Similar to Oyarzún and Richard, *Mujeres Creando* helps to understand gender not as an ontology but as a socio-cultural construct. In contrast with the Chilean critics, *Mujeres Creando*, call attention to the colonial history of this construct. *Mujeres Creando*, thus enact a reinterpretation of gender concepts that does not emerge from a mere inversion of signs. Emphasizing the experience of a multicultural society where racism and class contradiction continue to coalesce with gender stereotypes they dessentialize the notion of gender. They create a border space that helps to think transformation as a process that requires changing all the rules instead of becoming integrated into a multicultural diversity. Yet, where Richard places her bet with neo-vanguardism and where indigenous videomakers subvert capitalist market relations, *Mujeres Creando* use an urban punk aesthetic that runs the risk of becoming another object of urban consumption, as their

televised screening of the performances produce a shock effect but not necessarily a sustained reflection on the aesthetics and contents of the films, or even on the political oppression that the camera captivates, as Carlos Meza commented in his role as director of the cable channel P.A.T. that aired the videos by *Mujeres Creando* (2000, p. 20).

Despite the pitfalls of the approaches analyzed, *Mujeres Creando*, like the indigenous videomakers, contribute theoretical insights that require conceptualizing the construction of gender as deeply embedded in the coloniality of power. At the same time, they call attention to the binary thinking that has grounded the colonial project itself.

## Notes

1 Richard emphasizes that 'el Norte tiende a reservar el privilegio de la teoría a la académia metropolitana mientras la periferia latinoamericana descrita y analizada por esa teoría es vista como un simple campo de práctica habitado por quienes viven la experiencia mientras el latinoamericanismo del centro elabora su debida conceptualización' (1996, pp. 737–8)/'the North tends to reserve the privilege of academic theorizing for its metropolitan self. Meanwhile, the Latin American periphery theoretically described and analyzed is seen as a mere field of practice, inhabited by those living the experience while the Latinamericanism of the center elaborates its conceptualization' (pp. 737–8, my translation).

2 Frequently literacy is understood as the culmination of a process of intellectual and civilizational development where the voice is transformed into systems of representation that approximate the spoken word. Critics such as Jack Goody and Walter Ong have asserted that intellectual ability develops in correspondence to the technology of representation, permitting ever more complex thought. This view has been shown to be not only ethnocentric but also plain wrong. Rather, as Brian Street, Mignolo, Jacques Derrida, and others have shown, the notion of orality is flawed in multiple ways. Any system of communication implies oral forms as well as other systems of representation (mimetic and abstract) (Street 1984). The subalternization of alternative semiotic systems is itself an incomplete product of the colonial experience (Mignolo 1995, Salomon 2004).

3 This position remains influential for feminists such as Seyla Benhabib or Iris Young who are inspired by Habermasian philosophy of communication that is elaborated from the theory of speech acts rather than from the ethnomethodological approach to discourse analysis with insists that communication itself is always already embedded and constitutive of social relations, including those of power and inequality.

4 Monasterios (2006) offers a collection of essays on the work of *Mujeres Creando*.

5 The videotaped versions of these *acciones callejeras* are collected on two videos: *Prólogo* and *Acciones*. The individual titles are mine since the video segments on the video *Acciones* themselves are not titled.

6 The use of audiovisual technology by indigenous communities and movement organizations has become pervasive in almost all of Latin America. In collaboration with independent filmmakers indigenous videomakers and communicators script, film and edit documentaries and fiction shorts and distribute these through autonomous networks among diverse indigenous communities and at International indigenous film and video festivals. The argument presented here is based on research conducted primarily between 1999 and 2001 in Bolivia, Ecuador, Peru and Colombia. I thank in particular the members of CAIB and CEFREC in Bolivia for sharing their ideas, videos, and experiences with me. See also Himpele 2004, Wortham 2004, Turner 2002, and Schiwy 2003.

7 Cf. *Qati Qati/Whispers of Death*, Bolivia 1998; *Qulqi Chaliku/The Silver Vest*, Bolivia 1998); *El Oro Maldito/Cursed Gold*, Bolivia 1999; *Nuestra Palabra/Our Word. The History of San Francisco de Moxos*, Bolivia 1999, arguably also *El Espiritu de la Selva/Forest Spirit*, Bolivia 1998. Many indigenous-made documentaries from other regions in Latin America follow this tendency (Schiwy 2002, especially chapter two).

8 Fiction videos such as *Qati Qati* are distributed together with other indigenous fiction and documentary productions through the Bolivian Indigenous Network that connects over 400 villages in the Andean-Amazonian region (CEFREC 2001). The audience for these videos are primarily indigenous communities from Latin America as well as Native American and First Nation audiences from the US and Canada at international indigenous film and video festivals.

9 Relations with the multicultural market for indigenous video are thus under construction. Instead of easily integrating into themselves into the sale of diversity, market relations are challenged, and at least in part, rethought as to a possible balance between reciprocity and the free market (Schiwy 2003).

10 There is a vast amount of anthropological research on gender and Andean duality. Two foundational texts are Isbell (1976) and Harris (1978).

11 At the same time, the gendered division of labor is very strict, and in general women are seen as more able to assume male tasks (working the land) than men could assume female tasks (preparing food, washing clothes) because of the difference in value attributed to each. Also, women are able to find paid male labor, while men cannot find paid female labor – although they are able to take in that of female members of the extended family (Spedding 1997).

12 Rivera (1997) as well as Criales Burgos, *Mujer* for the Aymara context, de la Cadena 'Mujeres' and 'Matrimonio' for Quechua communities in Peru. Lehm and Equipo Ciddebeni (1996) on the Moxos. Jesús Avirama of the

Columbian indigenous organization CRIC stated that 'the emergence of foundations subject to the rhythm and whims of international fashion – focusing on the environment, women's issues, or development, for example – is troubling' (Avirama & Márquez 1995, p. 99.)

## References


Abercrombie, Thomas A. (1998) *Pathways of Memory and Power. Ethnography and History Among an Andean People*. Madison: University of Wisconsin Press.

*Acciones* (n.d.) Dir. Colectiva (Mujeres Creando). Videorecording. Bolivia, n.d.

Archondo, Rafael (1991) *Compadres al micrófono : la resurrección metropolitana del ayllu/Rafael Archondo*. La Paz: Hisbol.

Avirama, Jesús & Márquez, Rayda (1995) 'The Indigenous Movement in Colombia'. *Indigenous Peoples and Democracy in Latin America*. Ed. and trans. Donna Lee Van Cott. New York: St. Martin's Press and Inter-American Dialogue, pp. 83–106.

Butler, Judith (2004) *Undoing Gender*. New York: Routledge.

CEFREC (2001) 'Plan Nacional'. http:videoindigena.bolnet.bo.

Cervone, Emma, Garcés, Alicia, Larrea, Sissy, Morocho, Abelina, Prieto, Mercedes, Shiguango, Nely, Tapuy, Berta & Yangol, Dolores (1998) *Mujeres Contracorriente. Voces de Líderes Indígenas*. Quito: CEPLAES.

Chatterjee, Partha (1990) 'The Nationalist Resolution of the Women's Question' in *Recasting Women: Essays in Indian Colonial History*, eds Kumkum Sangari and Sudesh Vaid. New Brunswick: Rutgers Universty Press, pp. 233–53.

Choque Quispe & Eugenia, María (1998) 'Colonial Domination and the Subordination of the Indigenous Woman in Bolivia', trans. Christine Taff with Marcia Stephenson. *Modern Fiction Stiudies*, vol. 44, no. 1, pp. 10–23.

Criales Burgos, Lucila (1994) *Mujer y conflictos socio-culturales: el caso de las migrantes de Caquiaviri en la ciudad de La Paz*. La Paz: Aruwiyiri: Taller de Historia Oral Andina.

De la Cadena, Marisol (1992) 'Las mujeres son más indias: Etnicidad y género en una comunidad del Cuzco'. *Revista Isis Internacional* 16, p. XXXX

—— (1997) 'Matrimonio y etnicidad en comunidades andinas (Chitapampa, Cusco)'. *Más allá del Silencio*. Vol. 1 *Las fronteras de género en los Andes*. Comp. Denise Y. Arnold. La Paz: CIASE, ILCA, pp. 123–149.

Dubey, Madhu (1998) 'The 'True Lie' of the Nation: Fanon and Feminism', *Differences: A Journal of Feminist Cultural Studies*, vol. 10, no. 2, pp. 1–29.

Escobar, Arturo (forthcoming) *Hybrid Nature: Cultural and Biological Diversity at the dawn of the twenty-first century*. Durham: Duke University Press.

Fausto-Sterling, Anne (2000) *Sexing the Body. Gender politics and the construction of sexuality*. New York: Basic Books.

Fisher, Jo (1993) *Out of the Shadows. Women, Resistance and Politics in South America*. London: LAB.

Harris, Olivia (1978) 'Complementarity and conflict: An Andean view of women and men', in: *Sex and age as principles of social differentiation*, ed. J. La Fontaine, ASA 17, London: Academic Press.

Himpele, Jeff, ed. (2004) 'Gaining Ground: Indigenous Video in Bolivia, Mexico, and Beyond'. Dossier of 3 articles/interviews, *American Anthropologist*, vol. 106, no. 2, pp. 353–73.

Horswell, Michael J. (2003) 'Toward an Andean Theory of Ritual Same-Sex Sexuality and Third-Gender Subjectivity', in *Infamous Desire. Male Homosexuality in Colonial Latin America*, ed. Pete Sigal. Chicago: University of Chicago Press.

Isbell (1976). 'La otra mitad esencial: un estudio de complementariedad sexual andina', *Estudios Andinos* 12, pp. 37–56.

Jones, Ann Rosalind & Stallybrass, Peter. (1991) 'Fetishizing Gender: Constructing the Hermaphrodite in Renaissance Europe', in *Body Guards: The Cultural Politics of Gender Ambiguity* eds Julia Epstein and Kristina Straub. New York: Routledge, pp. 1–28.

Kaplan, E. Ann (1997) *Looking for the Other. Feminism, Film, and the Imperial Gaze*. New York: Routledge.

Lehm, Zulema & equipo CIDDEBENI (1996) 'El saber y el poder en la sociedad mojeña: aproximación desde una perspectiva de género', in *Ser mujer indígena, chola o birlocha en la Bolivia postcolonial de los años 90*, ed. Silvia Rivera Cusicanqui. La Paz: Subsecretaría de Asuntos de Género, pp. 393–453.

Mariscal, George (1991) *Contradictory Subjects: Quevedo, Cervantes, and Seventeenth Century Spanish Culture*. Ithaca: Cornell University Press.

McClintock, Ann (1995) *Imperial Leather. Race, Gender, and Sexuality in the Colonial Conquest*. New York: Routledge.

Mignolo, Walter D. (2000) *Local Histories/Global Designs. Coloniality, Subaltern Knowledges and Border Thinking*. Princeton Studies in Culture/Power/History, Princeton: Princeton University Press.

—— (1995) *The Darker Side of the Renaissance. Literacy, Territorialiy and Colonization*. Ann Arbor: Michigan University Press.

Mignolo, Walter D. & Schiwy, Freya (2003) 'Double Translation: Transculturation and the Colonial Difference', in *Translation and Ethnography: The Anthropological Challenge of Intercultural Understanding*, ed. Leland M. Searles. University of Arizona Press, pp. 3–30.

Mohanty, Chandra Talpade (1988) 'Under Western Eyes: Feminist Scholarship and Colonial Discourse', *Feminist Review*, vol. 30, pp. 61–88.

Monasterios, Elizabeth, ed. (2006) *Tecnocracia de género y feminismo autónomo: Mujeres Creando*. La Paz: Plural.

Montrose, Louis (1991) 'The Work of Gender in the Discourse of Discovery', *Representations*, vol. 33, pp. 1–42.

Mott, Luiz (1992) 'As amazonas: um mito e algumas hipótesis'. *América em tempo de conquista*. Org. Ronaldo V. Vainfas. Rio de Janeiro: Jorge Zahar, pp. 33–57.

Mujeres Indígenas de la CONAIE (1994) *Memorias de las Jornadas del Foro de la Mujer Indígena del Ecuador*. Quito: CONAIE and UNFPA.

Orduna, Victor (2000) 'La provocación de las lesbianas', *Pulso*, vol. 1, no. 33 (10–16 de marzo), pp. 18–20.

Oyarzún, Kemy (1992) 'Género y étnia: acerca del dialogismo en América Latina'. *Revista Chilena de Literatura*, vol. 41, pp. 33–45.

*Prólogo* (n.d.) Dir. Maria Galindo. Videorecording. Distr. Mujeres Creando. Bolivia.

*Qati Qati. Susurros de Muerte/Whispers of Death* (1999) Resp. Reynaldo Yujra. Prod. CEFREC/CAIB (La Paz). Fiction. 35 minutes. Aymara with Spanish Subtitles. CEFREC, Bolivia.

Quijano, Aníbal (2000) 'Coloniality of Power, Eurocentrism, and Latin America', *Nepantla. Views from South*, vol. 1, no. 3, pp. 533–580.

Quijano, Aníbal & Wallerstein, Immanuel (1992) 'Americanicity as a Concept, or the Americas in the Modern World-System'. *ISSI*, vol. 134, pp. 549–557.

Quispe Huanca, Felipe (1999) *El indio en escena*. Chukiyawu-Qullasuyu: Ed. Pachakuti.

Reinaga, Fausto (1972) 'Ideología y raza en América Latina' (1972). *Utopía y Revolución. El pensamiento político contemporáneo de los indios en América Latina*, ed. Guillermo Bonfil Batalla. México: Nueva Imagen, pp. 87–109.

Richard, Nelly (1996) 'Feminismo, Experiencia y Representación'. *Revista Iberoamericana*, vol. 62, pp. (176–177): 733–744.

Rivera Cusicanqui, Silvia (1997) 'La noción de 'derecho' o las paradojas de la modernidad postcolonial: indígenas y mujeres en Bolivia'. *Temas Sociales* (Revista de Sociología UMSA), vol. 19, pp. 27–52.

—— (1996) 'Prólogo: los desafíos para una democracia étnica y genérica en los albores del tercer milenio'. *Ser mujer indígena, chola o birlocha en la Bolivia postcolonial de los años 90*. La Paz: Ministerio de Desarrollo Humano, Secretaría de Asuntos Etnicos, de Género y Generacionales, Subsecretaría de Asuntos de Género, pp. 17–83.

Salomon, Frank (2004) *The Cord Keepers. Khipus and Cultural Life in a Peruvian Village*. Durham: Duke University Press.

Schiwy, Freya (2003) 'Decolonizing the Frame. Indigenous Video in the Andes', *Framework*, vol. 44, no. 1, pp. 116–132.

—— (2002) 'Reframing Knowledge: Indigenous Video, Gender Imaginaries, and Colonial Legacies'. PhD Dissertation. Duke University.

Shohat, Ella (1991) 'Imaging Terra Incognita: The Disciplinary Gaze of Empire', *Public Culture*, vol. 3, no. 2, pp. 41–70.

Spedding, Alison (1997) 'Investigaciones sobre Género en Bolivia: Un comentario crítico'. *Más allá del silencio. Las fronteras de género en los Andes*, ed. Denise Y. Arnold, La Paz: CIASE/ILCA, pp. 53–74.

—— (1997) ''Esa mujer no necesita hombre:' en contra de la 'dualidad andina' – imágenes de género en los Yungas de La Paz'. *Más allá del silencio. Las fronteras de género en los Andes*. Ed. Denise Y. Arnold, La Paz: CIASE/ILCA, pp. 325–44.

Street, Brian V. (1984) *Literacy in Theory and Practice*. Cambridge, London, New York, New Rochelle, Melbourne, Sydney: Cambridge University Press.

Turner, Terence (2002) 'Representation, Politics, and Cultural Imagination in Indigenous Video. General Points and Kayapo Examples', in *Media Worlds. Anthropology on New Terrain*, eds Faye Ginsburg, Lila Abu-Lughod, and Brian Larkin, Berkeley, Los Angeles and London: University of California Press, pp. 75–89.

Viezzer, Moema (1991) *Si me permiten hablar. Testimonio de Domitila una mujer de las minas de Bolivia*, 19th edn, México: Siglo Veintiuno Editores.

# Javier Sanjinés

## THE NATION: AN IMAGINED COMMUNITY?[1]

In revisiting the classics of social science, it is evident that even authors that acknowledge the division of societies into different classes, tend to treat societies as organic 'totalities', subject to rules of analysis that impart a sense of unity and homogeneity to events of the past. This tendency is also evident in historical analyses that neglect the deep ethnic and racial divisions that pervade political life, divisions that are particularly important in understanding societies of the Third World. In the same way, concepts so central to the study of social organization, like 'national culture', are based on a sense of social cohesion that simply does not reflect reality. In this way, the triad made up of the lettered practice – literature and journalism – the construction of the nation-state, and the organization of 'national culture', is based on a conflictive model that centers hopes for the future in the rational and teleological organization of a social utopia. This lineal model of modernity, originating in Europe and influenced by Hegel, assumes that no matter what the crisis in the present, modernity will overcome the obstacles it faces, and lead in the end to a future social utopia, be it capitalist or socialist. This inalterable course of history is based on the profound conviction that the crises suffered in different historical-economic cycles will transpire without throwing into doubt the overall lineal and progressive move toward social utopia.

Along this line of analysis, and when it comes to our understanding of the concept of 'national culture', our totalizing gaze of reality originates in the important and foundational works of the Hispanic- American nation, like *Facundo. Civilization and Barbarism* by Domingo Faustino Sarmiento. These works were also the basis for the beginning of the paradigm of civilization and barbarism in the middle of the nineteenth century. In effect, *Facundo* is based on the empirical observation that life in the towns seemed backwards, and this idea is also evidenced in other foundational texts of Latin American nation-states. These works reflected the stark contrast between the 'lettered cities', a term that the Uruguayan critic Ángel Rama used to refer to urban centers, and the rural zones in the interior of our countries. This empirical evidence was drawn from the fact that the cities and principal ports of Latin America were modern like the centers of power in European civilization, thanks to the close commercial relationship they shared. The diffusionist 'logic' held the cultural models imported from the center of international economic power in high esteem, and called for their transfer to the interior of Hispanic-American societies, replacing autochthonous cultural forms with a totalizing perspective, and a 'civilizing' gaze.

Beginning with Sarmiento's work for example, the rationalizing and organizing discourses of the nation-states, particularly the positivistic discourses of the second half of the nineteenth century, were based on the premise that Latin American unity was already practically achieved. In this way, writers put emphasis on education, reinforcing one of the most important characteristics of the altruistic and ennobling vision of history dominant at the time: the good will of learned educators (journalists and men of letters). This characteristic was key because learned educators wanted to integrate Latin American countries into the community of refined nations by promoting a much closer link of Latin America's natural resources to the dynamics of the world economy. It turns out that the rationalizing model of these learned men was also coherent with the project that sought to expand the ideals of the rising bourgeoisie. The most traditional oligarchical sectors also took to this rationalizing model, thus establishing the foundations of the oligarchical-liberal States. This progressive and untainted version of history, that held the lettered city as the only verifiable seat of civilization, also answered to an ideology whose utopia hid the 'backwards', fragmented character of reality.

There appeared however a few notable exceptions that objected to the triumphalist perspective of history: at the beginning of the twentieth century, a number of works started to doubt the boundless good will imparted to modernity, and probed more cautiously into the formation of our nations. One of these notable exceptions was *Os sertöes: campanha de Canudos* (1902) (*Rebellion in the backlands*, 1944) by the Brazilian writer Euclides de Cunha. The fictionalized essay was written while the First Republic in Brazil (1889–1930) was consolidating in terms of a positivistic model for the observation of reality, leaving behind the long stage of its institutional monarchy that began in 1808. But as the work of da Cunha testifies, the Republic was not created without bloodshed. The liberal politics of the Republic, impregnated with social Darwinism, did not survive without being put to the test by the violent opposition of rebel and millenarian movements such as Canudos, in the northeast state of Bahía. These movements stubbornly and fiercely opposed being assimilated into modernity as the secular Republic intended. For this reason, it would be useful to summarize the crisis of modernity that occurred in Latin America at the beginning of the twentieth century before I concentrate on da Cunha's impressive work.

In the first decade of the 1900s, there was a reaction against the positivist ideas that prevailed during the last half of the nineteenth century. A number of authors began to look at liberalism with a critical eye. Three historical events served as catalysts for this reaction (Williamson 1992, pp. 304–306). First, the defeat that Spain suffered at the hands of the United States in 1898. Indeed, the war of independence in Cuba increased the fear in Latin America that Anglo-Saxon dominance would bring an end to the values of the Hispanic world. This event led to the re-valuation of Latin America's Hispanic spiritual

traditions and made Latin American's aware of the need to put a halt to the modernizing, utilitarian materialism of the United States. *Ariel*, the notable work by the Uruguayan José Enrique Rodó, converged with the intellectual work of other great modernist writers, like the Nicaraguan Rubén Darío and the Cuban José Martí, giving clear evidence of the intellectual rejection of the United States, a movement that I will later describe as oppositional 'arielismo', that influenced the first decades of the last century. Secondly, as I said earlier, the rebellion of Canudos in 1896 demonstrated the deficiencies of the liberal Republic recently established after a long constitutional monarchy in Brazil. I give a very different treatment to this literary-historic event, that served as the backdrop to Mario Vargas Llosa's novel *La guerra del fin del mundo* (The war of the end of the world), published in 1981. Whereas Vargas Llosa was inclined towards imputing an unquestionable superiority to the Brazilian state, and paints the extermination of the barbarian *jagunços* as a 'tragic necessity' in the name of modernity, my work finds in da Cunha's essay an impressive account of the clash produced between modernity and coloniality in Latin America. We well know that there is no precise referential author of coloniality. Coloniality should be thought of in terms of the experience narrated in a long list of disparate accounts, such as the writings of Frantz Fanon and the chronicles of Felipe Guamán Poma de Ayala, among other examples. To these, and to other examples that would be too many to cite, I would add Euclides de Cunha. Although there is no clear original author of coloniality, it does have a precise temporal beginning: it appears as the result of the asymmetry of power created in the colonization of America in the sixteenth century, which served as the foundation of a modernity that still tries to hide its miseries and contradictions (Mignolo 2000). Is it not a contradictory fact of modernity today that development agencies like the World Bank and the International Monetary Fund promote a faith in the market and in economic growth, at the same time that they marginalize and segregate the population excluded from the 'benefits' of development? Doesn't this increase in production parallel the destruction of life and of natural resources? The complicated struggle between modernity and coloniality is reflected as well in the third historical-literary event observed in the crisis of modernity: I am referring to the literature of the Mexican Revolution, particularly the novel *Los de abajo* (The underdogs) written by Mariano Azuela in 1915. This novel paints an accurate picture of the social and political cataclysm that led to the Revolution. Having said this however, I will concentrate on da Cunha's work below.

Euclides da Cunha, a notable journalist, geological engineer and positivist researcher, was sent to cover the Canudos Rebellion as a newspaper correspondent from Rio de Janeiro. The Canudos Rebellion was an event that shook the consciousness of Brazilian citizens at the beginning of the twentieth century. As a witness to the peasants of the northeast's heroic defense while under assault by the Republican troops, da Cunha felt himself

seriously questioned. This made him confront his own 'civilizing' inclination for positivistic liberalism that made him believe in the innate inferiority of the autochthonous. This contrasted with the compassionate respect that his writing gradually acquired for the inhabitants of Canudos, true *damnés de la terre* who should be categorized as a degenerate social group and rejected according to the rigor of positivistic science. Said in another way: the evolutionism of da Cunha entered into conflict with his observations of reality. The journalist realized that the Canudos Rebellion was not the product of the *jagunços'* blind capriciousness for the return to the traditional constitutional monarchy, but the result of a religious vision anchored in ancestral myths that were absolutely incongruent with the world of modernity. Intrigued by the opposing forces that prevented Brazil from becoming a uniform entity, *Os sertöes* had a tremendous emotional force because of the tragedy in the contradictory and unresolved situation. This also made the work a revealing study of how racial determinisms come apart when faced with the humanity of the rebels, allowing us to see the complexities in a reality that resisted and still resists being studied as a homogenous unit, where modernity overcomes the retrograde and degenerated nature of those unable to enter into Western civilization. In *Os sertöes,* da Cunha did not reject progress, but he realized that the fruits of progress could not only benefit the elites. What is more, he felt tormented by the fact that it was difficult to explain how this people could integrate into modernity without destroying their identity; how would they achieve the construction of the nationality so longed for? Is it not true that this is still a big concern that remains unresolved at the beginning of the present century?

It seems to me that at the heart of these questions lies the presence of disparate cultures that did not converge to bring about a new civilizing project. The fact that these cultures did not coexist in harmony, flourishing reciprocally, also helps explain the inexistence of a 'national culture'. On the contrary, there was never any convergence, only opposition between the ancestral cultures and the successive variants of Western civilization that had acquired hegemony among the dominant groups. There is only one reason for this: the social groups that monopolized power (political, economic and ideological) since the beginning of the European invasion until today, social groups affiliated by descent or by circumstance to Western civilization, have sustained historical projects in which there is no room for local cultures to flourish. The dominant position of these groups, and the presence of their modernizing armies originating from the stratified order of colonial society, has been expressed in an ideology that only conceives of the future (development, progress, advancement, The Revolution itself) within the direction given to it by Western civilization. Cultural diversity, and more specifically, the presence of multiple local cultures, has been understood as an obstacle that impedes progress along the only certain path and toward the only valid goal. The coloniality of power and the coloniality of knowledge,

cognitive expressions inherited from the conqueror, do not permit one to see or to invent any other path: local cultures, like the Sertanera of the Brazilian northeast, are left for dead, or are expected to die before long, because their condition is one of unquestionable inferiority according to the colonizer's gaze, and has no future of its own.

Furthermore, given that Euclides de Cunha also considered the mestizo Sertanejo 'an instable hysteric', (1944, p. 97), he must have recognized that the peasants' stubborn defense of their customs called into question the scientific methods of observing reality. The biological sociology of the period was a limited and insufficient way to interpret the events. In effect, how was it possible following the positivist view, that a corrupt and degenerate ethnic group could oppose a modern army with such success, an army trained in the most advanced European technologies of warfare?

In *Os sertöes*, the tragic and mystical figure of Antonio Conselheiro, the 'inverse of a great man' (1944, p. 142), the'pietist that aspired to reach the Kingdom of God' (p. 139), the fearful *jaqunco* who 'reproduces the mysticism of the past' (p. 137), forced da Cunha's evolutionism to falter tragically; in effect, it is not *kronos,* lineal and progressive historical time that distinguished the defeat of Antonio Conselheiro and his Sertanejo rebels, but *kairos,* a time loaded with the painful truth of deep crisis: there were two Brazils, two nations divided by the struggle between the opposing forces of modernity and coloniality. In effect, the actions of Conselheiro were a product of the struggle between two different historical projects. The struggle did not simply refer to alternative proposals within the framework of a civilization in common. Proposals like that would hypothetically alter the reality of the moment, but go without questioning the deep values of the civilizing project. Rather, it referred to different projects that rested on different ways of conceiving the world, nature, society and human beings; projects that postulated different hierarchies of values; that did not have the same aspirations, and did not understand what it meant to be fully human in the same way. They were projects that expressed two different directions of social organization. Even given all this, cultural unification projects like 'national culture' never proposed unity based on the creation of a new civilization that was a synthesis of the previous cultures, but proposed a unity dependent on the elimination of one of them (the Sertanejo culture in the case of Brazil) and the generalization of the other, of the celebrated of modernity. In reference to this flight from local culture in favor of the exogenous, the imported, da Cunha affirmed,

> . . . After having lived for four hundred years on a vast stretch of seaboard, where we enjoyed the reflections of civilized life, we suddenly came into an unlooked-for inheritance in the form of the Republic. Caught up in the sweep of modern ideas, we abruptly mounted the ladder, leaving behind us in the centuries-old semidarkness a third of our

> people in the heart of our country. Deluded by a civilization which came to us second hand; rejecting, blind copyists that we were, all that was best in the organic codes of other nations, and shunning, in our revolutionary zeal, the slightest compromise with the exigencies of our national interests, we merely succeeded in deepening the contrast between our mode of life and that of our rude native sons, who were more alien to us in this land of ours than were the immigrants who came from Europe. For it was not an ocean which separated us from them but three whole centuries. . . .
>
> (p. 161)

As the passage above confirms, da Cunha discovered that the rebellion of Canudos did not have the return to monarchical-constitutional order as an end like the proponents of liberal republicanism believed. What the rebellion opted for was a resurgence of 'a religiosity that is diffuse and incongruent' with modernity (p. 161), demonstrating that the often mentioned national unity, the 'fraternal and horizontal' community that Benedict Anderson theorized as 'imagined' (Anderson 1983), is just another myth of modernity created to legitimate the political hegemony of the dominant sectors. For this reason, I now turn to demonstrating how the text of da Cunha can be used to critique Anderson's theory.

Anderson tries his best to present the notion of a 'deep horizontal camaraderie' as fundamental to the 'imagined community'. However, this notion obscures and distorts the experience of Latin America, where the ties between the different social and ethnic sectors were ties of 'dependence', not 'camaraderie', (Lomnitz 2001). In contrast to the historical experience of the European nations, Latin American dependence started with colonization. The way in which the new Latin American States of the nineteenth century treated the legacy of the sixteenth century definitively marked the direction the nation itself took. In other words, given that the ties of brotherhood and fraternity between different ethnic and social groups were not strong enough in Latin America to construct 'the nation', in the same way different ways of understanding nationalism surfaced during the postcolonial era, a result of intellectual borrowing from Europe that in the end was false and unstable.

There is no doubt of the importance of the religious act in the organization of local cultures. As I demonstrated in another essay on the work of José Carlos Mariátegui, the 'religious factor' is vital to the explanation of how the Andean world is organized. The strength of the religious myth in the Sertanera population proves that Anderson's affirmation of nationalism as a kind of cultural succession to the universalism of premodern religions is erroneous. Although Anderson situates the birth of nationalism at the end of the eighteenth and the beginning of the nineteenth centuries, the conditions that made way for the development of nation- states occurred much earlier, with

the expansion of Europe in the sixteenth century (Mignolo 2000). From Anderson's point of view, European expansion created the image of a civilizing development that was plural and independent, and this pluralism or relativism eventually transformed into a kind of secular historicism from where the individualized collective entities – the nations – competed with one anther.

One of the most surprising and interesting aspects of Anderson's book is the affirmation that nationalism developed first in the colonial world, to later expand to Europe. This way of looking at the geopolitics of the concept took historians of Latin America by surprise, as they were accustomed to thinking in terms of the European influences of liberalism and the Enlightenment, and not from the concrete reality of Latin America. But, in spite of such an original observation, it is difficult to accept Anderson's argument that the Hispano-American nations were constructed in terms of an extensive and horizontal camaraderie. I will not pause here to speculate whether nationalism was, as Anderson argues, a valid substitute for the centrality that religious structures had during the Colony. On the contrary, I will critique the claim that national construction was a 'fraternal and horizontal camaraderie' (1983, p. 25).

Claudio Lomnitz has noted that one of the principal weaknesses of the Anderson book is the argument that nationalism formed from a single imagined fraternal community (Lomnitz 2001). According to Lomnitz, what Anderson forgets is that in Latin America the division between a 'strong' and 'weak' citizenship has always existed, and the 'weak' (children, women, the indigenous, the uneducated) have been traditionally dependent and subjugated. Given that these distinctions deeply marked the heterogeneous nature of our reality, it is difficult to agree that the power of nationalism lied in the ties of fraternity that the State continues to instill in future citizens in classrooms, even today. Throughout history, using their written and oral communicative capacities, the 'strong' and first-class citizens have interpreted the 'others' by way of their cultural products, be they from journalism or literature. It is now a known fact that in the eighteenth century, a predominantly male 'public sphere' opened up giving rise not only to the novel, but also to literary criticism (Eagleton 1984). From there the importance that 'the lettered' acquired in Europe and in the Americas was in opening public spheres that would help to consolidate the building of nations. In this way, it is not strange that both the novel and journalism would have been the instruments capable of 'representing' the type of community that Anderson describes as imagined.

This critical look leads me to revise the definition that Anderson gives of the nation; to affirm, contrary to the concept of imagined community, that the deep fraternity among complete citizens – the criollos or criollo-mestizos-opened a relative 'public sphere', where the lettered role of journalists and writers was to mediate between the State and a half-formed citizenry, poor and weak, an embryo of citizenship that even today lives subjugated and

dependent. The role conferred on the lettered intellectuals also needs to be revised with greater care.

If the role of the lettered intellectual in the formulation of the romantic project of State-building was fundamental in the middle of the nineteenth century, the role of the intellectual was also important at the end of that century, and at the beginning of the twentieth century, at about the same time that da Cunha wrote *Os sertöes.* Lettered intellectuals played a key role in critiquing the modernizing 'barbarism' of North America that threatened to extinguish the spiritual values of Latin America. This anti-imperialist intellectual movement called 'arielismo', arising from the pen of modernist writers, like José Enrique Rodó and Rubén Darío, writers who resisted the overwhelming influence of Anglo-American culture. Their critiques were based on the exotic and highly cultured examples of opposition to the scientific positivism that organized the authoritarian states in the second half of the nineteenth century.

*Ariel*, written in 1900, is a meditation about the nature of civilization and allowed Rodó to contrast two forms of society, symbolized by the literary figures of Ariel and Calibán. The figure of Calibán, associated with the United States, represented a state in which mercantile utilitarianism, combined with the excessive appetites of the masses, produced a new barbarism that distanced Hispano-American societies from moral values and spiritual ideals. Contrasting this barbarism, Ariel, a spiritual figure, represented Hispano-American civilization, guided by an intellectual elite capable of subordinating the materialist inclinations to the mandates of reason and the well-tempered spirit. Although in this essay Rodó admired North American dynamism, he believed that Latin America should preserve the Greco-Latin values that approached the democracy of the masses and capitalism with caution.

In the 1910s and 1920s, the intellectual impact of *Ariel* was enormous. In effect, it awoke the Latin American desire to affirm their own culture. More specifically, it fostered resentment and contempt for the United States and its cultural expressions. As I affirm in another essay (Sanjinés 2003), this anti-imperialist but not necessarily popular model of national organization was constructed, in the case of Bolivia, by Carlos Montenegro's *Nacionalismo y coloniaje* (1943). This work is considered a foundation of 'revolutionary nationalism', where the role of the lettered was particularly clear given that Montenegro analyzed the history of the country through the prism of different literary genres (the epic, drama, tragedy, comedy and the novel). I think that *Nacionalismo y coloniaje* is an example of the way attachment to the high expressions of Western lettered culture impeded the appropriate understanding of the national being (Sanjinés 2003). I reach this conclusion because Montenegro, in contrast to the work of da Cunha, did not stop to look diligently enough at the colonialism that his book attacked and denounced. I think that his propensity for the West also impeded his observation of the

disparities and the disjunctions that characterize Bolivia, even today. Montenegro's 'arielismo' or anti-imperialism led him to fight against the social and economic oppression in which the country had fallen as a result of the surrender of its upper classes to Western models of observation, with an alternative intellectual project that was not daring enough to reflect the local fragmentations. This logic could have called into question European historicism and its epistemological premises.

This brief and critical look at Montenegro's book leads me to the question whether it is possible to continue invoking this type of 'arielismo', to continue defending Latin America without questioning the epistemological categories from which we want to build such a defense. If this were not the case, in what ways could the latent possibilities of subjugated peoples be developed? The factor that impeded the confrontation between Latin America and the United States and also prevented Latin America's ability to secure itself successfully in this confrontation was, as José Carlos Mariategui observed in the 1920s, the prolongation of elements of its colonial past, combined with a postcolonial model – the 'liberal' nationalism of the new republics in the nineteenth century – that marginalized and repressed the local cultures and the popular sectors. Now then, and following the logic of 'arielismo' explained above, one of the minor symptoms of emergent globalization of the Latin American economies was precisely the rejection of subaltern studies, postcolonial theory and multiculturalism on the part of certain intellectual sectors of Latin America. They consider them a type of colonization of thought by theories elaborated in the North American academy, from the perspective of what is often referred to as *area studies.* Echoing the concept developed by Edward Said, these intellectuals accuse postcolonial studies and subaltern studies of a kind of 'neoarielismo', in which the configuration of Latin America of its societies and cultures, is given in an eccentric and anomalous manner.

The connections that 'neoarielistas' make between Latin American cultures and the North American academy are simply an inefficient critique of the latter's supposed cultural domination. In affirming the value of 'lo latinoamericano' as an aesthetic-utopian opposition to the United States, 'neoarielismo' repeats the problem of being – as 'arielismo' was in the past – a reply that does not successfully challenge North American cultural hegemony. In other words, 'neoarielismo' reveals its incapacity to articulate Latin America in a hegemonic way. That is to say, it has no way to group all the heterogeneous and multifaceted elements that comprise the many cultures of the region, nor does it have the capacity to produce an interpellation that is genuinely 'national-popular', evoking the concept of Gramsci. Neoarielismo produces and reproduces a perpetual division between the culture of the intellectuals – including well-meaning leftist 'letrados' – and the bigger mosaic of the multifaceted cultures of the popular sectors. In this way, neoarielismo does not represent 'the popular' but rather the discomfort and

the distress of the intellectual groups of petty-bourgeois formation, the majority mestizo-criollos, threatened with displacement on the national scene by the strength of neoliberalism and cultural globalization on the one hand, and by an ethnically and socially heterogenous popular subject on the other, in whose name they once claimed to speak.

In this sense the neoarielista position, still dominant in the cultural and academic strata in Latin America, reproduces the anxiety constitutive of the original arielismo of Rodó and the other modernists who, as I already said before, manifest a profound anti-Americanism, together with a contempt or fear of the masses and democracy. Are there any viable alternatives to neoarielismo?

As John Beverley indicated (Beverley 2005), if the struggle between capitalism and socialism was essentially a fight to see which of the two systems could produce a better version of modernity, then history has handed down its verdict: capitalism. If we limit the possibilities of socialism to just the ability to achieve complete modernity – a fact that, from a different point of view, da Cunha's *Os sertöes* questions at the beginning of the twentieth century – we would be condemned to a defeated left. The possibility of reformulating a new Latin America 'from below', to put it this way, is tied to the question of how to imagine a new version of the socialist project, liberated from the teleology of modernity, and of the 'nation', imagined by the dominant sectors as the inevitably unitary phenomena of modernity. The challenge of ideological articulation that this task entails is to fuse the de-hierarchization of the cultural, the opening towards difference and to new forms of liberty and identity, with a clear sense of the need to displace capitalism and its institutionality, both bureaucratic and cultural. To achieve this task it seems to me that the most useful position is the posture represented by diverse forms of 'theory', like the subaltern and postcoloniality. These are more useful than the neutral, nationalist, criollo-mestizo position of neoarielismo. These 'theories' are concerned with the reconceptualization of those 'from below'. In order to discuss this subject briefly, I will return to the spine-chilling ending of da Cunha's work.

> '. . . The entrance of the prisoners into camp was a moving sight . . . The line of prisoners . . . came to a halt a hundred yards beyond – an ugly cluster of ragged, repulsive-looking human bodies . . . a legion of disarmed, crippled and mutilated, famished beings . . . Then there was the horrible hag, a wrinkled and skinny old witch . . . who alone raised her angry eyes darting sparks, to look the bystanders in the face . . . In her spindling arms she carried a small child . . . That child was a horrifying sight to behold. The left side of its face had been torn away some time ago by a splinter from a grenade, and the jawbones, white as could be, now stood out from the crimson edges of the wound, which had healed over.

> The right side of her face was wreathed in a charming smile – a pitiful half smile which was once extinguished in the vacuum, the gash, on the side. That was the most monstrous sight in all the campaign, to see that old woman reeling along, like one afflicted with locomotor ataxia, down that long line of unfortunates.
>
> (pp. 472–473)

Who were these turbulent and macabre *jagunços*? Were they a multitude?; maybe a people without a nation? Following John Beverley here (1999, 2004), I would be inclined to define them by combining the idea of 'multitude' with 'subalternity', the 'poor in spirit' that the Sermon of the Mountain mentions. But, I should recognize that there is an important difference between these two notions: the multitude, as Michael Hardt and Antonio Negri have theorized it (2000, 2004), evokes the head of Hydra with many faces, a collective subject arising from globalization and cultural deterritorialization. Subalternity, on the contrary, express a class, gender and occupation, that is to say, a specific identity, of flesh and blood, that loves, suffers and dies.

For Maquiavelli, the first modern thinker of national liberation movements, and for whom the idea of national unity was behind all his writings, the notion of a 'people without a nation' constituted the heterogeneous, the servile. This notion comes very close to that of multitude and responds to a way of doings politics that goes beyond the limits of the nation and of representation, traditionally related to the idea of hegemony. Multitude, a notion far removed from national unity, comes to be an amorphous social subject, arising outside of global capitalism and of the anachronistic system of national borders. But, in my estimation, this notion of multitude, that is referred to today to define social movements, does not explain the nature of the *jagunços* described above very well.

Were the *jagunços* an 'extending', 'expansive' form that designated a social subject that was far from being defined as proletariat, and that could not be limited to the category of 'remunerated workforce?' Were they, in other words, an excess that modernity could not control? Hardt and Negri, who use Paolo Virno's metaphor of the 'exodus' to describe the partition of the multitude from the nation-state, confirm this point of view. But, on the other hand and inversely, wasn't their potential for mobilization against power dependent on the very existence of the Republic and of the nation? My impression is that, outside the national territory, the *jagunços* would not have been more than an expression of multiculturalism, an aspect of the superstructure of capital. But in contrast to the notion of multitude, an idea that I consider to be rather slippery, it seems that ideologically speaking, the *jagunços* were looking to affirm their identity, including respect for their values, their religious beliefs, their languages, their territory and the defense of their rights and community.

To summarize, it seems to me that the reconceptualization of the nation from the point of view of 'those from below' is far from the fraternal imagined community of 'those from above'. This re-conceptualization of the nation draws more from the notion of the subaltern than the notion of multitude. To put it in another way, the notion of 'the people' is a notion that is closer to subalternity than multitude and depends on the recognition of the socio-cultural differences that separate the hegemonic sectors from the subaltern sectors. It is in this sense that Dipesh Chakrabarty, the historian of South Asia, affirms that:

> . . . Subaltern studies, as I think of it, can only situate itself theoretically at the juncture where we give up neither Marx nor the 'difference', for, as I have said, the resistance it speaks of is something that can happen only 'within' the temporal horizon of capital, and yet it has to be thought of as something that disrupts the unity of that time. . . .
>
> (2000, p. 95)

In effect, this passage from Chakrabarty allows us to conclude that the equation between the nation-state and the modern depends on the temporality that equates the people with modern citizenship. Subalternity, on the other hand, breaks with this temporal unity and in opting for the opposite, settles on the concept of 'ungovernability' – the capacity for resistance that the poor and needy defenders of Canudo exhibited – is precisely the space of resentment, disobedience, marginality and insurgence. In this line of thought, it is just a fantasy to think that the 'return of the plebeian' (García Linera 2000) could occur under the civilized form of 'civil society'. In its usual sense, the *bürgerliche Gesellschaft* of Hegel, tied to lineal sense of time and development, requires a formal education, technical and scientific knowledge, a nuclear family, a political party, business and private property, all categories that exclude large sectors of the population who do not attain full citizenship. This exclusion, this limitation, is precisely subalternity.

What then replaces the notion of 'civil society?' Would it be 'hybridity', as Hardt and Negri think? I doubt that this would be the correct alternative because the concept of hybridity, that separates and deterritorializes the binary opposition State/civil society, ends up surrendering to the market and globalization. Given that subalternity is in search of the opposite effect, we would have to say, as a means of conclusion to this work, that the crisis of nation as imagined community, measured in the politics of the multitude and under conditions of globalization that have weakened the State, requires paradoxically the legitimation of the territory and the nation-state. But this re-legitimation also requires that we rethink concepts like the nation, national identity, citizenship and democracy. In my opinion, the notion of multitude that Hardt and Negri propose in *Empire* as well as their most recent book

*Multitude,* does not contribute enough to this reclassificatory effort. In my opinion, we will have to be more careful in defining subalternity as 'historical agency'. Although the notion is insufficiently articulated in the works mentioned above, the concept of subalternity as historical agency would help us visualize the new society in which we aspire to live. In the last instance, I reiterate that the reconceptualization of the nation requires a way of thinking located at the limits of the temporality of Western history. As Euclides da Cunha says at the beginning of the twentieth century, the unresolved struggle between modernity and coloniality creates 'excesses' that are very difficult to control, and that go undetected if one surrenders uncritically to points of view, like Benedict Anderson's imagined community, that can only see the situation from the 'outside' of Western epistemology, and forget to weigh and assess the concept with the disjunctive qualities of the local.

## Note

1 This essay was originally published in Spanish in the book *Modernidad y Pensamiento Descolonizador*, published by the Universidad Para la Investigación Estratégica en Bolivia (U-PIEB) and the Instituto Francés de Estudios Andinos (IFEA), in August 2006.

## References

Anderson, Benedict (1983) *Imagined Communities. Reflections on the Origin and Spread of Nationalism*. London: Verso.

Beverley, John (1999) *Subalternity and Representation*. Durham, N.C: Duke University Press.

—— (2004) *Testimonio. On the Politics of Truth*. Minneapolis: University of Minnesota Press.

—— (2005) Prologue to Javier Sanjinés C., *El espejismo del mestizaje*. La Paz: PIEB/Embajada de Francia/IFEA.

Cunha, Euclides da, [1902] (1944) *Rebellion in the backlands (Os sertöes)*. Trans. Samuel Putnam. Chicago: University of Chicago Press.

Chakrabarty, Dipesh (2000) *Provincializing Europe: Postcolonial Thought and Historical Difference*. Princeton, N.J: Princeton University Press.

Eagleton, Terry (1984) *The Function of Criticism*. London: Verso/NLB.

García Linera, Álvaro, Gutiérrez, Raquel, Prada, Raúl & Tapia, Luis (2000) *El retorno de la Bolivia plebeya*. La Paz: Comuna.

Guha, Ranajit (1985) 'Nationalism Reduced to "Official Nationalism"', *ASSAA Review*, vol. 9, no. 1, pp. 103–108.

Hardt, Michael & Negri, Antonio (2000) *Empire*. Cambridge, Mass: Harvard University Press.

—— (2004) *Multitude. War and Democracy in the Age of Empire*. New York: The Penguin Press.

Lomnitz, Claudio (2001) 'Nationalism as a Practical System. Benedict Anderson's Theory of Nationalism from the Vantage Point of Spanish America' in *The Other Mirror. Grand Theory Through the Lens of Latin America*, eds. Miguel Ángel Centeno and Fernando López-Alves. New Jersey: Princeton University Press.

Mignolo, Walter (2000) *Local Histories/Global Designs. Coloniality, Subaltern Knowledges, and Border Thinking*. Princeton: Princeton University Press.

Sanjinés C., Javier (2003) 'Entre la historia y la literatura: Carlos Montenegro y la representación de la realidad', *Tinkazos,* no. 15, pp. 83–92.

Virno, Paolo (2004) *Gramática de la multitud. Para un análisis de las formas de vida contemporáneas*. La Paz: Malatesta/El juguete rabioso.

Williamson, Edwin (1992) *Penguin History of Latin America*. London: Penguin Books.

**Agustin Lao-Montes**

# DECOLONIAL MOVES

## Trans-locating African diaspora spaces

> The blackness is visible and yet is invisible . . . The blackness cannot bring me joy but often I am made glad in it. The blackness cannot be separated from me but often I can stand outside it . . . In the blackness, then, I have been erased, I can no longer say my own name, I can no longer point to myself and say 'I'. In the blackness my voice is silent. First, then, I have been my individual self. Carefully banishing randomness from my existence, then I am swallowed up in the blackness so that I am one with it.
>
> (Jamaica Kincaid)
>
> The American Negro must remake his past in order to make his future.
>
> (Arturo Alfonso Schomburg)
>
> Black studies require a complete reorganization of the intellectual life and historical outlook of the United States, and world civilization as a whole.
>
> (C.L.R. James)

The recent boom in the making and marketing of African Diaspora Studies still needs to fully integrate and center the histories, cultures, and politics of Afro-Latinidades. In this writing, I will place Afro-Latinidades in larger landscapes of world-history, more specifically in the context of the global African diaspora as a key geo-historical field within the modern/colonial capitalist world-system. In this inquiry, I will lay-out arguments about the analytical and political values of the African diaspora as a world-historical formation, while making an attempt to gender it analytics. Another main threat of this article will be the significance of Afroamerican politics and intellectual currents for the decolonization of power and knowledge.

In a seminal article Tiffany R. Patterson and Robin D.G. Kelley seek to develop 'a theoretical framework and a conception of world history that treats the African diaspora as a unit of analysis'.[1] They contend that even though black intellectual currents, cultural forms, and social movements have been transnational since the very dispersal of African peoples with the inception of

capitalist modernity and the institution of chattel slavery, languages of diaspora have only been used since the 1950s. In turn, Brent Edwards claims that not only the rhetoric of 'diaspora is of recent usage for African-Americans', but that it is still of limited political value given that it is not yet fully integrated into the discourse of Black social movements and political activism. Edwards argues that African diaspora discourses emerged in the 1960s partly as a response to Pan-Africanist views of the Black world in terms of racial sameness and cultural commonalities that assume basic cultural unity among black people. He advocates for 'a historicized and politicized sense of diaspora' and describes the African diaspora as a 'transnational circuit of politics and cultures beyond nations and even oceans' that given the contradictions and differences that characterize it would best be analyzed using the concept of *decalage*.[2] I will argue that geo-historical categories like the African Diaspora and the Black Atlantic are crucial to analyze the translocal networks that weave the diverse histories of peoples of African descent within the modern/colonial capitalist world-system.[3]

Patterson and Kelley argue that diaspora can be conceptualized both as process and condition. 'As a process it is constantly being remade through movement, migration, travel, and imagined through thought, cultural production, and political struggle. Yet as condition, it is directly tied to the process by which it is being made and remade . . . the African diaspora exists within the context of global race and gender hierachies', they write. Their analysis of the African diaspora as a *condition* linked to world-historical processes of capitalist exploitation, western domination (geo-political and geo-cultural), and modern/colonial state-formation; and as a *process* constituted by the cultural practices, everyday resistances, social struggles, and political organization of 'black people as transnational/translocal subjects' is analytically sound. I will add a third dimension, the African diaspora as a *project* of affinity and liberation founded on a translocal ideology of community-making and a global politics of decolonization. The African Diaspora can be conceived as a project of decolonization and liberation embedded in the cultural practices, intellectual currents, social movements, and political actions of Afro-diasporic subjects. The project of diaspora as a search for liberation and transnational community-making is grounded on the conditions of subalternization of Afro-diasporic peoples and in their historical agency of resistance and self-affirmation. As a project the African diaspora is a north, a utopian horizon to Black freedom dreams.[4]

There is a discussion in transnational Black studies about whether we should make a sharp distinction between Pan-Africanism and African diaspora perspectives. Some scholars contend that while Pan-Africanist internationalism was based on a politics of identity, the very emergence of African diaspora discourses concurred with the rise of a politics of difference. However, there are various versions of Pan-Africanism (ranging from Pan-African nationalism

to cosmopolitan Black Marxism),[5] as well as a diversity of African diaspora discourses.

## African diaspora/Black Atlantic and the contested terrain of blackness

In analyzing theories of global blackness some crucial questions are: What are the perceived presences of Africa and the meanings of Africaness? How should we analyze the ties that bind and the borders that divide Afro-diasporic (or Black) subjects? The very concepts of Africanity and Blackness have a wide range of significations, ideological implications, and political meanings. For instance, being black does not always imply African descent (e.g., at certain times and places the meaning of blackness in England may include people of South Asian descent), while the identity of Africanity should not be circumscribed neither to sub-Saharan Africa nor to blackness (in the narrow sense of very dark skin).[6] Hence the need for more complex genealogies to map the myriad of histories, identities, cultural-intellectual currents, and political projects that compose the African Diaspora and the Black Atlantic.

In Afrocentric discourses of Africanity, Africa tends to be imagined as the original homeland that provides the roots of the sameness of all African peoples.[7] In this light, the diaspora is constituted by people of African descent who live outside of the continent. The African continent is imagined as the primal source and ultimate homeland. In this identity logic the ties that bind are common origin, cultural affinity, and political destiny. Africanity is defined according to notions of tradition and authenticity that tend to correspond to patriarchal discourses of gender and sexuality. Nonetheless, not all Pan-Africanisms are Afrocentric, and to establish a simple equation of Afrocentrism, Black Nationalism, and Pan-Africanism would entail a reductive analytical move conflating diverse and distinct traditions of thought and politics.[8]

Pan-Africanism can be defined as a world-historical movement and ideological framework led by activists and intellectuals seeking to articulate a transnational racial politics of black self-affirmation and liberation. The timing of Pan-Africanism can be located in the period from the antisystemic slave revolts of the eighteenth century (epitomized by the Haitian revolution) and Black abolitionism during the long nineteenth century, to the rise of a new wave of antisystemic movements in the 1960s. The climax of such project (political, cultural, and intellectual) was during the early twentieth century Pan-African Congresses and the movements for decolonization of Africa in the 1950s–60s. There are diverse analyses and political projects involving various notions of justice, freedom, cultural democracy, and black liberation within this general rubric.

African diaspora discourses also vary in theoretical outlook and ethical-political project. A useful way to distinguish African diaspora discourses is by using Mishra's distinction between 'diasporas of exclusivism' and 'diasporas of the border'.[9] Likewise, James Clifford differentiate 'multicentered diasporas' characterized by 'transnational networks build from multiple attachments' from the 'centered diaspora model' in which diasporic identities standing from a history of uprooting and dispersal are based on a myth of return to an original homeland. The shift to diaspora discourse in transnational Black studies and in Black cosmopolitan networks (and to a lesser extent in Black racial politics), implied a broad division between Afrocentric/black nationalist narratives and multicentered/postnationalist understandings of diaspora. However, the distinctions are not that sharp, even though tracing these differences in broad strokes could be analytically useful and politically relevant.

Invocations of diaspora from afrocentric and black nationalist viewpoints tend to recycle Pan-Africanist internationalist analyses and politics. In contrast, postnationalist analyses of the African diaspora criticize Pan-Africanism for holding an essentialist view of African/Afro-disaporic cultures and a nationalist ideology which allegedly overlook differences (class, gender, sexual, ethnic) and minimize the possibility of alliances beyond racial divides. But, there are significant differences in each camp as revealed by a debate in which Kobena Mercer criticizes Paul Gilroy for theoretically keeping a basic core defining identities in the Black Atlantic (as expressed in Gilroy's concept of the 'changing same'), while Gilroy rebutted that Mercer 'rigorously antiessentialist' notion of diaspora as a 'site of multiple displacements . . . without privilege to race, cultural tradition, class, gender, or sexuality' lacks a sense of historicity in so far as it does not clearly link black histories to capitalism, modern racism, and cultures of resistance.[10]

Arguably, Stuart Hall's was able to transcend these terms of discussion by distinguishing between two moments of diasporic identification. The first moment he defines as one of retrieval against loss memory and of cultivating a collective identity in order to develop a sense of belonging and to be enabled to act politically. The second moment is when differences (class, gender, sexual) are liberated to deconstruct the multiple axes of domination (capitalism, patriarchy, racism, colonialism) that frame identifications (class, gender, sexuality, race, ethnic) and organize world-historical patterns of power.[11] For Hall, Africa is neither and origin nor an essential culture or civilization, but a symbolic marker of shared histories of displacement, oppression, resistances, counter-memories, and resemblances in cultural production.

As a political-cultural identity, Blackness is as contextual and contingent as Africanity. Whether the identifier blackness should be attributed to which kind of bodies and populations, as well as the political meanings and values of blackness, are historically contingent and contested matters. Blackness can be

used as a common denominator for the 'dark races of the world' that could promote proposals for 'World Black Revolution'.[12] But the denomination 'black' can also be restricted to the darkest bodies according to pigmentocratic criteria that signify blackness as a sign of the ultimate savagery and Africa as the dark continent without history. I conceptualize blackness as more than simply color, as a contested terrain of memory, identity, culture and politics, as an historical arena in which different political projects, historical narratives, cultural logics, and self-designations are enunciated and debated.[13] Some arenas of these variations of blackness are the politics of self-naming ('black' and/or 'Afro-descendant'), the question of color (should we distinguish black and brown?), and the entanglements of the local, national, and transnational dimensions of black histories. In this inquiry a key question is what's the relationship between nations and diasporas, and consequently between nationalist and diasporic discourses. Clifford argues that even though diasporas had always been part and parcel of modern nationalisms, 'diasporic cultural forms can never, in practice, be exclusively nationalists' given their history and condition as 'articulation of travels, homes, memories, and transnational connections' which place them in an 'entangled tension' with both host and sending places (nations, regions, continents). Therefore a diasporic community represents 'a stronger difference than an ethnic neighborhood' in so far as they have a 'sense of being a 'people' with historical roots and destinies outside of the time and space of the host nation'. The very constitution of diasporas are based on the principle of difference, and defined this way diasporic identities challenge nationalist pretensions to be the master discourse of identity and the primary framework for culture and politics. The argument here is not for displacing nations with diasporas, and/or for replacing nationalism with postnationalist discourses, but to look into how an Afro-diasporic perspective can allow us to rethink self, memory, culture, and power beyond the confines of the nation as unit of analysis (and the dominant form of political community) and to develop a politics of decolonization not confined to nationalism.[14] Analytical constructs like the African Diaspora and the Black Atlantic could allow us to rethink histories, cultures, and politics beyond the nation, while developing 'non-occidentalist post-imperial geo-historical categories'.[15] In light of the centrality of the African diaspora in formations and transformations of both western modernities and subaltern modernities, an afro-diasporic perspective should be an essential component of any critical theory of the modern world.

In short, I conceptualize the African diaspora as a multicentered historical field, and as a complex and fluid geo-cultural formation and domain of identification, cultural production, and political organization that is framed by world-historical processes of domination, exploitation, resistance, and emancipation. If the world-historical field that we now call the African

diaspora, as a condition of dispersal and as a process of displacement is founded on forms of violence and terror that are central to modernity, it also signifies a cosmopolitan project of articulating the diverse histories of African peoples while creating translocal intellectual/cultural currents and political movements. The Afroamerican diaspora it is not a uniform formation but a montage of local histories interweaved by common conditions of racial, political-economic, and cultural oppression and by family resemblances grounded no only in commensurable historical experiences of racial subordination, but also in cultural affinities and similar (often shared) repertories of resistance, intellectual production, and political action.[16]

## Gendering African diaspora discourses

Most accounts of the African diaspora tend to marginalize considerations of gender and sexuality.[17] The gendering of African diaspora discourse is necessary not only to draw a more complex and concrete picture (inclusive of women) of the histories of peoples of African descent in the modern world, 'to make visible social lives which are often displaced, rendered ungeographic' or as 'people without history' but most significantly to perform a feminist critique of the patriarchal forms, mediations, and practices that constitute modern/colonial regimes of power. Black feminists had redefined the theory, history, and politics of the African diaspora.[18] Black cultural critics such as Carol Boyce Davis had greatly contributed to redefine the parameters of black literature by netting a global diasporic field of black women writers. Black feminist scholars like Michelle Stephens and Michelle Wright had performed feminist critiques of Afro-diasporic cultural, intellectual, and political traditions not only led by male figures but also characterized by a masculine gaze and project. Their gendering of the African diaspora has redrawn its character.

Michelle Stephens' *Black Empire* focuses on how early twentieth century Pan-Africanist, US-based Caribbean intellectuals/activists (C.L.R. James, Marcus Garvey, and Claude McKay) developed a 'masculine global imaginary' wherein the African diaspora was conceived as a trans-nationalist project in search of sovereignty and peoplehood, and therefore partly as a battle between Afro-diasporic and western masculinities. As in nationalist discourses, in this masculine narrative of the African diaspora, women tend to be represented as affective and cultural custodians of the race while Africa tends to be feminized as a motherland to be protected and rescued. Stephens describes her work as 'a particularly gendered analysis of black transnationalism and internationalism, informed by a feminist critique of imperial formations and nationalist constructions'. She agrees with Jacqueline Brown's claim urging 'diaspora studies to attend more directly to the politics of gender rather than to 'women experiences' . . . we should interrogate how particular practices (such as

travel) and processes (such as diasporic community formation) come to be infused with gender ideologies (or become 'gendered')'.[19]

In her book *Becoming Black* Michelle Wright focalizes on 'African diasporic counterdiscourses of Black subjectivity' by doing critical readings of canonical figures (DuBois, Cesaire, Senghor, Fanon) in the Black male cosmopolitan intelligentsia, while contrasting their method and arguments on Black modernity to Black feminist (Audrey Lorde and Carolyn Rodgers) writings. She argues that mainstream Black intellectual traditions construct the Black subject as masculine, and argues that given that 'Blackness as a concept cannot be . . . produced in isolation from gender and sexuality' there is a need of feminist and queer rethinkings of the African diaspora against the 'hetero-patriarchal discourse' of nationalism where 'Black women do not exist'. Wright built her argument for a dialogic/diasporic method 'to recuperate the Black female as subject' from Audrey Lorde's understanding of Blackness standing from the figure of the mother. She contends that 'Lorde points to the African diaspora as a complex space in which different types of intersubjects exist' and assert that this means 'moving from the discrete boundaries of the nation to the infinitely more complex conflated space and time of the African diaspora'. Wright defines the African diaspora as 'a series of multivalent and intersected historical and cultural formations' and asserts that 'Black feminist and queer discourses are intimately bound up in producing an African diasporic discourse'. These Black feminist and queer perspectives on the African diapora respond to the fact that 'not all Black subjects would like to hear all subalterns speak' and reveal the particularly profound forms of subalternization experienced by women of color and black queers. In this vein, the African diaspora should be conceptualized as a contested terrain of gender and sexual politics where the very definitions of project, identity, and agency are at stake.

In sum, gendering African diaspora discourses implies important epistemic breaks and political imperatives including revisiting and challenging the masculinist character of mainstream ideologies of global Blackness, centering women histories and feminist perspectives, and recognizing the significance of gender and sexual difference among the multiple mediations that constitute Afro-diasporic selves. In general, feminist theory and politics provide important tools for the analysis and transformation of modern/colonial constellations of power and knowledge including the capitalist world-economy, empires, nation-states, cultural logics, families, formations of intimacy and the self.[20]

## Diasporas and borderlands: women of color/third world women feminisms

In the United States an intellectual current and social movement that self-defines as 'women of color' and/or 'third world feminism' championed

theoretical critiques and political opposition to global, national, and local modes of domination, revealing the workings of patriarchy through all social spaces and institutions (from the capitalist world-economy and the modern nation-state to formations of intimacy) while recognizing the agency of subaltern women in historical struggles and social movements, and in the forging of alternative worlds.[21] Women of color feminism stand from long-term intellectual and political coalitions between African-American and Latina women.

This strand of critique and politics engages in 'a critically transnational (internationalist) feminist praxis' based on 'an antiracist feminist framework, anchored in decolonization and committed to anticapitalist critique'.[22] The overall transformative project is defined as one of decolonization meaning 'profound transformations of self, community, and governance structures'. This 'unbounded promise of decolonization' entails combating all forms of oppression (class, race, gender, sexual, geo-political, epistemic) in all social spheres and at all scales (local, national, global). This search for decolonizing economy, polity, knowledge, culture, and subjectivity, involves creating a 'decolonial imaginary' to change our lens and inform transformative praxis.[23]

The critical theory and radical politics of women of color/third world women feminism converge in crucial ways with the analytics and decolonial project of intellectuals-activists who analyze and seek to transform capitalist modernity from the perspective of the coloniality of power.[24] Both analyze modernity from a world-historical decolonial perspective, and both see power as a complex pattern that integrates class exploitation and capital accumulation with ethno-racial, cultural-epistemic, and gender-sexual domination. In short, both women of color feminism and the coloniality of power perspective stand from a 'decolonial attitude' and act for a politics of decolonization.[25]

Women of Color/Third World Women feminisms had also elaborated concepts of diasporas as spaces of difference and places to build what Maria Lugones calls 'complex untity' or solidarity gained in the intersection of multiple chains of oppression and corresponding strategies of liberation.[26] This border/diasporic decolonial imaginary have informed politically and intellectually fruitful coalitions between US Black and US Latina feminists pursuing general goals of liberation and decolonization. In this specific sense of Afro-Latinidad as a feminist political identity, Afro-Latina difference serves as a crucial constituent within a coalitional political community and as a significant element within a field of intellectual production and critique.

One of the principal theoretical contributions of women of color feminism is the concept of 'politics of location'[27] that relates the 'multiple mediations' (gender, class, race, etc.) that constitute the self to diverse modes of domination (capitalism, patriarchy, racism, imperialism) and to distinct yet intertwined social struggles and movements.[28] Building from this formulation I

propose the concept of politics of translocation to link geographies of power at various scales (local, regional, national, global) with the subject positions (gender/sexual, ethno-racial, class, etc.) that constitute the self.[29] Afro-American diasporic subjects should also be conceptualized as translocal because even though we are connected to nationality we are also inscribed within larger geo-historical constellations (the Atlantic, the Americas, global Blackness, the modern/colonial capitalist world-system), at the same time that Black identities are mediated by a myriad of differences (class, gender, sexuality, place, generation). Afro-diasporic subjects can simultaneously be national (Afro-Cuban), local (Louisiana), regional (Afro-Latin American), and global (cosmopolitan Black intellectual/activist). In sum, the notion of African diaspora signifies an ocean of differences and a contested terrain inscribed by distinctive gendered ideologies, political agendas, and generational sensibilities.

In this sense we can analyze the African Diaspora as a Black Borderland, as a geo-historical field with multiple borders and complex layers.[30] Claudia M. Milian Arias attempt to 'reconceptualize two foundational models' namely Anzaldua's 'borderlands' and DuBois' 'double consciousness' as a way to construct links between Black Studies and Latino Studies based on a 'relational theory of race' is another important move. Her proposal of 'an open double consciousness' constitutes a useful extension of the analytical and political value of the concept in so far as it 'allows the mixture of blackness to correspond with brown *mestizaje*, alongside the mixture of ideologies that shape these figurations via gender, class, and sexuality'. Milian's comparison of DuBois' double consciousness with Anzaldua's 'alien consciousness' could also be related to Chela Sandoval's notion of 'differential consciousness' but not without recognizing that this last notion supposes and implies an oppositional and transformative praxis.[31]

To close this section I will argue that it is also important to direct the gaze beyond the epistemic and political horizons offered by an Afro-diasporic perspective. Patterson and Kelley point to the limits of African diaspora discourse by arguing that Black history and politics had always been based in more than racial considerations, and had always been articulated with other world-historical processes (South Asian indentured servitude), ideologies (socialism, Islam), and antisystemic movements (labor, feminism). An Afro-diasporic perspective is analytically insufficient and politically indeterminate if we do not specify its world-historical conditions of existence and do not explore its political and ideological possibilities. African diaspora discourses can also predicate exclusionary definitions of identity as we already saw in relationship to gender, but exclusions can also stand from civilizational (Afrocentric) and world-regional (Anglocentric) definitions of blackness and the diaspora. Hence the need to pluralize our concepts and cartographies of the African diaspora, to see its diversity, contradictions, and local

particularities, and to understand the limits and possibilities of Afro-diasporic politics.

## Afro-Latinidades: pluralizing African diaspora spaces

In mapping African diaspora spaces we need to historicize them specifying their diversity and complexity while analyzing their linkages. Earl Lewis concept of African-American communities as 'overlapping diasporas' is a useful tool to understand diversity and articulation within the African diaspora. I am introducing the concept of intertwined diasporas to signify no only the plurality of histories and projects articulated within the African diaspora, but also the world-historical entangleness of multiple genealogies of diasporic formation (African, South Asian, and East Asian diasporas composing a Caribbean diaspora space), and the transdiasporic character of world cities' populations (working classes and new immigrants as subaltern modernities).

Afro-Latinidades tend to be marginalized and even erased from most mappings of the African diaspora, at the same time that African diaspora perspectives need to play a more important role in Latino/American studies. This shows the marginalization of Afro-Latinidades from Latino studies while it reveals our invisibilization in most cartographies of the African diaspora. The same Eurocentric ideology that place blackness at the bottom of the great chain of being and imagine Africa as a dark continent outside of history, locate Blacks at the bottom or outside of Latino/Americanist world-regional and national definitions. On the other end, the geo-politics of knowledge that corresponds to the sequence of British and US hegemony in the modern/colonial capitalist world-system, informs cognitive mappings and historical accounts of the African diaspora and the Black Atlantic focused on the Anglo world. Nonetheless, in spite of this double subalternization of Afro-Latinidades from both Anglocentric accounts of the African diaspora and Latino/Americanist discourses, there is a long history of Afro-Latina/o diasporic consciousness and participation in African diaspora networks. A telling example is the trans-diasporic reciprocity of three cultural movements in three different nodes of a cosmopolitan network of black intellectuals, cultural creators, and political activists in the early twentieth century: the Harlem Renaissance, the Negritude movement, and Afro-Cubanismo. A telling relationship in this black cosmopolitan diasporic world was between writers Nicolas Guillen and Langston Hughes whose friendship, intellectual and political exchange, mutual translation of poetry, and reciprocal introduction to their respective national and linguistic contexts eloquently exemplify Afro-diasporic solidarity within a translocal web of black public spheres.

Another revealing example that should inform our project of remapping the African diaspora by inscribing Afro-Latina/o histories within it is the biography of Arturo Alfonso Schomburg. The life and legacy of Arturo Schomburg a Puerto Rican born mulatto who founded what still is the most important world archive of black history, was a pillar of the Harlem Renaissance and became president of the American Negro Academy, is a pregnant source for this discussion. The differential construction of Schomburg's biography by Puerto Rican, Black American, and Afro-Caribbean intellectuals it is revealing of how distinct diaspora discourses define their subject and space. In Puerto Rico Schomburg is barely known while in US Puerto Rican memory he is top on the official list of great Boricuas, at the same that US Black historians remember him as black archivist Arthur Schomburg. Some researchers argue that Schomburg abandoned Hispanic Caribbean militancy after 1898 and eventually let go of his Puerto Rican identity in favor of an Afro-diasporic one.[32] But if we dig into Schomburg's work and projects we will get a more nuanced view of his multiple locations and loyalties.[33] His long lasting commitment to Afro-Latinidades can be clearly seen in his struggle for inclusion of Afro-Cubans and Afro-Puerto Ricans in organizations like the Negro Society for Historical Research, and to include Afro-Hispanic writers in anthologies of Black literature. His research in Africans in early modern Spain pioneered the current revision of European history as multiracial. His advocacy for translation of Afro-Latino writers like Nicolas Guillen revealed his effort to articulate a plural African diaspora. Indeed, Schomburg could not give-up his Afro-Latino identity because his blackness was contested in light of his Puerto Rican origin and mixed color. Perhaps, it was partly because of his border subjectivity and liminal positioning that Schomburg was the Black figure in the US early twentieth century who kept good relations with competing characters such as W.E.B. DuBois, Marcus Garvey, Claude McKay, and Alain Locke. In short, Schomburg's project of Black cosmopolitanism, in understanding the diversity and complexity of the racial formations and cultural practices in different African diaspora spaces, challenged narrow notions of both Africanity and Latinidad. Schomburg represents the translocal intellectual enacting a diasporic project in which identity and community are conceived and articulated through and across differences.

Afro-Latinidades as transdiasporic subjects tend to transgress essentialist conceptions of self, memory, culture, and politics corresponding to all encompassing categories of identity and community such as simply 'Blacks' and 'Latinos'. Afro-Latinidades in their plurality and disporicity demonstrate the limits of categorical definitions of both blackness and latinidad at the same time that they reveal the limits of diaspora discourses themselves. This begs the question of the genealogical and categorical character of Afro-Latinidades.

## Afro-Latinidades and world-historical constellations of identity and difference

The composed denominator Afro-Latina/o is beginning to gain currency in academic discourse, media texts, and to some extent in popular parlance. Its semantic field is fairly broad ranging from designating the subject of a field of research about Latino/Americans of African descent and naming a political/racial identity for emerging social movements of Black Latinos across the Americas, to serving as the commercial title for a collection of salsa music in the African continent. In light of this broad range and diverse set of meanings, we write about Afro-Latinidades in plural.[34] But in searching to conceptualize Afro-Latina/o as a category we need minimal definitional clarity. Afro-Latinidad is an ethno-racial category that refers to the histories, memories, social locations, expressive cultures, social movements, political organization, and lived experiences of peoples of African descent in Latino/America.[35] Afro-Latinidad is a category of difference, in contrast to identity discourses based on hegemonic notions of nationality and race in Latino/America. Positing Afro-Latinidades as a designation of difference should entail an analysis of the conceptual and political values of related denominations (national, regional, ethnic, racial, civilizational) of identity/difference.

The hyphenated term Afro-Latino denotes a link between Africanity and Latinidad, two complex and contested world-historical categories of geography, identification, and cultural production which have their own particular yet intertwined genealogies.[36] More precisely, to deconstruct the categorical character of Afro-Latinidades we should analyze the historical relationship of three key discursive frameworks in modern/colonial definitions of historical space and collective identity, namely Africanity, Americanity, and Latinidad. Such constructs have been produced and signified through a world-historical process of capitalist development, imperial domination, and nation-state formation, that entailed the constitution of modern/colonial definitions of the self, based on gendered/eroticized hierarchies of peoplehood (racial, ethnic, national). This world-historical pattern of domination and resistance that we call the coloniality of power is the overall framework from where we analyze the joint historical production (or invention) of Africa (and the African diaspora), the Americas, and Europe as world-regional discourses of social space, memory, culture/civilization, and identity/self.[37]

I conceptualize Afro-Latinidades using a world-historical/decolonial perspective. If elaborated as a category for decolonial critique and as a critical political identity Afro-Latina/o difference could reveal and recognize hidden histories and subalternized knowledges while unsettling and challenging dominant (essentialist, nationalist, imperial, patriarchal) notions of Africanity, Americanity, and Latinidad.[38] Such lens would also allow us to conceptualize the Black Atlantic and Afroamerica as composed by intertwined diasporas

wherein Afro-Latinos had historically played important roles, at the same time that we conceive Latinidad as a trans-American/translocal diasporic category. Thus, Latino/Americanism should be redefined and challenged by accounting for the histories of Afro-diasporic subjects, while African diaspora discourses should become more nuanced and pluralized in light of Afro-Latina/o histories. Given that Afro-Latinidades are marginalized from hegemonic narratives of Africanity, Blackness, Latinidad, and Hispanicity and therefore from the corresponding world-regional (Black Atlantic, Latin America, Afroamerica, Afro-Caribbean) and national definitions of identity and community; Afro-Latina/o as a subalternized diasporic form of difference should be transformed into a critical category to deconstruct and redefine all of the above narratives of geography, memory, culture, and the self.

In this inquiry, a fruitful angle for analysis and critique is the ever changing and always contested politics of naming. For instance, we could ask who is included and excluded from the designation *African-American* that replaced *Black* that in turn displaced *Negro* as the politically preferred self-designation by US activists and intellectuals of African descent. Is confining African-American to the north a way of promoting the imperial reduction of America to the United States of North America? It is playing the liberal game of hyphenated ethnicization in detriment of critical race theory and radical anti-racist politics? Should we instead redefine the expression African-American to signify Africans in the Americas? On another register, should we choose between Afro-Latino and Afro-Hispanic, or does each of these hybrid signifiers denote particular meanings revealing specific genealogies?

## For a genealogy of *Afroamerica*

We can trace the genealogy of modern/colonial ethno-racial categories to the historical shift from the late medieval religious-linguistic notions of 'blood purity' at the Iberian Peninsula, to the early modern racial classifications (*indio, negro, mestizo, African, European*) developed in the contexts of the conquest of the Americas and the organization of chattel slavery as a main institution of capitalist modernity. Archival evidence indicates the presence of people of African descent on Columbus crew at the so-called discovery voyages. This should be no surprise given that Cordoba was one of the principal centers of the Islamic world and that sugar cane plantations based on African slave labor were first instituted in the Canary and Madeira islands circa 1450 by the Spaniards and the Portuguese.

In this Mediterranean contact zone centered on the Iberian peninsula that later was partly extended to the Atlantic world we also have written record of Afro-Hispanic intellectuals such as Juan Latino, an African born who became Latin grammarian and poet, and who in spite of marrying into nobility and

achieving great recognition continued expressing a Black African identity that he contrasted with hegemonic whiteness.[39] The very politics of location and self-naming of this fascinating character who became chair of poetry at the University of Granada should be an historical template for any genealogy of Afro-Latinidades. From *Ladino,* a common designation for Spanish subjects of the low stratum that proved proficiency of the language of empire (Castilian), he renamed as *Latino* to establish 'an old imperial bloodline and genealogy based on his own linguistic merits'[40] as master of Classic Latin. Despite escalating the ladders of race and class through acquired cultural capital, Juan Latino could not shed his embodiment of Afro-Hispanic difference. His relative whitening via linguistic latinization could not erase his black body from been inscribed within the modern/colonial somatic-visual regime of pigmentocracy that frames the onto-existential condition that Fanon calls 'the fact of Blackness'.[41] From our present perspective, to the extent that his story shows some key correspondences and contradictions in the relation between Latinidad, Hispanicity, and nascent notions of western whiteness, Juan Latino could be seen as an early incarnation of the specificity of Afro-Latina/o difference and as an early modern expression of Afro-diasporic subjectivity.

Given that the main focus of our analysis is *Afroamerica* we should ask, what are the spatio-temporal parameters of Afro-Latina/o difference?[42] The vast territory south of the Rio Grande that is known as Latin America and the Caribbean is where people were first massively shipped from sub-Saharan or Black Africa in the sixteenth century, and where there presently is a largest concentration of Afro-descendants in the Americas.[43] But in the hegemonic Anglophone world there is a tendency to marginalize Afro-Latinos from the historical memory and cultural-political mappings of the African diaspora. In the United States, when we use the term African-American, we conventionally refer to North American Blacks as a specifically US ethno-racial designation. However, the use of the suffix 'Afro' to signify world-regional and national denominations had been used in the southern side of the American hemisphere since the early twentieth century. Cuban intellectual Fernando Ortiz wrote about an Afrocuban culture in 1904 and by the 1930s was one of the founders of the *Asociacion de Estudios Afrocubanos*. In Mexico an *Instituto de Estudios Afroramericanos* was organized in the early 1940s and published a short lived magazine called *Afroamerica*.[44] The Asociacion and magazine were launched and supported by a trans-American group of intellectuals from (or for) the African diaspora that included Euro-Cuban Fernando Ortiz, Afro-Cubans Nicolas Guillen and Romuro Lachatenere, Brazilian Gilberto Freyre, Haitian Jacques Roumain, Mexican Gonzalo Aguirre Beltran, Martiniquean Aime Ceasire, Trinitarian Eric Williams, US Blacks Alain Locke and W.E.B. DuBois, and anthropologist Melvin Herkovits.[45]

The point is not to establish where the language of Afroamerica was first used or to simply show Black consciousness in Latin America, but to argue for the need of an Afro-diasporic perspective that would allow us to analyze the differences and particularities as well as the articulations and common grounds of the manifold histories of the African diaspora in the Americas. Such globalized and pluralized Afro-diasporic perspective should be a basis for refashioning both Black Studies and Latino Studies.

The most general common ground of Afro-diasporic subjects in the Americas is the subjection to modern/colonial regimes of racial classification/stratification as the outcome of a world-system based on racial capitalism and western racisms. The institution of chattel slavery was a key constitutive element of capitalist modernity and left profound marks on its basic structures and psyche. 'Race' became at once a universal system of classification that informed all the basic institutions and discourses of western modernity, as well as a basic mediation in national and local configurations of power, culture, and subjectivity. What is at stake here is not only how 'race' and racism built the modern world, but also what was the house that race built, or how racial divides enabled the production of black expressive cultures, intellectual currents, and social movements.[46]

In the Americas, processes of nationalization of memory, language, and identity, stand from a nationalist narrative in which white male Euro-American elites are assumed to represent the nation, while subaltern racial others (Blacks, Indians, 'Orientals') are marginalized or virtually erased from national imaginaries.[47] The continuation of these modern/colonial modes of ethno-racial domination and class exploitation after national independence in the Americas is an important feature of what Anibal Quijano terms the coloniality of power.

In this vein, the existential condition that DuBois characterizes as 'double consciousness' referring to the 'American Negro', of grappling with a split subjectivity (American and African) and of denial of substantive citizenship by nation-states because of been seen and classified as a problem by a dominant racist regime, should be extended to the whole of Afroamerica. In spite of local, regional, and national differences, this condition of relative exclusion from hegemonic definitions of national self and history that imply a devaluation of memory, a folklorization of culture, and submission to political-economic regimes of racial domination and class exploitation, frame a common diasporic ground for people of African descent in the Americas.[48]

These long-term histories of relative exclusion and subalternization inform historical processes of community-making, the constitution of black publics and expressive cultures, and the rise of black struggles for recognition, democracy, and social justice. Hence, we should redefine the concept of African-American, to signify a complex and diverse diasporic field that encompasses the histories, cultures, and identities of Afro-descendants in the

Americas. In this register, double consciousness refers to Afro-diasporic expressions of belonging and citizenship based on Afroamerican identifications with places and spaces located below (Palenque de San Basilio in Colombia) and beyond the nation (Afro-Andean geographies, Afroamerica). Afroamerica can be represented as a creolized polyphonic diaspora space, a translocal crossroads, a Black borderland. The play of differences within the Afroamerican diaspora calls for a politics of translation, not only in the narrow sense of linguistic translations, but speak to the need of cultural and political translations to facilitate communication and organization, to create the minimal conditions to construct the diaspora as a decolonial project.[49]

In mapping the multiple genealogies of Afroamerican communities we should account for both their heterogeneity and their multiple connections. For instance, Afro-North America can be defined as a shifting historical formation, as an on-going process continuously re-composed by a diverse constellation of African diasporas re-located from the US, the Caribbean, Latin America, Europe, and the African continent. In turn, the eastern region of Cuba is largely Haitian and West Indian, while Afro-descendant communities in Central America are largely composed by offspring from immigrants from the Anglophone Caribbean and by Garifuna people that the British had expelled from Saint Vincent in 1789 after realizing their inability to colonize them. Also, world cities like New York and Paris have been for many years diasporic crossroads and Afro-diasporic borderlands where Afro-descendants from different places meet, develop ties, and reach-out to other peoples and diasporas.

## Intertwined diasporas on 'the belly of the beast': Blacks, Latinos, Afro-Latinos

Afroamerican subjects-peoples are intertwined diasporas in their history, ethnic composition, cultural expressions, and political projects. Perhaps, the clearest example of the diasporicity and translocality of Afro-Latinidades are Afro-Latinos residing in the United States, who are situated in-between Blacks and Latinos in the US national space at the same time that they link Afro-North Americans with Afro-descendants south of the Rio Grande.[50] However, some short sighted analytical and political perspectives that are attempting to become common sense in both academy and public culture across the Americas keep feeding the tendency to divide Black and Latinos (and Black and Latino Studies) as sharply distinct and even opposing domains of identity, culture, and politics.

In analyzing Black-Latino coalitions we should observe Afro-Latina/o multiple identities and affiliations. To Arturo Schomburg we could add Denise

Oliver's double membership in the Black Panthers and the Young Lords. In their platform the Young Lords advocated Afro-Indio identity. Schomburg himself used the pen name Guarionex who was a Taino warrior chief.[51] Afro-Puerto Rican writer Piri Thomas in his classic Nuyorican novel *Down these means streets*, articulates with clarity how sharp distinctions between Blacks and Latinos produce disturbing dilemmas for mulatto subjects like him. Thomas narrates how after agonizing about whether he was 'Black' or 'Puerto Rican' he realized that he was both, an Afro-Latino. He realized that his blackness and his *mulataje* were not in contradiction but constitutive of both his Puerto Rican and Afro-Latino identities. In this context the concept of mulatto does not mean a racial hybrid between black and white and/or a brown product of mestizaje, but it is rather used to signify how Afro-Latina/o difference could transgress and transcend such ethno-racial binaries.[52]

If we view Blacks and Latinos as distinct groups, their relationship should be represented in its diversity and complexity. This means recognizing the 'patterns of cooperation, conflict, and ambivalence' as put by political scientist Mark Sawyer. There is a growing scholarship on Black and Latino relations that analyzes the actual and potential roles of Afro-Latina/os as 'bridging identities'.[53] This strand of research had taken important steps in identifying sources of conflict while analyzing bonds and potential forms of coalition-building. Researchers had shown how similar histories and conditions of Black and Latino subaltern sectors (and to some extent middle strata) account for shared sensibilities informing campaings against racial discrimination (for Affirmative Action, against mass incarceration of Black and Latino youth), urban injustices (in housing, education, and health care), and economic inequality (living wage, union organizing).[54] This should not deny how different forms of racism (Latino anti-Black) and xenophobia (nativism of Black and Latino US citizens), and how various political agendas and ideologies (ethnic-racial competition of Black and Latino political classes), are sources of Black-Latino conflict. The ambiguities and shifting character of Black-Latino coalitions are shown in the electoral race of Antonio Villaraigosa who was elected major of Los Angeles in 2004 with the majority of the Black vote but was not supported by Blacks in the prior election. Out task is to develop analytical frameworks to understand the articulations of power and culture embedded in different definitions of Blackness and Latinidad and distinct forms of Black and Latina/o politics.

The liberal ethnic optic that informs the terms of politics in the US, produces simplistic notions of justice, community, and coalition-building. If the main basis of cultural and political affinity is de-racialized ethnicity, class and gender differences are irrelevant, and labor and feminist organization of marginal importance. In this logic, coalitions that matter are ethnic and in the electoral arena, while social movement organizations such as community-labor coalitions, broad-based alliances for racial justice, feminist of color

alliances, Black-Latina/o Gay and Lesbian networks, and the myriad of institutions and informal networks that compose an emerging wave of collective action north and south of the Rio Grande are written out. The forms of power and difference (class, gender, race, ideology) that distinguish Latino identities and agendas are erased, hence producing a false sense of sameness and a superficial notion of community. This results in a minimal concept of democracy as formal representation, and of justice as a share of the pie for the ethnic community. Concerns on the relation between democracy, difference, freedom, and justice, that give substance to these ethical-political principles are absent. Fundamental differences among Latino political traditions, ideologies of power, and projects are also ignored.

For instance, Nicolas Vaca's critique of sixties discourse on alliances between US people of color and the connection between US minority struggles and third world liberation movements have implications for Black-Latino Studies and their the racial, class, gender and sexual politics. Feminist coalitions of women of color/third world women is implicitly dismissed as passé in this outlook. Women of color feminism critiqued and challenged the patriarchal character of the nationalist discourses of the sixties at the same time they frame their analyses of domination in a world-historical decolonial perspective. This clearly opposes Vaca's understanding of Latino community and politics as an ethnic race, as well as its view of the world as a sum of nations where Latinos are an ethnic group within the United States. Vaca's liberal gaze ignores domination (imperialism, racism, patriarchy) and exploitation (neo-liberal capitalism) at the global level and its connections with regimes of inequality (class, ethno-racial, gender, sexual) at national, regional, and local scales in the United States (Vaca 2004). In contrast, third world feminism anchors a politics of decolonization in a critical analysis of the entanglements of capitalism, imperialism, racism, and patriarchy from the local to the global.[55] Its coalitional politics of sisterhood promotes alliances among women of color (Black, Latina, Native American, Asian) as part of a broad-based movement for radical democracy and social justice. This is also the kind of decolonial critique and politics of decolonization enabled by Quijano's concept of the coloniality of power.

## Decolonial moves: Afro-Latinidades and the decolonization of power and knowledge

The global spread of neoliberal imperial doctrines and policies since the 1980s had been met with the rise of a new wave of antisystemic movements epitomized by the campaigns against neoliberalism organized by the Zapatistas, mass demonstrations of global reach (Seattle, December 1999; world anti-war,

February 2003), and the boom of social forums (world, regional, national). We should situate the growth of transnational Afro-Latina/o politics since the late 1970s and early 1980s in this world-historical context. The rise of explicitly black (or afro) cultural/intellectual currents and social/political movements in Brazil, Cuba, Colombia, Costa Rica, Guatemala, Ecuador, Dominican Republic, Honduras, Panama, Peru, Puerto Rico, Nicaragua, Uruguay, Venezuela, and Argentina, and their growing relations with US Afro-Latinos reveal the emergence of an Afro-Latina/o hemispheric movement. The colonization by transnational capital and states of previously under-exploited Afroamerican regions such as the Pacific Coast in Colombia, Esmeraldas in Ecuador, and Pinones in Puerto Rico, informs the rise of social movements affirming Afro-diasporic identities and combating racism while claiming place and ecological integrity, and vindicating black cultures and local knowledges against the sweeping negative effects of neoliberal globalization. The growth of Afro-Latina/o movements is also intimately related to the emergence of strong and vibrant Amerindian movements in Latino/America. The salience of such movements had moved institutions of global capital (e.g., Interamerican Development Bank, U.S Agency for International Development, and the World Bank) to acknowledge the conditions of inequality of most Afro-Latinos and to develop projects in Afro-Latina/o communities. These interventions by key institutions of transnational capitalism provoke debates that unleash the different social, economic, cultural, intellectual, and political issues at stake.

In spite of significant differences and contradictions, the drive for Afro-Latina/o self-affirmation had produced local and national organizations that provided effective leadership within popular movements, articulated regional identities and alliances (Afro-Andino), convened world-regional meetings (Black Latin American women conferences), and participated in hemispheric meetings (Afro-Americans in and after Durban). Afro-Latinos in the United States are protagonist actors in these hemispheric networks at the same time that they serve as bridge in US Black-Latino coalitions. An important example in the cultural front are the exchanges between Afro-Cuban and Afro-North American politicized hip-hop artists which had challenged in theory and praxis commodified versions of rap while advancing a radical aesthetics of hip-hop culture as an expression of the African diaspora in the domain of transnational youth cultures.

The scope and scale of such movements give them the potential of significantly contributing to questioning and challenging racist regimes and processes of domination throughout the Americas. An important feature of many of these emerging discourses of Afro-Latinidad is a diasporic-translocal perspective that links racial democracy to class struggle, and wherein Black women are championing feminist demands with campaigns against imperialism and neoliberal capitalism. In these explicitly subalternist Afro-diasporic politics the question of power is clearly tied to the question of knowledge. Similarly to

the social movements of the 1960s–70s that created Latina/o studies and refashioned African-American studies, Afro-Latina/o cultural practices and social movements are not only claiming a space in the academic world but also demanding authority and recognition for their vernacular modes of knowledge.[56] Afro-Latinidades are an important source for the decolonization of power and knowledge. Afro-Latina/o difference can pose a challenge to both Black Studies and Latino Studies to revitalize the critical and radical paths that gave them birth and could prevent them from loosing their transformative decolonial character. Black radical cosmopolitanism had been a fountain of decolonial knowledge and politics since its very inception. Paraphrasing Nelson Maldonado Torres, we contend that Africana Studies represents one of the main traditions of critical cosmopolitanism in modernity and had always been a field of production of critical theories based on a decolonial attitude.[57] In this register, critical traditions of both Black and Latino Studies converge in so far they are both based in a radical decolonial politics of liberation (anti-imperialist, and in often also anti-capitalist) framed by world-historical and transnational perspectives. Afro-diasporic feminist perspectives entail particularly complex analytical frameworks and political projects in which imperial power, ethno-racial domination, and class exploitation, are systemically link to gender and sexual oppression. Hence, if we understand diaspora not only as condition and process, but also as a radical project for the decolonization of power and knowledge, this cross-fertilization of critical Black and Latino Studies could be a crucial resource of liberation in both the epistemic as well as in the ethical-political fronts.

If we conceptualize decolonization as a long-term and uneven process that results from the combined historical effect of everyday resistances, social struggles, and antisystemic movements, and given the centrality of racial regimes in the coloniality of power and knowledge, Black struggles and racial politics are crucial in the longue duree of world decolonization. This has a long historical trajectory from the nineteenth century Haitian revolution, to the US Black Freedom movement of the 1960s, and the anti-Apartheid movement. The current rise of Afro-Latinidades places Afro-Latina/o difference at the heart of world processes of cultural and political contestation and construction of alternative futures. This clearly includes struggles over the reconfiguration of the structures, logics, and categories of knowledge. In this tune, an Afro-diasporic decolonial imaginary could serve as the foundation for a new alliance between Black Studies and Latino studies, a trans-diasporic alliance for which Afro-Latinidades should and must be a bridge.

## Notes

1 See Patterson and Kelley (2000) followed by several comments on the article.

2 For Edwards (2001, p. 65) the French word '*décalage* is the kernel of precisely that which cannot be transferred or exchanged, the received biases that refuse to pass over when one crosses the water. It is a changing core of difference; it is the work of 'differences within unity', an unidentifiable point that is incessantly touched and fingered and pressed'.

3 Edwards also articulates a useful distinction between the African Diaspora as a global category and the Black Atlantic as a transnational regional category. The long denomination modern/colonial capitalist world-system is use by several intellectuals as a theoretical representation of capitalist modernity as an historical totality in which coloniality serves as the underside of modernity. See among others, Grosfoguel (2003), Grosfoguel and Cervantes (2002), Quijano (2000), Mignolo (2000, 2006).

4 I use the concept of utopia as a horizon of alternative futures grounded on the possibilities of the present that serves as a source of hope and as a north indicating us in which direction to go. See Bloch (2000), Santos (2001), and Wallerstein (1998). For the concept of Black Freedom Dreams see Kelley (2003).

5 A classic example is the distinction between the theory and politics of Marcus Garvey (transnational racial nationalism) and C.L.R. James (Black Marxism). See Robinson (2000).

6 A relevant question here is whether North Africa is part of the definition of the African continent and the implications for definitions of Blackness and Africanity. A current example is from France where many of the youth who rebelled in November 2005 where of North African ancestry and self-defined as Black.

7 The meaning of Afrocentrism is by no means self-evident. There is a growing tendency of a reductive use of terms such as Afrocentrism and Black Nationalism and we actively need to challenge those facile dismissals of complex intellectual and political traditions. Here by Afrocentric discourses I mean those narratives which assume an essential unity of all peoples of African descent which can be traced to common African origins, an analysis based on a monolithic historical logic in which modern civilization is simply an offsping of the African continent. In the latter sense, Afrocentism is the flip side of the coin of Eurocentrism but using the same kind of monocentric logic of historical development. See Howe (1998). For alternative theories of history based on polycentric perspectives see Dussel (1996, 1998), Mignolo (1997), Prashad (2001), Shohat and Stam (1994).

8 A visible example is Gilroy (1993).

9 According to Mishra diasporas can follow a logic of identity that could be as exclusive (e.g., of other genders and races) as nations, or in contrast could follow a logic of difference that could serve as a premise for more flexible and inclusive practices of belonging. Mishra (1994), as quoted in Clifford (1997). The very idea of diasporas of the border challenges a sharp distinction between diasporas and borderlands and therefore between Latina/o Studies and Black Studies. See Milian (2006).

10 See Gilroy (1992) and Mercer (1988, 1990).

11 Hall analyzes the politics of difference of this second moment using Derrida's concept of differance as an epistemic and political principle for deconstructing categorical identities on the basis of alterity. The same theoretical and political logic is used by Rhadhakrishnan to formulate an argument about ethno-racial identities and diasporicity in the US. See Hall (1991a, 1991b), and Radhakrishnan (1996). Hall's analysis of world-historical identities in relation to global constellations of power and an epistemic and political logic of alterity also resembles analyses by Latin American critical theorists Enrique Dussel and Anibal Quijano. See Hall (1993), Dussel (1996), and Quijano (2000).

12 For the concept of the 'dark races of the world' see Du Bois (1935). I learned about and got the platform for a 'World Black Revolution' from my colleague and friend John Bracey.

13 This is captured with much poetic wisdom in James Baldwin's expression 'Black is a Country' that also serves as title to Nikil Pal Singh's book. See Singh (2004).

14 The question of nationalism is quite complicated and beyond the scope of this article. However, I want to state that I disagree with a tendency in postmodern/postcolonial theory to simply dismiss nationalism as passé. To address nationalisms we need to historicize nationalist discourses and movements and their articulations with other ideologies and movements such as socialism, feminism, and pan-Africanism given the vast variety of nationalisms. Two interesting attempts to develop a historical sociology of nationalisms and to distinguish their diverse political meanings are Lomnitz (2001) and Lazarus (1999).

15 Coronil (1996).

16 For the concept of family resemblances see Wittsgenstein (1968).

17 Clifford (op. cit.) observes that gender is outstandingly absent from diaspora discourse in general. Patterson and Kelley (op. cit) discuss the importance of gendering analyses of the African diaspora. I am bracketing the question of sexuality in this article. However, this should not mean a denial of the centrality of mediations of sexuality in world-historical constellations of power and hence in social movements, expressive cultures and forms of subjectivity. The sheer absence for the most, outside of feminist critique and queer theory, of an analysis of the sexual logics and libidinal economies inscribed in diaspora discourses in general and of Afro-diasporic trajectories in particular, imply an urgent need for an eroticization of critical theory and historical analysis.

18 See among others, Boyce Davis (1994), Hill Collins (2000), Gunning *et al.* (2004), McKittirick (2006), and Nassy Brown (2005).

19 This quote of Brown is from Stephens. See Nassy Brown (1998).

20 See among others, Stoler (2002), McClintock (1995), and Mies (1998).

21 See Moraga and Anzaldua (1983), Grewal and Kaplan (1994), Mohanty and Alexander (1996), Mohanty, Russo, and Torres (1991).

22 Mohanty (2003).
23 For the concept of decolonial imaginary see Perez (1999).
24 For the concept of the coloniality of power see Quijano (2000).
25 It is important to observe that significant currents of African-American and Latina feminism did not abandoned the elaboration of the anti/post-colonial critiques and the politics of decolonization to address questions of memory, self, and power in the United States. Most male scholars rejected the so-called colonial analogies that served as foundations of Latino studies in the 1960s/70s while feminist scholars developed critiques of the patriarchal forms of anti-colonial nationalisms while developing their own versions of decolonial theory and politics. See Perez (1999/), Sandoval (2000), and, Mohanty (2003). For the concept of decolonial attitude see Maldonado Torres (2006).
26 See Lugones (2003).
27 See Alarcon (1989), Grewal and Kaplan (1994), Frankenberg and Mani (1993).
28 For the concept of multiple mediations see Mani (1990).
29 I proposed a politics of translocation in the introduction to the co-edited volume *Mambo Montage*. See Lao-Montes and Davila (2001).
30 Clifford (op cit) distinguish 'borderlands' and 'diasporas' as two different spatial formations and as frameworks for identification and politics, at the same time that their meanings and dynamics intersect.
31 See Sandoval (2000). Also see Allen (2003) problematization of DuBoisian concept of double consciousness.
32 See among others, Des Verney Sinnette (1989), and James (1999).
33 See Sanchez (2001). Arroyo (2007) also engages in an analysis not only of the differential racial significations of Schomburg in different contexts and according to distinct criteria but also about his gender and sexual locations.
34 However, for the sake of style In this article I use Afro-Latina/o and Afro-Latinidades interchangeably.
35 The conceptual expression Latino/America signifies a geo-historical construct that designate Latino/America as a world-region that encompasses not only the nation-states south of the Rio Grande that emerged from the colonization and subsequent falls of the Spanish and Portuguese empires, but also include Latin American diasporas in the US. It should be clear that these geo-historical constructs are limited and exclusive both in the ways the region is concieved (e.g., Is Haiti part of Latino/America, which reveals both the question of the placing of the Caribbean as well as the role of Latinism as an ideology invented in the nineteenth century within French imperial discourse?), and in who are the subjects/citizens in question (e.g., Are Aymara people Latin Americans? Is Aymara a Latin American language?). See Mignolo (2006).
36 For world-historical groundings of modern/colonial categories of the self see Hall (1991a, 1991b), and Quijano (2000).

37 For the concept of the coloniality of power see Quijano (2000). For the modern invention of Africa see Mudimbe (1988). For the invention of the Americas see O'Gorman (1961, 1986), Dussel (1992), and Rabassa (1993).

38 In this formulation the concept of Afro-Latina/o difference, in so far is it designates subjects whose experience and knowledge are otherized and subalternized by hegemonic occidentalist discourses constitutes a form of Mignolo's category of colonial difference, See Mignolo (2000).

39 For the concept of contact zone as an imperial/colonial space of domination, hegemony, resistance, and transculturation see Pratt (1992).

40 As quoted in Piedra (1991). Also see Fra-Molinero (2005) & Lao-Montes (2005).

41 See Fanon (1967). For an excellent reading of the onto-existential meaning of Fanon's concept of the experience of blackness see Gordon (1995).

42 For the concept of Afroamerica see Luciano Franco (1961).

43 Andrews calculates 110 million Afro-descendants south of the Rio Grande (Andrews 2004).

44 See Ortiz (1906), and Luciano Franco (1961).

45 There is a strategic inconsistency in the differential way in which the intellectuals are introduced. The intention is to show the diverse composition of the group not simply in terms of nationality but also showing ethno-racial (and in the case of Herkovits intellectual) identities.

46 There is a vast literature on the subject. For a relatively recent attempt to develop a historical sociology to explain how racial formations are fundamental to modern institutions (states, world-economy, structures of knowledge) and cultural/political forms (identities, expressive cultures, social movements, political ideologies) see Winant (2001).

47 Clearly there are substantive differences, for instance between racial regimes in the United States and Latin America, and in different national contexts of racial hegemony which are complicated by local and regional particularities and by historical changes over time. However, after recognizing significant differences and historical contingencies, we would argue that the above described dynamic of racial domination and representation characterize the overall pattern of racial formation in the Americas.

48 For the transnational/translocal extension of the concept of double consciousness also see Gilroy (1993) and Sawyer (2005).

49 For the politics of translation see Santos (2004, 2005).

50 See Marquez (2000).

51 Taino is the name given to the people who inhabited Puerto Rico at the time of Columbus arrival.

52 For two fairly promising elaborations of such sort of concepts of 'mulatto', 'mulataje' see Arroyo (2004) and Buscaglia (2003). Also see Martinez-Echezabal (1990). The signifier 'mulatto', similarly to 'mestizo', is conventionally used to connote a false image of 'racial democracy' in Latin America, the Hispanic Caribbean, and among US Latinos. However, analogously as the way in which Anzaldua re-defined the 'new mestiza' to

develop a theory and politics of identification standing from the play of differences, the concept of mulatto can serve as an conceptual and political tool to challenge racial reasoning and to analyze 'race' through its multiple mediations and myriad of historical articulations.

53 See Sawyer (2005b).

54 See among others, Dzidzienyo and Oboler (2005), Betancur and Gills (2000), and Jennings (1994).

55 For the 'entanglements' of modern/colonial hierarchies within world-systemic logics see Grosfoguel (2003).

56 An important example is the effort for an 'Ethnic University' in the overwhelmingly Afro-Colombian Pacific coast of Colombia, that parallels the Indigenous University in the Ecuatorian highlands.

57 See Maldonado Torres (2006).

## References

Alarcon, Norma (1989) 'Traddutora, Traditora: A Paradigmatic Figure of Chicana Feminism' *Cultural Critique*, vol. 13, Fall.

Allen, Ernest (2003) 'DuBoisian Double Consciousness: The Unsustainable Argument', *Massachusetts Review*.

Andrews, George Reid (2004) *Afro-Latin America 1800–2000*. Oxford: Oxford University Press.

Arroyo, Jossianna (2007) 'Technologies: Transculturation of Gender, Race, and Ethnicity in Arturo A Schomburg's Masonic Writings' in *Technofuturos: Critical Interventions on Latina/o Studies*, eds Mirabal, Nancy Raquel and Lao-Montes, Agustin. New York: Lexington Books, pp. 141–172.

—— (2003) *Travestismos Culturales: literatura y etnografia en Cuba y Brasil*. Pittsburg: Nuevo Siglo.

Betancur John & Gills, Dave (eds) (2000) *The Collaborative City: Opportunities and Struggles for Blacks and Latinos in US Cities*. New York: Garland.

Bloch, Ernst (2000) *The Spirit of Utopia*. Palo Alto: Stanford University Press.

Boyce Davis, Carol (1994) *Black Women, Writing, and Identity: Migrations of the Subject*. New York: Routledge.

Buscaglia, Jose (2003) *Undoing Empire. Race and Nation in the Mulatto Caribbean*. Minneapolis: University of Minnesota Press.

Clifford, James (1997) 'Diasporas', in *Routes. Travel and Translation in the Late Twentieth Century*. Cambridge: Harvard University Press, pp. 244–278.

Coronil, Fernando (1996) 'Beyond Occidentalism: Toward Nonimperial Geohistorical Categories', *Cultural Anthropology*, vol. 11, no. 1, pp. 52–87.

Des Verney Sinnette, Elinor (1989) *Arthur Alfonso Schomburg: Black Bibliophile and Collector*. Detroit: Wayne University Press.

DuBois, W. E. B. (1935) *Black reconstruction: an essay toward a history of the part which black folk played in the attempt to reconstruct democracy in America, 1860–1880*. New York: Harcourt, Brace and Company.

Dussel, Enrique (1998) *Etica de la Liberacion en la edad de la globalizacion y exclusion*. Mexico: Trotta.

—— (1996) *The underside of Modernity*. New Jersey: Humanities Press.

—— (1992) *1492: el encubrimiento del otro: hacia el origin del 'mito de la modernidad': conferencias de Frankfurt, octubre de 1992*. Santafe de Bogota: Antropos.

Dzidzienyo Anani & Oboler, Suzanne (eds) (2005) *Neither Enemies Nor Friends: Latinos, Blacks, Afro-Latinos*. New York: Palgrave.

Edwards, Brent Hayes (2001) 'The Uses of Diaspora', *Social Text*, vol. 19, no. 1, pp. 45–73.

Fanon, Frantz (1967) *Black Skin, White Masks*. New York: Grove Press.

Fra-Molinero Baltasar (2005) 'Juan Latino and his Racial Difference' in *Black Africans in Renaissance Europe*, eds Earle, T.F. and Lowe, K.P.J., Cambridge: Cambridge University Press, pp. 326–344.

—— (2004) 'Juan Latino and his Racial Difference'

Franco, José Luciano (1961) *Afroamerica*, La Habana: Junta Nacional de Arqueologia y Antropologia.

Frankenberg, Ruth & Mani, Lata (1993) 'Crosscurrents, Crosstalk: 'Race', Postcoloniality, and the Politics of Location' *Cultural Studies*, vol. 7, no. 2, pp. 292–310.

Gilroy, Paul (1992) 'Cultural Studies and Ethnic Absolutism', in *Cultural Studies*, ed. Gossberg *et al.*, New York: Routledge, pp. 187–199.

—— (1993) *The Black Atlantic: Double Consciousness and Modernity*. Cambridge: Harvard University Press.

Gordon, Lewis (1995) *Fanon and the Crisis of European man: an essay on philosophy and the human sciences*. New York: Routledge.

Grewal, Iderpal & Kaplan, Caren (ed.) (1994) *Scattered Hegemonies: Postmodernity and Transnational Feminist Practices*. Minneapolis: University of Minnesota Press.

Grosfoguel, Ramon (2003) *Colonial Subjects: Puerto Ricans in Global Perspective*. Berkeley: University of California Press.

Grosfoguel, Ramon & Cervantes-Rodriguez, Ana Margarita (2002) *The Modern/Colonial Capitalist World-System in the Twentieth Century: Global Processes, Antisystemic Movements, and the Geo-Politics of Knowledge*. Boulder: Paradigm Press.

Gunning, Sandra, Hunter, Tera W. & Mitchell, Michele (eds) (2004) *Dialogues of Dispersal: Gender, Sexuality, and African Diasporas*. Oxford: Blackwell.

Hall, Stuart (1993) 'Cultural identity and diaspora', in *Colonial Discourse and Post-Colonial Theory*, eds Williams and Chrisman, London: Harvester, pp. 392–403.

—— (1991a) 'Old and New Identities', in *Culture, Globalization, and the World-System*, ed. Anthony D. King, Binghamton: State University of New York Press, pp. 19–40.

—— (1991b) 'The Local and the Global: Globalization and Ethnicity', in *Culture, Globalization, and the World-System*, ed. Anthony D. King, Binghamton: State University of New York Press, pp. 41–68.

Hill Collins, Patricia (2000) *Black Feminist Thought*. New York: Routledge.

Howe, Stephen (1998) *Afrocentrism: Mythical Pasts and Imaged Homes*. London: Verso.

James, Winston (1999) *Holding Aloft the Banner of Ethiopia: Caribbean Radicalism in Early Twentieth America*. New York: Verso.

Jennings, James (ed.) (1994) *Blacks, Latinos, and Asians in Urban America: Status and Prospects for Politics and Activism*. Westport, CT: Praeger.

Kelley D. G., Robin (2003) *Freedom Dreams: The Black Radical Imagination*. Boston: Beacon Press.

Lao-Montes, Agustin (2005) 'Blackening European Modernities/Dis-covering An-Other Europe: Toward a Genealogy of Afro-Hispanic Difference', Presented at Conference of 'Black European Studies', University of Mainz, Germany, November 5–7, 2005.

Lao-Montes, Agustin & Davila, Arlene (ed.) (2001) *Mambo Montage: The Latinization of New York*. New York: Columbia University Press.

Lazarus, Neil (1999) *Nationalism and cultural practice in the postcolonial world*. Cambridge: Cambridge University Press.

Lomnitz, Claudio (2001) *Deep Mexico, Silent Mexico: an anthropology of nationalism*. Minneapolis: University of Minnesota Press.

Lugones, Maria (2003) *Pilgrimages/Peregrinajes: Theorizing Coalition Against Multiple Oppressions*. New York: Rowman & Littlefield.

Maldonado-Torres, Nelson (2006) 'Toward a Critique of Continental Reason: Africana Studies and the Decolonization of Imperial Cartographies in the Americas', in *Not Only the Master's Tools: African-American Studies in Theory and Practice*, eds Gordon Lewis R. and Jane Anna Gordon, Boulder, Colorado: Paradigm Press, pp. 51–84.

Mani, Lata (1990) 'Multiple Mediations: Feminist Scholarship in the Age of Multinacional Reception', *Feminist Review*, vol. 35, Summer, pp. 24–41.

Márquez, Roberto (2000) 'Raza, Racismo, e Historia: Are All of My Bones from There?' *Latino Research Review*, vol. 4, winter, pp. 8–22.

Martinez-Echezabal, Lourdes (1990) *Para una Semiotica de la Mulatez*. Madrid: Ediciones Jose Porrua Turanzas.

McClintock, Anne (1995) *Imperial Leather: Race, Gender, and Sexuality in the Colonial Conquest*. New York: Routledge.

McKittrick, Katherine (2006) *Demonic Grounds: Black Women and the Cartographies of Struggle*. Minneapolis: University of Minnesota Press.

Mercer, Kobena (1988) 'Diaspora, Culture, and the Dialogic Imagination', in *Blackframes: Celebration of Black Cinema*, eds Mbye Cham and Claire Andrade-Watkins. Cambridge: MIT Press, pp. 50–61.

—— (1990) 'Black Art and the Burden of Representation', *Third Text*, vol. 10, spring, pp. 61–78.

Mies, Maria (1998) *Patriarchy and Accumulation on a World Scale: Women in the International Divison of Labor*. London: Zed Press.

Milian Arias, Claudia (2006) 'Playing with the Dark: Africana and Latino Literary Imaginations', in *The Blackwell Companion to Africana Studies*, eds Gordon, Lewis R. and Jane Anna Gordon, Cambridge: Blackwell, pp. 554–567.

Mignolo, Walter (2006) *The Idea of Latin America*. Cambridge: Blackwell.

—— (2000) *Local Histories/Global Designs: Coloniality, Subaltern Knowledges, and Border Thinking*. Princeton: Princeton University Press.

—— (1997) *The Darker Side of the Renaissance: Literacy, Territoriality, and Colonization*. Ann Arbor: University of Michigan Press.

Mishra, Vijay (1994) 'Theorizing the Literature of the Indian Diaspora: The Familiar Temporariness (V.S. Naipaul)'. Paper read at Center for Cultural Studies, University of California at Santa Cruz.

Mohanty, Chandra, Tapalde (2003) *Feminism without Borders: Decolonizing Theory, Practicing Solidarity*. Durham: Duke University Press.

Mohanty, Chandra, Tapalde & Alexander, M. Jacqui (eds) (1996) *Feminist Genealogies, Colonial Legacies, Democratic Futures*. New York: Routledge.

Mohanty, Chandra, Tapalde, Anna Russo & Torres, Lourdes (eds) (1991) *Thirld World Women and the Politics of Feminism*. Indianapolis: Indiana University Press.

Moraga, Cherrie & Anzaldua, Gloria (eds) (1983) *This bridge called my back: radical writings by women of color*. New York: Kitchen Table.

Mudimbe, V. Y. (1988) *The Invention of Africa: Gnosis, Philosophy, and the Order of Knowledge*. Bloomington: University of Indiana Press.

Nassy Brown, Jacqueline (2005) *Dropping Anchor, Setting Sail: Geographies of Race in Black Liverpool*. Princeton: Princeton University Press.

—— (1998) 'Black Liverpool, Black America and the Gendering of Diasporic Space', *Cultutal Anthropology*, vol. 13, no. 3, pp. 291–325.

O'Gorman, Edmundo (1986) *La invencion de America: investigacion acerca de la estructura historica del nuevo mundo y del sentido de su devenir*. Mexico, DF: Fondo de Cultura Economica.

—— (1961) *The Invention of America; an inquiry into the historical nature of the New World and the meaning of its history*. Blooomington: University of Indiana Press.

Ortiz, Fernando (1906) *Hampa Afro-Cubana: Los Negros Brujos*. Madrid: Librería de Fernando Fé.

Patterson, Tiffany Ruby & Kelley, Robin D. G. (2000) 'Unfinished Migrations: Reflections on the African Diaspora and the Making of the Modern World', *African Studies Review*, vol. 43, no. 1, pp. 11–46.

Perez, Emma (1999) *The Decolonial Imaginary: Writing Chicanas into History*. Bloomington: University of Indiana Press.

Piedra, Jose (1991) 'Literary Whiteness and the Afro-Hispanic Difference', in *The Bounds of Race,* ed. Dominick LaCapra, Ithaca: Cornell University Press, pp. 311–343.

Prashad, Vijay (2001) *Everybody was Kung-Fu fighting: Afro-Asian connections and the myth of racial purity*. Boston: Beacon Press.

Pratt, Mary Louise (1992) *Imperial Eyes*. New York: Routledge.

Quijano, Anibal (2000) 'Coloniality of Power, Eurocentrism, and Latin America', *Nepantla*, vol. 1, no. 3, pp. 139–155.

Rabasa, Jose (1993) *Inventing America: Spanish Historiography and the Formation of Eurocentrism*. Norman: Oklahoma University Press.

Radhakrishnan, Rajagopalan (1996) *Diasporic mediations: between home and location*. Minneapolis: University of Minnesota Press.

Robinson, Cedric (2000) *Black Marxism: The Making of a Radical Tradition*. Chapel Hill: University of North Carolina Press.

Saldivar, Jose David (1991) *The Dialectics of Our America. Genealogy, Cultural Critique, and Literary History*. Durham: Duke University Press.

Sánchez González, Lisa (2001) 'Arturo Alfonso Schomburg: A Transamerican Intellectual', in *African Roots/American Cultures: Africa in the Creation of the Americas*, ed. Sheila S. Walker, New York: Rowman & Littlefield.

Sandoval, Chela (2000) *Methodology of the Oppressed*. Minneapolis: University of Minnesota Press.

Santos, Boaventura de Sousa (2005) *Reinventar la Democracia. Reinventar el Estado*. Buenos Aires: CLACSO.

—— (2004) 'El Foro Social Mundial: hacia una globalizacion contra-hegemonica', in *El Foro Social Mundial: Desafiando Imperios*, eds J. Sen, A. Anand, A. Escobar y P. Waterman, Malaga: El Viejo Topo, pp. 330–343.

Sawyer, Mark (2005a) 'DuBois Double Consciousness versus Latin American Exceptionalism: Joe Arroyo, Salsa, and Negritude', *Souls*, vol. 7, nos. 3–4, pp. 85–95.

—— (2005b) 'Framing the Discussion of African American-Latino Relations: A Review and Analysis', in *Neither Enemies Nor Friends: Latinos, Blacks, Afro-Latinos*, eds Anani Dzidzienyo and Suzanne Oboler, New York: Palgrave.

Shohat, Ella and Robert Stam (1994) *Unthinking Eurocentrism: Multiculturalism and the Media*. New York: Routledge.

Singh, Nikhil Pal (2004) *Black is a Country. Race and the unfinished struggle for democracy*. Cambridge: Harvard University Press.

Sinnette, Elinor Des Verney (1989) *Arthur Alfonso Schomburg. Black Bibliophile & Collector*. Detroit: Wayne State University Press and New York Public Library.

Stoler, Anne Laura (2002) *Carnal Knowledge and Imperial Power: Race and the Intimate in Colonial Rule*. Berkeley: University of California Press.

Thomas, Piri (1997) (orig. ed. 1967) *Down These Means Streets*. New York: Vintage.

Vaca, Nicolas C. (2004) *The Presumed Alliance. The unspoken conflict between Latinos and Blacks and what it means for America*. New York: Harper and Rollins.

Wallerstein, Immanuel (1998) *Utopistics: or Historical choices of the twenty-first century*. New York: New Press.

Winant, Howard (2001) *The World is a Ghetto: Race and Democracy since World War II*. New York: Basic Books.

Wittgestein, Ludwig (1968) *Philosophical Investigations*. Oxford: Blackwell.

Wright, Michelle M. (2004) *Becoming Black. Creating Identity in the African Diaspora*. Durham: Duke University Press.

**José David Saldívar**

# UNSETTLING RACE, COLONIALITY, AND CASTE

## Anzaldúa's *Borderlands/La Frontera*, Martinez's *Parrot in the Oven*, and Roy's *The God of Small Things*

> What is termed globalization is the cultural process that began with the constitution of America and colonial/modern Eurocentered capitalism as a new global power.
>
> (Anibal Quijano, 'Coloniality of Power, Eurocentrism, and Latin America')

This comparative essay on Chicano/a and South Asian narratives has a somewhat sweeping character. It is a preliminary attempt to link *pensamiento fronterizo* (border thinking) in Chicano/a Studies and realist interpellations of the subject and the politics of unsettling the coloniality of power on a planetary scale. *Pensamiento fronterizo* emerges from the critical reflections of (undocumented) immigrants, migrants, *bracero/a* workers, refugees, *campesinos*, women, and children on the major structures of dominance and subordination of our times. Thus envisaged, *pensamiento fronterizo* is the name for a new geopolitically located thinking from the borderlands of Americanity and against the new imperialism of the USA.[1] *Pensamiento fronterizo* is a necessary and affiliated tool for thinking about what the Peruvian historical social scientist Aníbal Quijano calls the 'coloniality of power' and identity at the intersections (*los intersticios*) of our local *historias* and the double logics of capitalism and the cultures of US imperialism.[2]

Quijano's coloniality of power, I argue, can help us begin to account for the entangled relations of power between the global division of labor, racial and ethnic hierarchy, identity formation, and Eurocentric epistemologies. Moreover, the coloniality of power can help us trace the continuous forms of hegemonic dominance produced by colonial cultures and structures. As I use it, the coloniality of power is fundamentally a structuring process of identity, experience, and knowledge production articulating geo-strategic locations and subaltern (minor) inscriptions.

My emphasis will be on late twentieth-century postcolonial narratives (Chicano/a and South Asian) and early twenty-first century realist theories about identity, interculturality, and minoritized studies. So I'll begin by discussing three of the most important paradigms of minoritized study as forms of culture which have shared experiences by virtue of their antagonistic relationship to the hegemonic culture, which seeks to marginalize and interpellate them as minor.[3] Then I will examine the issue of border thinking and braided languaging practices in Gloria Anzaldúa's celebrated *Borderlands/La Frontera: The New Mestiza* and Victor Martinez's National Book-Award winning novel *Parrot in the Oven: Mi Vida*. Last, I will speculate on the issue of epistemic privilege and kinship trouble in Arundhati Roy's Booker Prize winning novel *The God of Small Things*.

Why propose a cross-genealogical (US Latino/a and South Asian) treatment of differently structured histories of border and diaspora identity and minoritized writing? I hope this will emerge as I go along, and indeed throughout this special issue of *Cultural Studies* (designed as it is by Walter Mignolo and Lawrence Grossberg to encourage in-depth, cross-cultural comparisons within the matrix of globalization's coloniality of power). But I'll begin by asserting some of the potential meanings and nuances of the minor as they have appeared on the scene of US subaltern studies in the past fifteen years.

## The politics of 'becoming minor'

In a landmark 1987 conference at the University of California, Berkeley, the literary theorists Abdul JanMohamed and David Lloyd called for a radical examination of the 'nature and context of minority discourse'.[4] JanMohamed and Lloyd were specifically interested in rethinking the relationship between a 'minor literature' and the canonical literatures of the majority. Schematically put, Lloyd and JanMohamed's theory and practice of minority discourse involves 'drawing out solidarities in the forms of similarities between modes of repression and struggles that all minorities experience separately but precisely as minorities' (1990, p. 9). Their project of minority discourse fundamentally supplemented Deleuze and Guattari's theorizing of a minor literature – a literature so termed by its 'opposition to those which define canonical writing'. A minor literature entails for them 'the questioning or destruction of the concept of identity and identification . . . and a profound suspicion of narratives of reconciliation and unification' (1990, p. 381). In other words, Lloyd and JanMohamed maintained that a 'minority discourse should neither fall back on ethnicity or gender as an *a priori* essence nor rush into calculating some 'nonhumanist' celebration of diversity for its own sake' (1990, p. 9). While some realists might take issue with Lloyd and JanMohamed's dismissal

of the cognitive work of our identities and their overreliance of the Eurocentric work of Deleuze and Guattari's (their erasure of the cognitive aspects of racialized minority experiences and identities), the political project of minority discourse remains on target: 'Becoming 'minor',' they write, 'is not a question of essence . . . but a question of position: a subject-position that in the final analysis can be defined only in political terms' (1990, p. 9).

My sense of the future of minoritized studies within the context of our globalized coloniality owes much to the theoretical work of my colleagues at Berkeley but it does not quite reproduce the nuances of the way Lloyd and JanMohamed use the term minor (following Deleuze and Guattari's famous study of Kafka).[5] In my own recent cross-genealogical work in Chicano/a and Americanity studies otherwise, on José Martí as a subaltern modernist, on the Cuban *testimonio* of Esteban Montejo and Miguel Barnet, and on 'Greater Mexico's' border modernism of María Amparo Ruiz de Burton and Américo Paredes for example, I have used the terms, subaltern and minor, to cast doubt not so much on our 'narratives of identity' but on the mainline narratives of the major, mainstream, and the hegemonic.[6] My emergent minority studies follows the lead of the Coloniality of Power and Americanity Group (especially Walter Mignolo, Enrique Dussel, and Quijano) and the South Asian Subaltern Group, particularly the work of historian Dipesh Chakrabarty. As Chakrabarty suggests in *Provincializing Europe: Postcolonial Thought and Historical Difference*, '[the minor] describes relationships to the past that the rationality of the [mainstream] historian's methods necessarily makes 'minor' or 'inferior' as something 'irrational' in the course of, and as a result of, its own operation'. The cultural and political work of the subaltern or minoritized historian, in Chakrabarty's words, is to 'try to show how the capacity (of the modern person) to historicize actually depends on his or her ability to participate in nonmodern relationships to the past that are made subordinate in the moment of historicization. History writing assumes plural ways of being in the world' (2000, p. 101).

This brings me to the third and most recent sense of minoritized studies: US minority studies as a comparative 'epistemic project' formulated by Mohanty, Moya, Hames-García, and Martín Alcoff. Against purely skeptical (postmodern and poststructuralist) attitudes toward identity, ethnic studies, and experience, they argue for a strong defense of critical multiculturalism and minority studies based on what they call 'realist' views.[7] (As a shorthand for this realist-inspired group of minority studies, I will focus in what follows on the collective project entitled *Reclaiming Identity*, edited by Paula Moya and Michael Hames-García.)

What Moya and Hames-García have done is to tease out – using Satya Mohanty's realist view of identity – a new way of doing literary, cultural, and comparative ethnic studies in the United States. *Reclaiming Identity* is at the very center of what the authors (after Mohanty) call a 'postpositivist realism',

an engaging method of philosophical, cultural and literary interpretation that situates 'identity' in both a 'radical universalist' and a 'multiculturalist' world view (1997, p. xii). Briefly stated, *Reclaiming Identity* (like Mohanty's *Literary Theory and the Claims of History* [1997] and Moya's *Learning From Experience* [2002]) is a sustained, eloquent, and rich exemplification of this innovative method, practice, and pedagogy. Moya puts their collective project this way: the realist view of identity can provide 'a reconstructed universalist justification for the kind of work being done by . . . ethnic studies scholars', (p. 2) by supporters of multicultural education, as well as for the salience of the identities around which such minoritized programs are organized.

Although the *Reclaiming Identity* project gracefully eschews righteous polemic, the work they are engaged in demonstrates beyond dispute what a critically focused research collective and interdisciplinary project – that is, philosophy, social science theory, and the philosophy of science – can bring to literary studies proper. Indeed, Mohanty ends his erudite *Literary Theory and the Claims of History* by calling for a new kind of literary studies: 'we should go beyond the bounds of a purely text-based literary theory to engage more directly the findings of the various scientific disciplines. . . . [W]e [need] to make serious contact with the growing knowledge about the natural and social world and come to terms with the empirical implications of our claims' (1997, pp. 251–52). Thus envisaged, for Mohanty, Moya and Hames-García literary theory must be a site in which scholars and activists 'examine, debate, and specify the social implications of advances in the natural and social sciences' (1997, p. 252).

Ranging across issues involving philosophy, literature, and social theory, the essayists explore realist accounts of identity and experience by making linkages among social location, experience, epistemic privilege, and cultural identity.[8] All contemplate a world where cultural identity is both socially constructed and substantively real. By attempting to transcend the limits of postmodernism/poststructuralism and essentialism, the authors in *Reclaiming Identity* take seriously that (1) identities are real and (2) that experiences are epistemically crucial. As philosopher Martín Alcoff emphasizes, *Reclaiming Identity* 'is an act of taking back . . . the term realism in order to maintain the epistemic significance of identity' (2000, p. 312).

Because I'm working under some spatial constraints, I will only focus in the remainder of this section on the essays by Mohanty, Moya, Hames-García, and Martín Alcoff. *Reclaiming Identity* blasts off with Mohanty's minoritized philosophical exegesis of Toni Morrison's celebrated novel *Beloved*. 'The community sought' in the novel he argues, 'involves as its essence a moral and imaginative expansion of oneself'. Moreover, Morrison's 'political vision of the oppressed . . . provides the context' in which her characters challenge each others' views 'on the limits of mother-love' in specifically historical, gendered, and ethnoracial terms. Thus envisaged, Morrison's character's perspectives,

Mohanty suggests, are 'not only affective but also epistemic'. By reading Morrison's *Beloved*, many of us are therefore put in the position of characters in the novel, like Paul D, who have inadequate understandings of the social world they live in. Briefly, Morrison teaches us in *Beloved*, among other things, how to read infanticide and the social roles of slave mothers, thereby widening the scope of the moral debates about slavery and the gendered division of labor in the modern world system of capitalism.

Do slave mothers, like Morrison's Sethe, have a 'special knowledge' (2000, p. 236)? Can a realist account of identity spell out the claim that members of a diaspora often have a privileged, albeit sharable knowledge about their social world? What are the valuable implications that the epistemic privilege of the politically oppressed and socially underprivileged people have? These are the major interpretive questions Mohanty grapples with in his essay. If diaspora implicitly refers to an identity, and Morrison elaborates it in narratological and descriptive terms, Mohanty argues persuasively that readers of *Beloved* have been slow to see how Morrison elaborates diasporic identity in unavoidably moral and theoretical terms. Thus instead of seeing Morrison's characters as 'empty signifiers' and therefore dismissing her take on identities on the grounds that they are after all rhetorically constructed and hence 'spurious', Mohanty argues that identities in *Beloved* are not only descriptive and affective but also evaluative and epistemic. Hence, realists need to distinguish between different kinds of constructedness and at the same time see the politics of identities as enmeshed in competing social and ethical-theoretical world views. Last, Mohanty sets the *Reclaiming Identity* project in motion by arguing for a notion of 'epistemic privilege' – that our experiences have real cognitive content and that deconstructive suspicions of experience (Joan Scott [1992] and Jonathan Culler [1982]) are unwarranted.

Building upon Mohanty's realist view of identity and his ideas about epistemic privilege, Moya and Hames-García complement and enlarge the realist view of the project by reading Cherríe Moraga's *Loving in the War Years* and Michael Nava's *The Hidden Law* as contributing to understandings of how the minoritized 'other' can change us, and how issues that challenge identity such as heterogeneity, multiplicity, and hybridity do not have to be seen as separate entities but as 'mutually constitutive'. If Moraga, as Moya suggests, 'understands identities as relational and grounded in the historically produced social categories that constitute social location' (2000, p. 69) and not as trapped in a cyborgian 'signifying function' a la Donna Haraway (1991), Nava's work, Hames-García argues, 'demands that we . . . take seriously the moral implications' of Henry Rios's experiences. For Hames-García, taking Henry's experiences seriously does not make him a 'strategic essentialist' a la Chakravorty Spivak (1988); rather Henry bases his claim on the 'moral sense of his right to participate in a Chicano community on the basis of his cultural upbringing and experience of racialization' (2000, p. 113).

In the book's conclusion, 'Who's Afraid of Identity Politics?' philosopher Martín Alcoff carefully defends the new postpostivist accounts of identity by discussing how approaches to the self developed by Hegel, Freud, Foucault, and Althusser have had on the most important postcontemporary conceptions of identity and subjectification. The answer to the problems of essentialism and anti-essentialism, Martín Alcoff argues, is not political scientist's Wendy Brown's theory of 'wounded attachments' (where the cycle of blame is never transcended) but new, better alternative formulations of identity produced by the essayists in *Reclaiming Identity*.[9] Near her essay's ending, Martín Alcoff writes, 'To say that we have an identity is just to say that we have a location in social space, a hermeneutic horizon that is both grounded in a location and an opening or site from which we attempt to know the world. Understood in this way, it is incoherent to view identities as something we would be better off without' (2000, p. 335).

Given this précis of what I take to be one of the central aims of the *Reclaiming Identity* project, I would like to end this section by raising two issues for further interrogation. The first concerns the issue of identity in relationship to what the historical social scientists Aníbal Quijano and Immanuel Wallerstein call 'Americanity' and what Quijano, Walter Mignolo, Agustín Lao-Montes, Ramón Grosfoguel, and others are calling 'the coloniality of power'.[10]

In their essay, 'Americanity as a concept, or the Americas in the modern world-system' (1992), Quijano and Wallerstein argue that the Americas were fundamental to the formation of the modern (colonial) world-system, and that Americanity is a fundamental element of modernity. For our purposes, Quijano and Wallerstein identify four new categories that originated in the so-called discovery of the Americas. They are: coloniality, ethnicity, racism, and the concept of newness itself. My first hesitation with the *Reclaiming Identity* project thus has to do with the way most of the contributors are generally silent about our identities in relationship to what Quijano and Wallerstein are grappling with in their work, namely, coloniality.

In other words, if Mohanty, Moya, Hames-García, and Martín-Alcoff are right that to have an identity means that we have to understand that 'we have a location in social space', wouldn't it be useful for us to ground these identities and locations in the history of the modern (colonial) world-system? Quijano and Wallerstein remind us that after all coloniality created a structure of hierarchy and drew new boundaries around and within the Americas. Moreover, coloniality was also essential to the formation of states, and Quijano in his more recent work such as 'Coloniality of Power, Eurocentrism, and Latin America' makes the additional claim that even in decolonization the stateness of decolonized states recentered the colonial structure of power. 'What is termed globalization', Quijano writes, 'is the cultural process that began with the constitution of America and colonial/modern Eurocentered

capitalism as a new global power. One of the fundamental axes of power is the social classification of the world's population around the idea of race, a mental construction that expresses the basic experience of colonial domination and pervades the more important dimensions of global power, including its rationality. The racial axis has a colonial origin and character, but it has proven to be more durable and stable than colonialism in whose matrix it was established. Therefore the model of power that is globally hegemonic today presupposes an element of coloniality' (2000, p. 533).

For Quijano and Wallerstein, ethnic identity fundamentally is 'the set of communal boundaries into which in part we are put by others [through coloniality], in part which we impose upon ourselves, serving to locate our *identity* and our rank within the state. . . . [Ethnic identities] are always contemporary constructs, and thus always changing. All the major categories, however, into which we ethnically divide today in the Americas and the world (Native Americans or Indians, Blacks or Negroes, Whites or Creoles/ Europeans, *Mestizos* or other names given to a so-called mixed-category) – all these categories did not exist prior to the modern world-system. They are part of what makes up Americanity. They have become the cultural staple of the entire world-system' (my emphasis, 1992, p. 550).

If our identities are real and affective, they do come from somewhere. Any postcontemporary account of subjectification (Butler, Laclau, Zizek [2000]) and any postpostivist realist account of identity (Mohanty, Moya, and Hames-García), I believe, would have to grapple with the 'colonial difference' that Quijano and Wallerstein, among others, are outlining for us. Perhaps to get back to Martín Alcoff's concluding riffs on the realist view of identity that is why it might not be so dizzying for some to view identities as something we might be better off without. Michel Foucault, for instance, noted in 'The Subject and Power' that the point is 'not to discover what we are but to refuse what we are' (1982, p. 212). But here, too, I'd stress that Foucault tends, especially in *The History of Sexuality*, to erase the crafty details of the colonial difference in his analysis of biopower. On the whole, however, I'm in strong agreement with Martín Alcoff's point about the political power of our identities. In our informational culture and society, our identities, Berkeley sociologist Manuel Castells insists in *The Power of Identity*, are crucial and important because 'they build interests, values, and projects, around experience, and refuse to dissolve by establishing a specific connection between nature, history, geography, and culture'. Identities, Castells concludes (in Marxist realist fashion), 'anchor power in some areas of the social structure, and build their resistance or their offensives in the informational struggle about the cultural codes constructing behavior and, thus, new institutions' (1997, p. 361). And it is this new subject or identity project of the informational mode of production, I believe, that many 'straight' marxists have refused to grapple with in their engagement with the powers of identity politics.

This issue of 'coloniality' then leads to another hesitation I have with the rich *Reclaiming Identity* project of Mohanty, Moya, and Hames-Garcia. In his recent book, *Local Histories/Global Designs* (2000), Mignolo draws on the social scientific work of Quijano and Wallerstein to criticize various recent desires for universalist theories among both neo-liberals and neo-marxists. Mignolo argues that parallel to the ethno-racialized classification of the Americas and the world (the embalming of identities) the colonial project in the Americas also classified languages and knowledges. The epistemology of the European Renaissance was, therefore, assumed to be the natural perspective for which knowledges could be described and suppressed. This same process, Mignolo suggests, was resituated after the Enlightenment, when the concept of reason opened up a new description and reason became associated with northern Europe and indirectly with whiteness (Hegel and Kant).

What are we to make of Mohanty and Moya's use of an apparently idealist Kantian 'universalism' in their postpostivist realist project? Shouldn't a realist view of identity severely criticize the abstract hegemonic universalisms in Kant and the Enlightenment? Is it possible to imagine an 'epistemic diversality or pluriversality', as Mignolo (drawing on the work of Glissant) suggests in his work on Zapatismo? For Mignolo, diversality is not 'the rejection of universal claims, but the rejection of universality understood as an abstract universal grounded in a monologic'. Further, he writes, a 'universal principle grounded on the idea of the di-versal is not a contradiction in terms but rather a displacement of conceptual structures' ('Zapatistas' Theoretical Revolution', 2002).

As an alternative to the Kantian universalism in Mohanty and Moya's post-positivist realist project, I propose that Gloria Anzaldúa, Victor Martinez, and Arundhati Roy's imaginative works belong to a 'diversalist' cross-genealogical field that I term (after Quijano) the coloniality of border and diaspora power. Coloniality, because of the many structural and ethno-racial similarities about identity formations binding them to a colonizing past. But border and diaspora power because there are certainly many discontinuities: – the outernational dimension of represented space – to dictate the cognitive metaphor of the 'world-system' text, which recalls as I have been suggesting the world political economy of Wallerstein and Quijano.

The category of the coloniality of power is not, of course, without its defects. But it has fewer than others, as well as having some local and global additional advantages. So let the coloniality of power be taken in my essay for what it is: a hypothesis designed to grapple with hierarchy based on what Quijano terms the 'social classification of the world's population around the idea of race'. The racial axis of *mestizaje* in Anzaldúa's *Borderlands/La Frontera*, of peasants in Martinez's poem, 'Shoes', and of caste in Roy's *The God of Small Things* have colonial origins in the Américas and South Asia, but Anzaldúa, Martinez, and Roy suggest that race, peasantry, and caste have proven to be more durable in our so-called postcolonial world.

By cobbling together Quijano's subalternist concept of the coloniality of power and Wallerstein's modern world-system, we can argue that the coloniality of power has survived in the Americas and South Asia (the Portuguese brought with them to India the idea of caste) for over 500 years and yet they have not come to be transformed into a world empire. The secret strength of the coloniality of power and the world system is the political side of economic organization called capitalism. Capitalism, Wallerstein astutely argues, has flourished precisely because the world-economy 'has had within its bounds not one but a multiplicity of political systems' (1974, p. 348).

## The borderlands of Chicano/a narrative and subaltern studies

Over the past decade an awareness has begun to develop of the affinities between the imaginative work of recent Chicano/a imaginative writers and the thought of US migratory postcolonial thinkers. Indeed, what is remarkable is that it should have taken so long for the interlocking of concerns between Chicano/a writers and postcolonial thinkers to be properly appreciated. Among the most prominent of such common concerns are: the location of knowledge from the perspective of the US empire's borderland contact zones; the critique of Occidentalist dominant perspectives in the current practices of US social sciences, humanities, and area studies; and the grappling with localized geopolitics of knowledge and what the theorist Mignolo calls 'border epistemologies'.[11] Furthermore, these affinities have not only been observed by scholars from the South (Latin America and South Asia) for example, but also are becoming part of the self-consciousness in what Gayatri Chakravorty Spivak has called the 'emerging dominant' (1995, p. 179) in American Studies.

This section is a study of the interplay between the performative, border epistemologies of two Chicano/a imaginative writers and the changing discourses of American vernacular literatures and cultures. Gloria Anzaldúa and Victor Martinez's writings about US Latino/a life explore, among other things, the linguistic intermixture of ethnic and mainstream languages (English, Spanish, and Spanglish) to illustrate the changing languages of America. What vernacular varieties of English or Spanish will dominate in twenty-first century America? Which *lingua rustica* will the some thirty million US Latinos/as (with over 10 million in California) hegemonize in their *testimonios*, novels, essays, and poetry? What new literary genres, produced by Chicanos/as, will emerge in American literature? If the 'dialect novel' was all the rage in late nineteenth century vernacular America[12] (Twain, Cable, Cahan, Du Bois), is there a borderlands English or Spanglish already underway in US Latino/a dominant California, Arizona, Florida, Texas, Illinois, and New York? On another level, I want to investigate the enabling condition of some recent Chicano/a narrative and poetry and the various ways in which they seek to create an

epistemological ground upon which versions of the world may be produced. As many US Latino/a writers themselves suggest, to read is to question and to understand the (bilingual) texture and the rhetorical resources of language. If Anzaldúa sees the aesthetic structure of knowledge as a form of *nepantilism*, a Mexica word signifying cultural in-betweenness, Martinez sees minority writing as a form of the California borderlands of subaltern studies informing mass youth US Latino/a culture.[13]

To begin, I will juxtapose Gloria Anzaldúa's key concept of US-Mexico border *nepantilism* (1987) against US historian Frederick Jackson Turner's well-known nineteenth century idea of the frontier. I do so to emphasize that while Turner and Anzaldúa may share some affinities of narrative and subaltern conventions and self-locations in the United States – each writer locates their stories in a tradition of border historiography – their contrasts, I think, run far deeper, for Turner's paradigms of the 'frontier' and Anzaldúa's *frontera* are not equivalent.

One of the most imperial images of the American West, Turner's so-called frontier thesis helped shape the study of Americanization both domestically, and after the War of 1898, globally. US historian William Cronin suggests that 'few historical arguments [about the significance of the frontier in American history] have risen so high and fallen so far in [US] scholarly reception' (1995, p. 692). In a more recent overview, US historian Kerwin Klein put Turner's significance this way: he 'introduced a new vocabulary into history by using old words in a new way, borrowing terms from other disciplines, and mixing these elements' (1997, p. 13). In other words, Turner had flair and a gift for mixing what social scientists call 'nomothetic' and 'idiographic' epistemologies and discourses.

Turner famously opens his 1893 essay by quoting from the 1890s census report that described empirically the disappearance of the frontier. Moreover, in a nomothetic vein, Turner theorized that US modernity and modernization were caused by the frontier, for 'free land and its continuous recession and the advance of American settlement westward, explain American development' (1920, p. 1). By emphasizing the movement westward, Northeastern, Euro-Americans not only encountered peoples and cultures 'less civilized' than they had experienced, but through this very contact, Turner argued, they had left behind their old world civilization and invented a new, North American one.

As Klein suggests, Turner's essay 'narrates a dramatic struggle between past and present'. Turner's compositional mode of emplotment rolls out from East to West; from the Puritan's errand into the wilderness to the Gilded Age's San Francisco. If Turner starts off quoting social scientific data (census reports), he quickly moves his essay into the mythos of romance. His invocations of the colonial frontier heroes (Daniel Boone, Andrew Jackson, and Abraham Lincoln) are, as Klein notes, perfect 'synecdoches for the American frontier spirit' (1997, p. 183).

All of the familiar themes of the US cultures of imperialism are cobbled together here in Turner's 'The Significance of the Frontier in American History' – the advancing of the frontier, the free land, or the nineteenth century's equivalent of the twentieth century US food stamp program, and the conquering of and the errand into the wilderness. Throughout Turner is gracefully straightforward: 'the frontier prompted the formation of a composite nationality for the American people' (1920, 40). And one of my favorite lines in the essay reveals Turner's poetic flair: 'In the crucible of the frontier, the immigrants were Americanized, liberated, and fused into one mixed race, English in neither nationality nor characteristics'(1920, p. 40).

If Klein sees Turner's essay moving in the direction of an Emersonian and Hegelian universalism, other US historians such as Richard White locate Turner's essay as part of an emerging incantatory imperialism. By strategically using a frontier iconography in his essay – log cabins, covered wagons, canoes, and the like – Turner argued for a Jeffersonian 'empire for liberty', surely one of our most interesting nationalist oxymorons for the cultures of US imperialism (White 1994). And like White, US Latino historian George Sánchez, too, chastises Turner for constructing 'a myopic vision' in his frontier essay – 'that of the East looking West, civilization looking toward chaos, Europe looking toward the rest of the world' (1993, p. 38). Conversely, against Turner's hegemonic vision, Sánchez suggests that the concept of the transnational *frontera* developed in postcolonial Chicano/a studies works against Turner's myopic imperialism. The transnational *frontera*, he argues, suggests 'limitations, boundaries over which American power might have little or no control. It implies a dual vision, that of two nations looking at each other over a strip of land they hold in common (1993, p. 38). US Latino/a border thinking, therefore, enacts a powerful contrapuntal corrective for mainline American studies.

In thinking about the emplotments of Turner's frontier essay and Anzaldúa's *frontera* thinking in *Borderlands/La Frontera*, it might be productive to consider what historian James Clifford has noted about the diaspora emplotments of Paul Gilroy's postcolonial *There Ain't No Black in the Union Jack:The Cultural Politics of Race and Nation* (1987). Diaspora cultures, Clifford writes, are 'produced by regimes of political domination and economic inequality'. These cultures, moreover, 'cannot claim an oppositional or primary purity. Fundamentally ambivalent, they grapple with the entanglement of subversion and the law, of invention and subversion – the complicity of dystopia and utopia' (1997, p. 265).

Does Anzadúa's Chicana paradigm of the US-Mexico borderlands share in expressing diaspora culture's dystopic-utopian tensions? Is there both bad news and good news built into the text? Can Anzaldúa's recodification of the utopian otherwise as *nepantilism* help us better ground or grapple with the tensions and ambivalences that Clifford theorizes in his reading of the work of Gilroy? What

are we to make of Anzaldúa's deportation stories, of her invocation of the US-Mexico War of 1846–48, of the post Jim Crow ethnoracial hierarchies in South Texas, of the international division of labor with undocumented women at the center of the *maquiladoras*, and of her dramatic swerve to Mexica *nepantilism* and new mestiza consciousness in *Borderlands/La Frontera*?

Border gnosis or border thinking, for Anzaldúa, is a site of criss-crossed experience, language, and identity. Mignolo's postcolonial reading of Anzaldúa is especially helpful in this context. She draws, Mignolo insists, 'a different map: that of reverse migration, the migration from colonial territories relabeled the Third World (after 1945), toward the First' (2000, 237). And this reverse US Latino/a migratoriness, in Mignolo's view, helps explain Anzaldúa's powerful 'languaging practices' which 'fracture the colonial language' (2000, p, 237).

If Anzaldúa's *Borderlands/La frontera* thematizes not the hegemonic Hegelian-Emersonian universalism of Turner's frontier thesis, but the epistemic diversal reason of Greater Mexico's local *nepantilism's* multiple broken tongues, 'such fractures', Mignolo argues, 'occur due to the languaging practices of two displaced linguistic communities' in Anzaldúa's work: 'Nahuatl, displaced by the Spanish expansion and Spanish displaced by the increasing hegemony of the colonial languages of the modern period (English, German, and French') (2000, p. 237).

This fracturing and braiding of colonial and postcolonial languages explains why Anzaldúa's *Borderlands/La Frontera* has the power to elicit such critical emphasis from Mignolo, one of the most innovative US Latino critics of postcolonial literatures of the Americas. Reading Anzaldúa as a Chicana feminist philosopher of fractured and braided languages is precisely what I want to address below as both one of the major postcolonial issues in *Borderlands/La Frontera* and indeed for US Latino/a studies in particular, and for the futures of minority studies in general.

Rather than a unified subject, representing a folk border culture in any holistic sense, we meet in Anzalduá's Chicana neologism, *autohistoriateoría,*[14] a braided, mestiza consciousness, and a feminist writer fundamentally caught between various hegemonic colonial and postcolonial languages and subaltern dialects, and vernacular expressions. Her lament that 'wild tongues' such as her own 'can not be tamed' for 'they can only be cut out' (1987, p. 76) might as well be addressed to Anzaldúa's complex postcolonial audience of radical women and (feminist) men of color. Throughout *Borderlands/La Frontera*, Anzaldúa expresses regret that even her bilingual mother in Hargill, has been partially complicit in valuing the English language of the hegemonic: 'I want you to speak English. Pa' hallar buen trabajo tienes que saber hablar el inglés bien. Que vale toda tu educación si todavía hablas inglés con un 'accent', my mother would say, mortified that I spoke English like a Mexican. At Pan

American University, I, and all Chicano students were required to take two speech classes. Their purpose: to get rid of our accents'(1987, p. 76).

In *Borderlands/La Frontera*, Anzaldúa not only self-consciously speaks English with an 'accent', she also writes in multiply accented, vernacular tongues. Read with its marked accentuation, Anzaldúa's work can be reinterpreted as expressing a late North American situation of multidialectism. Her negative dialectical answers to her earlier meditations that she will not 'tame a wild tongue', or 'train it to be quiet', or 'make it lie down' (1987, p. 76) are her feminist philosophical dictums of border language and thinking. At the very heart of Anzaldúa's Chicana feminist *autohistoriateoría* is her claim that a braided 'tongue' is centrally and dramatically at war with colonialism, US Empire, patriarchy, and androcentrism's project to silence women: 'Ser habladora was to be a gossip or a liar' (1987, p. 76).

Anzaldúa's response to being preoccupied with 'the unique positioning consciousness takes at these confluent streams'(1987, p. i) is apprehended linguistically in the text in the juxtaposition of multiple dialects or tongues – Tex Mex, *caló*, *choteo*, Spanish and English – with their dominant and subaltern varieties. Moreover, this linguistic juxtaposition allows us to see Anzaldúa's attempts to reflect post-Jim Crow ethnoracial practices in South Texas as well as attempts at *nepantilism* – however incomplete – to merge, transculturate, and braid different ethnoracial formations and languages in a single text. As she puts it, she struggles with an 'almost instinctive urge to communicate, to speak, to write about life on the borders, life in the shadows' (1987, p. i). In this regard, Anzaldúa's *conciencia de la nueva mestiza* seems to be a respectful and gendered updating of W. E. B. Du Bois's famous early twentieth century insights in *The Soul of Black* Folks (1903) about the cross-linguistic foundations of double consciousness and the shadows of the color line:

> One ever feels a two-ness, an American, a Negro; two souls, two thoughts, two unreconciled strivings; two warring ideals in one dark body, whose dogged strength alone keeps it from being torn asunder. The history of the Negro is the history of this strife . . . ,to merge his double self into a better and truer self. In this merging he wishes neither of the older selves to be lost. . . . He would not bleach his Negro soul in a flood of *white Americanism*, for he knows that Negro blood has a *message* for the world.
>
> (1986, pp. 364–365, my emphasis).

My point is that Anzaldúa, like Du Bois, sees her braided Chicana consciousness as a fractured, cracked, and braided construction, an effort to merge new cultural formations and ethnoracial subjectivities. Like Du Bois, she, too, highlights the inherent US linguistic wars both inside the body of the

nation and in the body of her soul, for like the US-Mexico border itself, it is 'an open wound, dividing a *pueblo*, a culture,/running down the length of my body,/[it] splits me, splits me/ me raja, me raja'( 1987, p. 24). Both Du Bois and Anzaldúa call for new ethnic, linguistic, and cultural exchanges between the South and the North. If, for Du Bois at the beginning of the twentieth century blackness and whiteness were inextricably woven together, then, for Anzaldúa at the century's end Chicana, Latina, African American, and Euro-American vernacular English and Spanish have been knitted together into what Du Bois called 'the very warp and woof of this nation'. This 'colonial difference' is crucial to emphasize for those of us tracking Chicano/a studies' shifting and shifty cross-genealogy from the matrix of globalization's coloniality.

In arguing for the centrality of human language rights in Anzaldúa's *Borderlands/La Frontera*, I mean to support Mignolo's critical, subaltern, US Latino/a, postcolonial evaluations of Anzaldúa's 'border *gnosis*' without losing sight of the importance of the author's multiple renaming processes and her radical recodifications of womanhood. As Chicana feminist scholars such as Norma Alarcón, Chela Sandoval, Yvonne Yarbro-Bejarano, Angie Chabram-Dernersesian, Sonia Saldívar-Hull, and Paula Moya have all rigorously and gracefully argued, *Borderlands/La Frontera* is fundamentally a Chicana feminist text; a first-rate *historia* of post-Jim Crow South Texas; a jolting new positioning of the native woman in Chicana Studies; a terrific study in comparative whiteness and brownness; and post-postivist realist call for identity and social justice.[15] Yet what is perhaps an equally powerful feature of Anzaldúa's text has also been one of its least analyzed – Anzaldúa's discussion of *nepantilism* as a braided, US Latino/a linguistic consciousness. *La conciencia de la nueva mestiza*, for Anzaldúa, is 'neither español ni inglés, but both'. It is a consciousness of *nepantla*, a Mexica term, signifying in betweeness, and which is 'capable of communicating the real values' of the US-Mexico borderlands to others (1987, p. 77).

In arguing for the centrality of her 'forked', 'wild', and active feminist tongues, Anzaldúa emphasizes that these tongues are informed with other, border-crossing tongues: 'los recién llegados, Mexican immigrants, north from Mexico', and the older tongues of the 'braceros' (p. 78). And to these vernacular tongues, she merges her Tex-Mex dialects that she uses with her brothers and sisters and the 'secret language of *pachuco*, a language of rebellion' (p. 78) in order to create a foundational consciousness of the new mestiza.

Read against recent legal attempts in California and Florida (states with large US Latino/a populations) to force an English-only linguistic absolutism, Anzaldúa's *Borderlands/La Frontera* offers readers a dialect centered anti-absolutism, for there 'is no one Chicano language just as there is no one Chicano experience'(1987, p. 80). In her own testimonial theorization of

experience, when in high school she was 'encouraged to take French classes because French [was] considered more 'cultured',' she ends by noting that 'Spanish speakers will comprise [by 2005] the biggest [minority] group in the USA' (1987, p. 81). However, she also argues that by the end of the twentieth-century, a braided 'Chicana/o' English 'will be the mother tongue of most' (1987, p. 81) Chicanas/os.

If I have focused on what may seem one of many issues, what Anzaldúa terms the practices and resistances of 'tam [ing] a wild tongue', my goal has been to highlight various things at once: to agree with Anzaldúa's insistence on the centrality of *nepantilism* as a minoritized and postcolonial linguistic project; and to explore *nepantilism* as the author's attempt to merging multiple subaltern and vernacular 'serpent tongues – my woman's voice, my sexual voice, my poet's voice' (p. 81).

The souls of the outernational new mestizas, Anzaldúa argues, have 'nothing to do with which country one lives in'. They are 'neither eagle or serpent, but both' (p. 85). It is precisely this going beyond the two-ness of national consciousness that Anzaldúa aspires to in *Borderlands/La Frontera*. If US literary historian Gavin Jones is right that at the heart of nineteenth century American literature was what he calls 'the cult of the vernacular' with real 'political and cultural functions', (1999) Anzaldúa's *autohistoriateoría* grounds her late twentieth century work in the differential vernacular serpent's tongue, a catechristic subalternist tongue which is capable of cracking, fracturing, and braiding the very authority of the master's English-only tongue.

This awareness of an interstitial in-betweenness empowers revisionist Chicano/a narratives and transmodernist poetry. Victor Martinez's *Parrot in the Oven: Mi Vida* (1996) is a splendid case in point. To better locate Martinez's double-voiced, vernacular novel, I will begin by exploring a poem the author wrote entitled 'Shoes' (1992), an everyday symbol that reappears in the novel about gangs, *klikas*, and youth cultures in California:

> Out of all of our enemies, all the catastrophes of nations
> scattered to rubble, plowed over with salt, we still have
> the warm friendliness, the unrelenting spirit
> of our shoes to console us.
> Two bubbles chopped square out of shapeless emptiness
> how this invention hisses in a hurry to correct time
> pumping little sneezes of sympathy for our tardiness.
> Although they owe us nothing, they walk
> in many of our dreams, conjuring music
> from a vaporous sidewalk or standing
> as pure reverence
> over the peaceful herds of our dead.
> They, who always return back to us faithfully

from every tropic, every desert,
to take us their jobs as stealth for the burglar,
spring under the killer's crouch, courage
for the guerrilla. They guard us
against thistles and thorns, protect us from stone
and unseen disasters of glass.
Wheels mean nothing to the shoe. They are the first
of peasants and would never think to kneel
before any god, or suck up to whatever tablet of the Law.
Ravenous for distance, they supply whole lives
with the loss of a mere heel
yet wear death, only once.

(1992, p. 12)

'Shoes', for Martinez, allows him to represent everyday things in the world, especially what he describes lyrically as 'the unrelenting spirit of our shoes' and how they often function 'to console us'. A flood of questions appears on the screen of transmodernist US 'border thinking': from what, specifically, do Martinez's shoes console us? From the 'elements of San Joaquin'; from the pesticides of California agribusiness? From the worldiness of the documented and undocumented farm worker world? From the *nepantilism* of our dwellings, the unhomeliness of mass, youth culture?

On an intertextual and transcultural frame of reference, Martinez's poem, 'Shoes', positions itself to comment audaciously on discussions of modernity and aesthetics, and by specifically alluding to such discussions embedded in Vincent Van Gogh's painting 'A Pair of Boots'. Why is Martinez interested in the debates surrounding modernist art? Does his poem grasp the structural and socially symbolic meanings of peasant 'shoes', and farmworker' boots'? In his landmark book, *Postmodernism, Or the Logic of Late Capitalism*, Fredric Jameson argues that Van Gogh's painting unleashes the 'whole object of agricultural misery, of stark rural poverty'(1991, p. 7). As an experienced former farm wage worker himself, Martinez's poem thematizes 'epistemic privilege' for the poem apprehends the brutalizing world of Agribusiness growers and their tussle with the wage earners, wage earners who, after 1965, were able to organize themselves through Cesar Chavez's United Farm Workers Committee.

If, as Jameson suggests, Van Gogh's painting can only evoke the peasants' alienation of labor, who are themselves literally worn down like a pair of boots, the modernist painter can only represent this through his 'hallucinatory surface of color' (p. 7) sometimes, 'garishly overlaid with hues of red and green' (p. 7). In other words, Van Gogh's 'A Pair of Boots', like Martinez's California farm worker poem 'Shoes', embodies deep dystopian and utopian tensions and ambivalences that we earlier saw in Gilroy's and Anzaldúa's narratives of the US-Mexico borderlands and the Black Atlantic diaspora. I am

even tempted to argue, after Jameson, that both Martinez and Van Gogh's works of art can be rewritten 'acts of compensation which end up producing a new Utopian realm of the senses' (p. 7) – especially, through the visual in Van Gogh's painting and the figurative, tropological in Martinez's writing.

In this way, Martinez suggests, 'shoes' always return to us, they form the very in-betweenness in our post-bracero, North-South global division of labor in California. On another level, if as Martin Heidegger once put it, Van Gogh's 'A Pair of Boots'vibrates the silent call of the earth . . . its enigmatic self-refusal in the fallow desolation of the wintry field', (qtd. in Jameson, p. 8), Martinez's 'Shoes' is his attempt to represent the very Heideggerian-like 'equipment' necessary for migrant farm workers in California to make do: 'They are', Martinez writes, 'the first/ of peasants and would never think to kneel/before any God, or suck up to whatever tablets of the Law'.

Before we move on to a reading of *Parrot in the Oven*, I want to underline Martinez's use of the word, 'peasant' in his poem. What is the poet trying to link up in his meditation of Mexican American farmworkers and peasants? Is Martinez, like the South Asian subaltern historians, trying to democratize US poetry by looking on subordinate social groups – farmworkers and *campesinos* – as the makers of their own minoritized destiny? My own sense is that by his looking at farmworker/*campesino* shoes, Martinez is attempting to stretch the very category of the political far beyond the borders assigned to them in European and American political thought. Farmworkers are not pre-political or pre-modern in any senses of the terms. Like Ranajit Guha (1988, 1997) before him, Martinez insists that farmworkers are real contemporaries of the coloniality of power in the modern Americas (not pre-modern or primitive rebels) and that they are a fundamental part of the modernity that coloniality brought to the Americas some five hundred years earlier.

Let's now turn to Martinez's *Parrot in the Oven: Mi Vida* (initially marketed by its New York publishers as a young adult novel) and contrapuntally read this young adult novel against his apparently more mature, modern, adult, philosophical poem, 'Shoes'? Do these works by Martinez have anything in common? Do they inform each other and help us do away with false dichotomies such as 'young adult' and 'adult' literature classifications? Why do mainline US publishers insist on infantilizing US Latino/a writers? Can a minoritized reading based on US Latino/a mass youth culture help us better ground Martinez's epistemological obsession with the gaps between the farm worker's earth and a post-developed California world? My firm sense is that Martinez's novel opens up fresh vistas on the relationship between mass culture and the social by transforming radically the genre of the so-called young adult novel itself.

If this emergent genre, like children's literature, is marginalized in the institutions of the academy, Martinez cross-cuts this subalternized form by focusing precisely on the ethnoracialized subalterns in California – especially,

the young *vatos firmes*, the Klikas, youth gangs, and their ritual initiations, what the Chicano hip pop artist Frost describes as the poetics of 'las chavas, las balas, and the Chevy Impalas' (1992). If historian Robin Kelley is right that 'most rap music is not about a nihilistic street life but about rocking the mike' (1997, p. 37), Martinez's *Parrot in the Oven: Mi Vida* takes it inventive linguistic lessons from the very youth culture it explores. What counts for Martinez is not just the Hernandez tussles in the barrio but the wild storytelling riffs and figures of speech of the young Chicano/a characters – especially Manny's ability to make comparisons in his world, his often hilarious facility to see likenesses between unlike things, what Kelley argues is fundamental to most urban rap music',the ability to kick some serious . . . linguistic inventiveness' (p. 37). This is what Martinez's rich *Parrot in the Oven* is fundamentally 'about'.

Like Martinez's 'Shoes', we can discern or discover the hermeneutical horizon of at least two levels or symptoms of reading. To begin with, *Parrot in the Oven* focuses on Manny Hernandez, a young homey from the barrio projects, who is determined to discover for himself what it means (existentially and cognitively) to be a *vato firme* – a guy to respect. This theme, the development or the education of the male hero's coming of age, is the *bildung* of the young adult novel. Moreover, Martinez continually meditates on the related spaces of home and leisure, and a la Paul Gilory and Robin Kelley, he sees the male body not only as an instrument of labor but also of pleasure. And, Manny, as we will see below, draws lots of pleasure through his intense labor of producing whirling figurative play.

As we begin reading *Parrot in the Oven* Manny lives in the barrio hood, somewhere in the projects of Sal Si Puedes, and attends the San Joaquin Valley's J. Edgar Hoover High. Like the farm workers in 'Shoes', he has to make do and has to grapple with his working class family life – an alcoholic father, Manny Sr., an abused, mother, Rebecca, who daily puts on a pair of worn out boots and mops the barrio casita's floors, and his brothers and sisters. Manny comes of age here in Sal Si Puedes in a poetic series of fast-paced chapter-vignettes. Stylistically and rhetorically, Martinez maintains the specificity of his setting and mass youth characterization through his artful everyday vernacular dialogues, and through intense language, what we earlier discussed as his startling elegant poetic imagery in 'Shoes'. Some of my favorite tropes include the following from Manny's consciousness:

> 'He could duck trouble better than a champion boxer could duck a right cross'. (p. 3)
> Dad is always 'cursing', 'simmering', and 'ready to boil over' (p. 5).
> Migrant farm workers are like 'whirlwinds' (p. 13).
> 'She was just trying to blossom herself up' (p. 59).
> 'I had a face Dad said would look handsome on a horse' (p. 80).
> 'She worked hard for beauty, teasing her hair as an ocean wave' (p. 92).

> 'Her shadow will be erased, and her soul will drift to heaven likea fluff of a dandelion in the wind. And then it will blossom in another garden, so bright the colors will hurt your eyes' (p. 89).

Against the tussles of everyday misery in Manny's barrio life, the world opens up its worldliness, through Martinez's poetic transpositions and metaphoric exchanges.

If Martinez's narrative focuses on the underside of the Hernandez family romance, *Parrot in the Oven* never lacks for compassion. Throughout, Manny wonders how his sisters and mother 'were able to stand it' (p. 12). Incredulously perhaps, Manny even makes fun of the profound alienation and pain of his father's abusive patriarchy by saying to himself 'deep down Dad liked me'. This has to be read contrapuntally, I suppose, against all the hard smacks given to him by his father. For even the title of the novel, *Parrot in the Oven: Mi Vida*, evokes a male folk patriarchal bruising: 'Perico, or parrot, was what Dad called me sometimes. It was from a Mexican saying about a parrot that complains how hot it is in the shade, while all along he's sitting inside an oven. People usually say this when talking about ignorant people who don't know where they're at in the world' (pp. 51–52), In other words, Manny's dad thinks his son is a *pendejo*, pure and simple.

Manny, the young adult novel protagonist, however, survives and even triumphs over his father's awkward love, California's under-endowed ugly, Proposition 13 public schools, and countless barrio feuds by working himself through a final climactic gang initiation beating – he is punched and whacked with storms of claps, kicks, and bites. When it is over, Manny's young body swells all over and Martinez writes: 'I could smell the acidy stink of the dirt, but strangely enough, there was no fear. Nor could I feel those blows, which felt instead like instead of me, they were hitting a slab of meat on a table

> . . . When they finally let me up, I sat there . . . swelling fast, flaring alive with throbs' (p. 194).

Martinez's *Parrot in the Oven* ends by thinking not only about the body's pains and pleasures from the 'sonic' forces surrounding it, but also by narrating the cholo body's place, pursuing barrio spaces into some of its jolting corners and subtle surfaces. For Martinez, place is intriguing, valuable, pleasurable, and indispensable. Here at the novel's end, Manny forces us to face place, to confront it, and take off its masks:

> When I opened the door to our house, the sun, out again, came rushing into the living room. Shadows lifted from the floor like a flock of birds rising into the horizon, and light guttered through the room, slapping away the dark for good . . . Magda and Pedi were lying asleep . . . Magda's hair was fanned out on a pillow, unteased. . . . Then I sat down on Dad's

cushioned chair and watched them . . . and the room . . . And it was a wondrous place . . . My home. The light in the room was closing in around me.

(pp. 214–215)

## Declaring oneself a 'Mobile Republic': South Asian kinship and identity

In concluding this essay, I want to stay with the thematizations of minoritized identities and the coloniality matrix of power I outlined in a broad trans-Americanity mapping of sorts, and examine briefly how postcontemporary South Asian writings in English of the memories of violence and identity may also help us think through the 'colonial difference' in a more global framework. I do not approach this question as a specialist in the history of the English novel in India. My relation to a globalized matrix of power is clearly at an early stage of thinking. However, what I have found in my preliminary readings of some of the most important English novels in India is this: at the center of many English novels in India are the histories and memories of violence and the coloniality of power – how humans produce absolutist others out of others. In this sense, narratives of the violence of colonialism in the English novel in India – Salman Rushdie's *Midnight's Children* or Amitav Ghosh's recent *The Hungry Tide*, for example – are also narratological studies of the politics of identity and the colonial difference. What animates many South Asian novels in English of the memories of violence of British coloniality, of the Partition of 1947, and beyond is the question of how to live within the context of global coloniality. At another level, South Asian (Indian) writers working in English (like Du Bois, Anzaldúa, and Martinez's double and mextiza/o consciousness I highlighted above) must continually grapple with the colonial histories that form the very English language they and their characters use.[16]

The complexities of South Asian identities and kinship are at the heart of Arundhati Roy's novel *The God of Small Things* (1997). Central to the novel is a vision of the continuity between knowing the world through experience and struggle and changing the central relations of the coloniality of power which sustain and make the world what it is. Additionally, subalternized characters in the novel, especially children, divorced women, and peasants defy bloodlines of kinship and caste to condemn the bloodsheds of their everyday world in Kerala. In so doing, they defy both the gods of dominance and of kinship to remember what they experienced and shared with the god of small things.

The radicalized sense of kinship sought in *The God of Small Things* involves an expanded standpoint positionality of oneself, in particular the ability to enlarge and enrich one's ability to experience.[17] Thus envisaged, readers can better understand the political terms of the debate over the coloniality of power, caste, and the normative principles of kinship within postcolonial Kerala that inform and shape the narrative: the debate between Ammu, the twins, Rahel and Estha, on the one hand, and Mammachi, Baby Kochamma, and the local police on the other, about the (archaic) nature of so-called Untouchables in postcolonial Kerala. Did Velutha that 'cheerful man without footprints . . . count' (1997, p. 208), Ammu asks her children? Was it possible for Ammu, Rahel and Estha 'bounded by the certain, separate knowledge' to have really 'loved a man [Velutha] to death'? (p. 307). 'How could [Ammu] stand the smell? . . . They have a particular smell, these Paravans' (p. 243) Baby Kochamma asks when she hears from the peasant Vallya Paapen what Ammu and Velutha had done. How we evaluate this debate over the coloniality of power, the love laws, kinship, and the politics of the erotic depends upon how we interpret Rahel and Estha's remarkable transformation and defiance at the novel's end and how we see their melancholic relationship between their ability to experience and understand, their capacity to grieve for their mother Ammu and the peasant Velutha, and even perhaps how in their grieving they de-institute kinship.

Ammu's defiant response to her family's insistence in maintaining caste rules coherent in Keralan culture and society is to make the twins Rahel and Estha 'promise' her that they will 'always love each other' – especially in the face of what Roy refers to as the local 'love laws' which pin down 'who should be loved. And how. And how much' (p. 168). With this straightforward speech act of promise, Ammu tampers throughout the novel with the stable heteronormative issues of family, bloodlines, and the bourgeois nation. The political vision of the subaltern which Roy's *The God of Small Things* seeks primarily through the standpoint positionality of women, children, and peasants provides the context in which family members such as Mammachi, Baby Kochamma, and the state police's support of caste and the coloniality of power can be challenged, made specific, and given meaning. These are the many idioms of dominance and subordination that Roy thematizes in the novel.

Ammu's capacity to know herself is directly related with her ability to feel with others and tussle with the normative rules of kinship in Kerala: 'It was what she had battling inside her. An unmixable mix. The infinite tenderness of motherhood and the reckless rage of a suicide bomber. It was this that grew inside her, and eventually led her to love by night the man her children loved by day' (p. 44). While Ammu disgraces her bourgeois family by divorcing from an alcoholic and abusive husband and returns home with her young twins to her parents' home in Ayemenem, she intensely feels 'that

there would be no more chances. There was only . . . a front verandah and a back verandah. A hot river and a pickle factory . . . And in the background, the constant, high, whining mewl of local disapproval' (p. 42). It is Ammu's braided 'unmixable mix[ed]' subaltern consciousness of 'tenderness' and 'rage' that drives her feelings toward her children, toward the Untouchable Velutha, and her disapproving mewling family and local culture and society. The urgent assurances that the peasant and card-carrying communist Velutha provides Ammu with profoundly change her and her children. Velutha, I sustain, makes possible a qualitative cognitive reorientation through his 'beauty' and his labor and gifts for her, the children, and the family's business. 'As she watched him she understood the quality of his beauty. How his labor had shaped him . . . Had left its stamp on him. Had given him his strength, his supple grace' (p. 316). Interestingly, Velutha is important not only because he is the god of small things in Kerala but also because of the qualitative joy he produces in others with his magician-like 'facility with his hands'. Velutha (since the age of eleven), Roy emphasizes, 'could make intricate toys – tiny windmills, rattles, minute jewel boxes out of dried palm reeds; he could carve perfect boats of tapioca stems and figurines on cashew nuts. He would bring them for Ammu, holding them on his palm (as he had been taught) so she wouldn't have to touch him to take them (pp. 71–72).

Apart from his graceful carpentry and toy-making skills, Velutha 'mended radios, clocks, water pumps. He looked after the plumbing and all the electrical gadgets in the house' (p. 72). Years later, Velutha's creative engineering skills are used at Ammu's family's business where he reassembled 'bottle-sealing machines, maintained 'new cannery machines' and automatic fruit and vegetable slicers (p. 72). Indeed, one of the main reasons for seeing Velutha as a pivotal character in the political debate about 'who counts' in Kerala and the world that *The God of Small Things* stages is that he reveals an enormous ability to create culture and society for everyone around him. He has an enormous imaginative and cognitive life of experiences that the coloniality of power in Kerala has denied him as a Paravan.

While there are several tragic deaths in *The God of Small Things* – the novel opens with the memories of the Mol family grieving around the drowned Anglo-Indian Sophie Mol's coffin, and Ammu dies alone in a grimy room in the Bharat Lodge in Alleppey at the viable and die-able age of 31, the novel revolves around the brutal death of Velutha and the postcolonial nation's inability to count him as one of its own.[18] After the forbidden sexual encounter between Ammu and Velutha is uncovered by the family, Baby Kochamma makes a complaint to the local police on false charges, and with the approval of the local Marxist party hegemony, Velutha is hunted down, beaten, and tortured to death at the police station: 'his skull was fractured in

three places. His nose and both his cheekbones were smashed, leaving his face pulpy, undefined. The blow to his mouth had split open his upper lip and broken six teeth. . . . Four of his ribs were splintered . . . The blood on his breath bright red. Fresh. Frothy' (p. 294).

*The God of Small Things* circles around Velutha's, Sophie Mol's, and Ammu's death and the subsequent 'social deaths'[19] of Rahel and Estha. After the twins are forced by Baby Kochamma to 'save' Ammu's sexual and caste reputation by condemning Velutha to false charges of kidnapping and child abuse, Roy shows how dominance (without hegemony) intrudes into the smallest spaces in Kerala. What Rahel and Estha experience, Roy writes, was 'a clinical demonstration in controlled conditions . . . of human nature's pursuit of ascendancy. Structure. Order. Complete monopoly . . . If [the police] hurt Velutha more than they intended to, it was only because any *kinship*, any connection between themselves and him, any implication that if nothing else, at least biologically he was a fellow creature – had been severed long ago. [T]he posse of Touchable Policemen acted with economy, not frenzy. Efficiency, not anarchy. Responsibility, not hysteria' (p. 293, my emphasis).

While Rahel and Estha almost never recover from these deaths, Velutha's life and brutal death force them to tamper with the inchorencies of 'kinship' and biology. Kinship is therefore not just a situation Rahel and Estha, Ammu and Velutha find themselves in, but a set of practices in postcolonial Kerala that are, as Roy suggests, controlled, performed, ritualized, and monopolized by those in power. Kinship trouble, we might say, is what Roy seeks to deinstitute in *The God of Small Things*.

In political and psychoanalytic terms, *The God of Small Things* traces Estha and Rahel's struggles to 'work through'[20] the implications of their complex cathectic relations with postcolonial Kerala and the Ayemenem House. Estha never fully recovers. He stops talking altogether. Occupying as little space as possible in Kerala, he walks 'along the banks of the river that smelled like shit and pesticides bought with World Bank loans' (p. 14). Rahel, too, returns from a self-imposed diaspora of sorts in the United States, where she suffers a bad marriage in Boston, divorces, and labors in a New York City ethnic restaurant. When she learns that Estha has returned to Ayemenem (they have been apart for 25 years, since December 1969), she comes home.

If for Rahel surviving the brutal Kerala past is partly predicated on her identity of diaspora, her attempt to form a coherent present also involves a transgressive 'acting out' with her twin brother Estha. The adult twins do so by making the love laws and its rules incoherent. Interestingly, Roy can not directly represent Rahel and Estha's sexual transgression. There was, after all, Roy explains 'very little that anyone could say to clarify what happened' to

Rahel and Estha. 'Nothing that . . . would separate Sex from Love. Or Needs from Feelings' (p. 310). What is only narratable is that Estha and Rahel had held each other closely, long after making love, and that 'that night was not happiness, but hideous grief' (p. 311).

Hideous grieving, intimate loving, working through the coloniality of melancholia – all these idioms are woven together in *The God of Small Things* through Rahel and Estha, suggesting the complexity involved of coming to know oneself and expanding one's capacity to experience with others. The figures of Rahel and Estha may well compel a reading that tampers with the normative spheres of kinship, bloodlines that sustain and monopolize the society and the nation by exposing the socially contingent character of kinship.[21]

Roy ends her postcolonial novel by suggesting how much theoretical and historical knowledge is involved in Ammu, Estha, and Rahel's learning to experience in Kerala. Their changing relationship with Velutha is based on an understanding of the brutality of caste, the love laws, and of the necessity and urgency to deinstitute them. *The God of Small Things* is one of the most intriguing of postcolonial texts precisely because of the ways it indicates the extent to which subaltern identity and experience depends upon a minor (or small) historiography. We cannot claim a political identification, Roy suggests, until we have reconstituted our small collective identities and reexamine who counts in our cultures and societies.

In conclusion, I suggested that *pensamiento fronterizo* is linked to a realist view of US minoritized studies. I suggested further that the recent directions in minoritized studies – subaltern studies, the coloniality of power, and postpositivist realist studies – could be taken as the most significant movements in US postcolonial studies rather than as blueprints or master discourses to be imposed worldwide. Thus, *pensamiento fronterizo* in minoritized studies demands a different conceptualization of the self, of power, and of cultural citizenship. I have also assumed a framework in which the minoritized and subalternized designs in Anzaldúa, Martinez, and Roy's narratives are linked to different stages of the modern world-system: the coloniality of power from the Renaissance to the present in Anzaldúa and Martinez's narratives, and the love laws and the British imperial difference in Roy's novel. All three minoritized designs in these Chicano/a and South Asian works argue for a border and diasporic thinking as a necessary epistemology upon which a diversalist knowledge can be articulated in a transmodernist world governed by global capitalism and new forms of coloniality. Finally, my essay is an argument for a critical and comparative cosmopolitanism from below; at the same time I see in Anzaldúa, Martinez, and Roy's imaginative writings a plea for a new politics of diversality – one that conceives border and diasporic thinking as a critical project.

## Notes

1 The concept of the coloniality of power was theorized by the Peruvian sociologist Aníbal Quijano. He argues that modern regimes of power are characterized by what he terms 'coloniality', which, as distinct from colonialism, is not simply defined by a formal redomination between empire and colony but primarily defined by global and national/cultural hierarchies (gendered, racialized, and sexualized) that are articulated differentially in time and space. See Quijano's (1992, 2000). See also Mignolo (2000), Lao-Montes (2001), and Grosfoguel (2002).
2 For a discussion of the twinned logics of US empire (as a spatial territory) and as the cultures of US new imperialism (as a deterritorialized logic of capitalism), see Harvey (2003).
3 See Althusser (1971) and Butler (1997).
4 See *The Nature and Context of Minority Discourse* (1990).
5 Deleuze & Guattari (1986).
6 See my 'Foreword' (2001), (2000a and b, 1996).
7 The postpositivist realism the *Reclaiming Identity* scholars defend emerges from within the philosophy of science, and is informed by the work of Charles Sanders Pierce, W.V.O. Quine, and Hilary Putnam, among others. I have profited from Putnam's autobiographical essay on the philosophy of science entitled 'A Half Century of Philosophy, Viewed From Within' (1997).
8 Mohanty hypothesizes in *Literary Theory and the Claims of History*: 'instead of conceiving identities as self-evidently based on the authentic experiences of members of a cultural or social group . . . , or as all equally unreal to the extent that they lay any claim to the real experiences of real people because experience is a radically mystifying term . . . , we need to explore the possibility of a theoretical understanding of social and cultural identity in terms of objective social location. To do so, we need a cognitivist conception of experience . . .' (1997, p. 216).
9 Brown (1995).
10 As I have suggested above, the coloniality of power functions to organize cross-genealogical dialogues and theoretical developments around issues central to the futures of minority studies: identity, subjectification, power regimes, espistemology, and transformative politics. Among the scholars engaged in those dialogues are Aníbal Quijano, Walter Mignolo, Agustín Lao-Montes, Ramón Grosfoguel, Enrique Dussel, Catherine Walsh, and Freya Schiwy.
11 For far-reaching studies of the emerging problems in the intellectual and institutional organization of academic thinking, see Walllerstein *et al*. (1996) and Mignolo (2000). While the Wallersteinian Gulbenkian Commission's report is a highly analytical narrative of the social sciences over the past 100 years, and gracefully uses world system theory, chaos and dynamical complexity theory, contingent universalism, and a timely call for ethnoracial

and gender diversity in the academy to overturn Max Weber's worn out call for a 'disenchantment with the world', Mignolo's study of the historical humanities in the modern world colonial system can be read as an exemplary corrective to the Gulbenkian Commission's call for universalizing the social sciences. Mignolo argues that the Gulbenkian Commission's position on universalism ends up subalternizing others. Briefly, the issue for Mignolo is not how to universalize the social sciences or the historical humanities, but how to better locate the 'colonial difference'embedded in our academic cultures of scholarship. Mignolo inists that we need to think in terms of local US Latino/a and global border knowledge (*gnosis*) rather than in terms of the disciplines.

12 For an understanding of how nineteenth-century America was obsessed about vernacular varieties of English, see Jones (1999).

13 *Nepantla* is a word used by a Nahuatl-speaking people in the sixteenth century to define their own socio-cultural situation in the face of the Spanish conquest. As Walter Mignolo suggests, the word, *nepantla*, was recorded by Diego Durán, a Dominican missionary who was writing an ethnographic history of the Nahuatl speakers from the Valley of Mexico. When Durán asked one of his informants what he thought about the difficult situation that had been created for them by the Spanish invasion, the informant is reported to have responded 'estamos nepantla', ('we are Nepantla'), that is, 'we are in-between'. Personal correspondence with the author, 15 January 1998. My emphasis on *nepantla* throughout the essay is meant to function as a reminder of the 'colonial difference' implicit in US Latino/a Studies, a translational and transnational memory that all cultural difference has to be seen in the context of power and of the relations of subalternity and domination.

14 Gloria Anzaldúa writes in 'Border Arte: Nepantla, El lugar de la Frontera', that border art 'depicts both the soul of the artist and the soul of the pueblo. It deals with who tells the stories and what stories and histories are told. I call this form of visual narrative *autohistorias*. This form goes beyond the traditional self-portrait or autobiography, in telling the writer/artist's personal story, it also includes the artist's cultural history' (p. 113). In a conversation with me at the University of California, Santa Cruz, on 17 October 1990, Anzaldúa described the form of *Borderlands/La Frontera* with the homegrown neologism, *autohistoriteoría*.

15 Anzaldúa's imaginative work has had the great fortune of having been treated by superb feminist and postcolonial critics. In addition to Mignolo, Saldívar-Hull, Sandoval,Yarbro- Bejarano, and Chabram-Dernesesian's work, readers can track an emerging debate in Chicana/o Studies between psychoanalytic and deconstructive work such as Norma Alarcon's and post-postivist realist work such as Paula Moya's. For Alarcón, Anzaldúa's 'lesbo-erotic' text not only 'recodifies the multiple names of Woman' and recuperates 'a new mestiza consciousness', but also resituates Coatlicue through the author's own 'nonconscious memory' (p. 50). Briefly, for Alarcón, Anzaldúa

represents 'the non-(pre)-oedipal mother' in *Borderlands/La Frontera* and in the process 'gives birth to herself as inscriber/speaker of/for mestiza consciousness' (p. 50). More recently, Paula Moya in *Learning from Experience*, has responded to Alarcón's and Chela Sandoval's reading of Anzaldúa by suggesting that in Alarcón's and Sandoval's proto-poststructuralist approaches to Chicana feminism in general and Anzaldúa's work in particular, they have 'run the risk of theorizing ... identity in terms of ambiguity and fragmentation so that the 'Chicana' becomes, in effect, a figure for marginality and contradiction in the postmodern world. I would argue that the term 'Chicana' should not denote a principle of abstract oppositionality' (p. 129). In contradistinction to Alarcón's and Sandoval's readings, Moya calls for a post-positivist realist approach to Anzaldúa's work based on issues of identity and experience. Thus envisaged, Anzaldúa's new mestiza consciousness for Moya can be interpreted as a form of 'epistemic privilege', that is, 'a special advantage with respect to possessing or acquiring knowledge about how fundamental aspects of our society ... ope-operate to sustain matrices of power' (p. 188, fn. 36). While this is not the place to respond to this debate in Chicano/a Studies, I would like to note that Anzaldúa's work engages us with another 'take' on the 'post', that is, what we might call, the 'post-human'. Throughout *Borderlands/La Frontera*, Anzaldúa asks an urgent question: how do we go about breaking down the barriers we pose between the human and the animal? In contradistinction to Weber and Descartes, Anzaldúa calls for a 'reenchantment with the world'. Specifically, her 'alien' allegory builds on passages such as the following one in her *autohistoriateoría*: 'I tremble before the animal, the alien, sub-or suprahuman, the one that has something in common with the wind and the trees ... , that possesses a demon determination and ruthlessness *beyond the human*' (p. 72, my emphasis).

16 I would like to thank my Berkeley colleague, Gautam Premnath for allowing me to read his superb dissertation entitled 'Arguments with Nationalism in the Fiction of the Indian Diaspora', which he completed at Brown University in 2003. I am especially indebted to Premnath's powerful suggestion that Arhundhati Roy politically declares herself and her characters to be 'mobile republics' in order to get at the fundamental failure of the Indian republic to come into its own. I read Premnath's work after I had completed the writing of this last section of the essay, and after I had formulated my arguments that Arundhati Roy's *The God of Small Things* fundamentally critiques postcolonial coloniality and nationalism through her dystopian deconstruction of kinship in Kerala and alternatively uses the erotic as a utopian form of political and cultural critique.

17 Here in this last section, it should become clear that I am in substantial agreement with Satya P. Mohanty that our identities are not mere social constructions and hence 'spurious', nor fixed unchanging essences in a brutalizing world. I agree, further, with Mohanty that 'we have the capacity to examine our social identities, considering them in light of our best

understanding of other social facts and our other social relationships' (1997, p. 201). My reading of Roy's *The God of Small Things* is indebted to what I take to be Mohanty's significant reformulation of experience and identity dispersed throughout his *Literary Theory and the Claims of History* (1997).

18 I read Roy's critique of the bourgeois nation in *The God of Small Things* as echoing Ranajit Guha's description of the South Asian Subaltern Group's project. In his essay, 'On Some Aspects of the Historiography of Colonial India' (1988), Guha defines the problematic of their project as 'the study of [the] historical failure of the nation to come into its own, a failure due to the inadequacy of the bourgeoisie as well as of the working class to lead it to a decisive victory over colonialism and a bourgeois-democratic revolution of either the classic nineteenth-century type under the hegemony of the bourgeoisie or a more modern type under the hegemony of workers and peasants, that is a "new democracy"', p. 43.

19 I refer, of course, to the term Orlando Patterson in *Slavery and Social Death* (1982) gives to the status of being a living being radically deprived of all rights.

20 See Dominick LaCapra's 'Representing the Holocaust: Reflections on the Historians' Debate' (1992).

21 My reading of kinship and positionality has profited from Judith Butler's *Antigone's Claim: Kinship Between Life and Death* (2000).

## References

Althusser, Louis (1971) 'Ideology and Ideological State Appartuses (Notes Towards an Investigation) in *Lenin and Philosophy and Other Essays*, trans. Ben Brewster. New York: Monthly Review Press.

Brown, Wendy (1995) *States of Injury: Freedom and Power in Late Modernity*. Princeton: Princeton University Press.

Butler, Judith (2000) *Antigone's Claim: Kinship Between Life and Death*. New York: Columbia University Press.

—— (1997) '"Conscience Doth Make Subjects of us All": Althusser's Subjection' in *The Psychic Life of Power: Theories of Subjection*. Stanford: Stanford University Press.

Deleuze, Gilles & Guattari, Felix (2002) 'What is a Minor Literature?' in *Kafka: Towards a Minor Literature*, trans. Dana Polan. Minneapolis: University of Minnesota Press.

Grosfoguel, Ramón (2002) *Colonial Subjects: Puerto Rico and Puerto Ricans in a Global/Comparative Perspective*. Berkeley: University of California Press.

Harvey, David (2003) *The New Imperialism*. New York: Oxford University Press.

JanMohamed, Abdul & Lloy, David (eds) (1990) *The Nature and Context of Minority Discourse.* New York: Oxford University Press.

Jones, Gavin (1999) *Strange Talk: The Politics of Dialect Literature in Gilded Age America*. Berkeley: University of California Press.

Lao-Montes, Agustín (2001) 'Introduction' in *Mambo Montage: The Latinization of New York City*, eds Augustín Lao-Montes and Arlene Dávila. New York: Columbia University Press.

Mignolo, Walter (2000) *Local Histories/Global Designs: Coloniality, Subaltern Knowledges, and Border Thinking*. Princeton: Princeton University Press.

—— *Local Histories/Global Designs: Coloniality, Subaltern Knowledges, and Border Thinking*. Princeton: Princeton University Press.

Mohanty, S. (1997) *Literary Theory and the Claims of History*. Ithaca: Cornell.

Patterson, Orlando (1982) *Slavery and Social Death*. Cambridge: Harvard University Press.

Putnam (1997) 'A Half Century of Philosophy, Viewed From Within' in *American Academic Culture in Transformation: Fifty Years, Four Disciplines*, eds Thomas Bender and Carl E. Schorske. Princeton: Princeton University Press, pp. 193–226.

Quijano, A. (1992) 'Modernity, Identity, and Utopia in Latin America', *Boundary*, vol. 2, pp. 140–155.

—— (2000) 'Coloniality of Power, Eurocentrism, and Latin America', *Nepantla*, vol. 1, no. 3, pp. 533–580.

Saldivar, J. D. (2001) 'Foreword: Migratory Locations: Subaltern Modernity and Inter-American Cultural Criticism' in Julio Ramos' *Divergent Modernities: Culture and Politics in Nienteenth-Century Latin America*. Durham, NC: Duke University Press.

—— (2000) 'Looking Awry at 1898: Roosevelt, Montejo, Paredes, and Mariscal', *American Literary History*, vol. 12, no. 3, pp. 386–406.

—— (2000) 'The Location of Américo Paredes's Border Thinking', *Nepantla*, vol. 1, no. 1, pp. 191–195.

——(1996) 'Las fronteras de Nuestra América:para volver a trazar el mapa de los Estudios Culturales Norteamericanos', *Casa de las Américas*, vol. 204, Julio–Septiember, pp. 3–19.

Wallerstein, I., Juma, C., Fox Keller, E., Kocka, J., Lecourt, D., Mudimbe, V.Y., Mushakojo, K., Prigogine, I., Taylor, P.J. & Trouillot, M.R. (1996) *Open the Social Sciences: Report of the Gulbenkian Commission on the Restructuring of the Social Sciences*. Stanford, CA: Stanford University Press.

**Manuela Boatcă**

# THE EASTERN MARGINS OF EMPIRE

## Coloniality in 19th Century Romania

Throughout the history of the modern world-system, its economic and political peripheries have consistently faced the charge of either a lack of modernity or a 'lag' in achieving it. The need to rethink modernity and to question its uniqueness has therefore often been the result of being defined along the lines of this deficit as 'less than', 'not yet', or simply 'non-'modern. As such, it has recurrently surfaced in peripheral locations, which thus became the privileged loci of enunciation (Mignolo 2000) of theories critical of modernity and the philosophy of history inherent to it. Latin American dependency theory, emerged in response to the developmentalist perspective advocated by U.S. theorists of modernization in the 1950s and 1960s, is in this respect the best-known, but by no means the only example. The metaphors of core and periphery, intially conceptualized in this context, have long informed social scientific thinking and have as such taken a variety of forms (center-periphery, metropolis-satellite, North-South). In most cases, they are however used without reference to a particular theoretical framework or are not even explicitly stated.

Yet it is precisely the existence of an economic, social, political, and not least intellectual core-periphery division that we have in mind when critiquing the uniqueness of modernity and examining its current 'global' character. Taking as a point of departure an heir of dependency theory, Immanuel Wallerstein's model of a world-system (Wallerstein 1974), I will therefore argue that what Aníbal Quijano has termed the 'European patent on modernity' (Quijano 2001, p. 543) is the result of a series of subsequent ideological projects mandating the Westernization of peripheral regions as a means of attaining world modernity. An assessment of how this exportation of the modernity paradigm has operated in an historical Eastern European periphery, nineteenth century Romania, as well as of this operation's present-day relevance, will provide a case study for the larger context in which such processes have been occurring.

### Primacy as the last privilege or: how many modernities are there?

Ever since the Enlightenment, modernity as emancipation – i.e., as the attempt to exit mankind's self-incurred immaturity by appealing to Reason, in

Kant's famous formulation – has been depicted as a critical project having its cultural roots in the Italian Renaissance, the Protestant Reform, and the philosophy of Continental Rationalism, as well as finding its first social, political and institutional reflection in the British Parliament and the French Revolution (Dussel 2000, p. 469). Modernity was thus conceptualized as originating in Europe and as necessitating only the study of the inner-European processes of secularization, industrialization, urbanization, nation-state formation, democracy building, and capitalism in order to understand and predict further developments. This perspective has not only informed and accordingly shaped the classical nineteenth century sociological approaches to the emergence of modernity and the rise of capitalism as formulated by Marx, Weber, Durkheim, and Sombart, but also the twentieth century US modernization theories and the more recent discourse on globalization. Although the growing empirical evidence has rendered the underlying convergence thesis – gradual Westernization as the non-Western societies' only path to modernization – increasingly implausible, the modifications that the dominant concept of modernity underwent in order to rise to the challenge of empirical reality proved insubstantial to the core of the matter: Hailed as a theoretical turnaround within Western social science, the merely numerical proliferation of modernity in approaches dealing with the emergence of 'other' (Rofel 1999), 'alternative' (Beck *et al.* 2001) or 'multiple' (Eisenstadt 2000) modernities in the non-Western world leaves both the chronological primacy and the exemplary character of Western modernity with respect to these divergent developments unaltered (Randeria *et al.* 2004, p. 15).

This enduring view has recently been criticized by Argentinean philosopher Enrique Dussel as being not only Eurocentric, but at the same time provincial and fragmentary (Dussel 2000, p. 470). According to him, the universal claim of European modernity is grounded in the central part that the economy, the states, and consequently the intellectual production of successive European locations played in world history from 1492 on (Dussel 2002). This coincides with Wallerstein's periodization of the emergence of the modern world-system as a single division of labor encompassing multiple political systems (Wallerstein 2000, p. 75f.), in which the accumulated surplus is unequally redistributed through the market to the benefit of the respective hegemon. The Spanish and Portuguese conquest of the Americas in the 'long sixteenth century' had marked the beginning of the displacement of earlier world-systems by a capitalist world-economy having Western Europe as its core. In economic terms, these conquests represented the 'comparative advantage' (Dussel 2002, p. 223)[1] that allowed successive European hegemons – Spain and Portugal were followed by the Netherlands and then Britain – a temporary monopoly in the world-market at the expense of (1) colonized regions as well as of (2) competitors still outside the world-system. With the incorporation of the Russian and Ottoman empires into the capitalist

world-system during the nineteenth century and the subsequent 'scramble for Africa' among European powers, modern Europe as the core of world history became the first geopolitical location ever to successfully englobe all other cultures as its periphery or semiperiphery (Wallerstein 2000, p. 140).

Eurocentrism, both as a general framework of knowledge and as a particular conception of modernity, was the result of the establishment of Western hegemony as a global model of military, economic, and epistemic power. The ongoing colonization of new areas enforced a classification of the planet with respect to its degree of Occidentalism, whose aim, as Walter Mignolo has put it, was 'to transform differences into values' (Mignolo 2000, p. 13), such that, of the various ethnocentrisms making up the vast array of coexisting cultures, European ethnocentrism alone claimed and imposed universal validity for its economic and cultural precepts. Peruvian sociologist Aníbal Quijano identified the foundational myths behind the propagation of Eurocentrism in *evolutionism* – the notion that human civilization proceeded in a linear and unidirectional way from an initial state of nature through successive stages leading to Western civilization – and *dualism* – the view that differences between Europeans and non-Europeans can be accounted for in terms of insuperable natural categories such as primitive-civilized, irrational-rational, traditional-modern (Quijano 2001, p. 543). With their help, the 'European patent on modernity' was thus constructed in colonial times as a consequence of the redrawing of geographical borders and their simultaneous transformation into temporal stages of rationality and modernity: 'The Europeans generated a new temporal perspective of history and relocated the colonized population, along with their respective histories and cultures, in the past of a historical trajectory whose culmination was Europe. From then on, there were inferior races, capable only of producing inferior cultures [. . .] From then on, they were the past' (Quijano 2001, pp. 543; 552). Modernization theory, mandating a specific type of economic and social development after the US model, was only the twentieth century embodiment of a long series of 'global designs' conceived and enacted from the particular local history of the Euro-American core, that had begun with Christianization in the sixteenth century and had been followed by the civilizing mission in the nineteenth, developmentalism in the twentieth and the neoliberal global market of the present (Mignolo 2000, p. 301). Allegedly universal knowledge therefore is never neutral or unpositioned, but reproduces the particular epistemological perspective of a local history that it subsequently does or does not manage to establish to the detriment of other local histories. Critical theories attacking modernity from within fail to pinpoint this additional dimension pertaining to coloniality,[2] and thereby become complicitous with the criticized global design, whose premises they unwillingly reproduce. Thus, throughout the history of the modern/colonial world-system, 'the construction of "pathological" regions in the periphery as opposed to the so-called

"normal" development patterns of the "West" justified an even more intense political and economic intervention from imperial powers. By treating the "Other" as "underdeveloped", as "backward", metropolitan exploitation and domination were justified in the name of the "civilizing mission"' (Grosfoguel 2002, p. 221).

In his criticism of Establishment social science as a product of Eurocentric liberalist thought, Wallerstein had emphasized the geopolitical distribution of cultures of scholarship, by noting that from 1850 to 1914, and probably 1945, most of the scholarship had originated in, and was about, five countries: France, Great Britain, the Germanies, the Italies, and the United States. 'This is partly pragmatic, partly social pressure, and partly ideological: these are the important countries, this is what matters, this is what we should study in order to learn how the world operates' (Wallerstein 1996, p. 3). This, then, was to be the domain of sociologists, political scientists, and economists. In terms of fields of study, the rest of the world was relegated to either anthropology or Oriental studies – the disciplines meant to arrive at an explanation as to why the non-Western countries were not or could not become modern. After 1945, the 'non-West' was handed over to the new discipline of area studies, which in turn undermined the traditional disciplinary boundaries. This kind of epistemological North-South divide amounts to establishing a fixed relation between the scientists' place of origin and the validity of their theories, or, in Mignolo's words, 'between knowing *about* and knowing *from*' (Mignolo 2000, p. 309). Consequently, the distribution of scientific and cultural production in First, Second, and Third Worlds mandates that someone originating *from* an economically and technologically underdeveloped country does not have the necessary frame of mind and culture of scholarship which would allow them to study other civilizations, and therefore cannot produce any kind of significant theoretical thinking because theory is defined according to First World standards. In line with this logic, valid knowledge is produced in First World countries where there are no ideological obstructions to scientific and theoretical thinking. Thus, the global design of the 'civilizing mission' is still at work in the distribution of scientific labor between the three worlds and continues to shape our understanding of modernity and the modern.

This is to say that, to the extent that the world-system became modern, it also became increasingly colonial, articulating 'colonial differences' such as racial, ethnic and class hierarchies as part of its self-definition. The resulting international division of labor between core and periphery was, then, not only of an economic and political nature, but of a cultural and epistemological one as well: while the core became the location of *modernity*, from where the world started being classified, described, and studied, the periphery engendered *coloniality*, where the modern world's definition power could be wielded. Latin America, the Caribbean, Africa, South Asia or the Middle East thus did not enter the modern world-system as part of 'modernity', but as its obverse

(or dark side) – coloniality – as the violently and illegitimately subdued, economically exploited, and culturally silenced 'Other'. Critical theoretical accounts produced within these local histories that have, at various moments in history, attempted to unveil the global designs behind the project of modernity from Renaissance Christianity to the contemporary global market have tended to remain silent in the world intellectual community both because of the lack of prestige of their epistemological location and for not having been articulated in a 'modern' language.

## Nineteenth century modernity: export and trade of a scarce good

Placing itself on a scale measuring degrees of rationality, modernity, and civilization as defined by and from the hegemonic location of the Western core was a dare Romania first faced in mid-nineteenth century. Situated at the periphery of the emerging modern world-system in the 'long sixteenth century', the three Romanian Principalities, Transylvania, Walachia, and Moldavia had long made the bone of contention between the Habsburg, Ottoman and Tsarist Empires surrounding them. With the end of Ottoman domination in 1821, the Romanian Principalities faced the passage from a protocolonial system, in which their economic surplus was used to finance the luxuries of the politically dominant metropole (Chirot 1976, p. 10), to a neocolonial regime as Western Europe's agrarian province. Hardly amounting to liberation, this was rather a new form of dependency, closely resembling the one experienced by classical colonies after political independence. In the particular geopolitical context of the region, this reshuffling of powers essentially entailed a shift of Romania's 'peripheral axis' away from the domination of an Eastern Empire and toward that of the Western core (Bădescu 2004, p. 82ff.)

Thus, although never formally colonized, nineteenth century Romania had entered European modernity through its back door – coloniality, and as such was subjected to the economical, political, but also epistemological redistribution of power that the modern world-system had put into effect. If race was not a prominent criterion of differentiation within Europe itself, unlike in its 'official' colonies overseas, the negative term of opposing pairs such as 'civilized – barbarian', 'rational – irrational', 'developed – underdeveloped' applied to its eastern regions nonetheless. Hence, the systematic process of constructing inferior 'Others' as a core mechanism of legitimation for political intervention in, economic exploitation and epistemological patronage of the periphery had also led to the emergence of 'pathological regions' in that area of the modern world-system whose 'North' was its West.

It was against this background of Western Europe's ambivalent relationship with its 'Other within', the lesser European East, that Romania had to position itself in the second half of the nineteenth century. As the Ottoman economic pressure was loosening, the Western, and particularly French, cultural influence gained ever more ground in the Principalities. Westernization, civilization, and economic progress were viewed as closely related and mutually reinforcing processes (Love 1996, p. 26). A French-inspired, liberal revolution in 1848 laying claim to national independence for all Romanians and stifled that same year by Russian and Turkish intervention had also addressed issues such as serf emancipation, abolition of the Belgian-inspired constitution and the privileges it warranted to the land-controlling class, equality of civic and political rights, freedom of speech and of the press, and the creation of a national army. Yet, unlike in the West, obstacles to cultural, political and economic modernization in the European periphery were, first, imperial military domination, and second, the expansion of international capital. This meant that, once politically independent, Romania had to resist economic conquest in order to safeguard its national identity. Development issues could therefore only be formulated in terms of the foreign domination to which the country was subjected at that time, such that incipient sociological concerns were aimed less at 'global designs' – i.e., at abstract evolutionary models applicable across space and time – and much more interested in the historical analysis of the nation – i.e., in 'local history'.

## The Western war for men's minds on the Eastern margins of empire

The 1848 revolutionaries, for their most part young intellectuals educated in Western universities, had advocated reforms in keeping with the country's traditions as well as the need for critical evaluation of the cultural imports. But their social thought, however concerned with the nation's wellbeing, was deeply rooted in the liberal ideology underlying their revolutionary activities, in their firm belief in progress as mankind's universal law and in civilization (chiefly understood in a Western European sense) as a superior stage of social evolution. Conservative thought, on the other hand, with its emphasis on organicity, tradition, collective values, and gradual change, was in itself critical of modernity. The acceptance it gained in Romania, where the awareness of peripherality invited critical rethinking, amounted to what has elsewhere been called a 'double critique' or 'border thinking' – i.e., a critical attitude toward two traditions that implies thinking from both, and at the same time from neither (Mignolo 2000, p. 67). By undertaking a critique from within modernity through the use of central elements of Western conservatism, and at the same time from its exteriority as an intellectual stance prompted by the

social realities of the system's periphery, Romanian conservative thought as first illustrated by the literary critic Titu Maiorescu, founder and leader of the most influential cultural society of the time, *Junimea* (*The Youth*), postulated the borderline between the Western core and the Eastern European periphery as a new locus of enunciation from which it was possible to rethink modernity.

In order to ensure that the benefits of Western culture could be appropriated in a country situated at the border between barbarianism and civilization, as he put it, a critical view of the modernizing process was necessary, Maiorescu argued. Given Romania's exposure to an array of proximate foreign powers, thorough social change – as it resulted from the economic and cultural opening toward the West of Europe and the corresponding adoption of modern institutional structures – represented a new kind of aggression, one on which the nation's survival came to depend. Dealing with the issue of the culture change in 'primitive areas' in the 1960s, evolutionary anthropologists critical of the US modernization school would similarly refer to the importation of Western ideology and political institutions by former European colonies lacking the corresponding technological and economical foundation as 'a war for men's minds' (Sahlins/ Service 1960, p. 117f.) waged by the West in the attempt to preserve world dominance after formal decolonization. One hundred years earlier, Maiorescu warned that, in the absence of constructive criticism, evolution – viewed not so much as a teleological process, but as the gradual development of given potentialities – could easily fail to result in the progress advocated by Enlightenment philosophy and the liberal doctrine in its wake.

His classically conservative stance on the positive function of criticism and of the continuity of traditions in times of disruptive social change delivered the means for framing his analysis of Romania's hasty modernization in terms of what would become a highly consequential approach, the theory of forms without substance (Boatcă 2003). A peasant country like Romania, he argued, had not been prepared by anything in its history to receive all the 'outer forms' of civilization in the absence of 'the deeper historical foundations which with necessity produced' (Maiorescu 1973a, p. 164) them and it lacked the means to support them – industrial production and a middle class. Contrary to the liberals' claims, imported superstructural forms did not foster progress, but only concealed the power structures inherent in the relationship between Western and Eastern Europe (Maiorescu 1973b, p. 239), the better to exploit the latter. Consequently, Romania's sole possibility of preserving national independence throughout the process of modernization depended on her providing a specific – cultural, economic, and political – foundation to match and sustain the adopted forms, a conclusion that evolutionary anthropology would reach with respect to the all the new states exposed to the ideological domination of the system's core powers after World War II (Sahlins/Service 1960, p. 119). Although he mainly referred to cultural and political

superstructural elements, Maiorescu clearly viewed both intellectual and economic progress as determining the issue of national sovereignty in the context of cultural dominance, thus warning against the dangers inherent in the 'modernization theory' of his own time. Much like the policy prescriptions of twentieth century US modernizationists, the liberal reforms implemented in mid-nineteenth century Romania disregarded the power structures within Europe, and placed the country in a dependency situation. 'As soon as a higher culture is located in the vicinity of a people, it is bound to have some bearing on it. [. . .] One cannot resist this call: union in terms of cultural principles is the necessary fate of every European people. The question is only whether one can accomplish it as an equal companion or as an obedient slave; whether by preserving and strengthening one's national independence or by submitting to the foreign power. And this question can only be solved by the vitality of the people's economic and intellectual life' (Maiorescu 1973, p. 239). The costs of 'modernization', Maiorescu noted one century in advance of Celso Furtado and Andre Gunder Frank, can only be assessed by considering both terms of the relationship, not by mandating modernity in self-contained societies. In the following decades, an amazing variety of sociological and economic theories of social development would use Titu Maiorescu's model in order to define a proper evolutionary path along the lines of either 'form' or 'substance'.

On the conservative side, it was the writer and columnist Mihai Eminescu who continued and expanded Maiorescu's approach into a coherent socio-political theory of Romania's dependency status. For him, the mechanisms of the country's renewed peripheralization – and as such, the means by which the 'war for men's minds' was waged – were not only economic, but also ideological. These, in his view, operated through the agency of a 'cosmopolitan element', first represented by *Christianity* (more particularly Catholicism) and later on, after the Enlightenment and the advent of the secular world-view, by internationally active *economic agents*. Cosmopolitanism – understood as 'an unseen power, alien everywhere and at home everywhere, trying to realize the ideal of a universal empire' (Eminescu 1876, p. 45) – provided both the ideological cohesiveness and a motive force for the imperial projects of European powers, of which Austria-Hungary, posing the most direct threat to the Romanian provinces, was Eminescu's main point of reference. In twenty-first century parlance, Eminescu therefore denounced the capitalist system's reliance on successive ideological strategies acting as 'global designs' and intent on providing a common identity to the otherwise historically and structurally heterogeneous (Quijano 2000) world-system in expansion during the nineteenth century.

Cosmopolitanism's emphasis on individualism, free trade, rational social organization based on universal and impersonal norms, and egalitarianism had found a well-suited agent in Romania's liberal government, Eminescu argued. Although they stood in sharp contrast to Romania's existing class structure,

social mobility, and economic level, most 'cosmopolitan principles' had already been forced upon Romanian society as part of the institutional reforms following the 1848 liberal revolution. Far from inducing development, these legislative changes wrought a serious breach in Romania's organic evolution: they disintegrated the traditional class system by displacing the indigenous bourgeoisie, destabilized the economy by enhancing consumption levels while diminishing production, and created gaps in the opportunity structure later to be filled by foreign economic agents. The Romanian Constitution, which, unlike its Belgian counterpart, from which it had heavily borrowed, failed to represent precisely the largest segment of the population, the peasantry, was symptomatic for this mechanical adoption of foreign institutions lacking in local social substance:

> 'Every constitution, as a state's fundamental law, has as its correlate a particular class on which it is based. The correlate of the Western states' constitutions is a rich and cultivated middle class, a class of patricians, of industrial manufacturers – who see in the constitution the means of representing their interests in line with their significance [. . .] Where are *our* positive classes? The historical aristocracy [. . .] has almost disappeared, there is no positive middle class, the gaps are filled by foreigners, the peasantry is too uncultivated, and, although it is the only positive class, no one understands it, no one represents it, no one cares about it'.
>
> (Eminescu 1876, p. 59)

For Eminescu, then, cosmopolitanism (in its liberal variant), although acting as a global design, was rooted in the local history of the Western societies that elaborated it. The ideology it sought to export to underdeveloped countries by means of rational models of capitalist organization was a success story, but one that consciously ignored the historical realities which it confronted in the Eastern European periphery. Social revolutions such as had taken place in 1848 all over Europe were a 'luxury' which small states, whose political or economic independence was constantly threatened, could not afford. Hence, advocating individual liberties in such a context could only act, as it already had, to the detriment of state power. Eminescu thus pleaded against a contractualist state, against individualism, free trade, and strictly formal modernization, and for a state representing the entire nation (instead of just separate individuals), for safeguarding nationality, and for protectionism.

Consequently, in the context of peripheral development, Romanian liberalism was not even a valid doctrine in need of revamping, but just 'pseudo-liberalism' (Eminescu 1879a, p. 301) – i.e., a form without substance, while 'true liberalism', like 'true liberty', the very basis of which was 'a middle class that produces something' (Eminescu 1877, p. 18),

represented the outgrowth of Western economic and social circumstances that found their formal expression in the state constitution. The absence of these economic correlates in Romania thus explained why the implementation of a liberal constitution and of democratic principles could not benefit Romanian society and instead ended up serving the interests of the geohistorical location that had engendered and propagated them – Western Europe:

> 'So we allowed foreign legislations? Well, we did not allow them for Romanians, the needs of whom they did not match, but for economic elements that they did match and that know how to put them to use. We created a public atmosphere for exotic plants which proves lethal to the indigenous one. For today we have the most advanced liberal institutions. Control, people's sovereignty, French codes, departmental and communal councils. Are we better off because of them? No, we are ten times worse off, for the new institutions did not match our degree of culture, the sum of work power available to us, the quality of our work, so we have to exhaust all these in order to sustain the modern state's costly and useless apparatus'.
>
> (Eminescu 1877, p. 20)

The main factors responsible for the increasing access foreigners gained to Romania's visibly growing state machinery had been, in Eminescu's view, the emergence of a favorable climate for social mobility and the creation of new socioeconomic positions especially in urban areas in the context of the rise of political liberalism. They, too, accounted for the resulting polarization of the country's class structure into a foreign urban minority and a large rural, native majority financing the former's consumerist habits. Eminescu explained the functioning of this mechanism by means of a three-layered model: the 'real land' – the large mass of the peasantry (four-fifths of the population), the country's sole productive force; the liberal institutions – the 'legal land' – providing the juridical apparatus needed for creating and justifying both the polarized structure and the economic exploitation; and, finally, the 'superimposed layer' of parasitical elements, rendered indispensable to the mass of the population by usurious practices (Eminescu 1881a, p. 75). The social and economic function of the superimposed layer turned out to be the creation of a structure of fiscal exploitation sheltered by Romanian legislation at the expense of Romanian economy. By labeling the foreign elite a 'xenocracy' (Eminescu 1881b, p. 323) in charge of the social and economic dimensions of the transition from a protocolonial to a neocolonial society, and further distinguishing between a 'xenocracy by conquest', i.e., a political one, as in the case of the Ottoman rule, and a 'xenocracy by insidiousness' – i.e., one employing ideological and economic mechanisms characteristic of a neocolonial model, Eminescu thus captured one of the most significant aspects of the

phenomenon of 'coloniality of power' – the contribution of neocolonial elites to peripheralization after formal juridical decolonization.

Not only was the country not approaching the Western standards of civilization, Eminescu claimed, but the very use of the notion of progress in Romania's current economic state was proof of the practical limitations and ideological sterility of imported political doctrines based on this notion – which, alongside liberalism, also included socialism. Since Romania's economic and social state could be placed nowhere on the alleged continuum leading from barbarism to civilization, Eminescu dubbed it 'semibarbarism', 'this state a hundred times worse than barbarism, not to speak of its detriment in relation to true civilization' (Eminescu 1881c, p. 375), thus questioning both Western ideology's postulate of progress and that of the unidirectionality of evolution. His theoretical model therefore transcended the single-country level of analysis and became a starting point for understanding peripheral evolution in general: as it diagnosed a 'pathological' condition with respect to organic evolution, it explained it within the larger context of the power relations embedded in the international division of labor and hence as an instance of the 'development of underdevelopment' (Frank 1966).

Eminescu's conservative solution to semibarbarism involved a recuperation of the potentialities inherent in the borrowed forms, and a bridging of the gaps created in the process. If an evolution from forms to substance was possible, it had to proceed from a national and historical basis, whose reproduction had been stunted by the exploitative action of the superimposed layer:

> 'A people's true civilization does not consist in heedless borrowing of foreign laws, forms, institutions, labels, clothes. It consists in the organic, natural development of its own powers, of its own faculties. There is no general human civilization, accessible to all people to the same degree and in the same way, but every people has its own civilization, although a lot of elements common to other peoples go into it as well'
>
> (Eminescu 1881d, p. 379).

This argument, serving both as a premise and as a conclusion to Eminescu's approach to social evolution, is above all further evidence of the remarkable productivity of the subaltern perspective. If theorists from the world system's periphery managed to identify and admit the failure of unilinear evolutionism in explaining underdevelopment in the periphery so much earlier than Western theorists, it was mainly because theirs was the local history overrun by global designs, not the one disseminating them. Theorizing *about* and *from* that local history, they were more sensitive to the spatial confrontation between a prescribed, uniformitarian evolutionary model and the social reality of the periphery than Western scientists, for whom the periphery was a mere object of study, if oftentimes a deviant one.

Against this background, insistence on the primacy of a peripheral country's national interest was a plea for the divergent character of evolution in general, for an acknowledgment of specific evolution in particular, and at the same time a form of resistance to the imposition of the global design of the 'civilizing mission', according to which the one general human civilization toward which evolution proceeded was European modernity. Thus, for Eminescu, the decision on whether or not industrialization was a choice for an agricultural country was not the predermined result of a rigid sequence of stages, but the logical consequence of the advantages entailed by an industrialized country's relation to capital. Therefore, if Romania should industrialize, it was not because this was the inevitable evolutionary path, but because this particular form of internal organization of work would allow it to participate in the productivity of foreign capital, as opposed to being exploited by it.

## Romanian conservatism as border thinking

Even more than Maiorescu's, the type of conservatism Eminescu embraced represents one of the clearest instances in which a Western political doctrine was resignified according to the historical realities of the world-system's periphery. By criticizing modernity from its exteriority, i.e., from the perspective of coloniality inscribed in Romanian local history, he thus discarded the reproductibility of Western modernity as a myth.

Consequently, to rule that the common denominator of such substantially different thinkers as Charles Maurras, the Slavophiles, Mihai Eminescu, and the 'agrarian' school of writers in the US South was 'the view that the foreigner was bad, modern society was bad, industry was bad, the soil was good, the past was noble, the nation had to be saved' (Chirot 1978, p. 36), as Daniel Chirot did in a sweeping survey of conservative reactions to orthogenetic evolutionism, is to wrongly equate Western conservatism with its reinterpretation outside the Euro-American core. This attitude, however, illustrates only too well the previously discussed Eurocentrism of critical approaches enunciated from within modernity, and their subsequent blindness to its obverse, coloniality.

That Chirot's reference to Eminescu's socio-political writings as the expression of a type of obscurantism rooted in the rejection of 'modernism and industrial society' (idem) is badly misplaced, clearly ensues from the preceding discussion on the Romanian writer's views on industrialization. The point to be made is that it is precisely subalternization of knowledge as a consequence of coloniality which renders particular ideologies not only politically, but also epistemologically functional. This was the case with the conservative doctrine in the East European periphery, transformed into a form of cultural and

ideological resistance to global designs, particularly liberalism. As in its Western variant, the emphasis conservatism placed on organic evolution was the counterpart of both liberalism's and Marxism's view of human history as essentially progressive, as already pointed out in the discussion of Titu Maiorescu's conservative sociology. Yet in addition to it, peripheral conservatism, present as well in Maiorescu's work, but more clearly in Eminescu's political articles, provided an account of organic evolution with respect to local histories rather than to the universal(izing) history which Western modernity postulated. It thereby not only identified the different logic of a particular *regional* history, but, more importantly, it analyzed the effects produced in peripheral areas by the tension between subaltern and hegemonic concepts of history, or between local histories and global designs. Briefly, while the 'tradition' and the 'evolution' advocated by Western conservatism were still rooted in modernity, the 'tradition' promoted by peripheral conservatism was located in time before modernity/coloniality, i.e., before the beginning of peripheralization through the encroachment of global designs.

Therein lies the decisive difference between Western conservatism and its reformulation in the Eastern European periphery. The former clung to tradition as a repository of feudal privileges whose disappearance in the course of the transition to capitalism it considered prejudicial to social evolution. In short, it was reactionary by virtue of its response to liberal ideology. In contrast, Eminescu pointed out that the very premises for a reactionary movement were absent in Romania, and that the meaning of 'conservative' was therefore lopsided (Eminescu 1879b, p. 165).

The conservatism, nationalism, and antiuniformitarianism along whose lines Chirot[3] and other Western critics defined Eminescu's work were categories of a Western culture of scholarship arisen in response to the needs of a particular geohistorical location, namely, Western Europe. Educated in the West, but theorizing about the East European periphery, the nineteenth century Romanian conservatives discussed above realized that Western cultural categories cannot be 'exported' uncritically without risking that the subalternization of knowledge be added to the economic peripheralization. They therefore were among the first Romanian thinkers to resignify the method of Western cultures of scholarship – in this case, conservatism and its evolutionary doctrine – precisely as a response to the uncritical borrowing of formal institutions, doctrines, and development policies by the liberal regime. In particular Mihai Eminescu, who made this perspective the very center of his theorizing, became the mouthpiece of what has elsewhere been called 'subaltern knowledges situated at the historical intersection of the traditional and the modern' (Grosfoguel 2002, p. 221) in the particular context of nineteenth century Romania.

Writing *from* the periphery, and not 'only' *about* it, both Maiorescu and Eminescu thus made an epistemological claim to the theoretization of social reality that would be both echoed and independently discovered in those peripheral regions of the world-system – most notably Latin America, but also China and Russia – which faced similar dependency contexts in the decades to come (see Love 1996). Concepts like Maiorescu's 'forms without substance' or Eminescu's 'superimposed layer' and 'xenocracy' – reminiscent of both Celso Furtado's 'myth of economic development' (Furtado 1974) and Andre Gunder Frank's 'lumpenbourgeoisie' (Frank 1974) – all represent attempts to outline specific realities of the modern world-system's periphery for which hegemonic social science, centered around European experience and its claim to universal truth, had no labels. This consistent groping for conceptual clarity on the part of theorists writing from colonial perspectives only goes to show that, since many of the concepts relevant to our analysis of modernity were coined in and about the core, their explanatory and predictive power should be assessed differently depending on the structural location of their origin.

During the following sequence of imperial control of Eastern Europe, the Communist one, these and related theoretical approaches were condemned precisely along the lines of their national dimension, which stood in disagreement with the internationalism that Communism propagated, as well as their conservative dimension, whose underlying evolutionism and advocacy of organicity blatantly contradicted the official government doctrine of revolutionary transformation. Accordingly, the works of Titu Maiorescu were banned for his alleged anti-progressivism, Eminescu's for nationalism and 'proto-fascism', and the political implications of the theory of 'forms without substance' silenced under the guise of applying solely to the field of literary criticism. Recuperation of this theoretical tradition still proves problematic in the post-Communist era, when political, economic, and intellectual alignment with the Western European norms, entailing the (however vague) promise of European integration, dictates the dismissal of approaches critical of globalization, wholesale Westernization, and cultural leveling out and therefore makes epistemic oblivion a prerequisite for political and economic acknowledgment.

The shift of axis that Romania once again faced with the Communist demise at the end of the twentieth century thus represents both a chance and a risk: On the one hand, a rich theoretical heritage tackling the issue of peripheralization in the face of economic and political dominance could prove invaluable when confronted with a novel modernization theory once again professing the adoption of forms without substance in the shape of IMF provisions and EU regulations. On the other hand, what Immanuel Wallerstein has termed the 'gigantic liberal-Marxist consensus' (Wallerstein 1991, p. 182), and which Eminescu had viewed as responsible for the importation of forms without substance in nineteenth-century Romania, is still very much active in

the region in the shape of a concerted Communist-cum-neoliberal epistemic control of knowledge production by old and new elites judging the intellectual production of the periphery in terms of categories – such as progress, development, modernity, globalization – created in the core. The chance to reassess and promote old solutions to a recurrent problem in the context of a vacuum of – or at least a shift in – political hegemony in post-Communist Eastern Europe is thus stunted by the continued epistemic discredit of forms of resistance containing a national component, accordingly denounced as dubious scholarship and political dynamite. This lack of definition power could not only become the new geohistorical edge deciding this – and other – colonialized regions' renewed drift into the periphery, but also a further missed opportunity to shape modernity from its borders.

Phrasing the issue in terms of one or several modernities, therefore, is asking the wrong question. The modernity that Western social sciences were called upon to analyze, but also to imagine, is a Western macronarrative, to be understood against the background of the history, cultural traditions and economic development of its place of origin – Western Europe. A bird's eye view of world modernity in turn requires taking into account the hitherto silent knowledges speaking from coloniality and able to translate between epistemological locations on account of having been trained in modern thought while living under (neo)colonial realities. The resulting picture will probably be neither modern nor colonial, neither postmodern nor postcolonial, but a synthesis incorporating both experiences while presupposing neither.

## Notes

1 Unlike David Ricardo, with whom the theory of 'comparative advantage' originated, Dussel does not apply the term to the sphere of economic production, but, following Wallerstein's analysis, to the entire complex leading to 'the rise of the West' to hegemonic positions within the world-system: '[. . .] the great scientific discoveries, precious metals (silver and gold), the new labor force incorporated into the system (Indians and, from the sixteenth to the eighteenth century, African slaves in the Americas), the new comestibles (the Inca potato, corn, the Mexican *tomatl* and *chocolatl*, etc.), the millions of kilometers incorporated by the conquest into European colonial agriculture, and the invention of new economic instruments. All of this allowed Europe to triumph in its competition with the Islamic world, Hindustan, Southeast Asia, and China (Dussel 2002, p. 223).

2 More generous than 'colonialism', the term *coloniality* as proposed by Aníbal Quijano for Latin America and now widely used in works dealing with all peripheral zones in the world-economy refers to a threefold process of classification gradually established since the beginning of the European colonial expansion in the sixteenth century and collateral to the emergence of modernity in Europe: in relations of exploitation between capital and

labor; in relations of domination between metropolitan and peripheral states; and last, but not least, in the production of subjectivities and knowledges (Quijano 2001, p. 553).

3 'This type of opposition to uniformitarian theories of change produced a great deal of anti-modern, nostalgic literature and some powerful rightist and nationalist political movements, but it produced very little reputable social science' (Chirot 1978, p. 36)

## References

Bădescu, Ilie (2004) *Sincronism european şi cultură critică românească*, Cluj Napoca: Dacia, first published 1984.

Beck, Ulrich, Bonß, Wolfgang & Lau, Christian (2001), 'Theorie reflexiver Modernisierung, Fragestellungen und Hypothesen', in *Die Modernisierung der Moderne*, eds Beck, Ulrich/Bonß, Wolfgang, Frankfurt/ Main: Suhrkamp, pp. 11–47.

Boatcă, Manuela (2003) *From Neoevolutionism to World-Systems Analysis. The Romanian Theory of 'Forms without Substance' in Light of Modern Debates on Social Change*, Opladen: Leske + Budrich.

Chirot, Daniel (1976) *Social Change in a Peripheral Society. The Creation of a Balkan Colony*. New York: Academic Press.

—— (1978) 'Neoliberal and Social Democratic Theories of Development: The Zeletin-Voinea Debate Concerning Romania's Prospects in the 1920's and Its Contemporary Importance', in *Social Change in Romania, 1860–1940. A Debate on Development in a European Nation, Institute of International Studies*, ed. Jowitt, Kenneth. Berkeley: University of California, pp.31–52.

Dussel, Enrique (2000) 'Europe, Modernity and Eurocentrism', *Nepantla: Views from South*, vol. 1, no. 3, pp. 465–478.

—— (2002) 'World-System and Trans-Modernity', *Nepantla: Views from South*, vol. 3, no. 2., pp. 221–244.

Eisenstadt, Samuel (2000) 'Multiple Modernities', *Daedalus,* vol. 129, no. 1, pp. 1–29.

Eminescu, Mihai (1876) 'The Austrian Influence on the Romanians Living in the Principalities', by Mihai Eminescu (1999), *Opera politică*, vol. I, pp. 44–61.

—— (1877) 'Icoane vechi şi icoane nouă', by Mihai Eminescu (1989), *Opere*, vol. X, Publicistică, Bucharest: R.S.R., pp. 17–31.

—— (1879a) [Editorial], by Mihai Eminescu (1989), *Opere*, vol. X, Publicistică: Bucharest, R.S.R., pp. 300–301.

—— (1879b) [Editorial], by Mihai Eminescu (1989), *Opere*, vol. X, Publicistică: Bucharest, R.S.R., pp. 165–168.

—— (1881a) [Editorial], by Mihai Eminescu (1985), *Opere*, vol. XII, Publicistică: Bucharest, R.S.R., pp. 75–76.

—— (1881b) [Editorial], by Mihai Eminescu (1985), *Opere*, vol. XII, Publicistică: Bucharest, R.S.R., pp. 320–324.

—— (1881c) [Editorial], by Mihai Eminescu (1985), *Opere*, vol. XII, Publicistică: Bucharest, R.S.R., pp. 375–376.

—— (1881d) [Editorial], by Mihai Eminescu (1985), *Opere*, vol. XII, Publicistică: Bucharest, R.S.R., pp. 378–379.

Frank, Andre Gunder (1966) 'The Development of Underdevelopment', *Monthly Review*, vol. 18, no. 4, S. 17–31.

—— (1974) *Lumpenbourgeoisie: Lumpendevelopment. Dependence, Class, and Politics in Latin America*, New York and London: Monthly Review Press.

Furtado, Celso (1974) *The Myth of Economic Development and the Future of the Third World*. University of Cambridge, Centre of Latin American Studies: Cambridge.

Grosfoguel, Ramón (2002) 'Colonial Difference, Geopolitics of Knowledge and Global Coloniality in the Modern/Colonial Capitalist World-System', *Review*, vol. XXV, no. 3, pp. 203–224.

Love, Joseph L. (1996) *Crafting the Third World. Theorizing Underdevelopment in Rumania and Brazil*. Stanford: Stanford University Press.

Maiorescu, Titu (1973a) 'În contra direcţiei de astăzi', in: *Critice*, Bucharest: Minerva, pp. 160–171 (first published 1868).

—— (1973b) 'Direcţia nouă', in: *Critice*, Bucharest: Minerva (first published 1872).

Mignolo, Walter (2000) *Local Histories/Global Designs. Coloniality, Subaltern Knowledges, and Border Thinking*. Princeton: Princeton University Press.

Quijano, Aníbal (2000) 'Colonialidad del Poder y Clasificación Social', *Journal of World-Systems Research*, vol. VI, no. 2, pp. 342–386.

—— (2001) 'Coloniality of Power, Eurocentrism, and Latin America', *Nepantla: Views from South*, vol. 1, no. 3, pp. 533–574.

Randeria, Shalini, Fuchs, Martin & Linkenbach, Antje (2004) 'Konfigurationen der Moderne: Zur Einleitung', in: *Diskurse zu Indien, ,,Soziale Welt' spezial issue*, eds Randeria, Shalini/Fuchs, Martin/Linkenbach, Antje, Munich: Nomos, pp. 9–34.

Rofel, Lisa (1999) *Other Modernities: Gendered Yearnings in China After Socialism*. Berkeley: University of California Press.

Sahlins, Marshall/Service, Elman R. (eds) (1960) *Evolution and Culture*, Ann Arbor: University of Michigan Press.

Wallerstein, Immanuel (1974) *The Modern World System, Vol. I, Capitalist Agriculture and the Origins of the European World-Economy in the Sixteenth Century*, New York: Academic Press.

—— (1991) *Unthinking Social Science*, Cambridge: Polity Press.

—— (1996) 'Open the Social Sciences', *Items. Social Science Research Council*, vol. 50, no. 1, pp. 1–7.

—— (2000) *The Essential Wallerstein*, New York: The New Press.

Zilkia Janer

# (IN)EDIBLE NATURE

## New world food and coloniality

Nature is the source of human subsistence but the transformation of nature into food is a cultural process that is not independent of power relations. The colonization of America comprised the systematic repression of indigenous ways of knowing and even after the elimination of political colonialism the relationship between European cultures and the others is still one of colonial domination (Quijano 1992, p. 438) The colonial repression of different knowledges also affects the culinary epistemology that informs food preparation and consumption. Three instances in which the effects of coloniality in the food cultures of the New World can be observed are: (1) the degradation of indigenous culinary knowledge as a response to the challenge that American nature and indigenous culinary practices posed to Europe, (2) the enduring hegemony of French cuisine as the highest standard of European culinary modernity-rationality against which all other cuisines are measured and (3) the practice of a fusion cuisine structured by European culinary values and that incorporates other cuisines only to reduce them to sources of natural ingredients devoid of a culture of their own. I finish with a consideration of what the decolonization of culinary knowledge might entail.

### The colonization of indigenous culinary epistemology

The colonization of Mesoamerica by the Spanish led to the confrontation of different discourses regulating cooking and eating practices. Such discourses classify foods into categories according to hegemonic social, religious and medical knowledge. Whether a food is considered edible or inedible, high or low status, festive or appropriate for fasting, good or bad for health, has more cultural than natural explanations. Amerindians received a number of new foods from Europe and resisted the subordination of their culinary ideas to the colonizers'. The Spanish, on the other hand, had to do without some of the food items and practices they were used to and struggled to insert New World foods into their established categories. Below I analyze how the confrontation of Spanish and Ameridian culinary practices in the colonial context resulted in the partial suppression of the Amerindian systems of knowledge that regulated

food production and consumption, and in a conceptual challenge and eventual adaptation of European religious and medical discourses.

Bread was the staple at the base of Spanish cuisine for centuries and it was present at all meals from breakfast to dinner and in all courses from main dish to dessert (González Turmo, 1999). No part of the bread was wasted: soft crumbs were scraped from the table and harder ones shaven from stale loaves to become the main ingredient in many traditional Spanish dishes like soups, fritters, *ajos* and *gazpachos* among others. Oftentimes bread also substituted for flatware helping to carry food to the mouth. The centrality of bread in Spanish diet is still present in popular expressions like *es más bueno que el pan* to refer to something that is really good as being better than bread, and *ganarse el pan* which equates making a living to earning your bread.

The Catholic calendar of feasts and fasts regulated what and when people ate. Feasts involved all kinds of excess, particularly the day before Ash Wednesday which started the forty days of abstinence culminating with the celebration of Christ's resurrection. The feast of the Eucharist, which is performed every Sunday during mass, is a practice that makes Spanish culture closer to Amerindian cultures than to European ones. The Eucharist involves the transformation of bread and wine – the staples of Spanish cuisine – into the body and blood of Christ. According to the Catholic doctrine of transubstantiation, this transformation is not symbolic but literal by virtue of a miracle. The Eucharist gave the common act of eating ordinary food a transcendental quality by turning it into a communion with Christ and a requirement for the salvation of the soul. It is also a sublimated version of ritual anthropophagy. The Spanish colonizers condemned the ritual anthropophagy of Amerindians without making a connection with their own practices which were under attack by dissenters.

Fasting was another practice through which the Catholic church structured the consumption of food. Fasting required the limitation of meals to one a day and the abstention from eating meat and animal products such as milk and eggs during the 40 days of Lent between Ash Wednesday and Easter and many other days throughout the year. Ritualized fasting has been considered a way of imposing the Christian cognitive system from Rome. Fasting contributes to the adaptation of individuals to the system of values and social interactions desired by ecclesiastical hierarchies, it establishes the public values of the community and mediates the experience of individuals (García Aranda 1996, p. 82). An infraction of the rule resulted in an impure status for both the individual and the community. The feast of the Eucharist and the fasting calendar thus determined membership in the community and the welfare of individuals and the community in this and the afterlife.

Medicine, particularly humoral physiology and dietary theory, authorized another theoretical food system that affected Spanish food culture. This system, first sketched by Galen in ancient Greece and elaborated upon by

many Arab and European writers, dominated medicine and dietetics in the Old World for centuries. According to humoral theory, four major fluids or humors dominate the human body: blood, phlegm, choler and black bile. Each of these humors is composed of two basic elements: heat and moisture make up blood, cold and moisture constitute phlegm, heat and dryness form choler and cold and dryness constitute melancholy (Albala 2000, p. 1205). For the body to be in good health, all four humors need to be in balance. Individuals were supposed to have their own constitutions in which a particular humor dominated. Foods were also supposed to have their own natural humor and thus they spoke of hot, cold, dry and moist foods. For good health, individuals were recommended to eat foods that would help them balance their natural constitution. Somebody with a choleric character, the one in which heat and dryness dominates, was advised to eat moist and cold foods like cucumbers or melon. To correct an excessively wet food like melon, it was served with cured ham which was considered hot and dry. Humoral theory is still at the base of many classic dishes like 'melon and prosciutto'.

Catholicism and humoral physiology provided the guidelines for what was considered the natural and right way to eat but when the Spanish arrived in America, they were forced to confront the constructed character of their culinary thought. Indigenous systems of knowledge are obviously hard to investigate since we do not have access to any sources unmediated by European categories and interpretation. Nevertheless a careful analysis of the available sources reveals that, at the very least, Amerindian culinary thought was structured by categories other than the European. A different set of available foods and a different culture account for a different way of categorizing, preparing and consuming food. A review of the uses of maize, cacao and chile illustrates this point.

Maize is a plant that originated in the Americas and it was the main staple in all Amerindian cuisines. Nixtamalization, the process of cooking maize with mineral lime, was developed in Mesoamerica. This process enhances the protein value of the maize for human beings and it has been suggested that the rise of Mesoamerican civilization was made possible by its invention (Coe 1994, p. 14). Nixtamalized maize is used to form a dough which is the base of indigenous Mesoamerican cuisine. The importance of maize is most noticeable in the central role it has in the Mayan creation narratives as recorded in the Popol Vuh. According to these narratives, the gods created the flesh and blood of humans out of maize after a few unsuccessful attempts using other materials. Eating is at the center of the relationship between the Maya and the gods. The gods were looking for subjects who would feed them and so they created humans using an edible and nutritious substance (Recinos 1960, p. 103–04). The Maya then ate maize to renew life and offered it in plant and human form to the gods in gratitude. An elaborate system of human sacrifice and a

sophisticated maize gastronomy were engendered and authorized by the religious discourse of the Popol Vuh.

The Franciscan Friar Bernardino de Sahagún, who wrote the monumental *Historia general de las cosas de la Nueva España* based on years of research aided by members of the indigenous intelligentsia, allows us to admire the complexity of the practice of human sacrifice. The selection of the subject and the rituals before and after the sacrifice varied according to the specific festival or deity being honored. Although with less detail, Sahagún also lists the many different ways in which maize was consumed: tortillas varied in shape, size, flavoring, filling and accompaniments according to the event and social status of the diners. Tamales, thick maize dough with a meat and/or vegetable filling, are the dish that bridges the gap between cuisine and human sacrifice. According to Claudia Alarcón (1999), tamales are a metaphor for creation since they are made much in the same way that humans were made. When offered to the gods, she considers tamales a symbolic representation of human sacrifice. It is not hard to see the structural similarity between this use of maize and the role of wheat bread in Spanish cuisine and religion. They share the use of food as a mediation between gods and humans and as sublimation of anthropophagy. It is harder to establish whether that similarity was already there and facilitated the integration of the two cultures, or whether it was imposed by Spanish narratives.

Cacao, the seeds of the fruit of a plant which originated in the Amazon region, is another food that played an important role in Mesoamerican culture. Mayans were the first to cultivate the seeds and transform them into a highly prestigious chocolate drink. Contending Amerindian nations fought either for control over the richest cacao-producing lands, or for the establishment of beneficial trading relationships with those who controlled them. By the late Post-Classic period, commerce meant mostly the cacao trade (Coe & Coe 1996, pp. 58–59). Cacao as a drink was enriched by the addition of many different flavorings like vanilla, chile, honey, flowers and anatto or achiote. The last flavoring also dyed the drink a deep red which made it look like blood. Aside from its economic and social importance, the cacao pod also had some ritual uses as a symbol of the human heart torn out in sacrifice (Coe & Coe 1996, p. 101).

Chiles are another fruit native to the Americas the traditional use of which allows us to appreciate how culinary practices are affected by discourses specific to different cultures. In the case of chiles, we do not have much information about how they were related to religion, medicine or any other discipline. However, their uses in Mesoamerican cuisines are so strikingly different from the way in which the rest of the world uses them nowadays that we can only conclude that the categories regulating their use came from a system of knowledge that is lost or at least misunderstood. Sahagún specifies the different chiles that were used in each dish. It is also known that fasting for

Amerindians meant abstaining from eating chiles and salt. Chiles as indispensable and versatile rather than as one-dimensional condiment is a characteristic of Mesoamerican cuisine that has neither been adopted by other cultures nor suppressed by more powerful ones. In the use of chiles we can still appreciate the trace of a different rationality even if we cannot fully grasp it.

The sixteenth century witnessed a true revolution concerning food cultures on both sides of the Atlantic, but the exchange of flora, culture and agriculture was asymmetrical. In terms of biodiversity, the asymmetry is considerable: out of 250,000 major plant species on the planet known today, 100,000 live in the Americas and only 12,000 in Europe (Hernández Bermejo & Lora González 1996, pp. 178–79). Produce now considered essential in European cuisine like tomatoes, potatoes, cacao, maize, and vanilla among many others, are native to America. In spite of the larger number and diversity of produce cultivated and consumed by Amerindians, newly arrived Spaniards experienced difficulty finding something to eat. Father Serra (cited in Coe 1994, pp. 27–28), an eighteenth century Franciscan missionary, explained it:

> At midday they brought us a meal of stewed and roast fowl. They brought *arepas* [thick maize tortillas], roast plantains, sweet manioc, sweet potatoes, etc. But we did not know how to eat without bread. Then I realized that bread was sustenance to someone who was brought up like me, and I remembered that when I was in Cádiz about to leave, a brother said to me, 'Brother John, you are going to the Indies: God keep you from losing sight of bread'.

According to the Spanish, lack of wheat bread was equal to lack of food in spite of the abundance of produce.

Not only the numerical proportion but also the cultural impact of the transatlantic exchange of food was unbalanced. The impact in the New World was already noticeable in the sixteenth century and it unequally affected the different social groups configured by the colonial system while the impact in Europe and the rest of the world was much slower (Garrido Aranda 1999, p. 198). Edible plants from the New World crossed the Atlantic without the indigenous knowledge about their cultivation, preparation and consumption. They were planted in scientific botanical gardens and many of them changed their use from nutritional to decorative (Garrido Aranda 1999, p. 205). Maize, like many new world foods, suffered a change in social status. As Amerindians were subjugated and their gods discredited, the importance of maize diminished. In Europe maize was adopted as food for the poor or as animal feed. Maize and potatoes have an important role in European history since they put an end to famine in the seventeenth and eighteenth centuries. However,

because the process of nixtamalization was not learned by Europeans, maize did not provide adequate nutrition.

Chiles also suffered a drastic change in their use when incorporated into European food culture. In the nineteenth century the use or avoidance of chiles almost became a moral issue (Coe 1994, p. 64). Outside of Mexico, they have been reduced to providers of 'heat' without attention to their different tastes, colors, textures and preparations. Chiles have acquired importance as decorative element and some of the indigenous medicinal uses are only now being validated by modern medicine. Capsaicin, the pungent alkaloid in chiles, is being used to treat pain and respiratory disorders and research on other uses is still ongoing (Andrews 2000, p. 287). The case of maize and chiles makes clear that the suppression of Amerindian knowledge was a regrettable loss for humanity.

Mesoamerican cuisines adopted the use of lard, meat and other animal products from the Spanish. The maize dough for tortillas and tamales is enriched and softened by lard and animal broth. The Mesoamerican diet, originally sparse in the use of meat, became more dependent on it. The heavy consumption of beef by colonial society has a material rather than a taste-related origin. Amerindians were displaced from maize producing lands to give place to the raising of cattle: cattle and a meat-based culinary culture literally colonized maize and a vegetable-based culinary culture. The cultivation of maize became increasingly difficult because of displacement and because of the destructive behavior of wild cattle. As a result the prices of maize became prohibitive and Spanish and Amerindians alike grew fond of beef which was plentiful (Romero de Solís 1996, p. 248).

A new culinary culture emerged in colonial Mexico as the repertory of available foods changed and as Creoles and Amerindians adapted some of each other's culinary practices. The creation of a new culinary culture required the revision of the systems of knowledge that authorized Spanish culinary practices according to the possibilities of food production and consumption in the colony. The Catholic practice of fasting had to be adapted to the new natural and social reality, and humoral theory had to be updated to include the new foods which sometimes seemed to challenge or escape its categories.

Chocolate, the foamy drink made with cacao seeds, was enthusiastically embraced by the Spanish after some initial hesitation. Before chocolate could become fully incorporated into Spanish and Creole food culture a few theoretical questions had to be sorted out. How does chocolate fit into humoral theory? Is it hot or cold? Is it healthy? Is chocolate appropriate for fasting? In 1570, Philip II sent his Royal Physician Francisco Hernández to the New Spain to classify the plants of Mexico as either hot or cold, and wet or dry (Coe & Coe 1996, pp. 122–23). His conclusions regarding cacao and chocolate were quite accommodating. He considered cacao leans to the cold and humid, making drinks made from it good in hot weather and to cure fevers but because the spices added to it are hot, it warms the stomach, perfumes the

breath and combats poisons. Chocolate could be adjusted to the needs of people with all kinds of humoral constitutions. This conclusion allowed the Spanish to continue enjoying chocolate without undermining the authority of the humoral system.

After gaining medical legitimacy, chocolate had to be conciliated with the fasting demands of the Catholic church. For centuries there was a theological controversy over whether chocolate was just a drink or a nourishing food that could not be taken during the fast. The controversy did not stop the practice of drinking chocolate during the fast and many arguments were developed to justify it: from the perspective that nothing liquid breaks the fast, to the point that it broke the fast if taken as food but not if taken as medicine. Chocolate was not the only Mesoamerican food that prompted an adaptation of Christian doctrine. Creoles demanded and acquired certain exemptions from fasting arguing a scarcity of appropriate foods in America. Because of the lack of olive oil they argued it would be impossible to cook without lard. Creoles were also in the habit of consuming milk products during the fast, which was not formally allowed by the church except with the purchase of a special dispensation. They argued that fish, a favorite food during Lent in Europe, was either of bad quality or too expensive and that other traditional Lenten foods like chestnuts, almonds and raisins were totally unavailable (Grupo Interdisciplinario de Cultura Alimentaria Andalucía-América 1996, pp. 168–72). Creoles had adapted to a different set of foods and successfully used the European bias against New World nature to help change fundamental religious tenets to accommodate their new food culture.

The food revolution prompted by the colonization of America had long lasting consequences not only in terms of the variety of foods available but also regarding the major discourses and disciplines that categorize foods and regulate their consumption. Unequal power relations resulted in the loss of some biodiversity – because the cultivation of many plants was abandoned – and in the loss of indigenous knowledge regarding the uses of native American plants. European systems of knowledge, particularly religious and medical, faced the challenge of a nature and culture that was organized independently of them. Some changes were performed in the European way of classifying the world but without breaking the overall cognitive systems that were supposed to give legitimacy to the colonial enterprise in the first place.

## Cooking Eurocentrism: a critical assessment of the hegemony of French cuisine

The subordination of indigenous and many other culinary knowledges made possible the establishment of the superiority of French cuisine as the culinary expression of European modernity-rationality. According to the official

website of the Cordon Bleu (2005) academy of culinary arts their instructors 'teach the techniques and methods of cuisine, pastry and bread baking which have been codified in France over the last 500 years, and which are applicable to any world cuisine'. The belief that knowledge of French technique enables cooks to prepare any world cuisine is based on the assumption that other cuisines lack their own techniques or that such techniques are expendable. Academics, cooks and diners alike seem resistant to revise the myth of the superiority of French cuisine in spite of the influence of postcolonial and postmodern analyses and their critique of Eurocentric metanarratives.

Based on the current popularity of a variety of national cuisines and of fusion or world cuisine we might feel tempted to argue that the French no longer have the monopoly of fine dining. However, the structure of the relationship between different cuisines in culinary schools curricula and in restaurant cooking reveals that French cuisine is still considered the superior one. The curriculum of schools with a general focus like the prestigious Culinary Institute of America (CIA) and the more up-to-date Institute of Culinary Education (ICE) is remarkably similar to the curriculum of schools that specialize on French cuisine like the Cordon Bleu or the French Culinary Institute. In spite of their claim to train generalist cooks, their instruction is almost exclusively French-style with some token additions from other cuisines.

The textbook used at the CIA is titled *The Professional Chef* (2002) but the qualifier 'French-style' should be added to the title since the book does not seriously engage any other cuisines. The textbook is organized by categories that are apparently not specific to any cuisine, but the contents reveal the biases of this structure. Out of seven parts, one is entirely devoted to stocks, sauces and soups. Stocks and sauces are fundamental to French cuisine but are almost irrelevant to many other. In Indian cuisine, for example, dependence on stocks and sauces is the mark of an incompetent cook. CIA graduates are likely to know dozens of sauces while being unable to distinguish a *khorma* from a *khalia*, or a *mole poblano* from a *mole oaxaqueño*. The other parts of the CIA course focus mostly on ingredients and techniques specific to French-style cooking. Students learn all about egg-based breakfasts, yeasted breads, and the use of the French knife but remain ignorant of the many sophisticated ways to use spices and chiles and of the advantages of using grinding stones. They will also not learn meat, poultry, fish and shellfish fabrication techniques that are essential for dishes other than French-style. How fish is cut up in India, for example, has more to do with creating pieces with the right degree of fattiness or leanness for specific preparations than with the creation of boneless fillets. It is understood that choices need to be made when putting together a curriculum but making a regional tradition of cooking pass as a globally valid one should not be acceptable.

The ICE (2005) divides its curriculum for the culinary arts diploma into six modules. The first four modules follow more or less the same structure as

the CIA textbook, and module 6 is an externship. What stands out is Module 5 which attempts to account for the actual variety of global culinary knowledges. The module is divided into four courses: (1) Cuisine of France, (2) Cuisine of Italy, (3) Cuisine of Asia and (4) Advanced culinary applications. There are two courses on European cuisines but only one to account for the varied cuisines of the Asian continent. The third course at least opens a window into other culinary systems which might allow students to realize the limits of their training. However, the ICE's description of their curriculum undermines the importance of that window: 'You will begin by creating classical, technique-driven dishes and progress to discovering the foods and flavors of global, ethnic, and contemporary American cuisines'. This statement implies that only French-style dishes are classical and technique-driven while dishes from other culinary systems are just an appendix that contributes foods and flavors, i.e. raw nature, but not culture or technique.

The belief in the technical, if not overall, superiority of French cuisine is carried into the restaurant business which results in the homogenization of high cuisines worldwide. Chefs that are trained in the French style prepare dishes from all kinds of cuisines using French techniques convinced that by doing so they are actually improving what they call traditional recipes. The effect of this is that when we dine in their 'Mexican' or 'Indian' restaurants we are still eating French-style dishes. Fusion or world cuisine restaurants which are not trying to conform to any single culinary system also relegate cuisines other than French-style to sources of 'exotic' ingredients or inspiration but rarely as a solid foundation of culinary technique and knowledge. A world cuisine determined by one local tradition passing as universal is the high-brow version of the McDonaldization of the world. I am not talking about the need to preserve so-called local traditions as if they were somehow frozen in a distant past. What I think is needed is the recognition of cuisines other than French as equal partners in the world of fine dining. All cuisines should be respected as living contemporary culture with their own rules, techniques and epistemology.

The hegemony of French cuisine can only be understood in the context of the modern/colonial world system and the cognitive framework that it created. Modern epistemology gave Europe the privilege of being the center of enunciation (Mignolo 2002). It established Europe as the model and point of view from which all other histories and epistemologies are evaluated. This epistemic privilege is also at work in historicist narratives that take the 'first in Europe and then elsewhere' structure of time (Chakrabarty 2001, p. 7). In the field of culinary history, the modern/colonial cognitive system has established the regional conceptual framework of French cuisine as the highest point of culinary development for the rest of the world to follow. Culinary conceptual frameworks alien to the French model have been labeled as 'ethnic' or 'traditional'.

The standard narrative of French culinary history is summarized by Neirinck and Poulain (2001). The starting point is the Middle Ages when spices were used liberally and cooking was determined by the principles of alchemy, humoral medicine and religion. The publication in 1651 of *Le cuisinier François* by Pierre La Varenne is considered the turning point that marks the beginning of French and modern cuisine. The use of spices was minimized in favor of local herbs, and sweet dishes were confined to the end of the meal. Carême and Escoffier, who are the main heroes of this narrative, continued the task of codifying the cuisine in writing with formulas that are considered to be rational and perfected over time. The codified culinary system has been exported worldwide through a genre of writing about food from the French perspective and through restaurants which are considered to be a unique French creation. A cycle of declines and nouvelle cuisines is acknowledged which is taken as a sign of the vitality of the cuisine.

Aside from the modern/colonial cognitive system that allows European culture to establish itself as the measure of everything human, the authority of French cuisine depends on three modern phenomena: the printed letter, standardization, and the restaurant. Alphabetic writing and the printed letter have been tools in the colonization of subaltern languages, memories and epistemologies (Mignolo 1995, p. 204). Modernity delegitimized knowledges that are not in writing as limited, variable and unimportant. Cultures that put their cognitive systems in print, like those with access to gunpowder or the atomic bomb, have been able to impose their views on the others. We can understand what French cuisine is all about after reading a few books, but understanding the cuisine of Nagaland in India, among many others, implies travels, interviews and challenging the very categories on which European culinary knowledge is based. All that work is considered unnecessary since modern narratives assure us that what Europe and the United States offer is already the best. The proliferation of cookbooks does not solve this problem since the genre itself imposes the categories and structures of European cooking failing to grasp the epistemologies that shape different culinary systems. We are impoverished by the modern bias in favor of the printed word.

Science, rationalization and standardization was the modern faith that French/European cooking counterpoised to cuisines that were regarded as guided and limited by religion and magic. But instead of creating a truly universal and constraint-free cuisine, the French created a cuisine driven by the need for efficiency in the restaurant kitchen. By limiting the number of dishes and creating a system in which many steps can be performed ahead of time, like the making of stocks and the *mise en place*, a very exportable and learnable cuisine was created. The system of French cuisine is ironically in a continuum with the system of fast food restaurants. The success of both has more to do with ease of production and predictability than with taste.

Restaurants are generally not considered 'proper modern restaurants' unless they conform to the model of French restaurants which are a result of a local history. The dominance of French-style restaurants is not related to taste. French-style restaurants exist all over the world because in the modern/colonial cognitive system they are considered a mark of civilization and development, but also because they are relatively easy to set up. Even with the increasing interest in other cuisines it is much easier to become a French cook than any other kind. Six months at the Cordon Bleu guarantee a successful career whereas there is no neatly packaged way to become an expert on cuisines like Mexican or Thai. Cuisines that have not codified their culinary knowledge in a way that makes it easy for outsiders to learn and efficient for a restaurant kitchen are dismissed. In the same way, other kinds of eating out establishments are considered as not quite restaurants instead of taken as alternative models of conviviality outside of the home.

When cuisines are described and hierarchized using French cuisine as a standard, those that are somehow sauce-based and that follow rules that are easy to understand using European concepts get a high mark, whereas cuisines that use spices or follow rules that are not easily translatable into French ones, are put down. If French cuisine was not backed-up by the prestige and power of modernity/coloniality it would be easier to accept it as what it is: one cuisine among many determined by its regional history. The assessment of French food given by two different visitors illustrates this point. Kosa Pan, the first Thai ambassador to France, visited Paris in 1686 when the culinary revolution started by La Varenne was already a few decades old. With his confidence as a representative of the flourishing kingdom of Siam he stated that wine 'helps give taste to the food which otherwise be insipid to our palates; here are few spices and much meat, and an attraction of quantity replaces piquant wholesomeness' (cited in Thompson 2002, p. 16). While remarking that abundance of meat and emphasis on quantity are contrary to the culinary system of Siam which emphasizes quality and in which meat is not given a central role, Kosa Pan does not fail to grasp the importance of wine in the French culinary experience. Muhammad As-Saffar (cited in Parkhurst Ferguson 2004, p. 185), a Moroccan scholar who visited Paris in the 1840s, offers another critical view of French cuisine: 'They are not creative in varying their menus with different things. Even if they have just eaten [something], they bring it on the next time. In general, their food lacks flavor, and even salt and pepper'. Similar opinions are shared by many people today but they are too often silenced by the weight of the modern/colonial cognitive system. Accepting the authority of French cuisine is not only to perpetuate a colonial legacy, but also an impoverishing provincialism.

## Cooking the Caribbean: fusion cuisine and transmodern epistemology

These days fusion cuisine, or the mix of ingredients and cooking techniques from different traditions, is often associated with the phenomenon of globalization. However, it is necessary to historicize the process of globalization and to acknowledge that its origins are not exclusively Western (Hopkins 2002). The Caribbean has played an important part in the early stages of globalization and has had a fusion cuisine ever since the sixteenth century. In the following pages I discuss the long history of fusion cuisine in the Caribbean and compare it with the more recent Caribbean fusion cuisine developed in metropolitan restaurants in terms of their potential to contribute to a transmodern epistemology.

I define Caribbean fusion cuisine widely in terms of time and space to include the cuisine practiced in the greater Caribbean since the sixteenth century and that continues developing today in the region as well as in the major cities where Caribbean peoples have migrated in large numbers. In contrast, I call metropolitan restaurant fusion the more limited but influential practice of professional chefs catering primarily to a non Caribbean clientele. The purpose of the comparison of these two systems of fusion is not to naively try to establish degrees of authenticity but rather to examine the political effects of cooking as social practice. Fusion, I argue, has been the way through which different cuisines were created before being codified as national cuisines and not a recent phenomenon that threatens the identity of regional traditions as some critics have suggested. However, the practice of fusion is not free from power relations as it establishes hierarchies between the different traditions that it merges. In this analysis of the history of Caribbean cuisine I seek to clarify the power structure that has shaped Caribbean and Metropolitan fusion practices and analyze their political implications.

When looking at Caribbean dishes designed by metropolitan chefs it seems like many of them have a naive vision of culinary traditions in which people simply eat what is locally produced. The abundance of fresh fish and the use of fruits in savory dishes so common in metropolitan restaurant Caribbean dishes have been the exception rather than the norm in dining tables across the Caribbean. Salted codfish from cold northern waters has been a more steady staple than fresh fish, and fresh fruits are eaten but are not routinely put into savory dishes. To account for the difference between the Caribbean cuisine of the metropolitan imagination and the cuisine actually developed and practiced in the Caribbean we need a more complex notion of culinary cultures. Aside from local ingredients a cuisine is determined by markets, social structures and systems of cultural values.

'This is what the ship brought in' is an old expression still used in parts of the Caribbean to express the need to work within the constraints of what is

available. Historically, the use of land and other natural resources has been determined by external market demands because of the logic of plantation agriculture. What is available for local consumption has been mostly imported, not locally produced. I use the expression to characterize Caribbean cuisine as a phenomenon which is neither national nor local. It is a cuisine created in the Caribbean region with elements from four continents and which extends across the Caribbean islands and many parts of the eastern littoral of the Americas. The ship brought in new ingredients and peoples together with the subordination or partial erasure of their culinary cultures. In other words, I see Caribbean cuisine as the result of the diasporic and genocidal history of the Caribbean. With the following account of the interactions between different ingredients and cooks in the Caribbean kitchen I want to conceptualize Caribbean cuisine as performance following the definition given by Joseph Roach (1996) of performance as a process of surrogation through which circum-Atlantic societies invented themselves.

Colonization and the plantation system changed the repertoire of available foods and brought together peoples with different culinary values and techniques. New World foods arrived in the rest of the world as exotic curiosities and it took a long time to incorporate them into the established culinary and dietary traditions. In contrast, in the Caribbean ingredients from Europe, Asia, Africa and the Americas were quickly incorporated because they arrived with people who presumably carried some of the knowledge about their possible uses. However, the fusion did not happen in a vacuum: socioeconomic hierarchies and the subordination of the islands as European overseas colonies were structuring constraints. For all the peoples involved, this culinary fusion has been a process of transculturation, defined as a process that includes the partial loss of a culture, the partial acquisition of another culture, and the eventual creation of a new one (Ortiz 1978, pp. 92–97). This is an ongoing process that continues today most notably with the incorporation and transformation of processed and fast foods.

Before the arrival of Europeans, Caribbean aboriginal diet was based on fish and shellfish, small game, tropical fruits, yucca, sweet potatoes, corn, beans, peppers, squashes and avocado. When the Spanish arrived, they tried unsuccessfully to cultivate their staple foods (wheat, olives and grapes) but they were extremely successful with the introduction of hogs. Some of the Lesser Antilles became mostly populated by wild hogs as the native peoples were wiped out by slave catching expeditions (Watts, 2000, p. 140). For some time colonists depended on imports and on the Indian *conucos*, or cultivation plots, for their food. However, hogs eventually destroyed the *conucos* and with the extermination of the native population that way of cultivation almost disappeared. Yucca is the ingredient that survived the longest and remained as a staple for a long time.

To solve the food crisis, colonists successfully introduced ingredients from the Americas (anatto, tomatoes, potatoes, vanilla, cacao), Europe (aromatic herbs, cabbage) and Africa (okra, ñames). They also brought ingredients from Europe that originally came from Asia (garlic, rice, eggplant, onions, citrus fruits, spices, apples, peaches, lettuce, cucumber, carrots) and ingredients from Africa that originally came from Asia as well (sugarcane, coconuts, bananas, cambur). In the nineteenth century additional ingredients were brought from Africa (akee, breadfruit) and Asia (mango, nutmeg, tamarind) (Lovera 1991). Thus, ingredients from all over the world constitute the base of traditional Caribbean cuisine since its early beginnings.

Who was doing most of the cooking and under what conditions? According to Spanish chronicles, the indigenous peoples and the colonists reacted to each other's food with repulsion. Out of necessity both groups ended up trying, adapting and liking unfamiliar foods. During the early phase when the colonists depended on indigenous *conucos* for their survival their taste was partially transformed. In free settlements of surviving indigenous peoples and free or escaped Africans some of the aboriginal cooking knowledge was probably acquired by the Africans. The first cooks in the Caribbean kitchen were the indigenous peoples and their cuisine survived their extermination in the food habits of the rest of the population. The next important group in charge of cooking, and therefore with the most impact in shaping the cuisine, were primarily Africans.

In the plantation system slaves were to a surprising degree in charge of food supply. They were assigned a ration of food normally consisting on manioc flour, rice or corn, and salt cod or beef. Plantation owners initially resisted but finally tolerated and even encouraged the practice of slaves cultivating small plots with subsistence crops during their 'free' time as a way to supplement and sometimes substitute for the ration. By the 1830s subsistence plots had become a space of relative slave autonomy in many islands. Some slaves produced a surplus to take to the market and colonies like Martinique became dependent upon slave produce for a substantial portion of their food (Tomich 2000). Jamaica is another example of a colony in which white society became dependent upon slaves' produce (Beckles 2000, p. 733).

Plantation agriculture, geared towards export, left the production of food for local consumption mostly in the hands of slaves. It follows that Caribbean eating patterns were to some extent determined by what slaves were able and willing to produce. Fruits and vegetables were understandably more common than seafood given that slaves had limited access to the sea which would have provided them with opportunities to escape. This would explain why a great number of traditional Caribbean dishes feature salt cod, which was standard food in the transatlantic voyage and part of the ration, rather than fresh fish.

Slaves were also in charge of food preparation working as cooks in the plantations. They had to cater to the taste memories of the masters: diverse

European tastes in some cases modified by indigenous eating habits. However, cooks had a certain level of space for creativity applying what they remembered from African cooking and inventing new recipes. Considering the resulting cuisine as just European or African cuisine adapted to the constraints of a new environment would be to deny the cook's agency in the process but also to overestimate the cooking knowledge carried by colonists and slaves. Diasporic peoples carry taste memories of dishes they have eaten but not necessarily know how to prepare them. Even in the case of those with cooking knowledge there were serious limitations because not all ingredients were available to reproduce the remembered dishes. Caribbean cuisine was invented primarily by African cooks who made choices in terms of how to recreate and create dishes and techniques based on a considerably large but new pool of ingredients and a number of imperfectly remembered traditions. In the substitution of ingredients and flavors in the attempt to recover remembered dishes Caribbean cuisine is constituted as performance in the sense that it 'stands in for an elusive entity that it is not but that it must vainly aspire both to embody and to replace' (Roach 1996, p. 3). Cuisine as performance is an attempt to cope with unspeakable loss. The creation of Caribbean cuisine was a first step in the quest for freedom. As Sidney Mintz (1996, p. 37) has argued, 'the taste of freedom was around before freedom itself'.

It is possible to talk about a cuisine shared by the whole Caribbean region in spite of the obvious and meaningful differences according to patterns of colonization, immigration and national histories. Mintz (1974), pp. xvii–xviii) has established the social and cultural integrity of the region based on shared features like its ecology, the extermination of its native populations, the plantation system, the successive introduction of massive new populations, and the persistence of colonialism. He explains that the combined effects of these points have been somewhat different and therefore he conceived the various societies of the Caribbean in terms of a continuum rather than in terms of a single abstract model.

Such cultural continuum has been observed by scholars of Caribbean music and languages. Kenneth Bilby (1985) has explained the Caribbean as a musical region which emerges in the middle ground between African and European cultures. Each island stands at a different point in the continuum, some closer to European music and some closer to African music, but still sharing some common characteristics. Mervin Alleyne (1985) illustrates the point in the case of the linguistic landscape of the Caribbean. The region presents a wide range of ways in which European and Creole languages are related, from islands that are multilingual, bilingual or monolingual to those characterized by diglossia and by the existence of different graded levels of language between Creole and European languages. In terms of culinary culture, the way in which

ingredients and techniques from four continents are combined varies while at the same time displaying some common characteristics.

There are a few techniques that give Caribbean cuisines a sense of unity. One of them is the generalized use of a paste of ground seasonings like *sofrito* in the Spanish speaking Caribbean and the *marinades* of the English speaking islands. The use of the African grinding stone to make dough from plantains and root vegetables is another technique central to the cuisine. In the areas that received a large number of Indian immigrants a distinctively Caribbean curry powder has been developed. What all these techniques have in common is that they ensure a consistency in the taste of the final dishes even when the ingredients are varied according to availability or preferences. As new ingredients and dishes as diverse as pasta and processed meats are incorporated into the Caribbean diet, the use of these techniques in their preparation gives them an unmistakable Caribbean character.

Probably the most salient Caribbean culinary technique is improvisation just like in salsa or jazz. Such music balances a fixed structure with an open one which is completed with individual and collective improvisation. Recipes for Caribbean dishes can only provide a basic structure that allows for considerable changes and substitutions. Caribbean cookbooks seem more arbitrary than cookbooks for more codified and standardized cuisines like the French or Chinese because they attempt to reproduce a performance which was already an attempt to recreate a memory. In Caribbean cooking, like in performance art, to repeat dishes in exactly the same way is not highly valued: fluidity, flexibility and creativity are defining characteristic of this culinary culture.

Puerto Rican *pasteles* – savory pies made with a dough of ground plantains and tubers, stuffed with pork, garbanzos and olives, wrapped in banana leaves and boiled – exemplify the centrality of improvisation in Caribbean cuisine. The dough can be made with plantains and green bananas and any or none of the following: calabaza pumpkin, potatoes, yucca, yautía, ñame and malanga. The ideal proportion between these ingredients has never been established and is subject to much discussion among proud cooks who claim their version is the best. The filling is equally variable and can be made with pork, chicken and more recently canned corned beef. *Pasteles* can finally be wrapped in plantain leaves, paper or aluminum foil, and boiled in a pot or in the microwave oven. The origin of such openness comes from the need to cook with whatever is available, yet all different versions of *pasteles* are recognizable as such. The openness of dishes like *pasteles* has been embraced as an opportunity for experimentation and innovation.

The radical variability of a single dish can also be observed across the Caribbean. Salt cod fritters are popular in all the islands although with different names: *accra* in Trinidad, *codfish cakes* in Barbados, *stamp and go* in Jamaica, *bacalaítos* in Puerto Rico, *acrats de morue* in Martinique and Guadalupe, and *marinades* in Haiti (Lambert Ortiz 1973, p. 16). All the recipes share salt cod,

flour and water as the indispensable ingredients. Differentiation comes from the kind and proportion of flavorings and from the use or exclusion of leavening agents. In spite of the wide range of differences they all are still identifiable as Caribbean salt cod fritters. The transformation of salt cod from basic ration food into a beloved snack is remarkable. The recurrence of salt cod in fritter form rather than in a stew or some other preparation makes one wonder what previous dish it was meant to replace.

Creatively designed to cope with the loss of culinary knowledge and ingredients, and to provide consistency even in cases of scarcity and unpredictable availability, cuisine provided Caribbean peoples with the first shared language across cultures. Evolutionary biology argues that cooking – the need to communicate new knowledge on how to transform nature into food – gave birth to language and it is the first activity that distinguished hominids from humans (Cordón 1980). I would argue that fusion cuisine was the founding stone on which Caribbean cultures were built.

Caribbean fusion cuisine enables the creativity of all cooks and its development contributed to the creation of a free Caribbean by providing the opportunity to practice freedom. In contrast, metropolitan restaurant fusion while constituting a tasty cuisine is also reinstating the hierarchies that have relegated the Caribbean to a position of subordination. The following examination of the definition of fusion given by experts and practitioners allows us to see the colonialist presuppositions of the fusion cuisine that is practiced today.

In the *Encyclopedia of Food and Culture*, Julie Locher (2003) defines contemporary fusion cuisine as different from the historical combinations of cuisines characterizing the former as proactive and the latter as reactive. This is a false opposition. On the one hand, it reduces the fusion cooks of the past to passive subjects that merely reacted to changes brought about by forces alien to them. In the case of the Caribbean I have explained that, even in the case of the slaves, cooks managed to create opportunities for creativity to the point that letting the initiative of the cook run free became a landmark of the cuisine. On the other hand, Locher's definition of contemporary fusion cuisine as proactive idealizes contemporary fusion cooks as agents free of constraints. In spite of the resources of metropolitan upscale restaurants the creativity of the chef is limited by the only slightly adventurous palate of most customers, their misconceptions about regional cuisines and the bias in favor of French technique.

Another problem with the above definition of fusion is that it inserts cuisine into a narrative of progress in which the new is more highly valued than the old. This is also evident in the use of the term 'Nuevo Latino' to refer to the contemporary fusion performed by restaurant chefs. There is a presupposition that cuisine in the Caribbean and Latin America is frozen in an old tradition and that innovation is the monopoly of upscale metropolitan

restaurants. The old/new and reactive/proactive oppositions are finally joined by the ethnic/French binary when Locher (2003) argues that French cuisine, which dominates in fusion cuisine, mainstreams ethnic ingredients, gives opportunities to immigrant and minority chefs and elevates the status of ethnic and regional cuisines. This comment takes the point of view of those who ignore the global wealth of ingredients and techniques, assumes that immigrant and minority chefs cannot cook cuisines other than the one of their countries of origin and takes for granted that ethnic and regional cuisines are essentially of low status without acknowledging the role of global relations of power in that hierchization. Restaurant fusion is supposed to rescue ethnic cuisines from their low position by inserting them into the matrix of French cuisine which is uncritically considered the highest form of culinary expression. Subordination to metropolitan taste and denial of the value of their culinary systems is the price so-called ethnic cuisines are paying to be known outside of their communities.

Another telling definition of culinary fusion comes from Norman Van Aken, an award-winning Florida chef and cookbook author. Van Aken (c.1988) states that his interest is on 'diving deeply back down in time to salvage the golden treasures and vibrant calypso flavors of old Key West and fusing them with a contemporary sensibility and an individual personality. The foundation must be the bedrock honesty of Conch, Black, Spanish and Cuban regional cooking'. According to Van Aken, Caribbean flavors are some pure 'honest' essence of the past that needs to be updated and rescued. This implies that Caribbean cooks have not developed the cuisine in centuries as if they were stuck in the past and not active agents in the constant reinvention of the cuisine. Van Acken further defines fusion as an interplay 'between regionalism and restaurant technical know how'. The presupposition of this statement is that regional cuisines lack their own techniques. The recipes produced by Van Acken and other fusion chefs more often than not consist on the application of French technique to a Caribbean dish or the addition of Caribbean ingredients to a continental dish. What is rarely seen is the application of a Caribbean technique to a continental dish. The role of the Caribbean in metropolitan restaurant fusion cuisine seems to be limited to the contribution of ingredients and of a few dishes in need of improvement. This hierarchization is reminiscent of the one that has relegated the Caribbean to a source of primary materials in the world economy. In both cases the Caribbean is valued for its raw nature while its culture is consistently undervalued.

Many metropolitan restaurant fusion chefs have a more personal relationship to the different culinary traditions that feed their fusion. However, they are also reinforcing the same old hierarchies whether they realize it or not. Douglas Rodríguez (1995), a star chef whose Cuban family moved him to New York before the revolution, often travels to Latin America looking for ideas and a creative connection with his heritage. He mentions that he likes to ask

questions to his staff about their native dishes and that such conversations gave way to new ideas constantly. In his travels and his conversations with his staff Rodríguez is feeding from the anonymous know-how of other cooks. For 'Nuevo Latino' restaurant customers the chefs are like cult figures but this does not necessarily translate into a better appreciation of Caribbean or Latin American culinary cultures. The above examples illustrate how metropolitan restaurant fusion treats the Caribbean as a source of underdeveloped ingredients and ideas, and does not consider Caribbean chefs as creators. This is no small irony considering that, as I have argued, cuisine was one of the first domains in which Caribbean peoples asserted their agency and exercised freedom.

Dussel (1993, p. 76) has proposed a transmodern liberation project in which both modernity and its negated alterity co-realize themselves in a process of mutual creative fertilization. Such a project should include a fusion cuisine different from the currently dominant one. A transmodern fusion cuisine would go beyond the inclusion of a few 'ethnic' dishes into a 'Non-Western' culinary hall of fame. It would value all culinary epistemologies equally, making French cuisine lose its privileged position. More importantly, it would allow all cuisines to develop according to their own logic and to challenge and transform the way in which global culinary knowledge is currently being produced.

## References

Alarcón, Claudia (1999) 'Tamales in Mesoamerica: Food for Gods and Mortals', *Petits Propos Culinaires,* 63. London: Prospect Books.

Albala, Kenneth (2000) 'Southern Europe', in *The Cambridge World History of Food*, eds Kenneth F. Kiple and Kriemhild Cone Ornelas, Vol 2, Cambridge: Cambridge University Press.

Alleyne, Mervin C. (1985) 'A Linguistic Perspective on the Caribbean', in *Caribbean Contours,* ed. Sidney W. Mintz, Baltimore: Johns Hopkins University Press.

Andrews, Jean (2000) 'Chilli Peppers', in *The Cambridge World History of Food,* eds Kenneth F. Kiple and Kriemhild Cone Ornelas, Vol 1. Cambridge: Cambridge University Press.

Beckles, Hilary McD. (2000) 'An Economic Life of Their Own: Slaves as Commodity Producers and Distributors in Barbados', in *Caribbean Slavery in the Atlantic World,* eds Verene A. Shepherd and Hilary McD. Beckles, Kingston: Ian Randle.

Bilby, Kenneth M. (1985) 'The Caribbean as a Musical Region', in *Caribbean Contours,* ed. Sidney W. Mintz, Baltimore: Johns Hopkins University Press.

Chakrabarty, Dipesh (2001) *Provincializing Europe: Postcolonial Thought and Historical Difference*. New Delhi: Oxford University Press.

Coe, Sophie D. (1994) *America's First Cuisines*. Austin: University of Texas Press.

Coe, Sophie D. & Michael, D. Coe (1996) *The True History of Chocolate*. London: Thames and Hudson.

Cordon Bleu (2005) 'About the Cordon Bleu', viewed 23 November 2005, <http://cordonbleu.com/International/English/cm1.cfm?fid = 13>.

Cordón, Faustino (1980) *Cocinar hizo al hombre*. Barcelona: Tusquets Editores.

Culinary Institute of America (2002) *The Professional Chef*. 7th ed. New York: Wiley.

Dussel, Enrique (1993) 'Eurocentrism and Modernity (Introduction to the Frankfurt Lectures)', *boundary 2*, The Postmodernism Debate in Latin America, vol. 20, no. 3, pp. 65–76.

Garrido Aranda, Antonio *et al.* (1999) 'La revolución alimentaria del siglo XVI en América y Europa', in *Los sabores de España y América,* ed. Antonio Garrida Aranda, Huesca: La Val de Onsera.

Grupo Interdisciplinario de Cultura Alimentaria Andalucía-América (1996) 'El ayuno como ritual de paso: El ayuno eclesiástico en España y América', in *Cultura alimentaria Andalucía-América*, ed. Antonio Garrido Aranda, Mexico: UNAM.

González Turmo, Isabel (1999) 'El pan: del plato al mantel', in *Los sabores de España y América,* ed. Antonio Garrido Aranda, Huesca: La Val de Onsera, pp. 59–92.

Hernández Bermejo, Esteban & González, Angel Lora (1996) 'El transporte recíproco entre América y Andalucía de especies agrícolas de interés alimentario', in *Cultura alimentaria Andalucía-América*, ed. Antonio García Aranda, México: UNAM.

Hopkins, A.G. (2002) 'Introduction: Globalization: An Agenda for Historians', in *Globalization in World History*, ed. A.G. Hopkins, London: Pimlico.

Institute of Culinary Education (2005) 'Culinary Arts Diploma Program Curriculum', viewed 23 November 2005, <http://www.iceculinary.com/career/culinary_outline.shtml>.

Lambert Ortiz, Elisabeth (1973) *The Complete Book of Caribbean Cooking*. New York: Ballantine Books.

Locher, Julie L. 2003. 'Fusion Cuisine' in *Encyclopedia of Food and Culture*, ed. Solomon H. Katz, New York: Thomson Gale.

Lovera, José R. (1991) *Gastronomía caribeña: Historia, recetas y bibliografía*. Caracas: CEGA.

Mignolo, Walter (2002) 'The Enduring Enchantment (Or the Epistemic Privilege of Modernity and Where to Go from Here)', *SAQ*, vol. 101, no. 4, pp. 927–54.

—— (1995) *The Darker Side of the Renaissance*. Ann Arbor: University of Michigan Press.

Mintz, Sidney W. (1996) *Tasting Food, Tasting Freedom: Excursions into Eating, Culture, and the Past*. Boston: Beacon Press.

—— ed. (1974) *Caribbean Transformations*. New York: Columbia University Press.

Neirinck, E. & Poulain, J. P. (2001) *Historia de la cocina y de los cocineros: Técnicas culinarias y prácticas de mesa en Francia de la Edad Media a nuestros días*. Barcelona: Editorial Zendrera Zariquiey.

Ortiz, Fernando (1978) *Contrapunteo cubano del tabaco y el azúcar*. Caracas: Biblioteca Ayacucho.

Parkhurst Ferguson, Priscilla (2004) *Accounting for Taste: The Triumph of French Cuisine*. Chicago: University of Chicago Press.

Quijano, Aníbal (1992) 'Colonialidad y modernidad-racionalidad' Cap 14 in *Los conquistados: 1492 y la población indígena de las Américas*, ed. Heraclio Bonilla, Ecuador, FLACSO, Tercer Mundo Editores and Ediciones Libri Mundi.

Recinos, Adrián (trans. ) (1960) *Popol Vuh: Las antiguas historias del Quiché*. México: Fondo de Cultura Económica.

Roach, Joseph (1996) *Cities of the Dead: Circum-Atlantic Performance*. New York: Columbia University Press.

Rodríguez, Douglas (1995) *Nuevo Latino: Recipes that Celebrate the New Latin American Cuisine*. Berkeley: Ten Speed Press.

Romero de Solís, Pedro (1996) 'Cultura bovina y consumo de carne en los orígenes de la América Latina', in *Cultura alimentaria Andalucía-América*, ed. Antonio García Aranda, México: UNAM.

Sahagún, Fray Bernardino de (2001) *Historia general de las cosas de la Nueva España* Vol I. Ed. Juan Carlos Temprano, Madrid: Dastin.

Thompson, David (2002) *Thai Food*. Berkeley and Toronto: Ten Speed Press.

Tomich, Dale W. (2000) 'The Other Face of Slave Labour: Provision Grounds and Internal Marketing in Martinique', in *Caribbean Slavery in the Atlantic World*, eds Verene A. Shepherd and Hilary McD. Beckles, Kingston: Ian Randle.

Van Aken, Norman (c.1988) 'Fusion', viewed 23 November 2003, <http://normans.com/index2.htm.> .

Watts, David (2000) 'Early Hispanic New World Agriculture, 1492 to 1509', in *Caribbean Slavery in the Atlantic World*, eds Verene A. Shepherd and Hilary McD. Beckles, Kingston: Ian Randle.

Madina Tlostanova

# THE IMPERIAL-COLONIAL CHRONOTOPE

## Istanbul-Baku-Khurramabad[1]

Mikhail Bakhtin in his studies of historical poetics of the Western European and Russian novel singled out a specific type of existential psychological chronotope connected with human self-identification and exceeding the frame of static mythic and folklore elements. The scholar named it a border chronotope or a threshold chronotope and linked with the problematic of existential transition, a critical transitory moment in the life of a character (Bakhtin 1986).

Obviously, Bakhtin was not interested in imperial/colonial relations, and even less with imperial differences[2] (Lieven 2000, Mignolo 2002, Mignolo & Tlostanova forthcoming, Tlostanova 2003) between Russia/Soviet Union and Western European imperial countries. That is why his border chronotopes are silent about imperial and colonial power differential. But what happens if we depart from Bakhtin's 'border chronotope' and look at this no doubt fundamental and useful concept through the lens of 'coloniality of power' (Quijano 2000) as it manifests itself in the works of transcultural writers coming from or writing about the cultures that have been marked with imperial/colonial difference. The imperial/colonial chronotope is characterized by in-between-ness, the protean nature, the constant state of transit, non-finality, parallel deterritorialization and dehistorizaion (i.e. falling out of space and time) – in short, by everything that Salman Rushdie called 'being elsewhere' (Rushdie 1991, p. 12), thus defining a possible territory of transcultural fiction, which is not limited politically or linguistically, but only in imaginative sense. Contrary to Rushdie, I think that it is not just the blurred category of imagination that is at work here, but a particular condition of transcultural subjectivity – that of restless non-belonging and a specific double consciousness, which generate complex relations with time and space and work for the creation of imperial/colonial chronotope that Bakhtin could not possibly write about. In this article I would like to dwell on the way the three contemporary transcultural writers coming from different traditions and places but equally marked with the colonial/imperial difference – Orhan Pamuk, Afanasy Mamedov and Andrey Volos – create each his unique chronotope of imperial or colonial city that in its turn defines the subjectivity of its inhabitants and the ways they cope with imperial/colonial differential.

## A few preliminary remarks

The degree of invented-ness of the colonial/imperial topos, of the imagined nature of space – is different in the works of various transcultural writers, but almost always it negates the conglomerate of locale, ethnic culture and time as the basis of poetological system typical for authenticity discourses. The way out of the dilemma of permanent transit has been looked for, both in the stale by now postmodernist paths and in the more attractive in-between routes, born at the juncture of the Western and non-western epistemology. The number of traditions, played on, questioned and interrelated in the trans-cultural works that I am going to discuss, most of which are not familiar to Western readers, is much wider and more complex than e.g. in case of the British empire and its (ex)colonies. As a result we have a complicated picture – on the one hand, these authors may demonstrate a certain nostalgic and at the same time parodic memory of their ethnic cultural background. On the other hand, there is a balancing between their inclination to several imperial and colonial traditions – e.g. a combination of the Ottoman and Russian-Soviet, or Austrian-Hungarian and Russian-Soviet imperial influence. Finally, the subaltern position of these very imperial histories in relation to capitalist modern empires and recently, the dictate of Americanization and globalization – lead to additional split-ness of identification in the works of trans-cultural authors, who cannot avoid reacting to the Western cultural expansion, which is also reflected in the way they interpret the imperial/colonial chronotope.

The 'imagined geography' of trans-culturation is an intentionally invented space, based on playing on various cultural topi, recreating and rethinking the artistic reality, distorting the angles under which it is placed in relation to the real world. It is built on the tendency to subjectification, to the more and more pronounced isolation from any real locales, to the unimaginable and ephemeral nature of the spaces, which gradually leads the authors further and further away from any spatial stability and materiality.

In the imperial/colonial chronotope the topos largely recreates the old model of utopia or dystopia adding to it the mutopian[3] element as well. The idea of nowhere-ness, lying in the basis of this chronotope, is close to the meaning of the word 'utopia' itself. What comes to mind here is not even the classical case of Thomas Moore's *Utopia*, but rather such trans-cultural works as Anglo-Australian author Samuel Butler's *Erewhon* (1872) – an anagram of the word 'nowhere' and a literate translation into English of the Greek 'utopia', where we encounter the theme of naming as the creation of the symbolic and real 'home' that lies in the basis of many literary works from various locales, sensitive to the imperial/colonial problematic. A classical example in this case would be of course the Caribbean aesthetics. In the local history of Eastern Europe, Russia, Caucasus and Central Asia the imperial/

colonial configuration was different, but here as well the toponymics retains the traces of various colonization layers, while the colonizers use the common strategy of erasing the previous cultural, linguistic and religious traditions even on the level of place-names.

The logic of interaction of cultural influences in the subaltern empires and their colonies is deeply rhizomic and based on the horizontal links and non-systemic differences, while any efforts to impose binarity on these locales from outside ultimately fail. At the same time the cultural, religious, ethnic incompatibility of the colonizers and the colonized in the space of Russian/Soviet or Ottoman empires has never been clearly asymmetrical in favor of the more modernized colonizer, as it was in case of Great Britain or France. On the contrary, in Russian empire it was often the logic of interaction of two or more subaltern and marginalized cultures, often on a similar or same stage of modernization, or it could be the logic of subordination of the more Europeanized people, e.g. the Baltic countries by a less European Russian colonizer. Finally, it could be the subordination by the in-confident Russian colonizer of the people with a much more ancient non-European history.

Time in the chronotope of in-between-ness changes its usual characteristics, such as linearity, one dimension, irreversibility, becoming multi-dimensional and moving with different speeds and in different directions, while the point of non-return (irreversibility) becomes highly arbitrary and can be easily negated. The Christian linear evolutionary idea of time, dominant in modernity, as well as the efforts to correlate it with the destiny of the whole mankind, is constantly presented as relative and arguable. This leads, on the one hand, to the revival of various concepts of cyclical time, both connected with traditional cultures and newly created, and on the other hand, sometimes, in the works of the same authors the concept of time correlates with the re-conceptualized but recognizable idea of time and history, coming from natural sciences. That is why a character from trans-cultural fiction easily combines in his concept of time the cyclical half-forgotten traditions, the logic of a net-game and the concepts of post-human existence.

The external and seemingly more objective time moves in several directions, so that linearity entangles and clashes with cyclical and backwards time models. Several time models also coincide in the minds of transcultural characters who cannot be easily attributed to the archaic cyclical model of time, because they live in the lacunas and gaps between the linearity of western modernity, the inadequacy of which they realize, and other time structures, which are being brought forward in their minds in various situations and often act together. A relatively subjective time which is born as a result does not have duration in the usual understanding of the word, or, in Bakhtin's definition, 'falls out of the normal flow of biographical time' (Bakhtin 1986, p. 280). Subjectification of external time leads to extreme relativity of personal time, to its arbitrary

acceleration or (less often) slowing down, sometimes, thickening, when an *other* acquires the ability to live out several lives – no matter how short or unhappy they are. Such characters live out several lives which seem to be crammed into one physical existence, pressed like a spring – in accordance with the fairytale beginning of B. Mukherjee's novel *Jasmine* (1991): 'My past happened many lifetimes ago' (Mukherjee 1991, p.5).

## The city chronotope

Let us now look at the chronotope of the imperial and colonial city in contemporary transcultural fiction from the point of view of imperial and colonial difference. The imperial city is often a sinister space where the imperial myths take shape and are realized in the life stories of various people. Here the colonial subject is defenseless and invisible. The imperial side of the city is viewed in utmost ruthless and phantasmagoric details by the individuals rejected and exiled by this space. They can be both colonial subjects and representatives of empire, carrying its deadening nature in themselves. Such a fearful and sickeningly attractive space is Moscow for the Bakinian character of Afanasy Mamedov and for the Western Ukrainian poet Otto von F. from Yuri Andrukhovich's book *Moscoviada*, or Istanbul – in Orhan Pamuk's *Black Book* and London in Rushdie's *Satanic Verses*.

Transcultural authors often juxtapose the colonial city topos and the space of the imperial capital. Depicting the colonial city as a crisscrossing of various imperial and colonized cultures, they do not necessarily base it on predictable accusations and resentment, but rather mark these portraits of colonial spaces with paradoxical nostalgia for the lost and imperfect, but still a paradise. Hence comes the idealizing of his childhood Baku by Mamedov and of Khurramabad (Dushanbe) by Volos, hence comes Bombay and Hong Kong nostalgia of Salman Rushdie and Paul Theroux.

Deleuze and Guattari, reflecting on the contrast of the State and the Nomadic War Machine, divided spaces into smooth and striated, giving an example of Chess and Go – the smooth space of Go in contrast with the striated space of Chess game, *nomos* against *polis* (Deleuze & Guattari 1992, p. 4). The chaotic post-imperial space – particularly in those territories of Eurasia where previously the nomadic empires existed for a long time, often acquires again the quality of smoothness and stops to be striated, but it retains definitely the traces of previous times, of crisscrossing of various imperial state machines, and it is important to try to understand the logic of these half-erased lines, which still determine the psychological types and reactions of the people living in these spaces.

The imperial city is the center of metropolis and its miniature model, a conglomerate of its main discourses, both verbal and non-verbal, connected

with human behavior, with architecture and with the very way of domesticating the space. The colonial city is a playful space of mimicry, of non-identical copy of metropolis, where not only the recognizable signs of colonization are palpably present in all their forms, but also the stability of original is effectively shaken, leading to its hybridizing. Both topi – the imperial and the colonial – undergo various artistic interpretations in the frame of the fantastic, the magic, the metamorphing, giving birth to imagined hybrid urban spaces, particularly if the time aspect of the urban chronotope corresponds to the moment of destruction, disintegration of empire and its reference system.

The global urbanization of the postmodern space in its relation to exodus and re-rooting of deterritorialized people in the imagined gigantic cosmopolis, also brings forward the rethinking of the city chronotope. Here the problem of skidding of the modernizing logic with its linear progressivist change of more archaic community forms to more modernized urbane ones comes forward. In the locales of civil wars and political turmoil in various parts of the world today one can encounter the peculiar phenomenon of de-urbanization and the reverse archaization of socio-cultural and economic reality, that also is reflected in fiction. Typical examples of such tendency would be the destroyed Yugoslavian towns, the Chechen capital Grozny, the ex-South African 'pearl' Johannesburg, the Tadzhic capital Dushanbe, etc.

The most interesting interpretations of imperial/colonial city chronotope emerge in the works of those writers whose cultural, linguistic, ethnic, imperial/colonial and religious positioning is marked with a paradigmatic insuperable in-between-ness. They cannot be classified unanimously within one local history, living on the crossroads of many instead, and not accepting any of the histories completely. For this reason their works cannot be so easily coincided with the well-known post-colonial fictional models. In the post-soviet space there are transcultural writers, whose identification is not firmly fixed in ethnic-cultural, linguistic or religious sense. Among them – A. Mamedov, A. Volos, M. Adamova and several others. Due to their in-between transcultural positioning they are far from ethnic-cultural extremism of any kind, their works cannot be regarded within the ethnic-national frame, interpreted according to political belonging or civil status of their authors. Very often, there are two or more cities living in them, creating a third one in the author's imagination. Rushdie, who can easily be regarded as a paradigmatic case of such sensibility, called himself and those like himself, the people marked with the insuperable sense of exile and loss – 'the world community of displaced authors' (Rushdie 1991, p.15). This becomes not only the acceptance of their often immigrant status, but also the sign of the deep spiritual internal exile, a metaphysical outside-ness out of which their art is born.

## The defeated capital. Orhan Pamuk's Istanbul

The polyphonic mythology of Istanbul – a mysterious ancient city between Europe and Asia, between the East and the West – lies in the center of Orhan Pamuk's novel *The Black Book,* overloaded with mysterious semiotic signs and marked with specific transcultural positioning of the author. In his 'autumn retrography' of the former Constantinople, in the winter Istanbul dream, the author is free from nostalgia of the great Ottoman Empire, but at the same time there is no feeling of inevitability and indisputability of the Western variant of modernization, chosen by Turkey with the collapse of the empire. Pamuk tries to make out in the ancient city the signs of alternative but never realized possibilities of another being, of other, almost lost epistemic traditions – Sufism, the Khurufites order doctrine, based on religious mysticism of the revelation type. A recurrent motif of the novel is an effort to formulate what would a different, non-western modernization of Turkey be like, a modernization, that in Pamuk's view, was strangled by Mustafa Kemal Ata Turk, whose image in the novel is compared indirectly with the famous dictators of the twentieth century. But in modern Istanbul even Ata Turk shrinks and turns into a kitsch plaster figure with blue light bulbs in place of eyes, put on sale in a junk store.

Another leitmotif in Pamuk's novel is a specific restlessness of his compatriots, their inability to finally master Istanbul's topos. They remain the aliens in the ancient Constantinople, who only manage to externally acquire the legacy of other ancient cultures, at the cross-roads of which stands the old city. For this reason Pamuk's characters are haunted with the sense of their own defeat, sadness, despair, peculiar stagnation (typical of all inhabitants of the defeated empires) and various post- and neo-imperial inferiority complexes. For the main character of Pamuk's novel Istanbul is a hostile place, floating from under his feet, as if in a nightmare. Pamuk sees his compatriots as stuck at the border, their modest world lacks a center and is not indicated on the maps, it is everywhere and nowhere at once, and they are not able either to be themselves or someone else.

The magic chronotope of Istanbul is based on the constant transit of the characters from Asia to Europe and back. The transition from Europe to Asia is connected with the metaphors of threshold, bridging, a complex mixture of various cultural influences and historical layers. European Istanbul is a synonym of Western modernization while the old Asian city is not just a way to the past, but to the impossible renaissance of the forgotten traditions – not necessarily archaic or authentic. Pamuk also strives to show that modernization and urbanization do not necessarily have to be in the form of painful breaking up, an artificial imposing of the Western models, as it happened in the ancient cosmopolitan city culture of Istanbul, which always – in its Byzantine and Turkish times – was marked by ethnic religious and

cultural tolerance. The millet system as the Ottoman variant of multicultural existence was destroyed together with the deterioration of territorial unity of empire and penetration of nationalist and socialist movements in the late nineteenth century. Istanbul of Pamuk's novel somehow retains a confluence of left radicalist, communist, nationalist sentiments and medieval mysticism of various Muslim heresies and secret orders, banned by Ata Turk in 1926.

The possibility of non-Western modernization stands in the center of the story of Bedya Ustod, who created the first Turkish mannequins for the museum of sultan Abdulhamid. His creations, competing with Allah – the exact copies of human beings, repeating even the typically Turkish gestures and mimics, were rejected by the religious elites of the country that had not started then yet its history of constant europeization. Later they were also rejected by the modernized style of the first years of the Republic – on account that their form was not Western enough and they desperately embodied the rejected national dream. They resembled the ordinary Turks too much, the people whom you could meet in the streets of Istanbul and thus – they did not correspond to the new myth of the West, that allowed even a common customer, buying a European dress, to feel himself a person from a far away and wonderful country. Pamuk ironically points out that it was for the sake of this dream of the West that the revolution in clothes, shaving off the beards and even changing of the alphabet – were introduced (Pamuk 2000, p. 81).

The semiotic nature of the city in this book lies not only in its buildings, squares or minarets, but also and more importantly in the faces and looks of the people living in Istanbul. The topography of the city is closely connected by the author with the topography of the human face and with the symbolic correlation of the alphabetic letters and the lines on the faces. The lines are connected with Arabic letters and for this reason, when the Turks rejected the Arabic alphabet in favor of the Latin one, they lost their secret and never acquired a different one instead. Now they are in need of a new way of discovering the mystery which would allow them to correlate the lines on the human faces with the 29 letters of the Latin alphabet. It is precisely the forgetting of the 'Sufi secret' that acts in the novel as a fantastic reason of the Ottoman's empire's defeat. In Pamuk's idea, when a civilization forgets about its mystery it means negating its own basis of thinking, and every people, copying others and forgetting about its own sources, inevitably dies (p. 537).

One of the crucial motifs in the interpretation of Istanbul's topos is the Western violation of the Eastern city which is recreated mostly in the metaphors connected with the magic meaning of geographical maps and the remaking of the real city under the influence of westernization. That is why on the pages of Pamuk's book we encounter the retired *pashas*, who all their lives long were trying to adjust the art and science of the West to the East, for many years creating on the maps the linden alleys in Berlin style – instead of

crooked Istanbul streets, or the straight boulevards with bridges like sun rays in Parisian manner; the photographers making the sky look Prussian blue and retouching the black earth, making it the color of the English green lawn (p. 242). The city becomes almost an animate character in Pamuk's novel with its grotesque descriptions of the old Istanbul lopsided bay windows, hanging over the street, the darkness of the abandoned waste lot, where time and space disappear, the upper floors of the buildings on both sides of the street – flowing towards each other (Pamuk 2000, p. 148).

The western culture is presented by Pamuk as simultaneously attractive and destructive for his Turkish characters. Thus even their love is presented as a juxtaposition and a complex interaction of various models of modernization – the wife and cousin of the main character is called Ruya which means a dream, an attractive reverie and not a Turkish one at that, but rather a product of cultural hybridizing with the West. She is easily lead by the socialist and left-radicalist theories, choosing a more dynamic, cruel, critical towards Turkey path of her step-brother and lover Jelal – a doppelganger of the narrator, whose identity he is striving to claim. As the illusive city itself, its inhabitants are balancing on the verge of real and imagined, the mundane and the mysterious. This is clearly expressed in the image of the narrator spying on himself and looking from the mysterious windows of the city at the man in a dark coat walking along its snow-covered streets – it is Galip meeting himself on the boulevards and side streets of old Istanbul.

For Pamuk the material reality itself and not just the internal worlds of human beings is influenced by various ideas and discourses and hence is quite vulnerable and fragile. That is why he says that people make murders copying other, earlier committed crimes, that they fall in love under the influence of already known love stories which are connected with each other as the enfilades of rooms in a palace, that is why Istanbul itself can change under the influence of the changed attitudes of its people. The motif of fragility and elusiveness of space and its dependence on the human will is central in Pamuk's book where the theme of violent westernization of Istanbul is expressed – among other things – in an incomprehensible change of the climate in the city, of its flora and fauna. The parrots left the city and their place was taken by the crows, when it started snowing in Istanbul. The modern Istanbul is also a scary city that forgot its mystery and borrowed the external elements of someone else's life. Hence the apocalyptic pictures of destruction and slow deterioration, constantly emerging in the character's imagination, in the reasoning of his interlocutors, in the artistic reality of the novel. Pamuk speaks again and again of the miserable crowd, the old cars, the bridges slowly sinking into water, the heaps of cans, the warped pavement, the incomprehensible large letters, the unclear bill boards, the inscriptions on the walls, the advertisement of alcohol and cigarettes, the minarets, that no one reads azan from any more, the mounts of stones, dust and dirt (pp. 169–170).

These haunting descriptions strangely resemble the pictures of the immigrant poor part of Babylondon, seen by Gabriel – a half fantastic character of Rushdie's *Satanic Verses*, and primarily this refers to the characteristically easy and almost imperceptible shift, a lacking boundary between the signs of material and spiritual deterioration and decline.

The key theme for the understanding of Istanbul's chronotope is the theme of original and the copy, mimicking, borrowing and independent creative work (the latter is impossible for the author, moreover, he even states that imitation in art is the real mastery). But in the interpretation of simulacra and copies Pamuk follows Baudrillard's and Deleuze's ideas with a clear variation. The novel is full of copies, they literally chase the main character everywhere – from the annoying commercial of olive paste 'Ender', the copies of which are multiplying and diminishing on the labels, to the flat in the building that the family used to own, as a stiff copy of the past, recreating the smallest details of the dust, the smell of forgotten perfume, the yellow newspapers. The city itself also is presented as a copy – good or bad – of the western original, resembling a museum exposition. But in Pamuk's de-centered world none of the copies equals the original word for word, and in fact none of the originals is possible in the long run, because each of them is a copy of something that existed before. Finally, in a certain sense, the theme of the copy is regarded within the mimicry problematic and that of imperial difference, which in its Turkish variant acquires a specific overtone – here we speak not of a colony in the real sense of the word, but of a defeated empire, conquered by the winning West not by means of colonial expansion, but rather by more subtle ways of cultural and epistemic colonization. Among these 'humanistic' means of modernization, that the author connects with deprivation of memory, of the past, of history, Pamuk points out the cinema, the music, the demonstration of the beautiful women's faces and landscapes, the bright bottles, the weapons, the airplanes, the clothes, etc. – they all attain better results than the more traditional methods of colonization, that he did not even give a name to, only commenting that they were used by the missionaries in Latin America and Africa (p. 165).

## Afanasy Mamedov's 'Bascow'

The chronotope of the imperial and colonial city plays an important role in the nostalgic novel *Khazar Wind,* written by Afanasy Mamedov and superimposing Moscow and his native Baku. If in Pamuk's book the ancient underground of Istanbul was the focus of the esoteric mystical knowledge, in Mamedov's work the underground clearly carries a negative infernal meaning, and is expressed in the image of Moscow metro where 'God disappears', as people and birds disappear, where the muscular sculptures at the station 'Revolutionary Square'

seem to be ready to come alive and jump off their granite places directly into the horrible 1937 and take all passengers with them, along the dark underground tunnels to their native Lubjanka' (Mamedov 2000, p. 242).

The metro-underground is similar to the fairytale wonderland that you can get into not only through the rabbit hole, but also through the sewage hatchway. The laws of time and space here change and time can freeze, but one can also go through an existential moment of spiritual enlightenment and revelation. That is what happens with Mamedov's character – the ascensionalist (the one who strives to the vertical) painter, who envisions his most successful canvas precisely in metro, together with seeing his own life under a new and unexpected angle, because every ascending along the vertical starts always from the absolute bottom symbolized by the underground.

But it is not the Moscow tube that is used by Mamedov as a fantastic transport, connecting the past and the present by a myriad of strange coincidences. It is tram No 6 from his Bakinian childhood, unexpectedly coming into the Moscow present and bringing him into the small flat at the outskirts of Moscow. The tram imagery is crucial here as well as in Pamuk's book, working for the creation of a specific atmosphere of a southern town by the sea, where even the trams lazily shine in the sun and move slowly, allowing the fast boys to jump off while the tram is still moving. Pamuk's main character desperately tried to read his city as a book and decipher its secret signs. Mamedov's autobiographical hero is also looking for the mysterious signs and correspondences, pointing in the direction of his previous Bakinian life in alien Moscow.

Mamedov creates a hybrid imagined space, as a collision of the real, native topos of Baku (the lost Eden of his childhood) and an other, alien topos of Moscow, where only small and carefully chosen isles can become native for the character. Finally, he creates an absolutely imagined, hybrid space in between, conceptualized mainly in visual terms, because the protagonist is an artist. Salman Rushdie would probably call this phantasmagoric hybrid world – 'Bascow' (a cross between Baku and Moscow). Such a subjectification leads to the character's strive to narrow down and limit his life space, e.g. when he recreates his ex-Bakinian flat that does not exist any more in a Moscow slum at Skhodnenskaya metro station, or when he chooses particular patches and little spaces in the alien Moscow topos, pierced here and there with Stalin's 'Vampires' (the word refers to the style in architecture that was associated with Stalin and called Stalin's Empire). A specific feature of this topos-creating activity is the unity, the magmatic plasticity of various times and spaces. That is why a tram from the Bakinian past materializes suddenly in Moscow present.

Baku and Moscow are not just two cities which live in the main character, they are two capitals – one is a colonial capital and the other is imperial, one is cosmopolitan in a specific Oriental way, almost as multicultural as Odessa or Tashkent, the other – with its official status of metropolis and a pseudo

European tint. The names and titles from his Bakinian childhood carry not only a sign of coloniality, of the outskirts of the Russian and later Soviet empire, but again, as in case of Istanbul, the remnant of a more ancient and non-western urban culture of a trade megalopolis, a multi-linguistic and tolerant port-city at the crossroads of civilizations, on the border of Europe and Asia. This city saw the caravans and the merchants, the Roman legions and the Zoroastrians. As in Pamuk's book, Baku is presented by Mamedov as almost a living being – with its lopsided old streets smelling of sweat and meat, its houses, growing together as the eyebrows of Eastern beauties, and the balconies, covered with vines as if with veils, where the long Bakinian evening tea-drinking takes place. The governor's park with the green theater, where the author used to be taken for a walk when he was a kid and where he had his first date under a palm tree, exists in this topos along with the Old Town – the fortress, Icheri-Shekher, the famous Sea Boulevard and the Torgovaya (Trade) Street, and the Soviet-imperial motif – the Bolshevik Kirov's monument over the restaurant 'Friendship', the old men with their Muslim beards under the palms, along with the tolling of the bells at the Armenian church that sounds so close from the Jewish quarter Juude-Meilesi – 'a real present for Shagal' (p. 110).

The Russian empire imagery is brought forward when the author describes the character's family dwelling and their favorite places – Agamalievs' flat with the door chain from tsar Nikolay's times, the Vorontsov's palace, the pre-revolutionary books that belonged to the grand-grandfather. When Afik is reading these books he is annoyed with their imperial sense of the 'big time', expressed not only in the fine paper and print, but also in the 'short-sighted and simple cheerfulness' – an unjustified self-confidence (p. 95). This link between his family and the Russian-Soviet imperial-colonial complex causes Afik's rejection of the present Islamic-Eastern variant of Azerbajdzan's re-colonization.

As in Pamuk's book, the transcultural topos of Baku which is called by the author simply the City (with a capital letter), as Mikhail Bulgakov did describing his Kiev, is clearly marked with specific tolerance, which couldn't be eliminated even in the Soviet decades, but was destroyed in just several months after the collapse of USSR and the conflicting building of the independent nation-state.

The winter miserable Baku in Mamedov's book comes unexpectedly similar to the winter myth of Istanbul in Pamuk's novel. It is also an Eastern city where there should not be any snow, but ironically it finds itself in a new and more Western climate zone due to its peculiar imperial/colonial configuration.

Discussing the presentation of Baku and Moscow topos by Mamedov it is important to take into account a paradigmatic duality of the main character, his inability to become a native in any culture – Azeri or Moscow, colonial or metropolitan. Brought up on the Western European and Russian-Soviet

intellectual and aesthetic canon, he cannot completely reject certain deeper Eastern epistemic roots. Although the main character calls his family an imperial one, rather it should be called cosmopolitan. It answers the definition of not quite Russian/Soviet variant of modernization, close to what Pamuk is describing in his book. Mamedov's character knowing almost no Azeri language and very little about its culture – tends to see it at least in the beginning in exoticist terms. Aestheticizing the Oriental difference, including his own, as if he was looking at it with the Western eyes, he is trying to remember his disappearing city, knowing that his life would continue from now on – bypassing Baku. But he is remembering it clearly in the wrong way, already changed and seen through the prism of stereotypes of Western exoticism and nostalgia: 'the flat roofs, the Maiden Tower – the symbol of Baku, the Nargen island, the women, cooking piti-bozbash in big iron pots, the girls with jugs on their shoulders, the minarets of Teze-Pira, the poetic side-streets and little yards, the blue communal night where everyone knew everything about everybody, the flowers, the tastes, the odors of the Bakinian life, the dark-blue shadow of the streets and the melting heat of the summer, the slow speech of Bakinian inhabitants . . . ' (p. 64).

In this sense the main character is entirely the product of this Bakinian city subculture, which is between the quasi-western modernization of the Russian and Soviet empire and the more archaic non-urban culture of the rest of Azerbajdzan. Hence the constant juxtaposition of a specific Bakinian microcosm and the 'regions' (provinces), the inhabitants of which are dreaming of making their way to the capital, even if colonial, that lives according to its own laws and in its own pace of modernization of an Eastern city. In the Bakinian part of the book the character acts as a colonizer of his own native city, exoticizing its topos, making it correspond to the norms acquired as a result of education and bringing up in a particular family and social environment. The character would acquire a completely different way of looking at things in Moscow, where the object of exotization and imperial demonization would be himself. He will mockingly play on the Moscow stereotypes about the people from Caucasus and Trans-Caucasia, whom they cannot tell apart either in ethnic-cultural or religious and linguistic sense. In the description of Moscow the optics changes as this city is regarded not through its imperial ethnic and cultural discriminatory elements, but rather through totalitarianism of the communist regime – the sensibility of a colonized subject here mingles with and flows into the sensibility of an individual, repressed by the ideological system.

As Mamedov was writing his novel for several years, the book turned out to be a diary of his own changing self positioning in relation to the Soviet Empire. In the beginning, the gloomy image of the Soviet Union – still intact – is hovering over the heroes of *Khazar Wind*. The people leaving the City in the late 1980s still do not see themselves as immigrants or refugees, but

only as lucky colonial subjects going to live in the metropolis and on top of that – having all the legal rights, equal with the titular nation – at least on paper. They do not yet understand that metropolis has its own subtle ways of repression and discrimination, which easily combine with formal egalitarianism. Urbanization as one of the important sides of modernization is recurrent in the novel and repeated in the experience of the village people coming to Baku, as well as on the larger scale, in the story of the migrants from the outskirts of the empire who are looking for luck and wealth in its center. Toward the end of the narrative the main character would become more and more aware of his double status – now he is an immigrant who never became a native in the unfriendly and cold Russia, and a person, whose childhood world is forever lost and nonexistent, who is expelled by the new and hostile Baku together with his family.

The disappearing city of the childhood is succeeded by the scary Baku of the civil war, following the Sumgait massacre. It is the city where one can always hear the machine guns and where people have to make it home before the curfew. There is an episode in the book which is important for the understanding of the relations between the colonized (Azeries and Armenians) and the Russian/Soviet empire, just before its collapse, half-heartedly trying to put the order back into the colony which it does not really need any more. The attitude of Slavic soldiers and officers to both the ethnic group they are persecuting and the group they are presumably protecting in this conflict clearly echoes the racism of the White man's burden type, which does not make difference between the Chinese, the Black and the Indian. The author casually informs us about a patrol tank riding along the old Bakinian street, destroying everything alive and man-made in its way and violating the beloved city. The two Slavic representatives of the empire, driving the tank, behave as if they already had all the keys from all the doors of the City and could not tell an Azeri from an Armenian calling all of them the 'Chureks' (corn bread, also in condescending Slavic slang – a non-European, Asiatic person) (p. 82).

Little by little Mamedov shows how in the new independent Azerbajdzhan the imperial-colonial configuration is changing once again – the pendulum of identification goes in the direction of Turkey and not the defeated Russian empire. Even the change of alphabet from Cyrillic to Latin demonstrates a clear change of the model to the Turkish variant of modernization. Connecting the disappeared Baku of the Russian and Soviet imperial times and Baku at the crack of the twenty-first century, the author mentions that the main character's grandmother went to a specific gymnasium where the local girls were made into the good second-rate copies of the Russian mademoiselles, and now in the new Baku this old school turns into a Turkish Lyceum and the new director equals Azeris and Turks, making the former be a copy of the latter.

A similar historical parallel is constructed by the author in connection with the crisscrossing and clashing of the Ottoman and Russian influences in the local Bakinian and Agamalievs' history. It is the Turkish genocide of the Armenians at the end of the nineteenth – beginning of the twentieth century that still lies deep in the genetic memory of the Bakinians, it is the arrival of Nuri-Pasha, Ata Turk Anver's brother, later on – the coming of the Scottish troops, and finally – the 11th Red Army – the succeeding colonizers that would be always remembered by the city. The new genocide of the looming twenty-first century leads to similar historical cataclysms and mass migrations, which will be forever imprinted as deep lines on the City's ancient face. Agamaliev's family is culturally European oriented and striving for assimilation, and therefore it always finds itself on the side of the Russian/Soviet empire, which with the same consistency grinds and destroys these people with its ruthless millstones. The grandfather of the main character *bey* Agamaliev is fighting the *basmachs* (the counter-revolutionary groups in Central Asia during the 1918–1920 Civil War), the people who are closer to himself than the new Soviet power, but this does not save him from Stalin's camps. Afanasy, who inherited the name of his grandfather that perished in Stalin's purges in 1937, is trying once again to acquire the colonial strategy of mimicry that did not save his ancestor. It is presented as a certain strategy of keeping out of sight, hiding in his hole, until the stormy times finish, waiting for the better moment. In the story of the main character's parents it is the Western model mediated by Soviet modernization, that comes forward. The same way as Pamuk's characters, Afanasy's parents were fascinated with Western cinema and in stuffy Bakinian nights easily repeated the great deeds of the foreign movie heroes, borrowing their clothes together with their beautiful names and their post-war popularity. These layers of previous cultural models again and again bring Afanasy to painful nostalgia, to the image of the sunny Baku of the 1950s that, alas, vanished forever.

## The city of happiness and joy. Andrey Volos's Khurramabad

*Khurramabad* tells the story of the mass exodus of Russians from the ex-Soviet colony of Tadzhikistan. It is written by a Russian writer, who should have been classified as a colonizer rather than a victim of the empire. And yet this is probably one of the most clearly anti-colonial and anti-imperial books in all post-soviet fiction. The most powerful stories in this book deal with the problem of the ex-colonizer's self-identification. But no less important is the metamorphosis of the alien land into the native one and the ex-motherland Russia's becoming alien for the new refugees. Thus, Volos touches upon the arbitrary and open connection of territory, ethnic-national identity, language and culture. The prototype of his imagined topos is quite real Dushanbe, the

capital of Tadzhikistan, while Khurramabad is a hybrid, based on the contrast of the cruelty of Volos's stories and the folklore toponym Khurramabad, the city of happiness, full of green trees and generous people, which was borrowed from the Turkish and Persian fairy tales.

Volos also touches upon the Oriental topos put under the artificial and deadly influence of Soviet modernization, although Khurramabad, or its real prototype Dushanbe, is an forcefully created urban topos, the same way as Grozny in Chechnya: for these mountain regions the urban culture has never been a typical element of social structure and partly because of that, as soon as the Soviet modernization went away, it gave please to de-urbanization, characteristic for many megalopolises throughout the world.

The writer sees the war in Tadzhikistan as a social, rather than ethnic-national or political upheaval. That is why in his stories there is always a motif of the quest for the others to blame – be they Russians, Armenians or even Tadzhiks themselves belonging to various fighting clans. The author stresses here the non-ethnic nature of belonging to a certain locale. In the absurd world of Khurramabad both the Tadzhiks and the Russians may become 'aliens' and 'natives' – may finds themselves among the thugs and marauders or in the self-defense regiment, meeting in the streets of the city, which is howling with horror and pain, the city where the air itself is full of violence, humiliation and robbery (Volos 2000, p. 367). The destruction of the urban civilization in Khurramabad during the civil war is also shown by Volos as a clash of a more modernized culture with the archaic one. The nationalistic opposition uses as its cannon-fodder the poor jobless youngsters from the villages, easy to manipulate by the ancient (and endemic for Tadzhikistan) clan social structure that just takes the form of the new political forces. The pictures of de-urbanization are terrible, absurd and even fantastic in this book – we see the people, who live in sky scrappers, but do not have running water, gas, electricity for months, spending days and nights in the lines for bread, making fires in their balconies and washing their hair with clothes washing detergents. But these pictures are also marked with almost documentary objectivity and a complete lack of sensationalism, at times bringing Volos's narrative to a truly tragic level.

In Khurramabad, a city where time stopped or started moving backwards, there are several minitopi around which the narrative is organized. It is the topos of the market as the center of any urban culture in the East, the topi of the city square and the cemetery, each of which presents a particular time layer corresponding to a certain stage of modernization and consequently, is closer or farther from the indigenous culture of this locale. *Khurramabad* literally starts in the cemetery and it will appear more than once in the book as a leitmotif of the contradictory connection with the past and with the alien land that became native for its Russian/Soviet inhabitants. The market in *Khurramabad* has two images. First, it is a real noisy Oriental bazaar with its

traditional division of roles, but seen through the exoticizing eyes of a Russian, who connects this imagery with Oriental fairytales from his childhood. The author constantly stresses this difference, juxtaposing the more or less objective descriptions of the bazaar and its interpretation by the newcomers for whom even the quarreling of the two Tadzhik onion sellers about the price sounds like wonderful poetry. Another face of the same market topos is presented in Khurramabad's city square which retains some of its initial characteristics and adds new imperial-colonial layers connected with distorted in Soviet time ancient symbolism of the market square. The city squares, along with their official role of the Soviet imperial centers, become for Volos the places of mass massacres, the un-ruled instincts, presented with no fairytale touches.

The Bakhtinian carnival meaning of the market square is replaced with communist symbolism, which strives to introduce the element of high official culture, building its own ideological sanctuaries – not Christian, not Muslim, but Soviet, as, e.g. a standard building of the central committee of the communist party, that had its clones in all Soviet republics/colonies. The Soviet Empire marked its political and cultural sanctuaries with certain signs, still found in many post-soviet spaces, modeling the architectural image of the colonial city. In the hot and dusty Khurramabad, this specific semiotization of reality is realized in the fountains. Before the Soviet rule the Central Asian culture associated fountains with oasis, with life-giving water, usually placing them at the crossroads of the caravan ways and in the center of towns and villages. In the Soviet time the fountain symbolism was frozen and stylized in the two official fountains of the city, marking the politicized square with Soviet establishments, and a 'democratic' fountain in front of the Opera theater where the author places the main character of another story – a Russian lumpen – alcoholic, nicknamed 'Beljash', who calls himself the 'boss of the fountain'.

Practically in every story there is the same compositional element at work – the flow of peaceful life and the images of wonderful Khurramabadian nature are suddenly disrupted with the scary, fantastic overtones, comparisons and metaphors, born in the minds of the frightened characters. This produces a strong impression on the reader because Volos generally works in a reserved and even seemingly mimetic narrative style, far from phantasmagoria or grotesque. The more shocking then comes the feeling of sudden split-ness, a crossed border, a point of non-return from the reality gone mad. The descriptions of Khurramabad before the civil war are full of gastronomic and still-life comparisons: 'the sugar bowl of the airport', 'the pink foam of the blooming almond trees', 'the glazed mountain peaks', 'the huge bowls of the stadium and the Komsomol lake' (p. 153).[4] While the later heaping images of violence, murder of innocent people, the looting – are presented in their bare, almost documentary laconic form, which, however, is often tinted with

expressionistic tones of a horrible metamorphosis. In front of the scared Volos's characters' eyes the city topos goes mad: 'This was so strange, . . . as if the trees would start walking or the buildings themselves would start moving along the streets, crushing the fleeing horrified people' (p. 159). Khurramabad is presented as an injured organism which can be hibernating or crucified with horror and pain in the midst of political turmoil, an organism, that can liven up with the tender colors and odors of the blooming trees and the sounds of the forever prevailing oriental bazaars in the spring, and finally, in the most telling episodes, the city is compared with mother's womb, where 'there is no hunger, no unhappiness, where you cannot call anything *your own* or *alien* because everything exists for you' (p. 371).

One of the best stories in the book – 'Little Grass Snake' – tells about a strange affection between the elderly Russian woman, refusing for a long time to leave the city because she has nowhere to go, and the poisonous snake, that crawled into her apartment by chance, looking for food and shelter and soon became a dear and close friend. Here the topos of Khurramabad is compressed into one injured building by the road, leading from the airport to the city center. The writer stresses the fragility of life balance, suddenly interrupted by the heavy tanks, that ironed the city, causing the people and animals living in and under the cracked land – loose their normal environment. The tanks of Empire, sent to repress the mutiny, are also presented in a personified way of the reality gone mad – not just as mechanisms, driven by people, but as fantastic green battle elephants, who seem to have their own will. 'Little Grass Snake' is based on a simple idea that when there is no platform for understanding left – either national or imperial, ethnic and religious – the only and last component, on which the main character is building her relations with the snake – a newcomer from an *other* world – switches on. It is an elementary unity of living beings, even if so different, 'and a human gets used to anything in the world, and moreover – to the living creatures' (p. 176), states Volos.

'Home' in Volos's book is presented as unattainable ideal for the people, who all of a sudden become the outsiders in this land. Home is the quintessence of stability, safety, protection. In Soviet times these people used to live on the thin crust of external artificially created life, and now they urgently need the material signs of their connection with reality, such as home. This is true about the main character of the story 'A House by the River', who almost lost his dream house and for whom the defense of his home turns out to be the dilemma of the moral choice – either to stay a human being with dignity, or to behave in the manner that is dictated to him by the crazy world around – i.e. to kill, to betray, to rob.

Unsuccessfully trying to answer the question of what makes a person an *other* or a *native* in the land, Volos's Russian characters, who are often the descendants of the Soviet unwilling colonizers, regard imperial Russia as an

alien space, while Tadzhikistan that becomes alien for them in one blink, the land where already two generations of their ancestors were buried, still remains for them a native land. Such are most of Volos's characters, who were not asked if they wanted to be replanted in the new soil or not. In this sense his view of the destiny of Russian settlers in Central Asia is rather unconventional, because instead of usual charges against the colonizers, the reader traces here the absurd logic of the Soviet empire, which was vainly trying to reach the certain leveling of the economic and social status of the colonies and the metropolis and at the same time to implant the imperial Soviet ideology by constant inflow of Slavic people, often with infringed rights (the prisoners, the so called special migrants, the people fleeing repressions, etc.) into the under-modernized outskirts of the empire.

In Volos's book topos is presented as a complex natural-urbanistic phenomenon – the streets of Khurramabad are inseparable from the smell of dust, from the earth and the air, and the author states many times that it is not the language, not ethnicity, not religion that define the individual's belonging to the locale. Each of the empire's step-children is trying to reject the forceful deterritorialization in his own way, repeating stubbornly that he will stay in Khurramabad and it is better if they kill him there, on his native land. The topos of Khurramabad itself has a certain magic of clearly non-ethnic nature, and leaves its mark on all its inhabitants, irregardless of their ethnic belonging and age. That is why Volos calls his Russian heroes 'skinny, dark, dried out Khurramabadians'.

Another important mini-topos in *Khurramabad* emerging in the story with a symbolic title 'An Other' is a train station. The main character San Sanych Dubrovin is reluctantly leaving Tadzhikistan for unknown Russia. The topos of 'no-where-ness' here corresponds to the mood of tedious waiting and frozen time, in a wider sense – of exile, exodus, the pain of rejection, for the story is set between the old and new life, between Tadzhikistan and the alien and hostile Russia. The author renders with graphic accuracy the sense of the halted time and the strange state of the character who is running away, remaining physically in the same place. San Sanych defines his state as exile, because even remaining in the same place he is already exiled, as everything around him all of a sudden became alien and dangerous. Volos carefully constructs the story on the contrast of the eternal – the nature, the mountains, the sky, the river, the previously existing peaceful life, and the absurdity of the present twisted reality. The fantastic suppositions, that he uses as the outset of many of his stories (e.g. in 'The Other' it is the railway, destroyed by an unknown opposition, thus delaying the main character for a month in the empty and miserable railway station, cut off the rest of the world) could be easily regarded as typical for existentialist parables, where the individual is put by the author deliberately in artificial conditions of survival and various hardships, but in fact, they are almost documentarily real.

The temporal aspect of the city chronotope is presented by Volos as several parallel coexisting times. The time of empire and its human remnants stopped, but the rest of the old city's life still continues behind the high clay walls. It stays almost untouched by the political events on the surface. And only a few neglected old Russian women, resembling absurdist characters in Ionesco's style, continue to sell in the streets of Khurramabad their strange useless goods, that stress the loneliness and uselessness of the owners: 'Everything they had was mysteriously single – a fork, a glass, a book with no cover, a boot with no laces, a torn wristlet, the watch itself, irreparably broken many years ago – and it was obvious that even if we gathered all these old women from all over the city, it would be impossible to find even two matching objects' (p. 370).

Russia is presented in Volos's book as an almost always absent, unfamiliar and hostile image of empire, an unfriendly step-mother for the characters, who rejects her step-children forever because they are stigmatized by their connection with Tadzhikistan. For the young characters of *Khurramabad*, who are not familiar with the empire and associate Russia only with an Arcadian picture from the ABC book, Russia at first acts an ideal topos, which is finally destroyed only in the last story with a meaningful title 'Zavrazhje' (the etymology of this word clearly incorporates not only 'ovrag' – ravine, but also 'vrag' – enemy). Volos draws an almost biblical exodus of his characters, in the beginning of which there stands a fairytale image of Khurramabad ('Ascend'), equipped with all necessary dreamlike elements, constantly balancing on the verge between the real and the imagined (e.g. the unreal mountains are perceived as being drawn on a piece of fabric or cut out of huge pieces of dusty papier-mâché). In the last story, on the contrary, the author turns to almost naturalistic optics, finally making his characters wake up and shake off their long-time enchantment, so that soon they realize that neither blood, nor religion or national identity are able to define the concept of the native, making them forever *others* in Zavrazhje, as well as in all other parts of the drunk, degraded, lacking religious or any other faith provincial Russia, giving an unfriendly greeting to its unwillingly prodigal sons. Russia in Volos's interpretation is an absent actor, an object of blind hatred or equally blind idealization, it is yet another alienated *othered* space. The images of post-Soviet Russia are presented as cruel, rejecting the border characters, who are revolving in the vortex of history, unable to reterritorialize, finding themselves unwillingly in the position of the hostages of empire, its prosecuted messengers with no rights and no mission, in accordance with Amos Oz's idea that a typically western quest for identity in this trans-cultural fiction changes into a certain negation of the character by the place, when the problem is not that the individual does not know himself, but that the place does not know him and does not want him to exist (Gordimer 1995, p. 45).

In Volos's position there is almost no nostalgia, typical for Mamedov, and yet the pictures of hunger, the civil war, the lines for bread, the deserted Khurramabadian parks comprise a topos drawn with love and despair.

## Conclusion

Chronotope acquires a central function in the works of the transcultural writers marked with both imperial and colonial difference. Andrey Volos's, Afanasy Mamedov's, Orhan Pamuk's works are among the best examples of transcultural fiction, incorporating and sharing many themes, motifs and metaphors, and drawing specific characters who become the new Ahasueruses of globalization, the new cosmopolites (often against their will), the complex selves with multiple national, ethnic, religious and linguistic attachments. Transcultural aesthetics and ontology is grounded in and simultaneously generates itself the imperial/colonial chronotope, within which there are more local chronotopes of imperial and colonial city/town, exodus, home and unhomeleness, etc. It is marked with a protean and unfinished nature, with constant transit, with falling out of space and time, with de-territorialization and de-historization, with existential restlessness, which both the ex-masters and the ex-subalterns share. A Turkish author Orhan Pamuk, a Muscovite with Bakinian roots Afanasy Mamedov and a Russian from Tadzhikistan Andrey Volos – all offer interesting and different spatial and temporal transcultural models, which are often based on the fairytale, fantastic imagery of utopian or dystopian kind, on the subjective, cyclical or many-directional time.

Within the city chronotopes presented in the works of these writers (the trans-imperial – Moscow and Istanbul, and the trans-colonial – Baku and Khurramabad) there are several minitopi organizing the space and the time of the imperial and colonial city – it is the market square, the cemetery, the underground, etc. Each of these books is also a story of painful modernization, fighting with and conquering the previous local traditions, bringing forward its own myths, meta-narratives and unresolved dilemmas of subjectivity. This happens in a semiotic way in case of Pamuk, takes a nostalgic Proustian form in case of Mamedov, finally, it is expressed in the specific double vision, circulating between the oriental fairytale and the cruelty of at times almost documentary Volos's narrative, while the empire itself acts for many new modern Ahasueruses as an absent and hostile space, where they do not feel at home.

Transcultural aesthetics generates a variety of imperial/colonial chronotopes, and in this article I dwelled on only three examples, leaving out many other interesting instances – from the Western Ukrainian Yuri Andrukhovich and American Paul Theroux to Australian Peter Carey and South African J.M. Coetzee and A. Dangor. The number and the impact of trans-cultural writings

has been constantly growing on the global scale lately and it is crucial to continue working on the conceptualizing of these phenomena, acutely reflecting our complex and constantly changing world.

## Notes

1 This article is based on a chapter from Tlostanova (2005).
2 By imperial difference I mean the difference between the capitalist Western empires of modernity (England, France, Germany) and the subaltern non-capitalist and non-western (not quite Western) empires, like the Ottoman Empire, Russia or Austria-Hungary. For more details see: Lieven (2000), Mignolo (2002), Mignolo & Tlostanova (forthcoming), Tlostanova (2003).
3 For the definition of mutopia see Csicsery-Ronay (1997).
4 See also the English translation, Volos (2001).

## References

Bakhtin, M. (1986) 'Formy Vremeni i Khronotopa v Romane. Ocherki po Istoricheskoy Poetike'. *Literaturno-kriticheskije Statji*. M. Khudozhestvennaya Literatura. [Forms of time and chronotope in the novel]

Csicsery-Ronay, I. (1997) 'Notes on Mutopia'. *Postmodern Culture*. An Electronic journal of interdisciplinary criticism (http://jefferson.village.virginia.edu/pmc), vol. 8, no. 1.

Deleuze, G. & Guattari, F. (1992) *Nomadology: The War Machine*. New York: Semiotext(e).

Gordimer, N. (1995) *Writing and Being*. New Heaven: Harvard University Press.

Lieven, D. (2000) *Empire. The Russian Empire and Its Rivals*. New Haven & London: Yale University Press.

Mamedov, A. (2000) *Khazarsky Veter*. M.: Text. [Khazar Wind], p. 242.

Mignolo, W. D. (2002) 'The Enduring Enchantment: (or the Epistemic Privilege of Modernity and Where to Go from Here)', *The South Atlantic Quarterly*, vol. 101, no. 4, pp. 927–954.

Mignolo, W. D. & Tlostanova, M. (forthcoming) 'The Logic of Coloniality and the Limits of Postcoloniality' in *The Postcolonial and the Global*, eds. R. Krishnaswamy and J. Hawley. Minnesota: University of Minnesota Press.

Mukherjee, B. (1991) *Jasmine*. London: Virago Press.

Pamuk, O. (2000) *Chernaja Kniga*. Trans. V. Feonova. Sankt-Peterburg: Amfora. [Black Book].

Quijano, A. (2000) 'Coloniality of Power, Eurocentrism, and Latin America', *Nepantla*, vol. 1, no. 3, pp. 533–580.

Rushdie, S. (1991) *Imaginary Homelands. Essays and Criticism. 1981–1991*. London: Granta Books.

Tlostanova, M. (2005) *The Sublime of Globalization? Sketches on Transcultural Subjectivity and Aesthetics*. Moscow: URSS.

——. (2003) *A Janus-faced Empire. Notes on the Russian Empire in Moderntiy, Written from the Border*. Moscow: Blok.

Volos, A. (2000) *Khurramabad*. Nezavisimaja Gazeta: Moscow.

——. (2001) *Hurramabad. Glas. New Russian Writing. Contemporary Russian Literature in English Translation*. Volume 26, Moscow: Novosti.

**Santiago Castro-Gómez**

# THE MISSING CHAPTER OF EMPIRE

## Postmodern reorganization of coloniality and post-Fordist capitalism[1]

This paper starts with a sense of puzzlement about this question: Is there only one world or are there various possible worlds? I want to reformulate this question in the following way: is it possible to share a single world where many worlds are possible? Or to put it yet another way, is it possible to share a world where different ways of knowing that world can coexist and complement each other? A world where *epistemological plurality* can be recognized and valued? Unfortunately, my answer to these questions would have to be a 'provisional no' because to this day, at least for the last 500 years, it has not been possible to recognize the epistemological plurality of the world. On the contrary, a single way of knowing the world, the scientific-technical rationality of the Occident, has been postulated as the only valid episteme, that is to say the only *episteme* capable of generating real knowledge about nature, the economy, society, morality and people's happiness. All other ways of knowing the world have been relegated to the sphere of *doxa*, as if they were a part of modern science's *past*, and are even considered an 'epistomelogical obstacle' to attaining the certainty of knowledge.

What made this possible? How was one form of rationality able to establish itself as the only legitimate way of knowing the world? By virtue of what kind of power were other ways of knowing expulsed from the map of epistemes and downgraded to the underdeveloped character of *doxa*? The 'Coloniality of power' is the category used by some social scientists and philosophers of Latin America to describe the phenomenon by which a rigid hierarchy between different knowledge systems exists in the world. This hierarchization is not new: its roots are based in the European colonial experience, and specifically in the idea that the colonizer possesses an *ethnic and cognitive superiority* over the colonized. It is for this reason that our question about the coexistence of diverse *legitimate* ways of producing knowledge should necessarily involve an analysis of the coloniality of power in the contemporary world. Our question would then be: Do we live in a word where the old epistemological hierarchies made rigid by modern colonialism have disappeared, or on the contrary, are we witnessing a postmodern reorganization of coloniality?

In their famous book *Empire*, Michael Hardt and Antonio Negri (from here forward H/N), offer a clear answer to this question. Their thesis is that the modern/colonial hierarchies have disappeared, and that there now exists a unique opportunity for the multitude to generate a plurality of possible worlds in opposition to the single world of Empire. However my thesis would be that Empire is only a postmodern renewal of the rigid epistemological hierarchies that existed under modernity, making it difficult to think of a radical democracy of the multitude as H/N propose. To defend this thesis I will present the following: first I will briefly outline the arguments that H/N offer to support the death of colonialism in the contemporary world. I will then give a critical analysis of their arguments, showing what problems are manifested in the genealogy of Empire by H/N. Finally, I will come to a case study that serves as an example of what constitutes the postmodern reorganization of coloniality in Empire.

## The era of empire

The general thesis of H/N is that both imperialism and colonialism have reached their end because they are both specifically *modern* devices of the exploitation of human labor, and today capital does not need these historical forms to reproduce itself. On the contrary, imperialism and colonialism, which were very useful to the expansion of capital for more that 400 years, actually became an *obstacle* for global capitalism. For this reason these forms were overtaken by the dynamics of the world market itself (Hardt & Negri 2001, p. 323).

Firstly, H/N associate colonialism directly with the formation of European nation-states in the seventeenth century. In the seventeenth century, the intellectual elites and politicians of Europe found themselves in a kind of civil war because the 'humanist revolution' of the sixteenth century[2] that established the 'plane of immanence', was threatened by the 'illustrious counterrevolution'. The intention of this counterrevolution was to exercise control over the constitutive desires of the 'multitude' (that is to say the early commercial bourgeoisie of Europe) and to establish rational standards in all areas of society. Finally, what the Enlightenment proposed was to legitimate, by way of science, the establishment of disciplinary apparatuses that permitted the normalization of bodies and minds to orient them towards productive work. But it is precisely in the *enlightened project of normalization* where colonialism fits so well. Constructing the profile of the 'normal' subject that capitalism needed (white, male, owner, worker, heterosexual, etc.) necessarily required the image of an 'other' located in the exteriority of European space. The identity of the bourgeois subject in the seventeenth century is constructed in opposition to the images of 'savages' who lived in America,

Africa and Asia that chroniclers and travelers had circulated throughout Europe. Therefore *present-day* values of 'civilization' are affirmed in contrast to the barbaric *past* in which all that are 'outside' live. The history of humanity is seen then as the uncontestable progress towards a mode of capitalist civilization in which Europe is the standard imposed on all the remaining forms of life on the planet. The transcendent apparatus of the Enlightenment constructs a unified European identity that requires the figure of the 'colonial Other' (Hardt & Negri 2001, p. 149).

Now in the nineteenth century, once the Fordist mode of production had consolidated its hegemony, colonialism continued to play an important role in the reproduction of capital, thanks to the struggle that arose between the different industrial empires of Europe. In this phase, colonialism is subordinated to the formation of European industrial society and the need to conquer outside markets as a source of resources. Here H/N yield to the way classical Marxist theory drew the limits of the concept of Imperialism. The 'era of imperialism', according to authors like Lenin, Rosa Luxemburg and Eric Hobsbawm, took place between 1880 and 1914, that is in the moment in which the larger part of the planet was under the political or commercial domination of the industrialized powers of Europe: the United Kingdom, France, Germany, Italy and the Netherlands. These countries competed fiercely for control of 'zones of influence' that could accelerate the process of industrialization, a competition that would culminate in the First World War. From this perspective, colonialism appears as a *subproduct* of the development of *industrial capitalism* in certain European nation-states. This situation persisted until well into the twentieth century, until the first two decades of the Cold War, when the larger part of the colonized countries declared their independence from Europe, in the moment when capitalism started to make the move from a Fordist economy to a *post-Fordist* mode of production.

H/N's thesis is that with the advent of postfordism, world capitalism enters into the last and definitive stage of its history: Empire. In the new phase, the type of production that now dominates the world economy is not that of commodities like in industrial society, but that of symbols and abstract language (Hardt & Negri 2001, pp. 286–297). It is not the manufacturing of physical objects but the manipulation of data images and symbols that characterizes the post-Fordist economy. This hegemony of immaterial work requires that production stop being tied to specific territories and that the factory is no longer the paradigmatic center of work. Globalization not only transplanted production outside the physical walls of the factory, radically transforming the relation between capital and work, it also converted colonialism into a historic relic of humanity. In the moment in which knowledge becomes the principal productive force of global capital, replacing the physical labor of slaves and the manual work of the factory, colonialism stops being necessary for the reproduction of capital.

In effect, colonialism was a historical formation that grew in a context where you could still talk about an 'inside' and an 'outside' of capital. In its expansive logic, capital needed to conquer markets, not capitalists, and that explains the processes of European colonization (Hardt & Negri 1000, pp. 228–233). But when the Empire had filled all social spaces with its logic, when production was no longer tied to specific territories, when the time of the 'open borders' of capital had ended, there is no longer an 'outside' where the categories of 'colonialism' and 'imperialism' can be applied.[3] The argument that capitalism has reached its end relies also on the thesis that the modern sovereignty of the nation state has declined and ceded to the postmodern sovereignty of Empire. If colonialism was a creation of the sovereignty of nation-states in Europe, then the decline of that sovereignty would necessarily mean the end of colonialism. The sovereignty that we are now living is not modern, but postmodern. Colonialism, as a functional element of the project of modernity, is a thing of the past. The colonial representations of the 'other' that affirmed European identity are no longer necessary, because Europe is no longer the 'center' of the world-system. In fact, Empire does not need to have more centers. According to H/N, 'our postmodern Empire doesn't have a Rome' (p. 310), that is to say that now we do not divide the world hierarchically into centers, peripheries and semi-peripheries, as Wallerstein would have wanted it. Without centers, without peripheries and without an outside, Empire doesn't need the representations of the 'other' to affirm its identity, because Empire doesn't have an identity. *Empire is smooth and spectral:* it is found everywhere, without being located anywhere at that same time. For this reason, affirm H/N, the 'dialectic of colonialism' has stopped being functional today.[4]

For H/N, the territorial dichotomies of center and periphery are obsolete, because in Empire it is no longer possible to demarcate large geographical zones as privileged sites of production. There certainly exists an 'uneven development', but the lines of division and hierarchy are now not found along national boarders (p. 324). There is also poverty and misery rooted in the large cities of Europe and the United States, the Third World inside the first, while in the countries of the 'South', like in India and Brazil, there exist post-Fordist elites that live better than those of the 'North'. Today, North and South are *global spaces* that no longer define an 'international order'. The principal economic actors of capitalist postmodernism are not nation-states but multinational corporations that do not operate on the basis of settling in specific territories. Uneven development *is not territorial*, since 'all the levels of production can exist simultaneously and together [in the same territory], from the highest levels of technology, productivity and accumulation, to the lowest' (p. 324).

To summarize: For H/N, the new hierarchy of global power is no longer understandable if we continue to think from the field opened and made visible

by the concept of Imperialism, where the only truly geopolitical actors are the nation-states that operate according to a center/periphery logic. Today, the structure of the postmodern world system does not operate primarily on the basis of inter-state relations and the struggle between metropolitan States for hegemonic control over the peripheries. Empire is not English, French, Arab or American, but simply capitalist. This explains the reordering of the old geopolitical divisions based on territories (North and South, center and periphery) in function of the new global hierarchy of power, and also explains why colonialism is a phenomenon of the past. In Empire, old inequalities and colonial segmentations between the countries have not disappeared, but have acquired another form. There are inequalities now that do not have an imperialist form because both imperialism and colonialism become obstacles for the expansion of capital (Hardt & Negri 2001, p. 323).

## The darker side of the force

I want to propose a critique of H/N that salvages some elements of their theory of postmodern capitalism, but which also points to the deficiencies in their analysis of colonialism. Formulated in positive terms, my thesis will be that the concept of Empire allows a critical analysis of global capitalism that supplements, and in some cases replaces, analyses using the concept of imperialism. The numerous critics of the book are correct in that there continue to be imperial rules and actors that are the same as those conceived under the concept of imperialism. However, there are *other rules and other global actors* becoming hegemonic in the post-Fordist economy that the concept of imperialism fails to grasp. It is here where the concept of Empire reveals its importance. Formulated in negative terms, my thesis will be that the genealogy of Empire, as it is reconstructed by H/N, makes the understanding of the typically *modern* phenomena that persist in Empire difficult, such as occidentalism, epistemological hierarchies and racism. From my point of view, the genealogy of Empire proposed by H/N is incomplete and should be complemented with what in this work I call the 'missing chapter of Empire'.

I want to begin by alluding to an article published by Walter Mignolo in the year 2002 titled 'Colonialismo global, capitalismo and hegemonía epistémica'. In this text, Mignolo affirms that the concept of Empire elaborated by H/N only shows one side of globalization, its postmodern side, completely ignoring its darker side (Mignolo 2002, p. 227). What is the 'darker side' of postmodernism? For a number of years, Mignolo has worked on the subject of colonial representations in modern occidental thinking. In his book, *The Darker Side of the Renaissance*, Mignolo appeals to the classic gesture of modern critical theory: it is not possible to understand the humanism of the

Renaissance if we ignore its historical *aprioris*, that is to say its historical conditions of possibility. In the pen of Wallerstein, Mignolo says that the capitalist economy-world that arose in the sixteenth century constitutes the global scene in which the humanistic thought of the Renaissance developed. But this economy-world comes marked from the beginning with what the sociologist Aníbal Quijano calls a 'structural heterogeneity'. The economic and political domination of the economy-world by Europe is sustained by colonial exploitation and is not conceivable without it. That is to say, the grand works of humanism of the Renaissance cannot be considered only 'spiritual' phenomena, independent of the modern/colonial world-system in which they materialized. The 'gold of the Indies' made the great flow of riches from America to the European Mediterranean possible, a situation that generated the conditions for the 'humanistic revolution' of the sixteenth century to flourish. Therefore, the 'structural heterogeneity' that Mignolo and Quijano talk about is based on the premise that the *modern and the colonial are simultaneous phenomena in time and space*. Thinking of the Renaissance as a European phenomenon, separated from the modern/colonial economy-world that sustains it, is equivalent to generating an incomplete and mystified image of modernity.

But this is precisely what started to occur in the eighteenth century. Mignolo affirms that Enlightenment (Aufklärung) thinking generates what the Argentinean philosopher Enrique Dussel calls 'the eurocentric myth of modernity'. This myth consists of the *elimination of the structural heterogeneity of modernity,* in the name of a lineal process in which Europe appears as a privileged place of enunciation and generation of knowledge. The traditional and the modern stop coexisting and now appear as successive phenomena in time. Coloniality is not seen as a constitutive phenomenon but rather as a *derivative* of modernity. This would be an *exclusively European* phenomenon originating in the Middle Ages, and that later spread around the world through Intra-European experiences like the Italian Renaissance, the Reformation, the Enlightenment and the French Revolution. In this way, the myth of eurocentrism identifies European particularity with universality *tout-court,* and identifies coloniality with the European *past*. The coexistence of diverse ways of producing and transmitting knowledge is eliminated because now all forms of human knowledge are ordered on an epistemological scale from the traditional to the modern, from barbarism to civilization, from the community to the individual, from the orient to the occident. Mignolo points out that this colonial strategy of producing silences and absences belongs to the 'dark(er) side' of modernity. By way of this strategy, scientific thought positions itself as the only valid form of producing knowledge, and Europe acquires an *epistemological hegemony* over all the other cultures of the world (Castro-Gómez 2005).

Now we can return to the question, why do H/N show only the postmodern side of Empire, without consideration of its 'dark(er) side'? Mignolo's answer is consistent with his previous work. As coloniality is the 'other face' constitutive of modernity, *postcoloniality is the structural counterpart of post-modernity.* But H/N only talk about the 'postmodern' face of Empire, ignoring its postcolonial manifestation. In this way, the structural heterogeneity is newly eliminated, privileging an *Eurocentric vision of Empire:*

> Empire is postmodern in the sense that modernity is transformed along with the *transformation of coloniality.* This step is not given by Hardt and Negri because to them postcoloniality is a phenomenon that is derivative (and not constitutive) of postmodernity. Their argument leads to the conclusion that for them, postcoloniality means overcoming or the end of coloniality. They do not think or suggest that postcoloniality is the hidden side of postmodernity (as coloniality is the hidden side of modernity), and in this sense, what postcoloniality means is *not the end of coloniality but its reorganization* . Therefore *the postcolonial* would be the new and up-to-date forms of coloniality that correspond to the postmodern stage of Occidental history.
>
> (Mignolo 2002, p. 228)[5]

Mignolo's argument – correct in my judgment – is that H/N outline a genealogy of Empire that does not take into account the structural heterogeneity of modernity. To them, modernity is a *European* phenomenon that later 'extends' to the rest of the world in the form of colonialism. In this way, for example, the authors begin the genealogy of Empire saying that everything begins in Europe, between the year 1200 and 1600 (Hardt & Negri 2001, p. 104).[6] Here it is clearly shown that for H/N, modernity gestates completely inside Europe and develops successively by way of Intra- European phenomena like the Renaissance, the Enlightenment and the creation of the modern State, the industrial revolution, etc., until modernity reaches its postmodern crisis in Empire. What happens in the rest of the world, outside of Europe, only interests H/N in that they consider the *expansion* of the sovereignty of the modern State outside of European borders.[7] Their point of reference, therefore is Europe and not the world-system, and is the reason why they see the 'humanistic revolution' only from its modern side, without recognizing its 'colonial face'. What Mignolo calls 'the dark side of the Renaissance' continues to be invisible to them.

But what would happen if the genealogy of Empire took the economic-world as its point of reference rather than the thinking and action of a few renowned men and European cultural movements? Mignolo points out what

would occur: it would be impossible to disregard the structural heterogeneity of the economic world. If the genealogy of Empire began with the rise of the world economy in the sixteenth century, then not only would we have a precise date of birth (12 October 1492) but also a specific scheme of functioning: the mutual dependence of coloniality and modernity. H/N however cannot take this step because it would seriously compromise their thesis that the 'humanistic revolution' of the XV and sixteenth centuries in Europe was a *constituent* social phenomenon. On the contrary, the thesis of Mignolo, Quijano and Dussel is that the humanism of the Renaissance was, first and foremost, a world phenomenon (and not European) because it unfolded inside the world-system, and second because it was a *constituted* process because its 'line of escape' was established in opposition to the theological culture of the European Middle Ages *but not against capitalism*. No revolutionary 'plane of inmance' was established in the sixteenth century as H/N propose, but the substitution of a plane of *local* transcendence for a plane of *world* transcendence.

The silencing of this 'dark side of the Renaissance' in the genealogy of Empire has grave analytical consequences. The first, outlined by Mignolo is that coloniality is considered a phenomenon *derived* from the sovereignty of the modern nation-state. And this interpretation leads to another that is even more problematic: once the sovereignty of the modern nation-state is put in crisis by globalization and the post-fordist economy, colonialism ceased to exist. Empire will mean the 'end' of colonialism because the devices of normalization and representation associated with the modern State are no longer necessary for the reproduction of capital. On the contrary, if one takes the economy-world of the sixteenth century as a point of reference to outline the genealogy of Empire, then you can no longer affirm that coloniality is a derivation of State, but a phenomenon *constitutive* of modernity as such. And this interpretation leads to another, which is the interpretation I will defend in the next section: Empire will not bring the end of coloniality but *its postmodern reorganization*. This imperialistic reorganization of coloniality is the other side (invisible to H/N) that Empire needs for its consolidation.

In summary, we can therefore say that the creators of the concept Empire have a eurocentric vision of the concept that fails to recognize its *colonial devices*.[8] The 'missing chapter of Empire' would have to elaborate a non-eurocentric genealogy to allow a critique of the new (postmodern) forms of coloniality. In the following, I will try to trace an outline of what such a critique might look like. Using the same concept of Empire created by H/N, I will show how coloniality does not disappear in postmodern capitalism, but is reorganized in a postcolonial way.

## The (post)coloniality of power

The question I want to answer in this final part is the following: what happens in the moment in which *immaterial production* – no longer the material production associated with industrialization- is placed at the center of the politics of development?

I want to show how the concept of Empire proposed by H/N is useful in specifying exactly what the change produced in the concept of development consists of. But this diagnostic should be complimented with what in this work I call 'the missing chapter of Empire'. The diagnostic that H/N offer is incomplete because they do not take into account one of the fundamental aspects of imperialistic power, recognizing its 'postcolonial face'. In effect, of all the structural changes that the authors analyze with great insight in their book (modern to postmodern sovereignty, imperialism to Empire, the Fordist to the post-Fordist economy, the disciplinary society to the society of control, etc.) there is one that stands out by its very absence: the change from coloniality to postcoloniality. I want to show what this change consists of, taking as an example the new global agendas of sustainable development.

During the sixties and the seventies, the nation-states, supported by studies in the social sciences and especially economics – defined development of Third World countries in reference to the indicators of industrialization. It was assumed that development depended on the promotion of industry, in such a way that underdevelopment necessarily corresponded to a pre-industrial stage of history. Overcoming underdevelopment was equated with promoting the *take off* of the industrial sector. It was believed that promoting industry would result in an increase in per capita income and improvement in the indices of literacy, education, life expectancy, etc. To the developmentalists, the call for promoting the transition from 'traditional' society to 'modern' society because they assumed that modernization, is a rehearsal of the old colonial idea according to which underdevelopment was an inferior phase to full development. Development and underdevelopment are *two Western ideas*. Thus, promoting modernization became the central objective of the Asian, African and Latin American States during these decades. In this context, state intervention was made urgent in key sectors like health, education, family planning, urbanization and rural development. All of this was part of a strategy designed by the state to create industrial enclaves that permitted a gradual elimination poverty and 'to bring development' to all sectors of society. The underdeveloped populations of the Third World were seen in this way as an object of planning and the agent of this *biopolitical planning* should be the state. The function of the state was to eliminate obstacles to development, that is to say eradicate, or in the best of cases discipline, all those whose profiles of subjectivity, cultural traditions and ways of knowing would not adjust to the imperatives of industrialization.

However, the Colombian anthropologist Arturo Escobar has shown that beginning in the 1980s, the idea of industrial development weakened and was replaced by another idea: *sustainable development*. According to Escobar,

> It seems the idea of development is loosing part of its strength. Its incapacity to carry out its promises, together with resistance from many social movements and many communities is weakening its powerful image; the authors of critical studies try to give form to this social and epistemological weakening of development by way of their analyses. You could argue that if [industrial] development is losing its push, it is because *it is no longer indispensable to the gobalization strategies of capital*.
>
> (Escobar 1999, p. 128)[9]

According to Escobar, capital is undergoing a significant change in its form and is gradually acquiring a postmodern face (Escobar 2004, p. 382). This means that certain aspects once considered residual variables of modern developmentalism (like the biodiversity of the planet, the conservation of the environment, and the importance of non-occidental systems of knowing) now become central elements of the global politics of development. For Escobar, 'sustainable development' is nothing more than the postmodern restructuring of modern development. This means that economic development is no longer measured by the *material* levels of industrialization, but in terms of the capacity of a society to generate and preserve *human capital*. While the development theories of the sixties and seventies only took into account the 'physical capital' (industrialized products) and the exploitation of 'natural capital' (primary resources), sustainable development places the generation of 'human capital' at the center of its concerns, that is to say the promotion of the knowledge, aptitudes and experiences that convert a social actor into an economically productive subject.[10] In this way, *the possibility of converting human knowledge into a productive force,* replacing physical work and machines, becomes the key ingredientof sustainable development.[11]

H/N's reflections also point in this direction. For them, hegemonic production is no longer centered on *material work*, that is to say hegemonic production is no longer based in the industrial sector and its disciplinary apparatuses. The hegemonic strength of work today does not comprise material workers but agents capable of producing and administering *knowledge and information*. In other words, the new type of work with strength in global capitalism is defined by its 'capacity to manipulate symbols'. This not only means that computers and new information technologies form an integral part of the labor activities of millions of people the world over, and that familiarity with these technologies of communication is a fundamental requisite for access to employment. It also means that the model for the *processing of symbols* characteristic of communication technologies is becoming the hegemonic

model for the production of capital. According to this model, the capitalist economy is being reorganized today based on the *knowledge* that sciences like molecular biology, genetic engineering, and immunology produce, as well as the knowledge that types of research like the human genome, artificial intelligence and biotechnology produce. For H/N and Escobar, postmodern capitalism is a biopolitical regime in the sense that it constructs both nature and bodies through a series of *biopractices* where it turns out knowledge is fundamental.[12]

Sustainable development is a good example of the way in which the capitalist economy is reorganized in a postmodern way. If we start from the assumption that nformation and knowledge are the basis of the new global economy (and no longer the industrial production controlled by the State), then the lack of access to those resources becomes the key factor in explaining underdevelopment. It is not in vain that Chapter 40 of Agenda 21 signed in Rio de Janeiro within the framework of the United Nations Conference on Environment and Development (1992),[13] establishes that 'in sustainable development, each person is at once a user and a carrier of information'. This means that the State is no longer the principle agent of the changes that drive economic development. The agents are now the social actors themselves, by way of their appropriation of the cognitive resources that would allow the promotion of an economy centered in information and knowledge. To be sustainable, economic growth should be capable of generating 'human capital', which means improving knowledge, expertise and the ability to manage social actors in order to use them more efficiently. The theorem of sustainable development can thus be formulated in the following way: without the generation of 'human capital', it will not be possible to overcome poverty because of the *increasing knowledge gap* between some countries and others. According to this theorem, a country could develop only when it learns to utilize and protect its intellectual assets because such assets are now the driving forces in an economy based on knowledge.

The centrality of knowledge in the global economy and in imperialistic politics of development is made more evident when we examine the subject of the environment. Beginning with the Conference in Rio already mentioned, the environment becomes the backbone of sustainable development. It was at the conference where this Conference that *The Agreement on Biological Diversity* was signed, obligating signatory nations to protect their *genetic resources* given that now genetic resources were considered part of the 'common heritage of mankind'. The United Nations' interest in the conservation and management if this 'heritage' is clear: genetic resources have economic value and mean benefits for those businesses that work with the latest technologies in the areas of biotechnology and genetic engineering. In this way, the handling of information and abstract languages – what H/N call 'immaterial production' – is placed at the center of the capitalist, postmodern *business*.

In effect, the identification, alteration and transference of genetic material by way of knowledge have economic applications in the fields of agriculture and health. In the agricultural sector, biotechnology works by incrementing the production of food by means of the production of transgenic plants that are most resistant to plagues and insects, and less vulnerable to chemical fumigation. In 1999, 90 percent of the soya beans produced in Argentina and 33 percent of the corn produced in the United States originate from transgenic crops, and that percentage is even higher for products like cotton, tomatoes, tobacco, sugar cane, asparagus, strawberries, papaya, kiwi, barley, cucumber and zucchini. The biotechnological transformation of agriculture is a profitable business for the food industry and is controlled by a handful of businesses specialized in biotechnical research. The same occurs in the health sector. The pharmaceutical industry is concentrated in the production of medicines with a biological basis that are used in the treatment of illnesses like cancer, hemophilia, and hepatitis B, not to mention the growing production of generic medication and pharmaceutical drugs. It is estimated that the market for medication derived from pant extracts or biological products generates profits that hover around four hundred thousand million dollars annually, earnings that are concentrated in the hands of a small number of multinational businesses that monopolize ground-breaking research.[14]

Therefore, the subject of biodiversity places us at the forefront of a strategic sector of the global economy that will certainly redefine the geopolitics of the twenty-first century because access to genetic information will determine the difference between success and economic failure. Multinational corporations are interested in genetic resources that can be altered and manipulated by expert knowledge. Interestingly enough the greatest diversity is found in countries located in the South, the underdeveloped countries. For this reason, these businesses have initiated a real 'lobbying' campaign to obtain patents for these resources, appealing to intellectual property rights (CDI). Before the Uruguayan round of the GATT[15] in 1993, no transnational legislation existed that pertained to intellectual property rights. Multinational businesses like Bristol Myers, DuPont, Johnson & Johnson, Merck and Pfizer, with vested interests in the biodiversity business, pressured for the introduction of the TRIP[16] accord into the negotiations. This agreement permits the monopolistic control of the planet's genetic resources by businesses.

Intellectual Property is a juridical concept with a transnational scope. It is protected by the United Nations through the OMPI (World Intellectual Property Organization), which protects and regulates the 'creations and innovations of the human intellect', such as artistic and scientific works.[17] According to this norm, when *immaterial products* involve some type of technological innovation that has commercial application, they can be patented by their authors and used as if they were private property.[18] A patent is

defined as the concession that the State grants to an inventor so he can commercially exploit his product in an exclusive way, for a certain amount of time. In the case of biodiversity and genetic resources, multinational corporations that work with the latest technologies can legitimately claim that any genetic alteration of the flora and fauna implies an inventive activity of the intellect that has a direct application in the agricultural or pharmaceutical industries, and therefore they are rightfully protected by patents. By claiming that genetically modified biological material is no longer a product of nature but of human intellect, the multinationals claim the right to patent and declare as their own the economic benefits from the commercialization of these products. Legitimated in this way by a supranational juridical regime, the *intellectual assets* administered by multinational corporations are converted into the key sector for the creation of wealth in postmodern capitalism.

But it is precisely here where the 'postcolonial face' of Empire is revealed. I am talking about the ways in which new representations of development reinforce the modern/colonial hierarchies in a postmodern register, establishing a difference between the valid knowledge of some, and the non-knowledge or *doxa* of the others. One example of this is the way in which global agendas of sustainable development approach the subject of 'traditional knowledge'. Multinational corporations are aware that by association with biodiversity and genetic resources, traditional knowledge and its 'officials' acquire a fabulous economic potential and represent numerous opportunities for commercialization. It is no wonder that in 2001 the OMPI created a 'intergovernmental committee for the protection of intellectual property, genetic resources, traditional knowledge and folklore', and that in 2003 UNESCO declared that '... communities, in particular indigenous communities, play an important role in the production, safeguarding, maintenance and recreation of the intangible cultural heritage, thus helping to enrich cultural diversity and human creativity'.[19] The 'safeguarding' of traditional knowledge, now transformed into the 'guarantors of sustainable development', does not come for free. What is sought is to put a whole series of knowledges used for hundreds of years, by hundreds of communities world-wide at the disposal of multinationals specialized in research on genetic resources. These knowledges become susceptible to appropriation by multinational corporations through patents. Naturally, this requires a change in the *representations of the other*. What does this change consist of?

We know that in the *modern* paradigm of development, non-occidental systems were seen as the enemies of progress. It was assumed that industrialization created the conditions to leave behind a type of knowledge based in myths and superstitions, replacing it with the technical-scientific knowledge of modernity. It was also believed that personal traits like passivity, lack of discipline and indolence, associated perhaps to defects of race, depended rather on the 'absence of modernity'. The absence of modernity

could be overcome in the same way that the State resolves structural problems like illiteracy and poverty. In this way, the modern paradigm of development was also a colonial paradigm. 'Other' knowledges had to be disciplined or excluded.

However, and as H/N see it, postmodern capitalism is presented as a machine of segmentary inclusions, not of exclusions. Non-occidental knowledge is welcomed by the global agendas of Empire because it is useful to the capitalist project of biodiversity. The tolerance of cultural diversity has become a 'politically correct' value in Empire, but only in the sense that diversity is useful for the reproduction of capital. The indigenous person, for example, is no longer seen as someone pertaining to the social, economic and cognitive past of humanity, but as the 'guardian of biodiversity' (Ulloa, 2004). Once considered obstacles to a nation's economic development, the indigenous are now seen as indispensable to the sustainable development of the world. Traditional knowledge is elevated to the category of 'the intangible heritage of humanity'. Arturo Escobar formulates it in this way:

> Once the semiotic conquest of nature is complete, the sustainable and rational use of the environment becomes imperative. Here is found the underlying logic of the discourses of sustainable development and biodiversity. This new capitalization of nature not only rests on the semiotic conquest of territories (in terms of biodiversity reserves) and communities (as the 'guardians' of nature); it also requires the semiotic conquest of local knowledges, in the sense that 'saving nature' requires the valuation of local wisdom about the sustainability of nature. Modern biology begins to discover that local systems of knowledge are useful complements.
>
> (Escobar 2004, pp. 383–384)

The point that we want to emphasize is that the 'semiotic conquest' mentioned by Escobar re-signifies the colonial and modern mechanisms that legitimated the exclusion of 'other' knowledges in a postmodern form. It is in this sense that we talk about the *postcolonial face of postmodernity*. The 'recognition' that is given to non-occidental systems of knowledge is pragmatic rather than epistemical. Although the wisdom of indigenous communities or black communities can now be seen as 'useful' for the conservation of the environment, the categorical distinction between 'traditional knowledge' and 'science', elaborated in the Enlightenment of the eighteenth century, is still in force. The former continues to be seen as anecdotal knowledge, not quantitative and lacking methodology, while the later continues, in spite of the transdisciplinary efforts of the last decades, to be taken as the only epistemically valid knowledge. Not a single document of global entities like UNESCO questions this assumption. On the contrary, the document of the

OMPI titled *Intellectual Property and Traditional Knowledge* establishes that traditional knowledge is tied to 'folkloric expressions' such as songs, narratives and graphic designs, reproducing the classic distinction between *doxa* and *episteme*. In no part of the document is a dialogue between occidental science and local wisdom proposed. No dialogue between a biologist trained at Harvard and a shaman from Putumayo is possible, only what amounts to a 'transfer' of knowledge in one direction. In this way, all that is sought is to document the doxa and preserve it (according to what is established by the Agreement on Biological Diversity signed in 1992) so that it can later be patented.[20]

The praxis of multinational corporations is a clear example of how we have not reached the 'end of colonialism' as H/N declare, but that colonialism reformulates itself in a postmodern way. Firstly, research in genetic engineering is very expensive. For that reason, a small number of companies from the richest countries in the world dominate the field, while their 'object of study', the biological wealth of the earth, is concentrated the poor nations of the subtropical and tropical regions of the world. It is estimated that more than 4/5 of the biological diversity of the planet is found in regions that used to be called 'Third World'. Colombia, surpassed only by Brazil, is the second most biodiverse country in the world. More species of amphibians, mammals and birds exist there than in any other nation. For the above reasons, supranational entities like the OMPI and regional treaties like the TLC are intended to eliminate national-level protections of biodiversity and open the door to big pharmaceutical and agribusiness corporations so they can move forward with research and, patent the genetic resources contained in natural products. All this of course is with the help of local communities according to those who look to seduce local communities with the promise of a share in the earnings from the sale of traditional knowledge. For this however, a patent is required that would allow those companies to control the knowledge and resources generated by this faboulous business. Indeed, 95 percent of the biological patents are controlled by five big biotechnical companies, and the earnings produced by the issuing of patents was fifteen thousand million dollars in 1990.

The patents are the juridical mechanism by which new forms of *colonial expropriation of knowledge* are legitimated. Vandana Shiva mentions the case of a bioprospecting contract between a conservationist institute from Costa Rica and the pharmaceutical multinational Merck in 1991. Merck, with earnings of four thousand million dollars a year and close to three thousand share-holders from all over the world, paid the ridiculously low sum of one million dollars to Costa Rica for the exclusive right to investigate, collect samples and catalogue the genetic resources in a number of Costa Rica's national parks. This was done without consulting or soliciting the opinion of the indigenous communities that live in that region, and without guaranteeing them any sort of benefit. According to Shiva, the market for the medicinal plants

discovered and patented by Merck, but facilitated by the indigenous communities and locals, is estimated today at some 43 thousand million dollars. Something similar occurs with the Free Trade Agreement (Tratado de Libre Comercio), which requires that countries rich in biodiversity like those of the Andean region provide legal guarantees for the implementation of 'biological corridors' where multinationals can appropriate genes and the ancestral knowledge of the population. In this way, and in signing the Agreement as proposed by the United States, the market for products derived from biodiversity and associated knowledge would stay under the monopolistic control of a handful of companies.

Therefore, we have argued that postmodern capitalism, based in the production of knowledge, has converted biodiversity into the new 'green gold' of the Indies. H/N's thesis that there is no 'outside of Empire' does not mean that all geographical territories have already been colonized by the market economy, and that therefore the era of colonialism has ended. It means, better yet, that capital now needs to find *posterritorial colonies* to continue its process of expansion. These new colonies, even if they continue to be seated in the old territories of modern colonialism, they no longer reproduce the same logic of that colonialism. Its logic is rather of a post-Fordist type, because it is no longer material riches that they seek, but *information* contained in the genes and in non-occidental systems of knowledge. It is for this reason that they no longer look to destroy but to preserve traditional wisdom, despite the fact they still see them as epistemically devalued forms. Now the 'value' given to the work of local communities has no material measure as in modern colonialism, but is measured in immaterial terms. Their work and their culture have value as long as they serve to produce 'sustainable knowledge'. However, this knowledge is expropriated by the new logic of Empire.

It is surprising then that H/N declare the death of colonialism so assuredly, in spite of being aware of this problem. Consider for example the following passage taken from the book *Multitude:*

> The global North is genetically poor in plant varieties and yet it holds the vast majority of the patents: while the global South is rich in species, but poor in patents. What is more, many of the patents in the power of the North are derived for the genetic primary material that is found in the species of the South. The wealth of the North generates benefits in the form of private property, while the wealth of the South does not generate any wealth because it is considered the heritage of all humanity.
>
> (Hardt & Negri 2004, pp. 216–217)

But instead of considering bioproperty as a form of postmodern reorganization of coloniality, H/N prefer to engage with hegemony of immaterial work. Nonetheless, the step from Fordist to post-Fordist production that is

emphasized by H/N does not only mean that immaterial production obtains hegemony over material production. It means, above all else, that we are entering a type of world economy that is no longer based entirely on mineral resources, but increasingly in plant and biological resources. Forty percent of all productive processes today are based in biological materials and the tendency is growing. This means that without the genetic resources located in the poor regions of the South, and without the premeditated expropriation of non-occidental systems of knowledge, the post- Fordist economy of Empire would not be possible. For this reason we declare that the colonialism of power has not died, but has only changed form. This does not mean that the strictly modern forms of coloniality have disappeared, but that other forms have appeared that share an affinity with the new imperatives of inmaterial production.

Returning then to the question that opened this work, is there only one world, or are there various possible worlds? It would have to be said that the conditions generated by Empire, the colonial hierarchies of knowledge established by modernity, persist and make it difficult to think of a world in which epistemic plurality is recognized and appreciated. Capitalism is a machine that captures the proliferation of possible worlds and expropriates the production of 'other' knowledges. For this reason, the multitude that H/N herald with such optimism is not possible or thinkable without an *epistemical democracy* in which science stops being a slave of capitalism and the diverse forms of producing and transmitting knowledge can coexist and complement each other. I am referring to a world in which non-occidental systems of knowledge can be incorporated into the curriculums of occidental universities on equal terms in areas like law, medicine, biology, economy and philosophy. A world in which for example the Yoruba cosmovision, the Buddhist cosmovision of Zen, or the cosmovision of the Cuna Indians, can serve to advance towards a more integral science, more organic, *more centered in the common* good rather than in the needs of capital. Perhaps then and only then, can we move forward towards a world in which many other worlds would be possible.

## Notes

1 This paper was previously published in Spanish in *La poscolonialidad explicada a los niños*, Editorial Universidad del Cauca, Instituto Pensar, Universidad Javeriana, 2005. It was presented in the International Symposium '¿Uno solo o varios mundos posibles?' organized by the Instituto de Estudios Sociales Contemporáneos (IESCO). Bogotá, 7–10 June 2005.

2 H/N say this humanistic revolution produced a type of immanent thought that found one of its most eminent representatives in father Bartolomé de las Casas. Las Casas is seen as a Renaissance thinker that stood up to the (sovereign brutality/unrivalled brutality) of the Spanish rulers. This utopian

and anticolonialist vein would even reach Marx. But the utopian vision of the Renaissance was also eurocentric. For Las Casas, the indigenous are seen as equal to the Europeans 'only in that they are potentially European' (Hardt & Negri 2001, p. 142). He believed that humanity was singular, he could not see that there are simultaneously many.

3 In each passage from the modern to postmodern there is less and less distinction between inside and outside. Following Jameson, H/N affirm that the modern dialectic of inside and outside has been replaced by a set of degrees and intensities. 'The binaries that define the modern conflict have faded away' (Hardt & Negri 2001, p. 202).

4 H/N talk about a 'dialectic of colonialism' belonging to the project of modernity that consists of the following: 'The identity of the European I is produced in this dialectical movement. Once the colonial subject is constructed as an absolute Other, he can be subsumed (annulled or integrated) into a more elevated unity/unit. Only by means of the opposition to the colonized does he really become himself, the metropolitan subject' (Hardt & Negri 2001, p. 152). That is to say that colonialism is a 'dialectic of recognition', just as Hegel saw it, but that today it no longer has meaning/purpose because Empire (the owner) no longer needs to affirm himself in opposition to his 'other' (the slave).

5 The emphasis is mine.

6 It is necessary to point out that H/N are correct when they identify the 'Renaissance' as a phenomenon that occurs in part *before* 1492, alluding to the experience of the Florentine Republic later theorized by Machiavelli. However it is necessary to qualify that experience because the formation of the world-system that began in 1492 contributed to the destruction of that first democratic experience in Europe. After 1492, the installation of a transcendental world design began, reflected for example in the imposition of only one language over vast plurilinguistical territories inside Europe itself.

7 They do not even acknowledge that during the thirteenth century, the time they choose to start their genealogy of Empire, Europe was only a small and unimportant province when compared with the great civilization that was developing in the Islamic world (Dussel 1999, pp. 149–151). It is not until the foundational event of 1492, with the appearance of an unprecedented commercial circuit across the Atlantic, that Europe becomes the 'center' of a truly world-wide process of capital accumulation.

8 H/N nonetheless declare that they are critics of eurocentrism. In the section titled 'Two Italians in India' in *Multitude*, H/N give an account of how Alberto Moravia and Pier Paolo Pasolini viewed India. Moravia tries to understand why India is so different from Italy, while Pasolini tries to understand why it is so similar. Neither of the two, however, can escape the necessity to take Europe as the universal criteria of measure, in this way falling into a Eurocentric vision of the world. H/N affirm that the only way to avoid eurocentrism is to renounce any kind of universal norm with which

to evaluate cultural differences. Italy and India are not different, but *unique*. To them, with the notion of 'singularity' developed by Gilles Deleuze, we can abandon the concept of 'Otherness' that has functioned as a cornerstone of eurocentrism. This entails thinking of cultural difference not as otherness but as singularity. According to H/N, 'Cultural difference should be conceived in itself as singularity, without substantiating itself in the concept of the 'other'.' In a similar way, all cultural singularities should be considered not as anachronistic survivals of the past, but as equal participants in our common present. While we continue to strictly consider European society as the norm against which to measure modernity, many areas of Africa, as well other subordinate areas of the world, will not be comparable; but when we recognize the singularities and plurality inside modernity, we will begin to understand that Africa is as modern as Europe. Not more, or less, but different (Hardt & Negri 2004, pp. 156–157). But Mignolo would say that this is a *eurocentric critique of eurocentrism* because the exaltation of 'singularity' corresponds precisely to the postmodern reorganization of colonial narratives of representation (Mignolo 2002, p. 228).

9 The emphasis is mine.

10 This means that the use and abundance of natural resources (natural capital) is no longer sufficient to develop. Now what is important is the *intelligent* use of those resources by social actors to make them more productive.

11 Sustainable development can be defined as 'a development that satisfies the necessities of the present, without putting in danger the capacity of future generations to attend to their own needs'. This definition was first used in 1987 in the World Commission of the Environment of the ONU, created in 1983. The economists concerned with sustainable development pointed out that the ability to satisfy the needs of the future depends on how much equilibrium is reached between the social, economic and environmental needs in the decisions that are made today.

12 Escobar affirms that 'we could be transitioning from a regime of 'organic' (premodern) and 'capitalized' (modern) nature to a regime of 'technonature' made by new forms of science and technology' (Escobar 2004, p. 387).

13 Agenda 21 was one of the 5 fundamental agreements reached in the Rio de Janeiro Conference. According to this agenda, the nations who signed the agreement made a commitment to guarantee the 'sustainable development' of their economies, in such a way that natural resources could be managed intelligently in order to satisfy the needs of this generation, without compromising the welfare of future generations.

14 Research in genetic engineering is very expensive and demands a large technological infrastructure. This is why concentrated mostly in the United States, Europe and Japan, but is financed in large part by private enterprises. In recent years we have observed the formation of huge economic monstrosities in this sector. A few specialized enterprises in biotechnology

gradually absorb smaller companies as they merge with other gigantic companies, until they form real monopolies on a transnational scale that control the market of agriculture and health for the entire planet. In the course of the next decades, it is estimated that half a dozen multinationals will control 90 percent of the world's food sources.

15 General Agreement on Trades and Tariffs.

16 This acronym makes reference to 'Trade Related Intellectual Property Rights'. As a part of the multilateral agreements of the GATT, the TRIP obliges signatory states to adopt a system of intellectual property for microorganisms and plant varieties. Under pressure from the multinationals by way of the United States' government (for example in accords like the Free Trade Agreement) the concession of patents over biological material is presented as the *only* mechanism for the protection of intellectual property, even though the GATT accords do not specifically address this. There are other ways of protecting intellectual property without resorting to patents.

17 The OMPI has 177 member States, is headquartered in Geneva and concerns itself with all matters related to the protection of intellectual property in the world. It supervises various international agreements, two of which (the Paris Agreement for the Protection of Intellectual Property and the Berna Agreement for the Protection of Literary and Artistic Works) constitute the foundation of the intellectual property sector.

18 In order for a patent to be granted, the intellectual product has to satisfy at least two criteria: that it is an invention, that is to say that it represents an (*innovation/novelty*), and that the innovation has 'practical utility', in such a way that it can benefit all of society.

19 http://unesdoc.unesco.org/images/0013/001325/132540s.pdf

20 This agreement requires member nations to protect regions rich in biodiversity, species threatened with extinction and local knowledge related to the conservation of the environment. In relation to this last point, the CDB establishes the following: 'in accordance with their national legislation, [every country] will respect, preserve and maintain the knowledge, innovations and practices of local and indigenous communities that involve traditional ways of life pertinent to the conservation and sustainable use of biological diversity and promote its wider application, with the approval and the participation of those who possess this knowledge, innovations and practices'. See: http://www.biodiv.org/doc/legal/cbd-es.pdf

## References

Castro-Gómez, Santiago (2005) *La hybris del punto cero. Ciencia, raza e ilustración en la Nueva Grenada (1750–1816)*. Bogotá, Colombia: Pontificia Universidad Javeriana.

Dussel, Enrique (1999) 'Mas allá del eurocentrismo: El sistema-mundo y los límites de la modernidad', in *Pensar (en) los intersticios. Teoría y práctica de la*

*crítica poscolonial*, eds Santiago Castro-Gómez, Oscar Guardiola-Rivera and Carmen Millán de Benavides, Bogotá, Colombia: CEJA.

Hardt, Michael & Negri, Antonio (2001) *Imperio*. Bogotá, Colombia: Ediciones desde abajo.

Hardt, Michael & Antonio, Negri (2004) *Multitud*. Guerra y democracia en la era del Imperio. Barcelona, Spain: Debate.

Mignolo, Walter (2002) 'Colonialidad global, capitalismo y hegemonía *epistémica*', in *Indisciplinar las ciencias sociales. Geopoliticas del conocimiento y colonialidad del poder*, eds Catherine Walsh, Freya Schiwy, Santiago Castro-Gómez. Quito, Ecuador: Universidad Andina Simón Bolívar/Ediciones Abya-Yala.

Shiva, Vandana (2001) *Biopiratería. El saqueo de la naturaleza y el conocimiento*. Barecelona, Spain: Icaria editorial.

Ulloa, Astrid (2004) *LA construcción del nativo ecológico. Complejidades, paradojas y dilemas de la relación entre los movimientos indígenas y el ambientalismo en Colombia*. Bogotá, Colombia: Instituto Colombiano de Antropología e Historia – ICANH.

**Walter D. Mignolo**

# DELINKING

## The rhetoric of modernity, the logic of coloniality and the grammar of de-coloniality[1]

> . . . colonialism is not simply content to impose its rule upon the present and the future of a dominated country. Colonialism is not satisfied merely with holding a people in its grip and emptying the native's brain of all form and content. By a kind of perverse logic, it turns to the past of the oppressed people, and distorts it, disfigures and destroys it.
>
> (Franz Fanon, *The Wretched*, 1961)

### Introduction

In May 2004, Arturo Escobar and I organized one of the meetings of the modernity/coloniality project at Duke and UNC. Each meeting of the group – since 1998 – has been devoted to the exploration of issues that emerged as interesting and/or problematic in previous meetings or during conversations, among its members, in between meetings. The guiding statement for the 30 May–1 June 2004 meeting was the following:

How does Horkheimer's 'critical theory' project look to us today, when global and pluri-versal 'revolutions' are taking place, out of the di-versity and pluri-versity of the many local histories that in the past 500 hundred years (some in the past 250 or perhaps only 50 years) couldn't avoid the contact, conflict, and complicity with the West (e.g., Western Christianity, its secularization and relation to/with capitalism and its obverse, Socialism/ Marxism)? What should 'critical theory' aim to be when the *damnés de la terre* are brought into the picture, next to Horkheimer's proletarians or today's translation of the proletariat, such as the multitudes? What transformations are needed in the 'critical theory' project if gender, race, and nature were to be fully incorporated into its conceptual and political framework? Finally, how

can 'critical theory' be subsumed into the project of modernity/coloniality and decolonization? Or would this subsumption perhaps suggest the need to abandon the twentieth century formulations of a critical theory project? Or, would it suggest the exhaustion of the project of modernity?

The questions formulated in the statement were not intended to drive the debate toward a 'manifesto of consensus', which would have killed the questions instead of leaving them as signposts for thought. I am sure that each of the participants in the three days workshop came out with their own answers, with reformulated questions or with other, related questions. The argument that follows started before the meeting but in its last version it carries the indelible mark of three days of intense, creative and productive dialogues.[2]

## I Epistemic de-linking

Under the spell of neo-liberalism and the magic of the media promoting it, modernity and modernization, together with democracy, are being sold as a package trip to the promised land of happiness, a paradise where, for example, when you can no longer buy land because land itself is limited and not producible or monopolized by those who control the concentration of wealth, you can buy virtual land!![3] Yet, when people do not buy the package willingly or have other ideas of how economy and society should be organized, they become subject to all kinds of direct and indirect violence. It is not a spiritual claim, or merely a spiritual claim that I am making. The crooked rhetoric that naturalizes 'modernity' as a universal global process and point of arrival hides its darker side, the constant reproduction of 'coloniality'. In order to uncover the *perverse logic* – that Fanon pointed out – underlying the philosophical conundrum of modernity/coloniality and the political and economic structure of imperialism/colonialism, we must consider how to decolonize the 'mind' (Thiongo) and the 'imaginary' (Gruzinski) – that is, knowledge and being.

Since the mid-seventies, the idea that knowledge is also colonized and, therefore, it needs to be de-colonized was expressed in several ways and in different disciplinary domains.[4] However, the groundbreaking formulation came from the thought and the pen of Peruvian sociologist Anibal Quijano. Quijano's intellectual experience was shaped in his early years of involvement in the heated debates ignited by dependency theory, in the seventies. Dependency theory, however, maintained the debate in the political (e.g., state, military control and intervention) and economy, analyzing the relationships of dependency, in those spheres, between center and periphery.[5] That knowledge could be cast also in those terms was an idea to which Enrique Dussel, in 1977, hinted at in the first chapter of his *Philosophy of Liberation* titled 'Geo-politics and Philosophy'. In a complementary way, in the late

eighties and early seventies, Anibal Quijano introduced the disturbing concept of 'coloniality' (the invisible and constitutive side of 'modernity'). In an article published in 1989 and reprinted in 1992, titled 'Colonialidad y modernidad-racionalidad' Quijano explicitly linked coloniality of power in the political and economic spheres with the coloniality of knowledge; and ended the argument with the natural consequence: if knowledge is colonized one of the task ahead is to de-colonize knowledge.[6] In the past three or four years, the work and conversations among the members of the modernity/coloniality research project',[7] de-coloniality became the common expression paired with the concept of coloniality and the extension of coloniality of power (economic and political) to coloniality of knowledge and of being (gender, sexuality, subjectivity and knowledge), were incorporated into the basic vocabulary among members of the research project.[8] One of the central points of Quijano's critique to the complicity between modernity/rationality, is the exclusionary and totalitarian notion of Totality (I am aware of the pleonasm); that is a Totality that negates, exclude, occlude the difference and the possibilities of other totalities. Modern rationality is an engulfing and at the same time defensive and exclusionary. It is not the case, Quijano added, that in non-European imperial languages and epistemologies (Mandarin, Arabic, Bengali, Russian, Aymara, etc.), the notion of Totality doesn't exist or is unthinkable. But it is the case that, particularly since the 1500s and the growing dominance of Western epistemology (from Theo-logy to secular Ego-logy (e.g., Descartes, 'I think, therefore I am'), non-Western concepts of Totality had to be confronted with a growing imperial concept of Totality. The cases of the Ottoman and Inca Empires are often quoted as examples of respect for the difference. I am not of course offering the examples of the Ottoman and the Inca Empires as idea for the future but just in order to show the regionalism of the Western notion of Totality. I am observing that from 1500 on, Ottomans, Incas, Russians, Chinese, etc., moved toward and inverted 'recognition': they had to 'recognize' that Western languages and categories of thoughts, and therefore, political philosophy and political economy, were marching an expanding without 'recognizing' them as equal players in the game.

Quijano's project articulated around the notion of 'coloniality of power' moves in two simultaneous directions. One is the *analytic.* The concept of coloniality has opened up, the re-construction and the restitution of silenced histories, repressed subjectivities, subalternized knowledges and languages performed by the Totality depicted under the names of modernity and rationality. Quijano acknowledges that postmodern thinkers already criticized the modern concept of Totality; but this critique is limited and internal to European history and the history of European ideas. That is why it is of the essence the critique of Totality from the perspective of coloniality and not only from the critique of post-modernity. Now, and this is important, the critique

of the modern notion of Totality doesn't lead necessarily to post-coloniality, but to de-coloniality. Thus, the second direction we can call the *programmatic* that is manifested in Quijano as a project of 'desprendimiento', of de-linking. At this junction, the analytic of coloniality and the programmatic of de-coloniality moves away and beyond the post-colonial.

Coloniality and de-coloniality introduces a fracture with both, the Eurocentered project of post-modernity and a project of post-coloniality heavily dependent on post-structuralism as far as Michel Foucault, Jacques Lacan and Jacques Derrida have been acknowledged as the grounding of the post-colonial canon: Edward Said, Gayatri Spivak and Hommi Bhabha. De-coloniality starts from other sources. From the de-colonial shift already implicit in *Nueva corónica and buen gobierno* by Waman Puma de Ayala; in the de-colonial critique and activism of Mahatma Gandhi; in the fracture of Marxism in its encounter with colonial legacies in the Andes, articulated by José Carlos Mariátegui; in the radical political and epistemological shifts enacted by Amilcar Cabral, Aimé Césaire, Frantz Fanon, Rigoberta Menchú, Gloria Anzaldúa, among others. The de-colonial shift, in other words, is a project of de-linking while post-colonial criticism and theory is a project of scholarly transformation within the academy. Quijano thus summarizes the de-colonial shift starting from the de-colonization of knowledge:

> La crítica del paradigma europeo de la racionalidad/modernidad es indispensable. Más aún, urgente. Pero es dudoso que el camino consista en la negación simple de todas sus categories; en la disolución de la realidad en el discurso; en la pura negación de la idea y de la perspectiva de totalidad en el conocimiento. Lejos de esto, es necesario *desprenderse de las vinculaciones de la racionalidad-modernidad con la colonialidad, en primer término, y en definitiva con todo poder no constituido en la decision libre de gentes libres.* Es la instrumentalización de la razón por el poder colonial, en primer lugar, lo que produjo paradigmas distorsionados de conocimiento y malogró las promesas liberadoras de la modernidad. La alternativa en consecuencia es clara: la destrucción de la colonialidad del poder mundial (italics mine).[9]

The last statement may sound somewhat messianic but it is, nonetheless, an orientation that in the first decade of the twenty-first century has shown its potential and its viability. Such 'destruction' shall not be imagined as a global revolution lead by one concept of Totality that would be different from the modern one, but equally totalitarian. The Soviet Union was already an experiment whose results is not an exemplar to follow. The statement shall be read in parallel to Quijano's observations about none-totalitarian concepts of totality; to his own concept of heterogeneous structural-histories (I will come back below to this concept), and to what (I will develop below) *pluriversality as*

*a universal project*. And, above all, it shall be read in complementarity with Quijano's idea of '*desprenderse*' (delinking).[10] In this regard, Quijano proposes a de-colonial epistemic shift when he clarifies that:

> En primer término, la descolonización epistemológica, para dar paso luego a una nueva comunicación inter-cultural, a un intercambio de experiencias y de significaciones, como la base de otra racionalidad que pueda pretender, con legitimidad, a alguna universalidad. Pues nada menos racional, finalmente, que la pretension de que la específica cosmovisión de una etnia particular sea impuesta como la racionalidad universal, aunque tal etnia se llama Europa occidental. Porque eso, en verdad, es pretender para un provincianismo el título de universalidad (italics mine).[11]

The argument that follows is, in a nutshell, contained in this paragraph. First, epistemic de-colonization runs parallel to Amin's delinkink. A delinking that leads to de-colonial epistemic shift and brings to the foreground other epistemologies, other principles of knowledge and understanding and, consequently, other economy, other politics, other ethics. 'New inter-cultural communication' should be interpreted as new inter-epistemic communication (as we will see bellow, is the case of the concept of inter-culturality among Indigenous intellectuals in Ecuador). Furthermore, de-linking presupposes to move toward a geo- and body politics of knowledge that on the one hand denounces the pretended universality of a particular ethnicity (body politics), located in a specific part of the planet (geo-politics), that is, Europe where capitalism accumulated as a consequence of colonialism. De-linking then shall be understood as a de-colonial epistemic shift leading to other-universality, that is, to pluri-versality as a universal project. I'll come back to this point in section IV ('The grammar of de-coloniality').

## II The rhetoric of modernity

Enrique Dussel provides a good point of entry in his Frankfurt Lectures.[12] He argues:

> Modernity is, for many (for Jurgen Habermas or Charles Taylor) an essentially or exclusively European phenomenon. In these lectures, I will argue that modernity is, in fact, *a European phenomenon but one constituted in a dialectical relation with a non-European alterity that is its ultimate content.* Modernity appears when Europe affirms itself as the 'center' of a *World* History that it inaugurates: the 'periphery' that surrounds this center is consequently part of its self-definition. The occlusion of this periphery

> (and of the role of Spain and Portugal in the formation of the modern world system from the late fifteenth to the mid-seventeenth centuries) leads the major contemporary thinkers of the 'center' into a Eurocentric fallacy in their understanding of modernity. *If their understanding of the genealogy of modernity is thus partial and provincial, their attempts at a critique or defense of it are likewise unilateral and, in part, false*.

It is a question of uncovering the origin of what I call 'the myth of modernity' itself. Modernity includes a rational 'concept' of emancipation that we affirm and subsume. But, at the same time, it develops an irrational myth, a justification for genocidal violence. The postmodernists criticize modern reason as a reason of terror; we criticize modern reason because of the irrational myth that it conceals.

There are several important issues packed together in these two dense paragraphs. My own argument, below, attempts to unfold and unravel some of the radical consequences of Dussel's statement for de-colonization (rather than emancipation) of knowledge and of being.[13] Let us begin, then, by seeking to understand how *de-colonization* and *liberation* subsume the 'rational concept of emancipation', as Dussel states it, and shift the geopolitical location of discourse; and from here walk our way toward the de-colonial shift.

The concept of 'emancipation', as Dussel implies, belongs to the discourse of the European enlightenment and it is used today within that same tradition. It is a common word in liberal and Marxist discourses. Thus, beginning with his foundational book *Philosophy of Liberation* (1977), Dussel makes the geopolitical choice to use the keyword 'liberation' instead of 'emancipation' in consonance with the social movements of 'national liberation' in Africa and Asia, as well as in Latin America[14] Attaching the word 'liberation' to 'philosophy' complemented the meaning that the word had on all revolutionary fronts of political decolonization, in Asia and Africa and their struggles for 'decolonization'. 'Liberation' referred to two different and interrelated struggles: the political and economic decolonization and the epistemological decolonization (e.g., philosophy in the case of Dussel; the social sciences in the case of Colombian sociologist Orlando Fals-Borda.[15] Thus, 'liberation' emerged in the process of de-centering the universal emancipating claims in the projects grounded in the liberal and socialist traditions of the European enlightenment. Seen in reverse, the fact that Ernesto Laclau,[16] for example, opts for 'emancipation' instead of 'liberation' might reveal that the two distinct projects are actually located on different geo-political terrains. The point here is less to determine 'which one is right;' but, rather, to understand what each offers and for whom. We must ask: Who needs them? Who benefits from them? Who are the agents and the intended targets of emancipating or libratory projects? What subjectivities are activated in these projects? Does the

distinction even matter when emancipation has a universal ring that seems to cover the interests of all oppressed people in the world?

The concept and the idea of 'emancipation' in the eighteenth century, was based on three 'major' historical experiences: the Glorious Revolution of 1668 in England, the independence of the colonists in America from the emerging British Empire in 1776; and the French Revolution in 1789. *In every historical account, the three initial historical moments were successful in achieving the meaning of emancipation.* Yet, the Glorious Revolution was led by the ascent of the British bourgeoisie and supported by the earlier uprising of the *levelers* in 1648. Likewise, the main actors of the US Revolution of 1776 were the Anglo-descendent colonizers just as the 'people' that ended up in the control of the French bourgeoisie in the French Revolution pertained also to that social stratum. While the Russian Revolution (1917) was, at least theoretically, the obverse of the Glorious, US and French revolutions, it responded to the same logic of modernity, although with a socialist/Marxist content instead of a Liberal one. While 'emancipation' was the concept used to argue for the freedom of a new social class, the bourgeoisie (translated into the universal term of 'humanity' and setting the stage to export emancipation all over the world, although Haiti presented the initial difficulties to emancipating universal claims) and was recovered in the twentieth century in Marxist discourse to argue for the 'emancipation of the working class' or still more recently, for the emancipating forces of the *multitude*,[17] 'liberation' provides a larger frame that includes the racialized class that the European bourgeoisie (directly or indirectly) colonized beyond Europe (or beyond the heart of Europe, as it was the colonization of Ireland) and, thus, subsumes 'emancipation'.). What remains still unsaid and un-theorized is the fact that the concept of 'emancipation' – in the discourses of the European enlightenment – proposes and presupposes changes within the system that doesn't question the logic of coloniality – the emerging nation-states in Europe were, simultaneously, new imperial configurations (in relation to previous monarchic empires, like Spain and Portugal). I am arguing here that both 'liberation' and 'decolonization' points toward conceptual (and therefore epistemic) projects of d*e-linking* from the colonial matrix of power. Because of the global reach of European modernity, de-linking cannot be understood as a new conceptual system coming, literally, out of the blue. Delinking in my argument presupposes border thinking or border epistemology in the precise sense that the Western foundation of modernity and of knowledge is on the one hand unavoidable and on the other highly limited and dangerous. The danger of what Ignacio Ramonet (*Le Monde Diplomatique*) labelled *la pensée unique* and that before him Herbert Marcuse labeled the 'one dimensional man'. La pensée' however, is not just neo-liberalism, as Ramonet implies. La pensée unique is Western in *toto*, that is, liberal and neo-liberal but also Christian and neo-Christian, as well as Marxist and neo-Marxist. La pensée unique is the totality

of the three major macro-narratives of Western civilization with its imperial languages (English, German, French, Italian, French, Spanish, Portuguese) and their Greco and Roman foundations. To de-link from the colonial matrix of power and the logic of coloniality embedded in la pensee unique, it is necessary to engage in border epistemology and in alternatives TO modernity or in a the global and diverse project of transmodernity. Why global and diverse? – because there are many 'beginnings' beyond Adam and Eve and Greek civilization and many other foundational languages beyond Greek and Latin. With and in each language comes different concepts of economy that of course Adam Smith was unable to think, and other political theories beyond Niccolo Machiavelli or Thomas Hobbes; and different conceptions of life which leads to philosophical practices that cannot be dependent from Greek canonical dictums in matters of thoughts!!! etc.etc. Conceptual (and theoretical) de-linking is, in the argument I am advancing the necessary direction of liberation and decolonization, while transformation within the colonial matrix of power is the splendor and limitations of any project of emancipation(s).[18] De-linking is not a problem for 'emancipating' projects because they are all presented as transformation within the linear trajectory of Western history and Western thoughts (once again, from Greek and Latin categories of thought, to German's, English's and French's).[19]

The distinctions I just established between emancipation on the one hand and liberation and decolonization (as de-linking projects) on the other, invites the rethink of the concept of 'revolution'. Yet, not every 'revolution' since the end of the eighteenth century to the second half of the twentieth century, then, belongs to the same universal and ascending order of 'modernity and the emancipation of Man'. The Túpac Amaru uprising in Peru (1781), the Haitian revolution (1804), and the decolonization of Africa and Asia in the twentieth century, introduced a different dimension, which was not entirely subsumed under and into the picture of Liberalism and socialism/Marxism. Tupac Amaru uprising as well as the Haitian revolution carried in them the de-linking seed. Contrary to any of the Spanish America or Anglo America independences, which were all independences within the system (and therefore, some kind of emancipation), Tupac Amaru and the Haitian Revolution introduced an-other cosmologies into the dominance and hegemony of Western cosmological variations within the same rhetoric of modernity and logic of coloniality. These struggles for decolonization were led by a mixture of native elite and the *damnés* (the racially defamed and politically, economically and 'spiritually' – in religion and knowledges – dispossessed.[20] Tupac Amaru uprising and the Haitian Revolution are part of the system of liberating and decolonizing movements that ended the modern structure linking empires to colonies (Spain, England, France, Portugal). Decolonization in Africa and Asia had in common with Tupac Amaru and the Haitian revolution, to 'liberate' from the ties to imperial power, although it was not clear that the 'liberation' from

categories of thoughts was also at stake. In this case it is appropriate to say that while de-colonization was clearly the goal, de-coloniality was not clearly seen or stated during the processes of cutting the Gordian knot with the empire. De-coloniality was clearly formulated, in the sixties and seventies, by radical Arabo-Islamic thinkers (Sayyid Qutb, Ali Shariati, Ayatollah Komeini); by philosophy of liberation in Latin America and by Indigenous intellectuals and activist in Laitn America, Australia, New Zealand and Canada.[21]

Emancipation and liberation are indeed two sides of the same coin, the coin of modernity/coloniality. While liberation framed the struggle of the oppressed in the 'Third World' and the history of modern coloniality that underline its history, decoloniality is an even larger project that encompasses both, as Fanon puts it, the colonized and the colonizer – and therefore, emancipation and liberation. De-coloniality turns the plate around and shifts the ethics and politics of knowledge. Critical theories emerge from the ruins of languages, categories of thoughts and subjectivities (Arab, Aymara, Hindi, French and English Creole in the Caribbean, Affrikaan, etc.) that had been consistently negated by the rhetoric of modernity and in the imperial implementation of the logic of coloniality. Conceiving emancipation as the profile of the revolutionary processes led by the European bourgeoisie and the White (Protestant and Catholic) Creoles from European descent in the Americas – as well by some 'native' elites in decolonized Asian and African countries – and conceiving liberation as the profile of the revolutionary processes in the colonies led by 'natives' (e.g., people of non-Christian faith and of non-White colors) against both the European colonizer and the local native elites that used the nation state to *link* with the political and economic projects of Western Europeans (and in the twentieth century US) states and private corporations – is another way to understand that 'modernity is not an exclusively European phenomenon but constituted in a dialectical relation with a non-European alterity'.

If modernity is understood essentially as a European phenomenon, then the 'emancipation' of people in the non-European world has to be planned, dictated and executed from Europe or the US itself only. 'Spreading democracy in the Middle East', President Bush repeated dictum is a case in point and an illustration of what Habermas's project on the completion of the incomplete project of modernity. It is not sure that Islamic or Indigenous progressive intellectuals, like Habermas himself, would like to go along with German ideals. In such a scenario, there is no possibility of an-other political economies and political theories. Religions would be tolerated as far as they do not interfere with THE political economy and THE political theory that rules the world. Every thing shall be dictated by and from that original point, in space and time, where power concentrates. The rest of the world would have to wait and see, to listen and follow the leaders like in the war in Iraq.[22]

Fortunately the World Social Forum, the Social Forum of the Americas and countless delinking social movements (not NGOs!). In an Habermasian type of scenario, liberation would be subservient to emancipation; and, decolonization, likewise, would still be covered over and managed by the emancipating rhetoric of modernity, either liberal or Marxist. In other words, if 'emancipation' is the image used by honest liberals and honest Marxists from the internal and historical perspectives of Europe or the US, then looking at the world history from *outside* of those locations (either from a country geo-historically located beyond both or from the perspective of immigrants from those countries to Europe and the US) means coming to terms with the fact that there is a still further need for 'liberation/de-coloniality' from the people and institutions raising the flag of 'emancipation'.[23] Thus, in this precise sense, emancipation cannot be the guiding light for liberation/de-coloniality but the other way round: liberation/de-coloniality includes and re-maps the 'rational concept of emancipation'. *In this complexity, we need a relentless critical exercise of awareness of the moments when the guiding principle at work is liberation/de-coloniality and when, on the other hand, the irrational myth directs social actors in their projects for political, economic and spiritual (epistemic, philosophical, religious) decolonization.*

Nobody has access to an ultimate truth, and, consequently, no one person (or collective, church or government) from the right or from left, can offer a solution for the entire population of the planet. That is why *abstract universals* (Christianity, Liberalism, Marxism, and Islamism) run out of fashion and become the different content of the same fundamentalist and imperial logic. For this reason, de-coloniality, as ethically oriented, epistemically geared, politically motivated and economically necessary processes, has the damnés as its central philosophical and political figure. As Fanon stated, decolonization is a double operation that includes both colonized and colonizer,[24] although enacted from the perspective and interests of the damnés. Otherwise, the damnés would be deprived of their 'right' to liberate and de-colonize and will have to wait for the generous gifts of the colonizer 'given them freedom'. In other words, if the colonizer needs to be decolonized, the colonizer may not be the proper agent of decolonization without the intellectual guidance of the *damnés*. There are two kinds of individuals at work in the colonizer's society: those that enact the 'irrational myth that justifies genocidal violence' and those that, within that society, oppose and denounce it. But denunciation within the colonizer's society, while important, is not sufficient in itself. It is necessary for dissenting actors belonging (e.g., having citizenship, not necessarily the right blood or skin color) to a colonizing society (e.g., the US today) to join projects of decolonization (political and epistemic) that are, at once, *articulated by the colonized* and yet *not the project of a colonized elite,* who use decolonization as a tool for personal benefit while reproducing, in the 'decolonized' country, the same 'irrational myth that justifies genocidal violence'. There are several

cases in Africa and South America that followed this path after 'decolonization' and likewise in the United States vis-à-vis Native Americans and people from African descent.

The colonized do not have epistemic privileges, of course: the only epistemic privilege is in the side of the colonizer, even when the case in point is emancipating projects, liberal of Marxist.[25] 'Colonizer side' here means Eurocentric categories of thought which carries both the seed of emancipation and the seed of regulation and oppression. Still, now are the histories and memories of coloniality; the wounds and a histories of humiliation that offer the point of reference for de-colonial epistemic and political projects and of de-colonial ethics. De-coloniality, then, means working toward a vision of human life that is not dependent upon or structured by the forced imposition of one ideal of society over those that differ, which is what modernity/coloniality does and, hence, where decolonization of the mind should begin. The struggle is for changing the terms in addition to the content of the conversation.

Delinking means to change the terms and not just the content of the conversation – the content has been changed, in the modern/colonial world by Christianity (e.g. theology of liberation); by liberalism (e.g., the US support to de-colonization in Africa and Asia during the Cold War) and by Marxism (also supporting de-colonization in Africa and Asia during the Cold War). Delinking requires that economic, politica, philosophical, ethical, etc., conceptualization based on principles that makes the Bible, Adam Smith and Karl Marx necessary (because Western categories of thougths have been globalized through the logic of coloniality and the rhetoric of modernity) but highly insufficient. In this section, then, I would like to explore further the different politics of knowledge organizing the darker side of modernity, the irrational myth that justifies genocidal violence within the layered historical frame established by processes of emancipation, liberation and decolonization. I will proceed by following Dussel's distinction of the critique of modernity from the perspective of liberation and decolonization.

If delinking means to change the terms of the conversation, and above all, of the hegemonic ideas of what knowledge and understanding are and, consequently, what economy and politics, ethics and philosophy, technology and the organization of society are and should be, it is necessary to fracture the hegemony of knowledge and understanding that have been ruled, since the fifteenth century and through the modern/colonial world by what I conceive here as the theo-logical and the ego-logical politics of knowledge and understanding.[26] We (I am referring to you and me, patient reader) are entering here in the unavoidable terrain of terminological de-naturalization. That is, one strategy of de-linking is to de-naturalize concepts and conceptual fields that totalize A reality. I take Theo-logy as the historical and dominant frame of knowledge in the modern/colonial world from the sixteenth to the

first half of the eighteenth century. Theo-logy was, as people like to say, not homogeneous. There were Catholics and Protestants, and also Eastern Orthodox. Catholics and Protestants were mainly linked to Latin Christianity while Eastern Christian to Greek Orthodoxy and to Slavic languages, etc. etc. The hegemony in the Western world (Western Europe and the Americas) during the sixteenth and seventeenth centuries was the common ground on which Catholics and Protestants played out their differences. The Theo-logical politics of knowledge and understanding was, then, the platform for the control of knowledge and subjectivity in Europe and the Americas, but not yet in China, India or the Arabic-Slamic world. When Western politics of knowledge began to be imposed in Asia and Africa, in the nineteenth century, Europe has already gone through an internal transformation. The sovereignty of the subject began to be felt at the beginning of the seventeenth century (Cervantes, Bacon, Shakespeare, Descartes) and the questioning of Theology open up the doors for a displament, within Europe, from the Theo-logical to the Ego-logical politics of knowledge and understanding.

But in the colonies, between the end of the sixteenth and the beginning of the seventeenth centuries, the concerns were quite different. Creoles from Spanish descent were concerned with the sovereignty of the colonial subject, that is, in asserting their sovereignty vis-à-vis the European modern subject as well as vis-à-vis the authority of the Church. At the end of the seventeenth century, the idea of science and of secular philosophy served very well the need of autonomy of the American Creoles from Spanish descent. A similar orientation could be traced within American Creoles from British descent in the British colonies of the North East. In all these cases, a displacement from the theo- and ego-logical hegemony toward a (de-colonizing) geo-politics of knowledge and understanding began to emerge. By geo-graphic (and body-graphic, as I will develop below)[27] I mean historical imperial/colonial location of new subjects of knowledge and understanding that had been negated, ignored and made invisible, precisely, by the imperial by the theo- and ego-logical politics of knowledge enacted agents and agencies of knowledge and understanding located in the domain of the empire rather than in the sphere of the colonies. Epistemic geo-politics implies a de-colonial shift and acquires its meaning, here, not in relation to an object (the earth), but in the frame of epistemic embodiments (geo-historical and body-graphical)[28] in the spatial organization of the modern/colonial world: the geo-politics of knowledge names the historical location (space and time, the historical marks and configuration of a space and a place, etc.) and authority of loci of enunciations that had been negated by the dominance and hegemony of both the theo-logical and ego-logical politics of knowledge and understanding.

But much before the Creoles from European descent, Latins or Anglos, Indigenous intellectuals expressed and articulated the need to de-ink. Chief example among them is Waman Puma de Ayala in the late sixteenth and early

seventeenth century. For several reasons, Waman Puma's argument and positionality both confronting the Spaniards and critiquing the Inca administration (Waman Puma belonged to a community under Inca's administration) is certainly very complex and I do not have room here to honor that complexity. For the purpose of my argument, Waman Puma's *Nueva Corónica y Buen Govierno* was a crucial moment whose relevance not only has been scholarly recognized and understood in his delinking argument,[29] but also his original move has been also understood by social movements like the Zapatista's in their relentless process of de-linking, from their theoretical revolution to their political and economic implementation in the Caracoles.[30] The basic structure of Waman Puma's arguments is that it is necessary, in the first place, a 'nueva corónica', that is, a chronicle of Andean civilization before the arrival of the Spaniards that complements the partial and very often crooked narratives of missionaries and men of letters who appointed themselves to write the chronicles that, according to them, indigenous people did not have. The missionary arguments wre simple: these people do not have alphabetic writing, therefore they cannot have history because for a Renaissance man of the sixteenth century, history was irretrievably linked to alphabetic writing in the Greco-Latin tradition (not Hebrew or Arabic or even Cirylic, of course). Thus, Waman Puma de Ayala 'nueva corónica' not only contradicts Spanish ones, but uses their one language in order to show that the Spanish histories were never told full.[31] The 'nueva corónica' furthermore is not a correction of a Spanish mistake within the same Spanish epistemic logic, but it is above all the introduction of a new logic to tell the story. It is, indeed, a truly epistemic delinking in history writing. Consequently, from a 'nueva corónica' that has delinked from the historiographical precepts of European historiography of the time, comes the proposal of 'buen gobierno'. Obviously, the 'buen govierno' that Waman Puma proposes is not based on Machiavelli but on the practices and histories of Andean social organization, but this time taking into account that – contrary to ancient times – the Spaniards were there to stay and the region was no longer what it was. The radical de-linking performed by Waman Puma put him at odds of course with Spanish authority and he paid with four centuries of silence. Inca Garcilaso de la Vega, instead, enjoys quick fame because he remains within the system and his proposal was closer to emancipation than to de-linking, that is, as radical liberation and epistemic de-colonization.

De-linking cannot be performed, obviously, within the frame of the theo and the ego-logical politics of knowledge and understanding. For, how can you de-link within the epistemic frame from where you want to de-link? De-linking is the reverse of 'assimilation': to assimilate means that you do not belong yet to what you are assimilating. It doesn't make sense to conceive assimilation within the frame one wants to assimilate!! For that reason, early de-linking projects (such as the one advanced by Samir Amin[32]), were not

radical de-linking but rather radical emancipation within the rhetoric of modernity and the logic of coloniality. In other words, de-linking could hardly be thought out from a Marxist perspective, because Marxism offers a different content but not a different logic.[33] The epistemic locations for de-linking comes from the emergence of the geo- and body-politics of knowledge[34]), of which Waman Puma shall become the reference point of all subsequent projects.[35]

If the theo- and ego- politics of knowledge and understanding are the hegemonic frame of Western modernity in its *internal diversity,* they are also the constraints of the 'pensée unique' (i.e., monotopic thinking), the process of delinking needs a different epistemic grounding that I describe here as the geo- and body- politics of knowledge and understanding.[36] These are epistemologies of the *exteriority* and of the *borders*. If there is no *outside* of capitalism and western modernity today, there are many instances of *exteriority*: that is, the outside created by the rhetoric of modernity (Arabic language, Islamic religion, Aymara language, Indigenous concepts of social and economic organization, etc.). The outside of modernity is precisely that which has to be conquered, colonized, superseded and converted to the principles of progress and modernity. Epistemic *geo*-politics as conceived by Dussel in his seminal *Philosophy of Liberation* (1977) can and should be read today as a de-linking manifesto. Dussel produced a fracture in the terrain on which theo- and ego-politics fought for the right to a 'new paradigm' (Khun) or a new 'episteme' (Foucault). The very historical foundation of the modern/colonial world in America (and I am using foundation here with careful awareness and not endorsing fundamentalisms), is characterized by the 'pulling out (extirpation) or removal of idolatry' which tells the story of the genocidal and epistemic violence of theology (e.g., 'extirpation' of knowledges and beliefs among the Indigenous population that Spanish missionaries believed, or at least said, were the work of the Devil). The continued disqualification and simultaneous appropriation of 'indigenous' knowledges to produce 'modern' pharmaceutical drugs is a contemporary example in which the rhetoric of modernity justifies not only the appropriation of land and labor forces but, lately and more intensively, the knowledge of 'Others'. Geo-politics of knowledge is one instance in which the mirage is broken up and denounced. (The other is the *body politics* of knowledge to which I will return later.)

Geo-politics of knowledge (e.g., emerging from different historical locations of the world that endured the effects and consequences of Western imperial and capitalist expansion) are necessary to break up the illusion that all knowledges are and have to originate in the imperial form of consciousness (e.g., the right, the left and the center). The geography of reason shifts. That is to say, the assumption that everything is thought out within the heart of the empire: repression, control, oppression as well as emancipation, liberation and decolonization. Whoever is not in the heart of the empire, but in its direct or

indirect colonies, has to wait for *imperial emancipations*. One of the reasons the Haitian revolution was an unthinkable historical phenomenon, as Trouillot[37] has shown, is precisely because of such assumptions. The geo-politic of knowledge is twice relevant, then. First, it is the affirmation of what has been denied by the agents that created, enacted and expanded the theo- and ego-politics of knowledge. Secondly, once geo-politics of knowledge is affirmed as the re-emergence of the reason that has been denied as reason, it makes visible what the theo- and ego-politics of knowledge occluded and still occludes, namely their own geo-political *location*, which is cloaked in the rhetoric of universality. Decolonization of knowledge shall be understood in the constant double movement of unveiling the geo-political location of theology, secular philosophy and scientific reason and simultaneously affirming the modes and principles of knowledge that have been denied by the rhetoric of Christianization, civilization, progress, development, market democracy.

## III Coloniality: the darker side of modernity

### *III. 1*

De-linking presupposes to know from where one should delink, as I suggested before. De-linking means 'desprenderse from the coloniality of knowledge controlled and managed by the theo-, ego and organo-logical principles of knowledge and its consequences. De-linking goes together with the de-colonial shift and the geo- and body-politics of knowledge provide both the analytics for a critique and the vision toward a world in which many worlds can co-exist. As a critique, the geo- and body-politics of knowledge reveals the totalitarian bent of theo-, ego- and organo- politics of knowledge, even when good intentions could be found in their content. As a vision, the geo- and body- politics of knowledge lead the way toward a 'pluri-versal world as a uni-versal project'. This vision differs, quite radically, from the 'polycentric world' that Samir Amin proposed as the path after de-linking. In its early version, de-linking was conceived as an economic and political de-linking from the Imperial States (e.g., Western European capitalists countries plus the US).[38] De-linking today shall be thought out and projected as a de-linking from the rhetoric of modernity and the logic of coloniality. But in order to proceed in that direction (part IV below), we need to spell out both the rhetoric of modernity and the logic of coloniality.

The rhetoric of modernity works through the imposition of 'salvation', whether as Christianity, civilization, modernization and development after WWII or market democracy after the fall of the Soviet Union. Thus, the geo-political – rather than postmodern – of modernity focuses not only on reason as the reason of terror (as Dussel pointed out) but also, and mainly, on 'the irrational myth that it conceals', which I understand here as the logic of

coloniality. If coloniality is constitutive of modernity, in the sense that there cannot be modernity without coloniality, then the rhetoric of modernity and the logic of coloniality are also two sides of the same coin. How are the rhetoric of modernity and the logic of coloniality entangled together? Let's explore the question, first, through the *concept* of modernity and then explore its relationship to the 'rational concept of emancipation'. For the purposes at hand, a general definition of modernity as proposed by Anthony Giddens about ten years ago should suffice:

> 'Modernity' refers to modes of social life or organization which emerged in Europe from about the seventeenth century onwards and which subsequently became more or less worldwide in their influence. This associates modernity with a time period and with an initial geographical location, but for the moment leaves its major characteristics safely stowed away in a block box.[39]

What would those 'modes of social life' be? Niall Ferguson helps by offering a snapshot:

While in the 1620s only gentlemen had taken tobacco, by the 1690 it was a custom, the fashion, all the mode – so that every plow man had his pipe . . . What people like most about these new drugs (tobacco among men, tea among ladies) was that they offered a very different kind of stimulus from the traditional European drug, alcohol. Alcohol is technically a depressant. Glucose, caffeine and nicotine, by contrast, were the eighteenth century equivalent of uppers. Taken together the new drugs gave English society an almighty hit; the Empire, it might be said, was built on huge sugar, caffeine and nicotine rush – a rush nearly everyone could experience.[40]

In the 1940s, Cuban anthropologist Fernando Ortiz made a similar, although sardonic, observation of the same phenomenon. Ortiz's is not an observation from inside the memories and sensibilities of the empire but, rather, from within the memories and sensibilities of the colonies. While Ferguson tells the story available within the ideological frame of the ego-politics of knowledge, Ortiz belongs to 'an-other history', literally, to the colonial history of the Caribbean looking East and somewhat up North. There is no warranty of being 'better' and being 'good' because of the simple fact of belonging to the memories of the colonies. It simply means that it is *an-other* frame of consciousness that perceives and senses the world that cannot be subsumed by and under the consciousness and sensibilities that have been produced in the social forms of life and institutions within the empire. The vision that emerges from the memories, wounds, humiliations, disavowal of Caribbean consciousness (e.g., Fanon 1952, Cesaire 1956, Winter 2006, etc.), where brutal exploitation of labor and massive slave trades took place, involving, of course, British merchants, is less glorifying and celebratory of

modernity than Giddens or Ferguson. But, above all, it is an-other way of knowing and not simply a critique of historical content that is argued within the same logic that underlies the narratives of Giddens and Ferguson. What is at stake, briefly, is the conflictive coexistence of the theo- and ego-politics of knowledge on the one hand and the geo (and body) on the other. From the 'underside' of modernity,[41] from, that is, the forms of consciousness shaped in and by the history of coloniality, Ortiz observed:

> Tobacco reached the Christian world along with the revolutions of the Renaissance and the Reformation, when the Middle Ages were crumbling and the modern epoch, with its *rationalism*, was beginning. One may say that *reason* starved and benumbed by theology, to revive and free itself, needed the help of some harmless stimulant that should not intoxicate it with enthusiasm and then stupefy it with illusions and bestiality, as happens with the old alcoholic drinks that lead to drunkenness.[ . . . ].
>
> The coincidental appearance of these four exotic products in the Old World, all of them stimulants of the senses as well as of the spirit, is not without interests. *It is as though they had been sent to Europe from the four corners of the earth by the devil to revive Europe when 'the time came', when that continent was ready to save the spirituality of reason from burning itself out and give the senses their due once more.*[42]

Contrary to alcohol, which incites violence, the stimulants in question create feelings of joy and celebration, on the one hand reported by Ferguson, but at the same time, as Ortiz notes, oblivion, forgetfulness and egotistic individualism as well as disregard in Europeans for other individuals in the colonies, particularly Blacks and Indians.

To further bring to light the silence of the colonies buried under the veil tended in and by the celebratory descriptions offered by Giddens and Ferguson (both of whom are British, I should remember), I turn to Afro-Antiguan Eric Williams. His characterization may offend enthusiastic supporters of Alain Badiou's critique of identity politics and his search for the singular universal. Another way to read into identity politics, although limited in its bend toward apartheid, is as the expression of *human interests* that have been historically denied because Blacks or Indians have not been considered humans and, therefore, could not have interests. Eric Williams reveals one aspect of modernity that is overlooked by both Giddens and Ferguson and perhaps taken for granted in the way of life of empire-building that characterized England in the second half of the seventeenth century:

> One of the most important consequences of the Glorious Revolution of 1688 and the expulsion of the Stuarts was the impetus *it gave to the principle of free trade*. In the same year the Merchant Adventurers of London were deprived of their monopoly of the export trade in cloth,

> and a year later the monopoly of the Muscovy Company was abrogated and trade to Russia made free. *Only in one particular did the freedom accorded in the slave trade differ from the freedom accorded in other trades – the commodity involved was man.*[43]

From Giddens to Williams, through Ferguson and Ortiz, we have the spectrum of the partial stories of modernity (e.g., the events as seen and narrated from the British perspective) and modernity/coloniality (e.g., the events seen and narrated from the Caribbean perspective). From the Caribbean, you see that modernity not only needed coloniality but that coloniality was and continues to be *constitutive* of modernity. There is no modernity without coloniality. From England, you see only modernity and, in the shadow, the 'bad things' like slavery, exploitation, appropriation of land, all of which will supposedly be 'corrected' with the 'advance of modernity' and democracy (e.g., today's US policy in Iraq) when all arrive at the stage in which justice and equality will be for all. Giddens and Ferguson offer a view of modernity and of empire from the consciousness of the ego-politics of knowledge while Williams and Ortiz see it from the consciousness of the geo-politics of knowledge. A lake looks different when you are sailing on it than when you are looking at it from the top of the mountains surrounding it. Different perspectives on modernity are not only a question of the eyes, then, but also of *consciousness* and of physical location and power differential – those who look from the peak of the mountain see the horizon and the lake, while those inhabiting the lake see the water, the fish and the waves surrounded by mountains but not the horizon. Sailing the lake of modernity are Giddens and Ferguson while looking at the lake from two different mountain peaks are Williams and Ortiz.

Alternatives **to** modernity, as these four brief examples show, cannot come (or cannot come only and perhaps mainly) from the theo- and the ego-politics of knowledge inhabited by those like Giddens and Ferguson, insofar as their perspective is restricted to a particular discourse. *Alternative modernities* are thinkable within the Ego politics of knowledge and understanding in the precise sense that it is the same principle of knowledge that is enacted in different locations (e.g., India, South Africa or Brazil). Alternatives **to** modernity, instead, presupposes delinking and building on the geo and body politics of knowledges and understanding. In order to fully understand this point, let's return to the rationality that has linked modernity with emancipation since rationality and emancipation are two elements of modernity that most progressive intellectuals would like to 'salvage' from the horror of modernity, from the complicity between the rhetoric of modernity and the logic of coloniality. It is in philosophy and in 'philosophical idealism' that the 'rational concept of emancipation' (to use Dussel's formulation) and the idea of modernity came together. Jurgen Habermas

attributes the conceptualization of modernization and modernity to Hegel who distinguishes the historical from the philosophical dimensions of modernity.[44] The disjunction between historical and philosophical modernity might explain why some theorists place modernity in the Renaissance and others in the Enlightenment. Historical modernity has, for Hegel, three landmark events: the Renaissance, the Reformation and the discovery of the New World. Philosophical modernity has a (different) three-part configuration of events that consists of the Reformation, the Enlightenment and the French Revolution. It is indeed interesting to note that for Hegel (as well as for Carl Schmitt (1952), historical modernity is conceived as a radical turn of events that begins around 1500 with the Renaissance and the discovery of the New World as the signposts for the moment in which the pre-global began to be re-articulated by the global. Schmitt prefers, as could be expected within the modern concept of time, to see a 'transition' from the pre-global to the global. The problem with the idea of 'transition' is that, once the new appears, the old vanishes out of the present, which is precisely the problem with the rhetoric of modernity for those who are not lucky enough to be in the *space* where *time* and *history* move forward.

The concept of emancipation belongs to the universe of discourse framed by the philosophical and historical concepts of modernity, which becomes apparent if we look at the particular intersection of Theo- and Ego-politics that later, in the eighteenth century, gave rise to the idea of emancipation – the Reformation. In terms of philosophical modernity, the Reformation was a crucial break-through for the emergence of critical self-reflexivity and it is easy to see how – and why – the concept of emancipation emerged from the 'transition' to 'freedom of subjectivity' and 'critical self-reflexivity' from lack thereof that began with the Reformation. The individual freedom sought to some degree within the Church by Luther became more and more autonomous through secularization until its detachment in Descartes dictum, 'I think, therefore I am', in Kant's transcendental subject and in Hegel's freedom of subjectivity and critical self-reflexivity.

Habermas underscores four connotations associated with Hegel's idea that 'the principle of the modern world is freedom of subjectivity': individualism, the right to criticism, autonomy or action (e.g., responsibility of what we do) and idealistic philosophy itself (e.g., Hegel's argument that in modern times philosophy grasps the self-conscious (or self-knowing) idea.[45] Habermas explains the importance of the Reformation in Hegel's concept of philosophical modernity:

> With Luther, religious faith became reflective: the world of the divine was changed in the solitude of subjectivity into something posited by ourselves. Against faith in the authority of preaching and tradition, Protestantism asserted the authority of the subject relying upon his own

> insight: the host was simply dough, the relics of the Saints mere bones. Then, too, the Declaration of the Rights of Man and the Napoleonic Code validated the principle of freedom of will against historically preexisting law as the substantive basis of the state [ . . . ]
>
> Furthermore, the principle of subjectivity determines the forms of modern culture. This holds true first of all for objectifying science, which *disenchants nature at the same time that it liberates the knowing subject*. 'Thus [writes Hegel], all miracles were disallowed: for nature was a now system of known and recognized laws; man is at home in it, and only that remains standing in which he is at home; he is free through the acquaintance he has gained with nature'.[46]

These two paragraphs contain most of the elements necessary to reveal the rhetoric behind what Dussel called 'the rational concept of emancipation'. Habermas' celebratory view of Hegel's concept of modernity allows me make visible its underside: (a) the limits of the concept of emancipation once it is detached from the historical experience and the social class that made it necessary, (b) the blindness to the other side of modernity, that is, coloniality. In spite of the fact that Hegel (and the enlightenment philosophers and economists) were reflecting on the particular experience of an ascending bourgeoisie that wanted 'freedom of subjectivity' from the Monarchic and Christian Catholic coercion, their exportation of 'freedom of subjectivity' and 'critical self-reflexivity' around the planet for the good of everyone repeated the same restrictive mechanisms. Certainly, Aymara, Quechuas, Nahuatls, African slaves in Haiti, etc., in the New World (and during the sixteenth century) also experienced coercion by Monarchic and Christian Catholic powers. But, was Hegel 'speaking' for all of them in the sense that Indians and people of African descent could or should identify with Hegel's freedom of spirit and disenchantment of nature? Individuals who have been enslaved or forced into a position of serfdom may not need philosophical 'freedom'. And Hegel's celebration of science and the disenchantment of nature may not have been enthusiastically acclaimed by Indigenous people and African-brought slaves. Nature was, precisely, one of the spheres of social life in which Africans, Afro-descendents and Indigenous people could maintain 'their freedom of subjectivity' and their 'critical self-reflexivity' as oppressed slaves or serfs of European powers administered by a Creole/Mestizo elite from European descent. It was, in fact, that sector of the population, the Creoles and Mestizo elite who led the way of independence from Spain and hooked themselves to the new economic, politic and epistemic imperial configuration imported from France, Germany and England, for whom Hegel made sense. At least in the Spanish colonies, the leaders of the independence and of the emerging nation-states opted for what seemed 'natural' – the 'application' of the principles of political theory and political economy that were emerging in

France, England and the US.[47] For the Creole/Mestizo elite, the term 'emancipation' applied, although only partially since emancipation from Spain put them in the economic hands of England, the political web of France and the philosophical net of Germany.

Although modernity is not simply a European phenomenon and is inextricably entangled with the colonies, as Dussel has noted, the rhetoric of modernity has been predominantly put forward by European men of letters, philosophers, intellectuals, officers of the state. The modern/colonial power differential was, of course, structured at all levels (economic, political, epistemological, militarily), but it was at the epistemological level that the rhetoric of modernity gained currency.[48] If we had time to go into the biography of the main voices that conceived 'modernity' as the series of historical events taking place from Italy to Spain and Portugal and from there to Germany, France and England, all of them would originate in one of the six European countries leading the Renaissance, the colonial expansion and capitalist formation, and the European Enlightenment. Dissenting voices from the colonies were not concerned about conceiving modernity and expanding it West. Dissenting voices, like that of Waman Puma de Ayala in the Spanish Viceroyalty of Peru in the early seventeenth century and of Quobna Ottobah Cugoano in British Ghana, were silenced or ignored. In the name of what or on what grounds? – of theo-politics of knowledge the first and the ego-politics of knowledge the second. Voices like Waman Puma and Quobna Ottobah anchored both the geo and body-politics of knowledge and they shall become – for the decolonial shift – what Plato and Aristotle were for the foundation of the theo- and ego-politics of knowledge. Epistemic decolonization is still of the essence since we are still living under the set of beliefs inherited from Theology and secularized by Philosophy and Science as well as the belief that 'capitalism' (and above all in its neo-liberal rhetoric and practice) and 'economy' are one and the same phenomenon. De-colonization (of the mind) must unveil the totalitarian complicity of the rhetoric of modernity and the logic of coloniality in order to open up space for the possibility, following the rhetoric of the World Social Forum as well as the Zapatistas, of 'another world' in which many worlds will co-exist.[49] Thus, Dussel's philosophy of liberation, via the geo-politics of knowledge, calls for 'liberation' from the ties and complicities maintained by earlier 'emancipation'. While modernity extolled emancipation, the indigenous population and people from African descent were waiting for their time, which has arrived, the time of liberation and decolonization (e.g., Frantz Fanon and Fausto Reynaga, as two clear examples). By opening up the question of the geo-politics of knowledge Dussel took a crucial step toward the grammar of decolonization. If we put the emancipating ideals of modernity in the perspective of coloniality, the historical frame here will not be constituted by events meaningful to Hegel but, rather, to the philosophy of liberation, to indigenous and Afro social

movements, to critical thought in the Caribbean, to the modernity/coloniality scholarly and political project, the Social Forum of the Americas (as well as the World Social Forum), etc. Within that frame, we can place the Tupac Amaru insurgency, the Haitian Revolution as well as the ambiguous and 'dependent independence' of the Mestizo/Creole elite in South America and the Caribbean Islands. While the latter was subservient to European imperial power, it still gave rise to dissident factions that would be voiced, for example, by José Carlos Mariátegui as well as in the contemporary modernity/coloniality project. (In order to preempt unnecessary questions, let me quickly clarify that the Creole/Mestizo perspective and consciousness (either pro-imperial or dissident like the philosophy of liberation or modernity/coloniality as a scholarly and political project) are the same as the perspective and consciousness of critical Indigenous and Afro-Caribbean or Andean projects. They are, however, compatible and complementary in that the memories are grounded in some shared 'ancestry', as Afro-Andean activist and intellectual, Juan Garcia, would have it.) From the inscription of these events in the memories and bodies, the 'experience', of people whose 'freedom of subjectivity' has been formed as a need from their experience of oppression, coloniality comes to the fore as the darker side of modernity.

### *III.2*

The conception of modernity as the pinnacle of a progressive transition relied on the *colonization of space and time* to create a narrative of difference that placed contemporary languages 'vernacular' (indeed, imperial) languages and categories of thought, Christian religion and Greco-Latin foundations in the most elevated position. Hence, men of letters in the European Renaissance invented the idea of the Middle Ages in order to locate themselves in the present of a history that they could trace back to Greece and the Roman Empire and, after the dark centuries, re-emerged in the radiant light of Antiquity. The idea of Western civilization that emerged at that juncture was based on pure and simple identity politics.[50] The colonization of time and the institution of the temporal colonial difference were crucial for the narratives of modernity as salvation, emancipation and progress. As Johannes Fabian shows in his classical book on *Time and the Other* (1982), the temporal colonial difference became apparent toward the end of the eighteenth century in the idea of *primitives* (which would replace the previous notion of *barbarians*) and in what Fabian calls the *denial of co-evalness*. Yet, to truly grasp the power of the denial of co-evalness in the narrative of modernity, it is necessary to step back to the Renaissance and understand first the colonization of space and the construction of *the spatial colonial difference*.

If the temporal difference was expressed through the notion of 'primitives', the spatial colonial difference worked through the concept of

*barbarians*, an idea taken from the Greek language and historical experience, but modified in the sixteenth century to refer to those who were located in an inferior space. The reconceived idea of barbarians arose as Western Christians in Latin and vernacular Western languages began to construct a narrative of themselves. Of course, Western Christians were not the only ones who, in the sixteenth century, were attempting to define their own identity and build a uni-versal identity politics based on the believed superiority of their religion over others. Jews and Moors (Arabs and Islamic) also believed with equally good reasons that their systems of belief were superior to Christianity. Beginning in the sixteenth century, Christianity, however, affirmed its complicity with capitalism. Christian Theology (theo-politics) and secular philosophy (ego-politics) took over the concept and the rhetoric of modernity. As they became hegemonic, Theology and Secular Philosophy grounded by Christianity formed the Master Voice through which the people, regions of the world and other religions would be classified, described and ranked. Jews, Moors, Chinese Buddhists, Japanese Sintoists, Aymaras and Quechua Pachaists (if I can invent a parallel term)[51] were placed in subservient levels in those hierarchies. The re-conceptualization of the 'barbarians' in the sixteenth century gave to the spatial colonial difference its evil actor. The later translation of the 'barbarians' into 'primitives' in the eighteenth century would incorporate the temporal dimension in the pre-existing spatial colonial difference. Both underlying ideas continue to work in contemporary discourse.

The basic frame for the sixteenth century iteration of the 'barbarians' can be found in the writings of the Dominican Friar Bartolomé de Las Casas. In the final section of his *Apologética Historia Sumaria* (*circa* 1552), Las Casas identified four types of barbarians. What the four types had in common, for Las Casas, was what he understood as 'barbarie negativa' (negative barbarism). That is, 'barbarians' were those who 'lacked' something in the area of government, knowledge of Latin and alphabetic writing because they lived in state of nature (that Hobbes and Locke would take as a starting point later on), had the wrong religion (like Jews, Moors, Chinese) or had no 'religion' at all (like Indigenous people in the Americas and Black Africans). Clearly, the *spatial colonial difference* was constructed not on the bases of *previous European history* (e.g., the European Middle Age), but from *non-European histories, or better yet, from people without history*. People without history were located in space, the non-European alterity in Dussel's terms. There was, however, a fifth type of barbarian that Las Casas distinguished from the previous four and described as *barbarie contraria* (oppositional barbarism). Las Casas identified oppositional barbarians as enemies of Christianity, those who envied it and wanted to destroy it. Oppositional barbarism is clearly defined as anti-Christianity, and as such resembles the conception terrorists today.

In the eighteenth century, the concept of 'primitive' was introduced in the narrative of modernity and translated the 'barbarians' into 'primitives' by

incorporating a temporal dimension of the former spatial colonial difference. 'Modernity' was defined no longer in simple contradistinction to the Middle Ages or against the spatially bound barbarians, but against 'tradition'.[52] By the end of the seventeenth century, when the ego-politics of knowledge was affirming itself and modernity/coloniality was entering the 'new age' of Enlightenment, in the linear history of Christian Europe, the exploitation of the reaches of the New World (mines and plantations) was in full bloom and with it the slave trade from Africa. Holland and England were beginning to extend their commercial tentacles through South Asia. And in both the Americas and Asia, there were people too. In the process of a growing 'modern-time consciousness', the 'behind' societies that did not respond to the styles and exigencies of European modes of life (per Giddens), were being translated from 'barbarians' (per the first stage of modernity/coloniality) into 'primitives'. 'Barbarians' coexisted in space, but primitives began to lag behind in time. The concept of 'primitives' as applied to people went hand in hand with the idea of traditions that applied to a whole set of beliefs and organization of society beyond Western Europe. Thus, 'primitives' and 'traditions' appeared as 'objects' outside Europe and outside modernity. Ironically, Constructivists were later celebrated when they 'discovered' that 'traditions' do not exist by themselves but have to been invented. Of course, they were invented! They were constructed precisely by the rhetoric of modernity. 'Tradition' is not outside modernity but in its *exteriority*: It is *an outside* invented by the rhetoric of modernity in the process of creating *the inside*. The outside of 'tradition' is invented in order to insure the inside as the locus of enunciation of knowledge. 'Tradition' is not a way of life that pre-dated 'modernity' but an invention of the rhetoric of modernity.

The spatial and temporal colonial differences joined forces to expel out of 'modernity' both non-Europeans and historical Europeans alike.[53] It was precisely at this junction that Karl Marx, working on the history of capital, invented the concept of 'original accumulation'[54] and looked at both accumulation within the history of Europe and in and from the colonies. By then, Marx had placed the Industrial Revolution at the very center of space and time and built on the already existing *temporal and spatial colonial differences*. As an added twist in the history of Europe, the 'discovery and conquest of America' were located closer to the Middle Ages in order to boost France, England and Germany to the triumphal present of modernity (as in Hegel's lesson in the philosophy of history).

It would be easy to follow this narrative up to the re-articulation of the *spatial* and *temporal* colonial differences after WWII, when the US entered as the new leader in the history of Western imperial powers. The concepts of development and underdevelopment are new versions of the rhetoric of modernity insofar as both concepts were invented to re-organize the temporal and spatial colonial differences. By categorizing the underdeveloped world

both as *behind* in time and *far* in space, the underdeveloped and the Third World became indistinguishable. Although the very idea of development and underdevelopment carries the weight of economy, it also incorporates the rest of human experience. 'Underdeveloped' in a highly industrialized world, also implies being 'behind' in spirit and knowledge. For that very reason, the underdeveloped world did not produce science or philosophy but culture, as Carl Pletsch convincingly argued many years ago (Pletsch 1982). But in the Cold War the rhetoric of modernity reached a crucial point of bifurcation: the re-distribution of the spatial and temporal colonial differences that started a quarter of century before, with the break through of the Russian Revolution and the *translation* of the Russian into the Soviet Empire and the rhetoric of time (developed and underdeveloped) as complemented by the rhetoric of ranking of geo-historical locations: First, Second and Third Worlds. The Russian Revolution was a family feud, a struggle within modernity, liberals vs. socialists: it was a consequence of the enlightenment, although socialist instead of liberal, pro-State instead of pro-private enterprises. Consequently, it was and it wasn't in the same paradigm than the Glorious, the US and the French Revolutions. And of course, even less within the same paradigm of the Haitian Revolution. What was the location of the Russian Revolution in the rhetoric of modernity and the logic of coloniality? We can only understand its location if we make note that another construction of difference was at work as early as the sixteenth century.

Take as evidence the fact that when Las Casas described the four types of 'negative barbarism', he did not place the inhabitants of the Ottoman and the Islamic empires in the same hierarchy as the people in the Inca and Aztec Empires, even though all co-existed at the beginning of the sixteenth century. A different difference must be at play. If we make an effort to put ourselves in Las Casas time and place (he lived in Spain and also in what are today Haiti, the Dominican Republic and Southern Mexico), we can assume he may have been aware that Suleyman the Magnificent, Sultan of the Ottoman Empire, was on equal footing with, if not above, Charles the V, Emperor of the Holy Roman Empire. And, because of the still vivid presence in the middle of the sixteenth century of signs of the sophistication of the Islamic Empire in Cordoba, Granada and Seville, he must have been aware of the accomplishments of that society. The Ottomans, then, posed a real threat to the superiority of Western Christians in mid-sixteenth century. The Aztecs and Incas, in contrast, had no history of fighting against Christianity like Islam had and as the Ottomans learned to have from the second half of the fifteenth and sixteenth centuries. And, above all, the society and economy of the Aztecs and Incas had already been dismantled and Spanish Christians were in their territory building European institutions and creating a Spanish/Christian like society. Thus, despite the many pages Las Casas devoted to argue that 'Indians' are human beings who are in a position to learn and adopt the Christian doctrine, he

couldn't avoid seeing in them the innocence of children who need guidance by 'conversion' and not physical punishment as in the just war defended by Sepulveda. Those inhabitants of regions East and South of Europe were not considered naïve or unequal but, merely, mistaken.

Thus, I would say that spatial/temporal difference must be seen simultaneously as both *imperial and colonial*. It was imperial in the way the agents of the Spanish crown and Church defined their relations and differences with Islam and the Ottomans; and, it was colonial in the way Spanish missionaries and men of letters defined themselves in relation to the Indians and the African slaves. Spain expelled the 'Moors' from their territory, but never colonized them, and recognized that they were among equals, although the Moors had the 'wrong' god from the point of view of the Christians. On the contrary, it was never considered, even by Las Casas, that the Aztecs and Incas ruling elites (with whom he did not have direct contact, like Cortés or Pizarro), were not *just* human beings but *equal* human beings. The Arabic and Islamic worlds of North Africa and the Middle East would be subjected to the *colonial difference* later on in the nineteenth century when France and England began the second wave of colonial expansion in Asia and Africa; but, from the sixteenth to the end of the eighteenth century, the Ottoman Empire and the Islamic world remained in the frame of *imperial difference*. We can likewise locate Russia within the imperial difference. It would have been difficult for Las Casas to pay attention to the rising Russian Empire. The ending domination of the Golden Horde coincided, chronologically, with the expulsion of the Moors from the Iberian Peninsula. Both what would become the Spanish and Russian was at their beginning. But events in Russia did not count in the life and interests of Christian Renaissance men of letters who were telling the stories that later on became canonical and hegemonic. Russia may have been out of Las Casas' radar even though Orthodox Christianity may have been among those threatening Christianity and wanting to destroy it. The emerging Russian Empire may have been peripheral to Las Casas' 'contrarian barbarism', but he may have known that during the first half of the sixteenth century, Moscow was redefined as 'The Third Rome' and as the center of an emerging empire, but Orthodox Christian.

The *imperial* difference works by using some of the features of the colonial difference and applying them to regions, languages, people, states, etc., that cannot be colonized. A degree of inferiority is attributed to the 'imperial other' that has not been colonized in that it is considered (because of language, religion, history, etc.) somewhat *behind* (time) in history or, if its present is being considered, *marginal* (space).[55] By the beginning of the nineteenth century, the idea of 'time' measured in terms of progress and the march of Western civilization, was gaining ground. George W. F. Hegel rewrote Las Casas and defined the new system of classification: 'History in general is therefore the development of Spirit in *Time*, as Nature is the development of

the Idea in *Space*'.[56] In his re-ordering of time/space and his effort to locate Germany (in space) as the first nation (in time), Hegel placed France and England next to Germany, as the 'heart' of Europe (similar to Kant's geo-political classification of the planet according to proximity to Reason, the Beautiful and the Sublime), with all the heavy implications that the word 'heart' has in his lessons in the philosophy of history. Latin countries occupied the margins to the South. The northeastern states of Europe – Poland, Russia and the Slavonic Kingdoms – came 'late into the series of historical States, and form and perpetuate the connection with Asia',[57] which as we know *is in the past*. Furthermore, Hegel underscored the time-space distribution and the role of places in universal history when he added, for example, that 'the Poles even liberated beleaguered Vienna from the Turks; and the Slavonics have to some extent been drawn within the sphere of Occidental Reason. Yet this entire body of peoples remains excluded from our considerations, because hitherto it has not appeared as an independent element in the series of phases that Reason has assumed in the World'.[58] They *were* and simultaneously they *were not*; now you see it, now you don't. Such is the mechanism of the imperial difference. Imagine the other side, what Poles and Russians felt and thought: The Hegelian heart of Europe was the object of desire; the desire to inhabit that present in time and that location in space, to be 'modern', precisely, as Giddens defined it in both time and space (e.g. seventeenth century and Europe).

I do not have time here to explore one of the latest stages of this same rhetoric of modernity in the twentieth century, but I would invite the reader to think of Samuel Huntington's *The Clash of Civilization* (1995) and *Who are we* (2004) as Huntington re-articulates the imperial/colonial difference with the Islamic world after the fall of the Soviet Union.[59] There is, in Huntington's description of 'Islamic civilization' the recognition of imperial glories, but, at the same time he voices the growing Western conceptualization – since Orientalism – of Arab inferiority based on their language, religions and ways of life. Add the fact that the invention of the idea of the Middle East, at the turn of the twentieth century, when oil became for industrialized countries what gold was in the sixteenth century for mercantile capitalism. Ten years after *The Clash of Civilization*, Huntington went on to re-map and refresh the colonial difference with Latin America (as he is hesitant to whether give to Latin America a place in the West). You can begin to see how refreshing of the imperial difference (Middle East) works in tandem with the re-drawing of the colonial difference (Latin America). Huntington remaps the ethno-racial pentagon (Hollinger 1995). Ten years ago, Hollinger was interested in asking who the Hispanics were and how they emerged as the fifth leg of the ethno-racial pentagon. Huntington is no longer interested in describing *who* Hispanics/Latino/as *are*, but in demonstrating that *they are* a *threat* and why they are so. If *The Clash of Civilization* re-inscribed Western hegemonic identity

politics, *Who are we?* does the same with Anglo-Saxon hegemonic identity politics.[60]

*III.3*

The spatial/temporal and imperial/colonial differences are organized and interwoven through what Peruvian sociologist Anibal Quijano has articulated as the colonial matrix of power, which was instituted at the inception of the 'modern' world (according to the narratives told by European men of letters, intellectuals and historians) or the modern/colonial world (if we define it through the critical consciousness of dissidents Creoles and mestizos, as well as from oppressed, exploited and marginalized history of Indians and Blacks in the Americas). The rhetoric of modernity with its various distinctions, I have been arguing here, goes hand in hand with the logic of coloniality, which allows me to make the strong claim that coloniality is constitutive of modernity; that there is no modernity without coloniality. Giddens (and Jürgen Habermas and Charles Taylor as quoted earlier by Dussel) tells half of the story, the imperial half that we also find in Las Casas, Hegel and Huntington. But what is the logic of coloniality and how does it work? A terminological question emerges here? Is 'the modern world' the same as 'modernity'? Is the 'colonial matrix of power' the same than 'coloniality'? As with any question of language, the answers are up for grab. The point should be to avoid the 'modern expectation' that *there is a word that carries the true meaning of the thing* instead of the form of consciousness and the universe of meaning in which the word *means*. Meaning is not a 'true value' but a reflection of cognitive (epistemic and hermeneutic) force and import within particular geo-political designs. As in Jorge Luis Borges' *The Garden of Forking Path*, once you select one of three courses of action, the second or the third unchosen paths become real as *possible worlds*.

Thus, I choose to understand the 'modern/colonial world' and 'colonial matrix of power' as part of the same historical complex, but not as synonyms. The 'colonial matrix of power' is the specification of what the term 'colonial world' means both in its logical structure and in its historical transformation. From the perspective of modernity, 'newness' is a motor of history and a constant celebration of 'modernity's progressive' power for the good of humankind. The 'discovery' introduced the idea of the 'new'. As a matter of fact, 'America' as a name took a while to be recognized. For at least 250 years, 'Indias Occidentales' was the administrative name for the Spanish Crown while non-Spanish men of letters and intellectuals, from Américo Vespucci to Pietro Martir d' Anghiera in the sixteenth century, and from Buffon to Kant in the eighteenth century, and to Hegel, preferred the term '*New* World'. It is in this narrative that the idea of 'revolution' has a strong appeal as it indicates radical changes *forward toward newness*, which is precisely the rhetoric of modernity.

The problem is that the celebration of newness and change shadows the consequences of such changes. We are not here once again in Borges' garden. By choosing path 1, for example, that of modernity, we would have left as mere possibility paths 2 and 3, which might include the path of coloniality, for example. Unfortunately, history does not follow the logic of possible worlds; and modernity/coloniality being constitutive go together no matter which path you choose.

Anibal Quijano and Immanuel Wallerstein[61] closed a long debate, in the seventies, as to whether there was a transition from feudalism to capitalism in America (a nonsense question that only could have been imagined by a model of history that takes European history as a model). The spatial epistemic break was invisible and unimaginable to the Latin American left. And in this case was the concept of coloniality, rather than Wallerstein history of capitalism that illuminated the structural moment in which the expansion of the West goes sidewise and not up. Quijano and Wallerstein stated that it was not the 'discovery' that integrated the Americas into an already existing capitalist economy. On the contrary, a capitalist economy, as we know it today, couldn't have existed without the 'discovery and conquest of Americas'. The massive appropriation of lands, massive exploitation of labor, and production of commodities on a new scale for a global market was possible with the emergence of the 'Americas' in the European horizon. The very idea of 'modernity' was invented in the narratives in which the emergence of Europe was articulated on a double front: separated from the Middle Ages, in the temporal axis and of the Americas, where the barbarians were located, in the spatial axis.

It was not the discovery, per se, that mattered, but its consequences – the transference of economic power from the Mediterranean to the Atlantic and the qualitative changes in the production of commodities and the transformation of the commercial circuits. While the European Renaissance was taking place in Italy within Western Christianity, sustained by three strong commercial centers (Venice, Florence and Genoa),[62] the simultaneous imperial foundation of Spain and the colonization of the Americas changed the course of Europe's own internal history. The European Renaissance and New World were two fundamental anchors of the modern/colonial world held together by the complicity between the rhetoric of modernity and the logic of coloniality. From the sixteenth century on, they co-exist and co-depend as well on the formation of 'capitalism' as we know it today. As a matter of fact, the modern/colonial world cannot be conceived except as *simultaneously capitalist. The logic of coloniality is, indeed, the implementation of capitalist appropriation of land, exploitation of labor and accumulation of wealth in fewer and fewer hands.*

How does 'capitalism' relate to and interact with the rhetoric of modernity and the logic of coloniality? Quijano (1990, 1995, 2000) has

been exploring the formation of the colonial matrix of power in four different and mutually articulated domains:

1 The appropriation of land and the exploitation of labor.
2 The control of authority (viceroyalty, colonial states, military structures).
3 The control of gender and sexuality (the Christian family, gender and sexual values and conduct).
4 The control of subjectivity (the Christian faith, secular idea of subject and citizen) and knowledge (the principles of Theology structuring all forms of knowledge encompasses in the Trivium and the Quadrivium; secular philosophy and concept of Reason structuring the human and natural sciences and the practical knowledge of professional schools; e.g., Law and Medicine, in Kant's contest of the faculties).

How are these four spheres of human experience interrelated? They are interrelated through *knowledge and racism* and *capital*.

The scheme might also be read in the reverse direction: the four domains are the particular structure that the conjunction of knowledge and capital assumed in the sixteenth century and beyond. How? *The control of knowledge in Western Christendom belonged to Western Christian men, which meant the world would be conceived only from the perspective of Western Christian Men*. There was 'diversity' within Christianity, of course, not only among Catholics and Protestants but also among Franciscans, Dominicans, Jesuits, Evangelists, etc. Yet, all recognized themselves as Christians and, better yet, as Western Christians (that is, those without much interaction with the Orthodox Church, hair of Byzantium and of Eastern Christians). There were, of course, numerous and prominent nuns, in Spain and in the New World, who like Sor Juana were intellectuals interested in the principles of knowledge. Sor Juana, though, is a good example of a woman who was chastised for entering the house of knowledge that 'belonged' to Men (the direct guardians on earth of God's knowledge). As her rejection demonstrates, for women in Europe as well as for Creoles or Mestizas in the New World, there was no space in the house of Western knowledge. Likewise, when the Moors were expelled from the Iberian Peninsula, Islamic knowledge was barred from the house of Christian knowledge. I have shown one telling instance in the case of Jose de Acosta's *Historia Moral y Natural de las Indias.*[63] By 1590, when he published the book, all knowledge that reached Western Christians (in and through Italy and Spain since the eighth century) was banned from the house of knowledge and not read. Only Greek or Latin and the languages of their Western Christian children (Italian, Spanish, Portuguese, French; and German and English as the Anglo-Saxon heir through the Holy Roman Empire inherited by Germany) could speak knowledge, meaning Hebrew, along with the Jews who were expelled from Spain and compared to Indians, and Arabic lost their residency in the house of knowledge.

The Western Christian men in control of knowledge were also White. Thus, in the sixteenth century a concept of *race* emerged at the intersection of faith, knowledge and skin color. In Spain, the emerging concept of religious racism justified the expulsion of Moors and Jews. In the New World, the surfacing of the 'Indians' (people speaking myriad languages among them Aymara, Quechua, Guaraní, Nahuatl, various dialects of Maya roots, as dissected and classified since the nineteenth century by Western linguists), created a crisis in Christian knowledge as to what kind of 'being' the 'Indians' would have in the Christian chain of beings? Since Indians did not fit the standard model set by White Christian Men and did not themselves have the legitimacy to classify people around the world, they were declared inferior by those who had the authority to determine who was who. There were defenders of the 'humanity' of the Indians among the Spaniards, as we noted above; but, generally, the recognition of their inferiority was shared. The conclusion was justified by the fact that, among other things, the Indians did not have 'religions' and whatever they believed was considered to be the work of the Devil. Also, they did not have alphabetic writing and so were considered people without history.[64] 'Superficial' traits became the visible markers of inferiority, the most apparent of which was a skin color that contrasted with the pale skin of most Spaniards, mostly missionaries and red haired soldiers as Hernán Cortés.

In the New World, then, racism was an epistemic operation that institutionalized the inferiority of the Indians and, subsequently, justified genocidal violence, as Dussel pointed out, and exploitation of labor, as Quijano underlined. Race was, in the colonies and before the industrial revolution, what class became after the industrial revolution in Europe. The implantation of the *encomienda* (an economic institution Spaniards had in place while pushing the Moors toward the south, and expropriating their lands) was one of the initial structure of both appropriation of land and exploitation of labor: the encomendero received in 'donation' from the King a substantial piece of land and a significant number of Indians workers as serf and slaves. The second fundamental economic structure more prominent among British, French and Dutch, was the *plantation* in the extended Caribbean (from today San Salvador de Bahia, in Brazil, to today Charlestown in South Carolina, including of course all the Caribbean islands). The genocidal violence that caused the death of millions of Indigenous people and created the need of renewed labor force generated, as we know, the massive slave trade of Black African, many of them Moors, but darker skinned in comparison with the Indians and the North African Muslims that were expelled from Spain. Thus, knowledge articulated the four spheres of social life in two ways, in terms of faith and physical complexion. Whatever did not fit the religious and moral standards set by Christianity, in terms of faith and physique, was cast out of the standard of humanity. Once people were classified, they were located in a

genealogy of beings, a caste, which is the term used in the fifteenth century and that became slowly translated into race.[65]

Thus, racism and the coloniality of being are one and the same cognitive operation entrenched at the philosophical level in the colonial matrix of power. The colonial matrix of power gives a historical depth and a logical consistency to Frantz Fanon's notion of the 'damnés' as a theoretical concept grounded in the history of the colonial matrix of power. The racial classification that constitutes the modern/colonial world (through the imperial and colonial differences) had in theology and the theo-politics of knowledge it's historical and epistemic foundation. The secular version of the late eighteenth and nineteenth century was simply a translation, as I've tried to show, from theo-politics into secular ego-politics of knowledge as the final horizon of knowledge. One may wonder, for instance, what people in the Islamic world or in China or India thought about racial classification in the West as it was being elaborated since the sixteenth century. Most likely, they were not aware that they were *being classified and what consequential role they would have in the order of thing that was being articulated in Western structures, principles and institutions of knowledge*. By the end of the twentieth century, however, the entire globe is responding in one way or another to Western racial classification.[66]

Let's leave knowledge there for the time being and explore the second fundamental element of the 'glue' holding together the four spheres of the colonial matrix of power: capital. I mentioned above Quijano and Wallerstein's thesis that capitalism as we know it today surfaced and materialized with the 'discovery and conquest' of America. Let me expand. The vocabulary of 'conquest' in the language in the rhetoric of modernity becomes the vocabulary of 'appropriation of land and exploitation of labor' in the logic of coloniality. There are two key nouns used in this paragraph: capital and capitalism. Capital refers to the resources (possession of land, buildings, tools, money) necessary for the production and distribution of commodities as well as for political interventions in the control of authority (as is again clear today). Capitalism, instead, refers to a philosophy that is based on a particular type of economic structure. It may not be redundant to insist in that economy (Greek *oikos*) is a word used to refer to the structure of production and distribution of foods, objects, commodities, etc. while 'capitalist economy' refers to a specific type of economic structure that today, under neo-liberalism, has spread all over the world. *Capital*, paradoxically enough, shall not be confused with capitalist economy in the sense that other economic structures could be envisioned in which 'capital' (a component of an economic structure) would not be the center piece, the object of desire and transcendent point of reference. In this view, Karl Marx's magnus opus, *Das Kapital*, is about capitalism rather than capital.

Making clear the distinction between capital and capitalism, will help us get out of the modernity trap in which Marx himself was caught (e.g., the idea of progress and the need of the bourgeois revolution to move to the next stage of progress, the socialist revolution). The rhetoric of modernity allowed for the colonial matrix of power to be kept secret (a shameful secret that aristocratic families sent to the attics). All the literature about the 'transition from feudalism to capitalism' in the history of Europe that was, in the sixties, transplanted in order to understand the transition from feudalism to capitalism in South America supported the myth of modernity as progress. The application to Latin America was absurd, of course, and did not work for the simple fact that there was no 'European feudalism' in Tawantinsuyu and Anahuac when the Spaniards arrived!

Let's imagine what 'world history' looked like in the second half of the fifteenth century. In Europe, Venice, Florence and Genoa constituted strong market centers in the Mediterranean and maintained commerce with Fez, Egypt and Timbuktu in North Africa, Baghdad in what is today the Middle East and with India and China in Asia. The Portuguese, on the other hand, were busy establishing commercial contacts on the coasts of Africa and on the Indian Ocean, not to speak about their presence in the Mediterranean. Heavy commercial activities were transforming, from within, the structure of Western Christendom post-Roman Empire into what would become self-fashioned as 'modern Europe'. Enter now, 'the discovery and conquest of the America'. Think about how, as we have mentioned, it changed the already existing commercial circuits led by Florence, Venice and Lisbon. In a matter of a few decades, a massive extension of land and the possibility of massive exploitation of labor to produce commodities for an already globalizing market were offered to the Europeans of the Atlantic coast, Spain, Portugal, Holland, France, and England. Capital was necessary to organize labor, production and distribution; and, the appropriation of land *enormously increased the size and power of capital*. It was land, rather than money, that made possible the qualitative jump of mercantile economy into mercantile capitalist economy. Capitalist here means that a theory of capitalism began to emerge out of the change in the scale of economic practices, which would later be articulated in the eighteenth century – with the Physiocrats in France and with Adam Smith in England. Thus, the story of 'the transition from feudalism' to capitalism will depend on whether you tell the story from the perspective of Europe alone or whether you believe that in the period of time between the twelfth to the eighteenth century there was also 'a world' beyond the European portion of the Roman Empire. That is, it depends on whether you believe that the story of Europe is the story of the world or that the history of Europe is about one fifth of the story of the world. What was going on across the planet, I ask again, between the twelfth and the eighteenth century of the Christian era (allow me, for simplicity, to use the Christian calendar)? We must choose between Story One

and Story Two to decide whether we accept the narrative of the 'transition from feudalism to capitalism' or unveil it as a mirage:

Story One: The Renaissance begins in 1453, the date of the fall of Constantinople to the Turks, a defeat for the Christian world that had much to do with propelling the 'renaissance'. Columbus needed to look for a new route to the East with the 'road blocked' by the Turks after the conquest of Constantinople and instead opened up the New World for exploration and conquest. Hence, from a political and economic point of view, the northwest and western ends of the Mediterranean began to see a flourishing in commerce and political transformations. As we mentioned, the Italian city-states in the Mediterranean as well as the Portuguese were important trade centers and a new class of merchants was gaining force over the power of the landlord and the Church who ruled the 'dark, middle ages' (from the fall of Rome in 426 to the fall of Constantinople in 1453). According to Story One, the renaissance was, politically, a period of emerging nation-states that rivaled one another to acquire stocks of gold (Italy, Portugal, Spain, Holland, France, England were among those nations) whether by exploratory expeditions to the New World, conquest, or by pursuing export trade. The mercantile interests of merchants became aligned with the sovereign to pursue policies that promised success in the acquisition of national treasure and the era of mercantilism and of statecraft was the product of their symbiosis. It is this story that traces the shift from feudalism to the 'big-bang' of human history, the industrial revolution.

Story Two: Western Christendom was, in the fifteenth century, one of the seven or eight major commercial circuits that existed at the time and was, relatively, marginal in the world-trade economy, as Abu-Lughod (1982) demonstrated in his discussion of the historical moment that preceded European hegemony. The emergence of a 'New World' coupled with the protestant reformation facilitated the translation of Western Christendom into Europe, one of the four continents. The sudden growth of European economy had as its counterpart the formation of new societies in which the massive appropriation of land created the conditions for European émigrés, for the destruction of existing civilizations, and for the transportation of African slaves to replace the labor force lost by the massive death of Indigenous people. Out of the genocidal violence of European merchants and the Church, which sometimes contributed to genocide and other times fought against it, and out of the intervention of the emerging European states, a new type of society emerged out of the ruins of the first wave of colonial expansion in the Americas. Story Two hints toward the colonial matrix of power and toward missing pieces of the story that disappear when the European renaissance is described as the internal history of Europe and not part of a larger global narrative which would include the disruptions of pre-existing societies in Africa and the Americas as well as concurrent events in the Arab world.

What prevailed was a partial history celebrating the discovery and conquest as European triumphs. Francisco de Gomara followed by Adam Smith and Karl Marx coincided in underscoring the discovery of America as a one of the greatest events in the history of humankind. Although the event was the same, De Gómara had religious motives for celebration while Smith and Marx had economic ones. Gomara cast the discovery in the frame of the theo-politics of knowledge while Smith and Marx framed it in the ego-politics of knowledge. According to Smith, who was looking retrospectively from the perspective of the eighteenth century, 'capital' and 'knowledge' joined forces to allow for the conceptualization of 'capitalism'. As such, the colonial matrix of power described above became the *foundation of capitalism* (e.g., the confluence of economic organization, social and institutional structures and social values) and capitalism, as the engine of the system that bears the name of 'neo-liberalism', a conservative and violent narrative advancing war and free trade to expand the Western world, continues to reproduce the colonial matrix of power, as we have seen in the military occupation of Afghanistan and Iraq and in Latin America through the enforcing the free trade of the Americas. Although 'against' capitalism (and indirectly empire), Marx also remains within the macro-imperial narrative because he misses the colonial mechanisms of power underlying the system he critiques. The unfolding the colonial matrix of power creates a fracture in the hegemonic imperial macro-narratives.

Frantz Fanon, on the contrary, introduced an-other consciousness and directed the evaluation of the 'discovery' toward the history African slavery that tied European imperial and capitalist powers to Africa and the colonies in the making of the modern/colonial world. To do so, he re-inscribed into the knowing process the 'secondary qualities' that both the theo- and ego- politics of knowledge suppressed when they divided body and soul (theo) or body and mind (ego). Fanon's was not just a general or universal inscription of the subjectivity of the modern subject. Rather, he brought back into the house of knowledge the subjectivity of the damnés, the denied and defamed subject that had been a subject beyond the possibilities of knowing. Likewise, the oppositional macro-narrative of Mestizos, like Mariátegui, who was critically aware in the 1920s of the consequences Spanish imperial formation of colonies in Indias Occidentales and of the dangers of the emerging imperial history of the US, and its politics toward Latin America (whose consequences are we witnessing today), brought to the surface that which festered beneath the rhetoric of modernity. Thus, while Gomara celebrated the triumph of Christianity, Adam Smith of free trade (which is being recast today by neo-liberalism) and Marx saw original accumulation as *a condition of capitalism,* that for him was coming into existence with the industrial revolution,[67] Fanon and Mariátegui (like Eric Williams above) made coloniality (although they did not use the word) the center of their critique. By so doing, Fanon and Mariátegui abandoned the geography of knowledge from the theo- and ego-politics of

knowledge, in which Gómara, Smith and Marx were dwelling, to found (in both senses or the word – to run into something un-known and to establish the basis for something different) the geo- and body politics of knowledge which would make possible a decolonized world not dominated by the theo- and ego-politics principles that still today guide the way of thinking of both the right (e.g., Samuel Huntington, and Frances Fukuyama) and the left (e.g. David Harvey, Michael Hardt and Anthony Negri).

I would like to advance the thesis that the emergence of the geo- and body-politics of knowledge introduced a fracture in the hegemony of the theo- and the ego-politics of knowledge, the two standard frames for the colonization of the souls and the minds since the Renaissance that comprises the right, the left and the center (e.g., Christianity in its various forms and secular Conservatism; Liberalism in its various forms; and socialism-Marxism in its various forms). Since I have already defined geo-politics, let me explain what I mean by body politics. The monarchic state of the sixteenth and the seventeenth century operated within the general theological frame. With the disentanglement of 'church and the state' following the bourgeois revolutions, as I have tried to explain, the nation-state entered the frame of the ego-politics of knowledge. In both the theo- and the ego-politics, the 'body-graphical' inscription of the knowing subject was cast out, made invisible, parallel to the invisibility of its the geo-political location in the modern imperial/colonial world. Thus, the body-politics of knowledge includes the re-inscription, per Fanon for example, of the history inscribed in the black body in a cosmology dominated by the white body underneath the theo- and ego- politics of knowledge.

## IV The grammar of de-coloniality: prolegómena to the de-colonial shift

### *IV.1*

The thesis advanced in the last paragraph lead us, directly to the grammar of de-coloniality. The time has come, and the process is already in motion, for the re-writing of global history from the perspective and critical consciousness of coloniality and from within geo and body-political knowledge. Part of the project of de-linking is, as Waman Puma clearly saw it at the beginning of the seventeenth century, the need to write 'nuevas corónicas'. That is, we must formulate a critical theory that goes beyond the point to which Max Horkheimer carried the meaning of critique in Kant. Horkheimer was still working within the frame of the ego-politic of knowledge and the radicalism of his position must be understood within that frame, and his critical concept of theory could offer no more than a project of 'emancipation' (epistemic, political, ethical, economic) within the conceptual frame of the modern/

colonial world. Traditional theory was, to summarize Horkheimer's position in a nutshell, constructed on the basis of givens, on the empirical acceptance, for instance, of laws in nature that science has only to discover. Critical theory, on the other hand, would interrogate the very assumptions that Nature is governed by 'laws'; and will also open the question on the consequences of such assumptions in and for a capitalist society. Critical theory should now be taken further, to the point and project of de-linking and of being complementary with decolonization. That is, as the foundations of the non-Eurocentered diversality of an-other-paradigm.[68] The Eurocentered paradigms of knowledge (its theo- and ego-political versions) has reached a point in which its own premises should be applied to itself from the repository of concepts, energies and visions that have been reduced to silences or absences by the triumphal march of Western conceptual apparatus.[69] The hegemonic modern/colonial and Eurocentered paradigm[70] needs to be *decolonized*. But how does epistemic decolonizaion works? What is its grammar (that is, its vocabulary, syntax and semantics)? There are at least two procedures here. One would be to show the partiality and limitations of the theo and ego politics of knowledge and understanding. The other is offered by the grow and expansion of the geo- and body-politics of knowledge and understanding. Both are de-linking procedures. It will not suffice to denounce its content while maintaining the logic of coloniality, and the colonization of knowledge, intact. The target of epistemic de-colonization is the hidden complicity between the rhetoric of modernity and the logic of coloniality. For critical theory to correspond with decolonization, we need to shift the geography of knowledge and recast it (critical theory) within the frame of geo- and body politics of knowledge. Thus, the first step in the grammar of decolonization could be cast, using an expression coming from the documents of the Universidad Intercultural de los Pueblos Indígenas del Ecuador, *learning to unlearn.*[71] Dussel and Fanon give us two solid starting points to do so – the first connected with epistemic geopolitics and the second with epistemic body politics.

When *critical theory* becomes de-colonial critique it has of necessity to be *critical border thinking* and, by so doing, the de-colonial shift (decolonization of knowdge and of being) marks the Eurocentered limits of critical theory as we know it today, from the early version of the Frankfurt School, to later post-structuralists (e.g. Derrida) and post-modernists (e.g. Jameson). Let's see how the de-colonial shift operates and why it cannot be subsumed as epistemic break (Foucault) or paradigmatic change (Khun). The de-colonial shift belongs literally to a different space, to the epistemic energy and the lack of archive that has been supplanted by the rumor of the dis-inherited or the *damnés* in Fanon's conceptualization.

Dussel identified in Marx's 'scientific program' a shift within the ego-politics of knowledge to unveil, contrary to Smith whose theory of political economy was framed within the perspective and consciousness of the

bourgeoisie, the logic of capital from the perspective of the labor force, that is, the proletariat.[72] By so doing, Marx embraced the perspective of the proletariat, although not necessarily its consciousness. However, as a German Jew (his early writings were devoted to the Jewish question), Marx may have felt the racial differential inscribed in his body and his persona. He translated the *racial differential* that made the Jews the *damnés* within Europe into the subaltern position of the proletariat in *class differential*. Marx's analysis resulted in a scientific explanation of the logic of oppression. It is perhaps the internal (to Europe) colonial wound that gave Marx (and also Spinoza and Freud) that critical edge, that discomfort and that anger that pushed them to reveal what the Christian bourgeoisie and its direct and indirect ideologues were either not seeing or covering up. Internal de-coloniality is really taking place among those thinkers, except that all of them were very entrenched in European memories and subjectivities and were unable to see the parallel between their situation and the external colonial wound (e.g., Indians, Africans, Arabs, Muslims, etc.). In that very specific domain, knowledge meant not so much related to seeking another abstract (and hegemonic) truth but a truth that was hidden by the classical (beginning with Smith's) theories of political economy. Within the ego-politics of knowledge, Marx contributed to the emancipation of the proletariat through the exposure of the logic of capital. Up to this point, Marx continues to be a fundamental contributor to critical theory. However, emancipation in the Marxian sense must be subsumed under liberation and de-colonization insofar as the emancipation of the proletariat in Europe (and the US) cannot be taken as a model-for-export. A similar observation might be made with respect to the *multitude,* understanding multitude not as a new proletariat but as a new working class (Paul Virno, Michael Hardt and Anthony Negri). In other words, the new and extended working class is not just oppressed because it is a working class but because the majority of the most exploited workers belong to the 'wrong' racial group. In spite of the fact that today whites are also subjected to similar exploitative rules, they are the quantitative minority of those laboring, for example, under reprehensible conditions in the multinational factories throughout the Third World. Although the structure of capitalism is different today, we should not forget that the colonial matrix of power organizing the exploitation of labor and underlying capitalism was based initially on the appropriation of lands with serfdom and slavery as the primary form of labor and *racism* as the fundamental argument justifying exploitation. The colonial matrix of power made possible the industrial revolution. True, in Northern Europe, when the industrial revolution took place, race was not a visible issue. The appropriation of land in the colonies was invisible, and the primary form of labor was waged. Thus, *class* became the dominant form of social classification. Isolated from the presence of the Moors, slightly tainted by Black-African slaves, and totally distant from the Indigenous population of the America, the class differential

was established among a population of White Anglo Protestant. Today, however, as immigration changes the demographics of industrial countries and industries move beyond previous borders to Mexico, China and the Philippines, racism, the foundation of the colonial matrix of power, is back with a vengeance and no longer eclipsed, as it was for a short while, by class differential as the ultimate form for the understanding of exploitation of labor. What is at stake, in the last analysis, is the correspondence of race and class. While class refers mainly to economic relations among social groups and is, thus, strictly related to the control of labor in the spheres of the colonial matrix of power, race refers mainly to subjective relations among social groups and is related to the control of knowledge and subjectivity. Thus, liberation and decolonization projects in the Americas today must have the colonial matrix of power, and not the industrial revolution, as a key point of reference.

Now, Fanon and Anzaldúa can provide another departure point for taking Horkheimer's original critical theory to the terrain of de-linking and to the de-colonial shift. That is, for taking critical theory to the negated side of the epistemic colonial difference: to the geo- and bio-logical negated locations of knowledge and understanding. Fanon brings both the geo- and body politics of knowledge and indirectly shows us the need to re-make Horkheimer's critical theory; to move critical theory from its emancipating to its liberating and de-colonizing dimension. Anzaldúa, articulates around the concept of borderland, brings together a geo- and body politics of knowledge that reveals both the racial and gender foundation of white foundation of hegemonic epistemology. Both Anzaldúa and Fanon move epistemology to the terrain where de-linking projects began to be articulated. Fanon points, as in the epigraph at the beginning of this discussion, toward the necessary diagnosis of the epistemic colonization (of souls, of minds, of spirits, of beings) and to the perverse logic of coloniality that, in his own words, distorts, disfigures and destroys (or tends to marginalize) every past that is not the past of the Eurocentered version of history. Let us start with Fanon's description of a colonized town in Algeria in *The Wretched of the Earth*:

> The town belonging to the colonized people, or at least the native town, the Negro village, the medina, the reservation, is a place of ill fame, people by men of evil repute. They were born there, it matters little where or how. It is a world without spaciousness; men live there on top of each other, and their huts are built on top of the other. The native town is a hungry town, starved of bread, of meat, of shoes of coal, of light [ . . . ]

The originality of the colonial context is that economic reality, inequality, and the immense difference of ways of life never come to mask the human realities. When you examine at close quarters the colonial context, it is evident

that what parcels out the world is to begin with the fact of belonging to or not belonging to a given race, a given species. In the colonies the economic substructure is also a superstructure. *The cause is the consequence; you are rich because you are white, you are white because you are rich.* This is why Marxist analysis should always be slightly stretched every time we have to deal with the *colonial problem.*[73]

And, that colonial problem is *not a minor one*. Quantitatively, there are far more people affected by *colonial* than by the *modern* problems. That is, the industrial revolution is caught and subsumed in the colonial problem and, thereby, moves to the periphery. Without questioning the relevance of Marx and Horkheimer contribution to emancipation, their insights do not cover the full story, in the same way that the Bible and the Q'uran are relevant for the believers but not necessarily for none believers. To replace sacred texts by secular texts does take us to de-coloniality, but to new forms of abstract and imperially geared universals. One of the benefits of secularization was, precisely, the 'emancipation' from the sacred insofar as the sacred became an obstacle for the emancipation of certain social groups. To turn into sacred figures the authors and texts that so brilliantly fought for the secularization of the sacred and for the emancipation of people held hostage to sacred truths, would be contradictory. Secularization is not by itself a safe place. Uncoupling the State from the Church is not a global way to go, necessarily in the sense that such uncoupling, as we have been witnessing since 9/11 doesn't promise or warranty justice, democracy and equality. At the same time, it would also be incongruous with the emancipating principles of 'modernity' to take secularization as *the* sacred truth and impose, by military force if necessary, the secular on societies who do *not necessarily have a problem* with giving priority to the sacred or with weaving together the sacred and the secular, the Mesquite and the State. Once we bring geo- and body politics into the realm of knowledge and understanding, we realize that secular modernity has its own politics, which do not necessarily coincide with the needs, visions and desires of everyone on the planet, and that new projects (ethical, political, epistemic) are emerging in which secular modernity is being transcended by multiple projects of epistemic decolonization grounded in the geo-and body politics of knowledge.

## *IV.2*

It is precisely at this point that Gloria Anzaldúa's conceptualization of 'the conciencia mestiza' (in terms of gender and race), becomes the platform of another de-colonial project emanating from the local histories of Chicano/as in the US; a project that continues and complements previous ones (e.g., Waman Puma, Mahatma Gandhi, Frantz Fanon, Rigoberta Menchú). Both the body-(Chicana, lesbiana) and the geo-politics (la frontera as subaltern epistemic

perspective) of knowledge are at work here deepening and enlarging the decolonial shift.

It is often mentioned that one of the many problems in Anzaldua's position, is that she quotes or, others will say, 'follows', Mexican's pro-Nazi philosopher Jose Vasconcelos. And of course, critics pointed out, it is a wrong path to follow, to go Vasconcelos' way. Indeed, Anzaldúa opens her crucial chapter on 'La Conciencia *de la* Mestiza. Towards a New Consciousness' quoting Vasconcelos. The chapter begins with an epigraph: 'Por la mujer de mi raza / hablará el espiritu', which is a twist on Vasconcelos famous dictum, a national dictum in Mexico, 'Por mi raza hablara el espíritu'. She quotes Vasconcelos after this epigraph by mentioning that he 'envisaged a *raza mestiza, una mezcla de razas afines, una raza de color – la primera raza sintesis del globo.* He called it a cosmic race, la raza cósmica, a fifth race embracing the four major races of the world. Curiously enough, Vasconcelos was proposing the formation of the fifth leg of the ethno-racial pentagon as an amalgamation and transcending of the previous four (White, African-Black, Asian-Yellow, Indian-Red). For Vasconcelos, this was a cosmic race, a super-human race that reminds Zaratustra. However, Vasconcelos's idea suffered two drawbacks. About forty years after his proposed ideal, in Mexico, the US government under Nixon's presidency proposed another version of the fifth leg of the ethno-racial pentagon: Hispanics. And Hispanics, far from being (or part of) the cosmic-race, fell at the bottom of the scale. Samuel Huntington has recently contributed to underscore the ranking of Hispanics that appeared under Richard Nixon.[74] The second mortal coup to the cosmic race was, from inside Latin/a/o history, came from Anzaldúa. After quoting Vasconcelos, preceded by the epigraph just mentioned, Anzaldúa goes on to specify that: 'From this racial (referring to Vasconcelos), ideological, cultural and biological cross-pollinization, an 'alien' consciousness is presently in the making: a new *mestiza* consciousness, *una conciencia de mujer*. It is a consciousness of the Borderlands'.[75] The title of the chapter, let's remember, is 'La conciencia *de la* Mestiza' and not for instance 'la conciencia mestiza'.

This second expression responds to the same logic that, for instance, the study of French anthropologist Jean-Loup Amselle on 'mestizo logics', which is a 'study' of identity in Africa and elsewhere. The same could be said of French ethno-historian, Serge Gruzinski, in his study of 'la pensée metisse' (mestizo thoughts), based on sixteenth century Mexico, but moving beyond to find other expression of such hybrid manifestations.[76] Both Amselle's and Gruzinski's are important disciplinary studies that remain within the ego-politics of knowledge that grounds the foundation of the social sciences in nineteenth century Europe. Like in Vasconcelos, mestizaje and hibridity are celebrated, 'out there', but neither of them let their epistemic frame get infected and mixed, like the blood and the mind of the bodies they are analyzing. The differences between Vasconcelos on the one hand and Amselle

and Gruzinski on the other is that the former celebrates 'mestizaje' to maintain the purity of the Creole national discourse; while the latter makes mestizaje an object of study maintaining intact the disciplinary purity of anthropological discourse. Anzaldúa, instead, proposes some thing else. Amselle and Gruzinski observe and describe a social phenomenon, but their 'consciousness' remains within the homogeneity of the disciplines. They do not question the disciplines but describe a phenomenon outside, so to speak. Anzaldúa turns the plate around and by underlining 'La conciencia *de la* mestiza', she radically shifts gears and introduces a fracture in the *ego-politics of knowledge*. As a matter of fact, hers is a radical contribution to the *Body politics of knowledge* that, like the geo-politics of knowledge we saw in Dussel, is shifting the attention from the enunciated to the very act of enunciation.

How does the *body-politics of knowledge* succeed in transforming the locus of enunciation and in changing the terms of the conversation? And how does it complement the *geo-politics of knowledge* in fracturing the epistemic hegemony of Western *theo and ego-politics of knowledge*? Let's me elaborate on some of the 'problematic' statements made by Anzaldúa:

> I think we need to allow whites to be our allies. Through our literature, arte, *corridos*, and folktales we must share our history with them so when they set up committees to help Big Mountain, Navajos or the Chicano farm-workers or *los Nicaraguenses* they won't turn people away because of their racial fears and ignorance. *They will come to see that they are not helping us but following our lead.*
>
> Individually, but also as a racial entity, we need to voice our needs. We need to say to white society: We need you to accept the fact that Chicanos are different, to acknowledge your rejection and negation of us. *We need you to own the fact that you looked upon us as less than human, that you stole our lands, our personhood, our self-respect*. We need you to make public restitution: to say that, to compensate for your own sense of defectiveness, you strive for power over us, *you erase our history and our experience because it makes you feel guilty – you rather forget your brutish acts.*[77]

First of all, there is an insisting 'us' vs. 'you' and 'them' that may bother those who see in it a manifestation of identity politics. One, in this case, would prefer a more subtle appeal to ideas and passing over who is white, or brown, or heterosexual or homosexual. Just to take an example of this more encompassing position, let's take Alain Baidiou *Manifesto for Philosophy* ([1989], 1992), and contrast with Anzaldúa's statement and with Dussel's 'geopolitics and philosophy'. The contrast or comparison is justified here on the fact that the three of them address the very principles of knowledge as philosophy (Dussel and Baidiou) as 'conciencia de la mestiza' (Anzaldua), and we all know that 'consciousness' has been a hot philosophical topic from Decartes to

Husserl; from Freud to Merleau-Ponty. Thus, disheartened because of the crisis of philosophy, Badiou wrote a 'manifesto' in defense of it. Let's look at the first paragraph:

> The dominant philosophical traditions of the century agree that philosophy, as a discipline, is no longer really what it used to be. It must be said that Carnap's critique of metaphysics as nonsense is very different from Heidegger's announcement of the supersession of metaphysics. It is also very different from the Marxist dream of a concrete realization of philosophy. Very different as well from what Freud ferrets out as illusion, indeed paranoia, from speculative systematicity. But the fact remains that German hermeneutics like Anglo-Saxon analytical philosophy, revolutionary Marxism and psycho-analytical interpretation concur to declare the 'end' of a millennial regime of thought. No further question of imagining a *philosophia perennis* perpetuating itself.[78]

In the following paragraph Badiou goes on to comment on Philippe Lacou-Labarthe, Jean-Francois Lyotard, Jacques Lacan, Jacques Derrida, etc. and to bring the 'Jews question' into consideration to conclude that if philosophy 'is incapable of conceptualizing the extermination of European Jews, it is the fact that it is neither its duty nor within its power to conceptualize it. It is up to an *other order of thought* to render *this* thinking actual' (1992, p. 30). Fair enough: we shouldn't ask of philosophy what philosophy can't deliver. Badiou mentions Emmanuel Levinas once, in passing, on page 67. But in comparison to Anzaldua, Badiou's is a restful paragraph. There is no division between 'us' and 'them'; the list of philosophers Badiou mentions are all European men, some are Jews, some are not. He is not making distinctions between Freud and Marx, on the one hand, and Heidegger and Carnap, on the other, beyond their different philosophical projects. And he takes as a natural given the fact that analytical philosophy is 'identified' with Anglo-Saxon tradition and herme-neutics with German tradition. There is no 'us' vs 'them', apparently, because there is no 'them' – only 'us'. Dussel, for example, cannot avoid situating his own philosophical project in relation to 'them' (the European philosophers) and Anzaldúa in relation to 'them' the white Anglo-Saxon. But for Badiou, this is not a problem.

This scenario should help in understanding Anzaldúa's claim, in the first paragraph quoted above: '*They will come to see that they are not helping us but following our lead*'. And she adds in the following paragraph '*We need you to accept the fact that Chicanos are different*'. There is no need for 'white Anglo-Saxon', in Anzaldua's conceptualization, or European men philosophers (with the exception of Levinas) to state that 'you, people of color and of the Third world, we (the European male philosophers) need you to accept the fact that

European male philosophers are different'. And if there is no need to make that assertion it is because an illegitimate universality of thought is assumed by male European philosophers, with the exception of Levinas. Thus, Anzaldúa's clear-cut, 'they are not helping us but following our lead', is the basic claim that established the foundation of the geo-politics (e.g., Third World perspective) and the body-politics (e.g., post-civil rights consciousness in USA: women and men of color, gay and lesbians) from where an *identity based on politics* (and not a *politics based on identity*) emerged.[79]

*IV.3*

The grammar of de-coloniality (e.g., de-colonization of knowledge and of being – and consequently of political theory and political economy) begins at the moment that languages and subjectivities that have denied the possibility of participating in the production, distribution, and organization of knowledge. The colonization of knowledge and of being worked from top down and that is the way it is still working today: looking from economy and politics, corporations and the state down. That is the way social sciences and financial and political think tanks work. On the other hand, the creative work on knowledge and subjectivity comes from the political society, from the institutionally and economically des-enfranchised (that is to say, intellectual work not at the service of the corporation or the state but geared toward the empowerment of the des-enfranchised, the des-inherited). In that sense, the grammar of de-coloniality is working, has to work, from bottom up.

That is, the practice of liberation and de-colonization is initiated with the recognition, in the first place, that the colonialization of knowledge and being consisted of using imperial knowledge to repress colonized subjectivities and the process moves from there to build structures of knowledge that emerge from the experience of humiliation and marginalization that have been and continue to be enacted by the implementation of the colonial matrix of power. Theo- and ego-politics of knowledge are exhausted and cannot generate an alternative to modernity because they rely on imposition of one perspective and one type of consciousness over others. To contribute to a world in which many worlds can co-exist, they must be decolonized and refashioned through the geo- and body politics of knowledge. For decolonization to be fully operative, we must create *alternatives to modernity and neo-liberal civilization*. We must begin to imagine such alternatives from the perspectives and consciousnesses unlocked in the epistemic, ethical and political domain of the geo- and the bio-political loci of enunciation and of action.

Such alternatives are not mere fantasies or the imagining of another utopia. Liberation and decolonization are currently being enunciated (in writing, orally, by social movements and intellectuals, by artists and activists) from nodes in space-time (local histories) that have been marginalized by the

temporal and spatial colonial differences. Although silenced in mainstream media, multiple fractures are creating a larger spatial epistemic breaks (e.g. geopolitics of knowledge) in the overarching totality of Western global and universal history that from Hegel to Huntington was successful in negating subjectivities from non-Western, non-capitalist, non-Christian nations. Indeed, it is comfortable for those who dwell in the dominant subjectivity to expect that the rest of the world be like 'us'. Thus, liberation and decolonization are shall be thought out in the same process and movement of delinking. De-linking from what? From the Totality of Western epistemology, grounded in Latin and Greek and expanded around the globe by means of the six imperial and vernacular European languages of modernity. The geo- and bio-political shift in epistemology presupposes 'border thinking' (which as a de-colonial project is always already 'critical' but beyond Horkhaimer's and post-modern uses of the term) and 'border thinking' is the connector between the diversity of locals that were subjected as colonies of the modern empires (Spain, England, the US) or that as empires had to respond to Western expansion (e.g., China, Russia, the Ottoman Empire until 1922). Border thinking is grounded not in Greek thinkers but in the colonial wounds and imperial subordination and, as such, it should become the connector between the diversity of subaltern histories (colonial and imperial – like Russia and the Ottoman empires) and corresponding subjectivities. That is, border thinking is one way to describe what the spatial epistemic breaks emerging all over the planet have in common and I will return to this idea later. We are not, of course, looking to retrieve an authentic knowledge from Chinese, Arabic or Aymara; but, rather, we want to include the perspective and in the foundation of knowledge subjectivities that have been subjected in and by the colonial matrix of power. The diversity of actual manifestations and practices of border thinking make up what I have described as an-other paradigm.

### *IV.4*

It is time to go back to Quijano's initial paragraph that set in motion this argument: the analysis of the continuing rhetoric of modernity and the logic of coloniality and the projects of decolonization of knowledge and of being and of de-linking. As the passage quoted above (section I) re-iterates, a specific group of individuals, the majority of whom were, as we know, white, Christian, European men, put into place the basic principles of knowledge (e.g. subject-object) which were complicit with the variegated concept of totality. There is, of course, nothing wrong in the fact that a given group of people put forward its own cosmovision. The problem arises when a limited number of people feel they are appointed by God to bring (their) good to the rest of the humanity. That is, as Quijano puts it, 'the provincial pretense to universality'. Thus, the already accepted claim that one of the directions for the decolonization of

knowledge is to provincialize Europe is clearly implied in the last sentence. The critique of the Eurocentered paradigm of knowledge, Quijano writes in the first of the three paragraphs, cannot be a total rejection of the concept of totality or of the European concept of subject. To make such move would be to use the same logic and pretend that a different universalism will be better than the one that is today hegemonic and dominant (and I mean both). Such is the problem and limitation, for example, of Islamic fundamentalism.

How can we proceed? Quijano suggests de-linking modernity/rationality from coloniality. First, as our discussion has indicated, we delink the rhetoric of modernity from the logic of coloniality. Then, the doors open to all forms and principles of knowledge that have been colonized, silenced, repressed, and denigrated by the totalitarian march of the genocidal dimension of modernity. That move takes us in the direction Dussel calls trans-modernity. An objection might be that this move by itself guarantees nothing and could be taken as a new version of the Neo-liberal project insofar as nothing escapes the market and there is no outside to the 'global neo-liberal, capitalist totality', 'no outside of capital(ism)' and so on and so forth.

We can counter this postmodern objection, which, of course, is still *within* modernity itself, by explaining that we have not been claiming an *outside* but an *exteriority* where the difference between 'the space of experience' and the 'horizon of expectations'[80] becomes apparent. The difference between the 'space of experience' and the 'horizon of expectations' is not the same for Koselleck, soaked to the skin in the memories and traces of European history, as for Lewis Gordon, flooded in the memories and traces of slavery in the Caribbean with all its past and current consequences and for Jacqueline Martinez, drenched with the memories and traces of Mexican-Americans and the meaning of homosexuality in that particular 'space of experience' and 'horizon of expectations'. Thus, that exteriority is a basic assumption in the modernity/coloniality scholarly and political project. Let me explain.

Habermas has relied on Koselleck to bring out one of the dimension of modernity, related to time. In his investigation in conceptual history, Reinhart Koselleck has identified and characterized 'modern time-consciousness' in terms of the increasing difference between the 'space of experience' and the 'horizon of expectation:'

> My thesis, said Koselleck, is that in modern times the difference between experience and expectation has increasingly expanded: more precisely, that modernity is first understood as a new age from the time that expectations have distanced themselves evermore from all previous experiences'.[81]

Commenting on this passage, Jürgen Habermas adds that:

> Modernity's specific orientation toward the future is shaped precisely to the extent that societal modernization tears apart the old European experiential space of the peasant's and craftsman's life-worlds, mobilizes it, and devalues it into directives guiding expectations. *These traditional experiences of previous generations are then replaced by the kind of experience of progress that lends to our horizon of expectation (till then anchored fixedly in the past) a "historically new quality, constantly subject to being overlaid with utopian conceptions"'.*[82]

If you read and think about both statements from the feeling, experiences, existence, history of Bolivia for example, and Latin America, instead of from Germany and Europe, I suspect that first you may not come up with these issues and problems as central and, secondly, if you pay attention to the fact that these issues have been put on the table by prominent German thinkers, then you have to accept that modernity goes together with the coloniality of knowledge: people in Bolivia, Nigeria, Argentina or India *have to think from the German experience from where Koselleck and Habermas are thinking*.

We have to recognize, however, that 'time has accelerated': cars are speedier, aircraft fly at an incredible amount of miles per hour, the internet has made the world shrink and post-modernity has been characterized by that time-space contraction of the life-world. However, one should ask whether people in La Paz, Bolivia are living the life world in an experiential space that gets further away from the 'horizon of expectations' of people in Munich, Germany. 'Further away' is indeed the conceptual trap in the sense that 'modernity' has been conceived as such precisely to produce the illusion that people living in the contemporary world are 'further away in time' and not 'living in a different socio-historical dimension'.

In Munich, you do not see or feel coloniality. In La Paz, Bolivia, you feel it all the way, all the time, in your bones: modernity is constantly reproducing coloniality. Which means that the rhetoric of progress, of salvation, of technology, of democracy goes hand in hand with the logic and practice of oppression, racial discrimination, political concentration of power in the hand of a Creole/Mestizo/an elite. As a consequence, the growing social movements led by leaders like Evo Morales (the cocaleros) and Felipe Quispe (the Aymara communities), have been giving the 'space of experience' and the 'horizon of expectations' a radical new twist, and the 'life world' of Bolivia has been transformed from the social roots, with the events of October 2003. Take another example. Pope John Paul II grew up in communist Poland. When he became a Pope, in 1980, he worked hard to dethrone communism. The explicit reason was the totalitarian bent of Soviet communism. The less explicit reason was that communism was an enemy of the Church and, in consequence, the manifestation of Evil. However, the interesting twist is that Pope John Paul II was short sighted and couldn't understand why Liberation

Theology in Brazil was fighting against totalitarian regimes that were not communist. As a matter of fact, Pope John Paul II was against Theology of Liberation for being to close to Marxism! The space of experience and the horizon of expectations had to be reframed within the geo- and body politics of knowledge and understanding; through the imperial and colonial differences and, above all, at the junction of the visible rhetoric of modernity and the invisible logic of coloniality.

These examples confront us with a few decisions regarding the creation, transformation and use of concepts. That is, confront us with the very issue of de-coloniality of knowledge and of being and in the ways in which the spaces of experience and the horizon of expectations of the modern world was confused with the march of history and civilization itself. One would say that indeed Koselleck's and Habermas's concepts and conceptualization of the life world of modernity is not really German or European but global as fast as the entire population of the globe, today, has been touched by modernity by 'societal, and I would add global, modernization that tears apart the old European experiential space of the peasant's life-world'. If we follow that route, we will have to use the experience of European peasants and from there we will *conceptualize and understand* the experience and life world of a peasant in China 2000 miles West of Beijing or of Aymara Indians (they are not peasants, they are Indians. Aymara intellectual and activist repeated in the sixties and seventies: I am not a peasant, damn it, I am an Indian!!). And at this point it may be a little bit difficult to make a Bolivian Indian, whose 'space of experience' is filled with 500 years of oppression, racialization, de-humanization with the experience of a peasant in the Black Forest or in the wonderland of Norway. I am not saying that it is not important to think of the peasant of southern Germany or central Norway; or even on the life-world of the modernized elite in Munich that is replacing the imperial memories and life style for a fast speed and technological way of making money. I am just saying that we cannot take for granted that what happens in Munich, and it is felt and thought by Germany, happens more or less similarly in other places and people will think more or less similarly. There are however reasons to think that, and one is the uses, for example, of Koselleck and Habermas, in Latin America or in China, which is, however, nothing else than the consequence of Western expansion since the sixteenth century. Western expansion includes the good, the bad and the ugly, although the 'good' in its various forms, it is a consequence of the bad and the ugly, as we are witnessing today in Iraq: first you destroy a country, then you provide help and promote reconstruction, third you promote freedom and democracy, and four you crash Islamic thinkers who would like to reconstruct Iraq and write the constitution on the basis of *sharia* and the Q'uran and not on the bases of the *democracy* and the Bible.

Two important observations are here necessary. I am not making deterministic assumptions here but thinking in terms of choices, options and responsibilities; that is, of the ethics of any project, political and/or scholarly and intellectual. Not every German, Black Jamaican or lesbian Chicana will follow the paths outlined by Marx, Fanon or Anzaldúa. Still, their choices and directions could not but be shaped by the cosmovision and the experiences that formed their intellectual and political projects. The second clarification is that I am not suggesting that Gordon and Martinez are preferable to Koselleck. I am simply saying that Koselleck's experience and formulation of the space of experience cannot be taken as the 'universal' frame to interpret and conceptualize all other spaces of experiences. By the same token, the same criteria apply to Gordon and Martinez. To universalize the Black or the Lesbian/Chicana experience would be to fall back into the same logic that caught Islamic fundamentalism and believe that 'my' space of experience and 'horizon of expectations' are beneficial for all.

Then, am I proposing a sort of 'cultural relativism' with its rhetoric of 'let me alone in my place'? Well, not exactly. To understand what I am suggesting it is necessary to take another step in the grammar of decolonization and enter into the *border space*, which is the *exteriority* of the modern and the postmodern. That border lies where, as Dussel has underlined, Western knowledge and subjectivity, control of land and labor, of authority, and ways of living gender and sexuality have been 'contacting' other languages, memories, principles of knowledge and belief, forms of government and economic organization since 1500 (often in relations to domination, exploitation and conflict). That 'contact' did not occur all at once with only one Western leading imperial power bringing every body under its telematic embrace. Still, the universalization of the regional is one consequence of Western imperial/colonial expansion. As a result, each local history of the planet, today, has to deal with the modern/colonial world, the rhetoric of modernity and the logic of coloniality. Each local history has its own language, memory, ethics, political theory, and political economy (as we have been witnessing daily in Iraq since March 2003 when the 'mission accomplished' statement was proffered in Washington), all of which are also marked by traces of the local in the relations of domination and exploitation within Western knowledge. The 'space of experience' and the 'horizon of expectations' are di-verse, or rather, pluri-verse – what each diverse local history has in common with others is the fact that they all have to deal with the unavoidable presence of the modern/colonial world and its power differentials, which start with racial classification and end up ranking the planet (e.g., First, Second and Third World was a racialization of politics, economy, cultures and knowledge). Thus, the pluri-versality of each local history and its narrative of decolonization can *connect* through that common experience and use it as the basis for a new common logic of knowing: border thinking. That is, the fact of having to imagine a

future that is not the future that those in Washington, or London, or Paris, or Berlin would like the people of the world to have can bring together all those who have been contacted in various ways by them.

Critical border thinking provides one method to enact the de-colonial shift and it operates as a connector between different experiences of exploitation can now be thought out and explored in the sphere of the colonial and imperial differences. Thus, critical border thinking is the method that connects pluri-versality (different colonial histories entangled with imperial modernity) into a uni-versal project of delinking from modern rationality and building other possible worlds. Critical border thinking involves and implies both the imperial and colonial differences.

Let's quickly look at some examples. Decolonizing knowledge and being from the perspective of Japan's or Russian's colonies will be quite different from the perspective of England's colonies. In the first two cases, de-colonization from the epistemic and existential conditions imposed by Japanese and Russian languages leaves still another layer to deal with, which is the epistemic and epistemic conditions growingly imposed world wide by Greco-Latin and the six vernacular imperial languages of Western empires. That is, Japanese and Russian languages and categories of thought became subordinated to the hegemony of Western epistemology and its imperial and global reach. Any project of decolonization must operate in full awareness of its location within the complex relations structured by imperial and colonial differences. At the same time, because the 'West is all over the rest' in a outwar expansion and the 'rest is all over the west' in an in-war mobilization lead by migrations, border thinking becomes crucial in any de-colonial project that will start from the weaker end of the imperial and colonial differences. When the languages and categories began to be activated in order to build a world in which many world will co-exist, by social actors aiming at de-colonization of knowledge and being and of de-linking from the imperial modernity, the splendors of human imagination and creativity will open up. Certainly, there is no safe place an any language that can be used, by social actors, to surrender to the languages and categories of thought of Western capitalism as it is the case also with the 'adaptation' of corporate values in the power sector of China, Japan, the Arabic world and Russia. De-linking requires analysis of the making and re-making of the imperial and colonial differences and it requires visions and strategies for the implementation of border thinking leading to de-colonization of knowledge and of being; from here, new concepts of economy and social organization (politics) will be derived. Solutions from the political theories of the West, from Aristotle and Plato to Machiavelli, Hobbes and Locke; to Marx and Gramsci and to Carl Schmitt and Leo Strauss have been exhausted and without border thinking any exercise in this arena could only lead to spinning the spin within the bubble of imperial modernity. De-linking means to remove the anchor in which the 'normalcy effect' has been produced as to hide the fact

that the anchor can be removed and the edifice crumbled. Trans-modernity would be the overall orientation of de-colonizing and of delinking projects; an orientation toward pluri-versality as universal project leading toward a world in which many worlds will co-exist. Border thinking, once again, is one of the methods that can help us moving to sustain a vision – a pluri-versal and not a uni-versal vision – and to implement a set of strategies to accomplish it. The future could no longer be owned by one way of life (la pensée unique of Ramonet), cannot be dictated by one project of liberation and de-colonization, and cannot be a polycentric world within Western categories of thoughts. A world in which many worlds could co-exist can only be made by the shared work and common goals of those who inhabit, dwell in one of the many worlds co-existing in one world and where differences are not cast in terms of values of plus and minus degree of humanity.

And that is how I understand Quijano's assertion, quoted above, that 'epistemic decolonization is necessary to make possible and move toward a truly intercultural communication; to an exchange of experiences and significations as the foundation of an-other rationality'. The exchange works as an alternative to Koselleck's 'space of experience', and an-other rationality replaces the 'horizon of expectations'. In fact, I submit that the horizon of expectations here will be precisely 'pluri-versality as a uni-versal project'. That is, the uni-versality of the project has to be based on the assumption that the project cannot be designed and implemented 'by one ethnic group', but has to be inter-epistemic and dialogical, pluri-versal. Thus, border thinking becomes the necessary critical *method* for the political and ethical project of filling in the gaps and revealing the imperial complicity between the rhetoric of modernity and the logic of coloniality.

Emancipating projects, as devised in Europe in the eighteenth century (Dussel's rational concept of emancipation), can be kept alive, but they must be 'extracted' from their appropriation by the rhetoric of modernity to justify the logic of coloniality (their use as irrational justification of ethnocidal violence). And, as I have tried to show here, they are far from being meaningful for every one on earth and should never again become 'an abstract universal of human emancipation'. We have come full circle back to the geo- and body politics of knowledge as alternatives to the hegemony and dominance of the theo- and ego-politics organizing the modern/colonial world (that is, as we have discussed, Europe and the US in their relations of conflict and domination framed by colonial and imperial differences). Liberation projects that have emerged and are emerging in the Third World and decolonizing projects arising from the critical consciousness of the damnés of their racialization and the ways they have been dispossessed of their humanity (mind and soul) (Fanon, C.R.L. James, Winter, Gordon, Maldonado Torres) will naturally subsume European projects of emancipation and open the possibility

of entering into a pluri-versal dialogue of equals in a common march toward a world in which 'Free Life' will be the horizon instead of 'Free Trade'.

## Coda

The struggle for epistemic de-colonization lies, precisely, here. The next step, the work we have to do next, is to link analysis from the perspective of coloniality and the grammar of de-coloniality (its ethical, political and theoretical consequences), with strategies, strategic plans toward the future. Such strategies will and are already taking place in different locals and histories (from the Zapatistas to the World Social Forum to progressive Muslims intellectuals and Southern European critical voices) and in diverse geo- and bio political genealogies of thought and action. Crucial to the strategies toward the future, toward a pluri-versal world linked to the assumption of the universality of the pluri-versal, is to avoid the modern and *imperial* temptation of the good and best uni-versal. Christianity, (neo) Liberalism, Marxism, Islamic fundamentalism, have given enough proof that not every body in the planet would submit to any one of the abstract universal at hand. De-coloniality is a planetary critical consciousness that emerged and unfolded, precisely out of the limits of abstract universal of its current manifestations and out of the dangers that, in the future, a 'new' abstract universal will attempt to replace the existing ones; or that the existing ones will renew themselves as 'new' (neo-liberalism, neo-Marxism, neo-Christianism, neo-Islamism, neo-Slavism, neo-Africanism, neo-Judaism, neo-Eurocentrism, neo-Confucianism, neo-Hinduism, etc.). Pluri-versality as a universal project is quite demanding. It demands, basically, that we cannot have it all our own way. The struggle for epistemic de-coloniality lies, precisely, here: de-linking from the most fundamental belief of modernity: the belief in abstract universals through the entire spectrum from the extreme right to the extreme left. For this reason, to imagine a new global left means falling back into the old house while just changing the carpet.

## Notes

1 Although this essay owes to all the participants in the modernity/coloniality project, its last stretch owes much to many conversations and exchanges of material with Anibal Quijano and Enrique Dussel as the leading figures of the project; with Ramón Grosfóguel and his contribution to shift the perspective of world-system analysis from its original disciplinary top-down orientation to the perspective of Puerto Rico and the Latino/as in the US in the modern/colonial world system; with José Saldívar, and his continuing contribution to walk in the border, to extend his original vision of the

'dialectics of our America' in the late eighties to the changing landscape of the beginning of the twenty first century; With Javier Sanjinés, Catherine Walsh, Freya Schiwy and Nelson Maldonado-Torres who are driving the project to new dimensions with unforeseen consequences. Javier Sanjinés opened up a door to the complex history and current situation in Bolivia. His work on 'mestizaje up-side down' has been instrumental to rethink a long legacy of 'mestizaje' as the oxymoronic figure to imagine the nation-state across the colonial difference. Catherine Walsh with her work with Indigenous and Afro communities in the Andes, and her reflection around the concept of 'ïnter-culturalidad' (introduced by Indigenous intellectuals), 'ancestralidad' (introduced by Afro-Andean intellectuals) and 'an-other thinking' that she takes from Abdelkhebir Khatibi in order to underline the de-colonial dimension of inter-culturalidad and ancestralidad. Freya Schiwy has brought to the project the problematic of gender and patriarchy and has theorized the role of 'indigenous subaltern intellectuals' using video instead of alphabetic writing to overcome the forces of coloniality that cast them as barbarian for their lack of writing. And to Nelson Maldonado-Torres for his ground-breaking reflections on the philosophical and political dimension of the category of *damnés*. The *damnés* confront us, on the one hand, with the coloniality of being (the damnés IS a product and a consequence of coloniality) and at the same time has an enormous de-colonizing potential. In this regard, the damnés opens up a new space and a new social actor, next to the subaltern and the multitude. Last but not least, three consecutive visits to Minsk (Belarus) and Moscow, between 2001 and 2004 opened up my vistas and prompted questions about the place of Rusia/Soviet empire in relation to Western Christian, liberal and capitalist empires. I owe much in this arena to Madina Tlostanova for her work on trans-cultural aesthetics from the perspective of Rusian/Soviet ex-colonies and for her analysis of Russia/Soviet Union as a 'Janus Faced Empire' (with one eye toward its inferior colonies and the other to its superior West). And during the past three years, I have been working and in close conversations with Arturo Escobar and graduate students, at Duke and UNC, gathered around a working group under the label of 'Globalization, Modernity/Coloniality and the Geopolitics of Knowledge. Last but not least, several conversations and collaborations with Boaventura de Sousa Santos – in the past four/five years – brought to the foreground his notion of 'an epistemology of the South' that he advanced in the mid-nineties and that materialized recently in his prominent work in and for the World Social Forum.

2 The participant-members of the research project were Anibal Quijano, Enrique Dussel, Catherine Walsh, Boaventura de Sousa Santos, Freya Schiwy, José Saldívar, Nelson Maldonado-Torres, Fernando Coronil, Javier Sanjinés, Margarita Cervantes-Salazar, Libia Grueso, Marcelo Fernández Osco, Edgardo Lander, Arturo Escobar and myself. The participant-invited guests from the Duke faculty whose works and interests are related, were

Miriam Cooke, Ebrahim Moosa, Roberto Dainotto, Ralph Litzinger and Leo Ching.

3 http://www.usatoday.com/tech/webguide/internetlife/2004-06-03-virtual-realty_x.htm

4 The idea of that knowledge is part of the colonizing processes, has already a history in Latin American scholarship and intellectual debates. Brazilian 'anthropologian' Darcy Ribeiro in the early seventies clearly stated that the imperial march toward the colonies goes with arms, books, concepts and pre-concepts. In philosophy and sociology, Enrique Dussel and Orlando Fals Borda claim the de-colonization of the social sciencies and of philosophy (which of course presupposed that social sciences and philosophy, that is knowledge, has been colonized. In colonial studies, French scholar Robert Ricard spoke of the 'spiritual conquest of Mexico' and a few years later, French scholar Serge Gruzinski followed suit with a book on 'la colonizatioin de l'imaginaire'. In her classic book on Waman Puma de Ayala, published in 1986, Rolena Adorno opened her argument by stating that her book was an act of decolonization of scholarship. I myself followed the path of my predecessor and in my book on the darker side of the renaissance cast colonization of knowledge in the domains of language, memory and space. It was clear by then that in the politics of scholarship we were not trying to take assault the state and to take power when thinking de-colonization but to assault knowledge and to take over epistemic power.

5 For an update on the pros and cons of dependency theory see Grosfugel (2000).

6 Quijano (1989); for a more extended version of the ideas explored in the nineties, see Quijano (2000) see also, in the same issue the article by Lander.

7 For a summary and contextualization, see Escobar (2004).

8 The bibliography generated by different members of the project around the question of knowledge (coloniality and de-coloniality of) is quite significant. And the elaboration of coloniality of and de-coloniality of being is already being debated. Among the many publications of coloniality and de-coloniality of knowledge, see Lander (2000), Walsh *et al.* (2002), Grosfoguel (2002) and Schiwy & Ennis (2002).

9 Quijano (1992).

10 The concept of 'delinking' (in French, 'la desconnection') was introduced by Egyptian sociologist Amin (1985), especially, 'The problematic of delinking', pp 44–84). The concept is a crucial one, although in Samir Amin's version its formulated at the level of economic and political (state) delinking. Without an epistemic delinking it is difficult to really delink from the modern notion of Totality. In the case of Amin, he was still caught in the mirage of Marxism and, therefore, of modernity. Thus, his delinking was proposed at the level of the *content* rather than *at the epistemic level that sustain the logic of coloniality*. I will bring together, in complementary fashion, Amin's 'delinking' with Quijano's 'desprendimiento'.

11 Quijano (2000, p. 447).

12 From his initial formulation Dussel (1995) has been revising the central idea. In this respect see also Dussel (2000). These two previous articles are the background for the introduction of the concept of 'Trans' modernity. See Dussel (2002).

13 I am using here 'de-colonization' and 'de-coloniality' as exchangeable in certain context, but always keeping in mind the historical distinction between (a) political de-colonization and liberation between 1947 and 1970, approximately, in Africa and Asia and (b) epistemic de-colonization. Ramon Grosfóguel described as 'second decolonization' and Catherine Walsh and Nelson Maldonado-Torres refers to as 'de-coloniality'. The pedagogical advantage of de-coloniality over de-colonization is twofold. On the one hand, it names the task of unveiling and undoing 'the logic of coloniality' and, on the other, it names a project and a process that should be distinguished from the diverse meanings attributed to 'post-coloniality'.

14 In Argentina, for example, the influential work of critical intellectual Arregui (1969). Hernández Arregui clearly and forcefully argue for the distinction between 'nationalism' in Europe and 'nationalism' in the Third World, and in the colonial history of Latin America and Argentina. He is one of the few critical intellectual to take colonization in Argentina seriously, and to avoid the trap of starting with the French Revolution and Argentinian independence from Spain in 1810. Hernandez Arregui shows clearly how the political independence from Spain meant the economic dependence from England and the British Empire, even if Argentina – and Latin America – were not 'colonized' as India. This is, on the other hand, a good example to avoid confusion between 'colonialism' and 'coloniality'.

15 See one of his initial statements, 'Ciencia propia y colonialismo intellectual: los nuevos rumbos' Bogotá: C Valencia Editors, 1971; and more recently, 'Research for Social Justice: Some South-North Convergences', 1995, http://comm-org.utoledo.edu/si/falsborda.htm#plenary;

16 See Ernesto Laclau 1996.

17 A new working class under neo-liberal economic re-structuration as Hardt and Negri argued (2000). However, the 'crowd' and the 'multitude' at least two stories and two genealogy of thoughts. In the 1960's and early 1970's Zavaleta Mercado, in Bolivia, was trying to make sense of a society in which 'Indians' and 'paisants'; 'Indians' and 'mine workers', mestizos, cholos formed a crowd difficult to distinguish clear in class formation. Zavaleta Mercado was admirer of Gramsci, but clever enough to understand that Bolivian society was quite different from Italian society, even from the South of Italy!! He then introduced the crucial concept, of difficult translation, 'sociedad abigarrada'. The 'crowd' and the 'multitude' were different also from the clear-cut notion of 'people' in European nation-State, where people were also identified by their citizenship. For both, Hernandez Arregui in Argentina and Zavaleta Mercado in Bolivia, the fact that the same terms (nationalism, people, multitude) meant quite different things in Europe and in their ex-direct colonies and current dependent nation-states,

was simply explainable because European nation-states were imperial while South American nation-states were colonial. How can abstract universals such as nationalism or multitude, could be the same when you look at the world from Argentina, Bolivia, from Italy or from the US? When you look at them from the perspective and the subjectivity of imperial or of colonial local histories?

18 See Laclau (2000).

19 The splendors and miseries of Hardt and Negri's *Empires* lies precisely in being caught within the limits of Western history and categories of thoughts.

20 See Maldonado Torres (2004) for the philosophical notion of damnés and its political implications and for a follow up on Maldonado-Torres ground breaking thesis, see my 'A topology of political agencies: the people, the subaltern, the damnés and the multitude' at the workshop on 'The Popular and the Subaltern' (University of Santa Barbara, March of 2004, forthcoming in the workshop proceedings). I have also brought into the discussion, in my argument, the ground-breaking the categories of 'form mass' , 'form class' 'multitude' and 'sociedad abigarrada' introduced by Bolivian sociologist and radical intellectual René Zavaleta-Mercado, in the seventies (see, among other works, 1988).

21 The World Social Forum, with all its limitations, offers without a doubt a new articulation of delinking projects after decolonization in Africa and Asia during the Cold War and the collapse of the Soviet Union. The First Social Forum of the Americas that took place in Quito in July of 2004 is, with all its limitatons, a point of no return and where delinking arguments and practices are already well underway. The II Cumbre de las Nacionalidades Indigenas, with all its limitations, that took place in Quito also the week before the Social Forum of the Americas, offers still another unmistakable example.

22 There is an argument that has been advanced by the European left that sees the Europe as a model for the world. The argument is an anti-US argument and it sounds like a new global design, from the left, to replace the long gone dreams of a planetary revolution of the proletarian (see George 2004).

23 Let me specify, for the critical and inquisitive reader who may be thinking 'but what is Europe, Europe is no homogeneous!!)' that when I say Europe I am referring to Hegel's conceptualization in his lesson in the philosophy of history. That is, the heart of the Greco-Roman legacy – Italy, Spain and Portugal in the South; France, England and Germany in the North; Greek and Latin language foundation; Italian, Spanish and Portuguese as the languages of the Renaissance; French, English and German, as the languages of the Enlightenment.

24 I am aware that colonized/colonizer composite has fallen into desuetude. I am just using it as a short cut for the continuous re-production of the rhetoric of modernity and the logic of coloniality. Certainly, Europeans are not one homogeneous group (neither Christians, nor Marxists). In the same vein, Indians or Afro in the Americas are not an homogeneous group either.

However, European diversity is grounded in Greek and Latin languages and Christianity. Indians and Afro are not. Aymara and Quechua on the one hand or Bantu and Wolof on the other, provide an epistemology (or if you wish a cosmology) that is very different to the cosmology (or epistemology if you wish) provided by Greek and Latin as has been framed in the dominant history of European imperial/colonial modernity.

25 On the epistemic imperial privileges see Mignolo (2002).

26 To simplify matters I will not explore the new stage, Organo-logy (e.g., the organization of knowledge and the knowledge of organization) within the chonological paradigmatic changes within Western epistemology. Organo-logy is displacing the centrality of the Ego in favor of the Organization: the individual is part of a team, of a corporation, of an organization and no longer the 'heroe' that overcomes the importance of the 'team'. The basketball final, in 2004, between Detroit Piston and Los Angeles Lakers is a good example of the displacement from ego-logy to organo-logy: there were no 'stars' in Detroit Piston's team, they won as a 'team' not as the effort of individual figures.

27 Delinking and changing the terms of the conversation means, among other things, to fracture the naturalized assumption that links words and things, as Foucault taught us. Geo-logy as sciences of the earth places the accent on the object of investigation, while geo-politics of knowledge and understanding put the enunciation at the center, an enunciation that could shape, describe and frame any possible 'object'. Thus, geo-politics of knowledge and understanding could articulate either emancipating projects (as the Creoles from Spanish and British descent did) or liberating and decolonizing projects, as we will see below in the early example of Waman Puma de Ayala, the Haitian revolution already mentioned, and more recent and consistent projects carried out by intellectuals in the academy and social movements.

28 What calls for thinking for example in Hanna Arendt, Jacques Derrida or Frantz Fanon? It is not just or only the floating spirit of abstract categories that come from heaven to the mind; they make you think, and then you realize that you exist. It is the other way round: you feel the embodiment geo-historically and biographically and it is from that embodiment that you realize that you exist, and you exist in a modern/colonial world that has distributed the population of the planet racially, sexually and by gender that you think. The geo- and ego-political revolution of our time lies precisely in (a) the affirmation of the reversal and (b) the unveiling of the geo- and bio-political embodiment that has been concealed in modern epistemology from the Renaissance, under the name of God (Theo-logy), the Reason of the emancipated individual (Ego-logy), and the supremacy of the Organization (e.g., in the sense of cybernetics, *kubernetes,* knowledge of the organization and the organization of knowledge) over the individual (Organo-logy). Cybernetic researchers quickly realized that 'the science of observed systems' cannot be divorced from 'the science of observing systems because it is we who observe. The cybernetic approach is centrally concerned with

this unavoidable limit of what we can know: our own subjectivity. In this way cybernetics is aptly called 'applied epistemology'. At minimum, its utility is the production of useful descriptions, and, specifically, descriptions that include the observer in the description. Cybernetic descriptions of psychology, language, arts, performance, or intelligence (to name a few) may be quite different from more conventional, hard 'scientific' views – although cybernetics can be rigorous too. Implemented in conjunction with imperial/global designs, the emancipating possibilities offered by *cybernetics* were used and applied 'instrumentally' in software and/or hardware, in the design of social and managerial of interpersonal systems. Last but not least, it is interesting to point out that in the mid-nineties, Sage Publications started a news journal: *Organization. The Interdisciplinary Journal of Theory and Society*. In the mid-nineties too, in Argentina, the monthly publication *Gestion* (Management) was started. Addressed to the executive world (and with an annual cost of $250), the journal was entirely devoted to the organization of corporation, business, offices, etc. in order to gain efficiency minimizing costs. If we look the administration of the universities in the US, from the late 80s on, we will see the same train. Thus, the corporate values and orientation of the university corresponds to the growing dominance of Organo-logy as overarching imperial metaphor.

29 Adorno (1986, 2000).

30 Rolena Adorno's seminal work on Waman Puma de Ayala opens with a statement that can hardly be misunderstood, although it has been conveniently forgotten by most of the critics that praised the book. It is clear and loud, though: 'In the pages that follow I have attempted to perform an act of decolonization in the forum of historical literary scholarship' (1986, p. 3). We could of course debate whether Adorno was succesful or not, but we cannot ignore what will remain as a turning point of her contribution to literary and historical scholarship. The Zapatistas have performed in a diffrerent terrain (that of the social movement) a theoretical revolution that clearly brings together decolonization with delinking (e.g., that is, decolonization without delinking it is just a different name for emancipation within the system, as the American or the French revolutions were). For the Zapatistas theoretical revolution, see Mignolo (2000) and for the history of the movement to the creation of Los Caracoles, see Munoz Ramirez (2003), Ornelas (2003), and above all the Zapatistas documents on www.ezln.org. Another radical example of epistemic and social delinking is the organization Via Campesina and above all the concept of 'soberania alimentaria' (www.ecoloxistesasturies.org/Temas/ Asturies/ Campo/ViaCampesinaSoberaniaAlimentaria.doc), Last but not least, similar processes are taking place in the World Social Forum (de Souza Santos, 2003).

31 Adorno 1986, pp. 12–35.

32 Amin 1985, pp. 41–84.

33 I developed this argument in the conclusion to *Local Histories/Global Designs* ('An other language, an other logic, an other thinking').

34 I have been using the expression body politics to describe the complementary dimension of the geo-politic of knowledge in the de-colonial shift. Ramon Grosfóguel suggested 'body-politics' instead which, on the one hand, avoid the confusion with the same expression used by Michel Foucault to mean a different social phenomena. On the other hand, it is more appropriate to make visible the color, gender and sexuality of the 'thinking body'; and making visible the white, male and heterosexual body-politics that lies, invisible, behind the hegemonic politics of knowledge of imperial European modernity.

35 I do not think that the reference to 'Juntas de Buen Gobierno' in the Zapatista's political theory and political economy are of recent invention without reference in the past.

36 Please bear in mind that epistemic theo-politics is not just a question of the past, buried in the history of the European Renaissance and the New World colonies. It remained well and alive next to the dominance of epistemic ego-politics and it is resurfacing now with vengeance in the brilliant theo-political critique of the ego-political foundation of the social sciences. See Millbank (1990). It is useful to think de-colonization of knowledge and of being as beyond Theology and Secular Reason (ego-logy and organo-logy), as far as de-coloniality comes from an spatial epistemological break, called *Pachakuti*, the turn around seen from the perspective of the inhabitants of Tawantinsuyu when the Spanish arrived with the intention of taking over gold, government and souls.

37 Trouillot (1995).

38 Amin's de-linking proposal did not contemplate the need of Soviet colonies to delink from the Soviet union, neither the situation of Japan's colonies. Delinking was thought out within the frame of liberal and capitalists empires, that is, in the history of Western expansion since 1500.

39 Gidden (1993).

40 Ferguson (2002).

41 See Martín Alcoff and Mendieta (2000).

42 Ortiz (1995). Also very revealing on the same point, looking at modernity from the perspective of coloniality (in the epistemological sense) or looking at the empires from the point of view of the colonies (in the historical sense), is Mintz (1986).

43 Williams (1994).

44 Habermas (1987).

45 Habermas 1987, p. 17.

46 Habermas, 1987, p. 17.

47 Botana (1997).

48 Why Judaism was not hegemonic instead of Christianity, is another story that shall be linked with the consolidation of a Jews state after 1948; and the

role that Jews play in complicity with existing structure of power (e.g., in Russia as well as in the US, see Chua (2003).

49 We should keep in mind that there the logic of coloniality and the rhetoric of modernity has been expanded all over the world. The question that needs attention to bring the rhetoric of modernity and the logic of coloniality at a world scale, and beyond the limited scope of the Christian and Liberal capitalist colonialism of Western Europe (Spain, Portugal, Holland, England and France), is the need to bring the Soviet revolution, the role of Japan and China in the global order, and the raise of Islamic fundamentalisms. How can we account for this complex configuration based on the principle that modernity combines the rhetoric of salvation, emancipation and progress with the logic of coloniality – of genocide, oppression, exploitation, expendability of human lives) – that it conceals? For reason of space I will leave China and Japan out of my consideration, and focus on the Soviet Union and post-Soviet Russia and on the rise of Islamic fundamentalisms. To account for the historical complexity in terms of the narratives based on the rhetoric of modernity and the logic of coloniality, we need the concepts of *colonial and imperial differences* as has been created and conceptualized by the rhetoric of modernity (Tlostanova 2003, Mignolo & Tlostanova 2006).

50 Take for example Badiou (1997) and Zizek (1998, Eurocentrism, book on god). In both cases, a critique of 'minorities identity politics' in favour of universalism, hides the fact that they are both inscribed in a 'hegemonic identity politics' that, because hegemonic, makes invisible the geo- and bio-historical inscriptions of the bodies from and with they think. It is a 'privilege position' to be able to criticize others for openly doing what they themselves are doing and hiding. For a critique of the imperial underpinnings of both Badiou's and Zizek's arguments see Mignolo (2002).

51 'Pacha' is a word of complex meaning, space/time but also life and energy that encompasses life in all its forms of living organisms of which 'humans' are only a small part. See Bouysse-Cassagne & Harris (1987).

52 Of course that 'tradition' was invented, but was invented by those who re-articulated during the Enlightenment the narratives of the Renaissance and needed 'tradition' instead of Middle Age and barbarians. But 'tradition' encompasses both space and time, and that is the power of the denial of co-evalness in eighteenth and nineteenth century narratives from European perspectives. Such perspectives, fully geo-politically grounded, hided its geo-political bases and presented themselves as universal narratives.

53 See Mignolo (2000).

54 Interestingly enough translated as '*primitive* accumulation' in English, while Spanish translations retained the biblical meaning in Marx's own language: 'original' as in the original sin.

55 Tlostanova 2003, p. 47.

56 Hegel (1822).

57 Hegel 1822, p. 102.

58 Hegel 1822, p. 350.

59 I have confronted Huntington's position in two separate essays. One, 'Huntington's Fears: 'Latinidad'in the Horizon of the Modern/Colonial world' was presented first orally in the conference 'Latino/as in the World System', Berkeley, April 2004. To appear in the conference proceedings, edited by Ramón Grosfóguel et al. The second, 'Imperial/Colonial Metamorphosis: From the Ottoman and Spanish Empires to the US and the European Union', paper read in the conference *Islam, Latinité, Transmodernité* (Istanbul, April 2005), published in the conference proceedings, edited by Candido Mendes (Rio de Janeiro: UNESCO and Universidad Candido Mendes, pp. 91–145, 2005).

60 It is curious and interesting that Zizek virulent attack of minority identity politics left the hegemonic identity politics intact. The reason may be that, as in the case of the theo- and ego-politics of knowledge their practitioners have been blind to their own geo-politics, as Bambach has shown in the case of Martin Heidegger (Bambach 2003). Nelson Maldonado-Torres in a powerful critique from the perspective of coloniality, reframes Bambach's critique an extended it to continental philosophy, including Levinas, Derrida and Zizek. See Maldonado-Torres (2004).

61 'Americanity as a concept, or the Americas in the Modern World-System', in ISSAI, 134, pp. 549–557.

62 For the commercial circuits circa the thirteenth century, from Beijing to Fez and Venice, see Abu-Lughod (1989). For the emergence of the Atlantic in its consequences in the previous commercial circuit, and the foundation of the colonial matrix of power, see Mignolo (2000).

63 de Acosta (2003).

64 Mignolo (2003a)

65 See the after-word to the second edition of *The Darker Side of Renaissance*, 2003.

66 The interesting anecdote of Bolivian candidate to Miss Universe, from Santa Cruz (El Nacional, The Economist), is revealing of the fact that the racism and the colonial matrix of power persist in Bolivia after 500 years, now integrated to new for of racial violence generated by market economy (Amy Chua 2003)

67 I develop this idea in more detail in the afterword to the second edition of *The Darker Side of the Renaissance*.

68 I introduce and develop the idea of 'an-other paradigm' in Mignolo (2003b).

69 Let me repeat so the reader cannot be confused by old habit of thinking taking for granted that the West is a geography and not a language-memory-conceptual apparatus than penetrated directly or indirectly billions of consciousness all over the world): in Greek, Latin and the six imperial modern/colonial European languages.

70 I use 'Eurocentered' as a descriptive term, very much in the sense that Carl Schmitt describes as 'Eurocentered international law' that legalized massive appropriation of land since the sixteenth century, that is, in what he calls the 'transition' from the pre-global to the global era . For example, Schmitt

(2001). Schmitt analysis clearly states that appropriation of land gave rise to a system of international law totally Euro-centered. His honesty is laudable, but his view remains limited to the perspective from modernity and German interests. The perspective from coloniality (and independently from Schmitt's concerns in the Germany after Hitler), and interests in de-coloniality, is provided by N'Zatioula Grovogui (1996). Schmitt and Grovogui would agree that massive land appropriation and the system of international law are a powerful combination of Imperial Europe, and then taken up by the US The difference is that they are both looking at the same phenomenon from different side of the fence: Schmitt from Germany and European History, Grovogui from Africa and African history. That is how de-coloniality begins to work, not through different interpretations from the same perspective of paradigm but from an-other paradigm.

71 Luis Macas and Jorge García in an oral presentation of the goal and curriculum of the Universidad Intercultural de los Pueblos y Naciones Indígenas del Ecuador, Universidad Andina Simón Bolívar, July 2002. For a general view see, http://icci.nativeweb.org/boletin/19/macas.html. The Universidad Intercultural is not an isolated phenomenon as it is already connected to the network of the Indigenous People in the Americas (http://www.aulaintercultural.org/breve.php3?id_breve = 184).

72 Enrique Dussel (2001). Dussel's point is that Marx's used the conceptual apparatus of science to unveil the logic linking plus-valued labor and capital-accumulation. In my argument, that is equivalent to saying that Marx unveiled the logic of coloniality in Europe, when capitalism was re-articulated by the emergence of the industrial revolution and of a new social class, the proletariat, that replaced massive slavery and serfdom during the sixteenth and the seventeenth centuries. Dussel's insight comes from looking at the history of Europe from the perspective of the colonies and, in that sense, supersedes Louis Althuser's 'coupure epistemologique'. For Althusser, Marx's break was to translated the ideological discourse of political economy into a scientific discourse (See Balibar (1979)). Although Althusser is not wrong in point that out, what I underlying is that Dussel's take on Marx belongs to a difference epistemic space: the space of de-coloniality rather than of post-structuralism.

73 *The Wretched of the Earth* (*Les damnés de la terre*), 1961, pp. 30, 40.

74 Huntington (2004).

75 Anzaldúa (1987).

76 Amselle (1999).

77 Anzaldúa 1987, p. 108.

78 Badiou (1992).

79 The unavoidable links between identity and epistemology (that is normally denied from the perspective of 'white epistemologies', male and female), has been clearly and forcefully argued by analytic and Latina philosopher Linda Alcoff (2005).

80 Koselleck (1985).

81 *Futures Past*, 1985.
82 Habermas 1987, p. 12.

## References


Abu-Lughod, Janet (1989) *Gefore European Hegemony: The World System, AD 1250–1350*. New York: Oxford University Press.

Adorno, Rolena (1986, 2000) *Guaman. Writing and Resistance in Colonial Perú*. Austin: The University of Texas Press.

Alcoff, Linda (2005) 'Identity Politics: North and South', paper debated at the workshop 'Shifting the Geo-graphy and the Bio-graphy of Knowledge', Center for Global Studies and the Humanities, Duke University, February.

Amin, Samir (1985) *Delinking. Towards a Polycentric World*, trans. Michael Wolfers. London: Zed Books.

Amselle, Jean-Loup (1998) *Mestizo Logics. Anthropology of Identity in Africa and Elsewhere*, trans. Claudia Royal. Palo Alto: Stanford University Press.

Anzaldúa, Gloria (1987) *Borderland/La Frontera. The New Mestiza*. Aunt – Lute: San Francisco: p. 7.

Arregui, Juan José Hernández (ed.) (1969) *Nacionalismo y liberacióon*. Buenos Aires: Peña Lillo.

Badiou, Alain (1992) *Manifesto for Philosophy*, trans and ed. Norman Madarasz. New York: State University of New York, p. 97

Badiou, Alain (1997) *Saint Paul. La fondation de l'universalisme*. Paris: College International de Philosophie/Press Universitaires de France.

Balibar, Etienne (1979) 'De Bachelard a Althuser: El concepto de corte epistemológico', in *La filosofía y las revoluciones científicas. Teoría y Praxis*. Proceedings of Mexican Second National Congress of Philosophy. Mexico: Editorial Grijalbo, pp. 9–48.

Bambach, Charles (2003) *Heidegger's Roots. Nietzsche, National Socialism and the Greeks*. Ithaca: Cornell University Press.

Botana, Natalio R. (1997) *La tradición republicana. Alberdi, Samiento y las ideas políticas de su tiempo*. Buenos Aires: Sudamericana.

Bouysse-Cassagne, Thérèse & Harris, Olivia (1987) 'Pacha: en torno al pensamiento aymara', in *Tres reflexiones sobre el pensamiento andino*, eds Thérèse Bouysse-Cassagne, Olivia Harris, Tristan Plat and Verónica Cereceda, La Paz: hisbol, pp. 11–60.

Césaire, Aimé (1956) *Discourse sur le colonialism*. Paris: Présence Africaines.

Chua, Amy (2003) *The World in Fire. How Exporting Free Market Democracy Breeds Ethnic Hatred and Global Instability*. New York: Double Day.

de Acosta, José (2003) *Natural and Moral History of the Indies*, trans. Frances López-Morilla, ed. Jane E. Mangan, with introduction and commentary by Walter D. Mignolo. Durham: Duke University Press.

Dussel, Enrique (1995) 'Eurocentrism and Modernity (Introduction to the Frankfurt Lectures)', in *The Postmodernism Debate in Latin America*, eds John

Beverley, José Oviedo and Michael Aronna. Durham: Duke University Press, pp. 65–77.

Dussel, Enrique (2000) 'Europe, Modernity and Eurocentrism', *Nepantla. Views from South*, vol. I, no. 3, pp. 465–478.

Dussel, Enrique (2001) 'El programa científico de investigación de Karl Marx', in *Hacia una filosofía política crítica*, ed. Enrique Dussel. Seville: Desclée, pp. 279–302.

Dussel, Enrique (2002) 'World-System and 'Trans' Modernity', *Nepantla. Views from South*, vol. 2, no. 3, pp. 221–245.

Escobar, Arturo (2004) 'Beyond the Third World: Imperial Globality, Global Coloniality, and Anti-Globalization Social Movements', *Third World Quarterly*, vol. 25, no. 1, pp. 207–230.

Fanon, Frantz (1952) *Peau Noire, Mosques Blancs*. Paris: Editions du Seuil.

Ferguson, Niall (2002) *Empire. The Rise and Demise of the British World Order and the Lessons for Global Power*. Basic Books: New York: p. 16.

George, Susan (2004) *Another world is possible if*.... Verso: London:.

Gidden, Anthony (1993) *The Consequences of Modernity*. Stanford University Press: Palo Alto: p. 1.

Grosfoguel, Ramón (2000) 'Developmentalism, Modernity and Dependency in Latin America', *Nepantla: Views from South*, vol I, no. 2, pp. 347–374.

Grosfoguel, Ramón (ed.) (2002) *Utopian Thinking*. Special issue of *Review*, vol. XXV, no. 3.

Gruzinski, Serge (1999) *La Pensée Métisse*. Paris: Fayard.

Habermas, Jurgen (1987) 'Modernity's Consciousness of Time and Its Need for Self-Reassurance' and 'Hegel's Concept of Modernity', in *The Philosophical Discourse of Modernity. Twelve Lectures*, trans. Frederick Lawrence. Boston: MIT, pp. 1–45.

Hardt, Michael & Negri, Anthony (2000) *Empire*. Boston: Harvard University Press.

Hegel, G. W. F. (1822) *The Philosophy of History* [1822], trans. J. Sebree. New York: Dover Publications, p. 72.

Huntington, Samuel (2004) *The Hispanic Challenge*. New York: Simon and Schuster.

Koselleck, Reinhart (1985) *Futures Past. On the Semantic of Historical Time*. Cambridge: Harvard University Press, pp. 270–280.

Laclau, Ernesto (1996) *Emancipation(s)*. London: Verso.

Laclau, Ernesto (2000) *Emancipation(s)*. London: Routledge.

Lander, Edgardo (2000) 'Eurocentrism and Colonialism in Latin American Social Thought', *Nepantla. Views from South*, vol. I, no. 3, pp. 519–532.

Lander, Edgardo (ed. ) (2000) *La colonialidad del saber. Eurocentrismo y ciencias socials. Perspectivas latinoamericanas*. Buenos Aires: CLACSO.

Maldonado Torres, Nelson (2004) 'The Topology of Being and the Geopolitics of Knowledge', *City*, vol. 8, no. 1, pp. 29–56.

Martín, Linda & Mendieta, Eduardo (2000) *Thinking from the Underside of History. Enrique Dussel's Philosophy of Liberation*. New York: Rowman and Littlefield Publishers, Inc.

Mignolo, Walter & Tlostanova, Madina (2006) 'Theorizing From the Borders. Shifting to Geo- and Body-Politics of Knowledge', *European Journal of Social Theory*, vol. 9, no. 2, pp. 205–221.

Mignolo, Walter (2002) 'The Enduring Enchantment (or the Epistemic Privilege of Modernity and where to go from Here'), in *Enduring Enchantments, South Atlantic Quarterly* special issue, vol. 101, no. 4, pp. 927–954.

Mignolo, Walter D. (2000) 'Coloniality at Large: Time and the Colonial Difference', in *Time in the Making*, eds Candido Mendez and Enrique Larreta. Rio de Janeiro: UNESCO/Universidad Candido Mendes.

Mignolo, Walter D. (2000) *Local Histories/Global Designs: Coloniality, Subaltern Knowledges and Border Thinking*. Princeton: Princeton University Press.

Mignolo, Walter D. (2002) 'Geopolitics of Knowledge and the Colonial Difference', in *Vicissitues of Theory*, ed. Kenneth Suring. Special issue of *South Atlantic Quarterly*, vol. 101, no. 1, pp. 57–96.

Mignolo, Walter D. (2003a) *The Darker Side of the Renaissance: Literacy, Territoriality and Colonization*. Ann Arbor: The University of Michigan Press.

Mignolo, Walter D. (2003b), preface to the Spanish edition of *Historias Locales/Diseños Globales*. Madrid: Editorial Akal.

Milbank, John (1990) *Theology and Social Theory. Beyond Secular Reason*. London: Blackwell.

Mintz, Sidney W. (1986) *Sweetness and Power: The Place of Sugar in Modern History*. London: Penguin Books.

Muñoz Ramirez, Gloria (2004) *El fuego y la palabra*. México: Planeta [online] Available at: http://www.revistarebeldia.org/html/descargas/rebeldia_23.pdf

N'Zatioula Grovogui, Siba (1996) *Sovereigns, Quasi Soverigns and Africans*. Minneapolis: University of Minnesota Press.

Ornelas, Raúl (2004) 'La autonomía como eje de la resistencia Zapatista. Del levantamiento armado al nacimiento de los caracoles', in *Hegemonias y emancipaciones en el siglo XXI*, Ana Esther Ceceña (comp.). CLACSO, Consejo Latinoamericano de Ciencias Sociales, Buenos Aires, Argentina, pp. 225–250 [online] Available at: http://bibliotecavirtual.clacso.org.ar/ar/libros/cecena2/ornelas.rtf

Ortiz, Fernando (1995) *Counterpoint of Sugar and Tobacco* (1940). Durham: Duke University Press, p. 206.

Quijano, Anibal (1992) 'Colonialidad y modernidad/racionalidad' (1989), reprinted in *Los conquistados. 1492 y la población indígena de las Américas*, ed. Heraclio Bonilla. Ecuador: Libri Mundi, Tercer Mundo Editores, pp. 437–448.

Quijano, Anibal (1992) 'Colonialidad y modernidad/racionalidad', in *Los conquistados. 1492 y la población indígena de las Américas*, ed. Heraclio Bonilla. Quito: Tercer Mundo-Libri Mundi, p. 447.

Quijano, Anibal (2000) 'Modernidad, colonialidad y América Latina', *Nepantla. Views from South*, vol. I, no. 3, pp. 533–580.

Schmitt, Carl (2001) *Le nomos de la tèrre*. Traduit de l'allemand par Lilyane Deroche-Gurcel. Paris: Presses Universitaires de France.

Schiwy, Freya & Ennis, Michael (eds) (2002) 'Knowledge and the Known: Andean Perspectives on Capitalism and Epistemology', Special Dossier, *Nepantla. Views from South*, vol. 3, no. 1, pp. 1–98.

Tlostanova, Madina (2003) *A Janus Faced Empire. Notes on the Russian Empire in Modernity, Written from the Border*. Moscow: Block.

Trouillot, Michel-Rolph (1995) *Silencing the Past. Power and the Production of History*. Boston: Beacon Press.

Walsh, Catherine, Schiwy, Freya & Cástro Gómez, Santiago (eds) (2002), *Indisciplinar las ciencias socials. Geopolíticas del conocimiento y colonialidad del poder. Perspectivas desde lo Andino*. Quito: Universidad Andina Simón Bolívar y Abya-Yala.

Williams, Eric (1994) *Capitalism and Slavery*. Chapel Hill: The University of North Carolina Press, [1944].

Wynter, Sylvia (2006) 'After Man. Towards the Human' in *Critical Essays on Sylvia Wynter*, ed. Anthony Bogues. Kingston and Miami: Ian Randle Publishers, 2006.

Zavaleta-Mercado, René (1988) *Clases socials y conocimiento*. La Paz-Cochabamba: Los Amigos del Libro.

Zizek, Slavoj (2004) 'The Topology of Being and the Geopolitics of Knowledge. Modernity, Empire, Coloniality', *City*, vol. 8, no. 1, pp. 29–56.

Zizek, Slavoj (1998) 'Á leftist plea for "Eurocentrism"', *Critical Inquiry*, vol. 24, pp. 988–1007.

# María Lugones

## The Coloniality of Gender

I am interested in the intersection of race, class, gender and sexuality in a way that enables me to understand the indifference that men, but, more importantly to our struggles, men who have been racialized as inferior, exhibit to the systematic violences inflicted upon women of color. I want to understand the construction of this indifference so as to make it unavoidably recognizable by those claiming to be involved in liberatory struggles. This indifference is insidious since it places tremendous barriers in the path of the struggles of women of color for our own freedom, integrity, and wellbeing and in the path of the correlative struggles towards communal integrity. The latter is crucial for communal struggles towards liberation, since it is their backbone. The indifference is found both at the level of everyday living and at the level of theorizing of both oppression and liberation. The indifference seems to me not just one of not seeing the violence because of the categorial separation of race, gender, class, and sexuality. That is, it does not seem to be only a question of epistemological blinding through categorial separation.

Women of Color feminists have made clear what is revealed in terms of violent domination and exploitation once the epistemological perspective focuses on the intersection of these categories. But that has not seemed sufficient to arouse in those men who have themselves been targets of violent domination and exploitation, any recognition of their complicity or collaboration with the violent domination of women of color. In particular, theorizing global domination continues to proceed as if no betrayals or collaborations of this sort need to be acknowledged and resisted.

In this project I pursue this investigation by placing together two frameworks of analysis that I have not seen sufficiently jointly explored. I am referring, on the one hand, to the important work on gender, race and colonization done, not exclusively, but significantly by Third World and Women of Color feminists, including critical race theorists. This work has emphasized the concept of intersectionality and has exposed the historical and the theoretico-practical exclusion of non-white women from liberatory struggles in the name of "Women." The other framework is the one introduced by Anibal Quijano and which is at the center of his work, that of the coloniality of power. Placing both of these strands of analysis together permits me to arrive at what I am tentatively calling "the modern/colonial gender system." I think this understanding of gender is implied in both frameworks in large terms, but it is not explicitly articulated, or not articulated in the direction I think necessary to unveil the reach and consequences of complicity with

this gender system. I think that articulating this colonial/modern gender system, both in the large strokes, and in all its detailed and lived concreteness will enable us to see what was imposed on us. It will also enable us to see its fundamental destructiveness in both a long and wide sense. The intent of this writing is to make visible the instrumentality of the colonial/modern gender system in subjecting us —both women and men of color—in all domains of existence. But it is also the project's intent to make visible the crucial disruption of bonds of practical solidarity. My intent is to provide a way of understanding, of reading, of perceiving our allegiance to this gender system. We need to place ourselves in a position to call each other to reject this gender system as we perform a transformation of communal relations. In this initial paper, I present Anibal Quijano's model that I will complicate, but one that gives us—in the logic of structural axes—a good ground from within which to understand the processes of intertwining the production of "race" and "gender."

## The Coloniality of Power

Anibal Quijano thinks the intersection of race and gender in large structural terms. So, to understand that intersection in his terms, it is necessary to understand his model of global, Eurocentered capitalist power. Both "race" and gender find their meanings in this model [patrón]. Quijano understands that all power is structured in relations of domination, exploitation and conflict as social actors fight over control of "the four basic areas of human existence: sex, labor, collective authority and subjectivity/intersubjectivity, their resources and products." (Quijano, 2001-2, p.1 )What is characteristic of global, Eurocentered, capitalist power is that it is organized around two axes that Quijano terms, "the coloniality of power" and "modernity." (Quijano, 2000b, 342)The axes order the disputes over control of each area of existence in such a way that the meaning and forms of domination in each area are thoroughly infused by the coloniality of power and modernity. So, for Quijano, the disputes/struggles over control of "sexual access, its resources and products" define the domain of sex/gender and the disputes, in turn, can be understood as organized around the axes of coloniality and modernity.

This is too narrow an understanding of the oppressive modern/colonial constructions of the scope of gender. Quijano's lenses also assume patriarchal and heterosexual understandings of the disputes over control of sex, its resources, and products. Quijano accepts the global, Eurocentered, capitalist understanding of what gender is about. These features of the framework serve to veil the ways in which non-"white" colonized women were subjected and disempowered. The heterosexual and patriarchal character of the arrangements can themselves be appreciated as oppressive by unveiling the

presuppositions of the framework. Gender does not need to organize social arrangements, including social sexual arrangements. But gender arrangements need not be either heterosexual or patriarchal. They need not be, that is, as a matter of history. Understanding these features of the organization of gender in the modern/colonial gender system—the biological dimorphism, the patriarchal and heterosexual organizations of relations—is crucial to an understanding of the differential gender arrangements along "racial" lines. Biological dimorphism, heterosexual patriarchy are all characteristic of what I call the "light" side of the colonial/modern organization of gender. Hegemonically these are written large over the meaning of gender. Quijano seems not to be aware of his accepting this hegemonic meaning of gender. In making these claims I aim to expand and complicate Quijano's approach, preserving his understanding of the coloniality of power, which is at the center of what I am calling the "modern/colonial gender system."

The coloniality of power introduces the basic and universal social classification of the population of the planet in terms of the idea of "race." (Quijano, 2001-2, p.1) The invention of "race" is a pivotal turn as it replaces the relations of superiority and inferiority established through domination. It re-conceives humanity and human relations fictionally, in biological terms. It is important that what Quijano provides is a historical theory of social classification to replace what he terms the "Eurocentric theories of social classes." (Quijano, 2000b, 367) This move makes conceptual room for the coloniality of power. It makes conceptual room for the centrality of the classification of the world's population in terms of "races" in the understanding of global capitalism. It also makes conceptual room for understanding the historical disputes over control of labor, sex, collective authority and inter-subjectivity as developing in processes of long duration, rather than understanding each of the elements as pre-existing the relations of power. The elements that constitute the global, Eurocentered, capitalist model of power do not stand in separation from each other and none of them is prior to the processes that constitute the patterns. Indeed, the mythical presentation of these elements as metaphysically prior is an important aspect of the cognitive model of Eurocentered, global capitalism.

In constituting this social classification, coloniality permeates all aspects of social existence and gives rise to new social and geocultural identities. (Quijano, 2000b, 342) "America" and "Europe" are among the new geocultural identities. "European," "Indian," "African" are among the "racial" identities. This classification is "the deepest and most enduring expression of colonial domination." (Quijano, 2001-2, p. 1) With the expansion of European colonialism, the classification was imposed on the population of the planet. Since then, it has permeated every area of social existence and it constitutes the most effective form of material and inter-subjective social domination.

Thus, "coloniality" does not just refer to "racial" classification. It is an encompassing phenomenon, since it is one of the axes of the system of power and as such it permeates all control of sexual access, collective authority, labor, subjectivity/inter-subjectivity and the production of knowledge from within these inter-subjective relations. Or, alternatively, all control over sex, subjectivity, authority and labor are articulated around it. As I understand the logic of "structural axis" in Quijano's usage, the element that serves as an axis becomes constitutive of and constituted by all the forms that relations of power take with respect to control over that particular domain of human existence. Finally, Quijano also makes clear that, though coloniality is related to colonialism, these are distinct as the latter does not necessarily include racist relations of power. Coloniality's birth and its prolonged and deep extension throughout the planet is tightly related to colonianism (Quijano, 2000b, 381)

In Quijano's model of global capitalist Eurocentered power, "capitalism" refers to the structural articulation of all historically known forms of control of labor or exploitation, slavery, servitude, small independent mercantile production, wage labor, and reciprocity under the hegemony of the capital-wage labor relation." () In this sense, the structuring of the disputes over control of labor are discontinuous: not all labor relations under global, Eurocentered capitalism fall under the capital/wage relation model, though this is the hegemonic model. It is important in beginning to see the reach of the coloniality of power that wage labor has been reserved almost exclusively for white Europeans. The division of labor is thoroughly "racialized" as well as geographically differentiated. Here we see the coloniality of labor as a thorough meshing of labor and "race."

Quijano understands "modernity", the other axis of global Eurocentered capitalism, as "the fusing of the experiences of colonialism and coloniality with the necessities of capitalism, creating a specific universe of intersubjective relations of domination under a Eurocentered hegemony. "(Quijano, 2000b, 343) In characterizing modernity, Quijano focuses on the production of a way of knowing, labeled rational, arising from *within this subjective universe* since the XVII century in the main hegemonic centers of this world system of power (Holland and England). This way of knowing is Eurocentered .By "Eurocentrism" Quijano understands the cognitive perspective not of Europeans only, but of the Eurocentered world, of those educated under the hegemony of world capitalism. "Eurocentrism naturalizes the experience of people within this model of power." (2000b, 343)

The cognitive needs of capitalism and the naturalizing of the identities and relations of coloniality and of the geocultural distribution of world capitalist power have guided the production of this way of knowing. The cognitive needs of capitalism include "measurement, quantification,

externalization (or objectification) of what is knowable with respect to the knower so as to control the relations among people and nature and among them with respect to it, in particular the property in means of production." This way of knowing was imposed on the whole of the capitalist world as the only valid rationality and as emblematic of modernity.

Europe was mythologically understood to pre-exist this pattern of power as a world capitalist center that colonized the rest of the world and as such the most advanced moment in the linear, unidirectional, continuous path of the species. A conception of humanity was consolidated according to which the world's population was differentiated in two groups: superior and inferior, rational and irrational, primitive and civilized, traditional and modern. "Primitive" referred to a prior time in the history of the species, in terms of evolutionary time. Europe came to be mythically conceived as preexisting colonial, global, capitalism and as having achieved a very advanced level in the continuous, linear, unidirectional path. Thus, from within this mythical starting point, other human inhabitants of the planet came to be mythically conceived not as dominated through conquest, nor as inferior in terms of wealth or political power, but as an anterior stage in the history of the species, in this unidirectional path. That is the meaning of the qualification "primitive." (Quijano, 2000b, 343-4) We can see then the structural fit of the elements constituting Eurocentered, global capitalism in Quijano's model (pattern). Modernity and coloniality afford a complex understanding of the organization of labor. They enable us to see the fit between the thorough racialization of the division of labor and the production of knowledge. The pattern allows for heterogeneity and discontinuity. Quijano argues that the structure is not a closed totality. (Quijnao, 2000b, 355)

We are now in a position to approach the question of the intersectionality of race and gender in Quijano's terms. I think the logic of "structural axes" does more and less than intersectionality. Intersectionality reveals what is not seen when categories such as gender and race are conceptualized as separate from each other. The move to intersect the categories has been motivated by the difficulties in making visible those who are dominated and victimized in terms of both categories. Though everyone in capitalist Eurocentered modernity is both raced and gendered, not everyone is dominated or victimized in terms of them. Crenshaw and other women of color feminists have argued that the categories have been understood as homogenous and as picking out the dominant in the group as the norm, thus "women" picks out white bourgeois women, "men" picks out white bourgeois men, "black" picks out black heterosexual men, and so on. It becomes logically clear then that the logic of categorial separation distorts what exists at the intersection, such as violence against women of color. Given the construction of the categories, the intersection misconstrues women of color. So, once

intersectionality shows us what is missing, we have ahead of us the task of reconceptualizing the logic of the "intersection" so as to avoid separability. It is only when we perceive gender and race as intermeshed or fused that we actually see women of color.

The logic of structural axes shows gender as constituted by and constituting the coloniality of power. In that sense, there is no gender/race separability in Quijano's model. I think he has the logic of it right. But the axis of coloniality is not sufficient to pick out all aspects of gender. What aspects of gender are shown depends on how gender is actually conceptualized in the model. In Quijano's model (pattern,) gender seems to be contained within the organization of that "basic area of existence" that Quijano calls "sex, its resources, and products." That is, there is an account of gender within the framework that is not itself placed under scrutiny and that is too narrow and overly biologized as it presupposes sexual dimorphism, heterosexuality, patriarchal distribution of power, and so on.

Though I have not found a characterization of gender in what I have read of his work, Quijano seems to me to imply that gender difference is constituted in the disputes over control of sex, its resources, and products. Differences are shaped through the manner in which this control is organized. Sex, he understands, as biological attributes that become elaborated as social categories. He contrasts the biological quality of sex with phenotype, which does not include differential biological attributes. "The color of one's skin, the shape of one's eyes and hair "do not have any relation to the biological structure." (Quijano, 2000b, 373) Sex, on the other hand seems unproblematically biological to Quijano. He characterizes the "coloniality of *gender* relations", that is, the ordering of gender relations around the axis of the coloniality of power, as follows:

> 1.In the whole of the colonial world, the norms and formal-ideal patterns of sexual behavior of the genders and consequently the patterns of familial organization of "Europeans" were directly founded on the "racial" classification: the sexual freedom of males and the fidelity of women were, in the whole of the Eurocentered world, the counterpart of the "free"—that is, not paid as in prostitution—access of "white" men to "black" women and "indias" in America, "black" women in Africa, and other "colors" in the rest of the subjected world.
>
> [*En todo el mundo colonial, las normas y los patrones formal-ideales de comportamiento sexual de los géneros y en consecuencia los patrones de organizacion familiar de los "europeos" fueron directamente fundados en la clasificacion "racial": la libertad sexual de los varones y la fidelidad de las mujeres fue, en todo el mundo eurocentrado, la contrapartida del "libre"-esto es, no pagado como en la prostitución, mas antigua en la historia—acceso sexual de los varones "blancos" a las mujeres*

*"negras" e "indias", en America, "negras" en el Africa, y de los otros "colores" en el resto del mundo sometido.*]

2. In Europe, instead, it was the prostitution of women, that was the counterpart of the bourgeois family pattern.
[ *En Europa, en cambio, fue la prostitución de las mujeres la contrapartida del patrón de la familia burguesa.*]

3. Familial unity and integration, imposed as the axes of the model of the bourgeois family in the Eurocentered world, were the counterpart of the continued disintegration of the parent-children units in the "non-white" "races", which could be held and distributed as property not just as merchandise but as "animals."This was particularly the case among "black" slaves, since this form of domination over them was more explicit, immediate, and prolonged.
[*La unidad e integración familiar, impuestas como ejes del patrón de familia burguesa del mundo eurocentrado, fue la contrapartida de la continuada desintegración de las unidades de parentesco padres-hijos en las "razas" no-"blancas," apropriables y distribuíbles no solo como mercancias sino directamente como "animales. En particular, entre los esclavos "negros," ya que sobre ellos esa forma de dominación fue la mas explícita, inmediata y prolongada.*]

4. The hypocrisy characteristically underlying the norms and formal-ideal values of the bourgeois family are not, since then, alien to the coloniality of power.
[*La característica hipocresía subyacente a las normas y valores formal-ideales de la familia burguesa, no es, desde entonces, ajena a la colonialidad del poder.* ](Quijnao, 2000b, 378) [my translation]

As we see in this complex and important quote, Quijano's framework restricts gender to the organization of sex, its resources and products and he seems to make a presupposition as to who controls access and who becomes constituted as "resources." Quijano appears to take it for granted that the disputes over control of sex is a dispute among men, about men's control of resources who are thought to be female. Men do not seem understood as the "resources" in sexual encounters. Women are not thought to be disputing for control over sexual access. The differences are thought of in terms of how society reads reproductive biology.

## Intersexuality

In "Definitional Dilemmas" Julie Greenberg (2002) tells us that legal institutions have the power to assign individuals to a particular racial or sexual category.

> Sex is still presumed to be binary and easily determinable by an analysis of biological factors. Despite anthropological and medical studies to the contrary, society presumes an unambiguous binary sex paradigm in which all individuals can be classified neatly as male or female (112)

She argues that throughout U.S. history the law has failed to recognize intersexuals, inspite of the fact that 1 to 4 percent of the world's population is intersexed, that is they do not fit neatly into unambiguous sex categories,

> "they have some biological indicators that are *traditionally* associated with males and some biological indicators that are *traditionally* associated with females. (my emphasis) The manner in which the law defines the terms *male*, *female*, and *sex* will have a profound impact on these individuals." (112,)

The assignations reveal that what is understood to be biological sex, is socially constructed. During the late nineteenth century until WWI, reproductive function was considered a woman's essential characteristic. The presence or absence of ovaries was the ultimate criterion of sex. (113) But there are a large number of factors that can enter in "establishing someone's 'official' sex:" chromosomes, gonads, external morphology, internal morphology, hormonal patterns, phenotype, assigned sex, self-identified sex. (112) At present, chromosomes and genitalia enter into the assignment, but in a manner that reveals biology is thoroughly interpreted and itself surgically constructed.

> XY infants with "inadequate" penises must be turned into girls because society believes the essence of manhood is the ability to penetrate a vagina and urinate while standing. XX infants with "adequate" penises, however, are assigned the females sex because society and many in the medical community believe that the essence of womanhood is the ability to bear children rather than the ability to engage in satisfactory sexual intercourse. (114)

Intersexed individuals are frequently surgically and hormonally turned into males or females. These factors are taken into account in legal cases involving the right to change the sex designation on official documents, the ability to state a claim for employment discrimination based upon sex, the right to marry. (115). Greenberg reports the complexities and variety of decisions on sexual assignation in each case. The law does not recognize intersexual status. Though the law permits self-identification of one's sex in certain documents, "for the most part, legal institutions continue to base sex assignment on the traditional assumptions that sex is binary and can be easily determined by analyzing biological factors." (119)

Julie Greenberg's work enables me to point out an important assumption in the model that Quijano offers us. This is important because sexual dimorphism has been an important characteristic of what I call "the light side" of the colonial/modern gender system. Those in the "dark side" were not necessarily understood dimorphically. Sexual fears of colonizers led them to imagine the indigenous people of the Americas as hermaphrodites or intersexed, with large penises and breasts with flowing milk. But as Gunn Allen and others make clear, intersexed individuals were recognized in many tribal societies prior to colonization without assimilation to the sexual binary. It is important to consider the changes that colonization brought to understand the scope of the organization of sex and gender under colonialism and in Eurocentered global capitalism. If the latter did only recognize sexual dimorphism for white bourgeois males and females, it certainly does not follow that the sexual division is based on biology. The cosmetic and substantive corrections to biology make very clear that "gender" is antecedent to the "biological" traits and gives them meaning. The naturalizing of sexual differences is another product of the modern use of science that Quijano points out in the case of "race." It is important to see that not all different traditions correct and normalize inter-sexed people. So, as with other assumption characteristics it is important to ask how sexual dimorphism served and serves Eurocentered global capitalist domination/exploitation.

## When egalitarianism takes a non-gendered or a gynecentric form

As Eurocentered, global capitalism was constituted through colonization, gender differentials were introduced where there were none. Oyeronke Oyewumi shows us that the oppressive gender system that was imposed on Yoruba society did a lot more than transform the organization of reproduction. Her argument shows us that the scope of the system of gender imposed through colonialism encompasses the subordination of females in every aspect of life. Thus Quijano's understanding of the scope of gendering in Eurocentered, global, capitalism is much too narrow. Paula Gunn Allen argues that many Native American tribes were matriarchal, recognized more than two genders, recognized "third" gendering and homosexuality positively and understood gender in egalitarian terms rather than in the terms of subordination that Eurocentered capitalism imposed on them. She enables us to see that the scope of the gender differentials was much more encompassing and it did not rest on biology. Gunn Allen also shows us a construction of knowledge and an approach to understanding "reality" that is gynecentric and that counters the knowledge production of modernity. Thus she points us in the direction of recognizing the gendered construction

of knowledge in modernity, another aspect of the hidden scope of "gender" in Quijano's account of the processes constituting the coloniality of gender.

## Non-gendered egalitarianism

In her *The Invention ofWomen*, Oyérónkẹ́ Oyewùmí, raises questions about the validity of patriarchy as a valid transcultural category. (20) She does so, not but contrasting patriarchy and matriarchy, but by arguing that "gender was not an organizing principle in Yoruba society prior to colonization by the West."(31) No gender system was in place. Indeed she tells us that gender has "become important in Yoruba studies not as an artifact of Yoruba life but because Yoruba life, past and present, has been translated into English to fit the Western pattern of body-reasoning." (30). The assumption that Yoruba society included gender as an organizing principle is another case "of Western dominance in the documentation and interpretation of the world, one that is facilitated by the West's global material dominance.(32) She tells us that "researchers always find gender when they look for it." (31).

> The usual gloss of the Yoruba categories *obinrin* and *okunrin* as"female/woman" and male/man," respectively, is a mistranslation. These categories are neither binarily opposed nor hierarchical. (32-33)

The prefixes obin and okun specify a variety of anatomy. Oyewumi translates the prefixes as referring to the anatomic male and the anatomic female, shortened as anamale and anafemale. It is important to note that she does not understand these categories as binarily opposed.

Oyewumi understands gender as introduced by the West as a tool of domination that designates two binarily opposed and hierarchical social categories. Women (the gender term) is not defined through biology, though it is assigned to anafemales. Women are defined in relation to men, the norm. Women are those who do not have a penis; those who do not have power; those who cannot participate in the public arena. (34) None of this was true of Yoruba anafemales prior to colonization.

> The imposition of the European state system, with its attendant legal and bureaucratic machinery, is the most enduring legacy of European colonial rule in Africa. One tradition that was exported to Africa during this period was the exclusion of women from the newly created colonial public sphere... (123)

> The very process by which females were categorized and reduced to "women" made them ineligible for leadership roles. ...The emergence of

> women as an identifiable category, defined by their anatomy and subordinated to men in all situations, resulted, in part, from the imposition of a patriarchal colonial state. For females, colonization was a twofold process of racial inferiorization and gender subordination. The creation of "women" as a category was one the very first accomplishments of the colonial state. It is not surprising, therefore, that it was unthinkable for the colonial government to recognize female leaders among the peoples they colonized, such as the Yorùbá. (124)The transformation of state power to male-gender power was accomplished at one level by the exclusion of women from state structures. This was in sharp contrast to Yorùbá state organization, in which power was not gender-determined. (125)

Oyewumi recognizes two crucial processes in colonization, the imposition of races with the accompanying inferiorization of Africans, and the inferiorization of anafemales. The inferiorization of anafemales extended very widely from exclusion from leadership roles to loss of property over land, and other important economic domains. Oyewumi notes that the introduction of the Western gender system was accepted by Yoruba males, who thus colluded with the inferiorization of anafemales. So, when we think of the indifference of non-white men to the violences exercised against non-white women, we can begin to have some sense of the collaboration between anamales and Western colonials against anafemales. Oyewumi makes clear that both men and women resisted cultural changes at different levels. Thus while

> In the West the challenge of feminism is how to proceed from the gender-saturated category of "women" to the fullness of an unsexed humanity. For Yoruba obinrin, the challenge is obviously different because at certain levels in the society and in some spheres, the notion of an "unsexed humanity" is neither a dream to aspire to nor a memory to be realized. It exists, albeit in concatenation with the reality of separate and hierarchical sexes imposed during the colonial period. (156)

We can see then that the scope of the coloniality of gender is much too narrow. Quijano assumes much of the terms of the modern/colonial gender system's hegemonic "light" side in defining the scope of gender. I have gone outside the coloniality of gender so as to think of what it hides, or disallows from consideration, about the very scope of the gender system of Eurocentered global capitalism. So, though I think that the coloniality of gender, as Quijano pointedly describes it, shows us very important aspects of the intersection of "race" and "gender," it follows rather than discloses the erasure of colonized women from most areas of social life. It accommodates

rather than disrupt the narrowing of gender domination. Oyewumi's rejection of the gender lens in characterizing the inferiorization of anafemales in modern colonization makes clear the extent and scope of the inferiorization. Her understanding of gender, the colonial, Eurocentered, capitalist construction, is much more encompassing than Quijano's. She enables us to see the economic, political, cognitive inferiorization as well as the inferiorization of anafemales regarding reproductive control.

## Gynecratric egalitarianism

To assign to this great being the position of "fertility goddess" is exceedingly demeaning: it trivializes the tribes and it trivializes the power of woman. (Gunn Allen,1986,p.14)

As she characterizes many Native American tribes as gynecratic, Paula Gunn Allen emphasizes the centrality of the spiritual in all aspects of Indian life and thus a very different intersubjectivity from within which knowledge is produced than that of the coloniality of knowledge in modernity. Many American Indian tribes "thought that the primary potency in the universe was female, and that understanding authorizes all tribal activities." (26)Old Spider Woman, Corn Woman, Serpent Woman, Thought Woman are some of the names of powerful creators. For the gynecratic tribes, Woman is at the center and "no thing is sacred without her blessing, her thinking." (13)

Replacing this gynecratic spiritual plurality with one supreme male being as Christianity did, was crucial in subduing the tribes. Allen proposes that transforming Indian tribes from egalitarian and gynecratic to hierarchical and patriarchal "requires meeting four objectives:

1. "The primacy of female as creator is displaced and replaced by male-gendered creators (generally generic)." (41)
2. "Tribal governing institutions and the philosophies that are their foundation are destroyed, as they were among the Iriquois and the Cherokee."(41)
3. The people "are pushed off their lands, deprived of their economic livelihood, and forced to curtail or end altogether pursuits on which their ritual system, philosophy, and subsistence depend. Now dependent on white institutions for their survival, tribal systems can ill afford gynocracy when patriarchy—that is, survival—requires male dominance." (42)
4. The clan structure "must be replaced in fact if not in theory, by the nuclear family. By this ploy, the women clan heads are replaced by elected male officials and the psychic net that is formed and maintained by the nature of nonauthoritarian gynecentricity grounded in respect for diversity of gods and people ise thoroughly rent."(42)

Thus, for Allen, the inferiorization of Indian females is thoroughly tied to the domination and transformation of tribal life. The destruction of the gynocracies is crucial to the "decimation of populations through starvation, disease, and disruption of all social, spiritual, and economic structures..." (42) The program of degynocratization requires impressive "image and information control." Thus

> Recasting archaic tribal versions of tribal history, customs, institutions and the oral tradition increases the likelihood that the patriarchal revisionist versions of tribal life, skewed or simply made up by patriarchal non-Indians and patriarchalized Indians, will be incorporated into the spiritual and popular traditions of the tribes. (42)

Among the features of the Indian society targeted for destruction were the two -sided complementary social structure; the understanding of gender; the economic distribution which often followed the system of reciprocity. The two sides of the complementary social structure included an internal female chief and an external male chief. The internal chief presided over the band, village, or tribe, maintained harmony and administered domestic affairs. The red, male, chief presided over mediations between the tribe and outsiders. (18) Gender was not understood primarily in biological terms. Most individuals fit into tribal gender roles "on the basis of proclivity, inclination, and temperament. The Yuma had a tradition of gender designation based on dreams; a female who dreamed of weapons became a male for all practical purposes. "(196)

Like Oyewumi, Gunn Allen is interested in the collaboration between some Indian men and whites in undermining the power of women. It is important for us to think about these collaborations as we think of the question of indifference to the struggles of women in racialized communities against multiple forms of violence against them and the communities. The white colonizer constructed a powerful inside force as colonized men were coopted into patriarchal roles. Gunn Allen details the transformations of the Iroquois and Cherokee gynecracies and the role of Indian men in the passage to patriarchy. The British took Cherokee men to England and gave them an education in the ways of the English. These men participated during the time of the Removal Act.

> In an effort to stave off removal, the Cherokee in the early 1800s under the leadership of men such as Elias Boudinot, Major Ridge, and John Ross, and others, drafted a constitution that disenfranchised women and blacks. Modeled after the Constitution of the United States, whose favor they

> were attempting to curry, and in conjunction with Christian sympathizers to the Cherokee cause, the new Cherokee constitution relegated women to the position of chattel. (37)

Cherokee women had had the power to wage war, to decide the fate of captives, to speak to the men's council, they had the right to inclusion in public policy decisions, the right to choose whom and whether to marry, the right to bear arms. The Women's Council was politically and spiritually powerful (36-37). Cherokee women lost all these powers and rights, as the Cherokee were removed and patriarchal arrangements were introduced. The Iroquois shifted from a Mother-centered, Mother-right people organized politically under the authority of the Matrons, to a patriarchal society when the Iroquois became a subject people. The feat was accomplished with the collaboration of Handsome Lake and his followers. (33)

According to Allen, many of the tribes were gynecratic, among them the Susquehanna, Hurons, Iroquois, Cherokee, Pueblo, Navajo, Narragansett, Coastal Algonkians, Montagnais. She also tells us that among the eighty-eight tribes that recognized homosexuality, those who recognized homosexuals in positive terms included the Apache, Navajo, Winnebago, Cheyenne, Pima, Crow, Shoshoni, Paiute, Osage, Acoma, Zuñi, Sioux, Pawnee, Choctaw, Creek, Seminole, Illinois, Mohave, Shasta, Aleut, Sac and Fox, Iowa, Kansas, Yuma, Aztec, Tlingit, Maya, Naskapi, Ponca, Maricopa, Lamath, Quinault, Yuki, Chilula, Kamia. Twenty of these tribes included specific references to lesbianism.

Michael J. Horswell (2003) comments usefully on the use of the term "third gender". He tells that third gender" does not mean that there are three genders. It is rather a way of breaking with the sex and gender bipolarity. "The 'third' is emblematic of other possible combinations than the dimorphic. The term "berdache" is sometimes used for "third gender." Horswell tells us that male berdache have been documented in nearly one hundred and fifty North American societies and female berdache in half as many groups. (27). He also comments that sodomy, including ritual sodomy, was recorded in Andean societies and many other native societies in the Americas. (27) The Nahuas and Mayas also reserved a role for ritualized sodomy. (Sigal, 104) It is interesting that Sigal (2003) tells us that the Spanish saw sodomy as sinful, but Spanish law condemned the active partner in sodomy to criminal punishment, not the passive. In Spanish popular culture, sodomy was racialized by connecting the practice to the Moors and the passive partner was condemned and seen as equal to a Moor. Spanish soldiers were seen as the active partners to the passive Moors. (102-104)

Allen's work not only enables us to see how narrow Quijano's conception of gender is in terms of the organization of the economy, and the organization

of collective authority, she also enables us to see that the production of knowledge is gendered, the very conception of reality at every level. She also supports the questioning of biology in the construction of gender differences and introduces the important question of gender roles being chosen and dreamt. But importantly, Allen also shows us that the heterosexuality characteristic of the modern/colonial construction of gender relations, is produced, mythically constructed. But heterosexuality is not just biologized in a fictional way, it is also compulsory and it permeates the whole of the coloniality of gender, in the renewed, large sense. In this sense, global Eurocentered capitalism is heterosexualist. I think it is important to see, as we understand the depth and force of violence in the production of both the "light" and the "dark" sides of the colonial/modern gender system, that this heterosexuality has been consistently perverse, violent, demeaning, a turning of people into animals, and the turning of white women into reproducers of "the race" and "the class." Horwswell's and Sigal's work complements Allen's, particularly in understanding the presence of sodomy and male homosexuality in colonial and pre-colonial America.

## The Colonial/Modern Gender System

Understanding the place of gender in pre-colonial societies is pivotal to understanding the nature and scope of changes in the social structure that the processes constituting colonial/modern Eurocentered capitalism imposed. Those changes were introduced through slow, discontinuous, and heterogenous processes that violently inferiorized colonized women. The gender system introduced was one thoroughly informed through the coloniality of power. Understanding the place of gender in pre-colonial societies is also pivotal in understanding the extent and importance of the gender system in disintegrating communal relations, egalitarian relations, ritual thinking, collective decision making , collective authority, and economies. And thus in understanding the extent to which the imposition of this gender system was as constitutive of the coloniality of power as the coloniality of power was constitutive of it. The logic of the relation between them is of mutual constitution. But it should be clear by now that the colonial, modern, gender system cannot exist without the coloniality of power, since the classification of the population in terms of race is a necessary condition of its possibility.

To think the scope of the gender system of Eurocentered global capitalism it is necessary to understand the extent to which the *very process of narrowing* of the concept of gender to the control of sex, its resources, and products constitutes gender domination. To understand this narrowing and to understand the intermeshing of racialization and gendering, it is important

to think whether the social arrangements prior to colonization regarding the "sexes" gave differential meaning to them across all areas of existence. That enables us to see whether control over labor, subjectivity/intersubjectivity, collective authority, sex—Quijano's "areas of existence"— were themselves gendered. Given the coloniality of power, I think we can also say that having a "dark" and a "light side" is characteristic of the co-construction of the coloniality of power and the colonial/modern gender system. Considering critically both biological dimorphism and the position that gender socially constructs biological sex is pivotal to understand the scope, depth, and characteristics of the colonial/modern gender system. The sense is that the reduction of gender to the private, to control over sex and its resources and products is a matter of ideology, of the cognitive production of modernity that understood race as gendered and gender as raced in particularly differential ways for Europeans/"whites" and colonized/"non-white" peoples. Race is no more mythical and fictional than gender, both powerful fictions.

In the development of twentieth century feminisms, the connection between gender, class, heterosexuality as racialized was not made explicit. That feminism centered its struggle and its ways of knowing and theorizing against a characterization of women as fragile, weak in both body and mind, secluded in the private, and sexually passive. But it did not bring to consciousness that those characteristics only constructed white bourgeois womanhood. Indeed, beginning from that characterization, white bourgeois feminists theorized white womanhood as if all women were white.

It is part of their history that only white bourgeois women have consistently counted as women so described in the West. Females excluded from that description were not just their subordinates. They were also understood to be animals in a sense that went further than the identification of white women with nature, infants, and small animals. They were understood as animals in the deep sense of "without gender," sexually marked as female, but without the characteristics of femininity. Women racialized as inferior were turned from animals into various modified versions of "women" as it fit the processes of Eurocentered global capitalism. Thus heterosexual rape of Indian women, African slave women, coexisted with concubinage, as well as with the imposition of the heterosexual understanding of gender relations among the colonized—when and as it suited Eurocentered, global capitalism, and heterosexual domination of white women. But it is clear from the work of Oyewumi and Allen that there was no extension of the status of white women to colonized women even when they were turned into similes of bourgeois white women. Colonized females got the inferior status of gendering as women, without any of the privileges accompanying that status for white bourgeois women. Though, the history presented by Oyewumi and Allen should make clear to white bourgeois women that their status is much inferior

to that of Native American women and Yoruba women before colonization. Oyewumi and Allen also make clear that the egalitarian understanding of the relation between anafemales, anamales, and "third" gender people has not left the imagination nor the practices of Native Americans and Yoruba. But these are matters of resistance to domination.

Erasing any history, including oral history, of the relation of white to non-white women, white feminism wrote white women large. Even though historically and contemporarily white bourgeois women knew perfectly well how to orient themselves in an organization of life that pitted them for very different treatment than non-white or working class women. White feminist struggle became one against the positions, roles, stereotypes, traits, desires imposed on white bourgeois women's subordination. No one else's gender oppression was countenanced. They understood women as inhabiting white bodies but did not bring that racial qualification to articulation or clear awareness. That is, they did not understand themselves in intersectional terms, at the intersection of race, gender, and other forceful marks of subjection or domination. Because they did not perceive these deep differences they did not see a need for creating coalitions. They presumed a sisterhood, a bond given with the subjection of gender.

Historically, the characterization of white European women as fragile and sexually passive opposed them to non-white, colonized women, including women slaves, who were characterized along a gamut of sexual aggression and perversion, and as strong enough to do any sort of labor. The following description of slave women and of slave work in the U.S. South makes clear that African slave females were not considered fragile or weak.

> First came, led by an old driver carrying a whip, forty of the largest and strongest women I ever saw together; they were all in a simple uniform dress of a bluish check stuff, the skirts reaching little below the knee; their legs and feet were bare; they carried themselves loftily, each having a hoe over the shoulder, and walking with a free, powerful swing, like *chasseurs* on the march. Behind came the cavalry, thirty strong, mostly men, but a few of them women, two of whom rode astride on the plow mules. A lean and vigilant white overseer, on a brisk pony, brought up the rear. (Takaki, 111)

> The hands are required to be in the cotton field as soon as it is light in the morning, and, with the exception of ten or fifteen minutes, which is given to them at noon to swallow their allowance of cold bacon, they are not permitted to be a moment idle until it is too dark to see, and when the moon is full, they often times labor till the middle of the night. (Takaki, 111)

Patricia Hill Collins provides a clear sense of the dominant understanding of Black women as sexually aggressive and the genesis of that stereotype in slavery:

> The image of Jezebel originated under slavery when Black women were portrayed as being, to use Jewelle Gomez' words, "sexually aggressive wet nurses" (Clarke et al. 1983, 99). Jezebel's function was to relegate all Black women to the category of sexually aggressive women, thus providing a powerful rationale for the widespread sexual assaults by White men typically reported by Black slave women. (Davis 1981; D. White 1985). Jezebel served yet another function. If Black slave women could be portrayed as having excessive sexual appetites, then increased fertility should be the expected outcome. By suppressing the nurturing that African-American women might give their own children which would strengthen Black family networks, and by forcing Black women to work in the field, "wet nurse" White children, and emotionally nurture their White owners, slave owners effectively tied the controlling images of jezebel and mammy to the economic exploitation inherent in the institution of slavery. (Hill Collins, 82)

But it is not just black slave women who were placed outside the scope of white bourgeois femininity. In *Imperial Leather*, Anne McClintock (1995) as she tells us of Columbus' depiction of the earth as a woman's breast, evokes the "long tradition of male travel as an erotics of ravishment (22)."

> For centuries, the uncertain continents—Africa, the Americas, Asia—were figured in European lore as libidinously eroticized. Travelers' tales abounded with visions of the monstrous sexuality of far-off lands, where, as legend had it, men sported gigantic penises and women consorted with apes, feminized men's breasts flowed with milk and militarized women lopped theirs off. (22)

> Within this porno tropic tradition, women figured as the epitome of sexual aberration and excess. Folklore saw them, even more than the men, as given to a lascivious venery so promiscuous as to border on the bestial. (22)

McClintock describes the colonial scene depicted in a drawing (ca. 1575) in which Jan van der Straet "portrays the "discovery" of America as an eroticized encounter between a man and a woman." (25)

> Roused from her sensual languor by the epic newcomer, the indigenous woman extends an inviting hand, insinuating sex and submission…Vespucci, the godlike arrival, is destined to inseminate her with his male seeds of civilization, fructify the wilderness and quell the riotous scenes of cannibalism in the background…The cannibals appear to be female and are spit roasting a human leg. (26)

In the 19th century, McClinctock tells us "sexual purity emerged as a controlling metaphor for racial, economic and political power." (47) With the development of evolutionary theory "anatomical criteria were sought for determining the relative position of races in the human series." (50)

> The English middle-class male was placed at the pinnacle of evolutionary hierarchy. White English middle class women followed. Domestic workers, female miners and working class prostitutes were stationed on the threshold between the white and black races. (56)

> Yen Le Espiritu (1997) tells us that

> "representations of gender and sexuality figure strongly in the articulation of racism. Gender norms in the United States are premised upon the experiences of middleclass men and women of European origin. These Eurocentric-constructed gender norms form a backdrop of expectations for American men and women of color—expectations which racism often precludes meeting. In general, men of color are viewed not as the protector, but rather the aggressor—a threat to white women. And women of color are seen as over sexualized and thus undeserving of the social and sexual protection accorded to white middleclass women. For Asian American men and women, their exclusion from white-based cultural notions of the masculine and the feminine has taken seemingly contrasting forms: Asian men have been cast as both hypermasculine (the "Yellow Peril") and effeminate (the "model minority"); and Asian women have been rendered both superfeminine (the "China Doll") and castrating (the "Dragon Lady"). (Espiritu, 135)

This gender system congeals as Europe advances the colonial project(s). It begins to take shape during the Spanish and Portuguese colonial adventures and becomes full blown in late modernity. The gender system has a "light" and a "dark" side. The light side constructs gender and gender relations hegemonic ally. It only orders the lives of white bourgeois men and women, and it constitutes the modern/colonial meaning of "men" and "women." Sexual purity and passivity are crucial characteristics of the white bourgeois females

who reproduce the class, and the colonial, and racial standing of bourgeois, white men. But equally important is the banning of white bourgeois women from the sphere of collective authority, from the production of knowledge, from most of control over the means of production. Weakness of mind and body are important in the reduction and seclusion of white bourgeois women from most domains of life, most areas of human existence. The gender system is heterosexualist, as heterosexuality permeates racialized patriarchal control over production, including knowledge production, and over collective authority. Heterosexuality is both compulsory and perverse among white bourgeois men and women since the arrangement does significant violence to the powers and rights of white bourgeois women and it serves to reproduce control over production and . White bourgeois women are inducted into this reduction through bounded sexual access.

The "dark" side of the gender system was and is thoroughly violent. We have began to see the deep reductions of anamales, anafemales, and "third" genders from their ubiquitous participation in ritual, decision making, economics; their reduction to animality, to forced sex with white colonizers, to such deep labor exploitation that often people died working. Quijano tells us

> The vast Indian genocide of the first decades of colonization was not caused, in the main, by the violence of the conquest, nor by the diseases that the conquerors carried. Rather is was due to the fact that the Indians were used as throwaway labor, forced to work till death. (My translation) (Quijano, 2000a.)

I want to mark the connection between the work that I am referencing here as I introduce the modern colonial gender system's "dark" side, and Quijano's coloniality of power. Unlike white feminists who have not focused on colonialism, these theorists very much see the differential construction of gender along racial lines. To some extent these theorists understand "gender" in a wider sense than Quijano, thus they think not only of control over sex, its resources and products, but also of labor as both racialized and gendered. That is, they see an articulation between labor, sex, and the coloniality of power. Oyewumi and Allen help us realize the full extent of the reach of the colonial/modern gender system into the construction of collective authority, all aspects of the relation between capital and labor, and the construction of knowledge.

There is important work done and to be done in detailing the dark and light sides of what I am calling the "modern colonial gender system." In introducing this arrangements in very large strokes , I mean to begin a conversation and a project of collaborative, participatory, research and

popular education to begin to see in its details the long sense of the processes of the colonial/gender system enmeshed in the coloniality of power into the present, to uncover collaboration, and to call each other to reject it in its various guises as we recommit to communal integrity in a liberatory direction. We need to understand the organization of the social so as to make visible our collaboration with systematic racialized gender violence, so as to come to an inevitable recognition of it in our maps of reality.

## References

Crenshaw, Kimberlé. 1995. "Mapping the Margins: Intersectionality, Identity Politics, and Violence Against Women of Color." In *Critical Race Theory* edited by Kimberlé Crenshaw, Neil Gotanda, Gary Peller, and Kendall Thomas. New York: The New Press.

Espiritu, Yen Le. 1997. "Race, class, and gender in Asian America." In Elaine H. Kim, Lilia V. Villanueva and Asian Women United of California, eds. *Making More Waves*. Boston: Beacon.

Gunn Allen, Paula. [1986] 1992. *The Sacred Hoop. Recovering the Feminine in American Indian Traditions*. Boston: Beacon Press.

Greenberg, Julie.A. 2002. "Definitional Dilemmas: Male or Female? Black or White? The Law's Failure to Recognize Intersexuals and Multiracials." *In Gender Nonconformity, Race, and Sexuality. Charting the Connections*. Edited by Toni Lester. Madison: University of Wisconsin Press.

Horswell. "Toward and Andean Theory of Ritual Same-Sex Sexuality and Third-Gender Subjectivity." In *Infamous Desire. Male Homosexuality in Colonial Latin America*. Edited by Pete Sigal. Chicago and London: The University of Chicago Press.

Lugones, María. 2003. *Pilgrimages/Peregrinajes: Theorizing Coalitions Against Multiple Oppressions*. Lanham: Rowman & Littlefield.

McClintock, Anne. 1995. *Imperial Leather. Race, Gender and Sexuality in the Colonial Contest*. New York: Routledge.

Oyewumi, Oyeronke. 1997. *The Invention of Women. Making an African Sense of Western Gender Discourses*. Minneapolis: University of Minnesota Press.

Quijano, Anibal. 2000b. "Colonialidad del Poder y Clasificacion Social", Festschrift for Immanuel Wallerstein, part I, Journal of World Systems Research, V. xi, #2, summer/fall 2000 [2000b]

——, 2000a. "Colonialidad del poder, eurocentrismo y America latina" in Colonialidad del Saber, Eurocentrismo y Ciencias Sicales. CLACSO-UNESCO 2000, Buenos Aires, Argentina, pp. 201-246.

——, "Colonialidad, modernidad/racionalidad" Peru Indigena, vol. 13., No.29, 1991, pp.11-29

——, "Colonialidad del poder, globalización y democracia. Revista de Ciencias

Sociales de la Universidad Autónoma de Nuevo León, Año 4, Números 7 y 8, Septiembre 2001-Abril 2002.

Sigal, Pete. 2003. "Gendered Power, the Hybrid Self, and Homosexual Desire in Late Colonial Yucatan." In *Infamous Desire. Male Homosexuality in Colonial Latin America*. Edited by Pete Sigal. Chicago and London: The University of Chicago Press.

Spelman, Elizabeth. 1988. *Inessential Woman*. Boston: Beacon.

Takaki, Ronald. 1993. *A Different Mirror*. Boston: Little, Brown, and Company.

# Arturo Escobar

## Afterword

One of the goals of this book has been to explore the relevance of the Modernity/Coloniality/Decoloniality research program to various world situations and issues not previously considered. Given its continued ties to Central/South America and the Caribbean, however, it makes sense to resituate within the most recent transformations under way in the continent. The character of these transformations needs to be ascertained simultaneously at the level of the state, of social movements, and at the state-social movement nexus. In keeping with MCD insights, the changes also need to be analyzed well beyond the political and economic realms, delving particularly into the potential for epistemic decolonization and the emergence of 'worlds and knowledges otherwise.' This potential and emergence are also being discussed in terms of post-liberalism and relationality. I would like to explore briefly in this Afterword the relation between these emerging concepts and decoloniality. I can only do so in a very cursory manner, as a way to signal some of the most recent intellectual-political trends that could be related to decoloniality.

Central/South America is the only region in the world where some counter-hegemonic processes of importance might be taking place at the level of the State, and certainly at the level of some social movements. The election of progressive regimes since the late 1990s (Argentina, Bolivia, Brazil, Chile, Ecuador, El Salvador, Nicaragua, Paraguay, Uruguay, and Venezuela) is the most visible sign of the transformation going on. Why is this happening in Latin America more clearly than in any other world region at present is a question I cannot tackle here, other than saying that it is related to the fact that Latin America was also the region that most earnestly embraced neo-liberal reforms since the late 1970s, where the model was applied most thoroughly, and where the results are most ambiguous, in the best of cases. For some, these processes might lead to a re-invention of socialism; for others, what is at stake is the dismantling of the neo-liberal policies of the past decades –the end the "the long neo-liberal night," as the period is known in progressive circles in the region—or the formation of a South American (and largely anti-American) bloc. Others point at the potential for *un nuevo comienzo* (a new beginning) which might bring about a reinvention of democracy and development or, more radically still, the end of the predominance of liberal society of the past two hundred years, that is, one founded on private property and representative democracy. *Socialismo del siglo XXI*, pluri-nationality and

pluri-ethnicity, direct and substantive democracy, *revolucion ciudadana*, endogenous development centered on the *buen vivir* (collective wellbeing) of people and nature, territorial and cultural autonomy, and post-liberal societies are some of the concepts most commonly used to name the ongoing transformations. Aníbal Quijano perhaps put it best when grasping the historical specificity of the moment: "It is a time of *luchas* (struggles) and of options. Latin America was the original space of the emergence of modern/colonial capitalism; it marked its founding moment. Today it is, at last, the very center of world resistance against this pattern of power and of the production of alternatives to it" (2008: 3).

This trend is often described as a "turn to the Left." However, as Walter Mignolo (2006) states, this label only reduces the transformation to the terms of Eurocentric political discourse; what Mignolo suggest is that some of the processes under way point in the direction of decolonial projects. To entertain this idea seriously requires placing the transformation in the context of a double conjuncture: the crisis of the hegemony of the neoliberal modernizing model of the past three decades; and the crisis of the project of bringing about modernity in the continent since the Conquest. It is in the space of thought and action opened up by this conjuncture of a two-faced crisis that what is happening in the continent can be most productively seen.

There is an acute sense, of course, that the potential opened up by the conjuncture will not necessarily be realized, and that the projects under way, especially in their State form, are not panaceas of any sort; on the contrary, they are seen as fragile and full of tensions and contradictions.[1] But the sense of an active stirring up of things in many of the continent's regions, from Chiapas and Oaxaca to Chile, and especially in large parts of South America, is strong. How one thinks about these processes is itself an object of struggle, and it is at this juncture that this volume is also situated. The MCD perspective, we believe, offers ways of thinking about the ongoing transformations that neither shortcut their potential by interpreting them through worn out categories –including 'Left' and 'Right'— nor that aggrandize their scope by imputing to them utopias that might be far from the desires and actions of the actors involved. MCD authors such as those in this volume believe that it is not enough to think from the space of the modern social sciences, and that it is necessary to incorporate other knowledge producers and forms of knowledge, such as the activist-intellectuals that inhabit the worlds of many of today's social movements and, in general, historical and contemporary expressions of decolonial thought (Mignolo 2007, Escobar 2008). In other words, the questions of where one thinks from, with whom, and for what purpose become themselves important elements of social science and humanities thinking; this also means that intellectual work, more than ever, is simultaneously theoretical and political.

The Central/South American/Caribbean specificity also has to do with the multiplicity of histories and trajectories that underlie the various projects in the continent at present, and with the fact that there are very diverse cultural and political projects that find in the transformations a convergence space. Two interpretive trends attempt to visualize these projects in the more farsighted way, that is, in terms of profound epistemic and cultural processes. Both refer to processes going on at the level of social movements more than at the State level. The first seeks to make visible 'non-liberal' and 'non-state' forms of politics and organization; the second finds in some of the movements in question the political activation of 'relational ontologies.' Both trends attempt to go beyond what has been thought so far from the established social sciences when studying social change in the continent; both create synergies, in the different ways, with the MCD framework. Allow me to describe both trends very succinctly.

## The question of post-liberalism

Arditti (2008) has argued that the many of the actions of both the progressive governments and social movements may be seen in terms of a post-liberal politics –in terms, for instance, of novel democratic processes. Focusing on a set of what could be termed exemplary struggles –particularly Zapatismo and the popular uprisings in Bolivia in the period 2000-2005, including the water and gas 'wars'—a group of intellectual activists are developing an account of these struggles in terms of what are seen as non-liberal and non-state forms of power (Zibechi 2006, Patzi 2004, Gutiérrez Aguilar 2008, Mamani 2005, 2006). The analysis is most eloquently centered on various autonomous struggles —largely but not solely indigenous, or only reconstituted as indigenous in recent years— particularly Aymara urban struggles in El Alto, Aymara communal rural uprising, and *cocalero* mobilizations). A guiding principle is that movements must be approached from below and from within, thus arriving at a view of veritable societies in movement, rather than discrete social movements, allegedly external to the flow of the social, and to the researcher. This inquiry allows these intellectuals to read the mobilizations in terms of the emergence of non-capitalist and non-statist forms of self-regulation that irradiate society and become structuring principles of social re/composition.

A main theoretical intervention in these analyses is a distinction between "communal forms" and "state forms" of power and social life. There is an explicit attempt at constructing a theoretical apparatus centered on making visible those forms of "self-regulation of social co-existence that go beyond the modern state and capital" (Gutiérrez Aguilar 2008: 18), that is, a type of society "characterized by non-capitalist and non-liberal social relations, labor

forms, and forms of organization" (Zibechi 2006: 52). Three of the main features of non-statist and non-liberal regulation identified in the repeated mobilizations and insurrections in Bolivia of the 2000-2005 period are: the practice of deliberative assemblies for all important decision making; the horizontality of organizations; and the rotation of assignments. Popular organization are found to be made up of "undivided organs" (*organos indivisos*), in contradistinction with the modern assumption of specialization as the basis of rational action.

What emerges from this framework is a characterization of the struggles in terms of self-organization aimed at the construction of non-state forms of power; these are defined as "forms of power that are not separate nor divided from society, that is, that do not create a separate group in order to make decisions, struggle, or deal with internal conflict" (Zibechi 2006: 40). In Aymara society, these power and functions (*capacidad*) appear distributed throughout the social body, immersed in the organization of daily life, and always subjected to the assemblies. As the Aymara sociologist Pablo Mamani puts it, they should be seen as "neighborhood micro-governments," and "diffuse anti-powers .... quasi-microbial, intermittent forms of power." What he finds in El Alto is an alternative territoriality to that of the state, which takes the place of instituted forms of power (Mamani 2006: 278). More technically, and borrowing from the work of the Chilean biologists Maturana and Varela, Zibechi describes the moblizations as non-statist and non-liberal logics that "work in the moments of insurrection to produce autopoietic multiplicities with self-learning and structural coupling to their environment. What obtains from the insurrection / communal logic is *una sociedad otra*); the objective is *organizarse como los poderes de una sociedad otra* (to organize around forms of power for an other society; Zibechi 2006: 75).

The overall argument could be summarized as follows: "In Bolivia, the communal-popular and national-popular forms fractured, after 2000, the liberal paradigm in an indubitable and abrupt way ... What was demonstrated was ... the possibility of transforming (*alterar*) social reality in a profound way in order to preserve, transforming them, collective and long-standing life-worlds and to produce novel and fruitful forms of government, association and self-regulation. In some fashion, the central ideas of this path can be synthesized in the triad: dignity, autonomy, cooperation" (Gutiérrez Aguilar 2008: 351). The challenge? To achieve emancipation from the instituted power relations of modernity: emancipation as a praxis of both overturning and flight (*trastocamiento y fuga*); that is, material *overturning* of the existing order and *flight* from the semantic and symbolic contents that confer material existence and meaning upon that which is instituted (*éxodo semántico*, or semantic exodus). The fundamental question becomes that of "being able to stabilize in time and space a mode of regulation outside of, *against and beyond*

the social order imposed by capitalist production and the liberal state" (Gutiérrez Aguilar 2008: 46). [2]

Aymara sociologist Félix Patzi Paco put this idea succinctly by saying that the social movements in Bolivia are about "the total transformation of liberal society" (Chapel Hill, November 17, 2005; 2004). What he meant was the end of the hegemony of liberal modernity, based on the notions of private property and representative democracy, and the rise of communal forms of social and economic organization based on indigenous practices. Patzi has developed a well-thought out (albeit controversial and contested) conceptualization of "the communal system" that would be at the basis of this proposal. I can only hint at Patzi's conceptualization here, beginning with the following characterization:

> By communal or communitarian concept we mean the collective property of resources combined with their private management and utilization. … Our point of departure for the analysis of communal systems is doubtlessly the indigenous societies. In contradistinction to modern societies, indigenous societies have not reproduced the patterns of differentiation nor the separation among domains (political, economic, cultural, etc.); they thus function as a single system that relates to both internal and external environments. ….The communal system thus presents itself as opposed to the liberal system (Patzi Paco 2004: 176).

As important as the economic dimension is the political dimension of the communal system; at this level, power is not centered on the individual or a group of persons, but in the collectivity. In the communal form of politics, "social sovereignty is not delegated; it is exercised directly" through various forms of authority, service, assembly, etc. (Patzi Paco 2004: 176). In the case of representation, the representatives "rule by obeying." Patzi's proposal, to sum up, involves the progressive replacement of the liberal system by a communally-based system, in terms of communal enterprises, communal forms of democracy, and cultural pluralism as the basis for a genuine (p. 190). It should be pointed out that underlying the communal forms is an entirely different view of life and the world, a collective life-world that values simultaneously autonomy and obligation and what could be called relational ontologies, the second trend I would like to discuss.

## Relationality and decoloniality

A key feature of what has been described as communal-popular forms of politics for cases such as Bolivia is their profound relationality; they eschew

the distinction between Nature (the domain of objects) and Culture (the domain of subjects) that is central to the modern/colonial world system. They are not based on the invention of separate spheres (economy, society, culture, nature, etc., as Patzi mentioned), but on the interconnectedness of all aspects of socio-natural life. A second important feature is that many movements of indigenous peoples, afrodescendants, and other territorially-based groups practice what can be described as non-representational politics —one in which the distinction between a representative and his/her constituency is obliterated through mechanisms that render the collective as the central locus of political action (as in the Aymara case just discussed, or the Zapatista or Oaxacan autonomous communities, but many other movements as well). In this way, the distinction between representation and what is represented, which is in turn patterned after the culture/nature divide, is also eschewed. Non-representational politics have become more prominent not because of its novelty but because it connects with relational worldviews sedimented in communal and collective experiences of grassroots groups. More generally, we can speak of relational ontologies, or relational worlds and knowledges, in the sense that these worlds are build on the basis of the interconnectedness and interdependencies of everything that exists, including all kinds of entities (human and not), on the continuity between knowing, doing, and being and between the biophysical, human, and spiritual worlds. In this way, and while of course in continued interaction with dominant modern practices, they defy the dualist ontology of dominant forms of modernity, and the binarisms on which the coloniality of nature, being, and knowledge is built.[3]

There is thus a larger and wide-spread process by which relational worldviews, embodied by many groups that contest institutions built on modern binary categorizations, are becoming visible as viable political alternatives. The conception of nature as a subject with rights present in the Ecuadorian constitution of 2008, and the conception of development in terms of the collective well-being of human-natural worlds (which is also present in the new Bolivian constitution) are not mainly inspired on modern environmentalist stances; rather they are embedded on indigenous relational notions. In the Andes this is known as *Sumaq Kawsay* (*buen vivir*), a relational principle which mandates an ethics of respect between humans and non-humans as fully agentive subjects. According to one of its proponents—David Choquehuanca, the Bolivian Minister for Foreign Affairs— *buen vivir* directly challenges the notions according to which the mandate of the state is to 'improve life'—usually at the expense of some humans and the non-humans that 'moderns' know as the environment. This is why the relational worldviews expressed in many communal-popular mobilizations can stake a claim as viable alternatives to modern political institutions.

The relational ontologies escape the division of nature and culture and politicize it by mobilizing non-humans (e.g., mountains, water, soil, the forest) as sentient entities, that is, as actors in the political arena (anti-mining protests, protests against dams, deforestation, etc.). Struggles against the destruction of life by conjuring up the entire the range of the living are sprouting in many countries in the region. These struggles evidence what could be called the political activation of relationality. Current indigenous and afro-Latin American mobilizations, in particular, might thus be seen as ontological-political projects. They push for non-representational politics and non-dualist understandings of socio-natural worlds and in this way their politics of difference often entail a *political ontology* (Blaser In press; de la Cadena 2008). Neither *Pachamama* nor *Sumaq Kawsay*, in other words, can be accommodated within modern/colonial frameworks without destabilizing them significantly; they are, indeed, unthinkable within modern social science frameworks, thus taking epistemic decolonization to the very heart of politics (e.g., Amawtay Wasi 2004; Walsh 2007). As Catherine Walsh put it recently (2009), the notion of "collective well being" opens up a new kind of ethical-epistemic decolonial politics and a philosophy of life that transgresses the modern-colonial capitalist order, calling for an otherwise logic of the State. At stake is the creation of new social, political and epistemic orderings, structures, conditions and articulations.

Some of the questions that emerge from the consideration of relationality include: How is the analysis reconfigured when 'nature' is conceived as subject? How does it impact our understanding of politics and the State? What is the relation between relational world-views, non-representational politics, and decoloniality? More generally, what is the connection between non-liberal/non-state forms and relational ontologies? It could be said that, in the last instance, the emergence of relationality as a set of intellectual tools and social/political practices points to a gradual epistemic decolonization, understood as a long-term process of re-signification and re/construction towards words and knowledges otherwise.

## Notes

1 See the thorough analysis of the social policies of the progressive regimes prepared by the Centro Latino Americano de Ecología Social, CLAES, in Montevideo (Gudynas, Guevara, and Roque 2008). According to the report, the development style of most, of not all, of the regimes –largely based on the export of natural resources as the source of economic growth and redistributive policies—has not changed much since the Left and Center-Left governments came into office.

2 It should be made clear, however, that Gutiérrez Aguilar nevertheless concludes that the struggles of 2000-2005 did not mange to propose "a system that could substitute the order of exploitation and political domination of capital"; in this way, "the anti-state and anti-capitalist character of a set of struggles consists, above all, in their commitment to displaying and making visible the *particularity* of the life-worlds from which emerges the very possibility of struggle and where it find nourishment" (p. 360). My thanks to Eduardo Gudynas for this observation.

3 For a more adequate treatment of relationality, including its provenance in both social movements and scholarly trends in geography, anthropology, science and technology studies, and political ecology, see Escobar (in press). Relational ontologies are the subject of an ongoing collective project with Mario Blaser and Marisol de la Cadena.

## References


Amawtay Wasi. 2004. Sumak Yachaypi. Alli Kawasaypipash Yachakuna. Aprender en la Sabiduría y el Buen Vivir. Learning Wisdom and the Good Way of Life. Quito: Banco Central de Ecuador.

Arditti, Benjamín. 2008. "Arguments about the Left Turns in Latin America: A Post-Liberal Politics?." *LARR* 43(3): 59-81

Blaser, Mario. In Press. *Storytelling Globality: A Border Dialogue Ethnography of the Paraguayan Chaco*. Durham: Duke University Press

De la Cadena, Marisol. 2008. "Taking Indigenous Politics in its Own Terms Requires an Analysis Beyond 'Politics'." Unpublished ms., Department of Anthropology, University of California, Davis.

Escobar, Arturo. In press. "Postconstructivist Political Ecologies." In Michael Redclift and Graham Woodgate, eds. International Handbook of Environmental Sociology, 2nd. edition. Cheltenham, UK: Elgar.

Escobar, Arturo. 2008. *Territories of Difference: Place, Movements, Life,* Redes. Durham: Duke University Press.

Patzi Paco, Félix. 2004. *El Sistema Comunal. Una Propuesta Alternativa al Sistema Liberal*. La Paz: CEA

Gudynas, Eduardo, Rubén Guevara, and Francisco Roque, eds. *Heterodoxos. Tensiones y posibilidades de las políticas sociales en los gobiernos progresistas de América del Sur*. Montevideo: CLAES. From http://www.globalizacion.org/

Gutiérrez Aguilar, Raquel. 2008. *Los ritmos del Pachakuti. Movilización y levantamiento indígena-popular en Bolivia*. Buenos Aires: Tinta Limón.

Pablo Mamani R. 2006. "Territorio y estructuras de acción colectiva: Microgobiernos barriales". *Ephemera* 6(3): 276-286 (in Spanish and English)

Pablo Mamani R. 2005. *Geopolíticas indígenas*. El Alto: CADES, pp. 7-43, 111-123.

Mignolo, Walter. 2007. "El pensamiento decolonial: desprendimiento y apertura". In Santiago Castro-Gómez and Ramón Grosfogel, eds. *El giro decolonial. Reflexiones para una diversidad epistémica más allá del capitalismo global*. Pp. 25-46. Bogotá: Instituto Pensar/IESCO

Mignolo, Walter. 2006. "Evo Morales en Bolivia: ¿giro a la izquierda o giro descolonial?." In José da Cruz, ed. *Democracias en Desconfianza. Ensayos en sociedad civil y política en América Latina*. Pp. 93-106. Montevideo: Editorial Coscoroba

Quijano, Aníbal. 2008. "Des/colonialidad del poder: el horizonte alternativo." Unpublished ms.

Walsh, Catherine. 2009. "Indigenous and Afro Struggles and the State: Interculturality, Decoloniality, and Collective Wellbeing in the Andes." Presented at the Conference, "Contested Modernities: Indigenous and Afrodescendant Experiences in Latin America," Lozano Long Institute of Latin American Studies, University of Texas, Austin, February 26, 2009.

Walsh, Catherine. 2007. "¿Son posibles una ciencias sociales/ culturales otras? Reflexiones en torno a las epistemologías decoloniales". *Nómadas* 26: 102-13.

Zibechi, Raúl. 2006. *Dispersar el poder. Los movimientos como poderes antiestatales*. Buenos Aires: Tinta Limón.

# BIBLIOGRAPHY


Cairo, Heriberto (ed) (2008). "Palestra: La colonialidad, la imperialidad y el debate sobre su superación." *Revista Tábula Rasa*, 8, http://www.revistatabularasa.org/numero8.html.

Castro-Gómez, Santiago (2000). "Traditional and Critical Theories of Culture." In *Nepantla.Views from South*, 1/3, 503-518.

Césaire, Aimé ([1955], 2000). *Discourse sur le colonialisme* [1955]. Translated by Joan Pinkham. New York: Monthly Review Press, 2000.

Escobar, Arturo (2008). *Territories of Difference. Place, Movements, Life, Redes*. Durham: Duke University Press.

Lander, Edgardo (2002). ¨Eurocentrism, Modern Knowledges and the ¨Natural¨ Order of Global Capital.¨ *Nepantla.Views from South*, 3-2, 245-268.

Dussel, Enrique (1995). "Eurocentrism and Modernity (Introduction to the Frankfurt Lectures), in *The Postmodern Debate in Latin America*, edited by John Beverley, José Oviedo and Michael Arona. Durham: Duke University Press, 65-77.

Dussel, Enrique (2002). "World System and 'Trans'-Modernity." *Nepantla.Views from South*, 3/2, 221-244.

Fernández-Osco, Marcelo (2008). "Ayllu: Decolonial Critical Thinking and (Other) Autonomy", in *Globalizaton and Autonomy Online Compendium*, http://www.globalautonomy.ca/global1/summary.jsp?index=RS_FernandezOsco_Ayllu.xml.

Kellner, Douglas (2001). "Critical Theory, Poststructuralism and Philosophy of Liberation." http://www.uta.edu/huma/illuminations/kell7.htm

Grzinick, Marina and Smid, Aina. *Obsession 1*. http://hackfemeast.org/web/?page_id=66.

Gordon, Lewis (2003). *Existentia Africana. Understanding Existential Thought*. London: Blackwell.

Gordon, Lewis (2004). "Fanon and Development." *Africa Development*, 29/1, 71-93.

Grosfoguel, Ramón (2008) "Transmodernity, Border Thinking and Global Coloniality, in *Eurozine*, http://www.eurozine.com/articles/2008-07-04-grosfoguel-en.html.

Mahbubani, Kishore (2008). *The New Asian Hamisphere. The Irresistible Shift of Global Power to the East*. New York: Public Affairs.

Martinez, Jacqueline (2000). *Phenomenology of Chicana Experience and Identity.*

*Communication and Transformation of Praxis*. Boulder and New York: Rowman and Little Field Publishers.

Mates, Reyes (2004). *Memory of the West. The Contemporaneity of Forgotten Jewish Thinkers*. Translated from the Spanishby Anne Day Dewey. Amsterdam: Rodopi.

Mignolo, Walter (2000). *Local Histories/Global Designs. Coloniality, Subaltern Knowledges and Border Thinking*. Princeton: Princeton U.P.

Mignolo, Walter (2003). "Los estudios culturales: geopolíticas del cnocimiento y exigencias institucionales" in *Los estudios culturales latinoamericanos hacia el siglo XXI* (Special issue of *Revista Iberoamericana*, 203, 401-416.

Mignolo, Walter (2008). "La opción descolonial: desprendimiento y apertura. Un manifiesto y un caso." In *Las vertientes americanas del pensamiento y el proyecto des-colonial*. Herberto Cairo and Walter Mignolo, eds. Madrid: Trama, 175-208;

Pacari, Nina (2008). "La incidencia de la participación política de los pueblos indígenas." In *Las vertientes Americanas del pensamiento y el proyecto descolonial*. Heriberto Cairo and Walter Mignolo, eds. Madrid: Trama Editorial, 45-58;

*Pasado y Presente* (1963-1973). Centro de Documentación e Investigación de la Cultura de Izquierdas en Argentina, http://www.cedinci.org/edicionesdigitales/pasadoypresente.htm;

Patzi, Félix (2008). "Sistema comunal: una propuesta alternativa al sistema liberal." In *Las vertientes Americanas del pensamiento y el proyecto des-colonial*. Heriberto Cairo and Walter Mignolo, eds. Madrid: Trama Editorial, 59-82

Quijano, Aníbal (2000a). "Colonialidad del poder y clasificación social." In *Festschrift to Immanuel Wallerstein. Journal of World System Research. XI/ 2*, 342-386.

Quijano, Aníbal (2000b). "Coloniality of Power, Eurocentrism and Latin America." *Nepantla. Views from South*, ½, 533-580.

Shiva, Vandana (2000). *Stolen Harvest. The Hijacking of the Global Food Supply*. Cambridge: South End Press.

Slabodsky, Santiago E (2009). "De-Colonial Jewis Thought and the Americas." In *Post-Colonial Philosophy of Religion*; Purshumottama Bilimoria and Andrew Irvine, eds. Dordrecht, The Netherlands: Springer

Rasmussen, David (2004). *The Handbook of Critical Theory*. London: Willey-Blackwell.

Tlostanova, Madina (2003). *The Sublime of Globalilzation?* Sketches on Transcultural Subjectivities and Aesthetics. Moscow: URSS Publishing.

Smith, Linda T. (1999). *Decolonizing Methodologies. Research and Indigenous People*. London: Zed Books.

# Index